WORLD
WAR II
A STATISTICAL SURVEY

By the same author

Armies in Revolution
The Social History of the Machine Gun
A Short History of Guerilla Warfare
Eye-Deep in Hell: Trench Fighting in World War I
The Sharp End: The Fighting Man in World War II
Cassino: The Hollow Victory
Brute Force: Allied Strategy and Tactics in the Second World War

WORLD WAR II

A STATISTICAL SURVEY

The Essential Facts and Figures for All the Combatants

JOHN ELLIS

Facts On File

World War II: A Statistical Survey
Copyright © 1993 by John Ellis

Facts On File, Inc.
460 Park Avenue South
New York NY 10016

Library of Congress Cataloging-in-Publication Data

Ellis, John, 1945–
    World War II : a statistical survey / John Ellis.
        p.   cm.
    ISBN 0-8160-2971-7
    1. World War, 1939–1945—Statistics.   I. Title.   II. Title: World
    War 2.   III. Title: World War Two.
    D744.E45   1993
    940.53—dc20   93–10627
                                                        CIP

A British CIP catalogue record for this book is available from the British Library.

Facts on File books are available at special discounts when purchased in bulk
quantities for businesses, associations, institutions or sales promotions. Please call
our Special Sales Department in New York at 212/683-2244 or 800/322-8755.

Text and Jacket Design, and Computer Composition by Philip Mann, ACE Limited.

Printed and bound in Great Britain.

10 9 8 7 6 5 4 3 2 1

This book is printed on acid-free paper.

9745714

Lies, damned lies and statistics . . .

This book is respectfully dedicated
to all those for whom the Second World War
was all too real.

CONTENTS

SECTION 2
COMMAND STRUCTURES

SECTION 3
ORDERS OF BATTLE

PART I COMBAT DIVISIONS

ALLIED
USA

CONTENTS

SECTION 4
TABLES OF ORGANISATION
AND EQUIPMENT

SECTION 5 STRENGTHS

PART I MILITARY MANPOWER

PART II ARMOUR

PART III AIR FORCES

COMPARATIVE STRENGTHS

BOMBING

SECTION 8
HARDWARE

PREFACE

I was prompted to assemble this book after experiencing considerable difficulties during the research for an earlier effort, *Brute Force: Allied Strategy and Tactics in the Second World War*. The central thrust of that book concerned the Allies' massive material preponderance during the latter stages of the war and making my case convincingly required a considerable amount of supporting quantitative data. But extracting such data – on comparative force levels, production figures, casualties and losses etc – proved to be much more difficult than I had first assumed.

Though tens of thousands of books have been written about the war, and more than a few of them purport to offer 'encyclopaedic' coverage, it was nevertheless very unusual to find works that contained any really systematic or comprehensive presentation of the kind of data I was seeking. Outside of a few official and semi-official works, as well as the odd 'buffs'' book, remarkably little attention has been paid to the administrative, industrial and logistical basis of military operations between 1939 and 1945. Personalities abound, with quite exaggerated importance often attached to the tactical and operational contribution of commanders like Montgomery or Rommel, Patton or Manstein, MacArthur or Nimitz, and almost none to the all-important bottom lines on military mobilisation, ship, aircraft or tank production, and the ability to get all the men and machines to the front.

But even those books that did contain some pertinent information hardly ever offered a sufficiently comprehensive range of comparative data that would, on the one hand, highlight the enormous gulf between the productive capacities of the Allies and their enemies and, on the other, draw attention to the important military role of a whole panoply of hitherto neglected belligerent nations. Books in English about the Second World War have tended to be somewhat parochial, over-emphasising the importance of one national contribution or another – the British campaign in North Africa is a prime example – at the expense of the overall Allied effort. Thus, while there is some justice in English complaints about very self-centred American accounts of the war, the former, too, have consistently harped on 'British' victories in the Middle East, Italy and Burma without giving remotely proper credit to the substantial Commonwealth, Dominion and Empire presence in Eighth and Fourteenth Armies. Similarly, both the Americans and the British have frequently downplayed the staggering Russian sacrifices on the Eastern Front – the front where Hitler actually lost the war – and many crucial Red Army victories, such as the destruction of Army Group Centre, are almost unknown in the West.

Nor have the enemies' efforts received even-handed coverage. Outside of a very well-informed technical database about German, Italian and Japanese ships, aircraft and tanks and an unhealthy fetishism with regard to certain Waffen-SS formations and accoutrements, knowledge of the enemy is limited to simplicistic generalizations about *'blitzkrieg'* methods, ill-informed sniggering about the Italians, knee-jerk racism regarding the Japanese and almost complete ignorance about the military role and sufferings of the Hungarians, Rumanians and Finns.

Hence this book which, though it probably has less narrative drive than a Mayan telephone directory, does at least attempt to present a fairly *complete* collection of the essential facts and figures about the Second World War. Inevitably, some of the data is fairly familiar. But, whilst old favourites like SS divisional combat records or the technical specifications of a P-51 Mustang or a Supermarine Spitfire are there, so too, for example, are thumbnail histories of every Hungarian and Rumanian division, every Polish division that fought with the Red Army and every Italian brigade that fought alongside the Allies after 1943. There are also details on Italian tank production and that of Hungarian bauxite, on cabinet changes in Denmark during the war, on the technical specifications of the V-1 rocket and of US landing craft, on the commanders of all Japanese army groups and armies, on the Russian order of battle in Manchuria in August 1945, etc, etc. We

have always known that the events of 1939-45 were a *world* war – this book endeavours to give this concept a database to stand on.

A few other specific points merit brief explanation.

It should be remembered that the word 'British', referring both to ground forces and to the RAF, is largely a linguistic convenience and usually 'British, Dominion, Commonwealth and Empire' would be a more accurate term. I have eschewed strict accuracy (perhaps mistakenly) in favour of familiarity and conciseness. I would, however, recommend all readers to give some attention to those parts of the Orders of Battle section that detail the Australian, New Zealand, Indian and South, East and West African contribution to the Allied cause.

The book contains no biographical entries as it was felt that this was one aspect of Second World War history that *had* been fully covered by the existing, alphabetically sequenced encyclopaedias/dictionaries/almanacs or whatever. This is not to say, however, that there are no names in this book, and the section on Command Structures is largely given over to them.

More surprising, probably, is the absence of an index. At first sight this might seem a remarkable omission, but in fact the decision stemmed from the slow realisation that one was simply not necessary. For it became clear that for most queries it would be self-evident which section and sub-section would contain the relevant information, and in those cases where there was the possibility of a misunderstanding, a detailed Contents list could provide exact page guidance just as easily as an index. It is to the *front* of the book, then, that those seeking to focus their enquiries should turn.

One semantic point should be clarified. In this book the word 'include' is used to mean that the constituent parts listed are not necessarily complete. The word 'comprise' is used when this *is* the case. Thus the Four Musketeers *included* Athos and Porthos but *comprised* Athos, Porthos, Aramis and d'Artagnan.

This book includes several question marks which indicate where I have been unable to track down the correct name or whatever. Each such mark represents a minor failure and I should be more than grateful to anyone who could, care of the publisher, provide an answer. I should be equally grateful (though rather more embarrassed) to anyone who can correct any of the (hopefully few) mistakes that must inevitably creep into a work of this nature. Any such further information or amendments will be duly acknowledged in subsequent editions.

My acknowledgments for the present edition are threefold. On a general level I should like to express my considerable debt to all those authors and publishers who produced the painstakingly researched books mentioned in the Bibliography, which provided vital databases and checklists for this present work. Specifically, I am extremely grateful to Mike Cox who, though not in the Bibliography, provided me with some priceless material from his quite staggering Orders of Battle database and who was a sure guide through some of the more arcane literature of the period. Last, but most emphatically not least, I would like to thank Philip Mann of ACE Design Consultants who actually computer typeset this book, translating my eccentric doodles, rickety tables and 'disorganigrams' into the austerely attractive and eminently functional layouts that adorn each page.

JOHN ELLIS
Manchester 1993

17

ABBREVIATIONS

Many of the abbreviations below are separated by full stops. For reasons of space it has sometimes been necessary to omit these in Tables, etc.

A.A..
A/aircraft } Anti-aircraft
ABDA   American British Dutch Australian
A/b   Airborne
A/car   Armoured car
Admin   Administrator/ion/ive
A.H.   Adolf Hitler
A.I.F.   Australian Imperial Force
Air Lan.
A.L. } Air Landing
A.O.I.   Africa Orientale Italiana ('Italian East Africa')
a.p.
A.P. } Armour piercing
Arm.   Armoured
Ar.   Arlete
Ass.   Assault
a/t   anti-tank
A.T.W.   Ahead-Thrown Weapon ('Hedgehog' or 'Squid')
Ausf.   Ausfuhrung (model, mark)
Ay.Tk.   Army Tank

B.A.R.   Browning Automatic Rifle
B.E.F.   British Expeditionary Force
Belg.   Belgian
B.G.   British Guiana
Bran.   Brandenberg
Brig.   Brigade
B.S.   Blackshirt
Byelo.   Byelorussian

C.A.   Chasseurs ardennais
Can.   Canadian
C.B.I.   China-Burma-India (Theater)
Chanc.   Chancellor (of the Exchequer)
C.I.G.S.   Chief of the Imperial General Staff
C.-in-C.   Commander-in-Chief
C.I.U.   Central Interpretation Unit
C/man.   Chairman
C. of Ops. Chief of Operations
C. of S.   Chief of Staff
Col.   Colonial
Comm.   Commisioner
            Commando
Coss.   Cossack
Coy.   Company

D.A.F.   Deutsche Arbeitsfront
d/b   demi-brigade
Det.   Detachment
D.-G.   Director-General
Dir.   Director
Dir. Int.   Director of Intelligence
D.L.M.   Division Légére Mécanisée
Div.   Division
D.P.   dual purpose

E.A.
E.Af. } East African
Esc.   Escort
F.B.I.   Federal Bureau of Investigation
F.E.   Far East
Field Tr.   Field Training
Fl.   Flieger
Fort.   Fortress
Fr.   Front
Fr. Guard   Frontier Guard
F.S.   Fortified Sector
F.T.   Fortress Training

G.C. & C.S. Government Code and Cypher School
G.C.H.Q.   Government Communications Headquarters
Gds.   Guards
Gds. Tk.   Guards Tank
G.F.   Giovani Fascisti ('Young Fascists')
G.O.C.   General Officer Commanding
GR D.   Grossdeutschland

h/drawn } horsedrawn
H.E..
h.e. } High explosive
H.G.Pz.   Hermann Goering Panzer Parachute Division
H.Kdo.   Heereskommando
How.   Howitzer

I.M.B.   Independent Mixed Brigade
Ind.Cst. Army Independent Coastal Army
Inf.   Infantry
It.   Italian

J.I.C.   Joint Intelligence (Sub-) Committee
J.P.S.   Joint Planning Staff

Kg.   Kampfgruppe
K.O.S.B.   King's Own Scottish Borderers
KwK.   Kampfwagenkanone (tank gun)

Ld.   Lord
L.E.   Légion Étrangère
Lit.   Littorio
L.R.   Long range
L/w.   Luftwaffe

M.   Moroccan
Mech.   Mechanised
Med.   Mediterranean
M.G.   Machine gun
Misc.   Miscellaneous
M.M.   Moroccan Mountain
Mob.   Mobile
Mot.   Motorised
Mt.   Mountain
Münch.   Münchenburg
M.V.S.N.   Milizia Volontaria per la Sicurezza Nazionale (Blackshirts)

N.A.   North Africa
N.R.   North Rhodesian

N.W.E.	North-West Europe
O.I.C.	Operational Intelligence Centre
O.K.H.	Oberkommando des Heeres (Army High Command)
O.K.L.	Oberkommando der Luftwaffe (Air Force High Command)
O.K.M.	Oberkommando der Marine (Navy High Command)
O.K.W.	Oberkommando der Wehrmacht (Armed Forces High Command)
O.R.	Other Rank
O.V.R.A.	Meaningless acronym for the Special Inspectorate of the Director-General of Public Security
Pack	Pack howitzer
PAK	Panzerabwehrkanone (Anti-tank gun)
P.G.	Panzergrenadier
PIAT	Projectile Infantry Anti-tank
Pol.	Polish
	Police (German)
P.O.W.	Prisoner of War
P.R.U.	Photo Reconnaissance Unit
Pz.	Panzer
QM.	Quartermaster
R.C.T.	Regimental Combat Team
R.D.S	Replacement Division Staff
R.D.X.	Research Department Explosive (including Torpex)
Recce	Reconnaissance
Rep.	Replacement
Res.	Reserve
R.H.A.	Royal Horse Artillery
R.H.S.A.	Reichssicherheitshauptamt (Chief Office for Reich Security)
R.I.C.	Régiment d'Infanterie Coloniale
R.L.E.	Régiment de la Légion Entrangère
Rplment.	Replacement
R.T.A.	Régiment de Tirailleurs Algerians
R.T.M.	Régiment de Tirailleurs Marocains
R.T.S.	Régiment de Tirailleurs Sénégalais
R.T.T.	Régiment de Tirailleurs Tunisiens
Rum.	Rumanian
S.A.	South African
S.D.	Sicherheitsdienst (Security Service)
Sd. Kfz.	Sonderkraftfahrzug (Special purpose vehicle)
Sec.	Security
S/Engine	Single-engined
Sk. J.	Ski Jäger
SNLF	Special Naval Landing Force
S.P.	Self-propelled
Sp. Admin.	Special Administration
Sp. Div.	Special Division Staff
SS	Schutzstaffel (literally Bodyguard Detachment. In this book usually the Waffen-SS or Armed SS)
S.S.F.	Special Service Force
StuG.	Sturm Infanterie Geschütz (Infantry assault gun/self-propelled)
StuH.	Sturmhaubitze (Assault howitzer/self-propelled)
T/engine	Twin-engined
Tk.	Tank
TOE	Table of Organisation and Equipment
Tre.	Trento
Tri.	Trieste
T.T.	Torpedo Tubes

UK	United Kingdom
US	United States
USSR	Union of Soviet Socialist Republics
V.F.	
Vf.	Verfügungs (decree)
V.G.	Volksgrenadier
V.L.R.	Very Long Range
V.M.	'Volks' Mountain (German 1 Mountain Division was renamed Volks-Gebirg in March 1945)
W.A.	West African
W.V.H.A.	Wirtschaftsverhaltungshauptamt (Chief Office for Economic Policy)
Y.F.	Young Fascists
zbV.	zu besondere Vorhaben (for special purposes)

SECTION 1

THE WAR IN MAPS

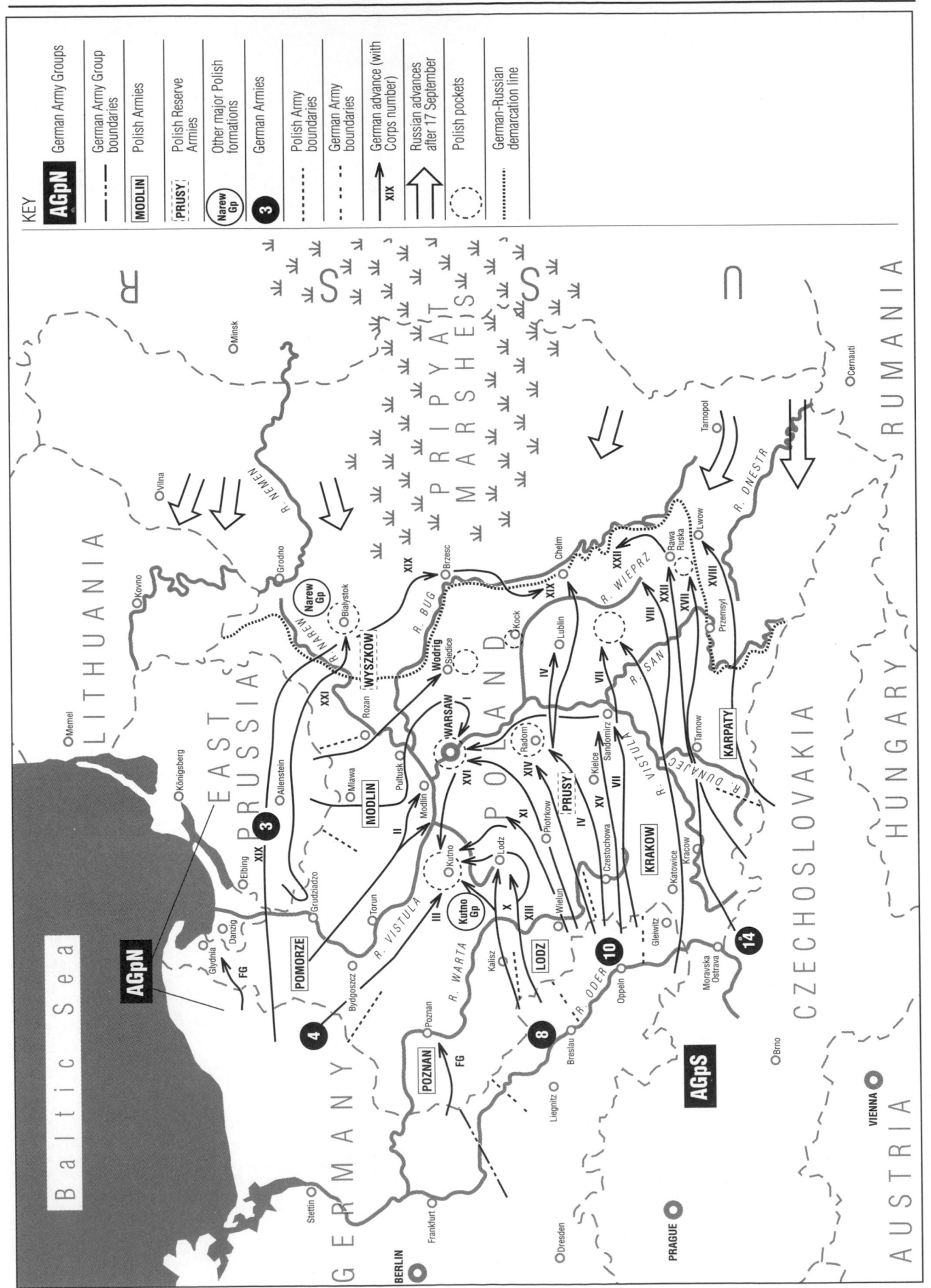

Map 1 Poland 1939: The Germans Sweep to Victory 1-27 September 1939

• **MAP 1** • POLAND 1939 •

NOTES TO MAP 1

Sadly for the Poles, the campaign of September 1939 was an extremely one-sided contest. Most military traffic was one-way, the German advance, and thus does not require the sort of stage-by-stage explanation that accompanies most of the campaign maps that follow.

Essentially the Poles were doomed from the start, firstly because they had placed too many of their units too far forward, secondly because their operations could not match the speed of the German advance, and thirdly because communications between headquarters and the front varied between the intermittent and the non-existent. The combination of these factors meant that many units near the frontier all too soon found German armoured formations swarming around in their rear and were obliged to fall back or be cut off, whilst the high command was never able to coordinate the funnelling in of reinforcements, or the realignment of troops in less threatened sectors, to counter-attack the exposed German spearheads. Moreover, such efforts as were made were dreadfully hampered by the devastating concentrations of fire from German aircraft and from their remarkably nimble artillery.

With this in mind, only the following few decisive events in the campaign need to be highlighted.

Key operational decisions

	Polish	German
3 Sept	Poznan Army's suggestion of attacking 8 Army's exposed northern flank rejected.	
6 Sept	All forces ordered to retire to Narew-Vistula-San line.	
7 Sept	High command moves from Warsaw to Brzesc. Line of the Narew deemed untenable. Northern units ordered to retreat to the Bug.	
8 Sept		OKH decides that Polish forces are retreating too swiftly to allow the planned encirclement west of the Vistula. Pincers now ordered to close down the line of the Bug.
9 Sept	The attack against 8 Army is finally sanctioned, around the River Bzura.	
10 Sept	Polish forces are divided into a new Northern Front and Southern Front. The former is ordered to retreat to a line Kock-Brzesc.	German forces are switched away from the drive on Warsaw to concentrate against the Bzura offensive.
11 Sept	All forces ordered to retreat to the south-east, the so-called Rumanian Bridgehead.	
15 Sept		Redirected forces join in the delayed major assault on Warsaw.
17 Sept	All forces are ordered to withdraw into neighbouring countries.	
20 Sept		German forces ordered to withdraw west of the demarcation line agreed with the Russians.

Surrender/destruction of main Polish concentrations

2 Sept Wielun; 5 Sept Tymbark (on R.Dunajec), Pietrkow; 6 Sept Tomaszow Mazowiecki, Krakow; 7 Sept Tarnow; 11 Sept Radom; 12 Sept Bialystok; 14 Sept Gydnia, Siedlce; 15 Sept Przemsyl; 17 Sept Kutno/R.Bzura, Brzesc; 19 Sept Vilna; 20 Sept Rawa Ruska; 21 Sept Lwow; 23 Sept R.Wieprz; 27 Sept Warsaw; 28 Sept Modlin; 6 Oct Kock.

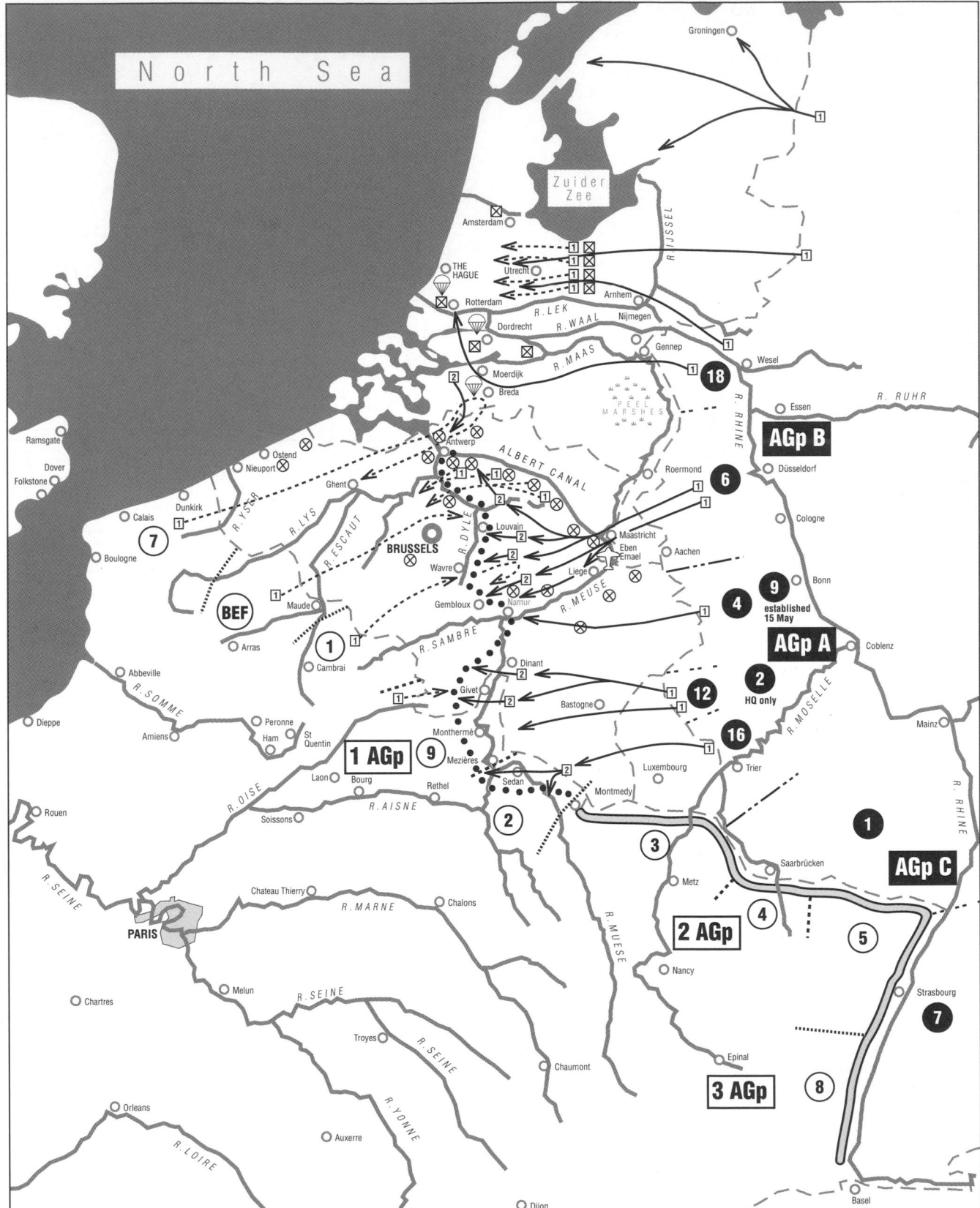

Map 2 France 1940 (i): Invasion of the Low Countries 10-15 May 1940

• **MAP 2** • FRANCE 1940 (i) •

KEY

1 AGp	French Army Groups
AGp B	German Army Groups
·················	French Army Group boundaries
— · · — · ·	German Army Group boundaries
(7)	French and British Armies
18	German Armies
- - - - - - - ·	French and British Army boundaries
-- -- --	German Army boundaries
⊠	Dutch divisions 10 May
⊗	Belgian divisions 10 May
▭	Maginot Line
1 - - - >	French and Allied movements
1 ——>	German movements
⛱ ⬥	German airborne landings
● ● ● ●	Limit of German advance 15 May

NOTES TO MAP 2

1 On 10 May German forces crossed the frontier into Holland, Belgium and Luxembourg, striking along three axes. In Holland they outflanked the Bregge Line by driving for the Waal-Maas estuary and Rotterdam and linking up with a parachute drop to seize the bridges; in northern Belgium they unhinged the Albert Canal defences by seizing key bridges at its southern end, using glider troops to capture the Eben Emael fortress; and in southern Belgium and Luxembourg they funnelled the mass of their armour through the supposedly impenetrable Ardennes, striving to crash the Meuse and so outflank the whole Allied defensive line. This would threaten to envelop those forces to the north, awaiting a latter-day Schlieffen-type offensive, as well as leave in the lurch those divisions tied up behind the Maginot Line, which the Germans chose not to attack.

The plan was totally successful. Rotterdam surrendered on the 13th and, though the bulk of Dutch troops were still available and were concentrated for the defence of the Hague and Amsterdam, the terror bombing of Rotterdam on the 14th precipitated general Dutch surrender the following morning. French troops from Seventh Army were unable to do much to distract the Germans and by the 13th were in full retreat. Belgian troops started pulling back from the Albert Canal on the 11th and withdrew to the River Dyle line to join the BEF and French First Army which had advanced there, according to plan, immediately on hearing of the German offensive. The Allies were fairly well ensconced by the 13th (though a sortie across the river by the French Cavalry Corps was soon driven back) and though the Germans took Liege on this day the momentum of their advance north of Namur began to falter. The advance through the Ardennes, however, was virtually unopposed.

2 Resistance along the line of the Dyle was still strong on the 15th and heavy German attacks north of Namur, especially against Louvain and Gembloux, were fought to a standstill. The Ardennes offensive, however, was paying enormous dividends. Spearheads crossed the Meuse at Dinant and Sedan (Generals Rommel and Guderian respectively) on the 13th and relentless probing during the next two days began to drive a wedge between French Second and Ninth Armies, and this threatened to split the whole Allied line asunder when Second Army was ordered to start falling back on the 14th. Sixth Army HQ was ordered up to the Aisne on this same day, together with divisions detached from duty on the Maginot Line, but by then it was too late.

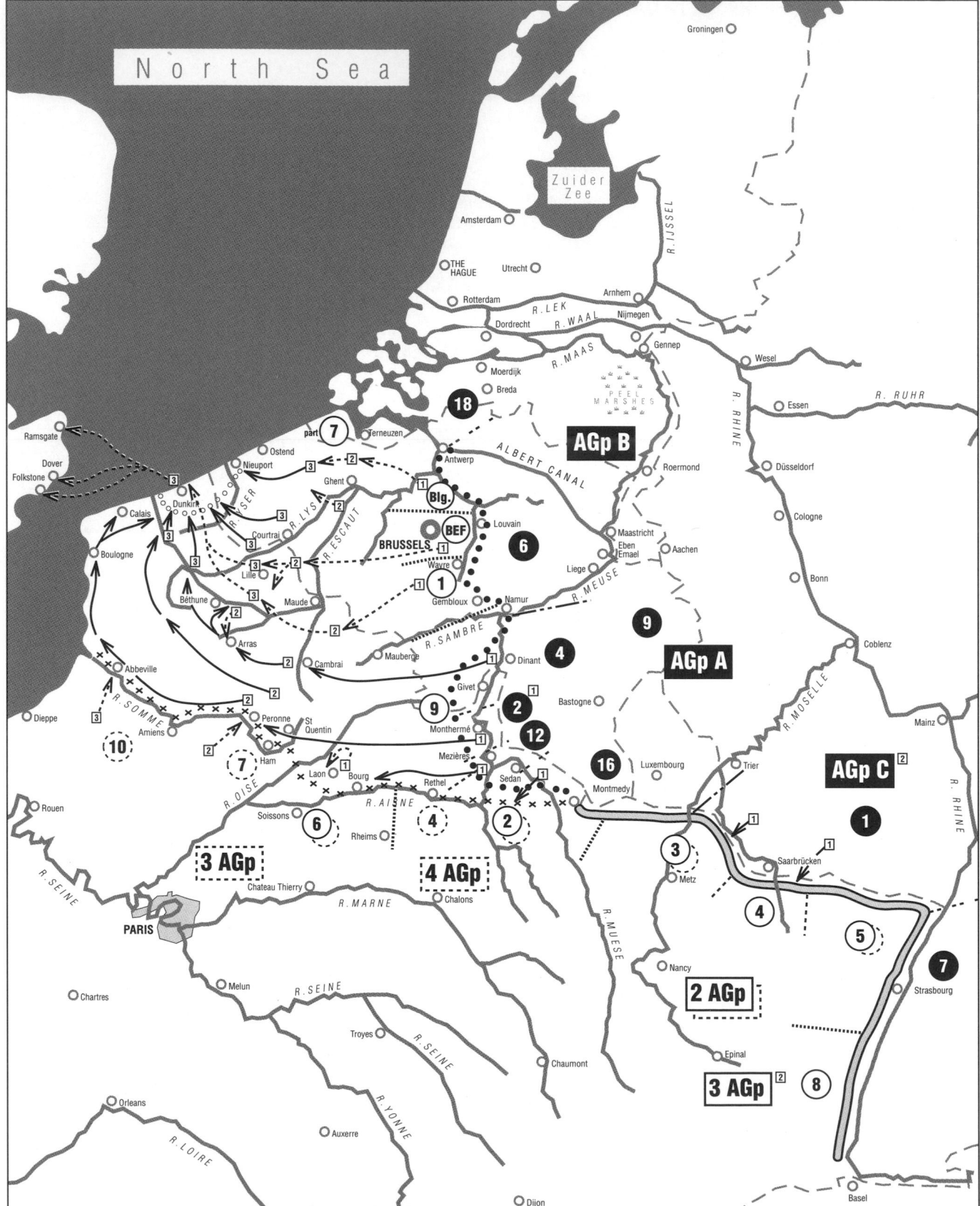

Map 3 France 1940 (ii): The Collapse in Belgium and North France 15 May-4 June 1940

• **MAP 3** • FRANCE 1940 (ii) •

KEY

1 AGp	French Army Groups 15 May
3 AGp	French Army Groups 4 June
AGp B	German Army Groups
....	French Army Group boundaries
— · — · —	German Army Group boundaries
⑦	French and British Armies 15 May
⑩	French and British Armies 4 June
⑱	German Armies
- - - - - - - ·	French and British Army boundaries
-- -- --	German Army boundaries
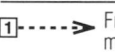	Maginot Line
 1 ---->	French and British movements
 1 ——>	German movements
● ● ● ●	Front line 15 May
○ ○ ○ ○	Dunkirk perimeter 1 June
 × × × ×	Limit of German advance 4 June

NOTES TO MAP 3

1 The German crossing of the Meuse and the ease with which their panzers began slicing through French Second and Ninth Armies convinced Allied commanders that the Dyle and even the Sambre were indefensible. They began falling back on the Escaut and the French frontier s.e. of Maude. The Belgians were to occupy the line Oudenarde-Ghent-Terneuzen and all forces north of the Sambre were in fact safely in position by the 19th. The Germans simply followed in their wake, taking Louvain on the 16th, Brussels on the 17th and Antwerp on the 18th.

South of Maubeuge, however, the Germans ran riot and French Ninth Army began to fall apart. Panzer spearheads reached Saint Quentin and Cambrai on the 18th and Peronne the next day, as well as crossing the Sambre also on the 18th. An attack by General de Gaulle against the German right flank, on the 17th and the 19th, failed, though Hitler remained extremely nervous about this flank right through until the 20th. In the meantime the Germans began funnelling in infantry divisions to take up positions along the Aisne and the Somme, introducing Second Army HQ into the line to oversee this process.

German First Army, opposite the Maginot Line, made local holding attacks on the 18th and 19th to pin French forces there and to further protect Army Group A's vulnerable southern flank.

2 German progress in the south was almost unchecked with Amiens and Abbeville falling on the 20th and advance parties reaching the Channel coast. The Germans had now split the Allied armies and Hitler felt able to cancel the projected offensive against the Maginot Line. The British, on the other hand, began assembling ships at Dover for a possible evacuation of the BEF from Dunkirk. Administrative troops began shipping out on the next day.

German forces on the coast turned north and cut off Calais on the 22nd (it surrendered on the 27th) and took Boulogne on the 23rd. A British tank foray at Arras, on the 21st, had had little impact on the German advance and subsequent efforts by the Allies to mount a concerted pincer attack from north and south of the panzer corridor came to nothing, the progressive disruption of their command structure being further aggravated by the death of General Billotte, commanding First Army Group.

Paralysis in the high command also had its effect in the north and on the 22nd the BEF pulled back to the French border which in turn obliged the Belgians to withdraw to the Lys. Ghent fell but French troops held out stubbornly to the s.w. of Lille. Over the next days pressure intensified on the Belgian front and the Lille salient. The French were pushed out of Valenciennes and Douai and the Belgians began to fall back from the Terneuzen-Ghent line whilst being heavily attacked on the Lys, around Courtrai.

On the 24th Hitler ordered that an offensive south, across the Aisne and the Somme (though this front had been fairly quiet since the 20th, when Third Army Group took over command of Sixth and Seventh Armies) would begin on the 31st. To facilitate the regrouping and replenishment of the panzers for this offensive he also ordered that no forces to the west were to push beyond the Aa Canal, even though some bridgehead there had already been secured. The elimination of the Dunkirk perimeter was to be left to the Luftwaffe. This decision provided the Allies with an invaluable breathing-space to begin fortifying their defensive perimeter, though there was no let-up on the Belgian front which was finally broken around Courtrai on the 25th.

3 The collapse around Courtrai prompted another Allied withdrawal, this time right back to the coastal perimeter around Dunkirk and Nieuport. This final dislocation was too much for the Belgians (who had fought exceptionally well) and they surrendered at midnight on the 27th. This was none too soon because the British had already set in motion Operation Dynamo, the evacuation of their forces at Dunkirk. The determination to get out was only strengthened by the lifting of Hitler's 'halt order' on this same day.

From then until 4 June British operations were concerned solely with facilitating mass evacuation and they succeeded in lifting off 225,000 British troops and 112,000 French. But many Frenchmen did not escape, not just the few thousand left in the Dunkirk perimeter but also the remnants of five divisions or so who were trapped in a pocket at Lille, sealed near Armentières on the 28th, and who absorbed the attention of some seven German divisions right up to their eventual surrender on 1 June. (French counterattacks from the south, however, towards Peronne and Abbeville, though ably led, were never more than pin-pricks.)

Dunkirk finally fell on 4 June and Hitler turned his armies southwards, having on the 31st postponed such an offensive for a further six days.

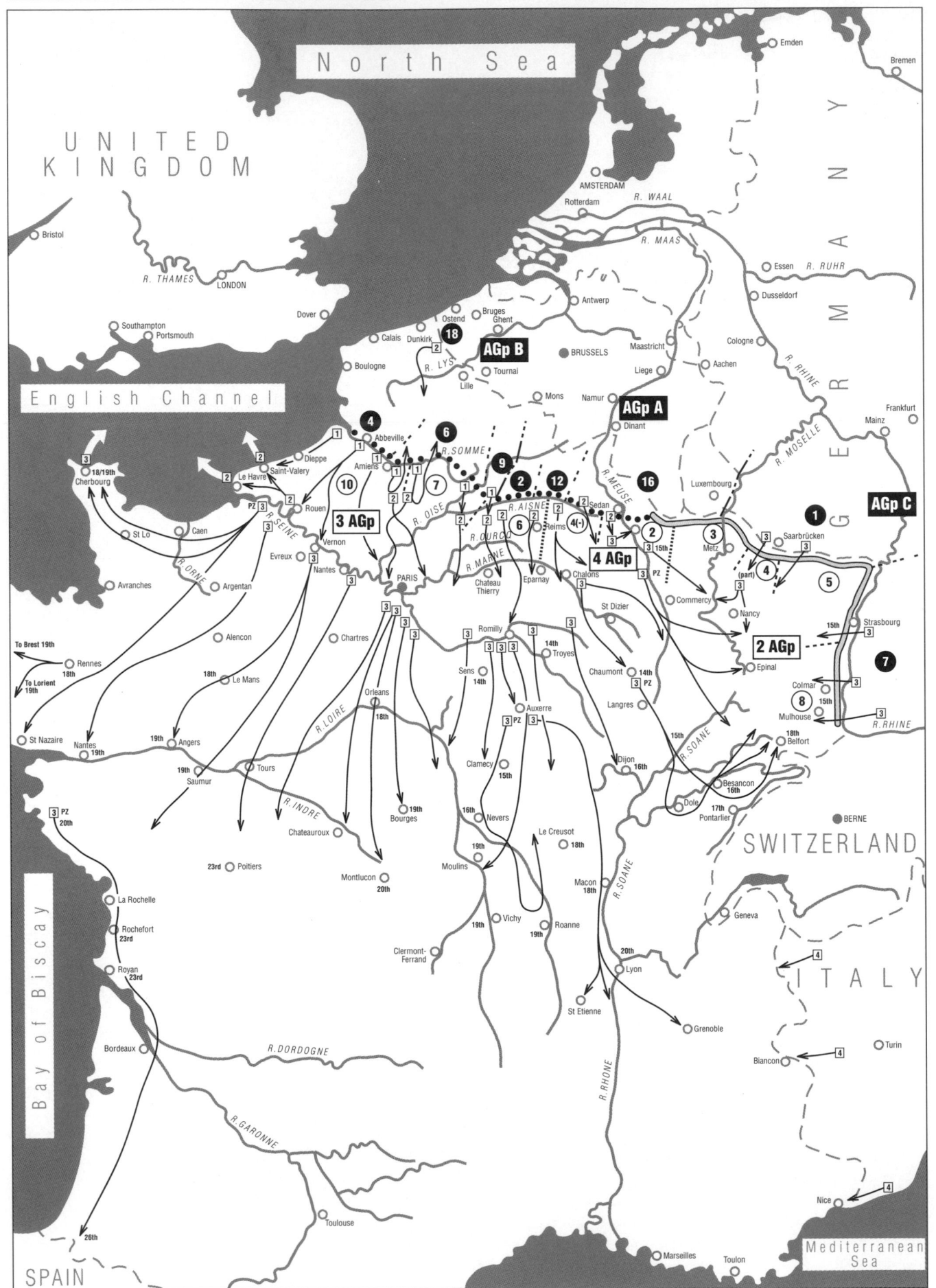

• **MAP 4** • FRANCE 1940 (iii) •

Map 4 France 1940 (iii): The French Collapse 5-25 June 1940

KEY

3 AGp	French Army Groups
AGp B	German Army Groups
··············	French Army Group boundaries
— ·· —	German Army Group boundaries
⑦	French and British Armies
⑱	German Armies
– – – – – – ·	French and British Army boundaries
-- -- --	German Army boundaries
▭▭▭▭▭	Maginot Line
1 - - - - ▷	British withdrawals
1 —▸	German and Italian advances
3 —▸ PZ	German armoured advances
● ● ● ●	Front line 5 June
20th	Date Germans arrived particular town

NOTES TO MAP 4

1 On 5 June the Germans turned southward and after a masterly regrouping of forces reopened their offensive with Army Group B leading off. French Third Army Group fought well but had put their whole trust in the original main line of resistance where units were to fight on even when cut off from their neighbours. There were thus very few reserves and when German spearheads did start storming through the gaps, heedless of their flanks, French resistance began to crumble. Advanced German units were on the Seine, near Rouen, by the 8th and on this day the whole of Third Army Group was ordered back behind the Seine and the Ourcq. A significant portion of it was cut off from the rest and had to retreat along the coast towards Dieppe.

The attack by German Sixth Army made slower progress, not least because of some tenacious defence, and the panzer force in this sector (Kleist) was withdrawn on the 8th to reinforce Ninth Army's push across the Aisne.

2 On 9 June the Germans also attacked along Army Group A's front where they pressed forward to the Aisne. On the very first day they drew up to the Ourcq and on the following day French Sixth Army was put under the command of Fourth Army Group which began to pull back to the Marne to regroup. Reims fell on 11 June, with German spearheads actually on the Marne to the east of Chateau-Thierry whilst in the evening they carved eastwards towards the Meuse, further unsettling the retreating Fourth Army Group. By the 12th the Germans had reached Chalons and were across the Marne at Chateau-Thierry and Eparnay.

Things went just as badly for the French in the west. When the Germans seized a bridgehead on the Oise near Paris, on the 10th, the government fled and on the 11th the Germans crossed the Seine in various places. On the 12th Paris was declared an open city. On the same day a large Allied force at Saint-Valéry-en-Caux, cut off after German forces wheeled right from Rouen and dashed to the coast, surrendered. A few thousand men were evacuated, as were a similar number from Le Havre which was taken on 13 June. German Fourth Army then halted briefly as the French endeavoured to fulfil an order of the day on the 12th to pull back along their whole line and take up new positions on a line Caen-Alencon-the Loire-Le Morvan-Côte d'Or-Champagnole-Les Russes. Also on the 13th German spearheads entered Romilly.

3 On the 14th German troops (from corps commanded by Eighteenth Army whose HQ was fed into the line on the 11th) entered Paris. On the same day German First Army attacked the Maginot Line to the east of Luxembourg and on the 15th Seventh Army attacked across the Rhine. By now French resistance was collapsing and on the 15th their GHQ retreated to Vichy where they requested an armistice on the following day. The British, who had been

disembarking troops back to France to resume the fight, soon gave up the idea and started re-embarking from Cherbourg on the 16th. On the 18th the French Navy left French ports or was scuttled, an armistice was signed on the 22nd and it came into force three days later.

Between the 14th and the 22nd, therefore, the German advance, despite individual instances of great French fortitude, was pretty much of a triumphal procession, the broad details of which are apparent from the map (dates are those when German forces first entered a town). Six main sectors can be discerned:

  a) a panzer sweep through Normandy and Brittany
  b) an infantry advance from the Seine to the Loire and the Indre
  c) a panzer assault from around Auxerre down the Rhone-Saone and Loire valleys
  d) an infantry encirclement of French troops manning the Maginot Line from east of Verdun to Saarbrucken, the pocket being closed north of Nancy
  e) another encirclement of French troops, on the Rhine and east of Saarbrucken, with German infantry pressing in from the north and east and panzers closing the trap from the south and the west
  f) a panzer dash to the Spanish frontier (using a panzer corps transferred from the Loire valley).

4 Italian attacks into certain alpine passes began on 21 June, and along the coast on the 23rd. They made almost imperceptible progress before the Franco-Italian armistice was signed on the 24th.

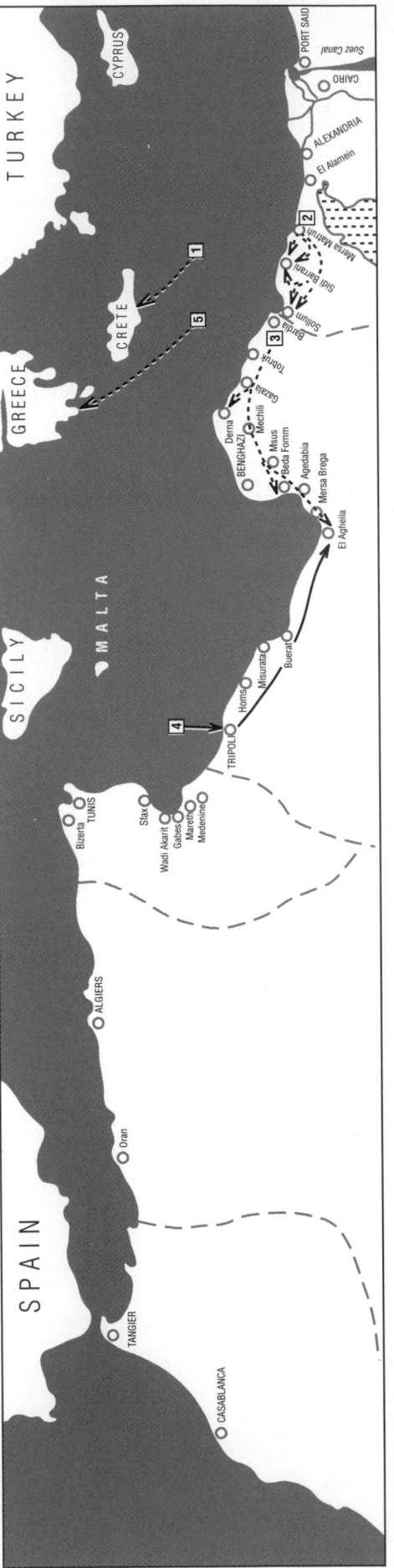

Map 5 North Africa (i): Wavell's North African Counter-offensive and the Greek Venture December 1940-March 1941

NOTES TO MAP 5

1 Crete was occupied by the British on 30 October 1940.

2 After a leisurely advance into Egypt, beginning on 13 September 1940, the Italians halted at Sidi Barrani. The British, under Wavell, launched a counter-offensive on 9 December, taking Sidi Barrani on the 10th and reaching Sollum on the 11th. The British were obliged to halt after losing one division of their small force for operations in the Sudan.*

3 Sollum was taken on 17 December, and the offensive proper resumed on 3 January 1941 with the arrival of a replacement division. Bardia fell on 4 January. After an advance by British armour towards Mechili, Tobruk was isolated and fell to an assault on the 21st. Subsequent operations split the Italian forces at Derna and Mechili, though the latter were allowed to escape on 26 January. Derna was abandoned on the 29th, but those troops retreating via the coast road were cut off at Beda Fomm on 5 February. They surrendered on the 7th and the Commonwealth forces reached El Agheila by the 9th. There they halted, Wavell being obliged to withdraw troops for operations in Greece.

4 On 12 February Rommel arrived in Tripoli, the first German troops following on the 14th. He assembled his German and Italian units opposite the Commonwealth positions at El Agheila.

5 British troops landed in Greece between 7 and 27 March.

* Not shown on this map are Commonwealth offensives from the Sudan into Abyssinia (August 1940-April 1941), Italian Somaliland (February-March 1941) and Eritrea (January-March 1941). Wavell later had to provide forces for operations against the Vichy French in Syria (June-July 1941) and against Iraqi nationalists under Rashid Ali (May 1941). Order of Battle details on all these campaigns can be found on pps. 155-6.

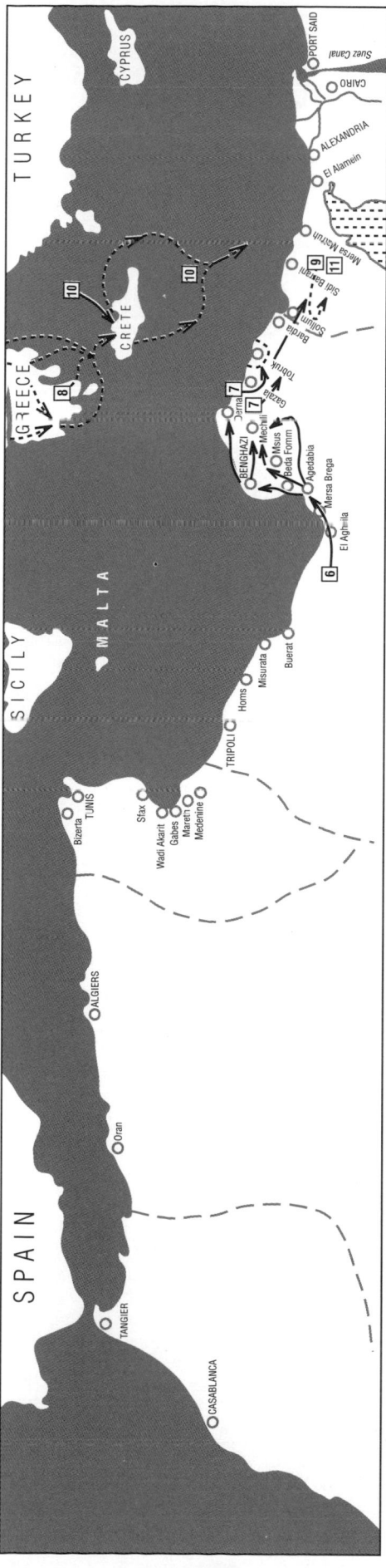

Map 6 North Africa (ii): British Forces Driven Back into Egypt March–June 1941

NOTES TO MAP 6

6 On 23 March 1941, Rommel launched a counter-offensive and easily took El Agheila on the 24th. Mersa Brega was a harder nut to crack but fell on 1 April, after which Rommel divided his force, sending separate columns towards Benghazi, Msus and Mechili. All three were successful, taking Benghazi on 4 April, Derna on the 7th and Mechili on the 8th.

7 Rommel immediately began to organise a drive towards Tobruk which began on 10 April. The first weak attacks were repulsed but the town was isolated, other Commonwealth forces retreating into Egypt. Further attacks on Tobruk, on 13–17 April, were again repulsed, as were those of 1 and 2 May. On 5 May, Rommel settled down to a siege of Tobruk.

8 On 6 April the Germans attacked Greece and Yugoslavia. On the 12th the Commonwealth troops in Greece began to fall back and on the 21st it was decided to evacuate the country completely. This began in earnest on the 24th, the last troops leaving on the 29th. Evacuated troops were landed on Crete.

9 On 15 May, in Operation BREVITY, Wavell attempted a minor offensive to improve his positions, as a preliminary to more ambitious operations. The main aim was to clear Halfaya Pass, just south-east of Sollum and thus gain access to the open Cyrenaican plateau. Halfaya Pass was taken but a drive beyond was repulsed on the 16th.

10 On 20 May German paratroopers landed in Crete. Commonwealth forces fared badly and evacuation was authorised on the 27th. All those able to escape had left by the 29th.

11 On 27 May Rommel retook Halfaya Pass but this did not deter Churchill from insisting that Wavell attempt his more ambitious counter-offensive, Operation BATTLEAXE, which began on 15 June. Only one of Wavell's three thrusts had any success and his armour was badly handled by German anti-tank guns. As Rommel began to concentrate his own armour for a counter-punch, on the 16th, Wavell decided to pull back.

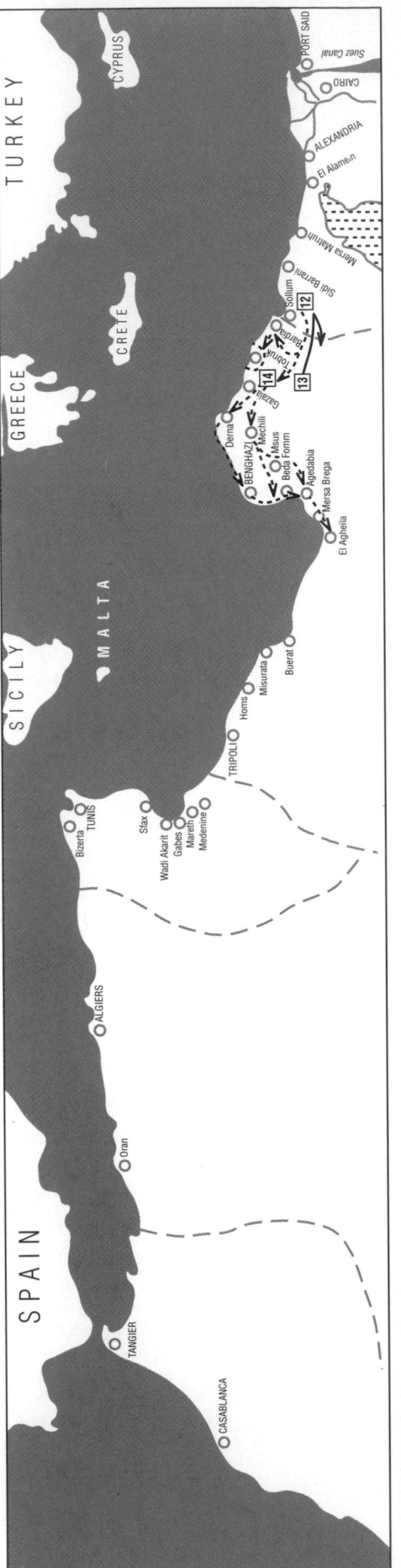

Map 7 North Africa (iii): The Reconquest of Cyrenaica November 1941-January 1942

NOTES TO MAP 7

12 From mid-June to mid-November 1941 both sides concentrated on building up their strength, the Commonwealth forces, now under Auchinleck, being determined to launch yet another offensive against the Sollum–Halfaya positions and raise the siege of Tobruk. This offensive, Operation CRUSADER, began on 18 November. Sollum and Bardia were to be masked while the main forces drove towards Tobruk. This main drive became hopelessly dispersed and British armour was brought to battle piecemeal around Sidi Rezegh.

13 British losses were heavy and their forces became extremely disorganised. On 24 November Rommel decided the time was ripe for an ambitious counter-offensive of his own and he sent both German armoured divisions off in a 'dash to the wire' along the Egyptian frontier. Eighth Army began to lose control and contemplated withdrawal, but Auchinleck insisted on a stand along the frontier and by the 28th Rommel had been checked.

14 In the meantime the siege of Tobruk had been lifted by the Sollum-Bardia masking force which had quietly moved along the coast. Though Rommel briefly reimposed it on 1 December, his heavy losses obliged him to withdraw a week later. By the end of the month his mobile forces had retraced their steps to El Agheila and the garrisons at Bardia and Halfaya were abandoned to their fate, being captured in the first half of January 1942.

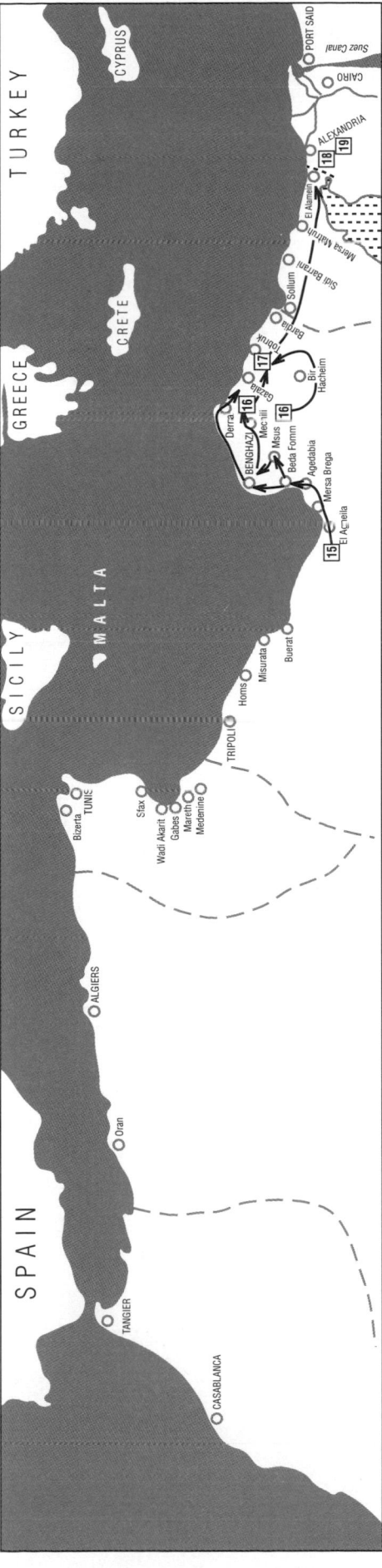

Map 8 North Africa (iv): Eighth Army Pushed Back into Egypt January-September 1942

NOTES TO MAP 8

15 British success was shortlived, however. On 21 January Rommel counter-attacked and soon pushed British forces back to Agedabia which fell the next day. On the 25th large numbers of British tanks were lost in fighting around Msus and on the 29th Benghazi was abandoned. On 1 February Eighth Army was ordered to withdraw to the Gazala line. Derna was evacuated on the 3rd and Rommel halted temporarily, between Mechili and the coast, on the 7th. Both sides now concentrated on building up their strengths.

16 On 26 May Rommel attacked, sending his armour to the south of Bir Hacheim to outflank the British. The latter had anticipated this move but their armour was nevertheless badly dispersed and Rommel crashed through into the rear of their line. Eighth Army blunted his momentum, though at the cost of very heavy casualties, and Rommel was forced to consolidate his armour in the 'Cauldron', half-way between Bir Hacheim and Gazala, on the 30th. Here he awaited the British tanks, which duly attacked on 5 June and were severely handled.

17 On 11 June Rommel counter-attacked out of the Cauldron, and smashed British ripostes in the Knightsbridge area. Between 13 and 16 June Eighth Army was forced to abandon any hope of forming a new line west of Tobruk and on the 17th lost yet more tanks in an abortive attack at Sidi Rezegh. Tobruk was now under siege again and surrendered on the 21st. Eighth Army withdrew to Mersa Matruh in confusion and despite a substantial inflow of reinforcements was unable to hold Rommel. Mersa Matruh was given up on the 27th and a firm position was not established until El Alamein was reached on the 30th.

18 Here Auchinleck determined to stand fast and between 1 and 4 July broke up the attacks of the exhausted German armour on Ruweisat Ridge. Fierce attacks and counter-attacks continued in this area until 22 July when Rommel decided that his forces were now too weak, and both sides paused to rest and regroup, protecting their positions with extensive minefields.

19 On 30 August Rommel attacked again, once more trying to swing to the south of the British line and cut their forces off from the rear. Auchinleck and his successor, Montgomery, had both been prepared for such a move and the bulk of the British armour was placed to the south of their line to fend off such a thrust. This it did, diverting the German attack north into heavy defences on Alam Halfa Ridge. On 2 September Rommel was obliged to pull back to his start line.

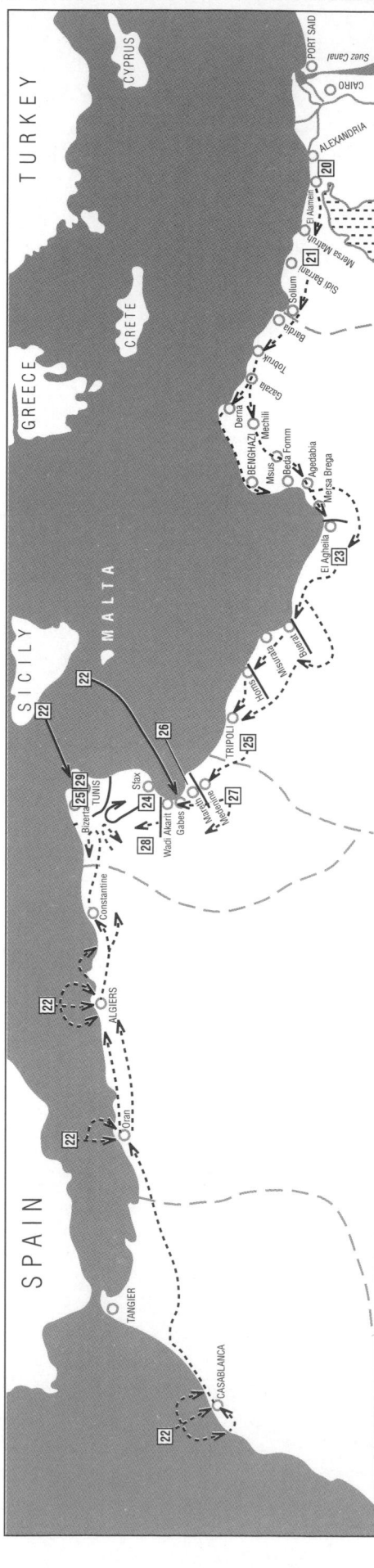

Map 9 North Africa (v): The Slow Squeeze October 1942-May 1943

NOTES TO MAP 9

20 On 23 October 1942 Montgomery attacked the German positions at El Alamein and after hard fighting managed to force Rommel to begin withdrawing on 2 November.

21 Eighth Army followed up in rather dilatory fashion, taking Tobruk on 12 November, Mechili and Derna on the 17th, and Benghazi on the 19th, but conspicuously failing to cut Rommel's retreat. El Agheila was reached on the 23rd but Rommel's line was not attacked until 13 December, upon which he promptly withdrew, easily evading Montgomery's attempt to outflank him.

22 Meanwhile, on 8 November, the Anglo-American First Army, in Operation TORCH, had landed in French North Africa. Resistance by Vichy forces was light but the Allies were unable to push through to Tunis itself before the Germans had lifted in substantial numbers of troops. Allied spearheads got to within 20 miles of Tunis, at Djedeida, on 28 November but were thrown back by German counter-attacks on the next day. German counter-attacks continued and by 25 December they had stabilised a front running between Cape Serrat–Medjez el Bab–Bou Arada–Maknassy–El Guettar, though neither side was in strength south of Bou Arada.

23 On 29 December advanced elements of Eighth Army came up against German defences at Buerat, where Rommel had arrived on the 17th. Montgomery halted to regroup and did not move again until 15 January 1943. Rommel was then forced to withdraw but once again evaded encirclement. On 19 January a fall-back position at Homs was outflanked and Rommel once again had to retire. The British entered Tripoli on 23 January and by 4 February their spearheads had crossed the Tunisian frontier. By 15 February the last of Rommel's rearguards had entered a new defensive line at Mareth.

24 In mid-January, after inconclusive attacks up and down the line, First Army resolved to seize the passes through the eastern Dorsales and establish themselves on a line Fondouk–Faid–Maknassy–El Guettar, to lay the ground for a major offensive in March. The Germans, however, decided to strike first, Rommel being particularly afraid that his positions at Mareth might be attacked from the rear. On 14 February he launched an armoured drive against Feriana and Sbeitla. On the 18th he stormed the Kasserine Pass and by the 22nd had spearheads at Thala and Sbiba. By then, however, his attack had lost virtually all momentum and on the 23rd he began to pull back. Yet again he easily evaded Allied pursuit.

25 On 26 February, after Rommel had begun to withdraw, the German forces in the Tunis perimeter, under von Arnim, belatedly attacked British positions in northern Tunisia. This thrust was held, whilst to the south, by 2 March, Eighth Army had advanced almost to the Mareth Line, where it established its own defensive line at Medenine.

26 On 6 March Rommel's forces attacked Eighth Army in the Medenine position but were easily repulsed.

27 On 20 March Montgomery began a major offensive against the Mareth Line. After he had developed an outflanking move, on the 23rd, and with increasing pressure from U.S. units around Maknassy and Fondouk, German forces withdrew to Wadi Akarit by the 27th.

28 On 5 April Montgomery attacked the Wadi Akarit positions and by the 7th Axis forces were in retreat. Eighth Army spearheads made contact with U.S. forces advancing from the east, on the Gafsa road. On the 10th Sfax was entered though Montgomery still proved incapable of actually cutting Rommel off. On the 14th his remnants took up their final defensive positions at Enfidaville.

29 On 20 April an attack on Enfidaville failed. The main push, however, was made by First Army, with reinforcements from the Eighth, attacking from Medjez el Bab. This was Operation VULCAN, which began on 22 April. Hopelessly outnumbered and almost totally bereft of supplies, the Axis perimeter was slowly pushed back. On 4 May more forces were withdrawn from Eighth Army, which had still made little progress against the Enfidaville positions, and on the 6th these were incorporated into Operation STRIKE, another direct thrust for Tunis along the Medjez el Bab road. Axis defences were overwhelmed and on 12 May von Arnim surrendered.

• **MAP 9** • NORTH AFRICA 1942–1943•

SWITZERLAND

AUSTRIA

YUGOSLAVIA

CORSICA

SARDINIA

Lake
Maggiore

Lake
Como

Lake Garda

MILAN

Brescia

Turin

Pavia

Parma

R. PO

Genoa

La Spezia

Modena

Ferrara

Bologna

Imola

R. RENO

Faenza

Ravenna

Rimini

RIVER SAVIO
RIVER MARECCHIO
RIVER MARANO

Pistoia

Pisa

R. ARNO

Leghorn

Florence

Arezzo

Sienna

Cecina

Lake
Trasimone

Perugia

Lake
Bolsena

Orvieto

Spoleto

Terni

Rieti

R. TIBER

ROME

Avezzano

Anzio

Cassino

Mignano

Mt. Comino

Sparanise

GUSTAV LINE

R. LIRI

R. VOLTURNO

Piedimonte

Benevento

Naples

Avellino

Salerno

Melfi

Potenza

Foggia

Borletto

Bari

Brindisi

Taranto

R. ORFANTO

R. FORTONE

R. BIFERNO

R. TRIGNO

R. SANGRO

Vasto

Termoli

Orsogna

Ortona

Pescara

RIVER MORO

R. PESCARA

R. CHIENTI

R. ESINO

Ancona

Pesaro

RIVER METAURO

GOTHIC LINE

Innsbruck
Brenner
Pass

Trento

R. ADIGE

Verona

Padua

Venice

Trieste

R. ADIGE

GOTHIC LINE

GOTHIC LINE

Trapani

Marsala

Corleone

Porto Empedocle

Licata

Gela

Scoglitti

Pachino

Avola

Syracuse

Augusta

Catania

Mt. Etna

Scaletta

Messina

Sant'Agata

Cefalu

Termini

Palermo

Caltanisetta

Enna

Caltagirone

Nicosia

Troina

Agira

KEY

10	Allied Armies
6 It	Axis and German Armies
- - ▶	Main Allied attacks/advance
⟶	German counter-attacks
6	See number in notes

36

• MAP 10 • ITALY 1943-45 •

Map 10 Italy 1943-45

NOTES TO MAP 10

1 On 9/10 July 1943, Alexander's 15th Army Group, comprising Seventh US and Eighth British Armies, landed in Sicily, at the beginning of the Operation HUSKY. The British met little opposition, taking Augusta on the 13th, but Patton's Seventh Army was heavily counter-attacked on the 11th and 12th. It resumed its advance on the 14th and on the 15th sent one corps westward and another north. Montgomery's Eighth army, meanwhile, took Caltigirone on the 16th but ran into heavy opposition south of Catania. Seventh Army pressed on along its twin axes, taking Porto Empedocle on the 17th and Caltanisetta on the following day.

2 On 19 July, Montgomery put the main weight of his attack further inland, towards Agira, and on his left flank Enna was taken on the 20th. Patton, against little opposition, made considerable progress on both axes, taking Corleone on the 21st, Palermo on the 22nd, and Trapani and Termini on the 23rd. On the 24th, Cefalu also fell but in the centre of the island an American thrust towards Nicosia and a British to Agira had made only limited progress by the 27th.

3 Agira and Nicosia fell on the 28th but this in no way presaged a major breakthrough. German positions in the north-east of the island were extremely strong. Troina held out against the Americans until 6 August at which time the British were still held south of Catania and Mount Etna. On the northern coast Sant'Agata did not fall until the 8th.

4 On 17 August, American troops entered Messina a few hours ahead of the British. The last ten days fighting had been extremely slow and bitter, and the satisfaction of having liberated Sicily was tempered by the fact that 40,000 German and 62,000 Italian troops had succeeded in evacuating across the Straits of Messina. Allied air and naval forces were unable to interdict this evacuation, whilst senior commanders gave little thought to mounting an immediate pursuit into mainland Italy.

5 On 3 September, Eighth Army landed at Reggio Calabria and by the 8th had pushed up to the top of the Italian 'instep', the Germans simply falling back in front of them. Montgomery then paused until the 13th.

6 On 9 September, Fifth US Army, under General Mark Clark, landed at Salerno and Kesselring, commanding Army Group C, ordered all units in southern Italy to fall back to nip out this bridgehead. The Italian government surrendered, having first opened negotiations on 25th July. On the same day, British paratroopers were shipped ashore at Taranto. These latter took Brindisi on 11 September and Bari on the 14th.

7 Between 13 and 15 September the Germans launched determined but understrength counter-attacks against the Allied bridgeheads. All were decisively repulsed thanks to heavy ground, air and naval gunfire.

8 On 13 September, Montgomery resumed his advance, making first contact with Fifth Army patrols on the 16th. On this same day, contact was also made with the Taranto force, whilst Potenza was taken on the 20th.

9 On 17th September, Kesselring ordered von Vietinghoff, commanding Tenth Army, to begin pulling back towards the Gustav Line. This withdrawal was slow and measured, however, involving numerous demolitions on roads and bridges, and it was not until the 27th that Allied vanguards pushed through into the plain of Naples. The city itself was occupied on 1 October. Fifth Army drew up to the Volturno by the 8th, having taken Avellino on 30 September and Benevento on 3 October.

10 On 22 September, British reinforcements landed at Bari and a mixed group of armour and infantry pushed on to Foggia, whose important airfields were taken on the 27th. On Eighth Army's left wing Melfi was also taken on the 27th and troops pushed northward to screen Foggia from the west. By 2 October, Eighth Army had moved up to the Biferno.

11 Between 10 and 30 September, the Germans evacuated their garrisons from Corsica and Sardinia.

12 On 2/3 October, Eighth Army began an assault crossing of the Biferno whilst commandos were landed at Termoli. German reinforcements were rushed across from the Volturno and it was only on the 7th, after fierce fighting, that the Germans decided to pull back across the Trigno. Eighth Army did not follow closely behind them and on the 11th Montgomery began regrouping his forward troops.

13 On 12/13 October, Fifth Army began a major assault across the Volturno. British units near the coast made little progress though the Americans, further inland, did somewhat better. Nevertheless, the Germans conceded ground only reluctantly and Piedimonte was not taken until 20 October and Sparanise until the 23rd. Not until 2 November did advance elements of Fifth Army reach the Garigliano, near the coast, whilst in the centre a major assault against Monte Camino and Mignano could not be launched until the 5th. By the 12th, this attack had still made very little progress. On the 15th, these attacks were halted by Clark.

14 On 14 October, Montgomery resumed his advance towards the Trigno and on the 22nd he attacked across it, securing a small bridgehead. This bridgehead came under serious pressure until 2 November when a more concerted assault across the river was made. By the 4th the Germans had begun pulling back towards the Sangro, getting the last of their troops across by the 19th.

Eighth Army was unable to cut off any of the retreating Germans and though a few of its units crossed the Sangro on 15 November, a full-scale offensive was not launched until the 28th. By the 30th the Germans had been driven off the first major mountain line north of the Sangro but Eighth Army did not close up to the Moro until 6 December. This river was crossed in strength between the 8th and the 10th. But fierce German resistance in Orsogna and Ortona, coupled with ever more appalling weather conditions, brought Allied attacks to a virtual standstill. Though Arielli, to the east of Orsogna was taken on the 23rd and Ortona was finally cleared on the 28th, after a week's vicious street-fighting, Orsogna continued to hold out. Eighth Army's offensive was closed down for the winter on the 28th and Montgomery left Italy to take charge of the cross-Channel assault, being replaced by General Oliver Leese.

15 On 5 December, Fifth Army resumed its attacks on Monte Camino and around Mignano. Monte Camino was finally secured on 6 December and on the 7th attacks began to the north of Mignano against Monte Sammucro and San Pietro. The former finally fell on 17 December, the latter on the following day. Not until 15 January 1944, however, did Fifth Army manage to draw up to the Gustav Line, running along the Garigliano though Cassino town and Monte Cassino.

On 18 January, Fifth Army began its assault on the Gustav Line, opening the first round of a six-month battle, soon to be known as the battle of Cassino. The main stages were:

a) An attack by British X Corps south of the Liri, on 18 January. A bridgehead across the river was established but it proved impossible to force a way into the Liri Valley proper.

b) An attack to the north of Cassino by the French Expeditionary Corps, beginning on 21 January. This was intended to exploit through to the north-east of Monte-Cassino, to outflank the German position there, but was unable to penetrate the Gustav Line.

c) An attack across the Garigliano just north of the Liri (the river here was technically known as the Rapido) by 36 US Division, launched on 20 January. This was another attempt to pave the way for exploitation up the Liri Valley but it did not even succeed in establishing a single bridgehead across the Garigliano and was called off on the 22nd.

d) An attack on Monte Cassino, from the north-east, by 34 US and later 36 US Divisions. This began on 24 January and drove to within a few hundred yards of the monastery before bad weather and terrible losses brought the attack to a halt on 12 February. Renewed diversionary attacks by the French, further to the north, also failed to make a decisive breakthrough. These lasted from 25 January to 3 February.

e) Monte Cassino now became the focus of Allied attention and two further assaults were launched by the New Zealand Corps, brought over from Eighth Army's sector. Both failed, taking place between 15 and 18 February and 15 and 23 March. During the first attack, Cassino Monastery was heavily bombed and during the second Cassino town, but in each case the bombardment only served to hinder the Allies.

16 One reason for the assaults across the Garigliano had been to direct German attention away from the coast where, on 22 January, VI US Corps came ashore at Anzio. Certain planners had envisaged a swift thrust from this beachhead towards Rome, but the cautious attitude of Clark and his local commander, as well as the speed with which the Germans activated another Army headquarters (Fourteenth) and supplied it with miscellaneous units, held the Allies within a restricted defensive perimeter. Fierce German counter-attacks between 16 and 21 February were repulsed but VI Corps found itself limited to a static defence posture until a decisive breach could be made elsewhere.

17 During April and May 1944, Alexander brought across most of the remainder of the Eighth Army from the Adriatic coast and began a build-up of forces for a full-scale offensive up the Liri Valley. This finally began on 11 May all along the Garigliano as far as Monte Cassino. At first progress was extremely slow, the Polish Corps being particularly severely handled on Monte Cassino itself. The decisive breakthrough was made by the French in supposedly impenetrable mountains between the Liri Valley and the coast, and once the Germans began to fall back here, on the 13th, the Gustav Line became untenable in the long term. Despite a delaying action on the Hitler Line, from 19 to 23 May, the Germans had little choice but to fall slowly back towards Rome.

On 23 May, the Anzio beachhead forces entered the battle in earnest, beginning a major attack that aimed to cut across Tenth Army's line of retreat. On the 26th, however, General Clark switched his main axis of attack north-westwards, towards Rome, and abandoned any real effort to cut off Tenth Army. With Eighth Army becoming badly bogged down in traffic jams in the Liri Valley, and the more mobile French denied permission to cut in front of Eighth Army, the Germans were able to slowly pull back ahead of the Allied spearheads. Though Rome fell to Fifth Army on 4 June, very few German troops were intercepted.

18 On 7 June, Alexander ordered Fifth and Eighth Armies to make haste towards Pisa and Florence, in an attempt to head the Germans off at the Arno and prevent then manning a strong defensive line covering the approaches to Bologna. In fact, it was the Germans who largely dictated the speed of the Allied advance, only allowing Eighth Army to take Avezzano on 10 June, Orvieto on the 14th, Terni on the 15th, Spoleto on the 16th and Perugia on the 20th. Between 19 and 27 June, it was held up in front of the Albert Line, around Lake Trasimeno, and though Fifth Army went on to take Cecina and Sienna on 1 and 3 July, the advance then slowed again in front of firm defences south of the Arno. Arezzo did not fall until 16 July, Leghorn until the 19th, whilst neither Pisa nor Florence were completely cleared until 12 August. The whole line of the Arno was not properly secured until the end of that month.

19 Eighth Army resumed its advance in early June 1944, the Germans pulling back from the River Pesara on the 7th. On 17 June, the Polish Corps took over operations in this sector with instructions to take Ancona as quickly as possible. Although baulked on the Chienti in the last week of June, the Polish advance was resumed on the 30th and Ancona itself fell on 18 July. The Cesano was crossed on 10 August and the Poles drew up to the south bank of the Metauro by the 22nd.

20 On 10 August Alexander dropped a plan for a dual thrust in the centre by both Fifth and Eighth Armies, towards Bologna, and opted for a more disparate effort, with Eighth Army attacking first, on the Adriatic coast, and Fifth Army following later in the centre, when German reserves had been drawn eastwards. Eight Army's assault across the Metauro, on the outskirts of the German Gothic Line, opened on 25 August. The Foglia was reached on the 29th, by which time Eighth Army was up against the Gothic Line proper. By 2 September the eastern half of this Line had been overrun, but then Eighth Army ran into fierce German resistance on the Gemmano and Coriano ridges, between the Gothic Line and the Marano, and it was not until the 17th that all resistance in front of the Marano finally ceased.

21 On 10 September, Alexander launched Fifth Army against the western end of the Gothic Line, though it was not until the 22nd that the vital Futa and Il Giogio Passes, on the route to Bologna, were finally secured. Futa Pass had been the first to fall, on the 17th, and rather than press for Bologna as originally planned, Clark attempted on the 20th to cut behind the Germans facing Eighth Army, through Imola and Faenza.

22 This axis seemed to offer opportunities because of Eighth Army's slow progress in the east. On the 18th and 19th, an attack across the Marano had failed and Kesselring had pulled behind the Marecchio on the 20th. Rimini fell to Eighth Army on the 21st and the leading troops crossed the Marecchio. The Uso was in turn crossed on the 25th but by 2 October, Tenth Army had established firm positions behind the Fiumicino. This was not crossed by Eighth Army until 9 October, whilst the Savio was not reached until the 21st and there the Germans held firm yet again.

23 Fifth Army's push towards Imola and Faenza, however, made only very limited progress and on the 28th Clark switched his main axis of attack back towards Bologna. By 2 October he was only twenty miles short of the city. The advance was resumed on the 15th and by the following day US vanguards were only ten miles short. But heavy casualties, appalling weather, difficult terrain and shortages of ammunition all combined to rob Fifth Army of its momentum and despite further small advances on 20 and 23 October, the Fifth Army offensive had to be closed down on the 28th.

24 Eighth Army's drive did not close down at the end of October, but its operations during the rest of 1944 were aimed more at drawing level with Fifth Army than with achieving any decisive breakthrough. The Savio was crossed on 7 November and the Lamone reached on the 16th. On 4 December, Ravenna was taken and on the 16th Faenza finally fell. By now, however, the Germans were safely behind the Senio and

• MAP 10 • ITALY 1943-45 •

with the complete breakdown of the weather, all Allied attacks were halted on the 29th.

25 In effect, both sides now took to winter quarters and no significant attacks were launched until the following spring. On the eastern coast, between 1 and 5 April, Eighth Army secured jumping-off positions to the south of Lake Comachio. The plan was to strike via the Argenta Gap, so-called because it avoided the endless series of rivers and canals (the Santerno, Sillaro, Fossa Quaderno, Idice, Fossa Cembalina, none of which are marked on the map) between the Senio and Bologna, but the first attacks were diversionary, launched between Lake Comachio and the sea. On 5 April, a further diversionary attack was carried out by Fifth Army along the western coast.

26 On 9 April, Eighth Army attacked in earnest, towards Ferrara via the Argenta Gap, and towards Bologna via Imola. By the 12th it had got bridges across the Santerno and was also pushing along the north bank of the Reno. On 14 April, Fifth Army joined in the offensive, on either side of the roads to Bologna from Florence and Pistoia. On 17 April, Argenta fell, the attack being assisted by amphibious flanking moves across Lake Comachio on 11 and 13 April. Other Eighth Army troops were across the Sillaro and moving towards Bologna. On 21 April, this city fell to Eighth Army and troops from Fifth Army also entered a few hours later. On the 22nd, Fifth Army took Modena and on the following day advanced units from both Armies reached the Po. On the 24th, Ferrara fell and Allied units began to stream across the Po in force. On the western coast, La Spezia also fell.

27 By now German resistance had almost totally collapsed and in the days before the German surrender in Italy, on 29 April (ratified by von Vietinghoff on 1 May), the Allies poured through northern Italy almost unopposed. On the 25th, Parma and Verona fell and on the following day Eighth Army crossed the Adige. On the 27th, Genoa was taken, on the 28th Brescia and on the 29th Padua and Venice. Yugoslav partisans entered Trieste on 1 May, followed by Eighth Army on the next day. Also on the 2nd, Fifth Army entered Milan and Turin, and on the 4th linked up with Seventh US Army at the Brenner Pass.

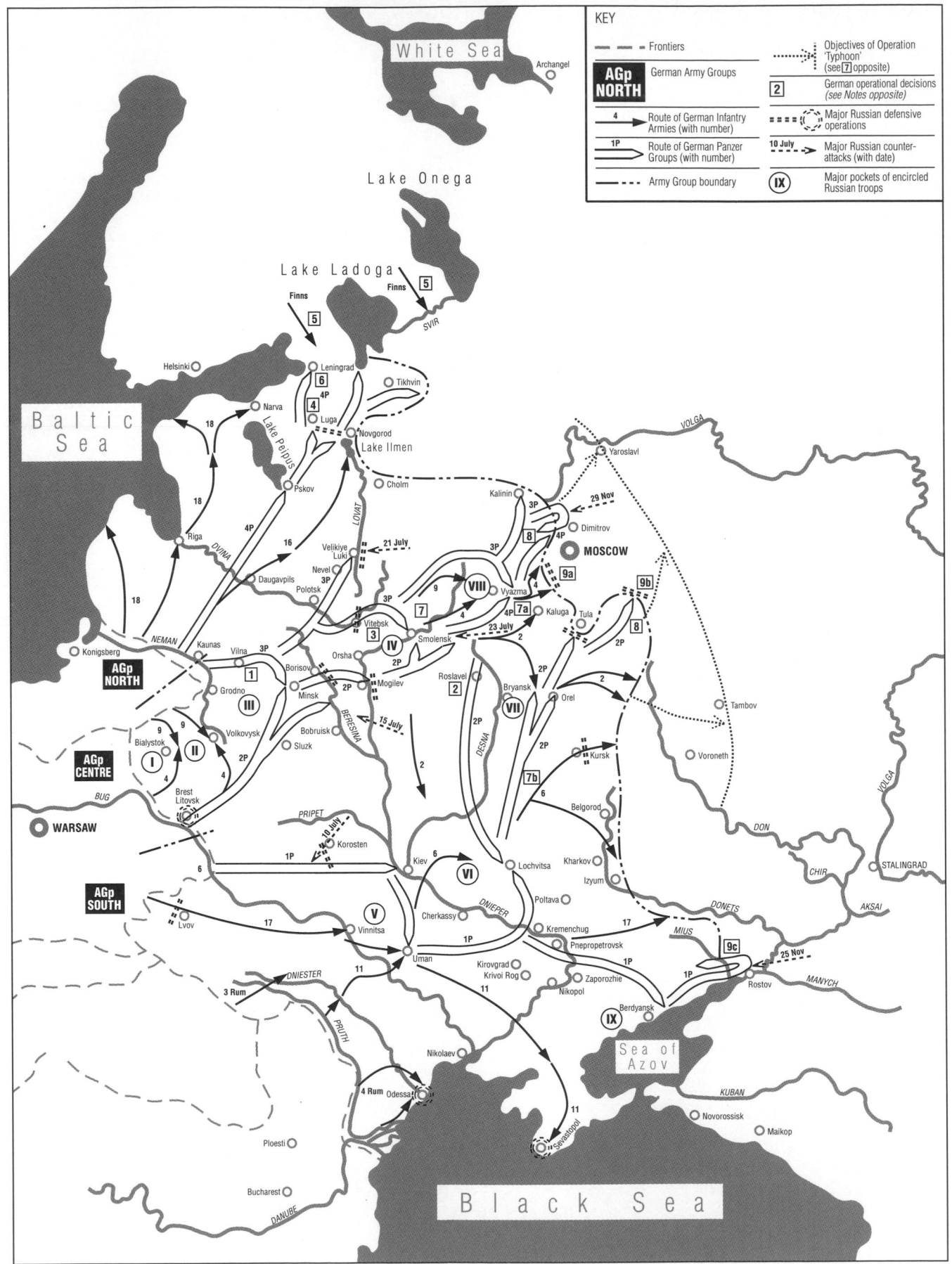

Map 11 The Eastern Front (i): Operation Barbarossa 22 June-4 December 1941

• **MAP 11** • THE EASTERN FRONT (i) •

NOTES TO MAP 11

Major pockets of encircled Russian troops

	Formed	Liquidated	Men	Captured Tanks	Guns
(I)	28 June	3 July			
(II)	28 June	5 July	290,000	2,585	1,449
(III)	27 June	9 July			
(IV)	18 July	5 Aug	310,000	2,500	3,000
(V)	2 Aug	8 Aug	100,000	317	858
(VI)	16 Sept	26 Sept	665,000	884	3,714
(VII)	6 Oct	25 Oct			
(VIII)	7 Oct	14 Oct	663,000	1,242	5,412
(IX)	10 Oct	18 Oct	100,000	212	672

Most important German operational decisions

1 **24 June.** 3 Panzer Group (Pz Gp) was refused permission to follow Army Group (A Gp) commander's suggestion that it go directly for Smolensk without completing encirclement of the Minsk pocket. The advance eastward did not begin until 3 July.

2 **19 July.** 2 Pz Gp was ordered south to assist A Gp South in eliminating Soviet forces in the Ukraine. Pz Gp commander prevaricated until 25 August. At this time XXXIX Pz Corps from Pz Gp 3 was sent north to assist in attack on Leningrad.

3 **23 July.** Hitler refused to sanction an advance towards Moscow until Smolensk pocket was liquidated.

4 **24 July.** XLI Pz Corps was halted to wait for LVI Pz Corps to breach Luga/Lake Ilmen gap. It was denied the opportunity to utilise an open road to Leningrad. The advance was not resumed until 8 August when the road was no longer open.

5 **4 September.** Marshal Mannerheim refused to allow Finnish troops either to cross the River Svir or to make more than a demonstration towards Leningrad.

6 **14 September.** Hitler refused to sanction an all-out attack on Leningrad and insisted on reducing it by siege.

17 September. 4 Pz Gp transferred to A Gp Centre (see **7** a).

7 **2 October.** Hitler having now sanctioned a drive towards Moscow, Operation TYPHOON began. First objectives were large encirclements around Vyazma and Bryansk.
a) 4 Pz Gp (see **6**) was to be used in this operation.
b) As was 2 Pz Gp, reallocated to A Gp Centre on 24 September.

8 **15 November.** Attempt to encircle Moscow was resumed, after TYPHOON had bogged down in late October.

9 a) **3 December.** 4 Army, of its own accord, began to make tactical withdrawals.
b) **5 December.** 2 Pz Gp, of its own accord, began to make tactical withdrawals.
c) **1 December.** Hitler was forced to allow 1 Pz Gp to quit Rostov and withdraw behind the River Mius.

NOTES TO MAP 13 (see p 43)

1 **19-23 November.** The Russians attacked to isolate 6 Army at Stalingrad.

2 **16 December to 27 January 1943.** The Russians crushed 8 Italian Army and attacked across the Rivers Chir and Aksai.

3 **14-27 January.** The Russians attacked across the Don to surround 2 German and 2 Hungarian Armies. The reduction of the Stalingrad pocket was completed between 1 January and 2 February.

4 **1-16 February.** The Russians pushed across the Donets and captured Kursk and Kharkov. More southerly formations were directed towards Rostov and Mariupol.

5 **27 January to 1 February.** 1 Pz Ay completed the evacuation of the Caucasus.

6 **10 February to 19 March.** The Russians pushed towards the Dnieper crossings but were halted by von Manstein's counter-attack on 19 February and then pushed back. The Germans retook Kharkov on 15 March and Belgorod on the 19th. The line stabilised on the Donets and the Mius. 17 Army was pinned in the Taman peninsula.

7 **12-18 January.** The Russians opened a narrow land corridor to Leningrad.

8 **15 January.** The Russians retook Velikiye Luki.

9 **12 February to 21 March.** A Russian offensive to retake Orel failed.

10 **15-28 February.** Russian attacks coincided with a German decision to evacuate the Demyansk salient.

11 **1-24 March.** The Germans evacuated the Rzhev-Vyazma salient.

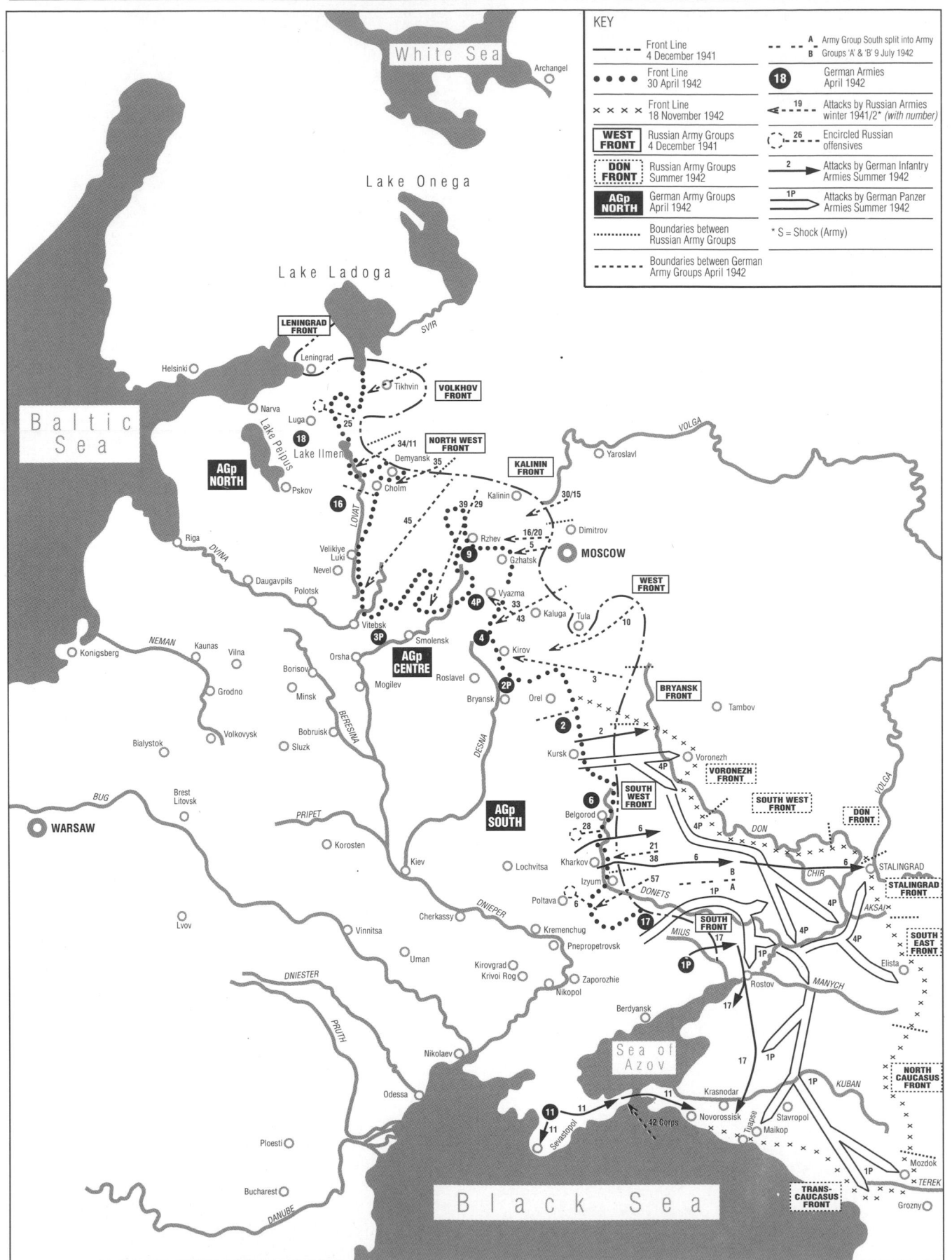

KEY

——— – – –	Front Line 4 December 1941
• • • •	Front Line 30 April 1942
× × × ×	Front Line 18 November 1942*
WEST FRONT	Russian Army Groups 4 December 1941
DON FRONT	Russian Army Groups Summer 1942
AGp NORTH	German Army Groups April 1942
··········	Boundaries between Russian Army Groups
– – – –	Boundaries between German Army Groups April 1942

A – – – B	Army Group South split into Army Groups 'A' & 'B' 9 July 1942
18	German Armies April 1942
◄— 19	Attacks by Russian Armies winter 1941/2* (with number)
⌇⌇ 26	Encircled Russian offensives
—— 2 ►	Attacks by German Infantry Armies Summer 1942
══ 1P ►	Attacks by German Panzer Armies Summer 1942
* S = Shock (Army)	

Map 12 The Eastern Front (ii): The Russian Moscow Counter-offensive December 1941-April 1942 and the German Stalingrad/Caucasus Offensive 28 June-18 November 1942*

* As the two offensives dealt with here are clearly separated geographically and chronologically it was not felt necessary to provide explanatory notes.

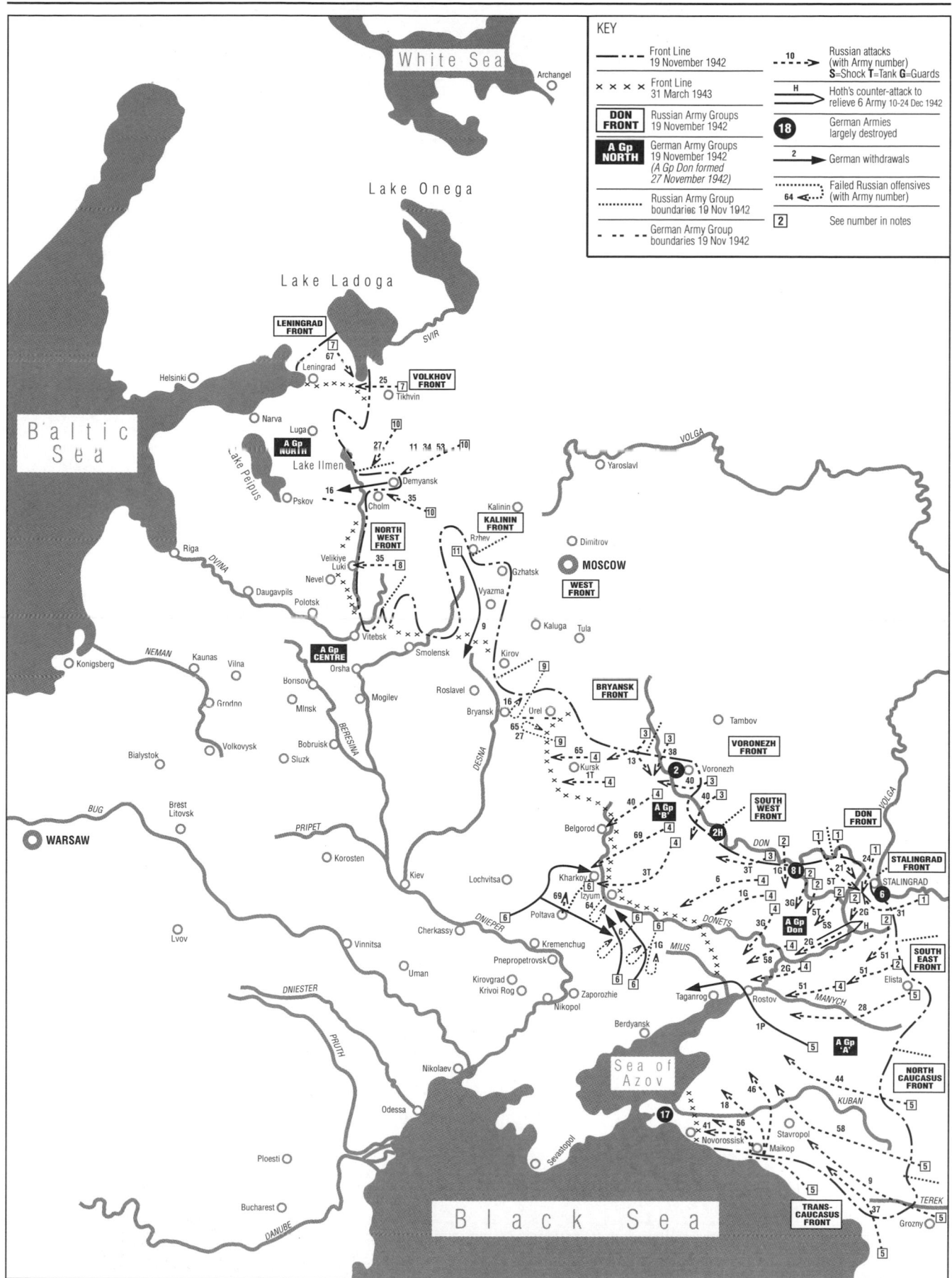

Map 13 The Eastern Front (iii): Russian Counter-offensives 19 November 1942-31 March 1943

(for Notes, see p. 41)

KEY

—·—·— Front Line 4 July 1943	— — — German Army Group boundaries 4 July 1943
× × × Front Line 23 December 1943	**18** German Armies
2 Balt. / **DON FRONT** Russian Army Groups 4 July 1943 (Supernumeraries= new designation October 43)	Russian attacks (with Army number) S=Shock T=Tank G=Guards GT=Guards Tank
A Gp NORTH German Army Groups 4 July 1943 (A Gp South from A Gps 'B' & Don, February 43)	→2 German withdrawals
········· Russian Army Group boundaries 4 July 1943	2 See number in notes opposite
	•••• The Wotan Line

Map 14 The Eastern Front (iv): The Russians Bounce the Dnieper 4 July–23 December 1943

• MAP 14 • THE EASTERN FRONT (iv) •

NOTES TO MAP 14

1 4-13 July 1943. 9 Army and 4 Pz Ay attacked to the north and south of the Kursk salient. Little progress was made.

2 12 July. The Russians counter-attacked against the Orel salient. It was abandoned by the Germans on 1 August.

3 17 July to 2 August. Probing attacks by South-West and South Fronts across the middle Donets and Mius. These were held but pulled German reserves south.

4 3-25 August. Voronezh and Steppe Fronts launched an offensive towards Kharkov and Belgorod. The latter fell on the 5th and the former was abandoned by the Germans on the 23rd. The advance was brought to a temporary halt on the 25th. On the 27th Hitler refused A Gp South requests for a withdrawal to the Dnieper.

5 7 August to 6 September. Repeated attacks by West and Bryansk Fronts towards Smolensk. Yelnya fell on 30 August.

6 11-23 August. Fruitless Russian attacks to widen the breach south of Lake Lagoda.

7 18 August to 8 September. South-West and South Fronts attacked in earnest across the middle Donets and Mius. Taganrog was cut off on the 20th, though the encircled corps broke out at the end of the month. On the 31st Hitler sanctioned the withdrawal of 6 Army and the right wing of 1 Pz Ay. On 8 September A Gp South again requested permission to withdraw behind the Dnieper. Again Hitler refused.

8 26 August to 9 September. Central Front attacked out of the Kursk salient. Progress was slow in the north but 60 Army in the south had spearheads across the Desna on 3 September. Konotop was taken on the 6th and Bakhmach on the 9th.

9 9 September to 9 October. Evacuation of the Taman peninsula authorised on 9 September. It began on the 15th and was completed by 9 October.

10 15-30 September. On the 15th Hitler authorised A Gp South to withdraw behind the Dnieper. Pursuing Soviet forces reached the river on the 21st and had closed up to it between Loev and Dneprpetrovsk by the 30th, obtaining numerous small bridgeheads. Central and Voronezh Fronts advanced to the Kiev area, Steppe Front to Kremenchug. South-West and South Fronts had pursued the Germans to the Wotan Line, between Zaporozhie and Melitopol. The Germans had retained bridgeheads of their own at Dneprpetrovsk and Zaporozhie.

11 23 September to 2 October. On 15 September A Gp Centre had also been given permission to withdraw behind the River Sozh (Panther Line) but it did not begin this movement in earnest until the 23rd, under heavy pressure from the Kalinin and West Fronts. Smolensk and Roslavl were given up on 25 September.

12 7-8 October. Central Front pressed in around Gomel.

13 7-9 October. Kalinin Front (renamed 1 Baltic Front) took Nevel.

14 10 October to 1 November. Russian offensive against the Wotan Line. Zaporozhie was taken by South-West Front (renamed 3 Ukrainian Front) on the 23rd. These Fronts closed up to the Dnieper, isolating the Crimea, by the end of October.

15 16-19 October. Voronezh Front (soon to become 1 Ukrainian Front) attacked from a bridgehead south of Kiev. All attacks were repulsed at high cost.

16 16-30 October. The Russians attempted to cut off German forces in the Dnieper bend, with 3 Ukrainian Front trying to pin them whilst Steppe Front (renamed 2 Ukrainian Front) cut round their rear. Dneprpetrovsk was taken and Krivoi Rog entered on the 23rd but a German counter-attack retook the latter on the 30th. The Germans stabilised the line.

17 3-26 November. 1 Ukrainian Front renewed the attack on Kiev from a new bridgehead to the north. The city fell on the 6th, Zhitomir on the 12th and Korosten on the 17th. Zhitomir was retaken by the Germans on the 18th but a week later bad weather halted further attempts to retake Kiev.

18 8 November to 23 December. 2 Baltic Front pushed into the German rear but failed to take Vitebsk.

19 10 November to 31 December. Central Front (renamed Byelorussian) greatly expanded its bridgehead on the River Sozh (having been baulked earlier, 20-25 October). The Germans evacuated Gomel on 24 November. The front stabilised on 26 December after minor German gains in a counter-attack.

Map 15 The Eastern Front (v): Liberating Leningrad, the Ukraine and the Crimea 24 December 1943-8 May 1944

• **MAP 15** • THE EASTERN FRONT (v) •

NOTES TO MAP 15

[1] 24 December to 25 January 1944. 1 and 2 Ukrainian Fronts attacked A Gp South towards Zhitomir and Kirovograd. Korosten fell on 29 December, Zhitomir on the 31st and Kirovograd on 8 January. A push southwards from Zhitomir was baulked by German counter-attacks in the second half of January.

[2] 14 January to 14 February. A Gp North fell back from Leningrad and Novgorod was taken on 20 January. The siege of Leningrad was officially lifted on the 27th and on the 28th the Germans pulled back to the River Luga.

[3] 25 January to 18 February. After regrouping, 1 and 2 Ukrainian Fronts mounted an offensive to cut off German forces in a pocket around Korsun. Spearheads met on 28 January and the pocket was sealed tight by 2 February. Attempts to relieve it, between 4 and 12 February, failed and on the 15th the troops there were ordered to break out southwards. Several thousand men escaped but almost all their equipment was lost.

[4] 30 January to 1 March. After a failed attack, 10–16 January, 3 and 4 Ukrainian Fronts resumed their offensive towards Nikopol and Krivoi Rog. The former fell on 7 February and the latter on the 22nd. By 1 March 3 Ukrainian Front had drawn up to the River Ingul.

[5] 15 February to 1 March. A Gp North pulled back to the Panther Line. Their front slowly congealed with the coming of the spring thaw.

[6] 4 March to 15 April. 1, 2 and 3 Ukrainian Fronts pressed forward. Between 4 and 11 March, 1 Ukrainian Front pushed south to the Bug, where it was held until 21 March, when it resumed its advance across the Dniester and the Pruth. An eastward thrust towards Brody and Tarnopol ended on 15 April, with the latter taken and the former surrounded. This date also marked the end of the southern advance. Further to the north Kovel had been surrounded by 2 Byelorussian Front, a temporary formation in existence between 24 February and 4 April. In this Front's southern sector Vinnitsa was taken on 20 March. 2 Ukrainian Front, from 5 March, directed its main weight towards Uman, which fell on the 10th. By the 28th 1 Pz Ay was surrounded but it managed to break out to Tarnopol by 9 April. By this time 2 Ukrainian Front was over the Pruth (27 March) and into Rumania, before its advance ran out of steam. 3 Ukrainian Front attacked over the Ingul on 6 March and though its spearheads bogged down short of the Bug, permitting the escape of 6 Army, other formations that had been assigned a holding role were able to break out towards Nikolaev. This city fell on 28 March, permitting a general advance towards Odessa which was taken on 10 April.

[7] 8 April to 9 May. 4 Ukrainian Front and Independent Coastal Army opened an offensive into the Crimea. The Germans withdrew into Sevastopol on 12 April and endured a siege lasting until 9 May. Though many thousands of Germans were evacuated, a full 80,000 were lost as well as all of 17 Army's heavy equipment.

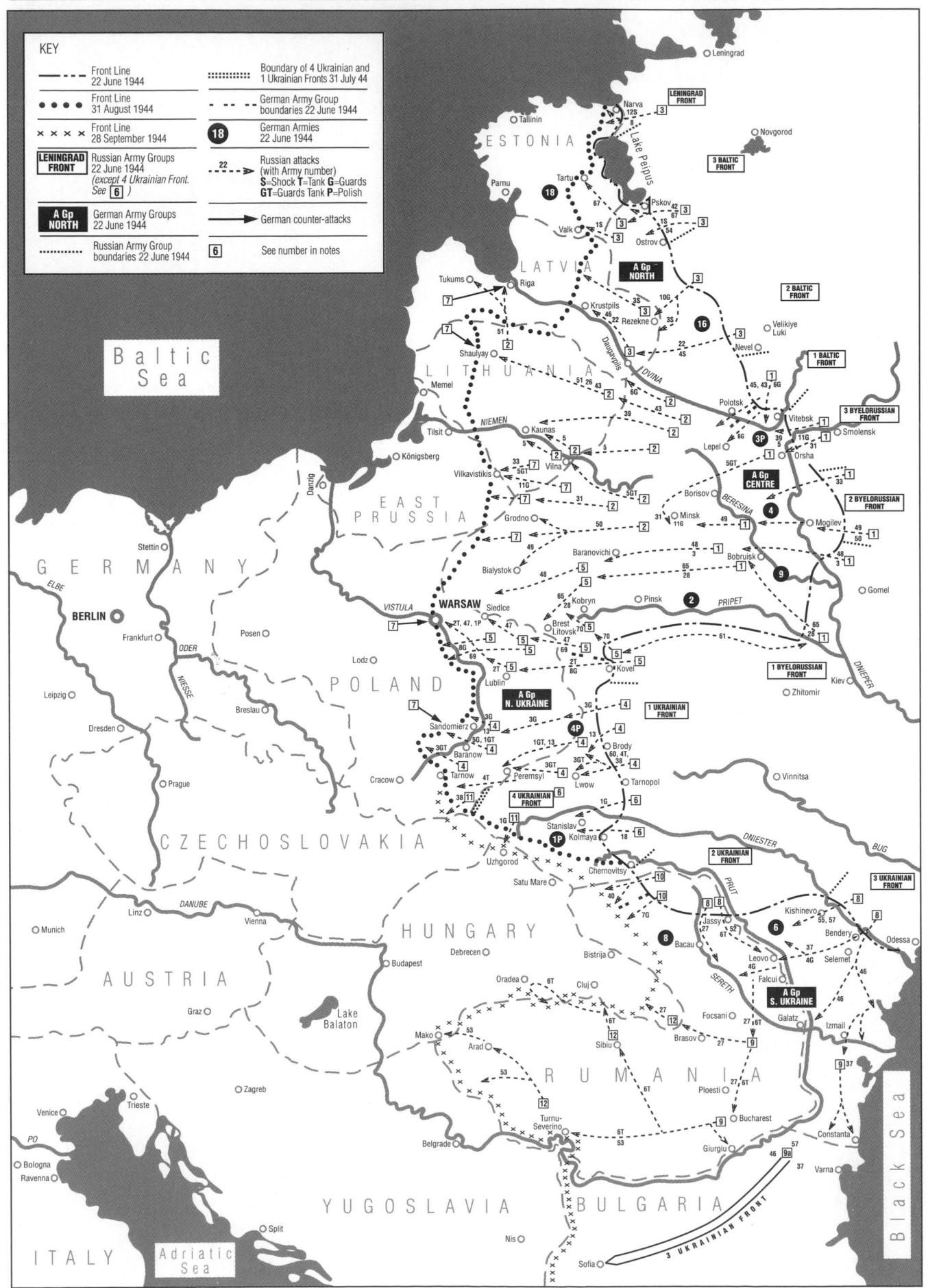

KEY

—·—·—	Front Line 22 June 1944	
●●●●	Front Line 31 August 1944	
××××	Front Line 28 September 1944	

LENINGRAD FRONT — Russian Army Groups 22 June 1944 (except 4 Ukrainian Front. See 6)

A Gp NORTH — German Army Groups 22 June 1944

·········· Russian Army Group boundaries 22 June 1944

·········· Boundary of 4 Ukrainian and 1 Ukrainian Fronts 31 July 44

– – – German Army Group boundaries 22 June 1944

18 German Armies 22 June 1944

22 Russian attacks (with Army number) S=Shock T=Tank G=Guards GT=Guards Tank P=Polish

→ German counter-attacks

6 See number in notes

• MAP 16 • THE EASTERN FRONT (vi) •

Map 16 The Eastern Front (vi): The Destruction of Army Group Centre, the Drive to the Baltic and the Vistula, and the Conquest of Rumania, 22 June-28 September 1944

NOTES TO MAP 16

* 2 Byelorussian Front (see Map v note [6]) was reconstituted on 18 April.

[1] 22 June to 11 July 1944. 1, 2 and 3* Byelorussian Fronts and 1 Baltic Front enveloped Minsk. The operation began with the creation of a pocket on each flank – at Vitebsk, eliminated 25-27 June, and Bobruisk, 26-29 June – and a drive westward in the centre, which took Mogilev on 28 June. Forces from the Vitebsk and Mogilev axes then encircled Minsk. Borisov fell on 1 July and Minsk on the 4th with the pocket to the east of the city being eliminated by the 11th. On the southern axis 1 Byelorussian Front pushed on westward, taking Baranovichi on 8 July. By the 11th A Gp Centre had had 28 divisions destroyed as fighting formations and had suffered upwards of 300,000 casualties.

[2] 12-31 July. 2 and 3 Byelorussian Fronts and 1 Baltic Front pressed on west and north-west. 3 Byelorussian Front encircled Vilna which fell on the 13th and then Kaunas, taken on the 30th. 2 Byelorussian Front followed a parallel axis to the south and took Bialystok on the 29th. 1 Baltic Front headed towards Daugavpils, where the going was slow, and Shaulyay, which was taken on the 27th. The Front then drove north to take Tukums on the 30th and reach the Baltic coast, west of Riga, on the following day.

[3] 10 July to 31 August. The northern Fronts, 2 and 3 Baltic and Leningrad, took up the attack on A Gp North. 2 Baltic led off on 10 July and took Rezekne on the 27th. Daugavpils fell on this same day as 2 Baltic Front lent its support to 1 Baltic. Krustpils was taken on 8 August. 3 Baltic Front began its offensive on 17 July, taking Ostrov on the 21st and Pskov on the 23rd. Progress thereafter was hampered by very difficult terrain, Tartu not falling until 25 August and Valk holding out against repeated Soviet assaults. Leningrad Front attacked on 25 July and smashed into Narva three days later.

[4] 12-29 July. 1 Ukrainian Front was unloosed against A Gp North Ukraine. A pocket formed around Brody was crushed between the 15th and the 22nd and Lwow fell on the 27th. Meanwhile, armoured spearheads had swept forward, taking Peremsyl on the 26th, as well as establishing bridgeheads over the Vistula at Sandomierz and Baranow, on the 28th and 29th.

[5] 18 July to 2 August. 1 Byelorussian Front added its weight to 1 Ukrainian Front's drive into Poland. To the south, Lublin was taken on 23 July and armoured formations then rushed into the suburbs of Warsaw, on the east bank of the Vistula, on the 31st. Bridgeheads over the Vistula, just south of Warsaw, were established in the first two days of August. On its northern flank, 1 Byelorussian Front encircled Brest-Litovsk which fell on 28 July.

[6] 26-31 July. Though the attack on Stanislav, taken on 27 July, was made as part of 1 Ukrainian Front's offensive, the participating armies were then handed over to 4 Ukrainian Front (whose HQ had been inactive since the fall of Sevastopol) which took over the Carpathian sector on 31 July.

[7] 2-31 August. Further progress into Latvia, Lithuania, East Prussia and Poland was very slow. The Russians were beginning to overload their communications system and fierce German counter-attacks brought the advance to a halt. One of these, on 20 August, retook Tukums and opened a corridor through Riga to re-establish contact between A Gps Centre and North. The Warsaw Uprising was suppressed between 1 August and 2 October.

[8] 20-29 August. Progress was far from slow in Rumania, however, where 2 and 3 Ukrainian Fronts opened an offensive against A Gp South Ukraine. Again the aim was encirclement. After the fall of Jassy on 22 August and Bendery on the 23rd, the pocket was sealed around Leovo on the 24th. Elements of 6 and 8 Armies retreating eastwards were cut off by a further envelopment on the Sereth, sealed on 26 August, and most of those trying to withdraw south were overtaken by Russian armoured forces dashing for the Foscani gap, reached on the 27th. Rumanian forces to the south-west of Odessa were also encircled against the Black Sea coast. These various pockets were eliminated by the 29th. The Russian task was considerably simplified by the defection of many Rumanian units, following that country's surrender on 23 August.

[9] 27 August to 8 September. Much of Rumania was speedily occupied by the Russians. Constanta fell on 29 August, Ploesti on the 30th and Bucharest the following day. Armoured units sped on to Turnu Severino and Sebiu, the former being taken on 6 September and the latter on the 7th.

[9a] 8-16 September. 3 Ukrainian Front was despatched into Bulgaria, which quickly declared war on Germany. Sofia was occupied without opposition on the 16th. (46 Army was transferred to 2 Ukrainian Front on 15 September).

[10] 30 August to 24 September. The right flank of 2 Ukrainian Front was brought into action, pushing towards Satu Mare and Bistrija. Progress was slower than expected, however, and the advance slowly ground to a halt.

[11] 9-24 September. 1 and 4 Ukrainian Fronts launched limited offensives to force the Carpathians and drive into Slovakia where a nationalist insurrection had broken out on 29 August. Progress was limited because of the extremely difficult terrain.

[12] 15-28 September. 2 Ukrainian Front was ordered to drive into Hungary but its attacks towards Cluj and Bistrija ran into heavy German opposition. Oradea was taken on the 26th but Soviet forces were driven out again only two days later. Better results were obtained on the left flank, however, with Arad falling on the 22nd and Mako, on the Hungarian border, on the 24th. 2 Ukrainian Front now halted to prepare a renewed attack to the south-east of Cluj.

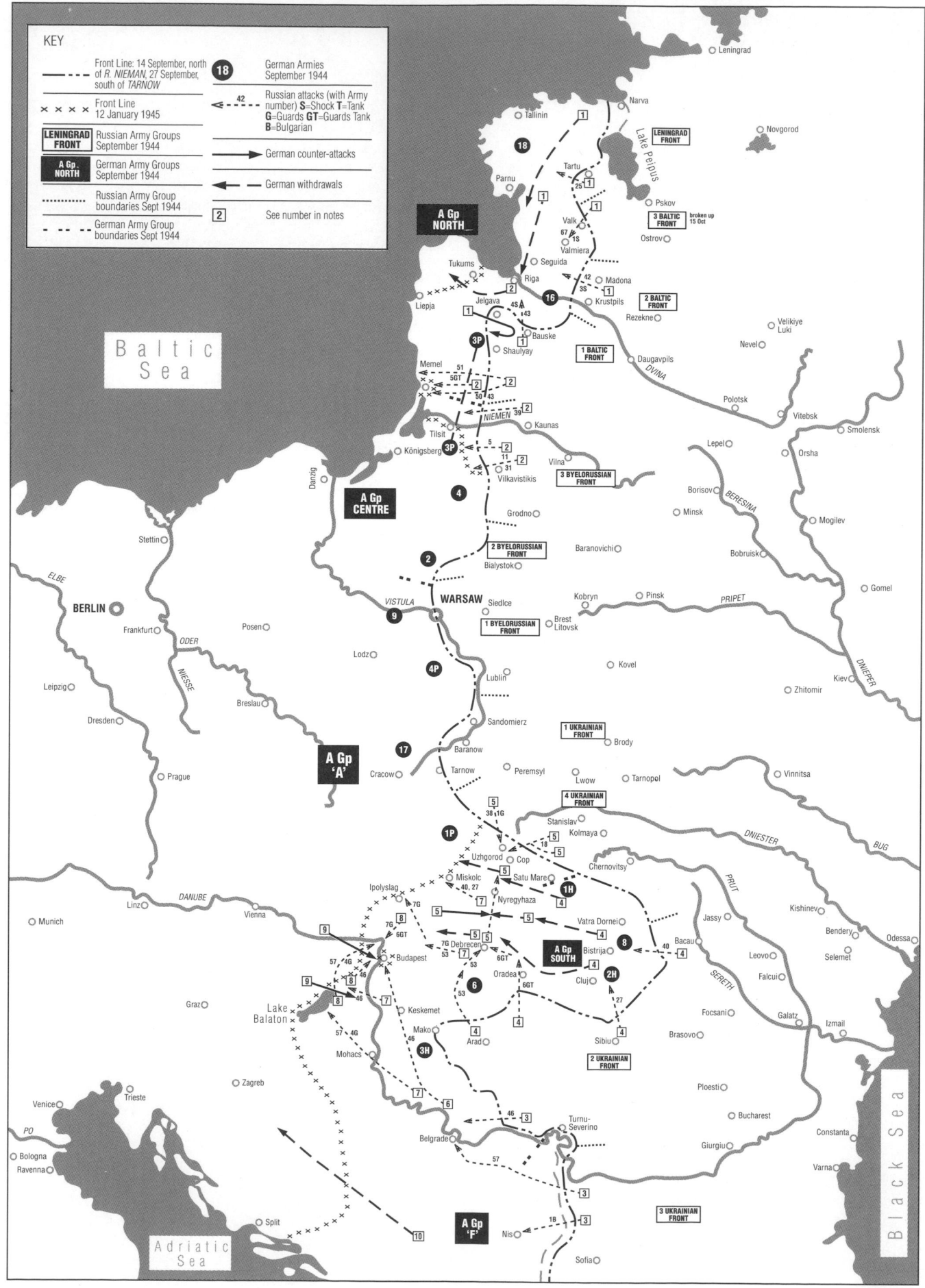

KEY

Front Line: 14 September, north of *R. NIEMAN*, 27 September, south of *TARNOW*

× × × × Front Line 12 January 1945

LENINGRAD FRONT Russian Army Groups September 1944

A Gp. NORTH German Army Groups September 1944

Russian Army Group boundaries Sept 1944

German Army Group boundaries Sept 1944

18 German Armies September 1944

42 Russian attacks (with Army number) **S**=Shock **T**=Tank **G**=Guards **GT**=Guards Tank **B**=Bulgarian

German counter-attacks

German withdrawals

2 See number in notes

• MAP 17 • THE EASTERN FRONT (vii) •

Map 17 The Eastern Front (vii): The Russians Clear the Baltic States and Hungary 14 September 1944 -12 January 1945

NOTES TO MAP 17

1 14-27 September 1944. The Russians attempted to crush A Gp North by cutting the Riga corridor and pushing their four northern Fronts towards the Baltic coast. They were less than successful. The Riga drive, by 1 Baltic Front, came to a halt on 24 September, having been sorely troubled by German counter-attacks between the 17th and 19th. Moreover, neither 2 and 3 Baltic nor Leningrad Fronts were able to reach the coast ahead of German formations withdrawing south (from 17 September). By the 27th all German formations had reached defensive positions around Riga and Russian attacks ceased.

2 25 September to 23 October. The Russians now attempted to cut off A Gp North on the Lithuanian coast and 1 Baltic Front regrouped for this purpose. On 5 October it attacked towards Memel, supported by 3 Byelorussian Front driving towards Tilsit, and by the 10th its northern army had reached the coast. Additional pressure around Riga by 2 and 3 Baltic Fronts forced that city's evacuation on the 11th and the bulk of A Gp North retreated into Courland, behind the Liepaja-Tukums line. Other elements were trapped inside Memel (which held out until 27 January), although 3 Pz Ay had succeeded in slipping one corps in front of 1 Baltic Front's westward thrust. By 23 October it had helped to stabilise a line on the southern bank of the lower Niemen, though this had been seriously threatened by an offensive by 3 Byelorussian Front between the 16th and the 22nd.

3 27 September to 15 October. 3 Ukrainian Front crossed into Yugoslavia, taking Nis and most of Belgrade on 15 October.

4 6-20 October. 2 Ukrainian Front attacked on its left flank towards Oradea and Debrecen which fell on the 12th and 20th respectively. On the 14th A Gp South decided on its own initiative to pull out of the Cluj-Bijistra-Vatra Dornei salient, pursued as it went by 2 Ukrainian Front's right flank armies.

5 20-30 October. Russian armoured elements sent forward from Debrecen took Nyregyhaza on 22 October but were then counter-attacked from both sides of the Theiss. Nyregyhaza was retaken on the 28th and the withdrawal of 8 and 1 and 2 Hungarian Armies over the Theiss continued. The link with Russian armies to the north was made by 4 Ukrainian Front which took Uzhgorod on the 26th. German problems had not been eased by their Hungarian allies who, in response to a defeatist broadcast by Admiral Horthy on the 15th, began to desert in large numbers.

6 30 October to 6 November. Russian 46 Army attacked north, between the Theiss and the Danube, towards Budapest. Keskermet fell on 31 October but the subsequent push to Budapest stalled and 46 Army was halted.

7 11 November to 14 December. After the failure of 46 Army, 2 Ukrainian Front decided to outflank Budapest from the north. The east bank of the Theiss was soon cleared but the offensive had to be discontinued on 26 November, some miles short of Budapest. It was resumed on 5 December and on the 14th Ipolyslag was taken. Meanwhile, 14 and 27 Armies had begun pushing into eastern Slovakia. By this time 3 Ukrainian Front had crossed the Danube and advanced to Lake Balaton, which was reached on 9 December, whilst 46 Army had turned west to take up a position between Lake Balaton and Budapest.

8 20-28 December. Now both Ukrainian Fronts joined in an attempt to encircle Budapest and closed the ring at Esztergom on 26 December. The drive into Budapest itself was halted on the 28th.

9 1 January to 7 February 1945. German counter-attacks on 1 and 17 January made substantial penetrations into the left flank of 3 Ukrainian Front but were unable to break through into Budapest, though Hitler refused to allow its garrison to attempt a break-out. German attacks ground to a halt and on 7 February the major formation, 4 SS Pz Corps (from A Gp Centre), was withdrawn. (Budapest held out until 13 February).

10 10 October to 31 December. A Gp E evacuated Greece and southern Yugoslavia.

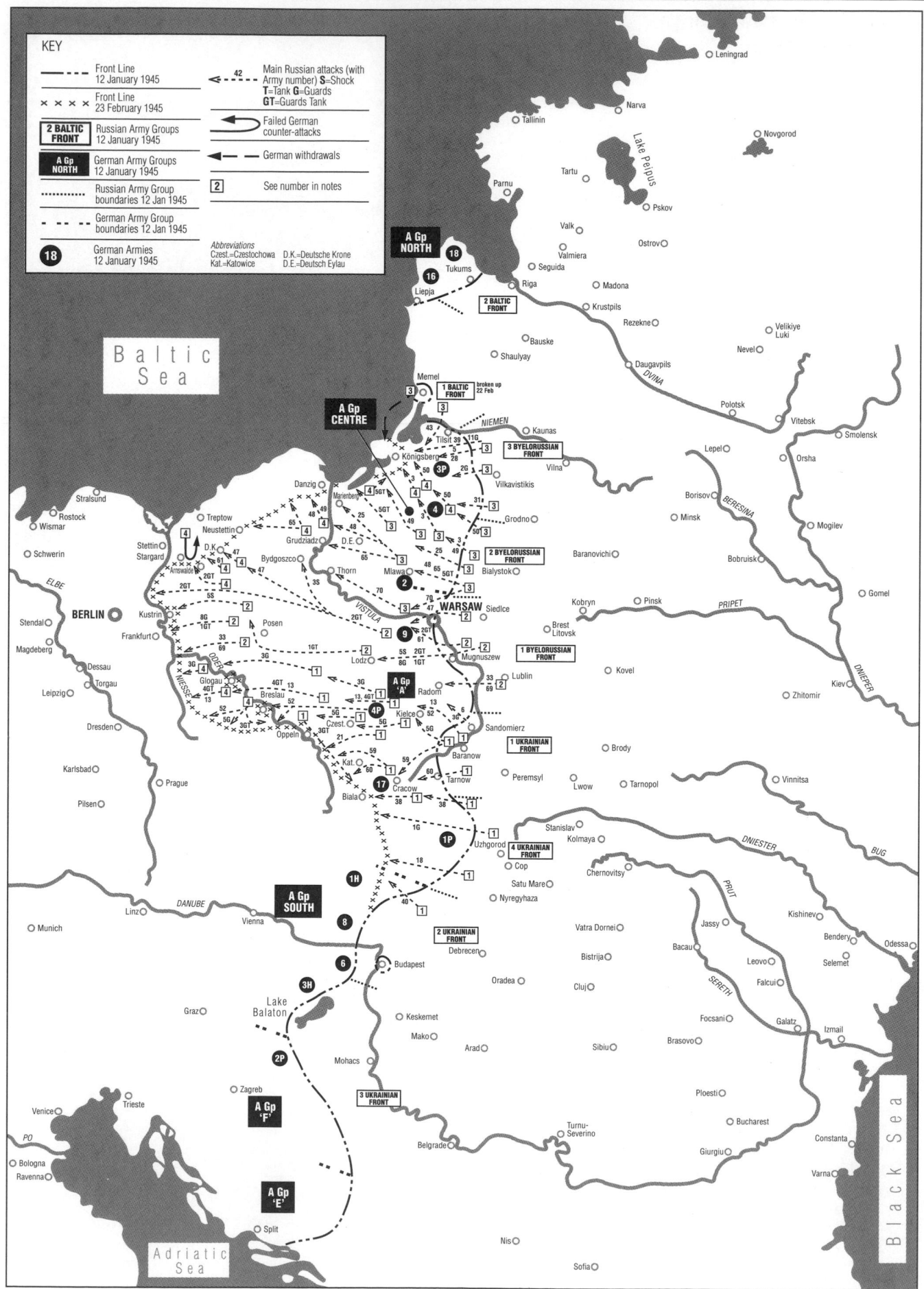

KEY

—— · —— ·	Front Line 12 January 1945
——————	Front Line
× × × ×	Front Line 23 February 1945
2 BALTIC FRONT	Russian Army Groups 12 January 1945
A Gp NORTH	German Army Groups 12 January 1945
·············	Russian Army Group boundaries 12 Jan 1945
— · — · — ·	German Army Group boundaries 12 Jan 1945
18	German Armies 12 January 1945

←---- 42	Main Russian attacks (with Army number) **S**=Shock **T**=Tank **G**=Guards **GT**=Guards Tank
↰	Failed German counter-attacks
←---	German withdrawals
2	See number in notes

Abbreviations
Czest.=Czestochowa   D.K.=Deutsche Krone
Kat.=Katowice   D.E.=Deutsch Eylau

• MAP 18 • THE EASTERN FRONT (viii) •

Map 18 The Eastern Front (viii): The Conquest of East Prussia and the Drive to the Oder-Niesse 12 January-23 February 1945

NOTES TO MAP 18

1 12-25 January 1945. 1 Ukrainian Front drove to the upper Oder. Kielce was cut off and fell on 15 January whilst the southerly push to Cracow saw that city fall on the 19th. Russian armour dashed along the Kielce-Breslau axis and on the 21st a bold armoured thrust was launched southwards into the German rear. By the 25th the Front had closed up to the Oder between Glogau and its upper reaches. To the south-east, Russian infantry pressed into the upper Silesia, 4 Ukrainian Front lending its support from 15 January to encircle this vital industrial area from the south. An army from 2 Ukrainian Front also joined in on 23 January.

2 14 January to 3 February. 1 Byelorussian Front drove to the middle Oder. In the north Warsaw was soon encircled and fell on 17 January. The southern pincer of this attack forced German troops north over the Vistula, thus uncovering the Posen axis. On 1 Byelorussian Front's southern flank, there was an attack towards Radom, taken on the 16th, but the main drive was in the centre where strong armoured formations thrust towards Lodz and Posen. The former fell on the 19th and the latter had been cut off by the 26th. The Germans now had no coherent front at all and the Russians were able to crash through to the Oder, only 35 miles east of Berlin. Between 31 January and 3 February 1 Byelorussian Front's left flank armies closed up to the Oder whilst those on the right edged slowly north-westward into Pomerania. (Posen held out until 23 February.)

3 13 January to 9 February. 2 and 3 Byelorussian Fronts attacked A Gp Centre in East Prussia. The latter's assault was particularly slow and bloody, driving through strong fortifications and difficult marshy terrain. On 27 January the Germans gave up Memel and transferred their forces there to the Samland peninsula, behind Königsberg. 2 Byelorussian Front started off aiming west and north-west and took Mlawa on 19 January. Thereafter, however, it was ordered to turn several of its armies north to assist in the reduction of the A Gp Centre pocket. Thorn was not taken until 9 February and Grudziadz, although encircled, continued to hold out. To the north Marienberg was taken on 24 January and the first armoured forces reached the Baltic two days later. Between 27 and 31 January the Russians fought off desperate Germans attempts to break out of this pocket westwards, across the Vistula towards Danzig.

4 8-23 February. Though their armies were by now severely weakened, the four Russian Fronts attempted to carry out ambitious High Command orders to eliminate A Gp Centre (now known as North) in the Königsberg Pocket, to clean out east Pomerania between Stettin and Danzig, and, in 1 Ukrainian Front's sector, to draw up to the Niesse alongside 1 Byelorussian Front. This latter operation was successfully completed by 23 February, though Glogau and Breslau, although encircled, continued to hold out. The other Fronts made only limited gains. 1 Byelorussian, on its northern flank, only managed to clear out Arnswalde and Deutsche Krone by the 23rd, though a much-vaunted German counter-attack from Stargard, on the 15th, made little impact. 2 Byelorussian Front lost four armies to 3 Byelorussian and was thus unable to pierce German defences between Neustettin and the mouth of the Vistula. 3 Byelorussian Front, despite considerable reinforcement, could not complete the reduction of the Königsberg pocket.

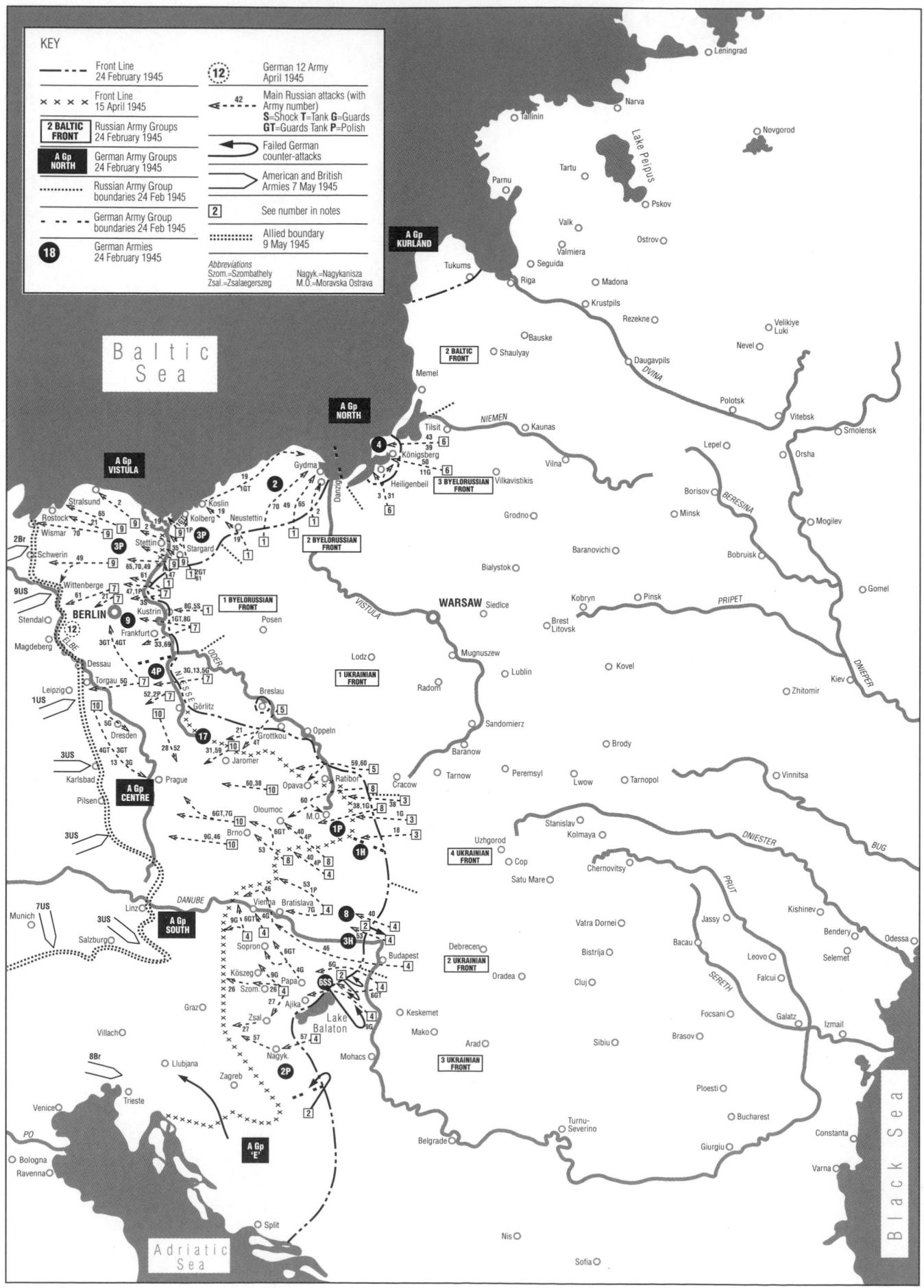

KEY

— — — ·	Front Line 24 February 1945
× × ×	Front Line 15 April 1945
2 BALTIC FRONT	Russian Army Groups 24 February 1945
A Gp NORTH	German Army Groups 24 February 1945
··········	Russian Army Group boundaries 24 Feb 1945
— · — ·	German Army Group boundaries 24 Feb 1945
18	German Armies 24 February 1945
(12)	German 12 Army April 1945
◄— 42	Main Russian attacks (with Army number) S=Shock T=Tank G=Guards GT=Guards Tank P=Polish
◄—	Failed German counter-attacks
⇨	American and British Armies 7 May 1945
2	See number in notes
···⊡···	Allied boundary 9 May 1945

Abbreviations
Szom.=Szombathely   Nagyk.=Nagykanisza
Zsal.=Zsalaegerszeg   M.O.=Moravska Ostrava

Baltic Sea

Black Sea

Adriatic Sea

• MAP 19 • THE EASTERN FRONT (ix) •

Map 19 The Eastern Front (ix): The Last Campaigns: Pomerania, Berlin, Austria and Czechoslovakia 24 February-9 May 1945

NOTES TO MAP 19

1 24 February to 31 March 1945. 1 and 2 Byelorussian Fronts cleared Pomerania, the latter attacking on 24 February, the former on 1 March. 2 Byelorussian Front made slow progress in its thrust to the Baltic through Neustettin, but further to its right great holes were punched in the German defences. The front then veered east, through Gydnia and Danzig, and reached the Gulf of Danzig on 25 March. The pockets at Gydnia and Danzig were cleared by 26 and 30 March respectively. 1 Byelorussian Front was also somewhat delayed at the start, Stargard not being cleared until 5 March, but by then other formations had swept through to Kolberg. This finally surrendered on the 18th, whilst other units cleaned out the east bank of the lower Oder. Further south, between 22 and 29 March, two armies cleared Küstrin.

2 17 February to 15 March. Hitler concentrated large armoured forces south of Budapest for a drive to the Danube and the re-occupation of the Hungarian capital. The central striking force was 6 SS Panzer Army, brought east after the abandonment of the Ardennes offensive. A preliminary attack on 17 February, by 6 Army, drove back Soviet bridgeheads north of the Danube, but the main attack around Lake Balaton, supplemented to the south by 2 Pz Ay and A Gp E, only made limited progress, and was called off by A Gp South on 15 March.

3 10 March to 5 April. Though the German offensive north of Lake Balaton disrupted Soviet plans somewhat (see **4** below) it did not dissuade the Soviet High Command from launching an ambitious offensive into Czechoslovakia, to the River Ultava and Prague. This offensive, by 4 Ukrainian Front, was, however, an utter failure, advancing barely seven miles in as many days. It began again on 24 March but still failed to reach even the preliminary objective of Moravska-Ostrava. It did, however, draw off German forces to facilitate 2 Ukrainian Front's advance to Bratislava and the Morava (see **4** below) and orders were given to prepare for a renewed offensive, with a two-front pincers meeting at Oloumoc.

4 16 March to 15 April. As the German attack at Lake Balaton petered out, the Russians immediately counter-attacked, resuming a drive to Vienna and Graz that had been planned since 17 February but which had been temporarily delayed by the German attack. 6 SS Pz Ay was caught before it could disengage north-westwards and was largely crushed against the north-western coast of Lake Balaton. Papa and Ajika were stormed on 25 and 26 March. 2 and 3 Ukrainian Fronts pressed on across the Raba, on the 28th, and had completely cleared western Hungary by 1 April, when Sopron fell and the Nagykanisza oil-fields were encircled. North of the Danube, in Czechoslovakia, 2 Ukrainian Front's right flank armies approached Bratislava and drew up along the River Morava. This city was taken on 4 April. Two days later elements of both Fronts, one army having been ferried across the Danube, were on the outskirts of Vienna. The centre of the city was evacuated by the Germans on the 10th, and the whole of it given up on the 13th. Other formations from 3 Ukrainian Front pushed into eastern Austria.

5 15-31 March. 1 Ukrainian Front cleared upper Silesia to the Czech frontier.

6 17 March to 21 April. 3 Byelorussian Front reduced Königsberg. The first stage of the assault was the reduction of the Heiligenbeil concentration to the west of the city. Heiligenbeil itself was stormed on 25 March and the whole pocket cleared by the 29th. The assault on Königsberg did not begin until 6 April though the city capitulated within

three days. German units in the Samland peninsula, to the west of Königsberg, were only eliminated after a second major assault, between 13 and 21 April.

7 16 April to 8 May. Having cleared Hungary, eastern Austria, Silesia and Pomerania, the Russians finally launched the long-awaited attack on Berlin. 1 Byelorussian and 1 Ukrainian Fronts took the star roles and jumped off on 16 April, each quickly carving out substantial bridgeheads across the Oder. Further progress was slower, however, 1 Byelorussian Front, in particular, being unable to break through the main German defences facing its centre until 19 April, whilst its northern and southern flanks were still heavily engaged near the Oder on the 21st. Momentum soon picked up in the centre, however, and the northern outskirts of Berlin were reached on the 20th. 1 Ukrainian Front had broken out of its bridgeheads much more quickly and its armoured units, though having much further to travel, were also in the southern outskirts of Berlin on the 20th. By the 25th the city was surrounded, on which day other elements of 1 Ukrainian Front dashed through to Torgau where they met up with American spearheads. Only this Front's south-east thrust, to Dresden, was disappointingly slow. As the ring around Berlin slowly tightened, Hitler committed suicide on the 30th and two days later the garrison capitulated. On 3 May 1 Byelorussian Front's right flank army dashed through to the Elbe. On 7 May Jodl signed the surrender to the western Allies and two days later formally ro surrendered to the Russians.

8 15 April to 1 May. 2 and 4 Ukrainian Fronts attacked into eastern Czechoslovakia. Attacking on 15 April, 4 Ukrainian Front still found the road to Moravska-Ostrava very hard going but, after the fall of Opava on 22 April, Moravska-Ostrava was finally cleared on the 30th. 2 Ukrainian Front started its own drive on 23 April, taking Brno on the 27th and then joining with 4 Ukrainian Front to push on Oloumoc.

9 20 April to 8 May. 2 Byelorussian Front cleared Mecklenberg. The commander, Rokossovsky, started his attack believing his mission was to encircle Berlin from the north. On the 23rd, however, his bridgehead having been slow to expand and 1 Byelorussian Front having by now established itself in some force on the northern outskirts of the German capital, he was ordered to strike directly west and north-west. The German commander in the area saw little profit in allowing himself to be trapped against the Baltic and proceeded to withdraw towards the British and the Americans. After taking Stettin on the 26th, therefore, Rokossovsky's attack made almost uninterrupted progress, taking Stralsund on 1 May, Rostock on the 2nd and Wittenberge on the 3rd.

10 6-9 May. On 1 May the Russian High Command directed 1 and 2 Ukrainian Fronts to encircle Prague from the north and south-east. The operation began on 6 May and Dresden was taken on the 7th. A Gp Centre refused to acknowledge the surrender in the West until Prague had been entered on all sides on the 9th. This marked the final collapse of German resistance in the East.

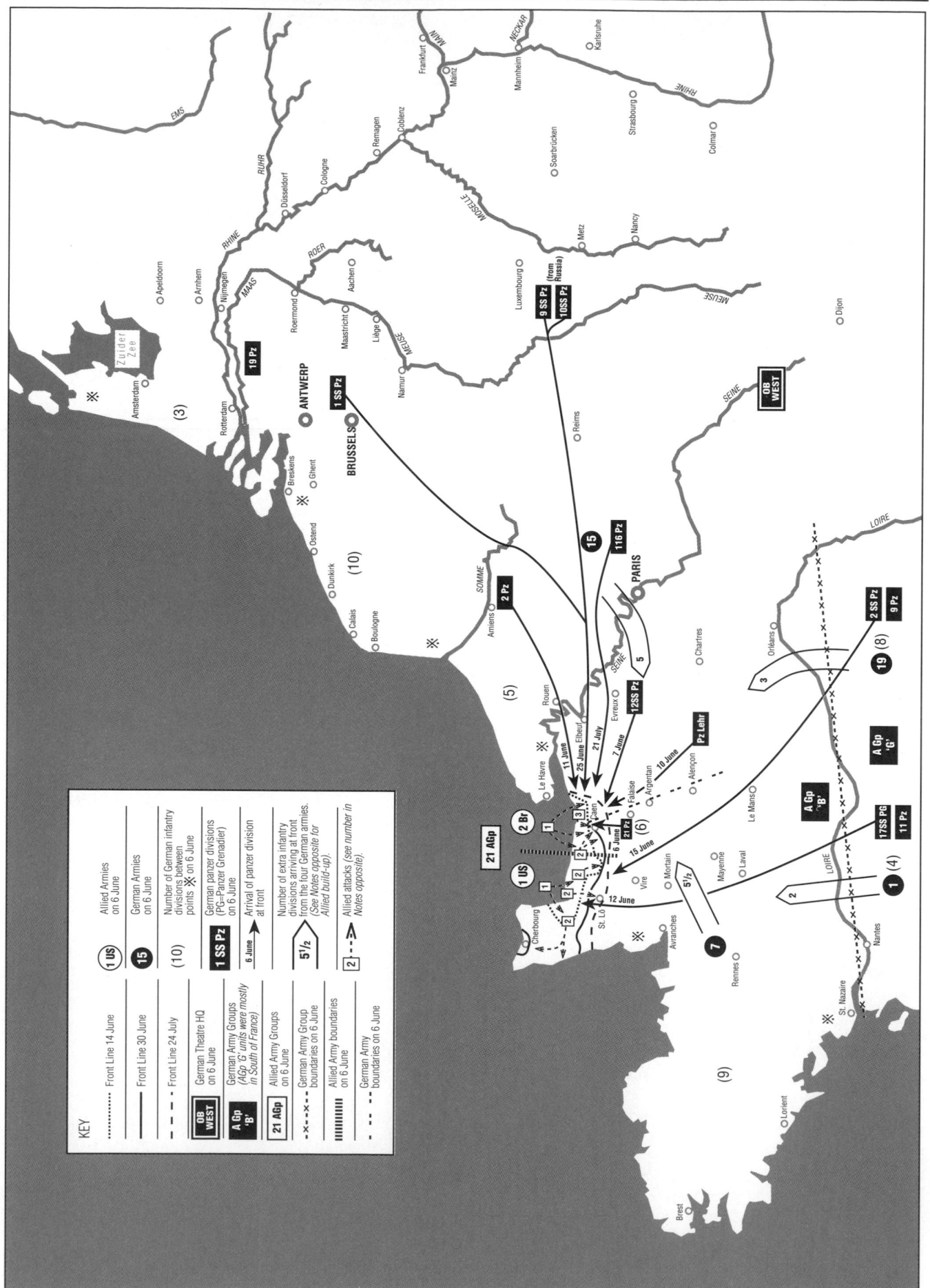

Map 20 North-West Europe (i): Attrition in Normandy 6 June–24 July 1944

KEY

⋯⋯⋯	Front Line 14 June
———	Front Line 30 June
– – –	Front Line 24 July
OB WEST	German Theatre HQ on 6 June
A Gp 'B'	German Army Groups (AGp 'G' units were mostly in South of France)
21 AGp	Allied Army Groups on 6 June
–×–×–	German Army Group boundaries on 6 June
‖‖‖‖	Allied Army boundaries on 6 June
– · – · –	German Army boundaries on 6 June
(1 US)	Allied Armies on 6 June
(15)	German Armies on 6 June
(10)	Number of German infantry divisions between points ※ on 6 June
1 SS Pz	German panzer divisions (PG–Panzer Grenadier) on 6 June
6 June ⬆	Arrival of panzer division at front
5½	Number of extra infantry divisions arriving at front from the four German armies. (See Notes opposite for Allied build-up).
2 -->	Allied attacks (see number in Notes opposite).

• **MAP 20** • NORTH-WEST EUROPE (i) •

NOTES TO MAP 20

1 On 6 June 1944, two US, two British and one Canadian division came ashore on five beaches in Normandy. There were also airborne landings by three divisions on the flanks of the beachhead. Resistance to these assaults varied greatly, but on none of the beaches did the Germans succeed in repulsing the Allies. In the British sector, however, armoured counter-attacks prevented Second Army from taking its first major objective Caen, and German defences began to stabilise to the north of this town.

2 Three main axes of attack developed, with the British pushing towards Caen and the Americans driving south to St Lô and west and north-west into the Cotentin peninsula. The latter was cut off on 17 June, at Barneville, and Cherbourg was closely invested by the 24th. Though Carentan was taken on 11 June, St Lô did not fall for another month, on 18 July, after extremely bitter and costly fighting among the Normandy hedgerows.

Caen was the target of three main British/Canadian assaults. The first was an attack by 7 Armoured Division towards Villers-Bocage, decisively repulsed by 2 Panzer Division on the 13th. The second was Operation EPSOM, an attack on the western flank, beginning on 25 June. A breakthrough of sorts was achieved to the south-west of Caen but the appearance of German armoured reinforcements persuaded the British commander to withdraw his spearheads on the 28th and hold a line along the Odon river. The third major effort, Operation CHARNWOOD was successful, at least insofar as Caen was finally taken. The attack began on 8 July and on the 9th most of the town was overrun. A breakout to the south proved impossible, however, and British forces paused for a renewed assault from the eastern side of the town.

3 The next British-Canadian attack was Operation GOODWOOD, launched on 18 July and preceded by a massive aerial bombardment of German positions. The front line was penetrated by three British armoured divisions but a congested axis of advance, as well as superb German defensive tactics, slowly robbed the attack of momentum. By 20 July it was virtually at a standstill. Considerable casualties had been inflicted on the Germans but a decisive breakthrough had not been achieved.

Note

During this period the Allied build-up into the Normandy battle area was as follows:

	Armoured Divisions	Armoured Brigades	Infantry Divisions	Infantry Brigades
7-10 June	1		3	
11-14 June	2	}7	5	}1
15-30 June	2		5	
1-15 July	-	}4	4	}1
15-24 July	4		1	
Total	9	11	18	2

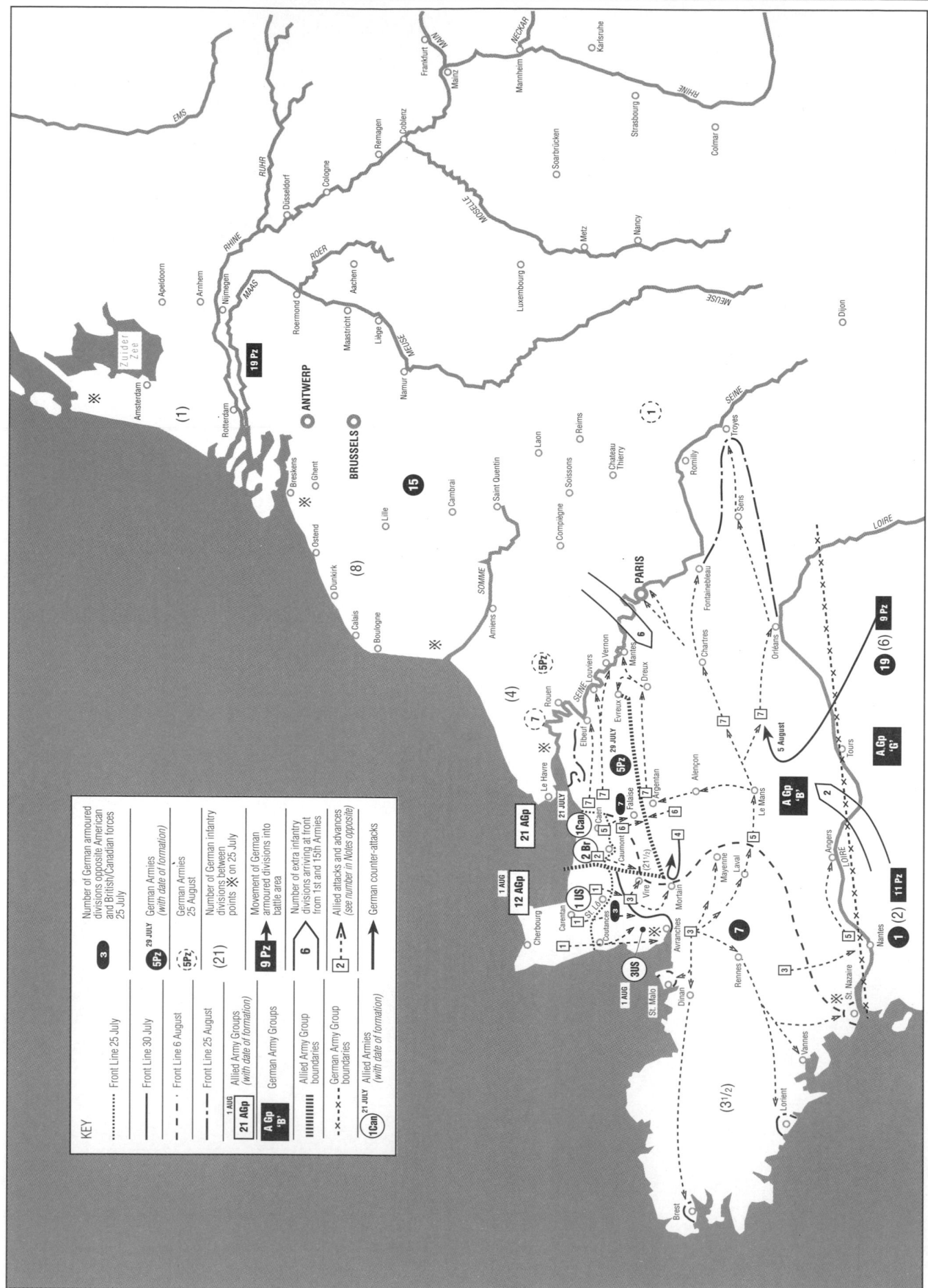

Map 21 North-West Europe (ii): Breakout from Normandy 25 July-25 August 1944

• **MAP 21** • NORTH-WEST EUROPE (ii) •

NOTES TO MAP 21

1 On 25 July First US Army opened Operation COBRA, an attempt to break through the western German defences in Normandy and pave the way for a drive into Brittany, to open up the ports, and for a drive around the southern German flank. Once the original line was ruptured, excellent progress was made, Coutances falling on 28 July and Avranches on the 30th.

2 The success of the American drive began to draw German armour away from the British-Canadian sector and Montgomery then launched an attack of his own, Operation BLUECOAT, on 30 July, to pin the panzers along his front and so increase the Americans' freedom of manoeuvre. Good progress was made on the right, towards Vire, although the British refused to cross the Army Group boundary and actually occupy the town, deserted though it was. Progress on the left was less satisfactory, leading to several sackings of commanders, but when the attack was halted on 3 August it had managed to draw three panzer divisions against it.

3 On 1 August 12 US Army Group and Third US Army came into being, the latter, under Patton, being given the mission of driving into Brittany. This he did *con brio*, taking Rennes on the 4th and Vannes on the 5th. On this same day US troops reached the outskirts of St Malo and Brest. By the 6th Lorient was also under attack and St Nazaire on the following day. (The latter two held out until the end of the war, but St Malo fell on 17 August and Brest on 19 September). Important progress was also made on First US Army's front, with Mortain falling on 3 August. Bradley, commanding 12 Army Group, now ordered Patton to swing his main forces eastwards, and this he did, taking Mayenne and Laval on the 5th and 6th and Nantes on the 8th. First US Army also made headway, taking Vire on 6 August.

4 On 7 August, at Hitler's insistence, the remnants of the German armour in Normandy were used up in a counter-attack against Mortain. The Germans fought desperately but were able to make almost no progress and were obliged to begin pulling back on the 10th.

5 On 7/8 August, First Canadian Army launched an attack south-west of Caen, Operation TOTALISE, with the aim of driving down towards Falaise to link up with the Americans and cut off German forces still fighting to the west. On 9 August, Third Army forces, having taken Le Mans on the previous day, turned north towards Alençon to make junction with the Canadians and seal off the Falaise/Argentan pocket. Alençon was taken on the 12th and US forces pushed on towards the outskirts of Argentan, which was largely cleared on the next day. By now other US units, having taken Angers on the 8th, were pressing on towards Orleans and Chartres.

6 On the 13th, however, Bradley ordered his left flank formations to halt at Argentan lest they blunder into British-Canadian units and end up in an Allied firefight. But First Canadian Army was making only slow progress towards Falaise, despite a concerted armoured attack, Operation TRACTABLE, on the 14th, and did not actually clear Falaise until the 17th. Their and US forces did not join hands until the 18th, by which time important elements of Seventh and Fifth Panzer Armies has managed to extricate themselves from the trap, through the so-called Falaise Gap. This Gap was not fully sealed off until 20 August.

7 In the meantime other US units had been racing across northern France towards the Seine. A westward drive from Argentan began on the 14th, reaching Dreux on the 17th, whilst to the south Chartres and

Orleans fell on the 16th and 17th respectively. On the 19th, Third Army units reached the Seine at Mantes Grassicourt and Fontainebleau was entered on the 20th. On the 21st Third Army had a bridgehead at Mantes whilst to the south Sens had been taken. On the 23rd, whilst 21 Army Group hurried westward towards the Seine, the Americans pushed north to take Evreux, and 2 French Armoured Division was brought forward to complete the liberation of Paris. This latter had begun on 19 August when resistance forces in the city rose and the German commander surrendered. On the same day, British units reached the Seine at Vernon and Louviers, whilst Canadian troops took Elbeuf.

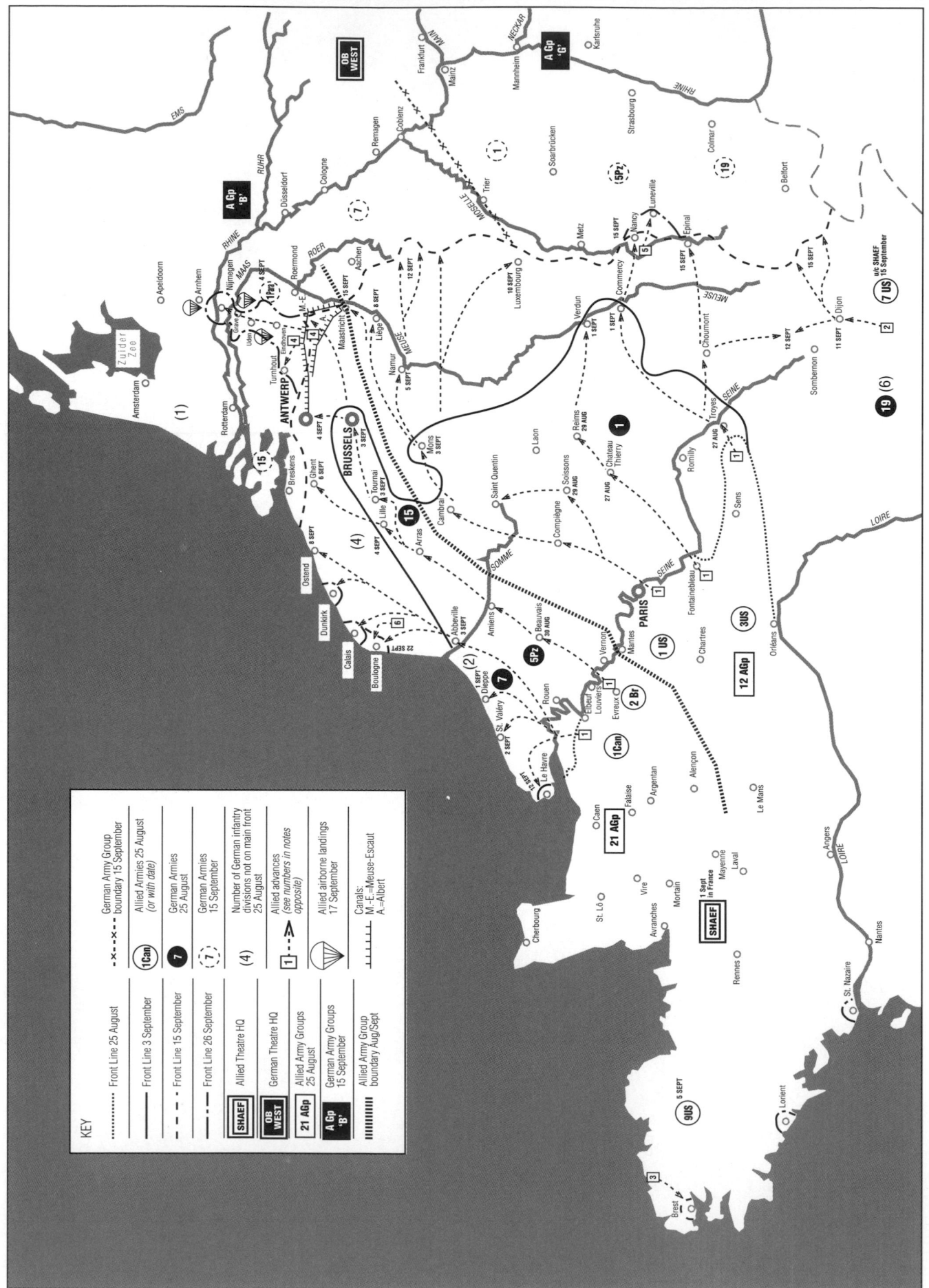

Map 22 North-West Europe (iii): The Allied Pursuit Falters 26 August–26 September 1944

KEY

··········	Front Line 25 August
——	Front Line 3 September
– – –	Front Line 15 September
–·–·–	Front Line 26 September
SHAEF	Allied Theatre HQ
OB WEST	German Theatre HQ
21 AGp	Allied Army Groups
A Gp 'B'	German Army Groups 15 September
▦▦▦	Allied Army Group boundary Aug/Sept
–x–x–	German Army Group boundary 15 September
(1Can)	Allied Armies 25 August (or with date)
7	German Armies 25 August
(7)	German Armies 15 September
(4)	Number of German infantry divisions not on main front 25 August
1 ⟶	Allied advances (see numbers in notes opposite)
◗	Allied airborne landings 17 September
	Canals: M.-E.=Meuse-Escaut A.=Albert

• MAP 22 • NORTH-WEST EUROPE (iii) •

NOTES TO MAP 22

1 On 25 August, Allied armies began pushing in earnest across the Seine. The German army was now in headlong retreat and operations were a simple pursuit, right up as far as Antwerp. Aachen and the upper Moselle. No detailed narrative is necessary, therefore, and the dates of the seizure of major towns are given on the map opposite.

2 On 11 September, Seventh US Army reached Dijon, having had a relatively straightforward passage all the way up from the southern coast. Prior to this, having landed in France on 15 August, Seventh Army had forced the surrender of Toulon and Marseille on the 28th but had been unable to prevent the substantial elements of 11 Panzer Division and other units breaking out of an encirclement south of Montélimar. On 1 September, French forces took Narbonne, on the 3rd Lyon, and on the 6th Châlons. American elements in Seventh Army took Besançon on the 8th, and a day later French units took Beaune and Le Creusot. Junction was made with Third Army on 12 September, north of Sombernon. Seventh Army came under SHAEF command, as opposed to Wilson's Mediterranean Supreme H.Q., on the 15th.

3 On 19 September. US forces under the newly arrived Ninth US Army finally succeeded in taking Brest.

4 On 17 September, in an attempt to 'bounce' the Rhine and slice his way into Germany, Montgomery dropped airborne troops around the main bridges between the Meuse-Escaut Canal and Arnhem. Their task was to seize and hold these bridges until the main British force could follow through to the Rhine, and across it towards the Ruhr. This main force, however, moved too slowly along its restricted axis of advance and by the time it had fought its way through to the airborne troops at Arnhem, the latter were too weak to do anything but withdraw back across the river. The last vital bridge, the 'bridge too far', remained in German hands. During its drive the main British force had taken Eindhoven on 18 September, Grave on the 19th, Nijmegen and the Waal Bridge on the 20th, and had drawn up to the south bank of the Rhine on the 24th. The corridor they had created remained in Allied hands, helped by the capture of Turnhout on 26 September.

5 On 20 September, Third US Army took Luneville.

6 On 22 September, the garrison in Boulogne surrendered.

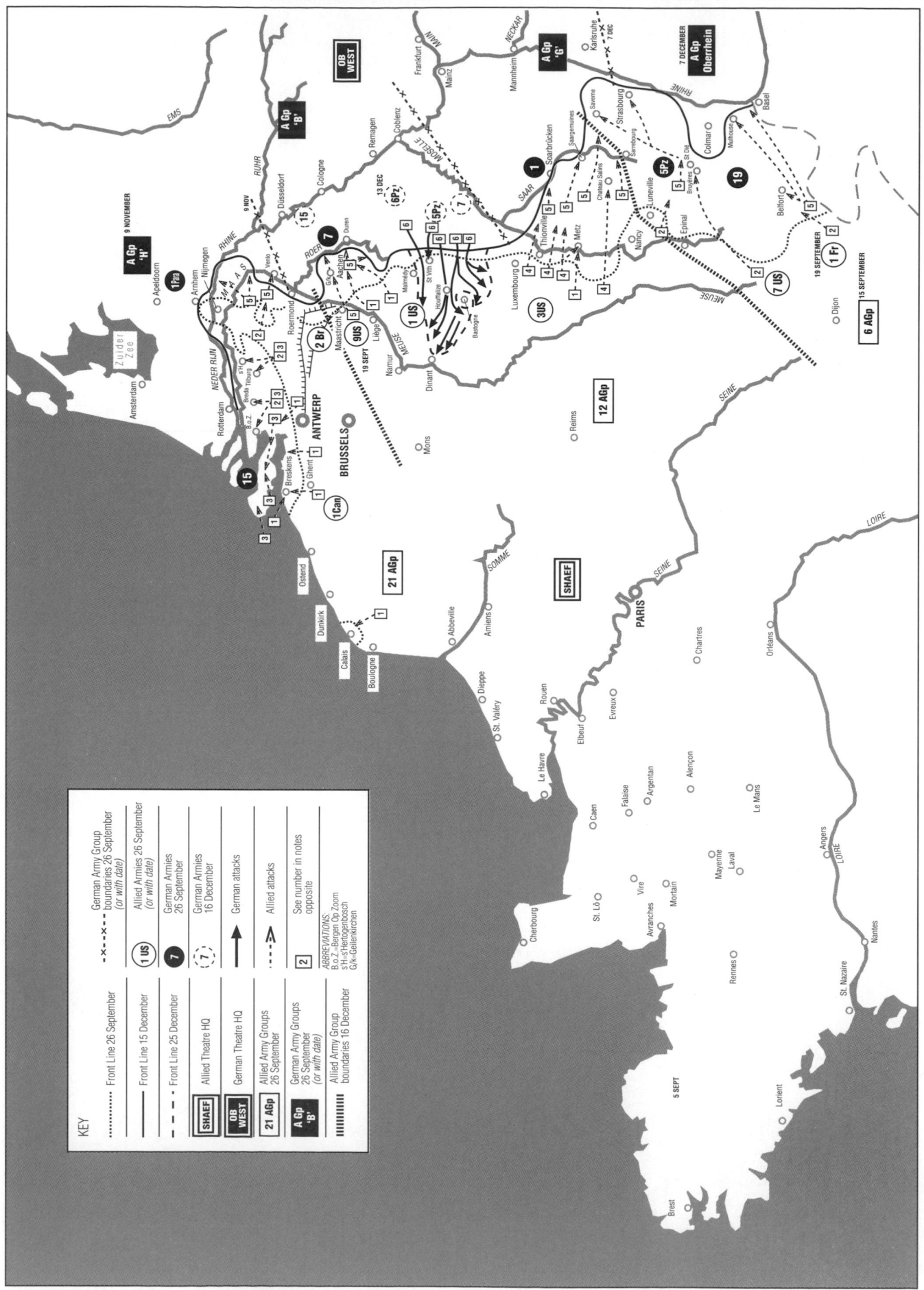

Map 23 North-West Europe (iv): Allied Frustration and German Counter-attack 27 September–25 December 1944

KEY

····· Front Line 26 September

——— Front Line 15 December

–·–·– Front Line 25 December

SHAEF Allied Theatre HQ

OB WEST German Theatre HQ

21 AGp Allied Army Groups 26 September

A Gp 'B' German Army Groups 26 September (or with date)

▨▨▨ Allied Army Group boundaries 16 December

–×–×– German Army Group boundaries 26 September (or with date)

1 US Allied Armies 26 September (or with date)

7 German Armies 26 September

7 German Armies 16 December

↑ German attacks

↑ Allied attacks

2 See number in notes opposite

ABBREVIATIONS:
B.o.Z.–Bergen Op Zoom
s'H–s'Hertogenbosch
G/k–Geilenkirchen

• MAP 23 • NORTH-WEST EUROPE (iv) •

NOTES TO MAP 23

1 After the failure of Montgomery's 'knife-like thrust' to Arnhem, Eisenhower, despite protestations to the contrary, adopted a 'broad front' strategy, putting in major attacks along the whole of the front. The most important of these were by the Canadians into the Breskens Pocket and to the north of Antwerp, to clear the Scheldt Estuary; by First US Army to capture Aachen, beginning 2 October; by Third Army towards Metz, beginning 27 September. All were dour, prolonged struggles. Breskens was not taken until 22 October, after a flanking seaborne assault on the 9th, (although the Canadians had had an earlier success when Calais surrendered on 30 September). Aachen was surrounded on 16 October and finally surrendered on the 21st. Metz continued to hold out.

2 Eisenhower persisted with his broad front strategy, throwing in more attacks at both ends of the line, in mid-October. In the north 21 Army Group began a drive towards Venlo on 13 October and towards Tilburg and the Maas on the 20th and the 22nd. The latter aimed at cutting off the islands in the Scheldt Estuary where German Fifteenth Army was tenaciously holding out. In the south the attacks towards Metz continued, supplemented by other Third Army drives further south and by the opening of offensives by Seventh US and First French Armies on the 15th and 16th respectively. That by Seventh US liberated Bruyère on 19 October.

3 In late October and early November the slogging match continued. In the north the Breskens pocket was not properly cleared until 3 November and in the Scheldt Estuary major offensives were required to clear Beveland, from 23 to 30 October, and Walcheren, from 1 to 8 November. Progress was equally slow inland, with Bergen-op-Zoom and s'Hertogenbosch falling on 27 October and Tilburg and Breda on the 28th and 29th respectively. The drive towards Venlo made only very limited progress.

4 On 8 November, Third Army began another offensive around Metz and to the south, aiming eventually for the Saar. Progress was made to the north and south of Metz, Chateau Salins falling on 9 November, but the city itself, although isolated on the 19th, continued to hold out until the 22nd.

5 In mid-November the rest of the Allied line flared into action. On the 13th, Seventh US Army forced the Germans out of St Dié, and on the following day First French Army renewed its drive towards Belfort, which fell on 21 November. Columns were also sent out towards the Swiss frontier, which reached a point north of Basel on the 19th, whilst Mulhouse was occupied on the 22nd. Seventh US Army made similarly impressive progress, taking Strasbourg and Saverne on the 24th and 26th respectively.

Third Army kept attacking throughout November and slowly pushed up to the Saar, taking bridges north of Saarbrücken on the 24th and Saargemuines on 6 December. First US and Ninth Armies jumped off again on 16 November, but were unable to push beyond the River Roer which was reached in early December. Progress by 21 Army Group was also extremely slow. By 4 December the Peel Marshes and the whole area south and west of the Maas had been cleared but further advances towards the Waal and the Rhine were limited.

6 On 16 December, with the Allied drive in the north having slowly ground to a halt, the Germans launched a powerful counter-attack in the lightly-held Ardennes, attempting to repeat their successes of May 1940. Other Allied operations, notably those of Third Army, were halted and on the 17th two airborne divisions were sent into the Ardennes. On the 19th, Montgomery took command of all Allied

forces north of the 'Bulge'. By the 20th the German advance was already seriously behind schedule, being most notably baulked at Bastogne and St Vith, where US garrisons were doggedly holding on. Houffalize fell on 21 December but progress to the north and south was still disappointing.

On the 22nd, the bad weather which had grounded Allied aircraft began to clear and though St Vith was lost on this day, local German commanders recommended to Hitler that the offensive be called off. Hitler refused and on the 23rd German forces lapped around both sides of Bastogne, pressing forward to the Meuse. By the evening of the 24th they had made their deepest penetration and thenceforth were obliged to fall back in the face of powerful Allied counter-attacks. All Hitler had succeeded in doing was once again gutting his panzer reserve.

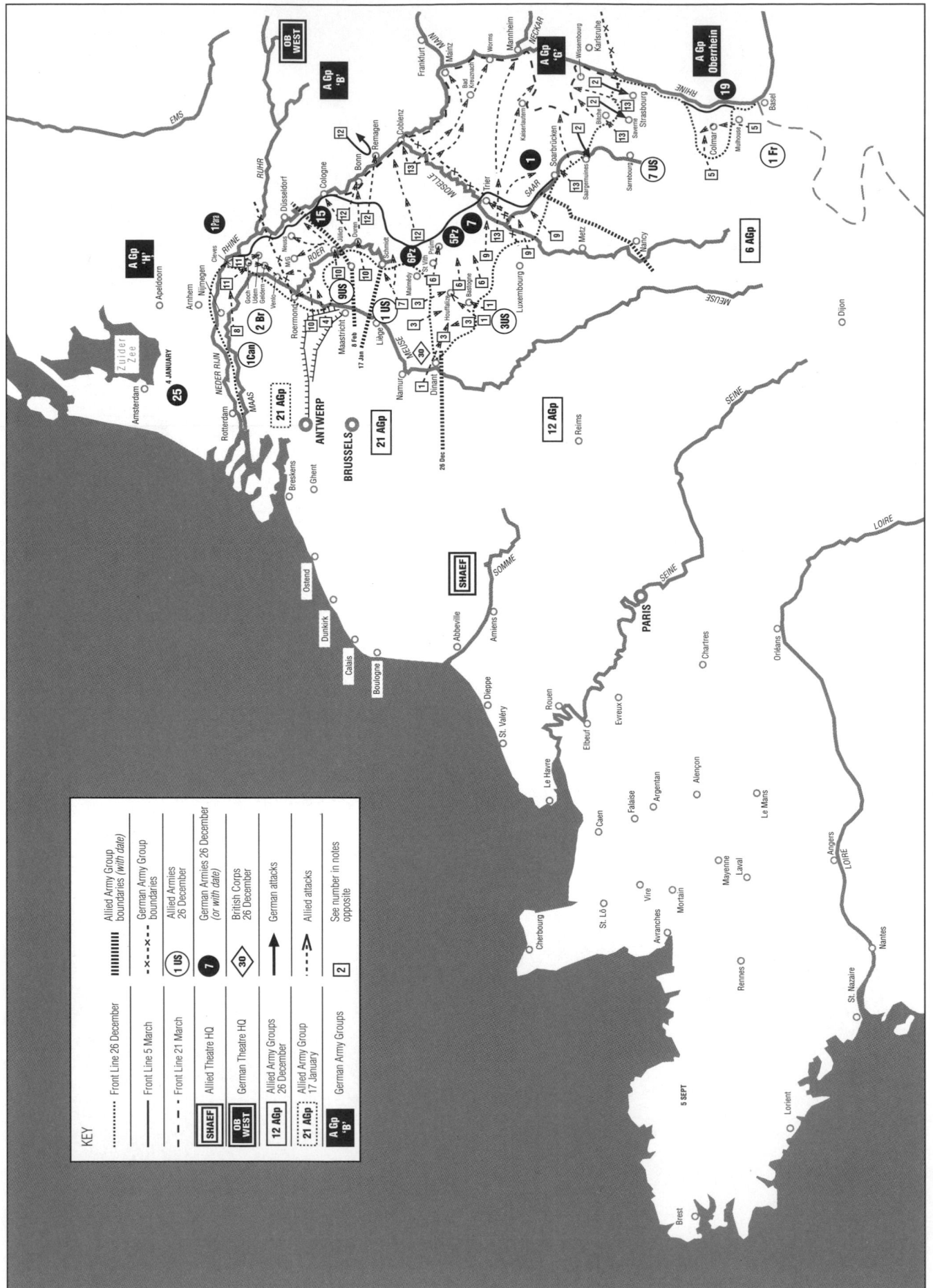

KEY

Front Line 26 December		Allied Army Group boundaries (with date)
Front Line 5 March		German Army Group boundaries
Front Line 21 March	1 US	Allied Armies 26 December
SHAEF — Allied Theatre HQ	7	German Armies 26 December (or with date)
OB WEST — German Theatre HQ	30	British Corps 26 December
12 AGp — Allied Army Groups 26 December	↑	German attacks
21 AGp — Allied Army Group 17 January	↗	Allied attacks
A Gp 'B' — German Army Groups	2	See number in notes opposite

Map 24 North-West Europe (v): The Allies Close to the Rhine 26 December 1944–21 March 1945

• MAP 24 • NORTH-WEST EUROPE (v) •

NOTES TO MAP 24

1 On 26 December, the Allies' own counter-offensive in the Ardennes began. Bastogne was relieved on the 26th and on the 27th British troops drove panzers out of Celles, just east of Dinant. After a short lull, Third Army began attacking towards Houffalize, on the 30th, whilst the British made further gains in the north-east corner of the salient.

2 On 1 January, Seventh US Army withdrew before a German counter-attack round Saargemuines, a withdrawal which continued until the 11th as German pressure mounted as far east as Strasbourg.

3 On 11 January, Third Army and XXX Corps joined up at St Hubert, whilst units of First US Army, having started on 3 January, fought their way down from the north of the salient. On 16 January, First US and Third Armies linked up at Houffalize.

4 To the north, on 16 January, Second British Army attacked into the Roermond Triangle, to eliminate this last major German bridgehead across the Roer.

5 On 20 January, First French Army launched an offensive in the Vosges, near Colmar, though bad weather made substantial progress impossible. Colmar itself was taken on 3 February. On the 5th the surviving German pocket to the west of Colmar was split in two, and finally eliminated on the 9th.

6 On 22 January, as Third Army battled away in the south of the Ardennes salient, First US Army launched a major offensive between St Vith and Houffalize. St Vith fell on the 23rd and by the 28th all gains made by the Germans had been eliminated. On 31 January, First Army units entered Germany, east of St Vith. Further progress was extremely difficult, however, Prüm not falling until 11 February.

7 On 4th February, First US Army began attacking towards the Roer Dams, south of Schmidt. This latter town fell on the 7th.

8 On 8 February, 21 Army Group began a new offensive, Operation VERITABLE, south-east of Nijmegen and on the first day penetrated into the Reichswald area. The Rhine was reached on the 9th and Cleves taken on the 11th. The Reichswald was cleared of the last German units on the 13th, after extremely vicious fighting.

9 On 17 February, Third Army attacked in the southern sector of its front and, having cleared the Saar-Moselle Triangle by the 23rd, pushed units across the former river on the 25th and on 2 March occupied Trier.

10 On 23 February, First US and Ninth Armies launched Operation GRENADE, an offensive across the middle Roer, and took Jülich on the 24th and Düren on the following day. Swinging north they then captured München-Gladbach and Neuss on 1 March. Other Ninth Army units, having taken over part of Second British Army's sector, attacked towards Roermond and Venlo, both of which fell on 2 March, after which some units pressed forward to link up with Canadian troops near Geldern, on 3 March. First US Army directed its main axis of advance towards Cologne, which was entered on 5 March.

11 The continuing British-Canadian offensive, having reached the Rhine, swung south to link up with the US First and Ninth Armies' push northward. Goch fell on 21 February and Udem on the 27th. After the link up with the Americans, Geldern was cleared of the enemy by 4 March. By this time Allied troops had closed up to the Rhine along most of its length between Cleves and Cologne.

12 From 6 March the main activity was in the southern half of the front as Third US Army and 6 Army Group also strove to close up to the Rhine. First US Army scored the first success, however, when some of its tanks reached the Rhine at Remagen, on the 7th, and discovered that the bridge there had not been blown. The Americans immediately began funnelling men across and at the same time other First Army units took Bonn, on the 9th. On that same day, Third Army reached the Rhine at Andernach just north of Koblenz. Heavy German counter-attacks at Remagen, on the 12th and 13th, were unsuccessful.

13 On 14 March, Third Army greatly expanded its attacks, sending one corps over the Moselle to the south-east of Koblenz and another just south of Trier. On the 15th, Seventh US Army joined in this offensive with attacks of its own around Saarbrücken and Bitche. This latter town fell on the 16th and Koblenz the next day. On the 18th Patton's men took Bad Kreuznach and on the 19th Worms was reached. Progress from the Trier bridgehead was almost as impressive, with Kaiserslautern falling on 20 March. Saarbrücken too fell on this same day, to Seventh US Army. Other Seventh Army units pressed towards Wissembourg, which was entered on the 22nd, by which time Third Army units had closed up to the Rhine everywhere north of Mannheim.

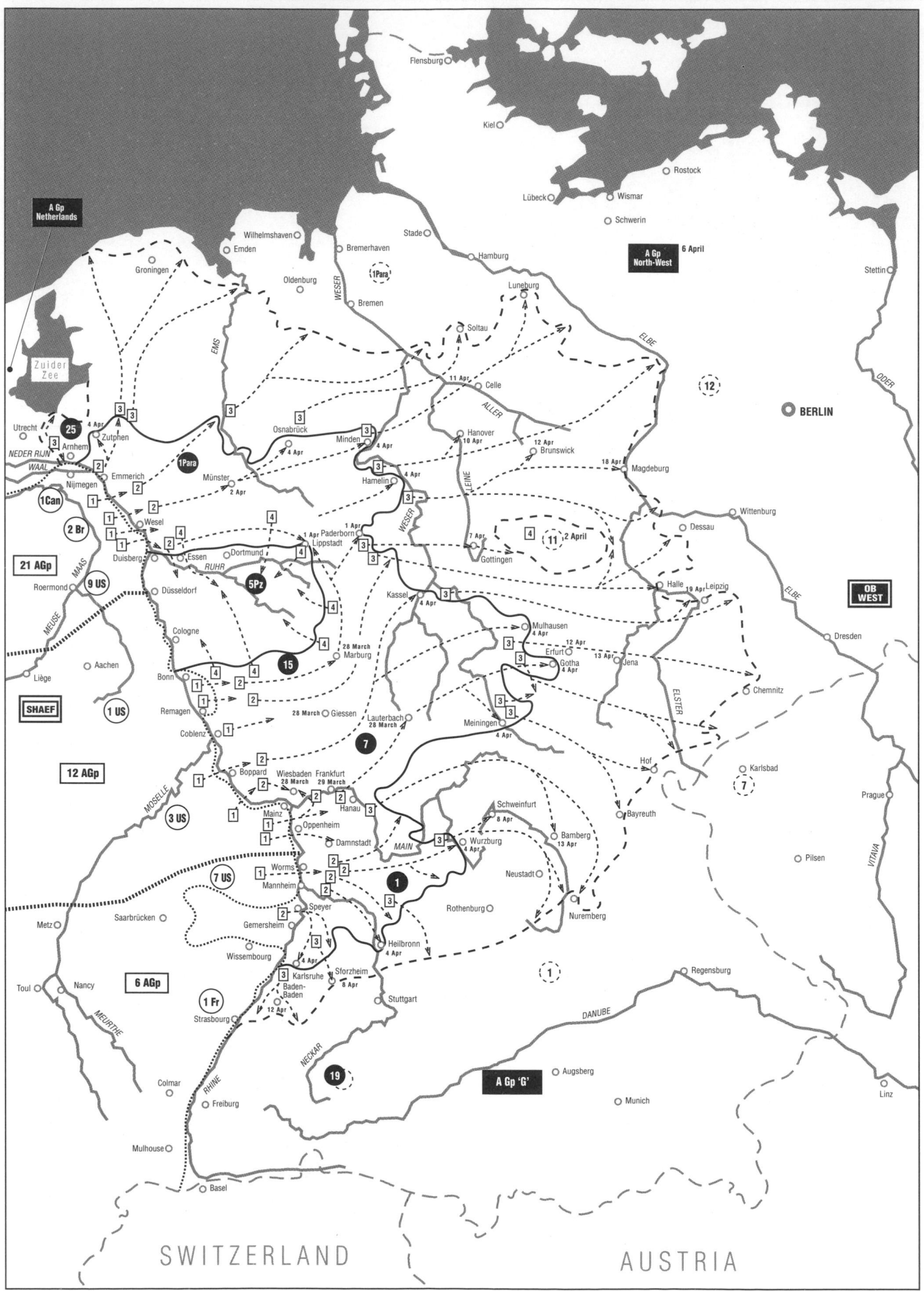

• MAP 25 • NORTH-WEST EUROPE (vi) •

Map 25 North-West Europe (vi): From the Rhine to the Elbe 22 March-19 April 1945

KEY

·············· Front Line 22 March

───────── Front Line 5 April

– – – – Front Line 19 April

| SHAEF | Allied Theatre HQ 22 March |

| OB WEST | German Theatre HQ 22 March |

| 12 AGp | Allied Army Groups 22 March |

| A Gp North-West | German Army Groups 19 April *(with date)* |

‖‖‖‖‖‖‖‖ Allied Army Group boundaries 22 March

(1 US) Allied Armies 22 March

● 15 German Armies 22 March

(11) German Armies 19 April *(with date)*

| 2 | --➤ Allied advances *(see numbers in notes)*

NOTES TO MAP 25

1 The various crossings of the Rhine began in late March. On the 22nd Patton slipped some units across near Oppenheim, adding other crossings near Boppard and elsewhere by the 25th. By this latter date Darmstadt had fallen and advanced units were approaching Hanau.

On 23 March, 21 Army Group's elaborate set-piece crossing, Operation PLUNDER, began. Second British Army led off, taking Wesel on the 24th. On this latter date Ninth US Army joined in and by the 25th the Army Group's bridgeheads were consolidated into one, some 30 miles wide.

On the 25th, First US Army launched its own offensive out of the Remagen bridgehead, with Seventh US Army joining in on the next day with attacks between Worms and Mannheim.

2 Over the next ten days the Allies made remarkable progress and by 4 April were across the Weser, on Eisenhower's main central axis towards Leipzig. British forces had also reached the Weser, at Minden, and Montgomery's southern army, Ninth US, had joined forces with First US Army at Lippstadt, cutting off a large proportion of Model's Army Group B in the Ruhr. First Canadian Army had also joined in the offensive, crossing the Rhine on 2 April and driving into Holland. In the south, after First French Army's crossing of the Rhine near Speyer, on 31 March, Allied forces were heading towards Stuttgart and Nuremberg. (The dates of the capture of major German towns in this period are given on the map opposite.)

3 The next fortnight's progress was almost equally good, with First Canadian Army clearing out Holland (Arnhem finally fell on 15 April) and Second Army advancing towards Schleswig-Holstein and the Baltic coast. Third Army, after nipping out the German salient in the Thüringian Forest, between Gotha and Meiningen, also headed towards Dresden and the Elbe, with its southerly units driving hard for the Czechoslovak frontier. 6 Army Group turned southwards, with its eyes on the successive barriers of the Neckar and the Danube. Ninth Army, which had been returned to 12 Army Group on 28 March, allocated certain of its forces to the reduction of the Ruhr Pocket, and did First US, but both also sent units eastwards, the former heading for Magdeburg, the latter for Dessau and Leipzig.

4 The reduction of the Ruhr Pocket was completed on 18 April and the commander of Army Group B, Model, committed suicide as his men surrendered. Another pocket, occupied by Eleventh Army, had meanwhile formed in First US Army's sector, in the Harz Mountains.

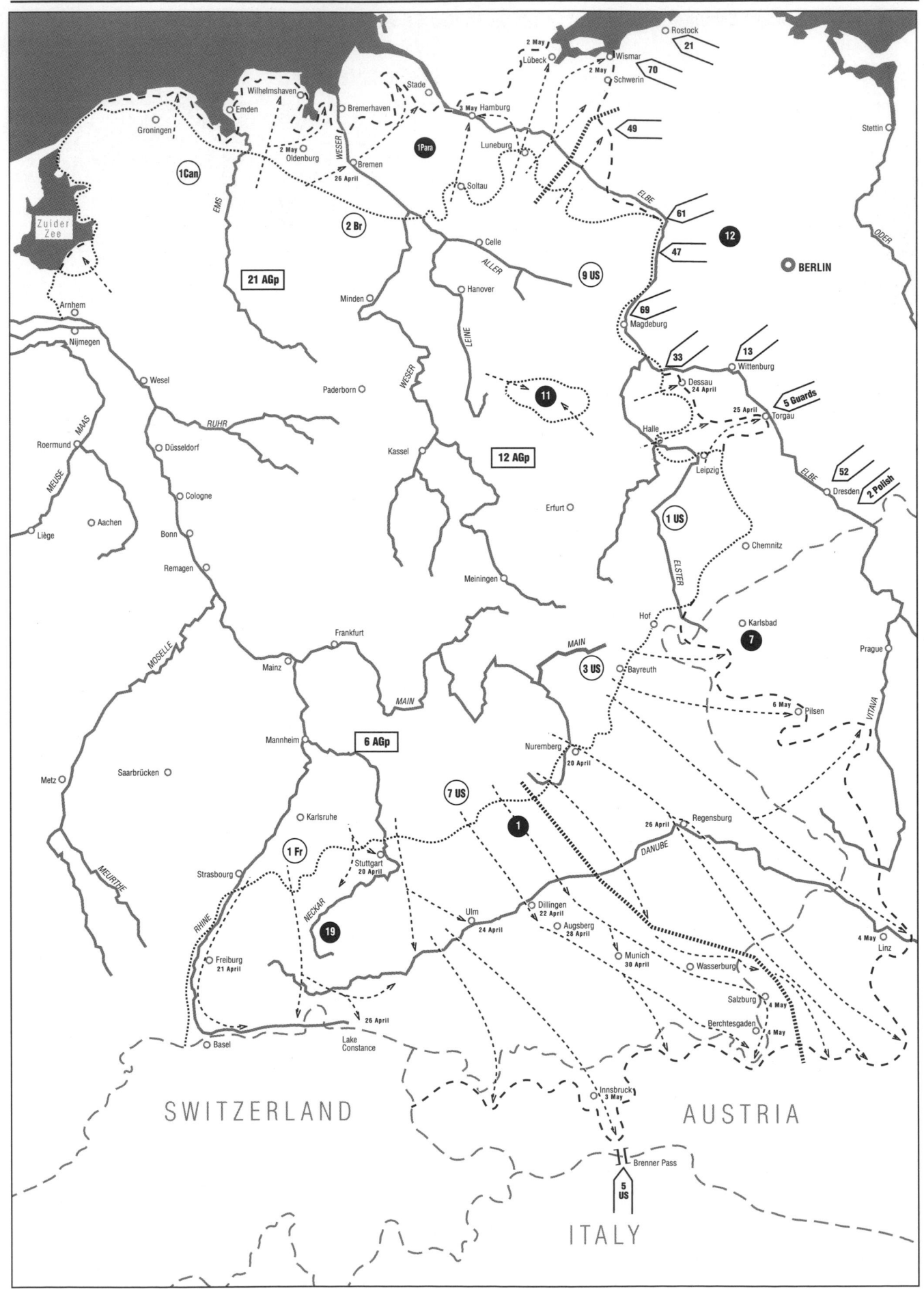

• MAP 26 • NORTH-WEST EUROPE (vii) •

Map 26 North-West Europe (vii): Mopping-up and Link-up with the Russians 19 April-7 May 1945

KEY

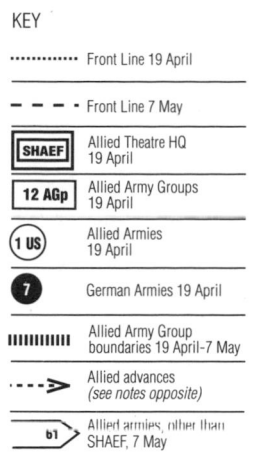

············	Front Line 19 April
– – – –	Front Line 7 May
SHAEF	Allied Theatre HQ 19 April
12 AGp	Allied Army Groups 19 April
1 US	Allied Armies 19 April
7	German Armies 19 April
||||||||||||	Allied Army Group boundaries 19 April-7 May
···-->	Allied advances (see notes opposite)
b1 >	Allied armies, other than SHAEF, 7 May

NOTES TO MAP 26

During the last fortnight or so of the war the major gains were made at the northern and southern ends of the front. In the centre, on First US and Ninth US Army's fronts, the Americans limited themselves to drawing up to the Elbe, in accordance with Eisenhower's agreement that the Russians should undertake all operations to the east of that river, including the capture of Berlin. The most notable event in this central sector was the first meeting of the Russian and Allied troops at Torgau, on 25 April. The only military operation of note was the liquidation of the Eleventh Army Pocket, by First US Army, between 11 and 23 April.

In the north, British troops advanced along two main axes, Bremen-Stadte and Hamburg-Lübeck-Wismar, whilst the Canadians completed the clearance of the Zuider Zee Pocket and advanced towards the western Baltic coast at several points. In the south, US Seventh and Third Armies conducted the most spectacular advances, into southern Germany and Austria. Third Army's main axis was Nuremberg-Regensburg, whilst Seventh Army advanced via Munich and Salzburg, Dillingen and Augsburg, and Ulm and Innsbruck. First French Army had lesser distances to cover, to the Swiss frontier, though their fast-moving troops netted large numbers of prisoners in two encirclements round Freiburg and round the Neckar.

On 5 May, German forces facing 21 Army Group surrendered to Montgomery whilst Army Group G surrendered to the Americans. On 7 May, the German armed forces as a whole surrendered to Eisenhower, though the last German resistance in the east did not cease until the 9th.

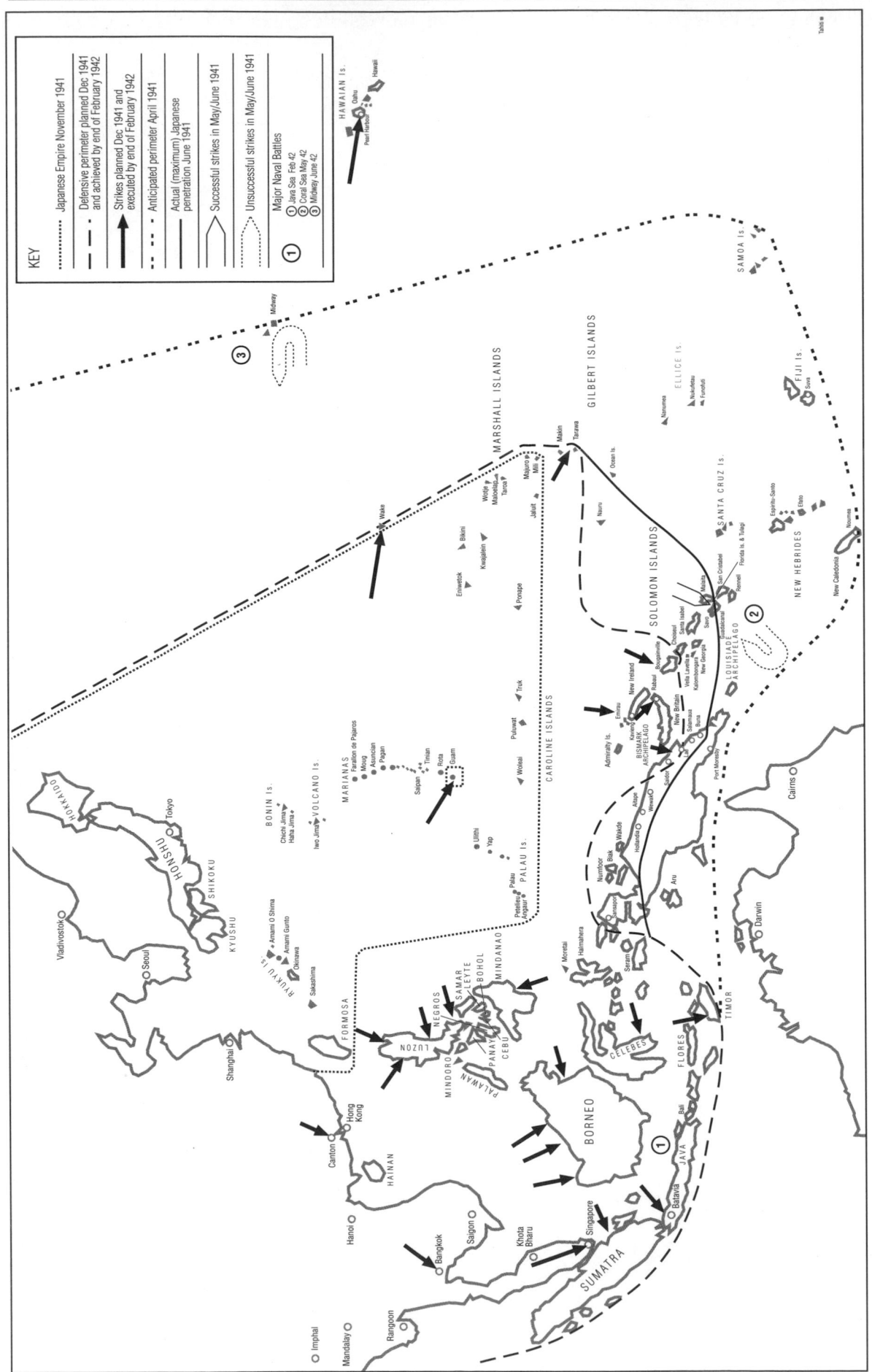

Map 27 The Pacific (i): The Japanese Offensive December 1941-June 1942

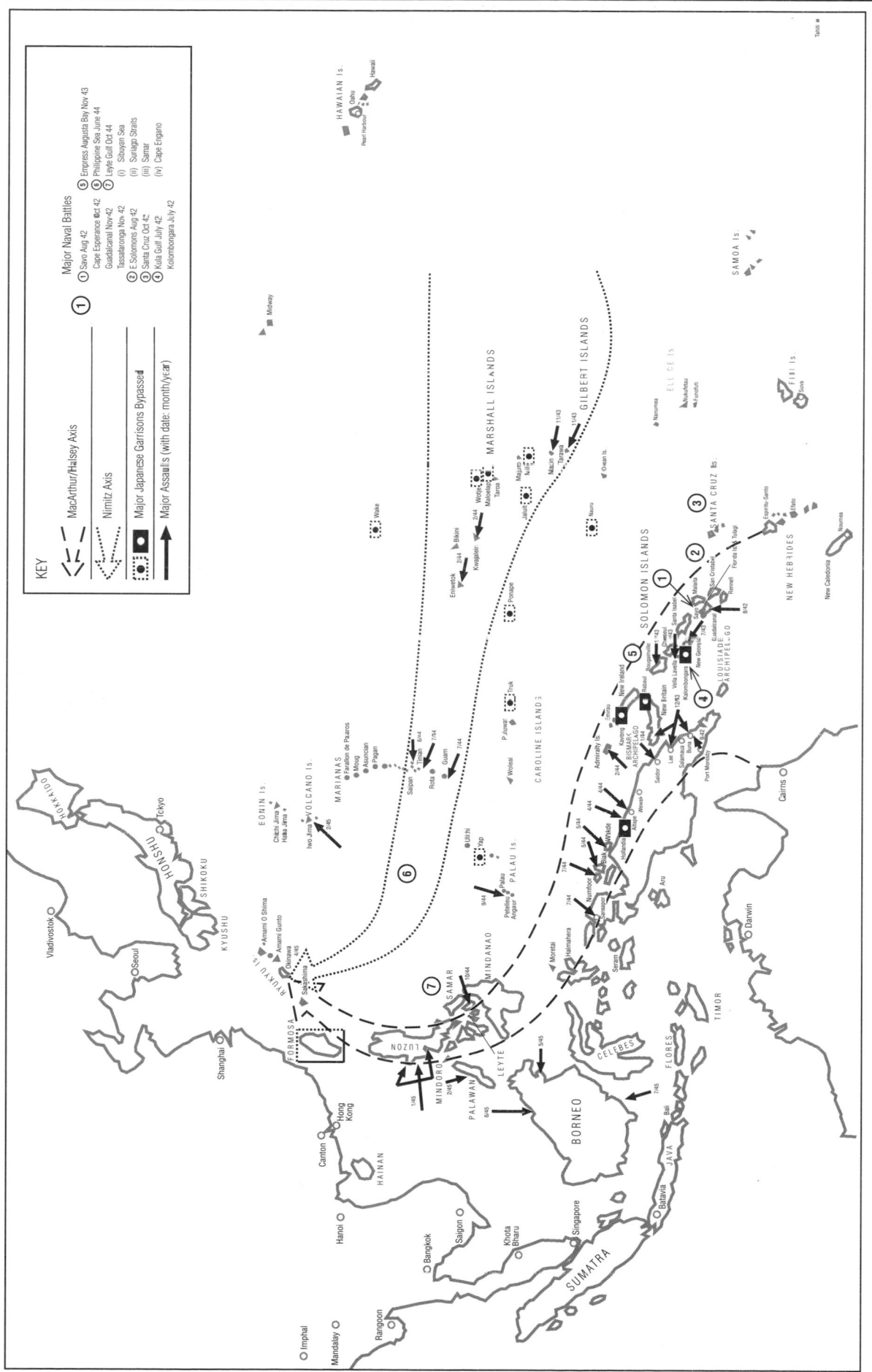

Map 28 The Pacific (ii): The American Counter-offensive August 1942–August 1945

SECTION 2

COMMAND STRUCTURES

• **TABLE 1** • US GOVERNMENT AND HIGH COMMAND 1941-45 •

This section addresses two basic tasks: firstly to at least outline the extremely complex administrative networks (*both* civilian and military) that were responsible for actually waging the war, and secondly to identify the key personnel involved. Organigrams, and detailed supplements thereto, are provided for the major belligerents (not forgetting the Allied combined commands) and all army groups, armies, air forces/fleets and naval fleets are included, together with their commanders. Such detail is not possible for all the belligerents but each of the rest is accorded a listing of the heads of state, key ministers and forces commanders. Where relevant, details are also included of governments-in-exile as well as of occupation or quisling administrations.

Table 1 US Government and High Command 1941-45

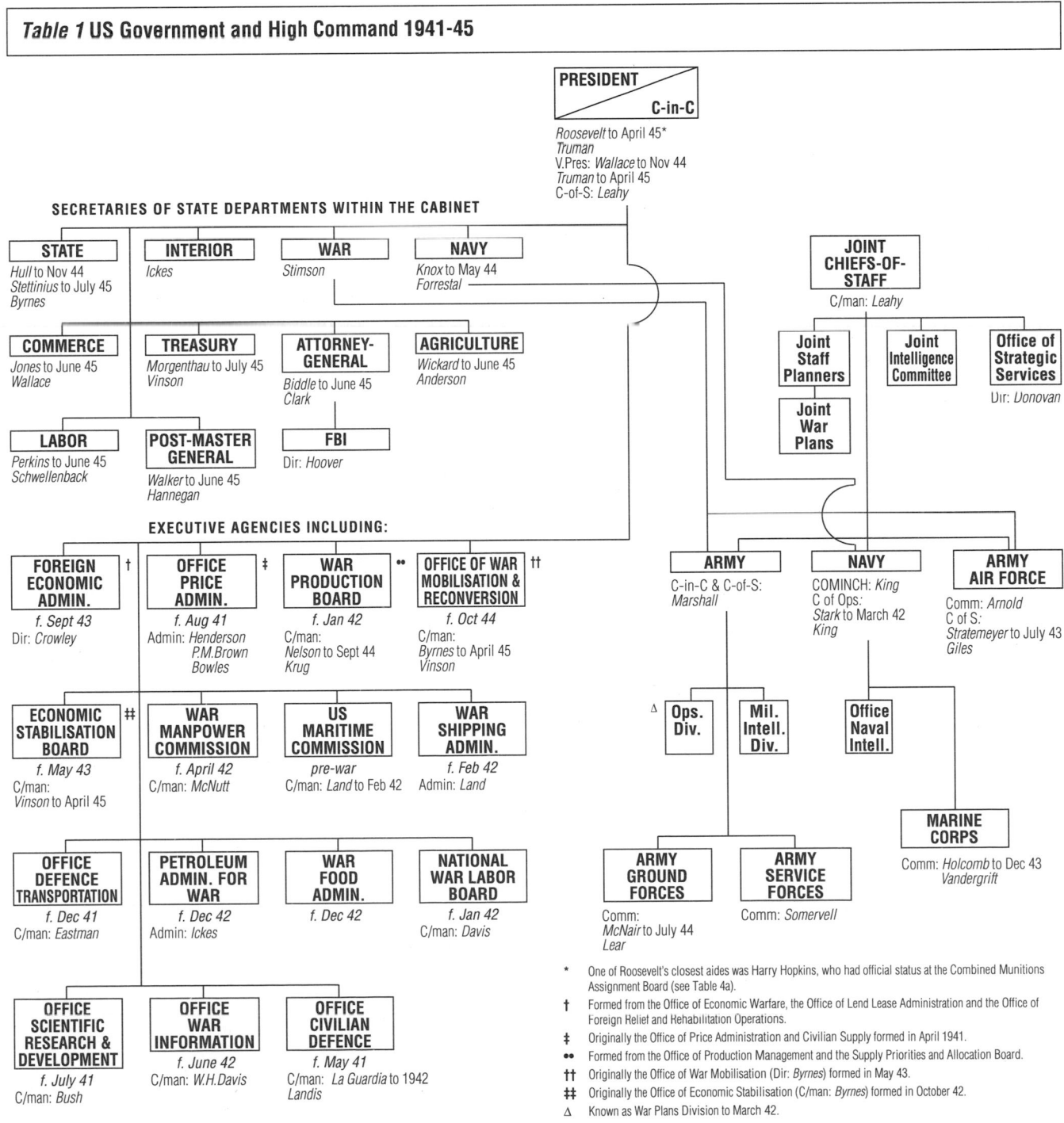

PRESIDENT / C-in-C
Roosevelt to April 45*
Truman
V.Pres: *Wallace* to Nov 44
Truman to April 45
C-of-S: *Leahy*

SECRETARIES OF STATE DEPARTMENTS WITHIN THE CABINET

STATE
Hull to Nov 44
Stettinius to July 45
Byrnes

INTERIOR
Ickes

WAR
Stimson

NAVY
Knox to May 44
Forrestal

JOINT CHIEFS-OF-STAFF
C/man: *Leahy*

COMMERCE
Jones to June 45
Wallace

TREASURY
Morgenthau to July 45
Vinson

ATTORNEY-GENERAL
Biddle to June 45
Clark

AGRICULTURE
Wickard to June 45
Anderson

Joint Staff Planners

Joint Intelligence Committee

Office of Strategic Services
Dir: *Donovan*

LABOR
Perkins to June 45
Schwellenback

POST-MASTER GENERAL
Walker to June 45
Hannegan

FBI
Dir: *Hoover*

Joint War Plans

EXECUTIVE AGENCIES INCLUDING:

FOREIGN ECONOMIC ADMIN. †
f. Sept 43
Dir: *Crowley*

OFFICE PRICE ADMIN. ‡
f. Aug 41
Admin: *Henderson*
P.M.Brown
Bowles

WAR PRODUCTION BOARD ••
f. Jan 42
C/man:
Nelson to Sept 44
Krug

OFFICE OF WAR MOBILISATION & RECONVERSION ††
f. Oct 44
C/man:
Byrnes to April 45
Vinson

ARMY
C-in-C & C-of-S:
Marshall

NAVY
COMINCH: *King*
C of Ops:
Stark to March 42
King

ARMY AIR FORCE
Comm: *Arnold*
C of S:
Stratemeyer to July 43
Giles

ECONOMIC STABILISATION BOARD ‡‡
f. May 43
C/man:
Vinson to April 45

WAR MANPOWER COMMISSION
f. April 42
C/man: *McNutt*

US MARITIME COMMISSION
pre-war
C/man: *Land* to Feb 42

WAR SHIPPING ADMIN.
f. Feb 42
Admin: *Land*

Δ **Ops. Div.**

Mil. Intell. Div.

Office Naval Intell.

OFFICE DEFENCE TRANSPORTATION
f. Dec 41
C/man: *Eastman*

PETROLEUM ADMIN. FOR WAR
f. Dec 42
Admin: *Ickes*

WAR FOOD ADMIN.
f. Dec 42

NATIONAL WAR LABOR BOARD
f. Jan 42
C/man: *Davis*

ARMY GROUND FORCES
Comm:
McNair to July 44
Lear

ARMY SERVICE FORCES
Comm: *Somervell*

MARINE CORPS
Comm: *Holcomb* to Dec 43
Vandergrift

OFFICE SCIENTIFIC RESEARCH & DEVELOPMENT
f. July 41
C/man: *Bush*

OFFICE WAR INFORMATION
f. June 42
C/man: *W.H.Davis*

OFFICE CIVILIAN DEFENCE
f. May 41
C/man: *La Guardia* to 1942
Landis

* One of Roosevelt's closest aides was Harry Hopkins, who had official status at the Combined Munitions Assignment Board (see Table 4a).

† Formed from the Office of Economic Warfare, the Office of Lend Lease Administration and the Office of Foreign Relief and Rehabilitation Operations.

‡ Originally the Office of Price Administration and Civilian Supply formed in April 1941.

•• Formed from the Office of Production Management and the Supply Priorities and Allocation Board.

†† Originally the Office of War Mobilisation (Dir: *Byrnes*) formed in May 43.

‡‡ Originally the Office of Economic Stabilisation (C/man: *Byrnes*) formed in October 42.

Δ Known as War Plans Division to March 42.

Supplement to Table 1: Other Major US Commands

THEATRE COMMANDS*

1 C-in-C. SOUTH-WEST PACIFIC AREA (COMSOWESPAC) was set up in April 42 as part of the reorganisation of command in the Pacific and the division thereof between the Navy and the Army. The major division was between the SOUTH-WEST PACIFIC (Army) and the PACIFIC OCEAN AREAS (Navy) (see below).

MacArthur

2 C-in-C. PACIFIC OCEAN AREAS (CINCPOA) was set up in April 42 (see above). It was subdivided into three subordinate (Navy) Areas which are listed below.

Nimitz

3 C-in-C. CENTRAL PACIFIC OCEAN AREA (COMCENPAC) was set up in April 42 (see above). It was by far the largest of the three subordinate (Navy) PACIFIC OCEAN AREAS and thus it too was commanded by

Nimitz

4 C-in-C. SOUTH PACIFIC AREA (COMSOPAC) was set up in April 42 (see above).

Ghormley to Oct 42

Halsey to June 44

Newton

5 C-in-C. NORTH PACIFIC AREA (COMNORPAC) was set up in April 42 (see above).

Theobald to Jan 43

Kinkaid to Oct 43

Fletcher

THE ARMY
Army Groups

These are listed in Tables 4c-e.

Armies

1 FIRST ARMY was in existence at the beginning of the war and arrived in England in Oct 43. From here it participated in the invasion of Normandy and fought in the North-West European theatre until the end of the war.

Bradley Oct 43 to Aug 44 (also commanding FIRST later TWELFTH ARMY GROUP headquarters [see Table 4e]).

Hodges

2 SECOND ARMY never went overseas.

3 THIRD ARMY was in existence at the beginning of the war and arrived in England in Jan 44. It landed in France in July 44 and fought through France and Germany to the end of the war.

Patton from Jan 44

4 FOURTH ARMY never went overseas.

5 FIFTH ARMY was activated in Algiers in Jan 43 and had responsibility for the administration and training of US troops in North Africa, though not for operations. Its first operational task was the Salerno landings in Italy in Sept 43 and it remained in this theatre until the end of the war.

Clark to Nov 44 (also commanding SEVENTH ARMY [see below] Jan to March 44).

Truscott

6 SIXTH ARMY was activated in Jan 43 and arrived in the Pacific in April, where it remained for the rest of the war. From April 43 to Sept 44 SIXTH ARMY was also known as TASK FORCE ALAMO.†

Kreuger

7 SEVENTH ARMY was activated in July 43 *en route* to Sicily, in whose invasion and conquest it participated. In Aug 44 it took part in the invasion of Southern France and fought in France and Germany until the end of the war.

Patton to Jan 44

Clark to March 44 (also commanding FIFTH ARMY (see above)).

Patch

8 EIGHTH ARMY was activated in June 44 and arrived in the Pacific in September. There it remained until the end of the war.

Eichelberger

9 NINTH ARMY was activated in April 44 and arrived in England in June. In September it became operational in France and fought there and in Germany until the end of the war.

Simpson

10 TENTH ARMY was activated in the Pacific in June 44 although it did not see action, *qua* Army, until April 45, on Okinawa.

Buckner to Jun 45

Geiger to July 45

Stilwell

11 FIFTEENTH ARMY was activated in Jan 45 in North-West Europe to undertake mopping-up and garrison duties in the wake of other US forces. It never contained more than six divisions.

Gerow

THE NAVY
Fleets

Whilst the ATLANTIC, PACIFIC and ASIATIC FLEETS existed at the beginning of the war, the numbered US Fleets (THIRD, FOURTH, FIFTH, SEVENTH, EIGHTH, TENTH and TWELFTH) did not appear as such until 1943 and 1944. Prior to that the ships in them had been organised in various formations, the most recent of which were the NAVAL FORCES attached to a particular area.

1 ATLANTIC FLEET (C-in-C = CINCLANT)

Ingersoll to Nov 44

Ingram

2 PACIFIC FLEET (C-in-C = CINCPAC)

Kimmel to Dec 41

Pye Dec 41 (acting)

Nimitz

3 ASIATIC FLEET was dissolved in June 42.

Hart (also C-in-C. ABDA naval forces [see Table 4b]).

4 THIRD FLEET was established in March 43 as a successor to SOUTH PACIFIC NAVAL FORCE, the latter having being formed in April 42. From June 44 operations in the South Pacific were not deemed sufficiently important to merit a Fleet headquarters and THIRD FLEET came under the command of COMCENPAC (see above) where it alternated with FIFTH FLEET (see below) in running operations in the Central Pacific Area. THIRD FLEET was in charge of these operations from Sept 44 to Jan 45 and from May 45 to the end of the war.

Ghormley to Oct 42

Halsey

5 FOURTH FLEET was established in March 43, having previously been known as SOUTH ATLANTIC FORCE. It remained under the command of ATLANTIC FLEET (see above). It was dissolved in April 45.

Ingram to Nov 44

Munroe

6 FIFTH FLEET was established in Aug 43 as CENTRAL PACIFIC FORCE, receiving its Fleet designation in April 44.‡ From June 44 it and THIRD FLEET had alternate charge of operations in the Central Pacific Area (see THIRD FLEET above). FIFTH FLEET was in charge from April to Sept 44 and Jan to May 45.

Spruance

7 SEVENTH FLEET was established in Feb 43, having previously been known as SOUTH-WEST PACIFIC FORCE. Throughout the war it operated under the overall command of General MacArthur.

Leary to Sept 42

Carpender to Nov 43

Kinkaid

* Details on American theatre commanders outside the Pacific, i.e. in combined Allied theatres, will be found in Tables 4c-e.

‡ The term Fifth Fleet had been used prior to that but only to refer to the *ships* within the Central Pacific and not to the entire amphibious force.

† To allow *Kreuger* to report to *Gen. MacArthur* directly and not to MacArthur's actual overall Army commander, *Blamey*, an Australian.

8 EIGHTH FLEET
[See Table 4c].

9 TENTH FLEET was established in May 43 and was a shore-based organisation responsible for controlling anti-submarine operations in the Atlantic areas under American command. It was commanded throughout the war by COMINCH (*King*). The Chiefs-of-Staff were
Low to Jan 45
McCann to June 45 (Fleet dissolved)

10 TWELFTH FLEET
[See Table 4e].

Seaboard Commands

The following shore-based commands existed during the war (known as SEA FRONTIERS from Feb 42) which were responsible for the protection of shipping within their offshore zone. Only those Sea Frontiers on the Atlantic seaboard are listed below as those on the Pacific and elsewhere had to face only very limited attacks on their shipping. The zones not listed are ALASKA SEA FRONTIER (f. April 44), HAWAIIAN SEA FRONTIER, MOROCCAN SEA FRONTIER (f. Feb 43), NORTH-WEST SEA FRONTIER (dissolved April 44), PHILIPPINE SEA FRONTIER and WESTERN SEA FRONTIER (which incorporated NORTH-WEST from April 44).

11 CARIBBEAN SEA FRONTIER
Hoover to Aug 43
Cook to May 44
Griffen

12 EASTERN SEA FRONTIER
Andrews to Nov 43
Leary

13 GULF SEA FRONTIER
Cronshaw to June 42
Kauffmann to April 43
Munroe to July 44
Anderson

14 PANAMA SEA FRONTIER
van Hook to Sept 43
Train to Nov 44
Kingman

Other

15 TASK FORCE (TF) 38 was the Fast Carrier Force around which THIRD FLEET (see above) was built. When these ships were being controlled by FIFTH FLEET (see above) they were known as TF 58.
McCain

16 TASK FORCE 58 [see TASK FORCE 38 above].
Mitscher

17 AMPHIBIOUS FORCES PACIFIC FLEET. This became a major command in Aug 43 when its most important constituent part, V AMPHIBIOUS FORCE was created to operate with FIFTH FLEET (see above) in the Central Pacific. The commander of 'V Phib' was also commander AMPHIBIOUS FORCES PACIFIC FLEET. Other constituents were III AMPHIBIOUS FORCE (originally AMPHIBIOUS FORCE SOUTH PACIFIC), SEVENTH AMPHIBIOUS FORCE (originally AMPHIBIOUS FORCE SOUTH-WEST PACIFIC), NINTH AMPHIBIOUS FORCE (originally AMPHIBIOUS FORCE NORTH PACIFIC) and AMPHIBIOUS TRAINING COMMAND (originally REAR ECHELON OF AMPHIBIOUS FORCE). The same alternation of command that characterised THIRD/FIFTH FLEET and TF 38/TF 58 operations (see above) also applied to the amphibious component which was either III or V AMPHIBIOUS FORCE (the former commanded by *Wilkinson*). However, it is to be noted that the commander of 'V Phib' remained commander of all amphibious forces in the Pacific and that during THIRD FLEET's tenure of command in the Central Pacific the only major amphibious enterprise was the invasion of the Palau Is. The commander of AMPHIBIOUS FORCES SOUTH PACIFIC from July 42 to Aug 43 and then of FIFTH AMPHIBIOUS FORCE and AMPHIBIOUS FORCES PACIFIC FLEET

for the rest of the war was
Turner

18 SERVICE FORCE PACIFIC FLEET was a mobile fleet train providing logistical back-up, notably fuel, ammunition and spares, for the Central Pacific advance.
Calhoun to March 45
W.W.Smith

19 SUBMARINES PACIFIC FLEET
Withers to May 42
English to Jan 43
Lockwood

20 NAVAL FORCES EUROPE
[See Table 4e].

21 NAVAL FORCES FRANCE
[See Table 4e].

22 NAVAL FORCES GERMANY
[See Table 4e].

The Marine Corps

Marine Corps organisation in the Pacific (the only theatre in which it fought) largely followed the pattern applied to THIRD/FIFTH FLEETS and AMPHIBIOUS FORCES PACIFIC FLEET (see above). Two AMPHIBIOUS CORPS were set up, the IIIRD, which began its life in the South Pacific, and the VTH which was formed in the Central Pacific. After the conquest of the former area the two Corps HQs then took it in turn to supervise landing operations in the Central Pacific. As with the AMPHIBIOUS FORCE (see above) control of the whole Marine Corps presence in the Pacific was initially taken by V CORPS, though in Oct 44 a separate overall commander was appointed.

23 FLEET MARINE FORCE PACIFIC was established early in the war as 2 JOINT TRAINING FORCE, later known as AMPHIBIOUS CORPS PACIFIC FLEET and from Sept 43 as V AMPHIBIOUS CORPS. It took its last change of title in March 44.
H.M.Smith March 44 to July 45
Geiger

24 III AMPHIBIOUS CORPS was formed in Oct 42 as I AMPHIBIOUS CORPS, being redesignated in April 44.
Vogel to July 43
Vandergrift to Nov 43
Barrett Sept to Oct 43 (acting)
Geiger to June 45
Rockey

25 V AMPHIBIOUS FORCE was formed in Sept 43 from AMPHIBIOUS CORPS PACIFIC FLEET.
H.M.Smith to Oct 44
Schmidt

26 C-in-C. AIRCRAFT, FLEET MARINE FORCE PACIFIC
Powell to Sept 44
Mulcahey to Feb 45
Moore

27 COMMANDANT MARINE CORPS
Holcomb to Dec 43
Vandergrift

THE ARMY AIR FORCE

Officially, the US Air Force throughout the war was a part of the Army though it was in fact granted a great deal of operational autonomy. As can be seen on the Table 1 organigram it even had its own place on the Joint Chiefs of Staff.

Area Commands

See Tables 4c-e for commands in North-West Europe, the Mediterranean and South-East Asia.

1 C-in-C. ARMY AIR FORCES PACIFIC OCEAN AREA was established in August 44 to oversee some of the land-based USAAF forces fighting with *Nimitz*. [See CINCPOA in Theatre Commands above.]
Harmon

2 C-in-C. US STRATEGIC AIR FORCES PACIFIC was established in June 45 to oversee TWENTIETH and newly arrived EIGHTH AIR FORCES (see below)
Spaatz

3 C-in-C. FAR EAST AIR FORCES was established in June 44 to oversee the operations of FIFTH and THIRTEENTH AIR FORCES (see below). SEVENTH AIR FORCE (see below) also came under command later in the war.
Kenney

4 C-in-C. US STRATEGIC AIR FORCES IN EUROPE [See EIGHTH AIR FORCE below].

Air Forces

5 FIRST AIR FORCE was established in Dec 40 as NORTHEAST AIR DISTRICT and was redesignated early in 1941. It served in the US throughout the war, being concerned mainly with air defence.
Krogstad to Mar 42
Bradley to July 42
Chaney to April 43
Royce to Sept 43
Hunter

6 SECOND AIR FORCE was established in Dec 40 as NORTHWEST AIR DISTRICT and was redesignated early in 1941. It served in the US throughout the war, being concerned mainly with training bomber crew.
Brooks to Feb 42
Martin to May 42
Johnson to Sept 43
Streett to Jan 44
Ent to Oct 44
Williams

7 THIRD AIR FORCE was established in Oct 40 as SOUTHEAST AIR DISTRICT and was redesignated early in 1941. It served in the US throughout the war, being concerned mainly with training all kinds of air crew.
Frank to June 42
Wash to Nov 42
Streett to Sept 43
Larson to May 45
Lynch May 45
Brereton

8 FOURTH AIR FORCE was established in Oct 40 as SOUTHWEST AIR DISTRICT and was redesignated early in 1941. It served in the US throughout the war, being concerned with air defence up to 1943 and then with training all kinds of air crew.
Fickel to April 42
Kenney to July 42
Giles to March 43
Kepner to July 43
Lynd to July 44
Parker to May 45
Morris to July 45
Hale

9 FIFTH AIR FORCE was established in Aug 41 as PHILIPPINE DEPARTMENT AIR FORCE and later as FAR EAST AIR FORCE. It received its numerical designation in Feb 42 but was not properly activated until September. It was stationed mainly in Australia, New Guinea and the Philippines and was closely associated with McArthur's drive in the South-West Pacific.
Brereton to Feb 42
Brett to Aug 42

Kenney to June 44
Whitehead

10 SIXTH AIR FORCE was established in Oct 40 as PANAMA CANAL and later CARIBBEAN AIR FORCE. It was numbered in Feb 42 and served primarily in the defence of the Panama Canal.
Davenport to Nov 42
Harmon to Nov 43
Wooten to May 44
Sorensen to Sept 44
Butler to July 45
Ford

11 SEVENTH AIR FORCE was established in Hawaii in Oct 40 as HAWAIIAN AIR FORCE and was redesignated in Feb 42. It provided air defence for Hawaii and after mid-1943 supported operations in the Western and Central Pacific.
Tinker to June 42
Davidson June 42
Hale to April 44
Douglass to June 45
White

12 EIGHTH AIR FORCE was formed in Jan 42 and moved to England between May and June. It was concerned mainly with strategic bombing operations into Germany and occupied Europe. In Feb 44 it was redesignated US STRATEGIC AIR FORCES IN EUROPE, with some authority over NINTH and FIFTEENTH AIR FORCES (see below), whilst its heavy bomber component, VIII BOMBER COMMAND, was upgraded to EIGHTH AIR FORCE. The latter was transferred to Okinawa in July 45 but never took part in the Pacific campaign.

EIGHTH AIR FORCE	VIII BOMBER COMMAND
Duncan to May 42	*Eaker* to Dec 42
Spaatz to Dec 42	*Newton* to July 43
Eaker	*Anderson*

US STRATEGIC AIR FORCES IN EUROPE	EIGHTH AIR FORCE
Spaatz	*Doolittle* to May 45
	Kepner to June 45
	Larsen to July 45
	Doolittle

13 NINTH AIR FORCE [See Table 4c]

14 TENTH AIR FORCE was formed in Feb 42 and moved to India between March and May. It served in India, Burma and China until March 43 and then, after the activation of FOURTEENTH AIR FORCE (see below) in India and Burma. It joined FOURTEENTH AIR FORCE in China in July 45.
Halverson to March 42
Brereton to June 42
Naiden to Aug 42
Bissell to Aug 43
Davidson

15 ELEVENTH AIR FORCE was established in Dec 41 as ALASKAN AIR FORCE, being redesignated in Feb 42. It was mainly concerned with air defence but did also take part in the offensive against the Aleutians and the Kurile Is.
Davis to Feb 42
Dunlap to March 42
Butler to Sept 43
Johnson to May 45
Davies to June 45
Brooks

16 TWELFTH AIR FORCE [See Table 4c].

17 THIRTEENTH AIR FORCE was established in Dec 42 and served in the South and South-West Pacific, being closely associated with

• **TABLE 2** • SOVIET GOVERNMENT AND HIGH COMMAND 1941-45 •

MacArthur's drive there.
   Twining to July 43
   Owens to Jan 44
   Harmon to June 44
   Streett to Feb 45
   Wurtsmith

18 FOURTEENTH AIR FORCE was established in March 43 in China and remained there until the end of the war.
   Chennault

19 FIFTEENTH AIR FORCE
[See Table 4c].

20 SIXTEENTH through NINETEENTH AIR FORCES were never formed.

21 TWENTIETH AIR FORCE was established in April 44 and flew strategic bombing missions against Japan from China and the Marianas. In 1945 it operated from the Marianas only.
   Arnold to July 45
   LeMay to Aug 45
   Twining

Other

22 AIR TRANSPORT COMMAND was established in May 41 as AIR CORPS FERRYING COMMAND and was redesignated in June 42.
   Olds to June 42
   George

Table 2 Soviet Government and High Command 1941-45

| Dept. C/man: *Molotov* |
| Members: *Beria* |
| *Malenkov* |
| *Voroshilov* to Nov 44 |
| *Voznozsensky* |
| *Mikoyan* } from Feb 42 |
| *Kaganovich* |
| *Bulganin* from Nov 44 |

SUPREME SOVIET *

COMMUNIST PARTY CONGRESS *

† **STATE COMMITTEE FOR DEFENCE**
C/man: *Stalin*

PRAESIDIUM

‡ **SUPREME COMMAND**
C-in-C: *Timoshenko* to July 41
Stalin ††

CENTRAL COMMITTEE
Gen Sec: *Stalin*
including

SOVIET OF PEOPLE'S COMMISSARS **
C/man: *Stalin*

ORGBURO   **POLITBURO**

COMMISSARIATS (including):

FOREIGN AFFAIRS
Comm: *Molotov*

DEFENCE
Comm: *Timoshenko* to July 41
Stalin

NAVY
to Feb 45
Comm: *Kuznetsov*
C-in-C: *Kuznetsov*

JUSTICE
Comm: *Rychkov*

INTERNAL AFFAIRS
Comm: *Beria*

N.K.V.D.
Comm: *Beria*

RED ARMY GENERAL STAFF ‡‡
C. of S: *Zhukov* to July 41
Shaposhnikov to June 42
Vasilevsky to Feb 45
Antonov
C. of Ops: *Zhlobin* to Aug 41
Vasilevsky to Nov 42
Antonov to May 43
Shtemenko
including

NAVY
from Feb 45
C-in-C: *Kuznetsov*

STATE CONTROL
Comm: *Mekhlis*

STATE PLANNING COMMISSION
C/man: *Saburov* to Dec 42
Voznesensky

ARMAMENT
Comm: *Ustinov*

AIRCRAFT INDUSTRY
Comm: *Shakhurin*

SMERSH Δ
formed April 42
Comm: *Chernyshov* to 43
Abakumov

TANK INDUSTRY
Comm: *Malyshev* to July 42
Zal'tsman to June 43
Malyshev

HEAVY ENGINEERING
Comm: *Pavshin*

AIR FORCE
C-in-C:
Zhigarev to April 42
Novikov
C-of-S: *Volodin* June 41
Vorozheykin to April 42
Khudyakov to July 42
Falakyev to May 43
Khudyakov

ARTILLERY
C-in-C: *Voronov*

REAR SERVICES
C-in-C: *Khrulev*

*   Dotted lines imply little real executive authority.
†   Also known by Russian initials as GKO (*Gosudarstvennyy komitet oborony*).
‡   Often known as Stavka (*Shtab glavnogo/verkhovnogo komandovaniya*).
** Often known as Sovnarkom (*Sovet Narodnykh Komissarov*).
†† From Aug 42 the First Deputy C-in-C. was Zhukov.
‡‡ Answerable to Stalin personally rather than to the Supreme Command as a collective i.e. to Stavka.
Δ   Reported directly to Stalin. The names given are of the Army representatives. From 1943 there was also a Navy representative, Gladkov.

> *Supplement to Table 2:* Other Major Soviet Commands

THE ARMY
Area Commands
These were groups of Fronts (or Army Groups) and existed only occasionally and for short periods.

1 NORTH-WEST THEATRE
   Voroshilov July 41

2 WEST THEATRE
   Timoshenko July to Sept 41
   Zhukov Feb 42

3 SOUTH-WEST THEATRE
   Budenny July to Sept 41
   Timoshenko Sept 41 and Nov 41 to May 42

Army Groups (Fronts)
Throughout the war the Russian High Command deployed forty-six different Fronts (in roughly chronological order these were: North, North-West, Reserve twice, West, South-West twice, South twice, Central twice, Bryansk twice, Karelia, Leningrad, Kalinin, Vilkhov, Transcaucasus twice, Caucasus, Crimea, North Caucasus twice, Voronezh, Stalingrad twice, South-East, Don, Steppe, Baltic, Byelorussian, 1, 2, 3 and 4 (twice) Ukrainian, 1 and 2 Baltic, 1 and 2 (twice) Byelorussian, 3 Baltic, 3 Byelorussian, 1 and 2 Far Eastern and Transbaikal. In fact, as with the Germans [see Table 5] many of these 'new' fronts were simply existing headquarters with a new name and it is possible to identify only thirty-two distinct headquarters. It is these that are listed below, though all their various nomenclatures are also given. All the Army Groups named, except for the last three, fought on Russia's western front.

1 NORTH FRONT was in existence in June 41 and became LENINGRAD FRONT in August. It remained in existence until late 1944.
   Popov to Aug 41 (NORTH)
   Zhukov Aug 41
   Voroshilov to Oct 41
   Khozin to June 42
   Govorov

2 NORTH-WEST FRONT was in existence in June 41 and fought until it was disbanded in Feb 44.
   Kuznetsov to June 41
   Subennikov to Aug 41
   Kurochkin to Feb 43
   Timoshenko to March 43
   Konev

3 RESERVE FRONT # 1 was in existence in June 41 and remained until October when it became a part of WEST FRONT (see below).
   Budenny to July 41
   Bogdanov to Aug 41
   Zhukov to Sept 41
   Budenny

4 WEST FRONT was in existence in June 41 and remained as such until it was reformed as 2 BYELORUSSIAN FRONT # 2 in April 44. It fought as such until the end of the war.
   Pavlov to June 41 (WEST)
   Eremenko June 41 (WEST)
   Timoshenko to Aug 41 (WEST)
   Konev to Oct 41 (WEST)
   Zhukov to Aug 42 (WEST)
   Konev to March 43 (WEST)
   Sokolovsky to April 44 (WEST)
   Petrov to May 44 (2 BYELO # 2)
   Zakharov to Nov 44 (2 BYELO # 2)
   Rokossovsky (2 BYELO # 2)

5 SOUTH-WEST FRONT # 1 was in existence in June 41 and

remained until May 42 when it was largely destroyed.
   Kirponos to Sep 41
   Timoshenko to Feb 42
   Kostenko

6 SOUTH FRONT # 1 was in existence in June 41 and survived until being absorbed into NORTH CAUCASUS FRONT # 1 (see below) in July 42.
   Tyulenev to July 41
   Ryabyshev to Oct 41
   Cherevichenko to Jan 42
   Malinovsky

7 KARELIA FRONT was formed in Aug 41 and remained in existence until late 1944, when its headquarters went east to form 1 FAR EASTERN FRONT.
   Frolov to Feb 44 (KARELIA)
   Meretskov (KARELIA; 1 FAR EAST)

8 CENTRAL FRONT # 1 was formed in July 41 and disbanded in August.
   Kuznetsov

9 BRYANSK FRONT # 1 was formed in Aug 41 and disbanded in November.
   Eremenko to Oct 41
   Zakharov

10 KALININ FRONT was formed in Oct 41 and lasted until Oct 43 when it became 1 BALTIC FRONT. This remained in existence until early 1945.
   Konev to Aug 42 (KALININ)
   Purkaev to July 43 (KALININ)
   Eremenko to Nov 43 (KALININ; 1 BALTIC)
   Bagramyan (1 BALTIC)

11 VOLKHOV FRONT was formed in Dec 41 and survived until Feb 44 when it was disbanded. It was also temporarily disbanded between April and June 42.
   Meretskov

12 BRYANSK FRONT # 2 was formed in Dec 41 and lasted to Oct 43 when it handed over its formations to CENTRAL FRONT # 2 (see below).
   Cherevichenko to April 42
   Golikov to July 42
   Chibisov July 42
   Rokossovsky to Jan 43
   Reiter to March 43
   Golikov to July 43
   Popov

13 TRANSCAUCASUS FRONT # 1 was formed in Dec 41, became CAUCASUS FRONT in Jan 42 and CRIMEA FRONT in April.
   Kozlov

14 NORTH CAUCASUS FRONT # 1 was formed in May 42 and was absorbed into TRANSCAUCASUS FRONT # 2 (see below) in September.
   Budenny

15 TRANSCAUCASUS FRONT # 2 was formed in July 42 and existed until late that year.
   Tyulenev

16 VORONEZH FRONT was formed in July 42 and lasted until Oct 43 when it became 1 UKRAINIAN FRONT which fought through to the end of the war.
   Golikov July 42 (VORONEZH)
   Vatutin to Oct 42 (VORONEZH)
   Golikov April 43 (VORONEZH)
   Vatutin to March 44 (VORONEZH; 1 UKRAINIAN)
   Zhukov to May 44 (1 UKRAINIAN)
   Konev (1 UKRAINIAN)

17 STALINGRAD FRONT # 1 was formed in July 42 and was renamed DON FRONT in September. In Feb 43 it became CENTRAL FRONT # 2, in

October BYELORUSSIAN FRONT and in Feb 44 1 BYELORUSSIAN FRONT. This it remained until the end of the war.

Timoshenko to July 42 (STALINGRAD # 1)
Gordov to Sept 42 (STALINGRAD # 1)
Rokossovsky to Nov 44 (DON; CENTRAL # 2; BYELO; 1 BYELO)
Zhukov (1 BYELO)

18 SOUTH-EAST FRONT was formed in Aug 42 and was that month renamed STALINGRAD FRONT # 2. In Jan 43 it became SOUTH FRONT # 2 and in October 4 UKRAINIAN FRONT. In May 44 it went into strategic reserve.

Eremenko to Jan 43 (SOUTH-EAST; STALINGRAD # 2)
Malinovsky to Aug 43 (SOUTH # 2)
Tolbukhin (SOUTH # 2; 4 UKRAINIAN)

19 SOUTH-WEST FRONT # 2 was formed in Sept 42 and fought to the end of the war, being renamed 3 UKRAINIAN FRONT in May 44.

Vatutin to April 43 (SOUTH-WEST # 2)
Malinovsky to June 44 (SOUTH-WEST # 2; 3 UKRAINIAN)
Tolbukhin (3 UKRAINIAN)

20 NORTH CAUCASUS FRONT # 2 was formed in Jan 43 and fought until September when it was disbanded.

Maslennikov to May 43
Petrov

21 RESERVE FRONT # 2 was formed in March 43. In July it became STEPPE FRONT and in October 2 UKRAINIAN. As such it fought through to the end of the war.

Reiter to July 43 (RESERVE # 2)
Konev to July 44 (STEPPE; 2 UKRAINIAN)
Malinovsky (2 UKRAINIAN)

22 BALTIC FRONT was formed in Oct 43 and that same month was renamed 2 BALTIC FRONT. It fought as such to the end of the war.

Popov to July 44 (BALTIC; 2 BALTIC)
Eremenko (2 BALTIC)

23 2 BYELORUSSIAN FRONT was formed in Feb 44 and disbanded in April.

Kurochkin

24 3 BALTIC FRONT was formed in April 44 and disbanded in November.

Maslennikov

25 3 BYELORUSSIAN FRONT was formed in April 44 and fought through to the end of the war.

Chernyakhovsky to Feb 45
Vasilevsky

26 4 UKRAINIAN FRONT was re-formed in Aug 44 and lasted to the end of the war.

Petrov to March 45
Eremenko

27 1 FAR EASTERN FRONT
[See KARELIA FRONT above].

28 2 FAR EASTERN FRONT was formed in 1941 and fought against the Japanese in Aug 45. It was known simply as FAR EASTERN FRONT up until the arrival of 1 FAR EASTERN FRONT (see above) in late 1944.

Apanasenko to April 43
Purkaev

29 TRANSBAIKAL FRONT was formed in 1941 and fought against the Japanese in Aug 45.

Kovalev to April 45
Malinovsky

THE AIR FORCE
Air Armies
These formations included most types of aircraft but were primarily concerned with tactical operations in direct support of the various Army Groups (Fronts).

1 1 AIR ARMY was formed in May 42 and served with WEST and 3

BYELORUSSIAN FRONTS (see above).

Kutsevalov to June 42
Khudyakov to May 43
Gromov to July 44
Khrykin

2 2 AIR ARMY was formed in May 42 and served with SOUTH-WEST # 1, STALINGRAD # 2, VORONEZH and 1 UKRAINIAN FRONTS (see above).

Krasovsky to July 42
Smirnov to March 43
Krasovsky

3 3 AIR ARMY was formed in May 42 and fought with KALININ and 1 BALTIC FRONTS (see above).

Gromov to May 43
Papavin

4 4 AIR ARMY was formed in May 42 and fought with SOUTH # 1, NORTH CAUCASUS # 2 and 2 BYELORUSSIAN # 1 and # 2 FRONTS (see above).

Vershinin to Sept 42
Naumenko to May 43
Vershinin

5 5 AIR ARMY was formed in May 42 and fought with NORTH CAUCASUS # 1 and 2 UKRAINIAN FRONTS (see above).

Goryunov

6 6 AIR ARMY was formed in June 42 and fought with NORTH-WEST FRONT until Nov 43 when it re-entered strategic reserve. It became active again in Feb 44 with 2 BYELORUSSIAN FRONT # 1 and in April 44 was assigned to 1 BYELORUSSIAN FRONT under the command of 16 AIR ARMY (see below). In Sept 44 it was withdrawn once more into strategic reserve, remaining there until the end of the war.

Kondratyk to Jan 43
Polynin

7 7 AIR ARMY was formed in Nov 42 and fought with KARELIA FRONT (see above) until being withdawn into strategic reserve at the end of 1944.

Sokolov

8 8 AIR ARMY was formed in June 42 and fought with STALINGRAD FRONT # 2 as well as with 1 and 4 UKRAINIAN FRONTS (see above).

Khryukin to July 44
Zhdanov

9 9 AIR ARMY was formed in Aug 42 and fought with 1 FAR EASTERN FRONT (see above) in Aug 45.

Senatorov to Sept 44
Vinogradov to June 45
Sokolov

10 10 AIR ARMY was formed in Aug 42 and fought with 2 FAR EASTERN FRONT (see above) in Aug 45.

Vinogradov to Sept 44
Slobozhan to May 45
Zhigarev

11 11 AIR ARMY was formed in Aug 42 and was stationed with 2 FAR EASTERN FRONT (see above) until absorbed into 10 AIR ARMY (see above) in Dec 44.

Bibikov

12 12 AIR ARMY was formed in Aug 42 and fought with TRANSBAIKAL FRONT (see above) in Aug 45.

Kutsevalov to June 45
Khudyakov

13 13 AIR ARMY was formed in Nov 42 and fought with LENINGRAD FRONT (see above) throughout the latter's existence.

Rybal'chenko

14 14 AIR ARMY was formed in June 42 and fought with VOLKHOV and 3 BALTIC FRONTS (see above) before being withdrawn into strategic reserve in late 1944.

Zhigarev

15 15 AIR ARMY was formed in July 42 and fought with BRYANSK and

2 BALTIC FRONTS up until the end of the war.
> *Pyatykhin* to May 43
> *Naumenko*

16 16 AIR ARMY was formed in Aug 42 and fought with DON, CENTRAL, BYELORUSSIAN and 1 BYELORUSSIAN FRONTS (see above) up until the end of the war.
> *Stepanov* to Oct 42
> *Rudenko*

17 17 AIR ARMY was formed in Nov 42 and fought with SOUTH-WEST # 2 and 3 UKRAINIAN FRONTS (see above) right up until the end of the war.
> *Krasovsky* to March 43
> *Sudets*

18 18 AIR ARMY was formed in Dec 44 as a successor to ADD, the Long-Range Aviation bomber force (see below). It fought against both the Germans and the Japanese.
> *Golovanov*

Functional Commands

19 ADD *(Aviatsiya dal'nego deystviya)*. Literally meaning Long-Range Aviation, this was the independent Soviet bomber force. It was formed in March 42 and survived until Dec 44 when it became 18 AIR ARMY (see above).
> *Golovanov*

20 IA-PVO *(Istrebitel'naya aviatsiya protivovozdushnoi oborony)*. Literally Fighter Aviation Air Defence, this force (comprising ninety-seven air regiments by 1945) was responsible for the defence of Russian cities, industrial locations and other strategic installations.
> *Klimov (?)*

THE NAVY

1 BALTIC FLEET
> *Tributs*

2 BLACK SEA FLEET
> *Oktiabrsky* to May 43
> *Vladimirsky*

3 NORTHERN FLEET (in the Arctic)
> *Golovko*

4 PACIFIC FLEET
> *Yumashev*

5 VVS-VMF *(Aviatsiya Voyenno-morskogo flota)* was the naval aviation arm, having come under navy control in 1938.
> *Zhavoronkov*

• **TABLE 3** • BRITISH GOVERNMENT AND HIGH COMMAND 1939-45 •

Table 3 **British Government and High Command 1939-45**

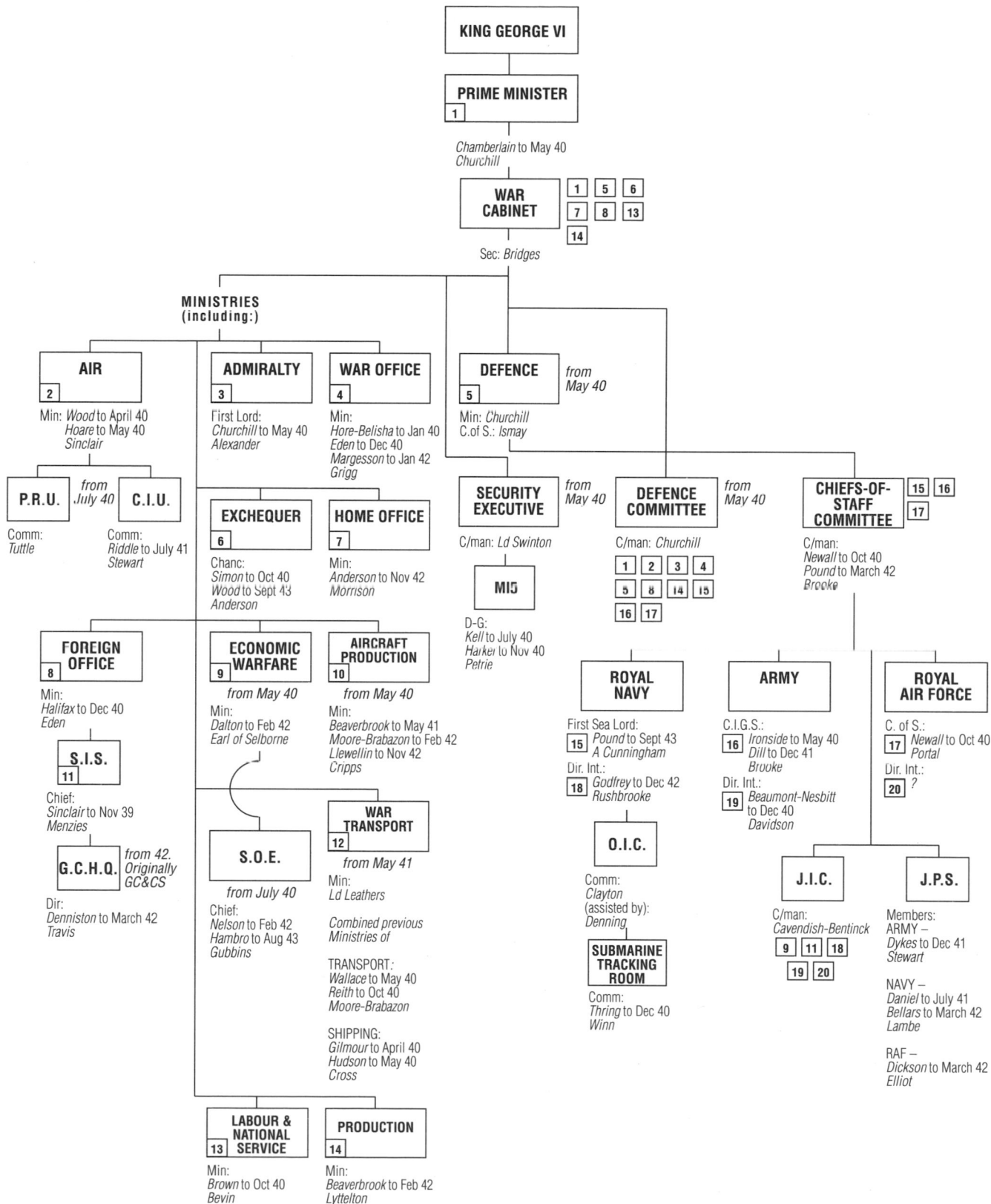

Supplement to Table 3 Other Major British Commands*

* Almost always containing sizeable Commonwealth and Empire contingents.

COMBINED OPERATIONS
Bourne June to July 40 (as Commander of Raiding Operations)
Keyes to Oct 41 (as Director Combined Operations)
Mountbatten to Oct 43
Laycock

THE ARMY
Theatre/Area Commands†
1 C-in-C. HOME FORCES
 Kirke to May 40
 Ironside to July 40
 Brooke to Dec 41
 Paget to Dec 43
 Franklyn
2 C-in-C. INDIA
 Cassels to Nov 40
 Auchinleck to June 41
 Wavell to June 43
 Hartley Jan-Feb 42 (acting)
 Auchinleck
3 C-in-C. MIDDLE EAST
 Wavell to June 41
 Auchinleck to Aug 42
 Alexander to Feb 43
 Wilson to Dec 43
 Paget
4 C-in-C. FAR EAST (f. Oct 40)
 Brooke-Popham to Dec 41
 Pownall to Jan 42 (post absorbed into ABDA COMMAND [see Table 4])
5 C-in-C. EAST AFRICA (E.AFRICA COMMAND f. Sept 41. Previously E.AFRICA FORCE)
 Cunningham to Aug 41
 Platt
 Wetherall Aug to Dec 41 (acting)
6 C-in-C. PERSIA/IRAQ (PERSIA/IRAQ COMMAND f. Aug 42. Previously TWELFTH ARMY [see below] under C-in-C. MIDDLE EAST [see above])
 Wilson to Feb 43
 Pownall to Sept 43 (command downgraded)
7 G.O.C. BURMA
 McLeod to Dec 41
 Hutton to March 42
 Alexander to Aug 42 (command abolished)
8 G.O.C. MALAYA
 Bond to April 41
 Percival to Feb 42 (command surrendered)
9 G.O.C. HONG KONG
 Grasett to July 41
 Maltby to Dec 41 (command surrendered)

Army Groups
See Tables 4b-e.

Armies
10 FIRST ARMY See Tables 4c-e.
11 SECOND ARMY was formed in June 43 and fought in N.W.Europe from June 44 to the end of the war.
 Anderson to Jan 44
 Dempsey
12 EIGHTH ARMY replaced WESTERN DESERT FORCE (f. June 40) from Sept 41. It fought in Egypt, Libya, Tunisia, Sicily and Italy right through to the end of the war.
 O'Connor to Feb 41
 Neame to April 41 (as C-in-C. CYRENAICA)
 Beresford-Peirse to Sept 41
 Cunningham to Nov 41
 Ritchie to June 42
 Auchinleck to Aug 42 (also C-in-C. MIDDLE EAST [see above])
 Montgomery to Dec 43
 Leese to Nov 44
 McCreery
13 NINTH ARMY was formed in Nov 41 from the forces that invaded Syria in June.
 Wilson to Aug 42
 Holmes
14 TENTH ARMY was formed in Feb 42 from PAIFORCE, itself a renaming of IRAQFORCE, which had been involved in operations in Iraq and Persia in May and Aug 41.
 Fraser to May 41
 Quinan
15 TWELFTH ARMY was formed in Burma in May 45 and took part in mopping-up operations there.
 Stopford
16 FOURTEENTH ARMY was set up in Oct 43 in N.W.Burma and took part in the liberation of that country over the next two years.
 Slim

Expeditionary and Other Forces
17 The BRITISH EXPEDITIONARY FORCE (B.E.F.) was sent to France in Sept 39, took part in the fighting there between May and June 40 and was largely evacuated by the end of the latter month.
 Gort to 1 June 40
 Alexander
18 The NORTH-WEST EXPEDITIONARY FORCE was the title given to forces in Norway from 13 May 40, though these forces had first landed there in mid-April with separate components known as SICKLEFORCE, MAURICEFORCE and AVONMOUTH/RUPERTFORCE. They were evacuated by the first week of June 40.
 Mackesy to 13 May 40
 Auchinleck
19 W FORCE was despatched to Greece in March 41 and was bundled out in April.
 Wilson (assumed command 4 April)
20 WESTERN DESERT FORCE see EIGHTH ARMY above.
21 IRAQFORCE see TENTH ARMY above.
22 PAIFORCE see TENTH ARMY above.
23 LAND FORCES IN GREECE were the formations sent there from Oct 44 and which remained until withdrawn by the Labour Government after the war.
 Scobie

Other
24 ANTI-AIRCRAFT COMMAND was formed in April 39 and was in existence throughout the war.
 Pile
25 C-in-C. MALTA (and Governor).
 Bonham-Carter to 1940
 Dobbie to 1942
 Gort to 1944
 Schreiber

† Details on commanders in combined Allied theatres will be found in Tables 4b-e.

ROYAL NAVY

1 C-in-C. HOME FLEET
Forbes to Dec 40
Tovey to May 43
Fraser to June 44
Moore

2 C-in-C. PORTSMOUTH
James to 1942
Little

3 C-in-C. WESTERN APPROACHES (moved from Plymouth to Liverpool Feb 41)
Dunbar-Nasmith to Feb 41
Noble to Nov 42
Horton

4 C-in-C. PLYMOUTH (f. Feb 41 on departure of C-in-C. WESTERN APPROACHES [see above])
Dunbar-Nasmith to 1941
Forbes to 1943
Leatham

5 C-in-C. THE NORE
Plunkett-Ernle-Ernle-Drax to Nov 41
D'Oyley Lyon to May 43
Tovey

6 C-in-C. SOUTH ATLANTIC
D'Oyley Lyon to Sept 40
Raikes to 1941
?

7 C-in-C. NORTH ATLANTIC
Woodhouse to Nov 39
North to Oct 40
Edward-Collins to 1943
?

8 C-in-C. ROSYTH
Ramsey to 1942
Ford to 1944
Whitworth

9 C-in-C. ORKNEYS AND SHETLANDS
Binney to 1942
Wells to 1944
Harwood

10 C-in-C. AMERICA AND WEST INDIES
Meyrick to April 40
Kennedy-Purvis to ?

11 C-in-C. MEDITERRANEAN
A.B.Cunningham to April 42
Pridham-Wippell to May 42 (acting)
Harwood to Feb 43
A.B.Cunningham to Oct 43
J.H.D.Cunningham

12 C-in-C. LEVANT (f. Feb 43)
Harwood to March 43
Leatham to June 43 (acting)
J.H.D.Cunningham to Oct 43
Willis to Dec 43
Tennant

13 C-in-C. FORCE H (f. June 40 with H.Q. at Gibraltar)
Somerville to Jan 42
Syfret to Jan 43
Burrough to March 43 (acting)
Willis

14 C-in-C. CHINA STATION
Noble to Sept 40
Layton to Dec 41 (absorbed by EASTERN FLEET [see below])

15 C-in-C. EASTERN FLEET (f. Oct 41. Arrived Singapore December).

From Nov 44 known as EAST INDIES FLEET.
Phillips to Dec 41
Layton to March 42
Somerville to Aug 44
Fraser to Nov 44
Power

16 C-in-C. BRITISH PACIFIC FLEET (f. Nov 44. Served with US Navy in the Pacific)
Fraser

17 C-in-C. SUBMARINES
Watson to Jan 40
Horton to Nov 42
Barry to Sept 44
Creasy

18 CHIEF OF NAVAL AIR SERVICES (5th SEA LORD)
Royle to March 41
Lyster to July 42
Dreyer to Jan 43
Boyd

19 C-in-C. WOMEN'S ROYAL NAVAL SERVICE
Mathews

ROYAL AIR FORCE

(Many of the most important operational air commands will be found in Table 4 dealing with the Combined Allied Commands.)

Functional Commands

1 BOMBER COMMAND
Ludlow-Hewitt to April 40
Portal to Oct 40
Pierse to Jan 42
Baldwin to Feb 42 (acting)
Harris

2 COASTAL COMMAND
Bowhill to June 41
Joubert de la Ferté to Feb 43
Slessor to Jan 44
Douglas to June 45
Slatter

3 FIGHTER COMMAND (known as AIR DEFENCE OF GREAT BRITAIN Nov 43 to Oct 44)
Dowding to Nov 40
Douglas to Nov 42
Leigh-Mallory to Nov 43
Hill

4 TRAINING COMMAND (split, in May 40, into FLYING TRAINING and TECHNICAL TRAINING COMMANDS [see below])
Longmore

5 FLYING TRAINING COMMAND (f. May 40)
Pattinson to July 41
Welsh to Aug 42
Babington

6 TECHNICAL TRAINING COMMAND (f. May 40)
Welsh to July 41
Babington to June 43
Barratt

7 MAINTENANCE COMMAND
Bradley to Oct 42
Donald

8 ARMY COOPERATION COMMAND (f. Nov 40. Disbanded June 43 when became part of 2 TACTICAL AIR FORCE [see Table 4e])
Barratt

9 FERRY COMMAND (f. July 41. Renamed 41 (Ferry) Group April 43)
Bowhill

10 TRANSPORT COMMAND (f. March 43)
Bowhill to Feb 45
Cochrane

Theatre/Area Commands

11 AOC-in-C. BRITISH AIR FORCES FRANCE (f. Jan 40 when it took command of the ADVANCED AIR STRIKING FORCE (Playfair) and the AIR COMPONENT (Blount)). Dissolved in June 40.
Barratt

12 AOC-in-C. MIDDLE EAST
Mitchell to May 40
Longmore to June 41
Tedder to Jan 43
Douglas to Jan 44
Park to Feb 45
Medhurst

13 C-in-C. RAF FAR EAST (not AOC-in-C, as between Nov 40 and Dec 41 the overall C-in-C. FAR EAST [see ARMY section above] was an Air Chief Marshal). The post disappeared in Feb 42 being amalgamated with AOC-in-C. INDIA (see below).
Babington to April 41
Pulford

14 AOC-in-C. INDIA (in Nov 43 this post was amalgamated into SOUTH EAST ASIA COMMAND [see Table 4d])
Higgins to Sept 40
Playfair to March 42
Peirse

15 AOC-in-C. WESTERN DESERT (the DESERT AIR FORCE, though this title was not formally assumed until May 43. Air HQ Western Desert was formed in Oct 41, largely from that of 204 Group, though this latter formation had been performing essentially those duties ever since its arrival in early 41, duties it took over from 202 Group. For details after Feb 43 see Table 4b).
Collishaw to July 41 (as commander 202 and 204 Groups)
Coningham to Feb 43

Other

16 WOMEN'S AUXILIARY AIR FORCE
Forbes to 1943
Walsh

Table 4a Allied Supreme Command 1942-45

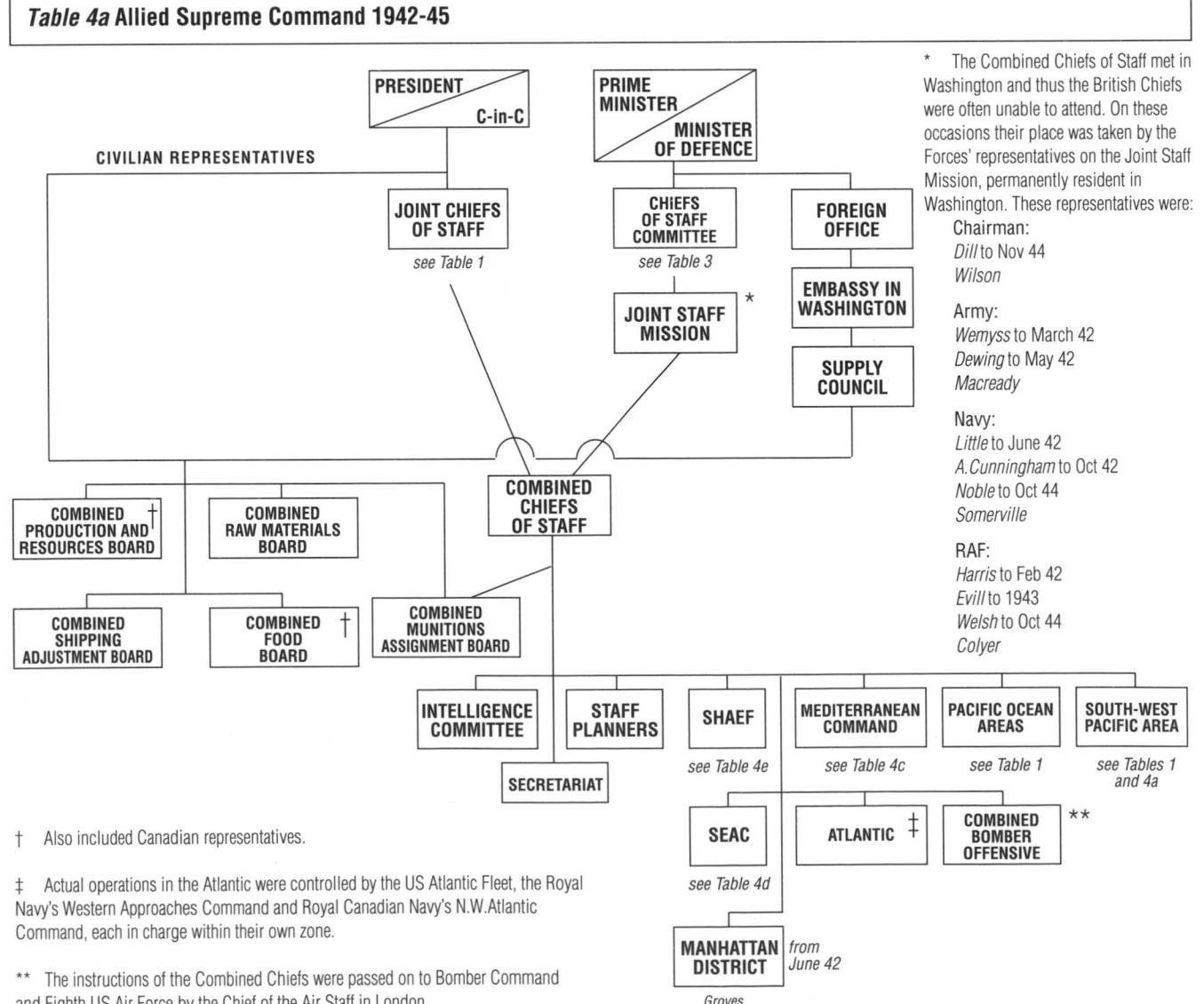

* The Combined Chiefs of Staff met in Washington and thus the British Chiefs were often unable to attend. On these occasions their place was taken by the Forces' representatives on the Joint Staff Mission, permanently resident in Washington. These representatives were:

Chairman:
Dill to Nov 44
Wilson

Army:
Wemyss to March 42
Dewing to May 42
Macready

Navy:
Little to June 42
A.Cunningham to Oct 42
Noble to Oct 44
Somerville

RAF:
Harris to Feb 42
Evill to 1943
Welsh to Oct 44
Colyer

† Also included Canadian representatives.

‡ Actual operations in the Atlantic were controlled by the US Atlantic Fleet, the Royal Navy's Western Approaches Command and Royal Canadian Navy's N.W.Atlantic Command, each in charge within their own zone.

** The instructions of the Combined Chiefs were passed on to Bomber Command and Eighth US Air Force by the Chief of the Air Staff in London.

Table 4b ABDA Command in S.W.Pacific 4 Jan-25 Feb 1942

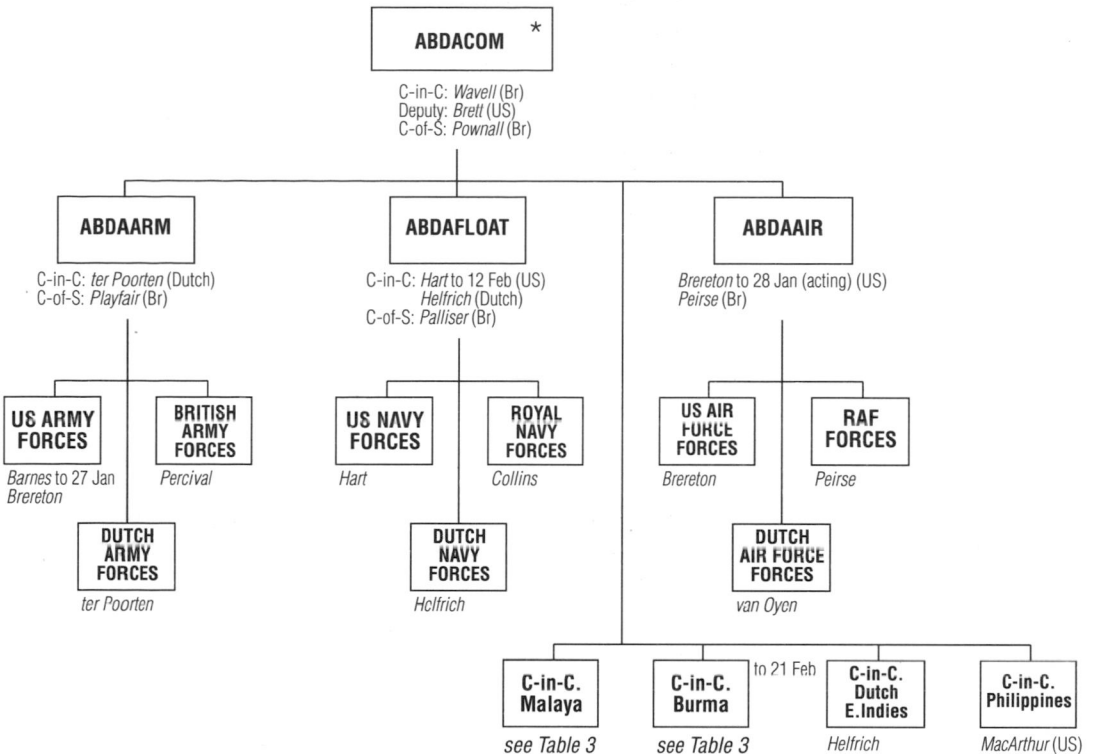

* American, British, Dutch and Australian Command with HQ at Lembang in Java.

Table 4c Allied High Command in the Mediterranean 1942-45

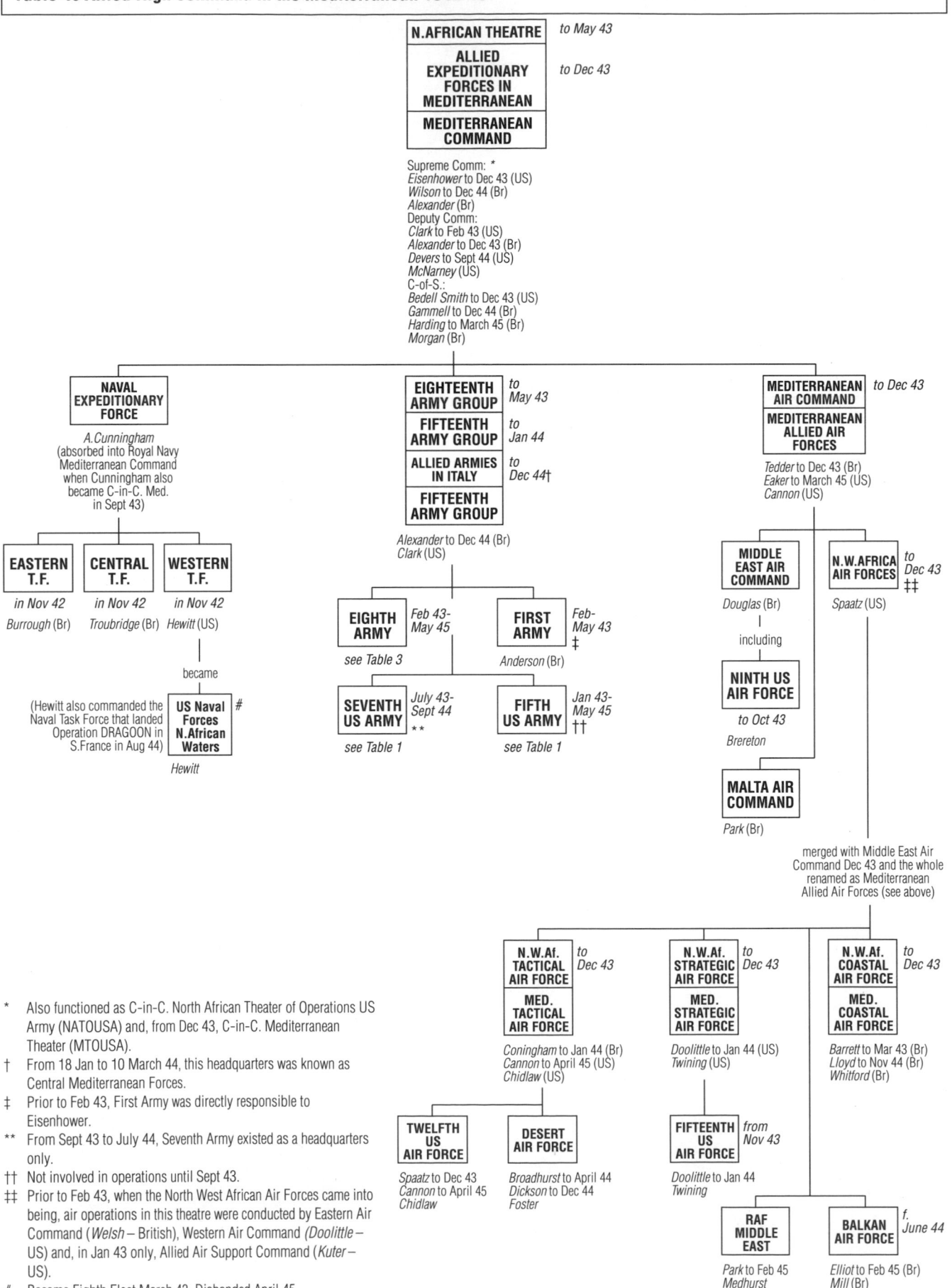

N.AFRICAN THEATRE	to May 43
ALLIED EXPEDITIONARY FORCES IN MEDITERRANEAN	to Dec 43
MEDITERRANEAN COMMAND	

Supreme Comm: *
Eisenhower to Dec 43 (US)
Wilson to Dec 44 (Br)
Alexander (Br)
Deputy Comm:
Clark to Feb 43 (US)
Alexander to Dec 43 (Br)
Devers to Sept 44 (US)
McNarney (US)
C-of-S.:
Bedell Smith to Dec 43 (US)
Gammell to Dec 44 (Br)
Harding to March 45 (Br)
Morgan (Br)

NAVAL EXPEDITIONARY FORCE

A.Cunningham
(absorbed into Royal Navy
Mediterranean Command
when Cunningham also
became C-in-C. Med.
in Sept 43)

EASTERN T.F.	CENTRAL T.F.	WESTERN T.F.
in Nov 42	in Nov 42	in Nov 42
Burrough (Br)	Troubridge (Br)	Hewitt (US)

became

(Hewitt also commanded the
Naval Task Force that landed
Operation DRAGOON in
S.France in Aug 44)

US Naval Forces N.African Waters #

Hewitt

EIGHTEENTH ARMY GROUP	to May 43
FIFTEENTH ARMY GROUP	to Jan 44
ALLIED ARMIES IN ITALY	to Dec 44†
FIFTEENTH ARMY GROUP	

Alexander to Dec 44 (Br)
Clark (US)

| EIGHTH ARMY | Feb 43-May 45 |
| see Table 3 | |

| FIRST ARMY | Feb-May 43 ‡ |
| Anderson (Br) | |

| SEVENTH US ARMY | July 43-Sept 44 ** |
| see Table 1 | |

| FIFTH US ARMY | Jan 43-May 45 †† |
| see Table 1 | |

| MEDITERRANEAN AIR COMMAND | to Dec 43 |
| MEDITERRANEAN ALLIED AIR FORCES | |

Tedder to Dec 43 (Br)
Eaker to March 45 (US)
Cannon (US)

| MIDDLE EAST AIR COMMAND | N.W.AFRICA AIR FORCES | to Dec 43 ‡‡ |
| Douglas (Br) | Spaatz (US) | |

including

NINTH US AIR FORCE	
to Oct 43	
Brereton	

| MALTA AIR COMMAND | |
| Park (Br) | |

merged with Middle East Air
Command Dec 43 and the whole
renamed as Mediterranean
Allied Air Forces (see above)

| N.W.Af. TACTICAL AIR FORCE | to Dec 43 |
| MED. TACTICAL AIR FORCE | |

Coningham to Jan 44 (Br)
Cannon to April 45 (US)
Chidlaw (US)

TWELFTH US AIR FORCE	DESERT AIR FORCE
Spaatz to Dec 43	Broadhurst to April 44
Cannon to April 45	Dickson to Dec 44
Chidlaw	Foster

| N.W.Af. STRATEGIC AIR FORCE | to Dec 43 |
| MED. STRATEGIC AIR FORCE | |

Doolittle to Jan 44 (US)
Twining (US)

FIFTEENTH US AIR FORCE	from Nov 43
Doolittle to Jan 44	
Twining	

| N.W.Af. COASTAL AIR FORCE | to Dec 43 |
| MED. COASTAL AIR FORCE | |

Barrett to Mar 43 (Br)
Lloyd to Nov 44 (Br)
Whitford (Br)

RAF MIDDLE EAST	BALKAN AIR FORCE	f. June 44
Park to Feb 45	Elliot to Feb 45 (Br)	
Medhurst	Mill (Br)	

* Also functioned as C-in-C. North African Theater of Operations US Army (NATOUSA) and, from Dec 43, C-in-C. Mediterranean Theater (MTOUSA).

† From 18 Jan to 10 March 44, this headquarters was known as Central Mediterranean Forces.

‡ Prior to Feb 43, First Army was directly responsible to Eisenhower.

** From Sept 43 to July 44, Seventh Army existed as a headquarters only.

†† Not involved in operations until Sept 43.

‡‡ Prior to Feb 43, when the North West African Air Forces came into being, air operations in this theatre were conducted by Eastern Air Command (*Welsh* – British), Western Air Command (*Doolittle* – US) and, in Jan 43 only, Allied Air Support Command (*Kuter* – US).

Became Eighth Fleet March 43. Disbanded April 45.

Table 4d Allied High Command in S.E.Asia 1942-45

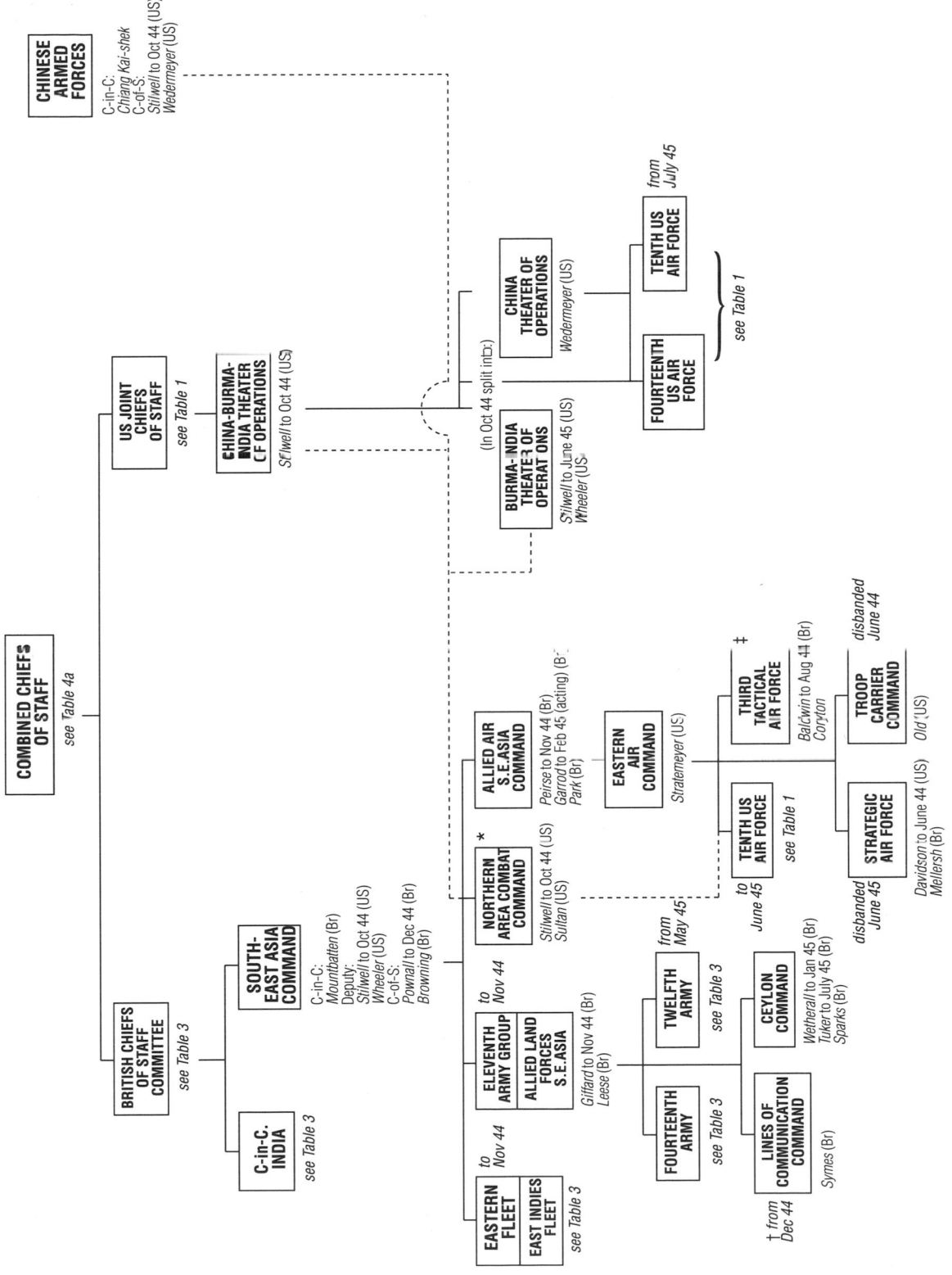

* Came under command Allied Land Forces S.E.Asia in Nov 44.
  Included Chinese forces for which further details can be found in
  the Orders of Battle Section on page 188. US Forces withdrew from
  SEAC in June 45.
† Became S.Burma District in June 45.
‡ Became RAF Burma in Dec 44.

Table 4e Allied High Command in N.W.Europe 1944-45

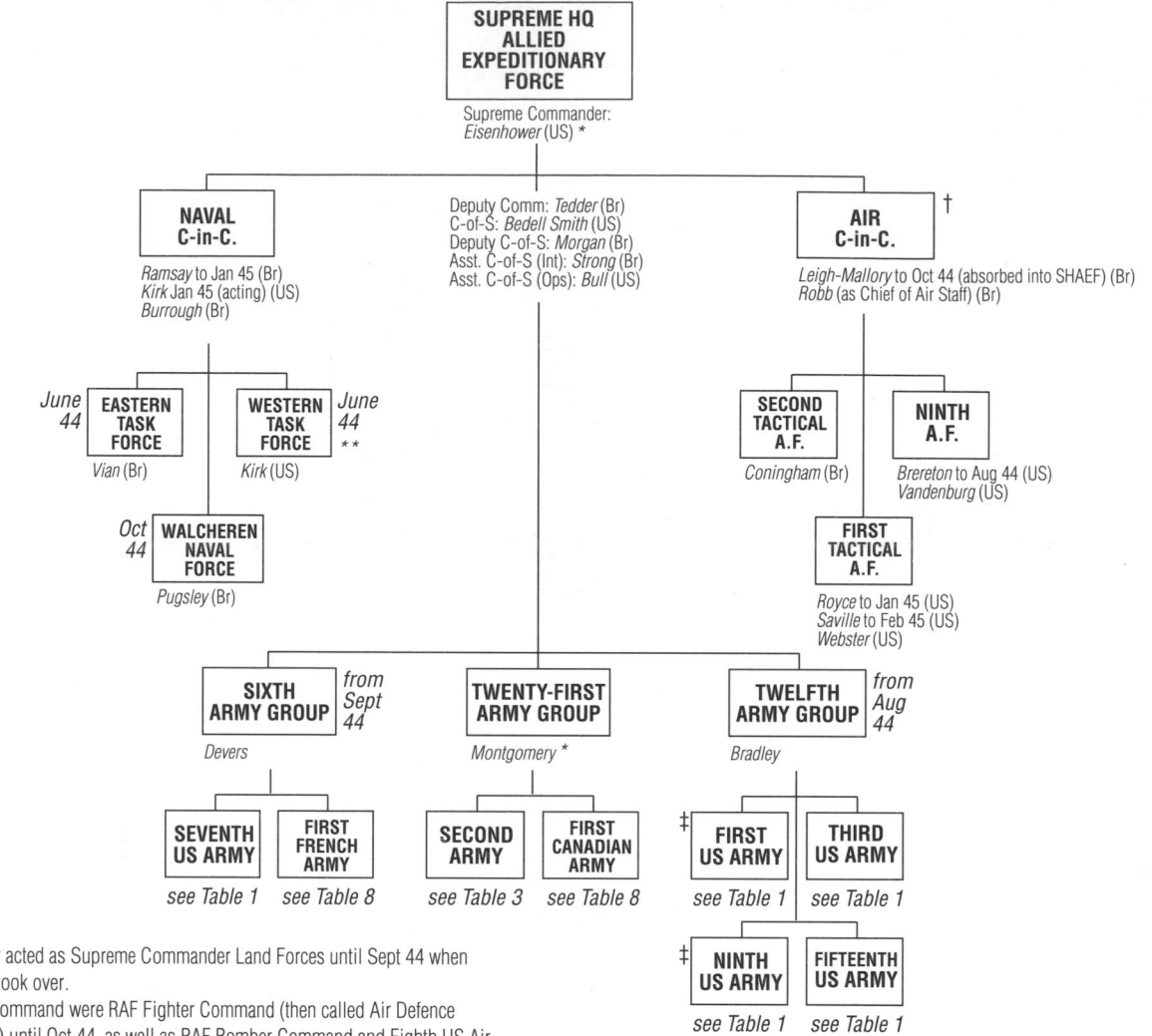

* Montgomery acted as Supreme Commander Land Forces until Sept 44 when Eisenhower took over.

† Also under command were RAF Fighter Command (then called Air Defence Great Britain) until Oct 44, as well as RAF Bomber Command and Eighth US Air Force until Sept 44.

‡ First US Army fought under Twenty-First Army Group until Aug 44 and from Dec 44 to Jan 45. Ninth US Army was similarly under command from Dec 44 to March 45.

** US Naval forces all formed part of US Twelfth Fleet formed in March 43 from Naval Forces Europe. From March 42 to the end of the war the Commander was Admiral Stark. Subordinate to Stark were Naval Forces France (*Kirk*) formed in Sept 44 and Naval Forces Germany (*Ghormley*) formed in April 45.

• **TABLE 5** • ALLIED N.W.EUROPE/GERMAN HIGH COMMAND 1939–45 •

Table 5 **German Government and High Command 1939-45**

Legend:

DAF: *Deutsche Arbeitsfront* or German Labour Front.
RSHA: *Reichssicherheitshauptamt* or Chief Office for Reich Security.
SD: *Sicherheitsdienst* or Security Service.
SS: *Schutzstaffel* or Protection Department.
WHVA: *Wirtschaftsverwaltungshauptamt* or Chief Office for Economic Policy.

Top-level structure:

FÜHRER — "Hitler"
REICH CHANCELLOR
MINISTER OF WAR
C-in-C. WEHRMACHT *

OKW
- Chief of Staff: *Keitel*
- Chief of Operations Staff: *Jodl*
- Deputy Chief of Operations Staff: *v. Buttlar* to Dec 44 / *Winter*
- Chief of Plans: *Warlimont*
- Chief of Foreign and Counter-Intelligence: *Canaris* (absorbed by RSHA Feb 44)
- Chief of Military Economy and Armaments: *Thomas* to July 44†

OKH
- C-in-C *v. Brauchitsch* to Dec 41 / *Hitler*
- C-of-S *Halder* to Sept. 42 / *Zeitzler* to July 44 / *Guderian* to March 45 / *Krebs*
- ‡ O.Qu. *Stülpnagel* to May 40 / *Mieth* to Sept 40 / *Paulus* to Jan 42 / *Blumentritt* to Sept 42 / *Heusinger* to July 44 / *Wenck* to Feb 45 / *Krebs* to March 45
- ‡ Chief of Ops: *v. Greiffenberg* to Oct 40 / *Heusinger* to Sept 42 / *?* to July 44 / *v. Bonin*

OKL
- C-in-C: *Goering* to April 45 / *v. Greim*
- C-of-S: *Jeschonnek* to Aug 43 / *Korten* to July 44 / *Kreipe* to Oct 44 / *Koller*
- Chief of Ops: *v. Waldau* to April 42 / *Jeschonnek* to March 43 / *Meister* to Oct 43 / *Koller* to Oct 44 / *Christian* to April 45 / *Schulz*
- Chief of Supply and Procurement: *Udet* to Nov 41 / *Milch* to March 44 / *Milch/Saur* to Aug 44 ** / *Saur***

OKM
- C-in-C: *Raeder* to Jan 43 / *Dönitz* to May 45 / *v. Friedeburg*
- C-of-S: *Schniewind* to June 41 / *Fricke* to Feb 43 / *Meisel*
- C-in-C. U-Boats: *Dönitz* to Jan 43 / *v. Friedeburg*
- C-in-C. High Seas Fleet: *Boehm* to Nov 39 / *Marschall* to July 40 / *Lütjens* to May 41 / *Schniewind* to July 44 / *Meendsen-Bohlken*

Theatre commands:

OKW: Denmark / Norway / Finland / Africa / Balkans (from July 41) / W.Europe (from March 41) / Italy

OKH: Poland / W.Europe (to March 41) / Balkans (to July 41) / E.Front

* Because of uncertainty and jealousy over the relative status of the Wehrmacht High Command and those of the three services, individual theatres of war were placed under the command of either the OKW or the OKH. The division of authority was as follows

---

REICH MINISTRIES including:
- FOREIGN — *von Ribbentrop* to May 45 / *Schwerin von Krosigk*
- INTERIOR — *Frick* to Aug 43 / *Himmler*
- MUNITIONS *from March 40* — *Todt* to Feb 42 / *Speer*
- TRANSPORT — *Dorpmüller*
- AVIATION — *Goering* / State Secretary: *Milch* to May 44 (post abolished)
- PROPAGANDA — *Goebbels* to May 45 / *Naumann*
- EASTERN OCCUPIED TERRITORIES *from July 41* — *Rosenberg*
- INSPECTORATE ROAD SYSTEM — *Todt*
- LABOUR MOBILISATION *from March 42* — *Sauckel*
- FOUR-YEAR PLAN *from Oct 36* — *Goering*

STATE FUNCTIONARIES including:
- CHANCELLERY — *Hess* to May 41 / *Bormann*
- DAF — *Ley*

PARTY OFFICES including:
- TREASURER — *Schwarz*
- YOUTH — *von Schirach* to Aug 40 / *Axmann*
- ORGANISATION — *Ley*
- FOREIGN — *Rosenberg*
- PRESS — *Dietrich* to March 45
- SS — *Himmler* including:
  - RSHA — *Heydrich* to June 42 / *Kaltenbrunner*
  - WVHA — *Pohl*
  - GESTAPO — *Müller*
  - SD — *Heydrich* to Oct 39 then split into:
    - FOREIGN — *Schellenberg*
    - HOME — *Ohlendorf*

** From March to August: 44 Milch retained some responsibility for aircraft procurement as joint chairman (with Speer) of the Fighter Staff (*Jägerstab*) of which Saur was the Director. In August, however, all responsibility was handed over to Speer's Ministry.

• All officials and officers marked thus were normally present at Hitler's daily briefing discussions (*Lagebesprechungen*). Also present though not named in Table 5 were the Service Liaison Officers, a representative of the Navy Chief-of-Staff and a permanent Navy representative on the OKW.

† In May 42 many of the responsibilities of Thomas' department (the *Wehrwirtschafts und Rüstungsamt*) were handed over to Speer's Ministry of Arms and Munitions. After Thomas' departure the OKW remnant was renamed the Field Economic Department (*Feldwirtschaftsamt*), responsible largely for the collation of economic information on occupied and foreign territories.

‡ The O.Qu.I and the Chief of the Operations Department are often indiscriminately referred to as the Army Chief of Operations. In fact, the former (*Oberquartermeister I*) was the Chief-of-Staff's deputy and closest adviser also responsible for all matters pertaining to training, organisation and operations. The Chief of the Operations Department was just one of his deputies, up until Sept 40 when that department was made directly subordinate to the Chief of Staff.

Supplement to Table 5 Other Major German Commands

THEATRE COMMANDS

The letters OB below are an abbreviation of *Oberbefehlshaber*, or Commander-in-Chief. In fact, German usage of the term usually denoted the headquarters rather than the individual.

OB WEST (f. March 42. France, Belgium and the Netherlands)
    von Runstedt to July 44
    von Kluge to Aug 44
    Model to Sept 44
    von Runstedt to March 45
    Kesselring
OB SÜDWEST (f. Oct 41. Italy)
    Kesselring to March 45
    von Vietinghoff Oct 44 to Jan 45 (acting)
    von Vietinghoff to April 45
    Schultz
OB SÜDOST (f. Dec 42. Balkans, Greece and the Aegean))
    Löhr to Aug 43
    von Weichs to March 45
    Löhr
OB NORDWEST (f. March 45. The Netherlands)
    Busch

THE ARMY

Army Groups (Heeresgruppen)

During the war twenty-eight German Army Group headquarters were established (Army Group [A Gp] A three times, A Gp Afrika, A Gp B twice, A Gp C twice, A Gp Centre twice, A Gp Don, A Gp E, A Gp F, A Gp G, A Gp H, A Gp Kurland, A Gp North three times, A Gp North Ukraine, A Gp Oberrhein, A Gp Ostmark, A Gp South four times, A Gp South Ukraine, A Gp Vistula/ Weichsel, but in many cases a 'new' Army Group was simply an existing one renamed.)

In fact, there were only thirteen separate headquarters involved and it is these that are listed below, though all their various nomenclatures are also given.

1 A Gp SOUTH (#1) fought in Poland in Sept 39. It transferred to the Western Front in the following month as A Gp A (#1) and fought as such in May-June 1940. In April 41 it transferred East as A Gp SOUTH (#2) and participated in Operation Barbarossa in June. In June 42 it became A Gp B (#2) and the headquarters were withdrawn from Russia in Feb 43. It moved to Italy/France in July and to France alone in Nov. It remained in the West until destroyed in April 45 in the Ruhr.
    von Runstedt to Dec 41 (SOUTH #1; A #1; SOUTH #2)
    von Reichenau to Jan 42 (SOUTH #2)
    von Bock to July 42 (SOUTH #2; B #2)
    von Weichs to July 43 (B #2)
    Rommel to July 44 (B #2)
    von Kluge (B #2). Also OB WEST (see above)
    Model. Also OB WEST to Sept 44
2 A Gp NORTH (#1) fought in Poland in Sept 39, went West in October and invaded France in May 40 as ARMY GROUP B (#1). It moved East in Sept 40 where it became A Gp CENTRE (#1). In Jan 45 it became A Gp NORTH (#3) and was deactivated in April.
    von Bock to Dec 41 (NORTH #1; B #1; CENTRE #1)
    von Kluge to Oct 43 (CENTRE #1)
    Busch to June 44 (CENTRE #1)
    Model to Aug 44 (CENTRE #1). Also in command of A Gp NORTH
      UKRAINE.
    Reinhardt to Jan 45 (CENTRE #1)
    Rendulic to March 45 (NORTH #3)
    Weiss (NORTH #3)

3 A Gp C (#1) fought in France in May-June 40 and then went East in Sept to become A Gp NORTH (#2). It fought as such until Jan 45 when it became A Gp KURLAND.
    von Leeb to Jan 42 (C #1; NORTH #2)
    von Küchler to Jan 44 (NORTH #2)
    Model to March 44 (NORTH #2)
    Lindemann to July 44 (NORTH #2)
    Friessner to July 44 (NORTH #2)
    Schörner to Jan 45 (NORTH #2)
    Rendulic Jan 45 (KURLAND)
    von Vietinghoff to March 45 (KURLAND)
    Hilpert (KURLAND)
4 A Gp A (#2) was formed in the Caucasus in June 44. It was redesignated as A Gp SOUTH UKRAINE in April 44 and then as A Gp SOUTH (#4) in Sept. In the last days of the war it became A Gp OSTMARK.
    List to Sept 42 (A #2)
    Hitler to Nov 42 (A #2)
    von Kleist to March 44 (A #2)
    Schörner to July 44 (A #2; SOUTH UKRAINE)
    Friessner to Dec 44 (SOUTH UKRAINE; SOUTH #4)
    Wöhler to April 45 (SOUTH #4)
    Rendulic (SOUTH #4; OSTMARK)
5 A Gp DON was formed in Nov 42 and became A Gp SOUTH (#3) in Feb 43. In April of the following year it was A Gp NORTH UKRAINE, in September A Gp A (#3) and in Jan 45 A Gp CENTRE (#2).
    von Manstein to March 44 (DON; SOUTH #3)
    Model to Aug 44 (SOUTH #3; NORTH UKRAINE)
    Harpe June to Aug 44 (acting) (NORTH UKRAINE)
    Harpe to Jan 45 (NORTH UKRAINE; A #3)
    Schörner (CENTRE #2)
6 A Gp WEICHSEL (or VISTULA in English) was organised in Jan 45 in East Prussia.
    Himmler to March 45 (in practice *Wenck* [Feb] and *Kinzel* [March])
    Heinrici to April 45
    Student
7 A Gp E was formed in Dec 42 with its commander also serving as OB SÜDOST in the Balkans. In Aug 43 its responsibilities were limited to Greece and the Balkans and it lost its OB SÜDOST responsibilities to A Gp F (see below). It regained these responsibilities in March 45 but became subordinate to OB SÜDWEST in the following month.
    Löhr
8 A Gp F was formed in Aug 43 and its commander took over as OB SÜDOST from A Gp E (see above). It gave up responsibility for Hungary in April 44 (to A Gp SOUTH UKRAINE) and the role of OB SÜDOST reverted to A Gp E in March 45. Shortly afterwards the A Gp was disbanded.
    von Weichs
9 A Gp AFRIKA was set up in Feb 43 to coordinate the operations of First Italian Army and Fifth Panzer Army. It surrendered to the Allies in Tunis in May 43.
    Rommel to March 43
    von Arnim
10 A Gp C (#2) was formed in Italy in Nov 43 and directed operations there until the end of the war. Its commander also functioned as OB SÜDWEST.
    Kesselring to March 45
    von Vietinghoff Oct 44 to Jan 45 (acting)
    von Vietinghoff
11 A Gp G was formed in Sept 44, being an upgrading of Army Detachment G formed the previous April. When formed it was stationed in the South of France and remained in the West until the end of the war.
    Blaskowitz to Sept 44
    Balck to Dec 44

Blaskowitz to Jan 45
Hausser to April 45
H. Schulz

12 A Gp H was formed in Nov 44 and existed as such until March 45 when it was renamed OB NORDWEST.
Student to Jan 45
Blaskowitz

13 A Gp OBERRHEIN was formed in the West in Nov 44 only to be broken up in Jan 45 when its sector was taken over by A Gp G (see above).
Himmler to Jan 45
Hausser

Panzer Armies

1 FIRST PANZER ARMY (PZ AY) was formed in Nov 40 though until Oct 41 it was known as PZ GP I. It served in Yugoslavia in April 41 thereafter moving to the Eastern Front where it remained until the end of the war.
Kleist to Nov 42
Mackensen to Nov 43
Hube to April 44
Raus to Aug 44
Heinrici to March 45
Nehring

2 Formed in Nov 40, SECOND PZ AY was known as PZ GP II until Oct 41. It served in the East throughout the war, being with A Gp F from Sept 43 to Dec 44 with no major formations under command.
Guderian to Dec 41
R. Schmidt to July 43
Model to Aug 43
de Angelis

3 THIRD PZ AY was formed in Nov 40, being known as PZ GP III until Dec 41. It served in the East throughout the war.
Hoth to Oct 41
Reinhardt to Aug 44
Raus to March 45
von Manteuffel

4 FOURTH PZ AY was formed in Feb 41 and was known as PZ GP IV until the following December. It served in the East throughout the war.
Hoepner to Jan 42
Hoth to Nov 43
Raus to April 44
Nehring to May 44
Harpe to June 44
Balck to Sept 44
Gräser

5 FIFTH PZ AY was formed in Dec 42 in Tunisia where it was destroyed in May 43. It was reformed in July 44 (from PZ GP WEST) and remained in the West until it surrendered in April 45.
von Arnim to March 43
von Vaerst to May 43
von Schweppenberg Feb to July 44
Eberbach to Aug 44 (briefly known as PZ GP EBERBACH)
Dietrich to Sept 44
von Manteuffel to March 45
Harpe

6 SIXTH SS PZ AY was formed in Sept 44 to take part in the Ardennes counteroffensive. It remained in the West until Feb 45 when it transferred to the Eastern Front.
Dietrich

7 ELEVENTH SS PZ AY was formed in Jan 45 on the Eastern Front. In March 45 it was renamed ARMY DETACHMENT STEINER.
Steiner

8 PZ AY AFRIKA was formed in Aug 41 as PZ GP AFRIKA, becoming a PZ AY in Jan 42. Also known as GERMAN/ITALIAN PZ AY, it changed its name once more in Feb 43, to FIRST ITALIAN ARMY. It surrendered in May 43.
Rommel to Jan 43
Crüwell March 42 (acting)
Stumme Sept to Oct 42 (acting)
Messe

Armies

1 FIRST ARMY was formed in Aug 39 in the West and served there throughout the war.
von Witzleben to Oct 40
Blaskowitz to May 44
von der Chevallerie to Aug 44
von Knobelsdorff to Dec 44
von Obstfelder to March 45
Foertsch

2 FIRST PARACHUTE ARMY was formed in July 44 in Holland and served in the West until the end of the war.
Student to Nov 44
Schlemm to March 45
Blumentritt to April 45
Student

3 SECOND ARMY was formed in Oct 39 from the redesignated EIGHTH ARMY (see below) and after serving in France in May 40 and the Balkans in April 41, it served on the Eastern Front for the remainder of the war. In late April 45 it was renamed ARMY COMMAND EAST PRUSSIA.
von Weichs to June 42
von Salmuth to Feb 43
Weiss to March 45
von Saucken

4 THIRD ARMY was formed in Aug 39 and served only in the Polish campaign, being then redesignated SIXTEENTH ARMY (see below).
von Küchler

5 FOURTH ARMY was formed in Aug 39 and served in Poland and on the Eastern Front. Destroyed there in March 45, its headquarters were used to create TWENTY-FIRST ARMY (see below).
von Kluge to Dec 41
Kübler Jan 42
Heinrici to Aug 44
Tippelskirch May-July 44 (acting)
Hossbach to Jan 45
Müller

6 FIFTH ARMY was formed in Aug 39 but never saw combat. In Nov 40 it was redesignated EIGHTEENTH ARMY (see below).

7 SIXTH ARMY was formed in the West in Oct 39 and served there until it moved East for Operation Barbarossa. Destroyed at Stalingrad in Feb 43, it was reformed in March and remained in the East for the rest of the war.
von Reichenau to Dec 41
Paulus to Feb 43
Hollidt March 43 to April 44
de Angelis to July 44
Fretter-Pico to Dec 44
Balck

8 SEVENTH ARMY was formed in Aug 39 and served in the West until it surrendered in the Ruhr in April 45.
Dollman to June 44
Hausser to Aug 44
Eberbach Aug 44
Brandenberger to March 45
von Obstfelder

9 EIGHTH ARMY was formed in Aug 39, served in Poland and was then redesignated as SECOND ARMY (see above). The Army was reformed in Aug 43 and served on the Eastern Front for the remainder of the war.
Blaskowitz to Dec 39

Wöhler Aug 43 to Dec 44
Kreysing

10 NINTH ARMY was formed in May 40 and fought in France in that month before serving on the Eastern Front for the rest of the war.
Blaskowitz to May 40
Strauss to Jan 42
Model to Nov 43. Also in command of SECOND PANZER ARMY July to Aug 43.
Harpe to May 44
Jordan to June 44
von Vormann to ? Under command SECOND ARMY in July 44.
von Lüttwitz to Jan 45
Busse

11 TENTH ARMY was formed in Aug 39 and fought in Poland after which it was redesignated SIXTH ARMY (see above). It was reformed in Italy in Aug 43 and served there until the end of the war.
von Reichenau to Oct 39
von Vietinghoff Aug 43 to Feb 45
Lemelsen Oct 44-Feb 45 (acting)
Heer

12 ELEVENTH ARMY was formed in Oct 40 and took part in operations on the Eastern Front until Nov 42 when it was redesignated A Gp DON (see 5 under Army Groups above). The Army was reformed in Feb 45 from A Gp OBERRHEIN (see above) and served in the West.
von Schobert to Sept 41
von Manstein to Nov 42
Lucht from Feb 45

13 TWELFTH ARMY was formed in Oct 39 and took part in the Balkans campaign in April 41. In June 41 it was redesignated ARMED FORCES HQ SOUTH EAST and in Dec 42 became A Gp E and OB SÜDOST (see above). The Army was formed again in April 45 on the Eastern Front. In its first formation, the appellation Twelfth Army does not seem to have been retained in parenthesis between June 41 and Dec 42.
List to June 42
Löhr to Dec 42
Wenck from April 45

14 There was no THIRTEENTH ARMY.

15 FOURTEENTH ARMY was formed in Aug 39 and served in Poland before being redesignated as TWELFTH ARMY (see above). It was reformed in Nov 43 in Italy and served there until the end of the war.
List to Oct 39
Mackensen Nov 43 to June 44
Lemelsen
Ziegler Oct to Nov 44 (acting)
Tippelskirch Jan 45 (acting)

16 FIFTEENTH ARMY was formed in Jan 41 and remained in the West throughout the war.
?
von Salmuth to Aug 44
von Zangen

17 SIXTEENTH ARMY was formed in Oct 39 and served in the West until May 41 when it moved East and remained on this front until the end of the war.
Busch to Oct 43
C.Hansen to ?
Laux to Sept 44
Hilpert to April 45
Volckamer von Kirschensittenbach

18 SEVENTEENTH ARMY was formed in Dec 40. It served on the Eastern Front throughout the war. The Army was largely destroyed in the Crimea in May 44 and its headquarters did not reappear in the line until late July and then only with a handful of divisions. It was only in September that it could be said to be commanding an Army proper.
von Stülpnagel to Oct 41

Hoth to Jan 42
Ruoff to June 43. Known as ARMY DETACHMENT RUOFF July to Sept 42.
Jaenecke to May 44
Allmendinger May 44
Schultz

19 EIGHTEENTH ARMY was formed in Nov 39 and served in the West until July 40. It then moved East to take part in Barbarossa and remained on this front until the end of the war.
von Küchler to Jan 42
Lindemann to March 44
Loch to Sept 44
Boege

20 NINETEENTH ARMY was formed in Aug 43 and served in the West until the end of the war.
Wiese to Jan 45
Rasp to April 45
Brandenberger

21 TWENTIETH MOUNTAIN ARMY was formed in June 42 and served in Finland and Norway until the end of the war.
Dietl to June 44
Rendulic to Jan 45
Boehme

22 TWENTY-FIRST ARMY was formed in the East in April 45 from the remnants of FOURTH ARMY (see above).
Tippelskirch

23 TWENTY-FOURTH ARMY was formed in Dec 44 but only commanded units in the line in late April 45.
Schmidt

24 TWENTY-FIFTH ARMY was formed in Jan 45 as part of ARMY GROUP H (see above) in the West.
Blumentritt
Kleffel March to April 45 (acting)

25 The ARMY OF NORWAY was formed in Dec 40. It served as part of TWENTIETH MOUNTAIN ARMY (see above) from Oct 44 and was dissolved in December.
von Falkenhorst

26 The ARMY OF LAPLAND was formed in Jan 42 becoming TWENTIETH MOUNTAIN ARMY (see above) in June.
Dietl

THE AIR FORCE

Air Fleets (Luftflotten)

Luftflotten were the major operational formation employed by the Luftwaffe and contained units of all types of aircraft. They were built around one or more *Fleigerkorps*, these latter being in turn subdivided into *Geschwadern* (90-120 aircraft), *Gruppen* (30-70 aircraft: normally one *Gruppe* occupied a single airfield) and *Staffeln* (c. 10 aircraft).

1 LUFTFLOTTE 1 was formed in Feb 39 and served in Poland and then on the Eastern Front throughout the war. In 1945 it was downgraded to LUFTWAFFEKOMMANDO KURLAND.
Kesselring to Jan 40
Stumpff to May 40
Wimmer to Aug 40
Keller to June 43
Korten to Sept 43
Pflugbeil

2 LUFTFLOTTE 2 was formed in Feb 39 and served in France in May 40 as well as in the subsequent Battle of Britain. It went East for Barbarossa in early June 41 and then was transferred to the Mediterranean in December. There it remained to the end of the war though in October 44 it was downgraded to LUFTWAFFEKOMMANDO SÜD whilst from November its commander was merely known as LUFTWAFFEGENERAL ITALIEN.

Felmy to Jan 40
Kesselring to June 43
von Richthofen to Nov 44
von Pohl

3   LUFTFLOTTE 3 was formed in Feb 39 and served in the West throughout the war, taking part in the invasion of France, the Battle of Britain and the Normandy campaign. In September 44 it was downgraded to LUFTWAFFEKOMMANDO WEST and subordinated to LUFTFLOTTE REICH (see below).

Sperrle to Aug 44
Dessloch to Oct 44
Holle to ?
Schmid to April 45
Harlinghausen

4   LUFTFLOTTE 4 was formed in March 39 and served in Poland and the Balkans and on the Eastern Front.

Löhr to July 42
von Richthofen to June 43
Dessloch to Aug 44
? to Oct 44
Dessloch to April 45
Deichmann

5   LUFTFLOTTE 5 was formed in Norway in April 40 and served there and in Finland throughout the war. In Sept 44 it was downgraded to LUFTWAFFEKOMMANDO NORWEGEN.

Milch in April 40
Stumpff to Jan 44
Kammhuber to Oct 44
von Schleich

6   LUFTFLOTTE 6 was formed in July 43 and served on the Eastern Front until the end of the war.

von Greim to April 45
Dessloch

7   LUFTFLOTTE REICH was formed in December 43 to defend Germany against the Allied Combined Bombing Offensive.

Stumpff

Two other headquarters accorded *Luftflotte* status were:

8   LUFTWAFFEKOMMANDO OST which was formed in May 42 on the Eastern Front, serving there until being redesignated LUFTFLOTTE 6 (see above) in July 43. Its commander was *von Greim*.

9   LUFTWAFFEKOMMANDO SÜD was formed in Jan 42 to cover the Balkans, Greece and Crete. By November 44 it had been subordinated to LUFTFLOTTE 4 (see above). The commanders were *von Waldau* to March 43, *Fiebig* to Sept 44 and *Fröhlich*.

Other

For certain periods during the war some of the *Fliegerkorps* operated independently of any *Luftflotte* headquarters. The most important of these were:

10   FLIEGERKORPS X in Denmark and Norway in April 40, commanded by *Geisler*. This formation then served with LUFTFLOTTEN 5 and 2 until Jan 41 when it was transferred to the Mediterranean, operating autonomously there until the arrival of LUFTFLOTTE 2 (see above) in December. The commanders in 1941 were *Harlinghausen* to March, and *Geisler* again. (See also FLIEGERFÜHRER ATLANTIK below).

11   FLIEGERKORPS XI was a specialist air-landing formation, commanded by *Student*, that participated in the invasion of Crete in May 41.

12   FLIEGERKORPS VIII did not go with LUFTFLOTTE 2 (see above) when it left for the Mediterranean in Dec 41 but operated independently on the Eastern Front until May 42 when it was subordinated to LUFTFLOTTE 4 (see above). Its commander was *von Richthofen*.

13   FLIEGERKORPS IV was made independent of LUFTFLOTTE 4 (see

above) between Nov 43 and July 44 when it served, in theory at least, as the strategic bombing formation on the Eastern Front. Its commander was *Meister*.

Other commands of some importance were:

14   FLIEGERFÜHRER AFRIKA, a command formed in July 41 and operating from bases in Libya. It was absorbed into FLIEGERFÜHRER TUNIS (see below) in Jan 43 before which it was commanded by *Fröhlich* to March 42, *von Waldau* to Aug 42 and *Seidemann*.

15   FLIEGERFÜHRER TUNIS was established in Nov 42 to counter the Allied TORCH landings. It was commanded by *Harlinghausen* to Feb 43.

16   FLIEGERFÜHRER ATLANTIK was established in March 41 under the command of LUFTFLOTTE 3 (see above) and existed until March 44 when it was renamed FLIEGERKORPS X under that headquarters, commanded by *Holle*. Commanders in the interim were *Harlinghausen* to Jan 42 and *Kessler*.

THE NAVY

See organigram for Table 5.

Table 6 Italian Government and High Command 1940-43

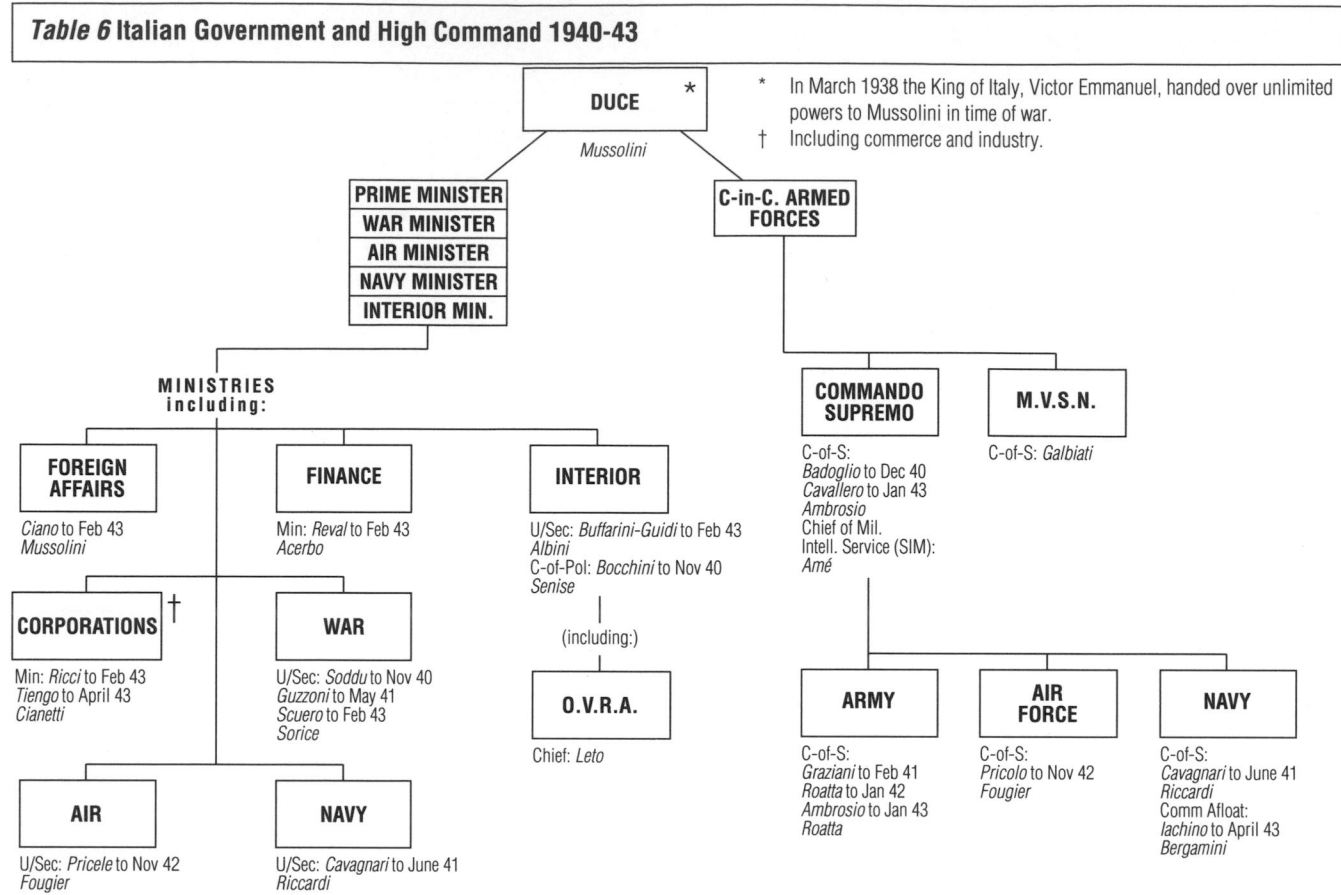

* In March 1938 the King of Italy, Victor Emmanuel, handed over unlimited powers to Mussolini in time of war.

† Including commerce and industry.

DUCE *

Mussolini

PRIME MINISTER / WAR MINISTER / AIR MINISTER / NAVY MINISTER / INTERIOR MIN.

C-in-C. ARMED FORCES

MINISTRIES including:

COMMANDO SUPREMO

C-of-S:
Badoglio to Dec 40
Cavallero to Jan 43
Ambrosio
Chief of Mil.
Intell. Service (SIM):
Amé

M.V.S.N.

C-of-S: *Galbiati*

FOREIGN AFFAIRS

Ciano to Feb 43
Mussolini

FINANCE

Min: *Reval* to Feb 43
Acerbo

INTERIOR

U/Sec: *Buffarini-Guidi* to Feb 43
Albini
C-of-Pol: *Bocchini* to Nov 40
Senise

(including:)

CORPORATIONS †

Min: *Ricci* to Feb 43
Tiengo to April 43
Cianetti

WAR

U/Sec: *Soddu* to Nov 40
Guzzoni to May 41
Scuero to Feb 43
Sorice

O.V.R.A.

Chief: *Leto*

ARMY

C-of-S:
Graziani to Feb 41
Roatta to Jan 42
Ambrosio to Jan 43
Roatta

AIR FORCE

C-of-S:
Pricolo to Nov 42
Fougier

NAVY

C-of-S:
Cavagnari to June 41
Riccardi
Comm Afloat:
Iachino to April 43
Bergamini

AIR

U/Sec: *Pricele* to Nov 42
Fougier

NAVY

U/Sec: *Cavagnari* to June 41
Riccardi

Supplement to Table 6 Other Major Italian Commands

THEATRE COMMANDS

1   C-in-C. ARMY GROUP WEST which fought very briefly in France in June 40.

Prince of Piedmont

2   C-in-C. LIBYA and NORTH AFRICA

Balbo to June 40
Graziani to Feb 41
Gariboldi to July 41
Bastico

3   C-in-C. ABYSSINIA

Duke of Aosta to May 41
Gazzera

4   C-in-C. GREECE and ALBANIA

Guzzoni to Dec 39
Geloso to June 40
Prasca to Nov 40
Soddu to Dec 40
Cavallero to May 41

THE ARMY

Armies

Commanders are given only for those periods during which the Armies were involved in combat operations.

1   FIRST ARMY fought very briefly in France in June 40 and again in Tunisia between Feb and May 43.

Pintor June 40
Messe Feb to May 43

2   SECOND ARMY fought a few skirmishes in April 41 during the Axis invasion of Yugoslavia and remained there as an occupation force.

Ambrosio to Jan 42

3   If a THIRD ARMY headquarters ever existed it never took part in combat.

4   FOURTH ARMY fought very briefly in France in June 40 and some units clashed with the Germans during their occupation of Italy, following the Italian surrender, in Sept 43.

Guzzoni June 40
Vercellino Sept 43

5   FIFTH ARMY was stationed in western Libya during the British offensive of 1940-41. Most of its units were destroyed in this offensive and the Army headquarters took no further active part in the African campaign. It was stationed in Italy at the time of the Italian surrender and some units clashed with German occupation troops.

Gariboldi to Feb 41
Carraciolo di Feroleto Sept 43

6   SIXTH ARMY was stationed in Sicily during the Allied invasion in July 43.

Guzzoni July 43

7   SEVENTH ARMY was in reserve during the Italian invasion of France in June 40 and thereafter served in Italy. Some units clashed with the Germans during the occupation of Italy, following the Italian surrender, in Sept 43.

Duke of Pistoia June 40
Prince Adalberto, Duke of Bergamo to 2 Sept 43
Arisio

8   EIGHTH ARMY headquarters arrived in Russia in July 42 to take over command of Italian forces there from the Corpo di Spedizione Italiano in Russia (CSIR). It left Russia in March 43.

Messe July 41 to July 42 (commanding CSIR)
Gariboldi

9   NINTH ARMY provided the occupation forces in Albania as well as

• **TABLE 6** • ITALIAN HIGH COMMAND/OTHER MAJOR ITALIAN COMMANDS •

taking part in the invasions of Greece in Oct 40 and March 41.
> *Vercellino* to Feb 41
> *Pirzo-Biroli* to Oct 41

10 TENTH ARMY was destroyed in Libya during Wavell's offensive of 1940-41.
> *Berti* to Dec 40
> *Gariboldi* Nov to Dec 40 (acting)
> *Tellera*

11 ELEVENTH ARMY took part in the invasions of Greece in Oct 40 and March 41 and was stationed there thereafter as an occupation force.
> *Geloso* to April 41

THE AIR FORCE

Area Commands

1 SQUADRA 1 was stationed in northern Italy and remained there throughout the war. As well as undertaking maritime duties along the southern French coastline it was also responsible for training aircrew for the other commands.

2 SQUADRA 2 was based in Sicily until Dec 40 and carried out maritime duties in the central Mediterranean. During the remainder of the war it was stationed in north-east Italy where it was responsible for home defence. Its only offensive activities of any importance were during the occupation of Yugoslavia in April 41.

3 SQUADRA 3, based in Rome, carried out maritime duties in the western Mediterranean. From Nov 42 it was mainly concerned with home defence, being heavily involved in the defence of Sicily in July and Aug 43.

4 SQUADRA 4, based at Bari from May 41, was active in the Yugoslav campaign and the occupation of the Greek islands. Thereafter it undertook maritime duties in the central and eastern Mediterranean and the Adriatic as well as providing aircraft for the defence of Sardinia and Sicily.

5 SQUADRA 5* existed before the war as AERONAUTICA DELLA LIBIA and was retitled in July 40. It fought in North Africa right up until the surrender in Tunis in May 43, when the command ceased to exist, though for much of 1941 and 1942 the poor quality of Italian aircraft meant that most of the front-line activities had to be left to the Germans.

6 AERONAUTICA DELL'ALBANIA (AALB) was responsible for air cover in the Balkans and over the Adriatic. It participated in both Greek campaigns in 1940 and 1941 as well as in the occupation of Yugoslavia.

7 AERONAUTICA DELL'EGEO (AEGE) was responsible for maritime duties in the Aegean Islands, particularly escorting convoys from Greece to Libya.

8 AERONAUTICA DELLA GRECIA (AGRE) was established in Aug 41 to control air operations over the Greek mainland. From April to August these had been the responsibility of AERONAUTICA DELL'EGEO (see above).

9 AERONAUTICA DELLA LIBIA (ALIB). See SQUADRA 5 above.

10 AERONAUTICA DELLA PROVENCE (APRO) was set up in April 43 in southern France. Formed originally from close-support units it later became a training formation for bomber aircrew.

11 AERONAUTICA DELLA SARDEGNA (ASAR) was based in Sardinia and was responsible for the defence of the central Mediterranean, Vichy North Africa and the approaches to Sicily. It was heavily involved throughout the war, in attacks on the Malta convoys and in the defence of Tunisia and Sicily. For these last two tasks it was heavily reinforced by units from SQUADRA 3 and 4 (see above).

12 AERONAUTICA DELLA SICILIA (ASIC) took over operations against the Malta convoys from SQUADRA 2 (see above) in Dec 40 and fought in the Central Mediterranean, Tunisia and Sicily throughout the war, being virtually wiped out during the defence of the latter island.

13 AERONAUTICA DELLA TUNISIA (ATUN)† was formed in Nov 42, in the wake of Operation TORCH, to protect convoys sailing between Sicily and Tunisia. It was absorbed by SQUADRA 5 (see above) in Feb 43, but was briefly reconstituted between April and the Axis surrender in May.

* Commanders were Aimone-Cat to Nov 41, Marchesi to Oct 42 and Bernasconi.

† Commanders were Gaeta to Feb 43 and later Boschi.

14 AFRICA ORIENTALE ITALIANA (AOI) was the formation covering Italian colonies in Eritrea, Abyssinia and Somaliland. It disappeared with the collapse of Mussolini's East African Empire in Nov 41.

15 CORPO AERO ITALIANO (CAI) was a unit based at Brussels that participated in several raids against Britain between its arrival in Sept 40 and its departure in April 41.

16 CORPO DI SPEDIZIONE ITALIANO IN RUSSIA (CSIR) was the aerial component of the Italian contingent on the Eastern Front. See EIGHTH ARMY above.

Functional Commands

17 AVIAZIONE PER IL REGIA ESERCITO (AVRE) comprised the units working with the Army, to whose formations they were directly attached. By the second half of 1942 they were to be found only in the Balkans, engaged in counter-insurgency operations.

18 REGIA MARINA (RM) was the equivalent of RAF COASTAL COMMAND (see Table 3) and was equipped with flying boats and sea planes.

19 SERVIZI AERI SPECIALI (SAS) was responsible for air supply to Italian contingents abroad, one section being equipped with military transports and the other with commandeered civil aircraft.

THE NAVY

See organigram for Table 6.

Table 7 Japanese Government and High Command 1941-45

```
                                    EMPEROR
                                    Hirohito
```

IMPERIAL HQ
ARMY | **NAVY**

NAVY
C-of-S: *Nagano* to Feb 44
Shimada to Aug 44
Oikawa to May 45
Toyoda

COMBINED FLEET
(including:)
C-in-C: *Yamamoto* to April 43
Koga to March 44
Toyoda to May 45
Ozawa
C-of-S: *Ugaki* to April 43
Fukodome to April 44
Kusaka

ARMY
C-of-S: *Sugiyami* to Feb 44
Tojo to July 44
Umezu

BOARD OF MARSHALS AND ADMIRALS *

SUPREME MILITARY COUNCIL *

LIAISON CONFERENCE †

SECRETARIAT **

PRIME MINISTER
Tojo to July 44
Koiso to April 45
Suzuki

MINISTRIES including:

FOREIGN AFFAIRS
Min: *Togo* to Sept 42
Tani to April 43
Shigemitsu to April 45
Suzuki
Togo

NAVY
Min: *Shimada* to July 44
Yonai

WAR
Min: *Tojo* to July 44
Sugiyama to April 45
Anami

CABINET PLANNING BOARD
became

COMMERCE AND INDUSTRY
became

Nov 43.

MUNITIONS
Min: *Tojo* to Aug 44 (in practice his deputy *Kishi*)
Fujihara to Dec 44
Yosida to April 45
Toyoda

(including:)

AIR ORDNANCE BUREAU
Chief: *Endo*

GENERAL MOBILISATION BUREAU
Chief: *Shiina*
Takamine

INTERIOR
(including:)

TOKKO (Secret Police)

---

* Advisory only with little real authority.

† Renamed Supreme Military Council August 44. Attended by Prime Minister, Ministers for War and Navy, Army and Navy Chiefs-of-Staff, and such Ministers as required at individual meetings.

** Comprising Cabinet Secretary (*Hoshino* to late 44), and Chiefs of Army and Navy Military Affairs Bureaux at the respective Ministries.

• **TABLE 7** • JAPANESE HIGH COMMAND/OTHER MAJOR JAPANESE COMMANDS •

Supplement to Table 7 **Other Major Japanese Commands**

THE ARMY

Army Groups

As can be seen from the Campaign organigrams in the Orders of Battle section, Japanese Army Groups (usually referred to as Area Armies) were much smaller than their equivalents in the other major armies of the Second World War. In many cases they were no bigger than an Allied or a German Army, having only ten or even less divisions.

1 FIRST AREA ARMY was formed in July 42 in eastern Manchuria, where it formed part of the KWANTUNG ARMY (see below). It was not engaged in significant operations until the Russian invasion of Aug 45.

Yamashita to Oct 44

Kita

2 FIRST GENERAL ARMY was formed in April 45 to participate in the defence of the Japanese islands. It comprised ELEVENTH, TWELFTH and THIRTEENTH AREA ARMIES also recently formed.

Sugiyama

3 SECOND AREA ARMY was formed in July 42 in western Manchuria, where it formed part of the KWANTUNG ARMY (see below). In Oct 43 it departed for eastern New Guinea and the East Indies, where it remained for the remainder of the war. In June 45 it was redesignated Second Army.

Anami to Dec 44

Idmura

4 SECOND GENERAL ARMY was formed in April 45 to participate in the defence of the Japanese islands. It comprised FIFTEENTH and SIXTEENTH AREA ARMIES, also recently formed.

Hata

5 THIRD AREA ARMY was formed in Manchuria in late 1943 to take over from the departing SECOND AREA ARMY (see above). It was not engaged in significant operations until the Russian invasion of Aug 45.

Ushiroku

6 FIFTH AREA ARMY was formed in Jan 45 to coordinate the defence of the Kurile Is., Sakhalin and Hokkaido.

Higuchi

7 SIXTH AREA ARMY was formed in Aug 44 in China.

Okamura

8 SEVENTH AREA ARMY was formed in May 44 to coordinate the defence of Malaya and the major islands of the Dutch East Indies.

Doihara to July 45

Itagaki

9 EIGHTH AREA ARMY was formed in Nov 42 to coordinate Japanese defences in the south-east Pacific (western New Guinea and the Solomons). It was cut off from the rest of the Empire by autumn 44 but remained in being until the end of the war.

Imamura

10 TENTH AREA ARMY was formed in Feb 45 to coordinate the defence of Formosa and the Ryukyus (including Okinawa).

Ando

11 ELEVENTH, TWELFTH, THIRTEENTH, FIFTEENTH and SIXTEENTH AREA ARMIES were formed in Jan and Feb 45 to participate in the defence of the Japanese home islands. They never saw combat as the dropping of the A-bombs precipitated the Japanese surrender.

12 FOURTEENTH AREA ARMY was formed in the Philippines in Aug 44. Though pretty much destroyed by June 45, the command remained in existence until the end of the war.

Kuroda to Oct 44

Yamashita

13 SEVENTEENTH AREA ARMY was formed in Feb 45 to coordinate the defence of Korea.

Itagachi

14 EIGHTEENTH AREA ARMY was formed in July 45 in Siam, being a redesignation of 39th Army.

Nakamura

15 BURMA AREA ARMY was formed in March 43 and fought until the end of the war.

Kawabe to Aug 44

Kimura

16 CHINA EXPEDITIONARY ARMY was formed in early 1938 and was in existence until the end of the war.

Hata to Nov 44

Okamura

17 KWANTUNG ARMY was formed in Manchuria in 1905 and considerably expanded in 1932 when the Japanese took over this province. It remained in existence until the end of the war when it was destroyed during the Russian invasion of Aug 45.

Umezu Sept 39 to Sept 44

Yamada

18 SOUTHERN ARMY was constituted before the war to oversee the Japanese offensive into the Pacific that began with the attack on Pearl Harbour. It remained in existence until the end of the war, later embracing other Army Groups within it.

Terauchi

Armies/Garrisons

During the course of the war, thirty-six Japanese Armies served overseas (FIRST through SIXTH, ELEVENTH through TWENTIETH, TWENTY-THIRD, TWENTY-FIFTH, TWENTY-SEVENTH through THIRTY-FIFTH, THIRTY-SEVENTH [ex-BORNEO GARRISON ARMY], THIRTY-EIGHTH [ex-INDOCHINA GARRISON ARMY], THIRTY-NINTH [ex-SIAM GARRISON ARMY], FORTIETH, FORTY-FIRST, FORTY-FOURTH, FORMOSA ARMY, KOREA ARMY and NORTHERN ARMY). Many of these, however, were not involved in countering the Allied offensive, whilst those that were were often in combat only for a short time. The following list, therefore, includes only armies or garrison forces that fought against the Allies and names commanders only for the period of actual combat. Further details on dates and units involved will be found in Orders of Battle, The Pacific: US and Japanese Forces Island by Island, starting on page 192.

GUADALCANAL (part SEVENTEENTH ARMY)

Ichiki to Aug 42

Kawaguchi to Oct 42

Hyakutake (c.o. SEVENTEENTH ARMY)

NEW GUINEA (part SEVENTEENTH ARMY to Nov 42, then EIGHTEENTH ARMY and, from Oct 44, SECOND ARMY)

Yokoyama to Aug 42

Horii to Nov 42

Adachi (c.o. EIGHTEENTH ARMY) and *Teshima* (c.o. SECOND ARMY)

THE SOLOMONS (SEVENTEENTH ARMY)

Hyakutake

GILBERT ISLANDS (under Naval command: both FOURTH FLEET and CENTRAL PACIFIC AREA [see below]). Only small Marine and Pioneer units involved.

Makin: *Lts. Ishikawa* and *Kurokawa*

Tarawa: *Shibasaki*

MARSHALL ISLANDS (under Naval command as above)

Akiyama

MARIANA ISLANDS (most THIRTY-FIRST ARMY)

Obata (c.o. THIRTY-FIRST ARMY)

PALAU ISLANDS (part THIRTY-FIRST ARMY)

Inoue

PHILIPPINE ISLANDS (FOURTEENTH AREA ARMY)

Leyte: *Suzuki* (c.o. THIRTY-FIFTH ARMY)

Luzon: *Yamashita* (c.o. FOURTEENTH AREA ARMY)

IWO JIMA (under direct command of Imperial General Headquarters)
Kuribayashi
OKINAWA (most THIRTY-SECOND ARMY)
Ushijima (c.o. THIRTY-SECOND ARMY)
BORNEO (THIRTY-SEVENTH ARMY)
Bara

THE NAVY

Fleets

In Dec 41 the Imperial Japanese Navy consisted of six Fleets, numbered One to Six, which were administrative entities defined either by their function or by the area in which they were stationed. Thus
FIRST FLEET was the main Battle Fleet, incorporating the CARRIER STRIKE FORCE.
SECOND FLEET was responsible for Scouting.
THIRD FLEET was responsible for Blockade and Transport.
FOURTH FLEET looked after the Japanese Mandated Islands.
FIFTH FLEET was stationed in northern waters.
SIXTH FLEET controlled the submarine force.

These Fleets remained in existence for much of the war, all under the command of the so-called Combined Fleet which had its headquarters first in Tokyo and later in Truk, Palau and Singapore. By March 44, however, FIRST and FOURTH FLEETS controlled hardly any ships at all and the two largest formations, SECOND and THIRD FLEETS were combined into FIRST MOBILE FLEET. In the meantime, two extra formations had been created, EIGHTH FLEET, also known as the OUTER SOUTH SEAS FLEET, formed in July 42, and the GENERAL ESCORT COMMAND, responsible for convoy protection, established in Nov 43.

Except for the last named, however, none of these commands had much operational responsibility, this being the task of both the AREA FLEETS and of the *ad hoc* task forces formed to undertake a particular mission. The AREA FLEETS were set up in the summer of 1942 when Japanese conquests had reached their furthest extent. They were responsible for day-to-day operations within a particular Pacific area and were thus primarily concerned with reconnaissance and patrol work, for which they were largely dependent on their air component (see AIR FORCES below). The AREA FLEETS created were the NORTH-EAST AREA, the CHINA AREA, the SOUTH-WEST AREA* and the SOUTH-EAST AREA. A CENTRAL PACIFIC AREA FLEET was set up in March 44, whilst the home islands were the responsibility of geographical NAVAL DISTRICTS based in major coastal towns.

Task Forces

But the formations probably of most interest to the student of military history are the *ad hoc* Task Forces and it is these that are listed in some detail below.

1 The First Phase of Japanese Expansion Dec 41 to March 42
Central Pacific
PEARL HARBOUR STRIKE FORCE (inc. FIRST AIR FLEET)
Nagumo
GUAM INVASION FORCE
Inouye
WAKE INVASION FORCE
Kajioka
Malaya
SECOND FLEET MALAY FORCE†
Kondo
SOUTHERN EXPEDITIONARY FLEET
Ozawa
Philippines
DAVAO ATTACK FORCE (also Jolo Is.)
Tanaka

FIRST SURPRISE ATTACK FORCE (Aparri Is.)
Hara
SECOND SURPRISE ATTACK FORCE (Vigan Is.)
Nishimura
THIRD SURPRISE ATTACK FORCE (Bataan and Camiguin Is.)
Hirose
FOURTH SURPRISE ATTACK FORCE (Legaspi Is.)
Kubo
NORTH COVER FORCE (Lingayen Is.)
Takahashi
DISTANT COVER FORCE (Lingayen Is.)
Kondo ‡
Dutch East Indies
DISTANT COVER FORCE and SOUTHERN EXPEDITIONARY FLEET
(Sumatra and W.Java)
as above
NORTH-EAST INDIES FORCE (E. Java, Celebes, Ambon and Dutch
Borneo)
Takahashi
SUPPORT FORCE MAIN BODY
Takagi
BALI INVASION FORCE
Kubo
New Britain
INVASION FORCE, INVASION SCREENING FORCE and DISTANT
COOPERATING FORCE all subordinated to FOURTH FLEET commanded
by *Inouye*.
Indian Ocean
FIRST CARRIER FLEET
Nagumo
SECOND SOUTHERN EXPEDITIONARY FLEET
Ozawa
2 The Second Phase of Japanese Expansion April to June 42
MO Operation (an attempted invasion of New Guinea which brought
about the Battle of the Coral Sea).
CARRIER STRIKE FORCE
Takagi
MAIN BODY SUPPORT FORCE
Goto
PORT MORESBY TRANSPORT FORCE
Abe
PORT MORESBY ATTACK FORCE
Kajioka
PORT MORESBY COVER FORCE
Marumo
TULAGI INVASION FORCE
Shima
MI Operation (leading to the Battle of Midway).
All units under the direct command of COMBINED FLEET
Yamamoto
FIRST FLEET MAIN BODY
Yamamoto
FIRST MOBILE/CARRIER STRIKE FORCE
Nagumo
SECOND FLEET STRIKE FORCE MAIN BODY
Kondo
ESCORT FORCE
Tanaka
OCCUPATION SUPPORT FORCE
Kurita
AL Operation (Aleutians).
FIFTH FLEET MAIN BODY
Hosogawa
SECOND STRIKE FORCE/CARRIER FORCE

‡ Back from Malayan waters.

* The SOUTH-WEST AREA FLEET seems to have been sub-divided into a MALAYA AREA FLEET, a DUTCH EAST INDIES AREA FLEET and a PHILIPPINES AREA FLEET.

† The main damage to the British, the sinking of the *Prince of Wales* and the *Repulse*, was done by the Navy's land-based 22 Air Flotilla, commanded by *Matsunaga*.

Kakuta

ATTU OCCUPATION FORCE

Omori

KISKA OCCUPATION FORCE

Ono

3   Guadalcanal Aug 42 to Feb 43

Operations in the Solomon Is. were under the control of the OUTER SOUTH SEAS FORCE, an operational off-shoot of EIGHTH FLEET (see above) commanded by *Mikawa*. In some of the larger naval battles, however, which it was hoped might bring the Japanese a 'decisive' victory, command was exercised directly by the Combined Fleet.

Battle of Savo Island

FORCE (Name unknown)

Mikawa

Battle of the Eastern Solomons (under command COMBINED FLEET)

MAIN BODY SUPPORT FORCE

Kondo

THIRD FLEET CARRIER STRIKE FORCE

Nagumo

VANGUARD FORCE CLOSE SUPPORT

Abe

THIRD FLEET DETACHED CARRIER STRIKE FORCE

Hara

EIGHTH FLEET REINFORCEMENT FORCE

Mikawa

CONVOY ESCORT FORCE

Tanaka

Battle of Cape Esperance

EIGHTH FLEET BOMBARDMENT FORCE

Goto

CONVOY ESCORT FORCE

Joshima

Battle of the Santa Cruz Islands (under command COMBINED FLEET)

THIRD FLEET CARRIER STRIKE FORCE

Nagumo

SECOND FLEET ADVANCE FORCE

Kondo

SECOND FLEET ADVANCE FORCE MAIN BODY

Abe

SECOND FLEET CLOSE SUPPORT FORCE

Kurita

EIGHTH FLEET GUADALCANAL ATTACK FORCE

Mikawa

EIGHTH FLEET BOMBARDMENT FORCE

Takama

Battle of Guadalcanal (Naval)

ATTACK FORCE MAIN BODY

Kondo

ADVANCE RAIDING FORCE

Abe

SWEEPING FORCES

Hashimoto and *Takama*

SCREENING FORCE

Kimura

BOMBARDMENT UNIT

Nishimura

SUPPORT FORCE MAIN BODY

Kurita

EIGHTH FLEET SUPPORT GROUP

Mikawa

DESTROYER ESCORT FORCE

Tanaka

Battle of Tassafaronga

SUPPLY FORCE

Tanaka

4   The Solomon Islands July to November 43

In March 43 operational command in this sector had passed from *Mikawa* to *Samejima*.

Battle of Kula Gulf

REINFORCEMENT FORCE

Akiyama

Battle of Vella Gulf

Group of four destroyers

Sugiura

Battle of Kolombangara

Cruiser/destroyer group

Izaki

Battle of Vella Lavella

SUPPORT FORCE and TRANSPORT FORCE

Ijuin

Battle of Empress Augusta Bay

TOROKINA INTERCEPTION FORCE

Omori

After this battle ships from *Kurita*'s SECOND FLEET were despatched to bolster the OUTER SOUTH SEAS FORCE but these were largely destroyed in American carrier raids on Rabaul.

Battle of Cape St. George

BUKA REINFORCEMENT UNIT

Kagawa

5   Other Battles before June 44

Battle of the Komandorski Islands (Japanese attempt to reinforce the Aleutian Is.)

FIFTH FLEET NORTHERN FORCE

Hosogaya

Battle of the Bismarck Sea (Japanese attempt to reinforce New Guinea)

A Convoy

Kimura

6   Japanese Bids for a Decisive Fleet Action June to Oct 44

Battle of the Philippine Sea (Operation A-GO: under command COMBINED FLEET)

MOBILE FLEET ADVANCE FORCE

Kurita

MOBILE FLEET 'A' FORCE

Ozawa (also commanding MOBILE FLEET)

MOBILE FLEET 'B' FORCE

Joshima

DESTROYER FORCES

Hayakawa and *Kimura*

Battle of Leyte Gulf (under command COMBINED FLEET)

MOBILE FORCE MAIN BODY

Ozawa

MOBILE FORCE FIRST STRIKING FORCE (inc. STRIKING FORCE 'A')

Kurita

STRIKING FORCE 'C'

Nishimura

SOUTH-WEST AREA FORCE (at Manila)

Mikawa

SECOND STRIKING FORCE

Shima

SOUTH-WEST AREA GUARD FORCE

Sakonju

7   Other Japanese Forays

Attack on Mindoro

SAN JOSE INTERVENTION FORCE

Kimura

Operation TEN GO (Attempt to support Okinawa land forces by beaching a battleship and using her guns as artillery)
SURFACE SPECIAL ATTACK FORCE
Ito

THE AIR FORCES

There were two Japanese air forces, that belonging to the Japanese Army and that to the Navy. Each formed an integral part of its parent service (analagous to the position of the US Marine Corps Air Service within the Marine Corps rather than that of the USAAF within the Army), and thus had only limited operational autonomy.

Army Air Force

At the beginning of the war, the Army fielded five AIR DIVISIONS, only two of which, the THIRD and FIFTH, were involved in the early conquests. The former was mainly active in the Dutch East Indies and the latter in Burma. By the summer of 1942, however, the sprawling nature of the new Pacific empire necessitated the creation of more self-sufficient commands and the first AIR ARMIES were established. These were the*

1 FIRST AIR ARMY with headquarters in Tokyo covering Japan, Korea, Formosa, the Kurile Is. Here it remained until the end of the war.
2 SECOND AIR ARMY with headquarters in Hsingking covering Manchuria. Here it remained until the end of the war although in mid-44 it lost the bulk of its planes to the defence of the Philippines.
3 THIRD AIR ARMY with headquarters in Singapore covering Burma, Thailand, southern Indo-China, Malaya, Sumatra, Java and Borneo. Here it remained until the end of the war.

Three more AIR ARMIES were formed during the rest of the war:

4 FOURTH AIR ARMY (f. Aug 43) with headquarters first at Rabaul and then at Manila. For most of 1944 this Army was responsible for the defence of the Philippines, the Celebes and western New Guinea. By early 1945 it had virtually ceased to exist.
5 FIFTH AIR ARMY (f. Feb 44) with headquarters in Nanking and responsible for China. There it remained throughout the war, though in June 45 two-thirds of its aircraft were transferred to Korea.
6 SIXTH AIR ARMY (f. 1945) with headquarters in Japan and responsible with FIRST AIR ARMY (see above) for the defence of the home islands.
7 AIR GENERAL ARMY (f. April 45) and taking under command FIRST, SECOND, FIFTH and SIXTH AIR ARMIES (see above).

Navy Air Force

The Navy Air Force was organised along similar lines to its parent force in that it had overlapping administrative and operational commands, often with the same commander, stationed in a particular sector. Just as in the surface Navy the major administrative component of the air arm was the AIR FLEET, of which there were two in Dec 41:

1 FIRST AIR FLEET provided the aircraft for the Japanese carrier force and participated in all of the great carrier battles of the Pacific war. By late 1943, however, almost all the carrier pilots were dead and the Fleet was reformed as a land-based formation, though still to function as COMBINED FLEET's main strike force. In early 1944 it went to the Mariana Is., a few months later to the Philippines and in Jan 45 to Formosa.
2 ELEVENTH AIR FLEET provided the Navy's land-based units at the beginning of the war and was still responsible for the defence of the whole of the Pacific at the end of 1942. With the formation of additional Air Fleets in 1943 (see below), the ELEVENTH was made responsible only for eastern New Guinea and the central Pacific. In fulfilling this task it had been virtually destroyed by March 44.

During the war itself the following additional Air Fleets were formed, not, it will be noted, in the same chronological sequence as the numerical.

3 TWELFTH AIR FLEET was formed in 1943 and remained responsible throughout the war for the defence of the north-eastern Pacific.
4 THIRTEENTH AIR FLEET was formed in 1943 and was based in the Dutch East Indies and Malaya, where it was originally responsible for the defence of the whole of South-East Asia and the South-West Pacific, including the Philippines and western New Guinea. Towards the end of 1944 it was joined in the Philippines by FIRST AIR FLEET (see above).
5 SECOND AIR FLEET was formed in early 1944 and remained in Japan throughout the war.
6 THIRD AIR FLEET was formed in early 1944 and remained in Japan throughout the war.
7 FOURTEENTH AIR FLEET was formed in early 1944 from the remnants of ELEVENTH AIR FLEET (see above) and fought in the Central Pacific. It seems to have been largely destroyed by spring of the following year.
8 FIFTH AIR FLEET was formed in early 1944 and remained in Japan throughout the war.
9 TENTH AIR FLEET was formed in 1944 and remained in Japan throughout the war. It provided the men and machines for the Navy Air Force's contribution to the *kamikaze* offensive.

The major operational component of the Navy air force was the so-called BASE AIR FORCE, which was pretty much an AIR FLEET (see above) minus its base and rear echelon personnel. At least seven BASE AIR FORCES were formed, numbered 1 to 7, and those that were stationed outside of the home islands are listed below, together with their corresponding AIR FLEET and the surface fleet AREA FLEET (see above) to which they were attached.

AIR FLEET	BASE AIR FORCE	AREA FLEET
Eleventh	First	South-East
Twelfth	Second	North-East
Thirteenth	Third	South-West
Fourteenth	Fourth	Central Pacific
First (reformed)	Fifth	Combined Fleet

* It has not proved possible to provide a full list of either Army or Navy air force commanders. Prominent Army names were *Kinoshita, Obata* and *Tominaga* whilst important Navy commanders included *Fukudome, Kakuta, Kusaka, Onishi, Tsukuhara* and *Ugaki.*

• TABLE 8 • GOVERNMENTS AND HIGH COMMANDS ALBANIA-BULGARIA •

> **Table 8** Governments and High Commands in other Occupied and Belligerent Countries

ALBANIA

Albania was invaded by the Italians in April 39 and King Victor Emmanuel 'accepted' the crown upon the abdication of King Zog. A puppet government was established, headed by

Verlaci to Dec 41
Kruja to Jan 43
Libohova to Feb 43
Bushati to May 43
Libohova to Sept 43

but real power was exercised by the Italian Governor-General

Jacomoni to March 43
Pariani.

After the Italian surrender in Sept 43 the country came under German control although the new government, headed by the President of the Council of Regency, Frasheri, was allowed a reasonable amount of autonomy.* Indeed, much of the subsequent fighting in Albania was between rival guerilla groups (the Committee of National Liberation, the National Front and the Legality Movement) and it was the first, led by the Communist Enver Hoxha, that slowly gained ascendancy. In Oct 44 the Germans evacuated the country and Hoxha, who had established a Provisional Government in May, took power.

Δ Of enormous influence over the King was his chief military aide van Overstraeten.

* The Prime Ministers were Mitrovica to June 44, Fiqri to Aug 44 and Biçaku.

AUSTRALIA

PRIME MINISTER

Menzies to Aug 41
Fadden to Oct 41
Curtin to July 45†
Chifley

DEFENCE MINISTER

As above except that Beasley was Defence Minister under Chifley

TREASURER

Casey to 1940
Fadden to Oct 41
Chifley

EXTERNAL AFFAIRS

Gullett to Aug 40
Stewart to Oct 41
Evatt

From Oct 41 the Australian Government also included Ministers for the ARMY, the NAVY, AIR, MUNITIONS, WAR ORGANISATION OF INDUSTRY, AIRCRAFT PRODUCTION, NATIONAL SERVICE and HOME SECURITY, though one man often held more than one portfolio.

C-in-C. AUSTRALIAN MILITARY FORCES

Blamey from March 42

CHIEF OF THE GENERAL STAFF

Squires to March 40
White to Aug 40
Sturdee to Oct 42
Northcott

FIRST NAVAL MEMBER

Colvin to July 41
Royle

CHIEF OF THE AIR STAFF

Williams to Feb 40
Goble to Dec 39 (acting)
Burnett to May 42
G. Jones‡

FIRST ARMY was formed in April 42 and served as an administrative headquarters in Australia before taking over from the Americans in the South-West Pacific in Oct 44.

Lavarack to March 44

† The Curtin government was re-elected in the General Election of Aug 43

‡ Of equal rank and authority was Air Vice-Marshall Bostock who was in command of the combat squadrons. Relations between the two men were appalling.

Sturdee

SECOND ARMY was formed in April 42 and served as an administrative headquarters in Australia.

Mackay to Oct 43
Morshead to July 44

BELGIUM
1939-40

KING
C-in-C. ARMED FORCES

Leopold III Δ

PRIME MINISTER

Pierlot

FOREIGN MINISTER

Spaak

FINANCE MINISTER

Gutt

DEFENCE MINISTER

Denis

ARMY CHIEF OF STAFF

van der Bergen to Jan 40
Michiels

The Belgians capitulated on 28 May 1940.

Government-in-Exile

As above except that Gutt took over DEFENCE as well until he relinquished it to Pierlot in Oct 42. The C-in-C. FREE BELGIAN FORCES was van Strydonck de Burkel. The Government returned to Belgium in Sept 44. A new Government took office in Feb 45, led by van Acker.

BULGARIA

Anxious to avoid German occupation and with its eyes on Yugoslav and Greek territory, Bulgaria joined the Tripartite Pact in March 41. However, its armed forces never fought alongside the Axis except as garrison troops in parts of Serbia and Macedonia. Nor were any whole Axis formations stationed in the country. The Russians invaded in Sept 44 and that same month the Communist Fatherland Front seized power. Thereafter the Bulgarian Army fought with the Russians right to the gates of Vienna.

KING

Boris III to Aug 43
Simeon II (with Council of Regency)

PRIME MINISTER

Filov to Sept 43
Bozhilov to June 44
Bagryanov to Sept 44
Muraviev Sept 44
Georgiev

FOREIGN MINISTER

Popov to April 42
Filov to Sept 43
Kirov to Oct 43
Shishmanov to June 44
Bagryanov June 44
Dagranov to Sept 44
Stainov

FINANCE MINISTER

Bozhilov to June 44
Savov to Sept 44
Girginov Sept 44
Stoyanov

WAR MINISTER
Daskalov to April 42
Mihov to Aug 43
Rusev to May 44
Velchev
C-in-C. ARMED FORCES (from Sept 44)
Marinov
C-in-C. FIFTH ARMY (from Sept 44; fought with Russians)
Stanchev

CANADA
PRIME MINISTER
King *
EXTERNAL AFFAIRS MINISTER
King
FINANCE MINISTER
Ralston to July 40
Ilsley
NATIONAL DEFENCE MINISTER
Rogers to July 40
Ralston to Nov 44
McNaughton
By 1944 the Government also included Ministers for AIR, NAVAL SERVICES, MUNITIONS and NATIONAL WAR SERVICES.
CHIEF OF THE GENERAL STAFF
Crerar to Dec 41
Stuart
CHIEF OF THE NAVAL STAFF
Murray to 1940
Nelles
Jones
CHIEF OF THE AIR STAFF
Leckie 1944-45
C-in-C. FIRST ARMY (f. April 42)
McNaughton to Feb 44
Crerar
C-in-C. NORTH-WEST ATLANTIC (f. March 43)
Murray

CHINA
PRESIDENT
Li Sen to Aug 43
Chiang Kai-shek
PRESIDENT OF THE EXECUTIVE YUAN †
DIRECTOR OF THE KUOMINTANG
CHAIRMAN OF THE NATIONAL MILITARY COUNCIL‡
CHAIRMAN OF THE SUPREME NATIONAL DEFENCE COUNCIL‡
Chiang Kai-shek
FOREIGN MINISTER
Soong
WAR MINISTER
Ho Ying-chin to 1944
Cheng Chieng
FINANCE MINISTER
Kung to 1944
Yui
CHIEF OF THE SUPREME STAFF
Ho Ying-chin
CHIEF OF OPERATIONS
Hsu Yung-chang

The Sino-Japanese War began in July 37 and in the following year China was divided into nine war areas. By 1944 this number had grown to twelve and three regional field headquarters were set up to coordinate operations.

At the end of the year a Headquarters Chinese Ground Forces was established and four subordinate regional commands. By this stage of the war the whole Chinese war machine was being overhauled, the intention being to reduce the number of divisions from 327 to 84, 39 of which were to be retrained and reequipped by the Americans. But only a dozen had actually undergone 'Americanisation' by the end of the war.‡‡

Rather more details are available about the Chinese effort in Burma where they participated in the British collapse in 1941/42 and later fought alongside American troops. Three armies participated in the retreat from Burma:
FIFTH ARMY
Tu Lü Ming
SIXTH ARMY
Kan
SIXTY-SIXTH ARMY
Chang Cheng
The following forces took part in *Stilwell's* (commanding CHINESE ARMY IN INDIA) two-pronged attack into Burma in 1944/45:
NEW FIRST ARMY (also known as 'X' Force)
Sun Li-jen
NEW SIXTH ARMY (also known as 'X' Force)
Liao Yao-hsiang
YUNNAN EXPEDITIONARY FORCE (also known as 'Y' Force)
Wei Li-Huang

CZECHOSLOVAKIA
In 1938 much of Czechoslovakia was ceded to Germany, Hungary and Poland under the terms of the Munich Agreement and from March 39 the rump was divided into the semi-autonomous republic of Slovakia and the German Protectorate of Bohemia-Moravia. A Czechoslovak government-in-exile was established in Oct 39, with its headquarters first in Paris and later in London. This was first known as the Czechoslovakian National Committee and from July 40 as the Provisional Government. But in the government actually established in Czechoslovakia, at Kosice in March 45, the London faction was heavily outnumbered by Soviet nominees.

Slovakia
PRESIDENT
Tiso
PRIME MINISTER
Tuka
DEFENCE MINISTER
C-in-C. ARMY
Catlos to Sept 44

Bohemia-Moravia
REICH PROTECTOR
Neurath to Sept 41
Heydrich to May 42
Dalüge to Aug 42
Frick
STATE SECRETARY
K.H.Frank
PRESIDENT (Czech)
Hacha
PRIME MINISTER (Czech)
Elias to May 42
Krejci to Jan 45
Bienert

Provisional Government (London)
PRESIDENT
Benes
PRIME MINISTER

‡‡ This perforce rather sketchy outline of Chinese military organisation should not blind one to the importance of their military contribution to the Allied cause. The list of Japanese divisions in the Orders of Battle section, starting on page 139 shows how many Japanese divisions were continually tied down in China.

* *King* was returned to power in the General Election of 1940 and survived a plebiscite on conscription in 1942.

† The executive arm of the civil government.

‡ The exact distinction between these two bodies is unclear except that the latter's duties seem to have been more administrative than operational.

Sramek
FOREIGN MINISTER
Masaryk
FINANCE MINISTER
Outrata to Oct 41
Feierabend
DEFENCE MINISTER
Ingr *

Provisional Government (Kosice)
PRESIDENT
Benes
PRIME MINISTER
Fierlinger
FOREIGN MINISTER
Masaryk (and communist deputy *Clementis*)
DEFENCE MINISTER
C-in-C. ARMED FORCES
Svoboda

DENMARK
Denmark was occupied by the Germans in April 40 but they at first adopted a remarkably conciliatory approach, even allowing a perfectly authentic General Election in 1943. In August of that year, however, a state of military emergency was declared and the powers of the local German commander much enhanced. The country was not liberated until May 45.
KING
Christian X
PRIME MINISTER
Stauning to May 42
Buhl to Nov 42
Scavenius
FOREIGN MINISTER
Munch to May 42
Scavenius
FINANCE MINISTER
Buhl to July 42
Andersen to Nov 42
Koefoed
DEFENCE MINISTER (in 1940)
?
C-in-C. ARMY (in 1940)
Pryor
C-in-C. NAVY (in 1940)
Rechnitzer
GERMAN C-in-C.
Lüdke to Oct 42
von Hanneken

FINLAND
PRESIDENT
Kallio to Nov 40
Ryti to Aug 44
Mannerheim
PRIME MINISTER
Kajander to Dec 39
Ryti to Jan 41
Rangell to March 43
Linkomies to Aug 44
Hackzell to Sept 44
Castren to Nov 44
Paasikivi
FOREIGN MINISTER
Erkko to Dec 39

* Some sources state that *General Viest* was the Defence Minister until he went out to Slovakia in Sept 44 to take command of the national uprising that had just begun.

† In conjunction with *Koivosto* from Jan 41.

Tanner to March 40
Witting to March 43
Ramsay to Aug 44
Enckell
FINANCE MINISTER
Tanner to Dec 39
Pekkale to May 42†
Tanner to Aug 44
Hiltonen to Nov 44
Helo to April 45
Tuomija
DEFENCE MINISTER
Niukkanen to March 40
Walden to Nov 44
C-in-C. ARMED FORCES
Österman to Nov 39
Mannerheim to Dec 44
Heinrichs
CHIEF OF STAFF
Heinrichs to Dec 44

FRANCE
1939-40
PRESIDENT
Lebrun
PRIME MINISTER
Daladier to March 40
Reynaud to 16 June 40
Pétain
FOREIGN MINISTER
Bonnet to March 40
Reynaud to 18 May 40
Daladier to 5 June 40
Reynaud to 16 June 40
Baudouin
FINANCE MINISTER
Reynaud to March 40
Lamoureux to 5 June 40
Bouthilier
WAR MINISTER and MINISTER OF NATIONAL DEFENCE
Daladier to 18 May 40
Reynaud to 16 June 40
Weygand
AIR MINISTER
La Chambre to March 40
Laurent-Eynac to 16 June 40
Pujo
MINISTER OF MARINE
Campinchi to 16 June 40
Darlan
MINISTER OF MUNITIONS
Dautry
INSPECTOR GENERAL OF THE ARMY
CHIEF-OF-STAFF TO THE MINISTER OF NATIONAL DEFENCE
C-in-C. ARMED FORCES (in wartime)
C-in-C. ALLIED ARMIES IN FRANCE
Gamelin to 19 May 40
Weygand
CHIEF-OF-STAFF ARMY GHQ
Bineau to Jan 40
Doulenc
CHIEF-OF-STAFF AIR FORCE GHQ
Vuillemin
Mendigal Jan 40 (acting)

C-in-C. NAVY
Darlan
INSPECTOR-GENERAL OF TANKS
Keller
C-in-C. NORTH-EAST FRONT•
Georges (Chief-of-Staff:*Roton*)
FIRST ARMY GROUP
Billotte to 22 May 40
Blanchard (evac. 1 June 40)
SECOND ARMY GROUP
Prételat to 18 June 40
Condé
THIRD ARMY GROUP
Besson
FOURTH ARMY GROUP (f. 6 June 40)
Huntziger
FIRST ARMY
Blanchard to 22 May 40
Prioux
SECOND ARMY
Huntziger to 4 June 40
Freydenberg
THIRD ARMY
Condé to 18 June 40
FOURTH ARMY
Requin
FIFTH ARMY
Bourret
SIXTH ARMY
Touchon
SEVENTH ARMY
Giraud to 18 May 40
Frère
EIGHTH ARMY
Garchery to 22 May 40
Laure
NINTH ARMY
Corap to 15 May 40
Giraud
TENTH ARMY (f. 30 May 40)
Altmayer
ARMY OF THE ALPS
Orly
MILITARY GOVERNOR PARIS (from 15 May 40)
Héring
COOPERATION AIR FORCE was set up on the NORTH-EASTERN FRONT (see above) as a replacement for FIRST AIR ARMY and was in charge of the NORTHERN and EASTERN ZONES OF AIR OPERATIONS (see below).
Mouchard to Feb 40 (as FIRST AIR ARMY)
Têtu
NORTHERN ZONE OF AIR OPERATIONS was part of the FIRST AIR ARMY and later the COOPERATION AIR FORCE (see above). It was to operate in conjunction with FIRST ARMY GROUP (see above).
d'Astier de la Vigerie
EASTERN ZONE OF AIR OPERATIONS was organised in the same way as the NORTHERN ZONE (see above) but was to cooperate with SECOND ARMY GROUP (see above).
Pennès to Oct 39
Têtu to Feb 40
Bouscat
ALPINE ZONE OF AIR OPERATIONS was formed in Feb 40 from THIRD AIR ARMY and was to fight in conjunction with THIRD ARMY GROUP (see above).
Houdemon

NORTH AFRICAN ZONE OF AIR OPERATIONS was formed in Feb 40 from FIFTH AIR ARMY.
Bouscat to Oct 39
Pennès

Occupied France*
MILITARY GOVERNOR
O. von Stülpnagel to May 42
H. von Stülpnagel to July 44
Kitzinger
SUPREME SS AND POLICE CHIEF (from April 42)‡
Oberg
CHIEF OF FRENCH POLICE
?
Bousquet to Dec 43
Darnand
SPECIAL OPERATIONS EXECUTIVE (see organigram to Table 3) had six sections concerned with France•, two of which deserve particular mention. One was F Section which worked largely independently of the Free French (see below) and endeavoured to test all shades of French opinion. The other was RF Section which was set up specifically to work for the Free French intelligence organisation, the BUREAU CENTRAL DES RENSEIGNEMENTS ET ACTIONS (see below).

F SECTION	RF SECTION
Humphreys to Dec 40	*Piquet-Wicks*
Marriott to Nov 41	*Sweet-Escott*
Buckmaster	*Hutchinson*
	Dismore

FRANC-TIREURS ET PARTISANS was founded in May 41 and was the military wing of the Communist-dominated (though far from monolithic) FRONT NATIONAL. The C-in-C. of the F.T.P. was
Tillon
MOUVEMENTS UNIS DE RESISTANCE was set up in March 43 by *Jean Moulin*, the Free French Delegate-General in occupied France, and was a Gaullist co-ordinating committee uniting some of the numerous resistance groups there. In May 43 it was superseded by the CONSEIL NATIONAL DE LA RESISTANCE, the chairman of both bodies being
Moulin to July 43
Bidault
The ARMEE SECRETE was the military wing of the MOUVEMENTS UNIS DE LA RESISTANCE (see above) and in March 44 was replaced by the FORCES FRANCAISES DE L'INTERIEUR. The main commanders were
Delestraint to June 43
Koenig from May 44

Vichy France△
After the signing of the armistice with Germany on 22 June 1940, the French Government and National Assembly moved down to Vichy and in July the Assembly voted to give full powers to *Pétain* as head of state, thus ending the III Republic. But *Pétain* was very much a figurehead and real power was exercised by the VICE-PRESIDENT OF THE COUNCIL OF MINISTERS or, from April 42, the CHIEF OF GOVERNMENT.
PRESIDENT
Pétain
CHIEF OF STATE (effective)
Laval to Dec 40 (as VICE-PRESIDENT COUNCIL OF MINISTERS)
Flandin to Feb 41 (as FOREIGN MINISTER)
Darlan to April 42 (as VICE-PRESIDENT COUNCIL OF MINISTERS)
Laval (as CHIEF OF GOVERNMENT)
C-in-C. ARMED FORCES△
Darlan to Nov 42

Provisional Government
General de Gaulle reached England in June 40 and there established the

• Further details on the location and composition of French formations in May/June 1940 will be found in Maps 2-4 and in the Orders of Battle section on page 146.

* At first there was some meaningful distinction to be drawn between the regimes in the northern occupied zone of France and in Vichy France to the south. But the distinction became purely legalistic after the Germans moved into Vichy France also, in Nov 42.

‡ *Oberg* replaced *Thomas*, who had been *Heydrich's* representative in France since 1940, and took under command *Knochen*, the Gestapo chief. The latter also remained in France until the Liberation.

• All six in the charge of *R.E.Brook*.

△ The government's puppet role became yet more pronounced after the Germans occupied the whole of France in Nov 42. Amongst other acts they demobilised the whole of the Vichy armed forces.

• TABLE 8 • GOVERNMENTS AND HIGH COMMANDS FRANCE–HUNGARY •

headquarters of a government-in-exile known as FREE FRANCE. From July 42 this was known as FRANCE COMBATTANTE though by then (from Sept 41) there existed an executive organ, known as the FRENCH NATIONAL COMMITTEE whose 'ministers' were known as Commissioners. *De Gaulle* moved to North Africa in Jan 43, in the wake of Operation Torch, and in June the F.N.C. was superseded by the FRENCH COMMITTEE OF NATIONAL LIBERATION which was intended to also rally support amongst those elements who had remained in North Africa whilst it was under Vichy control. In July 44 this Committee was formally declared to be the PROVISIONAL GOVERNMENT of France and in September it moved to Paris. Recognised by the Allies in Oct 44, it created a provisional Consultative Assembly in November, though elections were not held until after the war.

HEAD OF FRENCH NATIONAL COMMITTEE
CHAIRMAN OF FRENCH COMMITTEE OF NATIONAL LIBERATION
PRESIDENT OF COUNCIL, PROVISIONAL GOVERNMENT
C-in-C. FREE FRENCH ARMED FORCES
    de Gaulle
    Giraud was co-chairman of the F.C.N.L. until Aug 43.
FOREIGN MINISTER/COMMISSIONER
    Dejean to Oct 42
    Massigli to Sept 44
    Bidault
FINANCE MINISTER/COMMISSIONER
    Pleven to Nov 43
    Mendès-France to Sept 44
    Lepercq to Nov 44
    Pleven
WAR MINISTER/COMMISSIONER
    Legentilhomme
    Le Troquer
    Diethelm
CHIEF OF THE GENERAL STAFF (Provisional Government in France)
    Juin
C-in-C. FRENCH ARMY (from Jan 43)•
    Giraud to April 44
    de Gaulle
C-in-C. FRENCH LAND FORCES NORTH AFRICA (Jan to May 43)
    Juin
C-in-C. FRENCH EXPEDITIONARY CORPS IN ITALY (Sept 43 to July 44)
    Juin
C-in-C. FIRST FRENCH ARMY (f. Dec 43. Known as Army B until Aug 44)
    de Lattre de Tassigny

GREECE
1939-41
KING
C-in-C. ARMED FORCES
    Georgios II
PRIME MINISTER
    Metaxas to Jan 41
    Korizis to 20 April 41
    Tsouderos
FOREIGN MINISTER
    Metaxas
FINANCE MINISTER
    Apostolides
WAR MINISTER
    ?
C-in-C. ARMY Δ
    Papagos

Occupied Greece
From May 41 the country was divided into Bulgarian, Italian and German

zones of occupation, the Italian zone being by far the largest. In May 43 the Germans abolished the distinction between their and the Italian zones but still relied heavily on Italian troops until the latters' surrender in September. The Germans themselves did not quit Greece until Oct 44.*

MILITARY GOVERNOR (Italian Zone)
    Geloso
PRIME MINISTER
    Tsolácoglou to Nov 42
    Logothetopoulos to April 43
    Rallis

NATIONAL LIBERATION FRONT (E.A.M.) was a communist-dominated resistance organisation established in Sept 41 and was run by a six-man central committee. Its military wing was the NATIONAL POPULAR LIBERATION ARMY (E.L.A.S.) which was set up in April 42 but which was very much a paper force for some months. The commanders of E.L.A.S. were†
    Aris (pseud. of *A. Klaras*) to Jan 43
    Saraphis

The NATIONAL DEMOCRATIC GREEK LEAGUE (E.D.E.S.) was formed in Sept 41 and was the most important non-communist resistance grouping during the war. It was largely destroyed during the second round of internecine fighting in Dec 44.† Its leaders were
    Plastiras (political)
    Zervas (military)

Government-in-Exile
PRIME MINISTER
FOREIGN MINISTER
    Tsouderos to April 44
    Venizelos April 44
    Papandreou
FINANCE MINISTER
    Tsouderos to Sept 41
    Varvaressos to April 44
    Manzadones to June 44
    Kanellopoulos to Aug 44
    Svolos

1944-45
In Feb 44 E.A.M. established a provisional government but in September they altered their tactics and permitted some of their nominees to join the government-in-exile, this latter returning to Greece the following month. All sides agreed to place their forces under British command, the latters' troops having come ashore with the government. This was to ensure a peaceful transfer of power but within a few weeks the British were conducting military operations against E.L.A.S.

KING
    Georgios II (under the Regency of *Archbishop Damaskinos*)
PRIME MINISTER
    Papandreou to Dec 44
    Plastiras to April 45
    Voulgaris
FOREIGN MINISTER
    Papandreou to Jan 45
    Sophianopoulos
FINANCE MINISTER
    Svolos to Jan 45
    Sideris to April 45
    Mantzarinos
C-in-C. GREEK AND BRITISH FORCES
    Scobie

HUNGARY
Hungary joined the Tripartite Pact in Nov 40 but remained reluctant to fight

as part of the Axis. In April 41, however, she was forced to allow the passage of German troops en route for Yugoslavia and a new government subsequently agreed to participate in Operation Barbarossa. But Hungarian support became increasingly lukewarm and in March 44 the Germans marched into Hungary and set up a puppet government. But these men were distasteful to Regent *Horthy*, who had maintained his position, and in August he dismissed them. The Germans intervened again and this time supported the creation of an overtly fascist regime which was not ousted until the Russians imposed their own nominees in April 45.

REGENT
   Horthy
PRIME MINISTER
   Teleki to April 41
   Bárdossy to March 42
   Kállay to March 44
   Sztójay to Aug 44
   Lakatos to Oct 44
   Szálasi
FOREIGN MINISTER
   Csáky to Feb 41
   Bárdossy to March 42
   Kállay to July 43
   Ghyczy to March 44
   Sztójay to Aug 44
   Hennyey to Oct 44
   Keményi
FINANCE MINISTER
   Reményi-Schneller
DEFENCE MINISTER
   Bartha to Sept 42
   Nagy to June 43
   Csatay to Oct 44
   Beregffy
CHIEF OF THE GENERAL STAFF
   Werth to Sept 41
   Szombathelyi to April 44
   Vörös to Oct 44
   Beregffy

FIRST ARMY was the original Hungarian Home Army and received its numerical designation upon the creation of SECOND ARMY (see below) in early 1942. It did not see any action, however, until May 44 when it entered the front in Galicia. Thereafter it fought against the Russians until the end of the war.
   Náday March to April 44
   Lakatos to May 44
   Beregffy to Aug 44
   Miklós to Oct 44
   László

SECOND ARMY was formed in April 42 and arrived on the Eastern Front in July.* It was all but destroyed in the Russian offensive to the north of Stalingrad in Jan 43 and was withdrawn back to Hungary in March. It was reformed in Aug 44 but had all but disappeared by the end of the year.
   Jany to March 43
   Vörös Aug to Oct 44
   Major

THIRD ARMY was formed in Sept 44 and immediately entered the front in Transylvania. It fought against the Russians until the end of the war but was never more than a skeleton formation.
   Heszlenyi
C-in-C. AIR FORCE
   Rakosi to 1944
   Banfalvy

Provisional Government

This was a coalition of Russian nominees formed in Dec 44 and usually referred to as the Debrecen Committee. In April 45 it returned to Budapest to become the recognised government.
PRIME MINISTER *Miklos*; FOREIGN MINISTER *Gyöngyössy*; FINANCE MINISTER *Vasary*; DEFENCE MINISTER *Vörös*.

INDIA
GOVERNOR-GENERAL
   Linlithgow to Oct 43
   Wavell
C-in-C. INDIA
   Cassels to Nov 40
   Auchinleck to June 41
   Wavell to June 43
   Auchinleck

Executive Council of the Governor-General
including:
HOME AFFAIRS MEMBER
   Maxwell to 1944
   Mudie
FINANCE MEMBER
   Raisman to 1945
   Rowlands

Other
FLAG OFFICER INDIAN NAVY
   Fitzherbert to 1943
   ?

THE NETHERLANDS
1939-40
QUEEN
   Wilhelmina
PRIME MINISTER
FINANCE MINISTER
   de Geer
FOREIGN MINISTER
   van Kleffens
DEFENCE MINISTER
   Dijxhoorn
C-in-C. ARMED FORCES
   Reynders to Feb 40
   Winkelman
C-in-C. FIELD ARMY
   Voorst tot Voorst
C-in-C. NAVY
   Furstner
The Dutch surrendered on 14 May 1940.

Occupied Holland
No puppet government was ever established in the Netherlands, though in 1942 the Germans did threaten to make the Nazi *Mussert* head of state. The key German appointments were
REICH COMMISSIONER
   Seyss-Inquart
C-in-C. HOLLAND
   Christiansen

Government-in-Exile
PRIME MINISTER
   de Geer to Sept 40
   Gerbrandy

* The first Hungarian troops to fight in Russia were the Carpathian Group, built around the Mobile Corps. These men fought through the Ukraine to the Donets in the first weeks of Barbarossa but because of heavy casualties and mechanical losses had to be withdrawn back to Hungary in Nov 41.

• **TABLE 8** • GOVERNMENTS AND HIGH COMMANDS HUNGARY–POLAND •

FOREIGN MINISTER
van Kleffens
FINANCE MINISTER
de Geer to Sept 40
Welter to Nov 41
Albarda to Sept 42
van den Broek to Feb 45
Huysmans
DEFENCE MINISTER*
Dijxhoorn to Nov 41
van Boeyen to late 42

There was no Dutch Government in the Netherlands until May 45, after the resignation of the *Gerbrandy* administration in London.

NEW ZEALAND
PRIME MINISTER
Savage to April 40
Fraser |
EXTERNAL AFFAIRS MINISTER
Savage to April 40
Langstone to 1942
Fraser
FINANCE MINISTER
Nash to 1942
Fraser to Sept 43
Nash
DEFENCE MINISTER
Jones

Other Ministries that came into being during the war were SUPPLY AND MUNITIONS, MAORI WAR EFFORT, INDUSTRIAL MANPOWER, WAR EXPENDITURE, ARMED FORCES AND WAR COORDINATION, NATIONAL SERVICE, and PRIMARY PRODUCTION FOR WAR PURPOSES.
CHIEF OF THE GENERAL STAFF
?
Puttick 1941-45
CHIEF OF NAVAL STAFF
?
CHIEF OF THE AIR STAFF
?
Goddard 1941-3
Izett

NORWAY
1940
KING
Haakon VII
PRIME MINISTER
Nygaardsvold
FOREIGN MINISTER
Koht
FINANCE MINISTER
Torp
DEFENCE MINISTER
Ljungberg
C-in-C. ARMY
Laake to 11 April 40
Ruge
C-in-C. NAVY
Diesen
C-in-C. AIR FORCE
?

The King and his Government left Norway on 6 June 1940.

* From Nov 41 NAVAL AFFAIRS were administered by a separate Ministry. Throughout the war the Minister in charge was *Admiral Furstner*.

| *Fraser* was acting Prime Minister from the beginning of the war as *Savage* was terminally ill. The Labour administration was returned to power in the General Election of Sept 43.

† Including most of the Polish air force which was not a separate service but was divided between the Army and the Navy.

Occupied Norway
PRIME MINISTER (from Feb 42)
Quisling to May 45
REICH COMMISSIONER
Terboven
C-in-C. NORWAY
Falkenhorst to Dec 44
Böhme

Government-in-Exile
King and Ministers as 1939/40 except that *Lie* replaced *Koht* Feb 41, *Hartmann* replaced *Torp* March 42, and *Torp* replaced *Ljungberg* at the same time.
C-in-C. ARMED FORCES
?
Hansteen to July 44
Crown Prince Olav

The King and his Government did not return to Norway until after the German surrender in May 45.

POLAND
1939
PRESIDENT
Moscicki
PRIME MINISTER
Skladkowski
FOREIGN MINISTER
Beck
FINANCE MINISTER
Kwiatkowski
DEFENCE MINISTER
Kasprzycki
C-in-C. ARMY†
Rydz-Smigly
CHIEF OF STAFF ARMY
Stachiewicz

CARPATHIA ARMY was redesignated MALOPOLSKA ARMY on 6 Sept and had been largely destroyed by 20 Sept.
Fabrycy
CRACOW ARMY merged with LUBLIN ARMY (see below) on 16 Sept.
Szylling
LODZ ARMY was disbanded on 8 Sept and its command elements used to form WARSAW ARMY (see below).
Rommel
LUBLIN ARMY was formed on 4 Sept, merged with CRACOW ARMY (see above) on 16 Sept and capitulated on the 20th.
Piskor
MODLIN ARMY was absorbed by WARSAW ARMY (see below) between 10 and 12 Sept.
Krukowicz-Przedrzymirski
POMERANIA ARMY was destroyed on 17/18 Sept.
Bortnowski
POZNAN ARMY merged with POMERANIA ARMY (see above) on 9 Sept.
Kutrzeba
PRUSSIA ARMY had been destroyed by 10 Sept.
Dab-Biernacki
WARSAW ARMY was formed on 8 Sept using command elements from LODZ ARMY (see above). It surrendered on 28 Sept.
Rommel
C-in-C. AIR FORCE (Army Component)
Zajac

Occupied Poland
After the defeat of Sept 39 Poland was dismembered. Part of the country

was directly annexed by Germany, the *Gaus* of Danzig and Warthe; part was annexed by Russia, the provinces of Lwow, Stanislawow, Tarnopol, Volnynia, Polesia, Bialystok, Nowogrodek and Wilno; the rest was put under the control of a German Government General.△ After the invasion of Russia in 1941, the first four of the annexed provinces were added to the Government General and the other four constituted an area of occupied Russia known as Ostland.

GOVERNOR GENERAL
    H.Frank to Aug 44
STATE SECRETARY
    ?
C-in-C. HOME ARMY (Polish Underground)
    Rowecki
    Komorowski (pseud. *'Bor'*) to Sept 44
    *Okulicki**
CHIEF DELEGATE (of Government-in-Exile)†
    Ratajski Dec 40 to Aug 42
    Piekalkiewicz to Feb 43
    Jankowski

Government-in-Exile

The Polish government left Poland for Rumania on 19 Sept 1939. It then moved to Paris and had to move to London after the French collapse. It never returned to Poland as power there was handed over by the Russians to a government formed of their own nominees.

PRESIDENT
    Raczkiewicz
PRIME MINISTER
    Sikorski to July 43
    Mikolajczyk to Nov 44
    Arciszewski
FOREIGN MINISTER
    Zaleski to Aug 41
    Raczynski to July 43
    Romer to Nov 44
    Tarnowski
FINANCE MINISTER
    Koc to Jan 41
    Strasburger to July 43
    Grosfeld to Nov 44
    Kwapinski
DEFENCE MINISTER
    ?
    Kukiel
C-in-C. ARMED FORCES
    Sikorski to July 43
    Sosnkowski to Sept 44
    Komorowski (pseud. *'Bor'*)

Provisional Government

In April 1943 the Russians broke off relations with the Polish government in London and established their own Union of Polish Patriots in Russia. In July 44 a Committee of National Liberation was formed, meeting in Lublin, and this declared itself to be the Provisional Government in Dec 44.

PRESIDENT
    Bierut
PRIME MINISTER
    Osobka-Morawski
FOREIGN MINISTER
    Rzymowski
FINANCE MINISTER
    Dabrowski
DEFENCE MINISTER
C-in-C. ARMED FORCES

    Zymierski

Polish Forces Fighting Outside Poland

C-in-C. POLISH FORCES IN RUSSIA
    Anders to July 42
    Berling (from Feb 43)
II POLISH CORPS (in Italy)
    Anders

1 POLISH ARMOURED DIVISION (in North-West Europe)
    Maczek

RUMANIA

For much of the war Rumanian politics were dominated by *General Ion Antonescu* who came to power in Sept 40 when *King Carol* abdicated in favour of his son. *Antonescu* signed the Tripartite Pact in Nov 40 and in June 41 marched with the Germans, in considerable force, into Russia. But the endless slaughter on the Eastern Front and the clear signs that Germany was losing the war encouraged the King, in Aug 44, to dismiss *Antonescu*, announce a truce with the Allies and declare war on Germany. Thereafter substantial Rumanian forces fought with the Russians right through to the end of the war. In March 45, in the face of growing social disorder in Rumania, the Russians forced the King to dismiss the government and install a group of Soviet nominees.

KING
    Carol II to Sept 40
    Mihai I
PRIME MINISTER
    Argetoianu to Nov 39
    Tartarescu to July 40
    Gigurtu to Sept 40
    Antonescu to Aug 44‡
    Sanatescu to Dec 44
    Radescu to March 45
    Groza
FOREIGN MINISTER
    Gafencu to June 40
    Gigurtu to July 40
    Manoilescu to Sept 40
    Sturdza to Dec 40
    Antonescu to Aug 44
    Niculescu-Buzesti to Dec 44
    Visoianu to March 45
    Tatarescu
FINANCE MINISTER
    Constantinescu to July 40
    Savu to Sept 40
    Cretzianu to Jan 41
    Stoenescu to Oct 42
    Neagu to Aug 44
    Potopeanu to Dec 44
    Romniceanu to March 45
    Alimanisteanu
DEFENCE MINISTER
    Iacobici to Sept 40
    Antonescu to Aug 44
    Racovita
    Vasiliu-Rascanu
CHIEF OF THE GENERAL STAFF
    Enescu
    Iacobici
    Radescu to March 45
    Sanatescu
FIRST ARMY only saw action after the cease-fire with Russia and was in

△ Called *Reststaat Polen* until Aug 40.

* The Home Army was dissolved in Dec 44.

† The ultimate Polish authority inside occupied Poland.

‡ *Antonescu* styled himself the Conducator, yet another variation on the Fuhrer theme.

• **TABLE 8** • GOVERNMENTS AND HIGH COMMANDS POLAND-YUGOSLAVIA •

action against the Germans until the end of the war.
>*Atanasiu*

There was no SECOND ARMY, or at least one never saw action.

THIRD ARMY** took part in Operation Barbarossa but was withdrawn from the front towards the end of 1941. It returned late in the next year and was reduced to remnants by December, reappeared and was severely handled again in Dec 43, and came back into the line for the last time in May 44. It saw no further action after the fall of *Antonescu* in Aug 44.
>*Dumitrescu*

FOURTH ARMY** took part in Operation Barbarossa but was out of the line for the whole of 1942. It reappeared for the first few months of 1943 and then disappeared once more until May 44. Though largely destroyed in the fighting in Bessarabia it was reformed after the ceasefire with Russia in Aug 44 and fought with them right through until the end of the war.
>*Ciuperca* to Nov 42
>*Constantinescu* to ?
>*Racovita* to Aug 44
>*Stetlea*
>*Avramescu*
>*Doscalesco*

SOUTH AFRICA
PRIME MINISTER
EXTERNAL AFFAIRS MINISTER
DEFENCE MINISTER
C-in-C. UNION DEFENCE FORCES
>*Smuts*

CHIEF OF THE GENERAL STAFF
>*van Ryneveld*

C-in-C. AIR FORCE
>?

YUGOSLAVIA
After the military collapse in April 41, Yugoslavia was comprehensively dismembered by the Axis. Half of Slovenia was annexed by the Germans, the other occupied by the Italians. One province in the north-west went to Hungary and the whole of Macedonia to Bulgaria. Montenegro became an autonomous state under Italian administration whilst much of Dalmatia was simply annexed. Croatia and Serbia (the latter from Aug 41) were allowed their own puppet administrations, though in Serbia real power was in the hands of the German and Italian occupation forces. The legitimate Yugoslav government fled to London, moving to Cairo in Sept 43. Resistance to the Axis in Yugoslavia itself was conducted by Serbian royalists, the Cetniks, and by the Communist Party, the Partisans. It was the latter, with Russian support, who took power in March 45.

1939-41
KING
>*Peter II* (under the Regency of Prince Paul to March 41)

PRIME MINISTER
>*Cvetkovic* to March 41
>*Simovic*

FOREIGN MINISTER
>*Cincar-Markovic* to March 41
>*Nintchic*

FINANCE MINISTER
>*Sutej*

DEFENCE MINISTER
>*Pesic* to March 41
>*Nedic*

CHIEF OF THE GENERAL STAFF
>?
>*Kalafatovic*

C-in-C. AIR FORCE

>*Simovic* to March 41
>*Mirkovic*

Croatia
KING
>*Duke of Spoleto* (never actually visited Croatia)

PRIME MINISTER
>*Pavelic*

DEFENCE MINISTER

C-in-C. ARMED FORCES
>*Kvaternik* to Oct 42

REICH MINISTER
>*Kasche*

GERMAN C-in-C.
>*Glaise-Horstenau*

Serbia
PRIME MINISTER*
>*Nedic*

ITALIAN C-in-C. (of SECOND ARMY)†
>*Ambrosio* to Jan 42
>*Roatta* to Feb 43
>*Robotti*

Government-in-Exile
KING
>*Peter II*

PRIME MINISTER
>*Simovic* to Jan 42
>*Jovanovic* to June 43
>*Trifimovic* to Aug 43
>*Puric*

FOREIGN MINISTER
>*Nintchic*

FINANCE MINISTER
>*Sutej* to Aug 43
>*Cicin-Sain*

DEFENCE MINISTER
>*Ilic* to Jan 42
>*Mihailovic* to July 44‡

Occupied Yugoslavia
See entries under Croatia and Serbia, above, for details on collaborators and occupation forces.

C-in-C. CETNIKS
>*Mihailovic*

PRESIDENT AVNOJ•• (formed Nov 42)

PRESIDENT EXECUTIVE COMMITTEE OF NATIONAL LIBERATION (formed Oct 43)

SECRETARY-GENERAL YUGOSLAV COMMUNIST PARTY

C-in-C. ARMY OF NATIONAL LIBERATION
>*Tito*

PRESIDENT SUPREME COUNCIL (formed Oct 43)
>*Ivan Ribar*

CHIEF OF OPERATIONS, SUPREME STAFF (formed Sept 41)††
>*Jovanovic*

Liberated Yugoslavia (This government was formed in March 45).
KING
>*Peter II* (under a Regency Council. Return to Yugoslavia to be decided by plebiscite. In fact the King abdicated in Nov 45).

PRIME MINISTER

DEFENCE MINISTER
>*Tito*

** When these headquarters were out of the line there were still numerous Rumanian divisions attached to German *Gruppen* and Armies.

* Appointed in Sept 41.

† Responsible for all Italian-occupied areas in Yugoslavia.

‡ In July 44 *Tito* was recognised as commander of the Yugoslav Army.

•• Anti-Facist Council of National Liberation.

†† The membership of the Supreme Staff underwent numerous kaleidoscopic permutations but two consistent and important political officials were *Rankowic* and *Kardelj*.

FOREIGN MINISTER
  Subasic
FINANCE MINISTER
  Zejevic

SECTION 3

ORDERS OF BATTLE

The following section is divided into two basic groups of data. In the first will be found, by country, lists of all the divisions (infantry, armoured, parachute, mountain etc.) that saw any kind of prolonged combat during the war. Each divisional entry features a brief resumé of its combat history, focussing mainly on the theatres in which it saw service*. In a few cases (e.g. the Italian Gruppi di Combattimento that fought with the Allies after September 1943) formations nominally smaller than divisions are listed but it will be appreciated that for the most part available space has simply not permitted the inclusion of formations below divisional level. Available books giving this kind of order of battle detail are listed in the Bibliography.

The second half of this section assembles sets of more conventional orders of battle, comprising organigrams giving army group/army/corps/division breakdowns of the forces available to both sides at particular dates during the major campaigns. In most instances these 'snapshot' orders of battle are supplemented by theatre Ebb and Flow Charts which detail the divisions present at the start of a campaign and then go on to list, month by month, which divisions left or arrived in the theatre. The monthly totals of divisions present are listed but it is also a fairly simple matter to work out which divisions these actually were.

Details on the size of the various types of division will be found in Section 4.

*   Wherever possible the Combat Record entry for all divisions excludes prolonged periods spent in theatre but out of the line. This particularly applies to a division's first arrival in theatre.

PART I COMBAT DIVISIONS
ALLIED

USA

ARMOURED DIVISIONS (total = 16)

DIVISION	FORMED	COMBAT RECORD
1	1940	N. Africa Nov 42–May 43; Italy Oct 43–May 45
2	1940	N. Africa Nov 42–May 43; Sicily July–August 43; N.W.Europe June 44–May 45
3	1941	N.W.Europe June 44–May 45
4	1941	N.W.Europe July 44–May 45
5	1941	N.W.Europe July 44–May 45
6	1942	N.W.Europe July 44–May 45
7	1942	N.W.Europe Aug 44–May 45
8	1942	N.W.Europe Jan–May 45
9	1942	N.W.Europe Dec 44–May 45
10	1942	N.W.Europe Sept 44–May 45
11	1942	N.W.Europe Dec 44–May 45
12	1942	N.W.Europe Nov 44–May 45
13	1942	N.W.Europe Jan–May 45
14	1942	N.W.Europe Oct 44–May 45
16	1943	N.W.Europe Feb–May 45
20	1943	N.W.Europe Feb–May 45

CAVALRY DIVISIONS (total = 1)

DIVISION	FORMED	COMBAT RECORD
1	pre-1940	Pacific Dec 43–Aug 45

Details on whereabouts in the Pacific US divisions served will be found in Part II of this section, starting on page 192.

INFANTRY DIVISIONS (total = 66)

DIVISION	FORMED	COMBAT RECORD
1	pre-1940	N. Africa Nov 42–May 43;Sicily July-Aug 43; N.W.Europe June 44–May 45
2	pre-1940	N.W.Europe June 44–May 45
3	pre-1940	N.Africa Nov 42-May 43; Sicily July-Aug 43; Italy Sept 43-July 44; N.W.Europe (via S. France) Aug 44–May 45
4	1940	N.W.Europe June 44–May 45
5	pre-1940	N.W.Europe July 44-May 45
6	pre-1940	Pacific Jan 44-Aug 45
7	1940	Pacific May 43-Aug 45
8	1940	N.W.Europe July 44-May 45
9	1940	N. Africa Nov 42-May 43; Sicily July-Aug 43; N.W.Europe June 44-May 45
24	1941	Pacific April 44-Aug 45
25	1941	Pacific Dec 42-Aug 45
26	1941	N.W.Europe Sept 44-May 45
27	1940	Pacific June 44-Aug 45
28	1941	N.W.Europe July 44-May 45
29	1941	N.W.Europe June 44-May 45
30	1940	N.W.Europe June 44-May 45
31	1940	Pacific March 44-Aug 45
32	1940	Pacific Sept 42-Aug 45
33	1941	Pacific Dec 44-Aug 45
34	1941	N. Africa Nov 42-May 43; Italy Sept 43-May 45
35	1940	N.W.Europe July 44-May 45
36	1940	N. Africa April-May 43; Italy Sept 43-July 44; N.W.Europe (via S.France) Aug 44-May 45
37	1940	Pacific July 43-Aug 45
38	1941	Pacific Dec 44-Aug 45

115

INFANTRY DIVISIONS continued

DIVISION	FORMED	COMBAT RECORD
40	1941	Pacific April 44-Aug 45
41	1940	Pacific Jan 43-Aug 45
42	1943	N.W.Europe Jan-May 45
43	1941	Pacific July 43-Aug 45
44	1940	N.W.Europe Sept 44-May 45
45	1940	Sicily July-Aug 43; Italy Sept 43-July 44; N.W.Europe (via S.France) Aug 44-May 45
63	1943	N.W.Europe Jan-May 45
65	1943	N.W.Europe Jan-May 45
66	1943	N.W.Europe Dec 44-May 45
69	1943	N.W.Europe Jan-May 45
70	1943	N.W.Europe Jan-May 45
71	1943	N.W.Europe Feb-May 45
75	1943	N.W.Europe Dec 44-May 45
76	1942	N.W.Europe Jan-May 45
77	1942	Pacific July 44-Aug 45
78	1942	N.W.Europe Nov 44-May 45
79	1942	N.W.Europe June 44-May 45
80	1942	N.W.Europe Aug 44-May 45
81	1942	Pacific Sept 44- Aug 45
83	1942	N.W.Europe June 44-May 45
84	1942	N.W.Europe Nov 44-May 45
85	1942	Italy March 44-May 45
86	1942	N.W.Europe March-May 45
87	1942	N.W.Europe Dec 44-May 45
88	1942	Italy Feb 44-May 45
89	1942	N.W.Europe Jan-May 45
90	1942	N.W.Europe June 44-May 45
91	1942	Italy June 44-May 45
92	1942	Italy Oct 44-May 45
94	1942	N.W.Europe Sept 44-May 45
95	1942	N.W.Europe Sept 44-May 45
96	1942	Pacific Oct 44-Aug 45

DIVISION	FORMED	COMBAT RECORD
97	1943	N.W.Europe March-May 45
99	1942	N.W.Europe Nov 44-May 45
100	1942	N.W.Europe Oct 44-May 45
102	1942	N.W.Europe Sept 44-May 45
103	1942	N.W.Europe Oct 44-May 45
104	1942	N.W.Europe Sept 44-May 45
106	1943	N.W.Europe Dec 44-March 45
Americal	1942	Pacific Oct 42-Aug 45

MOUNTAIN DIVISIONS (total = 1)

DIVISION	FORMED	COMBAT RECORD
10	1943	Italy Jan-May 45

93 and 98 Infantry Divisions also served, in the Pacific, but they saw almost no combat.

AIRBORNE DIVISIONS (total = 4)

DIVISION	FORMED	COMBAT RECORD
11	1943	Pacific May 44-Aug 45
17	1943	N.W.Europe Dec 44-May 45
82	1942	Sicily July-Aug 43; Italy Sept 43-March 44; N.W.Europe June 44-May 45
101	1942	N.W.Europe June 44-May 45

13 Airborne Division also served in N.W.Europe but never saw combat.

MARINE CORPS DIVISIONS (total = 6)

DIVISION	FORMED	COMBAT RECORD
1	1941	Pacific Aug 42-Aug 45
2	1941	Pacific Sept 42-Aug 45
3	1943	Pacific Oct 43-Aug 45
4	1943	Pacific Jan 44-Aug 45
5	1943	Pacific Feb-Aug 45
6	1944	Pacific March-Aug 45

USSR

Given that it has not been possible to determine exactly when and where Russian divisions served on the Eastern Front as a whole, and given also the remarkable frequency with which Russian divisions were destroyed and/or reformed or redesignated, it has been necessary to organise this USSR sub-section somewhat differently from those for other belligerents. But if the information presented is, necessarily, a little bureaucratically arcane, it does most emphatically serve to show the prodigious amount of manpower that the Red Army fed into combat.

TANK CORPS

Tank corps were the nearest Red Army equivalent of armoured/panzer divisions.

GUARDS TANK CORPS (total = 12)

The following Guards Tank Corps were created, all of them honorific redesignations of existing line tank corps. Unlike most other types of formation (see below) none were destroyed or reformed.

GUARDS TANK CORPS	ORIGINAL LINE CORPS	YEAR REDESIGNATED
1	26	1942
2	24	1942
3	7	1943
4	17	1943
5	4	1943
6	12	1943
7	15	1943
8	2	1943
9	3	1944
10	30	1943
11	6	1943
12	16	1943

LINE TANK CORPS (total = 31)

The following Line Tank Corps were created (list includes those mentioned in column 2 above, some of which were later reformed with their original designation and existed in addition to the redesignated Guards Tank Corps). No redesignated tank corps were ever destroyed.

* If not redesignated.

† Fate of redesignated unit is given in appropriate Table.

TANK CORPS	YEAR FORMED	YEAR DESTROYED	YEAR* REFORMED	IF REDESIGNATED		
				YEAR	NEW DESIGNATION †	YEAR ORIGINAL REFORMED
1	1942	—	—	—	—	—
2	1942	—	—	1943	8 Gds. Tk. Corps	—
3	1942	—	—	1944	9 Gds. Tk. Corps	—
4	1942	—	—	1943	5 Gds. Tk. Corps	1943
5	1940	—	—	1942	5 Mech. Corps	1942
6	1942	—	—	1943	11 Gds. Tk. Corps	1943
7	1942	—	—	1943	3 Gds. Tk. Corps	1943
8	1942	—	—	—	—	—
9	1942	—	—	—	—	—
10	1942	—	—	—	—	—
11	1942	—	—	—	—	—

TANK CORPS	YEAR FORMED	YEAR DESTROYED	YEAR* REFORMED	IF REDESIGNATED		
				YEAR	NEW DESIGNATION †	YEAR ORIGINAL REFORMED
12	1942	—	—	1943	6 Gds. Tk. Corps	—
13	1942	—	—	1943	4 Gds. Mech. Corps	1943
14	1942	1942	1942	1942	6 Mech. Corps	—
15	1942	—	—	1943	7 Gds. Tk. Corps	—
16	1942	—	—	1943	12 Gds. Tk. Corps	—
17	1942	—	—	1943	4 Gds. Tk. Corps	1943
18	1942	—	—	—	—	—
19	1942	—	—	—	—	—
20	1942	—	—	—	—	—
21	1942	1942	—	—	—	—
22	1942	—	—	—	—	—
23	1942	—	—	—	—	—
24	1942	—	—	1942	2 Gds. Tk. Corps	1943
25	1942	—	—	—	—	—
26	1942	—	—	1942	1 Gds. Tk. Corps	1942
27	1942	—	—	—	—	—
28	1942	—	—	1942	4 Mech. Corps	1942
29	1943	—	—	—	—	—
30	1943	—	—	1943	10 Gds. Tk. Corps	1943
31	1943	—	—	—	—	—

MECHANISED CORPS

These were an approximate equivalent of the German panzer-grenadier divisions.

GUARDS MECHANISED CORPS (total = 9)

The following Guards Mechanised Corps were created, either by amalgamating smaller units or by redesignating existing line corps. No Guards Mechanised Corps were destroyed.

GUARDS MECHANISED CORPS	ORIGINAL CORPS	YEAR FORMED	HOW FORMED	
			AMALGAMATED	REDESIGNATED
1	—	1942	✓	—
2	—	1942	✓	—
3	4	1942	—	✓
4	13 Tk.	1943	—	✓
5	6	1943	—	✓
6	—	1943	✓	—
7	2	1943	—	✓
8	3	1943	—	✓
9	—	1944	✓	—

GUARDS MOTORISED DIVISIONS (total = 2)

Also formed were 2 and 3 Guards Motorised Divisions (from 107 and 82 Motorised Divisions: see below) which were in existence February-October 1942 and March 1942-June 1943 respectively, before being dissolved.

LINE MECHANISED CORPS (total = 30)

The following Line Mechanised Corps were formed (list includes those mentioned in Guards Mechanised Corps column 2 above, some of which were later reformed with their original designation and existed in addition to the redesignated Guards Mechanised Corps). No redesignated mechanised corps were ever destroyed.

MECHAN-ISED CORPS	YEAR FORMED	YEAR DESTROYED/ DISBANDED	YEAR* REFORMED	IF REDESIGNATED		
				YEAR	NEW DESIGNATION †	YEAR ORIGINAL REFORMED
1	1940	1941	1942	—	—	—
2	1940	1941	1942	1943	7 Gds. Mech. Corps	—
3	1940	1941	1942	1943	8 Gds. Mech. Corps	—
4	1940	1941	1942	1942	3 Gds. Mech. Corps	1943
5	1940	—	—	—	—	—
6	1940	1941	1942	1943	5 Gds. Mech. Corps	1943
7	1940	1941	1942	—	—	—
8	1940	1941/2	1942	—	—	—
9	1941	1941	1943	—	—	—
10	1941	‡	?	—	—	—
11	1941	1941	—	—	—	—
12	1941	1941	—	—	—	—
13	1941	1941	1942	—	—	—
14	1941	1941/2	—	—	—	—
15	1941	‡	?	—	—	—
16	1941	1941	—	—	—	—
17	1941	1941	—	—	—	—
18	1941	1941/2	—	—	—	—
19	1941	1941/2	—	—	—	—
20	1941	1941	—	—	—	—
21	1941	1941/2	—	—	—	—
22	1941	1941/2	—	—	—	—
23	1941	1941	1941	1941	23 Rifle Corps	—
24	1941	1941	—	—	—	—
25	1941	1941/2	—	—	—	—
26	1941	1941/2	—	—	—	—
27	1941	1941	—	—	—	—
28	1941	1941	1942	1942	Cadre for reforming 48 Army	—
30	1941	1941	—	—	—	—
39	1941	1941	—	—	—	—

LINE MOTORISED DIVISIONS (total = 24)

Also in existence were the following motorised divisions.

MOTORISED DIVISION	YEAR FORMED	YEAR DESTROYED /DISBANDED	YEAR REFORMED	NEW DESIGNATION †
15	pre-1941	1941	1941	15 Rifle
36	pre-1941	1943 (?)	?	?
57	pre-1941	—	—	—
69	pre-1941	1941	1942	69 Rifle
82	pre-1941	1942	1942	3 Guards Motorised
95	pre-1941	1942	—	—
101	pre-1941	?	?	101 Rifle
103	1941	1941	1942	103 Rifle

MOTORISED DIVISION	YEAR FORMED	YEAR DESTROYED /DISBANDED	YEAR REFORMED	NEW DESIGNATION †
106	1941	1941	1941	106 Rifle
109	pre-1941	1941	1941	109 Rifle
139	pre-1941	1941	1941	139 Rifle
163	pre-1941	1941	1941	163 Rifle
198	1941	1941	1942	198 Rifle
202	1941	?	1943 (?)	202 Rifle
204	1941	1941	1941	204 Rifle
205	1941	1941	1941	205 Rifle
209	1941	1941	1945 (?)	209 Rifle
213	1941	1941	1942	213 Rifle
216	1941	?	?	216 Rifle
218	1942	1942	1943	218 Rifle
219	1941	1941	1942	219 Rifle
220	1941	1941	1941	220 Rifle
236	1941	?	?	236 Rifle
266	1941	1941	1942	266 Rifle

CAVALRY DIVISIONS

GUARDS CAVALRY DIVISIONS (total = 17)

The following Guards Cavalry Divisions were formed, some possibly from scratch and some by redesignating existing line cavalry divisions. No Guards Cavalry Divisions were destroyed.

GUARDS CAVALRY DIVISION	ORIGINAL LINE DIVISION	YEAR FORMED	HOW FORMED	
			FROM SCRATCH	REDESIGNATED
1	5	1941	—	✓
2	—	1941	?	—
3	—	1941	?	—
4	—	1941	?	—
5	—	1942	?	—
6	14	1941	—	✓
7	31	1942	—	✓
8	—	?	?	—
9	12 Cossack	1942	—	✓
10	13 Cossack	1942	—	✓
11	—	1942	?	—
12	—	1942	?	—
13	—	?	?	—
14	21 Mt. Cav.	1943	—	✓
15	55	1943	—	✓
16	112	1943	—	✓
17	—	1944	?	—

LINE CAVALRY DIVISIONS (total not known)

It has not been possible to draw up a complete list of Line Cavalry Divisions but the following numbers are known to have existed:
2-9, 11-15, 17 Mt., 18 Mt., 20 Mt., 21 Mt., 24-26, 28-32, 34-38, 40, 41, 43-55, 57, 58, 61, 62, 64-66, 68, 70, 72, 73, 75, 76, 78-83, 87, 91, 94, 97, 108, 110, 112, 115, 116.

* If not immediately redesignated.

† Fate of redesignated unit is given in appropriate Table.

‡ May never have been destroyed/ disbanded and was still in existence 1945.

MOUNTAIN DIVISIONS (total = 22)

As with tank and mechanised corps some mountain divisions were redesignated and renumbered and then reformed, as completely separate units, under the original designation and number.

* If not redesignated.

† Fate of redesignated unit is given in appropriate Table.

• 32 to 42 Guards Rifle Divisions were formed from 1 to 10 Airborne Corps.

MOUNTAIN DIVISION	YEAR FORMED	YEAR DESTROYED/DISBANDED	YEAR* REFORMED	IF REDESIGNATED		
				YEAR	NEW DESIGNATION †	YEAR ORIGINAL REFORMED
128 Gds	1943	—	—	—	—	—
9	pre-1941	—	—	1943	9 Rifle	—
20	pre-1941	—	—	1944	20 Rifle	—
28	pre-1941	1941	1942	—	—	—
30	pre-1941	—	—	1942	52 Guards Rifle	—
47	pre-1941	1942	1942	1943	47 Rifle	—
58	pre-1941	—	—	—	—	—
63	pre-1941	—	—	1942	53 Guards Rifle	1943
75	pre-1941	1941	1941	—	—	—
76	pre-1941	—	—	1942	76 Rifle	—
77	pre-1941	—	—	1942	77 Rifle	—
79	pre-1941	—	—	—	—	—
83	1941 (?)	—	—	1943	128 Guards Mountain	1944
96	pre-1941	—	—	1941	96 Rifle	—
100	?	?	?	?	?	?
138	pre-1941	1942	—	1942	138 Rifle	—
173	pre-1941	1941	1941	1943	77 Guards Rifle	1943
192	pre-1941	41 & 42	42 & 43	—	—	—
194	1941	—	—	—	—	—
242	1941	1941	1942	—	—	—
302	1941	—	—	1942	302 Rifle	—
318	1942	—	—	—	—	—

RIFLE (INFANTRY) DIVISIONS

GUARDS RIFLE DIVISIONS (total = 121)

The following Guards Rifle Divisions were formed, almost all by honorific redesignation of existing line rifle divisions. No Guards Rifle Divisions were destroyed and only two were disbanded. These were 1 Guards Rifle and 12 Guards Rifle in 1942. They were reformed in 1943 and 1942 respectively.

Δ (ii) indicates a division that had been destroyed/disbanded and reformed with original number.

GUARDS RIFLE DIVISION	ORIGINAL LINE DIVISION	YEAR FORMED
1	100	1941
2	127	
3	153	
4	161	
5	107	
6	120	
7	64	
8	316	
9	78	
10	52	
11	18	1942
12	258	
13	87	
14	96 Mountain	

GUARDS RIFLE DIVISION	ORIGINAL LINE DIVISION	YEAR FORMED
15	136	(1942)
16	249	
17	119	
18	133	
19	336	
20	174	
21	361	
22	363	
23	88	
24	111	
25	—	
26	93	
27	—	
28	180	
29	32	
30	238	
31	328	
32	•	
33	•	
34	•	
35	•	
36	•	
37	•	
38	•	
39	•	
40	•	
41	•	
42	•	
43	201	
44	5	
45	70	
46	170	
47	154	
48	264	
49	—	
50	124 (ii) Δ	
51	76	
52	63	
53	130	
54	119 (ii) Δ	
55	30 Mountain	
56	—	1943
57	153	
58	344	
59	197 (ii) Δ	
60	278 (ii) Δ	
61	159	
62	127 (ii) Δ	
63	136	
64	327	

GUARDS RIFLE DIVISIONS continued

GUARDS RIFLE DIVISION	ORIGINAL LINE DIVISION	YEAR FORMED
65	—	(1943)
66	293	
67	304	
68	96	
69	120	
70	138 Mountain	
71	23	
72	29	
73	38(ii) Δ	
74	45	
75	95(ii) Δ	
76	157	
77	173(ii) Δ	
78	204	
79	284(ii) Δ	
80	298	
81	422	
82	321(ii) Δ	
83	97(ii) Δ	
84	110(ii) Δ	
85	118(ii) Δ	
86	98(ii) Δ	
87	300	
88	99	
89	160(ii) Δ	
90	325	
91	257	
92	—	
93	—	
94	—	
95	226(ii) Δ	
96	258(ii) Δ	
97	343	
98	—	
99	—	1944
100	—	
101	14	
102	—	
103	13 Guards A/b	
104	11 Guards A/b	
105	12 Guards A/b	
106	16 Guards A/b	
107	8 Guards A/b	
108	—	1943
109	—	1943
110	—	1943
112	?	?
114	14 Guards A/b	1944
116	?	?

GUARDS RIFLE DIVISION	ORIGINAL LINE DIVISION	YEAR FORMED
117	—	1943
118	7	1945
119	—	1943
120	308	1943
121	342	1943
122	249	1945
128	83	1943
130	—	1943

Δ (ii) indicates a division that had been destroyed/ disbanded and reformed with original number.

LINE RIFLE DIVISIONS (total = 413)

The following Line Rifle Divisions were formed (including those mentioned in column 2 of the preceding table). Details on redesignation and reformation are as in previous tables (e.g. Line Tank Corps) with the additional proviso that some divisions were reformed more than once.

RIFLE DIVISION	YEAR FORMED	YEAR DESTROYED /DISBANDED	YEAR* REFORMED	IF REDESIGNATED		
				YEAR	NEW DESIGNATION †	YEAR ORIGINAL REFORMED
1 MPMR	pre-1941	—	—	1941	1 Guards Mot. Rifle	—
1		1941	1942	1942	58 Guards Rifle	1944
2		1941	1942	—	—	—
3		—	—	—	—	—
4		—	—	—	—	—
5		—	—	1942	44 Guards Rifle	1942
6		—	—	—	—	—
7		—	—	—	—	—
8		1941	1942	—	—	—
9	1943	—	—	—	—	—
10	pre-1941	—	—	—	—	—
11		—	—	—	—	—
12		1941	1941	—	—	—
13		—	—	—	—	—
14		—	—	1944	101 Guards Rifle	1945
15	1941	—	—	—	—	—
16	pre-1941	1941	1941	—	—	—
17		1941	1941	—	—	—
18		—	—	1942	11 Guards Rifle	1942
19	pre-1941	—	—	—	—	—
20	1944	—	—	—	—	—
21	pre-1941	—	—	—	—	—
22		—	—	—	—	—
23		1941	1941	1943	71 Guards Rifle	1943
24		1941	1942	—	—	—
27		1941		—	—	—
29		41 & 41	41 & 41	1943	72 Guards Rifle	1943
30	1943	—	—	—	—	—
31	pre-1941	—	—	—	—	—
32		—	—	1942	29 Guards Rifle	1942
33		—	—	—	—	—
34		—	—	—	—	—
35		—	—	—	—	—
37		—	—	—	—	—

* If not redesignated.

† Fate of redesignated unit is given in appropriate Table.

LINE RIFLE DIVISIONS continued

* If not redesignated.

† Fate of redesignated unit is given in appropriate Table.

RIFLE DIVISION	YEAR FORMED	YEAR DESTROYED /DISBANDED	YEAR* REFORMED	IF REDESIGNATED		
				YEAR	NEW DESIGNATION †	YEAR ORIGINAL REFORMED
38	pre-1941	1941	1942	1943	73 Guards Rifle	1943
39		—	—	—	—	—
40		—	—	—	—	—
41		41 & 42	41 & 42	—	—	—
42		1941	1942	—	—	—
43		—	—	—	—	—
44		1941	1941	—	—	—
45		1941	41 & 42	1943	74 Guards Rifle	1943
46		41 & 42	41 & 42	—	—	—
47	1943(?)					
48	pre-1941	1941(?)	—	—	—	—
49		1941	1941	—	—	—
50		—	—	—	—	—
51		1941	1941	—	—	—
52		—	—	1941	10 Guards Rifle	1942
53		—	—	—	—	—
54		—	—	—	—	—
55		1941	1941	—	—	—
56		—	—	—	—	—
59		—	—	—	—	—
60		1941	1941	—	—	—
61		—	—	—	—	—
62		1942	1943	—	—	—
64		—	—	1941	7 Guards Rifle	1942
65	1941	—	—	1944	102 Guards Rifle	—
66	pre-1941	—	—	—	—	—
67	pre-1941	—	—	—	—	—
68	pre-1941	—	—	—	—	—
69	1941	—	—	—	—	—
70	pre-1941	—	—	1942	45 Guards Rifle	1943
71	1941	—	—	—	—	—
72	1941	1941	1941	—	—	—
73	pre-1941	1941	1943	—	—	—
74	pre-1941	—	—	—	—	—
76	1942	—	—	1942	51 Guards Rifle	1943
77	1942	—	—	—	—	—
78	pre-1941	—	—	1941	9 Guards Rifle	1942
80	pre-1941	—	—	—	—	—
81	pre-1941	—	—	—	—	—
82	1942	—	—	—	—	—
84	pre-1941	—	—	—	—	—
85	1941	1941	1941	—	—	—
86	1941	—	—	—	—	—
87	pre-1941	1941	1941	1942	13 Guards Rifle	1942
88	pre-1941	—	—	1942	23 Guards Rifle	1942
89	1941	1941	1942	—	—	—
90	pre-1941	—	—	—	—	—
91	pre-1941	1941	1942	—	—	—

RIFLE DIVISION	YEAR FORMED	YEAR DESTROYED /DISBANDED	YEAR* REFORMED	IF REDESIGNATED		
				YEAR	NEW DESIGNATION †	YEAR ORIGINAL REFORMED
92	pre-1941	1942	1942	—	—	—
93	pre-1941	—	—	1942	26 Guards Rifle	1942
94	1941	—	—	—	—	—
95	1942	—	—	1943	75 Guards Rifle	1943
96	1941	—	—	1942	14 Guards Rifle	1942
96(ii)	1942	—	—	1943	68 Guards Rifle	1943
97	pre-1941	1941	1942	1943	83 Guards Rifle	1943
98	1941	1941	1941	1943	86 Guards Rifle	1943
99	pre-1941	1942	1942	1943	88 Guards Rifle	1943
100	pre-1941	—	—	1941	1 Guards Rifle	1942
101	?	—	—	—	—	—
102	1941	41 & 42	41 & 42	—	—	—
103	1942	1942	?	—	—	—
104	pre-1941	—	—	—	—	—
105	1941	—	—	—	—	—
106		41(x2) 42	41(x2) 42	—	—	—
107		—	—	1941	5 Guards Rifle	1942
108		—	—	—	—	—
109		41 & 42	41 & 42	—	—	—
110		1941	1941	1943	84 Guards Rifle	1943
111	pre-1941	—	—	1942	24 Guards Rifle	1942
112	1941	1941	1942	—	—	—
113	pre-1941	1941	1941	—	—	—
114	1941	—	—	—	—	—
115	pre-1941	—	—	—	—	—
116	1941	1941	1941	—	—	—
117	pre-1941	1941	1942	—	—	—
118	1941	1941	1941(?)	1943	85 Guards Rifle	1943
119	1941	—	—	1942	17 Guards Rifle	1942
119(ii)	1942	—	—	1942	54 Guards Rifle	1943
120	1941	—	—	1941	6 Guards Rifle	1942
120(ii)	1942	—	—	1943	69 Guards Rifle	1943
121	1941	—	—	—	—	—
122	pre-1941	—	—	—	—	—
123		—	—	—	—	—
124		1941	1941	1942	50 Guards Rifle	1943
125		—	—	—	—	—
126		1941	1941	—	—	—
127		—	—	1941	2 Guards Rifle	1942
127(ii)	1942	—	—	1943	62 Guards Rifle	1943
128	1941	—	—	—	—	—
129	1941	1941	1941	—	—	—
130	pre-1941	1941	1942	1942	53 Guards Rifle	1943
131	pre-1941	1941	1942	—	—	—
132	pre-1941	—	—	—	—	—
133	1941	—	—	1941	18 Guards Rifle	1942
134	1941	1941	1942	—	—	—
135	pre-1941	1941	1942	—	—	—
136	pre-1941	—	—	1942	15 Guards Rifle	1942
136(ii)	1942	—	—	1943	63 Guards Rifle	1943

LINE RIFLE DIVISIONS continued						
RIFLE DIVISION	YEAR FORMED	YEAR DESTROYED /DISBANDED	YEAR* REFORMED	IF REDESIGNATED		
				YEAR	NEW DESIGNATION †	YEAR ORIGINAL REFORMED
137	pre-1941	—	—	—	—	—
138	1942	—	—	1943	70 Guards Rifle	1943
139	1941	1941	1942	—	—	—
140	pre-1941	41(x2) 42	41&42(x2)	—	—	—
141	pre-1941	1941	1942	—	—	—
142	1941	—	—	—	—	—
143	1941	1941	1943	—	—	—
144	pre-1941	—	—	—	—	—
145	1941	1941	1942	—	—	—
146	pre-1941	1941	1942	—	—	—
147	pre-1941	1941	1942	—	—	—
148	1941	—	—	—	—	—
149	1941	1941	1942	—	—	—
150	pre-1941	1942	1942	—	—	—
151	1941	1941	1941	—	—	—
152	pre-1941	1941	1942	—	—	—
153	1941	—	—	1941	3 Guards Rifle	1942
153(ii)	1942	—	—	1943	57 Guards Rifle	1943
154	1941	—	—	1942	47 Guards Rifle	1943
155	pre-1941	1941	1942	—	—	—
156	1941	1942	1943	—	—	—
157	pre-1941	—	—	1943	76 Guards Rifle	1943
158	pre-1941	1941	1942	—	—	—
159	pre-1941	1941	1941	1943	61 Guards Rifle	1943
160	1941	1941	1941	1943	89 Guards Rifle	?
161	1941	—	—	1941	4 Guards Rifle	1942
162	1941	41 & 42	42 & 42	—	—	—
163	1941	—	—	—	—	—
164	pre-1941	1941	1941(?)	—	—	—
165	1941	1941	1941	—	—	—
166	1941	1941	1942	—	—	—
167	1941	1941	1942	—	—	—
168	pre-1941	—	—	—	—	—
169	pre-1941	—	—	—	—	—
170	1942	1942	1942	—	—	—
171	pre-1941	1941	1941(?)	—	—	—
172	1941	41 & 42	41 & 42	—	—	—
174	pre-1941	—	—	1942	20 Guards Rifle	1942
174(ii)	1942	—	—	1942	46 Guards Rifle	1943
175	1941	41 & 42	41 & 42	—	—	—
176	1941	—	—	1943	129 Guards Rifle	1944
177	1941	—	—	—	—	—
178	1941	—	—	—	—	—
179	pre-1941	—	—	—	—	—
180	1941	—	—	1942	28 Guards Rifle	1942
181	pre-1941	41 & 42	42 & 43	—	—	—
182	1941	—	—	—	—	—
183	1941	—	—	—	—	—

RIFLE DIVISION	YEAR FORMED	YEAR DESTROYED /DISBANDED	YEAR* REFORMED	IF REDESIGNATED		
				YEAR	NEW DESIGNATION †	YEAR ORIGINAL REFORMED
184	1941 (?)	41 & 42	42 & 42	—	—	—
185	pre-1941	—	—	—	—	—
186	pre-1941	—	—	—	—	—
187	pre-1941	1941	1941(?)	—	—	—
188		—	—	—	—	—
189		—	—	—	—	—
190		1941	1941(?)	—	—	—
191		—	—	—	—	—
193		1941	1942	—	—	—
195		1941	1942	—	—	—
196		1941	1942	—	—	—
197		1941	1942	1943	59 Guards Rifle	1943
198	1942	—	—	—	—	—
199	1941	1942	1943	—	—	—
200	1941	1941	1942	—	—	—
201	1941	—	—	1942	43 Guards Rifle	1943
202	1942(?)	—	—	—	—	—
203	1941	?	1942	—	—	—
204	1941	—	—	1943	78 Guards Rifle	1943
205	1941	41 & 42	41 & 42	—	—	—
206	1941	1941	1942	—	—	—
207	1942	1942	1943	—	—	—
208	1941	41 & 42	41 & 43	—	—	—
209	?	—	—	—	—	—
211	1941	1941	1942	—	—	—
212	1941	1942	1943	—	—	—
213	1942	—	—	—	—	—
214	1941	1941	1942	—	—	—
215	1941	1941	1942	—	—	—
217	1941	1941	1941	—	—	—
218	1943	—	—	—	—	—
219	1942	—	—	—	—	—
220	1941	—	—	—	—	—
221	1942	1942	1943	—	—	—
222	1941	—	—	—	—	—
223		—	—	—	—	—
224		1942	1942	—	—	—
225		—	—	—	—	—
226		1942	1942	1943	95 Guards Rifle	1943
227		1942	1942	—	—	—
228		1941	1941	—	—	—
229		1942	1942	—	—	—
230		1942	1943	—	—	—
231		1942	?	—	—	—
232		1941	1942	—	—	—
233		1941	1942	—	—	—
234		—	—	—	—	—
235		1941	1942	—	—	—
236	?	—	—	—	—	—
237	1941	1941	1942	—	—	—

* If not redesignated.

† Fate of redesignated unit is given in appropriate Table.

* If not redesignated.

† Fate of redesignated unit is given in appropriate Table.

LINE RIFLE DIVISIONS continued

RIFLE DIVISION	YEAR FORMED	YEAR DESTROYED /DISBANDED	YEAR* REFORMED	IF REDESIGNATED		
				YEAR	NEW DESIGNATION †	YEAR ORIGINAL REFORMED
238	1941	—	—	1942	30 Guards Rifle	1942
239		—	—	—	—	—
240		1941	1941	—	—	—
241		—	—	—	—	
243		—	—	—	—	—
244		1941	1942	—	—	—
245		—	—	—	—	—
246		—	—	—	—	—
247		—	—	—	—	—
248		41 & 42	42 & 42	—		
249		—	—	1942	16 Guards Rifle	1942
250		—	—	—	—	—
251		—	—	—	—	—
252		1942	1942	—	—	—
253		1942	1942	—	—	—
254		—	—	—	—	—
255		1942	?	—	—	—
256		—	—	—	—	—
257		—	—	1943	91 Guards Rifle	1943
258		—	—	1942	12 Guards Rifle	1942
258(ii)	1942			1943	96 Guards Rifle	—
259	1941	—	—	—	—	—
260		1941	1941	—	—	—
261		1942	1942	—	—	—
262		—	—	—	—	—
263		—	—	—	—	—
264		1941	1942	1942	48 Guards Rifle	?
265		—	—	—	—	—
266	1942	1942	1942	—	—	—
267	1941	1942	1942	—	—	—
268		—	—	—	—	—
269		—	—	—	—	—
270		1942	1942	—	—	—
271		1944	1944	—	—	—
272		—	—	—	—	—
273		1941	1942	—	—	—
274		—	—	—	—	—
275		1942	1944	—	—	—
276		1942	1942	—	—	—
277		1941	1942	—	—	—
278		1941	1942	1943	60 Guards Rifle	?
279		1941	1942	—	—	—
280		1941	1942(?)	—	—	—
281		—	—	—	—	—
282		1941	1942	—	—	—
283		—	—	—	—	—
284		1941	1942	1943	79 Guards Rifle	?
285		—	—	—	—	—

RIFLE DIVISION	YEAR FORMED	YEAR DESTROYED /DISBANDED	YEAR* REFORMED	IF REDESIGNATED		
				YEAR	NEW DESIGNATION †	YEAR ORIGINAL REFORMED
286	1941	—	—	—	—	—
287		1941	1941	—	—	—
288		—	—	—	—	—
289		1941	1941	—	—	—
290		—	—	—	—	—
291		—	—	—	—	—
292		1942	?	—	—	—
293		—	—	1943	66 Guards Rifle	?
294		—	—	—	—	—
295		—	—	—	—	—
296		1942	—	—	—	—
297		—	—	—	—	—
298		1941	1942	1942	80 Guards Rifle	?
299	1941	1941	1942	—	—	—
300	1941	—	—	1943	86 Guards Rifle	?
301	1941	1941	1942	—	—	—
302	1942	—	—	—	—	—
303	1941	1941	1942	—	—	—
304	1941	—	—	1943	67 Guards Rifle	1943
305	1941	1942	1942	—	—	—
306	1941	—	—	—	—	—
307	1941	—	—	—	—	—
308	1942	—	—	1943	120 Guards Rifle	1943
309	1941	1941	1942	—	—	—
310		—	—	—	—	—
311		—	—	—	—	—
312		1941	1942	—	—	—
313		—	—	—	—	—
314		—	—	—	—	—
315	1942	—	—	—	—	—
316	1941	—	—	1941	8 Guards Rifle	1942
316(ii)	1942	1942	1943	—	—	—
317	1941	1942	1942	—	—	—
319	1942	1943	1943	—	—	—
320	1941	1942	1942	—	—	—
321		1942	1942	1943	82 Guards Rifle	1944
322		1941	1942	—	—	—
323		—	—	—	—	—
324		—	—	—	—	—
325		—	—	1943	90 Guards Rifle	1943
326		—	—	—	—	—
327		—	—	1943	64 Guards Rifle	1943/4
328		—	—	1942	31 Guards Rifle	1942
329		?	1944	—	—	—
330		—	—	—	—	—
331		—	—	—	—	—
332		—	—	—	—	—
333		—	—	—	—	—
334		—	—	—	—	—
335		1942		—	—	—

LINE RIFLE DIVISIONS continued

RIFLE DIVISION	YEAR FORMED	YEAR DESTROYED /DISBANDED	YEAR* REFORMED	IF REDESIGNATED		
				YEAR	NEW DESIGNATION †	YEAR ORIGINAL REFORMED
336	1941	—	—	—	—	—
337		—	—	—	—	—
338		—	—	—	—	—
339		—	—	—	—	—
340		—	—	—	—	—
341		1942	—	—	—	—
342		—	—	1943	121 Guards Rifle	—
343		—	—	1943	97 Guards Rifle	1944
344		—	—	1942	58 Guards Rifle	1942
345		1942	—	—	—	—
346		—	—	—	—	—
347		—	—	—	—	—
348		—	—	—	—	—
349		1942	—	—	—	—
350		—	—	—	—	—
351		1942	1942	—	—	—
352		—	—	—	—	—
353		—	—	—	—	—
354		—	—	—	—	—
355		1942	1944(?)	—	—	—
356		—	—	—	—	—
357		—	—	—	—	—
358		—	—	—	—	—
359		—	—	—	—	—
360		—	—	—	—	—
361		—	—	1942	21 Guards Rifle	1945(?)
362		—	—	—	—	—
363		—	—	1942	22 Guards Rifle	1945(?)
364		—	—	—	—	—
365		1942	1945(?)	—	—	—
366		—	—	1942	19 Guards Rifle	—
367		—	—	—	—	—
368		—	—	—	—	—
369		—	—	—	—	—
370		—	—	—	—	—
371		—	—	—	—	—
372		—	—	—	—	—
373		—	—	—	—	—
374		—	—	—	—	—
375		—	—	—	—	—
376		—	—	—	—	—
377		—	—	—	—	—
378		—	—	—	—	—
379		—	—	—	—	—
380		—	—	—	—	—
381		—	—	—	—	—
382		—	—	—	—	—
383		—	—	—	—	—

RIFLE DIVISION	YEAR FORMED	YEAR DESTROYED/ DISBANDED	YEAR* REFORMED	IF REDESIGNATED		
				YEAR	NEW DESIGNATION †	YEAR ORIGINAL REFORMED
384	1941	1942	1943(?)	—	—	—
385		—	—	—	—	—
386		1942	—	—	—	—
387		—	—	—	—	—
388		1942	1945(?)	—	—	—
389		—	—	—	—	—
390		1942	1942	—	—	—
391		—	—	—	—	—
392		—	—	—	—	—
393		1942	1945(?)	—	—	—
394		—	—	—	—	—
395		—	—	—	—	—
396		1942	1945(?)	—	—	—
397	1942	—	—	—	—	—
398	1941	1942	—	—	—	—
399	1942	—	—	—	—	—
400	1941	—	—	—	—	—
402	1941	—	—	—	—	—
404	1941	1942	—	—	—	—
406	1941	—	—	—	—	—
407	1941	—	—	—	—	—
408	1942	1942	—	—	—	—
409	1941	—	—	—	—	—
411	1941	1942	—	—	—	—
413	1941	—	—	—	—	—
414	1942	—	—	—	—	—
415	1941	—	—	—	—	—
416	1942	—	—	—	—	—
417	1942	—	—	—	—	—
418	?	—	—	—	—	—
421	1941	1942	—	—	—	—
422	1942	—	—	1943	81 Guards Rifle	—
443	1941	1942	—	—	—	—
446	?	—	—	—	—	—
469	1941	1942	1944	—	—	—

* If not redesignated.

† Fate of redesignated unit is given in appropriate Table.

UNITED KINGDOM

ARMOURED DIVISIONS (total = 7)

DIVISION	FORMED	COMBAT RECORD
Guards	1941	N.W.Europe Aug 44–May 45
1	pre-1939	France May 40; N.Africa Nov 41-May 43; Italy May 44-Jan 45. Disbanded Jan 45
2	1940	N.Africa Jan 41-May 41. Overrun May 41 and not reformed
6	1940	N.Africa (Tunisia) Nov 42-May 43; Italy March 44-May 45
7	1940	N.Africa June 40-May 43; Italy Sept-Dec 43; N.W.Europe July 44-May 45
10	1941	N.Africa April-Dec 42. Disbanded July 44
11	1941	N.W.Europe June 44-May 45
79	1942	N.W.Europe June 44-May 45

8, 9 and 42 Armoured Divisions were also formed but none of them saw combat.

INFANTRY DIVISIONS (total = 25)

DIVISION	FORMED	COMBAT RECORD
1	pre-1939	France May 40; N.Africa March-May 43; Italy Dec 43-Jan 45. Then to Palestine
2	pre-1939	France May 40; Burma April 44-April 45. Then to India
3	pre-1939	France May 40; N.W.Europe June 44-May 45
4	pre-1939	France May 40; N.Africa March-May 43; Italy Feb-Dec 44. Then to Greece
5	pre-1939	France May 40; Sicily July-Aug 43; Italy Sept 43-July 44 and Feb-March 45; N.W.Europe March-May 45
6	1939	Syria June-July 41; became 70 Division Oct 1941
12	1939	France May 40. Disbanded July 40
15	1939	N.W.Europe June 44-May 45
18	1939	Malaya Jan 42. Captured and not reformed
23	1939	France May 40. Disbanded July 40
36	1944	(was 36 Indian Division) Burma Sept 44-May 45
42	pre-1939	France May 40. Became 42 Armored Division Nov 41
43	pre-1939	N.W.Europe June 44-May 45
44	pre-1939	France May 40; N.Africa July 42-Jan 43. Disbanded
46	pre-1939	France May 40; N.Africa (Tunisia) Jan-May 43; Italy Sept 43-April 44, July 44-Jan 45 and April-May 45
48	pre-1939	France May 40
49	pre-1939	Norway May 40. Disbanded. Reformed Aug 42. N.W.Europe June 44-May 45
50	pre-1939	France May 40; N.Africa June 41 and Feb 42-May 43; Sicily July-Aug 43; N.W.Europe June-Dec 44. Then UK
51	pre-1939	France May 40. Captured. Reformed Aug 40. N.Africa Aug 42-May 43; Sicily Jul-Aug 43; N.W.Europe June 44- May 45
52	pre-1939	France May 40; N.W.Europe June 44-May 45
53	pre-1939	N.W.Europe June 44-May 45
56	1940	N. Africa March-May 43; Italy Sept 43-April 44 and July 44-May 45
59	pre-1939	N.W.Europe June-Aug 44. Disbanded Oct 44
70	1941	Disbanded as such Oct 43. Basis of Chindits
78	1942	N.Africa (Tunisia) Nov 42-May 43; Sicily July-Aug 43; Italy Sept 43-July 44 and Sept 44-May 45

8, 9, 38, 45, 54, 55, 61, 66, (all formed 1939), 47 (f.1940),76 and 77 (f.1941) and 80 (f.1943) Divisions also existed but none of them saw combat and only 8 Division ever left the UK. 7 Division (security duties in Palestine) was redesignated 6 Division (see above) in Nov 1939.

AIRBORNE DIVISIONS (total = 2)

DIVISION	FORMED	COMBAT RECORD
1	1941	N.Africa April-May 43; Sicily July 43; Italy Sept-Nov 43; N.W.Europe Sept 44
6	1943	N.W.Europe June and Sept 44; March 45

ARMOURED BRIGADES (total = 16)

Formations smaller than divisions are not usually included in this section but British Armoured Brigades included the same armoured component as an Armoured Division and they were, moreover, widely employed in most theatres. It should be borne in mind that the periods of combat cited below refer only to when the brigades were fighting independently or were attached to an infantry division. Those brigades which at certain times also formed part of an armoured division in combat are marked with an asterisk.

BRIGADE	FORMED	COMBAT RECORD
1 Arm.	1940	N.Africa May 41-June 42. Disbanded Nov 42
*1 Ay.Tk.	pre-1939	France May 40; N.Africa June-July 41 and Nov 41-Oct 42. Dismembered Nov 44
*4 Arm.	1940	Sicily July-Aug 43; Italy Sept 43-Jan 44; N.W.Europe June 44-May 45.
4 Lt. Arm.	1942	(temporary redesignation of 4 Arm Brig) N.Africa June 42-May 43
6 Gds. Tk.	1943	N.W.Europe July 44-Feb 45
*7 Arm.	1940	N.Africa Nov 41-Feb 42; Italy April 44-May 45
*8 Arm.	1941	N.Africa Nov 42-May 43; N.W.Europe June 44-May 45
*9 Arm.	1941	N.Africa March-Nov 42; Italy May 44-May 45
21 Ay. Tk.	pre-1939	N.Africa March 42-May 43; Italy May 44-May 45
23 Arm.	1940	N.Africa June 42-May 43; Sicily July-Aug 43; Italy Sept 43-May 44. Then to Palestine.
24 Arm.	1940	N.Africa Sept 42-Feb 43. Became Dummy Tank Unit
25 Ay. Tk.	pre-1939	N.Africa Feb-May 43; Italy April-Dec 44. Became Armoured Assault Brigade R.E.
27 Arm.	1940	N.W.Europe June-July 44. Disbanded
32 Ay. Tk.	1941	N.Africa Sept 41-June 42. Destroyed at Tobruk
34 Arm.	1945	N.W.Europe Feb-May 45
34 Ay. Tk.	1941	N.W.Europe July 44-May 45

BRITISH EMPIRE and COMMONWEALTH
India

ARMOURED DIVISIONS

Four Indian armoured divisions were raised, 31, 32, 43 and 44, but none saw any combat. 31 Armoured Division served in the Middle East, whilst 32 and 43 Divisions were merged to form 44 Division which remained in India until being converted into 44 Airborne Division in 1944.

INFANTRY DIVISIONS (total = 17)

DIVISION	FORMED	COMBAT RECORD
3	1944	Burma March-June 44. (Cover name for Wingate's Chindits)
4	pre-1939	N.Africa Dec 40; Italian E.Africa Jan-April 41; N.Africa April 41-May 43; Italy Dec 43-Oct 44
5	pre-1939	Italian E.Africa Jan-April 41; N.Africa May-Aug 42; Burma Nov 43-Aug 45
7	1940	Burma Sept 43-Aug 45
8	1940	Italy Sept 43-May 45
9	1940	Malaya Dec 41-Feb 42. Destroyed
10	1940	Iraq May-June 41; N.Africa June-July 42; Italy March 44-May 45
11	1940	Malaya Dec 41-Feb 42. Destroyed
14	1941	Burma Sept 42-May 43. Became Training Division
17	1941	Burma Sept 42-Aug 45
19	1941	Burma Oct 44-Aug 45
20	1942	Burma Oct 43-Aug 45
21	1944	Burma May-July 44. (Emergency HQ only)
23	1942	Burma Sept 42-Aug 44. Became India Command Reserve
25	1942	Burma March 44-Aug 45
26	1942	Burma Feb-Sept 43. Became 14 Army Reserve
36	1942	Burma Feb-Sept 44. Became 36 British Inf. Division

Also formed were 2, 6, 12 and 39 Infantry Divisions, which saw no combat.

AIRBORNE DIVISIONS

44 Airborne Division, formed in 1944, did not see any but the most fragmentary combat.

ARMOURED BRIGADES (total = 3)

See preamble to UK Armoured Brigades on preceding page.

BRIGADE	FORMED	COMBAT RECORD
50 Tk	1941	Burma Nov 44-March 45
254 Tk	1942	Burma Oct 43-Aug 45
255 Tk	1942	Burma Oct 44-Aug 45

Also formed were 251 and 267 Armoured Brigades. The former was broken up in November 1943 to reinforce the Chindits and the latter never left India.

Australia

ARMOURED DIVISIONS

Two armoured divisions, 1 and 3, and two motorised divisions were formed but none served as such outside Australia.

INFANTRY DIVISIONS (total = 7)

DIVISION	FORMED	COMBAT RECORD
3	pre-1939	Pacific April 43-Aug 45 (Militia)
5	1940	Pacific Aug 43-Aug 45 (Militia)
6	1940	N.Africa Jan-Feb 40; Greece/Crete April-May 41; Pacific Sept 42-Aug 45
7	1940	Syria June-July 41; Pacific Aug 42-Aug 45
8	1940	Malaya Dec 41-Feb 42. Destroyed
9	1940	N.Africa March-Oct 41; Pacific Sept 43-Aug 45
11	1941	Pacific April 44-Aug 45 (Militia)

Also formed were 1, 2, 4, 10 and 12 Infantry Divisions, none of which left Australia.

ARMOURED BRIGADES (total = 2)

See preamble to UK Armoured Brigades on preceding page.

BRIGADE	FORMED	COMBAT RECORD
1	1943	Pacific May 43-Aug 45
4	1943	Pacific Nov 43-Aug 45

Canada

ARMOURED DIVISIONS (total = 2)

DIVISION	FORMED	COMBAT RECORD
4	1942	N.W.Europe July 44-May 45
5	1941	Italy Nov 43-March 45; N.W.Europe March-May 45

INFANTRY DIVISIONS (total = 3)

DIVISION	FORMED	COMBAT RECORD
1	1939	France June 40 (One brigade); Sicily July-Aug 43; Italy Sept 43-March 45; N.W.Europe March-May 45
2	1940	Dieppe Aug 42; N.W.Europe July 44-May 45
3	1941	N.W.Europe June 44-May 45

ARMOURED BRIGADES (total = 2)

See preamble to UK Armoured Brigades on preceding page.

BRIGADE	FORMED	COMBAT RECORD
1 Arm.	1943	Sicily July-Aug 43; Italy Sept 43-March 45; N.W.Europe March-May 45
2 Arm.	1943	N.W.Europe June 44-May 45

African Colonies

INFANTRY DIVISIONS (total = 5)		
DIVISION	FORMED	COMBAT RECORD
11 African	1940	Italian E.Africa Jan-Nov 41
12 African	1940	Italian E.Africa Jan-Nov 41
11 E.African	1943	Burma June 44-Aug 45
81 W.African	1943	Burma Dec 43-Aug 45 (one brigade fought as Chindits)
82 W.African	1943	Burma Nov 44-Aug 45

South Africa

ARMOURED DIVISIONS (total = 1)		
DIVISION	FORMED	COMBAT RECORD
6	1943	Italy April 44-May 45

INFANTRY DIVISIONS (total = 2)		
DIVISION	FORMED	COMBAT RECORD
1	1940	Italian E.Africa Jan-April 41; N.Africa June 41-Dec 42
2	1940	N.Africa Aug 41-June 42. Destroyed Tobruk

3 South African Infantry Division never left S.Africa.

New Zealand

INFANTRY DIVISIONS (total = 2)		
DIVISION	FORMED	COMBAT RECORD
2	1939	Greece/Crete April-May 41; N.Africa Nov-Dec 41 and June 42-May 43; Italy Nov 43-May 45
3	1940	Pacific Nov 42-Aug 45

Also formed were 1, 4, 5 and 6 Infantry Divisions. The first three never left New Zealand, whilst the last, raised in the Middle East, was disbanded before seeing any combat.

ARMOURED BRIGADES (total = 1)		

See preamble to UK Armoured Brigades on page 125.

BRIGADE	FORMED	COMBAT RECORD
4 Arm.	1942	Italy Nov 43-May 45

OTHER ALLIES (POST 1940)
France

This list does not include divisions involved in the May/June 1940 campaign. For these see the relevant Order of Battle organigram below.

ARMOURED DIVISIONS (total = 3)		
DIVISION	FORMED	COMBAT RECORD
1	1943	N.W.Europe Aug 44-May 45
2	1943	N.W.Europe Aug 44-May 45
5	1943	N.W.Europe Nov 44-May 45

INFANTRY DIVISIONS (total = 8)		
DIVISION	FORMED	COMBAT RECORD
1 Motorised	1943	Italy April-Aug 44; S.France Aug 44
2 Moroccan	1943	Italy Nov 43-Aug 44; S.France Aug 44; N.W.Europe Sept 44-May 45
3 Algerian	1943	Italy Jan-Aug 44; S.France Aug 44; N.W.Europe Sept 44-May 45
4 Mor. Mt.	1943	Italy March-Aug 44; S.France Aug 44
9 Colonial	1944	N.W.Europe Sept 44-May 45
10	1944	N.W.Europe Jan-May 45
14	1944	N.W.Europe Feb-May 45
27 Alpine	1944	N.W.Europe Feb-May 45

1 Infantry Division also served but saw no combat.

Poland

This list does not include divisions involved in the September 1939 campaign. For these see the relevant Order of Battle organigram below.

ARMOURED DIVISIONS (total = 1)		
DIVISION	FORMED	COMBAT RECORD
1	1942	N.W.Europe Aug 44-May 45

INFANTRY DIVISIONS (total = 2)		
DIVISION	FORMED	COMBAT RECORD
3	1942	Italy Dec 43-May 45
5	1941	Italy Feb 44-May 45

6 and 7 Infantry Divisions were also raised in the Middle East but never saw combat.

ARMOURED BRIGADES (total = 1)		

See preamble to UK Armoured Brigades on page 125.

BRIGADE	FORMED	COMBAT RECORD
2 Arm.	1942	Italy March 44-May 45

Italy

For Italian divisions that fought against the Allies see the much more extensive Italian listing below.

The first pro-Allied regular forces formed were the 1 Raggruppamento Motorizzato in September 1943. This saw combat from November 1943 and was renamed the Corpo Italiano di Liberazione in April 1944. In September/October 1944 this corps was broken up into the Gruppi Combattimento listed hereafter.

INFANTRY DIVISIONS (total = 2)

DIVISION	FORMED	COMBAT RECORD
184 Nembo	1943	Italy April-Aug 44. (See Gruppo Folgore below)
'Utili'	1944	Italy April-Aug 44.

GRUPPI DI COMBATTIMENTO (total = 4)

With an official establishment of 432 officers and 8,578 ORs these formations were a valuable addition to the always overstretched Allied order of battle in Italy whilst their combat contribution has been consistently underrated. (Column 3 denotes the pre-Armistice division around elements of which the Gruppo was formed.)

GRUPPO	FORMED	ORIGINAL DIVISION	COMBAT RECORD
Cremona	1944	44	Italy Sept 44-May 45
Legano	1944	58	Italy Sept 44-May 45
Friuli	1944	20	Italy Sept 44-May 45
Folgore	1944	184 Nembo	Italy Sept 44-May 45

Brazil

INFANTRY DIVISIONS (total = 1)

DIVISION	FORMED	COMBAT RECORD
1 Exped.	1943	Italy July 44-May 45

Czechoslovakia

ARMOURED BRIGADES (total = 1)

See preamble to UK Armoured Brigades on page 125.

BRIGADE	FORMED	COMBAT RECORD
Czech Independent Armoured Brigade Group	1943	N.W.Europe June 44-May 45

RUSSIA'S ALLIES
Poland

INFANTRY DIVISIONS (total = 9)

DIVISION	FORMED	COMBAT RECORD
1 Koszuiszko	1943	E.Front Oct 43-May 45
2 Warsaw	1943	E.Front July 44-May 45
3 Pomeranian Romuald Traugutt	1943	E.Front July 44-May 45
4 Pomeranian Jan Kilinski	?	E.Front July 44-May 45
5 Saxon	1944	E.Front Jan-May 45
7 Lusatian	1944	E.Front Jan-May 45
8 Dresden Bartosz Glowacki	1944	E.Front Jan-May 45
9 Dresden	1944	E.Front Jan-May 45
10 Sudetian	1944	E.Front Jan-May 45

Also formed were 11, 12 and 13 Infantry Divisions though these saw no combat.

Polish armour was organised into five tank brigades, 1 serving with First Polish Army, 2, 3 and 4 in I Tank Corps, with Second Polish Army, and 16 Independent Tank Brigade.

Rumania

Between Rumanian defection to the Allies in August 1944 and the official armistice with the Russians in October, a large part of the Rumanian army, including divisions reforming, training units and combat divisions, fought against the Germans and Hungarians. After October, however, many units were forced to disband and only the following divisions fought on, under Red Army direction, until the end of the war: 1 Cavalry, 9 Cavalry, 8 Motorised, 1 Guards (from April 45), 2, 3, 4, 6, 9, 10, 11, 18, 19, 21 Infantry, 2 and 3 Mountain. They were also joined by the Rumanian Communist Tudor Vladimirescu Division.

THE AXIS, JAPAN AND AXIS ALLIES

Germany

PANZER DIVISIONS (total = 38)

DIVISION	FORMED	COMBAT RECORD
1	pre-1939	Poland Sept 39; France May-June 40; E.Front June 41-Dec 42; Balkans June-Oct 43; E.Front Nov 43-May 45
1SS	1943	E.Front Oct 43-May 44; France June-Dec 44; E.Front Jan-May 45
2	pre-1939	Poland Sept 39; France May-June 40; Greece April 41; E.Front July 41-Dec 43; N.W.Europe June 44-May 45
2SS	1943	E.Front Oct 43-March 44; N.W.Europe June 44-Jan 45; E.Front Jan-May 45
3	pre-1939	Poland Sept 39; France May-June 40; E.Front June 41-May 45
3SS	1943	E.Front Oct 43-May 45
4	pre-1939	Poland Sept 39; France May-June 40; E.Front June 41-May 45
5	pre-1939	Poland Sept 39; France May-June 40; Greece April 41; E.Front July 41-May 45
5SS	1943	E.Front Oct 43-April 44 and July 44-May 45
6	1939*	France May-June 40; E.Front June 41-April 42 and Dec 42-May 45
7	1939*	France May-June 40; E.Front June 41-May 42 and Dec 42-May 45
8	1939*	France May-June 40; Yugoslavia April 41; E.Front June 41-May 45
9	1940*	Holland and France May-June 40; Yugoslavia April 41; E.Front June 41-March 44; N.W.Europe June 44-May 45
9SS	1943	E.Front March-June 44; N.W.Europe June 44-Jan 45; E.Front Feb-May 45
10	1939	Poland Sept 39; France May-June 40; E.Front June 41-April 42; N.Africa (Tunisia) Dec 42-May 43. Destroyed
10SS	1943	E.Front March-June 44; N.W.Europe June 44-March 45; E.Front March-May 45
11	1940	Yugoslavia April 41; E.Front June 41-May 44; S.France Aug 44; N.W.Europe Sept 44-May 45
12	1940	E.Front June 41-May 45
12SS	1943	N.W.Europe June 44-Jan 45; E.Front Jan-May 45
13	1940	E.Front June 41-May 45 (From Jan 45 as *Feldherrnhalle* 2)
14	1940	Yugoslavia April 41; E.Front June 41-Feb 43. Destroyed Stalingrad. Reformed April 43; E.Front Nov 43-May 45
15	1940	N.Africa April 41-May 43. Destroyed. (Reformed as 15 Panzer Grenadier)
16	1940	E.Front June 41-Feb 43. Destroyed Stalingrad. Reformed March 43. Italy Sept-Nov 43; E.Front Nov 43-May 45
17	1940	E.Front June 41-May 45
18	1940	E.Front June 41-Nov 43. (Became 18 Artillery Division)
19	1940	E.Front June 41-May 45
20	1940	E.Front June 41-May 45
21	1941	E.Front June 41-May 45 *(sic!) N Africa, 41-3; NW Europe 1944*
22	1941	E.Front March-Dec 42. Disbanded
23	1940	E.Front March 42-May 45
24	1942	E.Front June 42-Feb 43. Destroyed Stalingrad. Reformed March 43. E.Front Oct 43-May 45

DIVISION	FORMED	COMBAT RECORD
25	1942	E.Front Oct 43-March 44 and Sept 44-May 45
26	1942	Italy Sept 43-May 45
27	1942	E.Front Sept 42-Jan 43. Disbanded
116	1944	N.W.Europe July 44-April 45
Panzer Lehr	1943	N.W.Europe June 44-April 45
Gross † Deutschland	1942	E.Front June 42-May 45
Hermann • Göring	1943	N.Africa (Tunisia) Jan-May 43 (part); Sicily July-Aug 43; Italy Sept 43-July 44; E.Front July 44-May 45

Several other Panzer divisions were formed in 1945 though none achieved more than regimental strength and none saw much prolonged combat. These formations were Panzer Divisions Kurmark, Clausewitz, Donau, Schlesien, Thüringen, Westfalen, Kurland, Holstein, Münchenburg, Jüterbog.

MOTORISED & PANZER-GRENADIER DIVISIONS (total = 29)‡

The designation 'motorised' was changed to 'panzer-grenadier' in March 1943.

DIVISION	FORMED	COMBAT RECORD
1SS	1941	E.Front June 41-Aug 42 and Feb-Aug 43. (Becomes 1SS Pz Oct 43)
2	pre-1939	Poland Sept 39; France May-June 40. (Becomes 12 Pz Dec 40)
2SS	1940	E.Front June 41-June 42 and Jan-Oct 43. (Becomes 2SS Pz Oct 43)
3	1940	E.Front June 41-Feb 43. Destroyed Stalingrad. Reformed March 43. Italy Sept 43-Aug 44; N.W.Europe Sept 44-April 45
3SS	1939	E.Front June 41-Oct 42 and Feb-Oct 43. (Becomes 3SS Pz Oct 43)
4SS	1939	France May-June 40; E.Front June 41-May 43; Greece Dec 43-Sept 44; Yugoslavia Sept-Nov 44; E.Front Nov 44-May 45
5SS	1940	E.Front June 41-Oct 43. (Becomes 5SS Pz Oct 43)
9SS	1942	(Becomes 9SS Pz Oct 43)
10	1940	E.Front June 41-May 45
10SS	1942	(Becomes 10SS Pz Oct 43)
11SS	1943	E.Front Nov 43-April 45
12SS	1943	(Becomes 12SS Pz Oct 43)
13	pre-1939	Poland Sept 39; France May-June 40. (Becomes 13 Pz Oct 40)
14	1940	E.Front June 41-July 43. (Becomes 14 Inf again)
15	1943	Sicily July-August 43; Italy Sept 43-Sept 44; N.W.Europe Sept 44-May 45
16	1940	Yugoslavia April 41; E.Front June 41-March 44. (Becomes 116 Pz March 44)
16SS	1943	Italy July 43-April 44; Yugoslavia April-June 44; Italy June 44-March 45; E.Front March-May 45
17SS	1943	N.W.Europe June 44-May 45
18	1940	E.Front June 41-July 44 and Jan-May 45

† Nominally a panzer-grenadier division but with a panzer division's firepower.

• Officially known as a parachute panzer division and under Luftwaffe control.

* Formed from Light divisions: 6 Pz. from 1 Light, 7 from 2, 8 from 3, 9 from 4

‡ Motorised/ Panzer-grenadier: Other panzer-grenadier divisions formed but which never achieved more than regimental strength or saw only a few days combat were 26, 27, 28, 32 and 38SS, Führer Grenadier.

MOTORIZED & PANZER-GRENADIER DIVISIONS continued

DIVISION	FORMED	COMBAT RECORD
18SS	1944	E.Front Aug-Dec 44 and Feb-May 45
20	pre-1939	Poland Sept 39; France May-June 40; E.Front June 41-May 45
23SS	1943	E.Front April-May 45
25	1940	E.Front June 41-Oct 44; N.W.Europe Oct 44-Feb 45; E.Front Feb-May 45
29	pre-1939	Poland Sept 39; France May-June 40; E.Front June 41-Feb 43. Destroyed Stalingrad. Reformed March 43. Sicily July-Aug 43; Italy Sept 43-May 45
34SS	1943	Yugoslavia Nov-Dec 43; E.Front Dec 43-May 45
36	1940	E.Front June 41-July 43. (Becomes 36 Infantry again)
60	1940	Yugoslavia April 41; E.Front June 41-Feb 43. Destroyed Stalingrad. Reformed March 43 (as PG *Feldherrenhalle*). E.Front Jan-July 44. Destroyed. Reformed Aug 44. E.Front Oct 44-May 45
90	1943	Italy Nov 43-May 45
Brandenburg	1943	E.Front Dec 44-May 45

CAVALRY DIVISIONS (total = 5)†

DIVISION	FORMED	COMBAT RECORD
1	pre-1939	Poland Sept 39; E.Front June-Nov 41. (Became 24 Pz Feb 42)
1 Cossack	1943	Yugoslavia Oct 43-May 45
2 Cossack	1944	Yugoslavia Nov 44-May 45
8SS	1942	E.Front Oct 42-Nov 43; Yugoslavia Nov 43-April 44; E.Front April 44-Feb 45. Destroyed Budapest
22SS	1944	E.Front Oct 44-Feb 45

INFANTRY DIVISIONS (total = 280)

DIVISION	FORMED	COMBAT RECORD
1	pre-1939	Poland Sept 39; France June 40; E.Front June 41-May 45
2	pre-1939	(Became 2 Mot 1936)
3	pre-1939	Poland Sept 39; France May-June 40. (Became 3 Mot Oct 40)
4	pre-1939	Poland Sept 39; France May-June 40. (Became 14 Pz Aug 40)
5	pre-1939	France May 40; E.Front June-Dec 41. (Became 5 Jäger Dec 41)
6/6VG	pre-1939/1944	France May-June 40; E.Front June 41-July 44. Destroyed. Reformed as VG E.Front Aug 44-May 45
7	pre-1939	Poland Sept 39; France May-June 40; E.Front June 41-May 45
8	pre-1939	Poland Sept 39; France May-June 40; E.Front June 41-Jan 42. (Became 8 Jäger)
9/9VG	pre-1939/1944	France May-June 40; E.Front June 41-Aug 44. Destroyed. Reformed as VG Sept 44. N.W.Europe Dec 44-May 45
10	pre-1939	Poland Sept 39; France June 40. (Became 10 Mot Oct 40)
11	pre-1939	Poland Sept 39; France June 40; E.Front June 41-May 45

DIVISION	FORMED	COMBAT RECORD
12/12VG	pre-1939/1944	Poland Sept 39; France May-June 40; E.Front June 41-July 44. Destroyed. Reformed as VG Sept 44. N.W.Europe Sept 44-April 45
13	pre-1939	(Became 13 Mot 1936)
14	pre-1939	Poland Sept 39; France May-June 40. (Became 14 Mot Oct 40)
14SS*	1943	E.Front March-July 44. Destroyed. Reformed Nov 44. E.Front April-May 45
15	pre-1939	E.Front June-Nov 41 and Feb 43-May 45
15SS*	1943	E.Front Nov 43-May 45
16	pre-1939	Poland Sept 39; France May-June 40. (Became 16 Pz)
16	1944	(Second Division formed from 158 Reserve and 16 L/w.) N.W.Europe July-Sept 44. Destroyed
17	pre-1939	Poland Sept 39; France May-June 40; E.Front June 41-June 42 and Feb 43-May 45
18	pre-1939	Poland Sept 39; France May-June 40. (Became 18 Mot Oct 40)
18VG	1944	N.W.Europe Oct 44-May 45
19	pre-1939	Poland Sept 39; France May-June 40. (Became 19 Pz Oct 40)
19SS*	1944	E.Front March 44-May 45
20	pre-1939	(Became 20 Mot 1938)
20SS*	1943	E.Front Feb 44-May 45
21	pre-1939	Poland Sept 39; France May-June 40; E.Front June 41-May 45
22	pre-1939	(Became 22 Air Landing 1937)
23	pre-1939	Poland Sept 39; France June 40; E.Front June 41-July 42. (Became 26 Pz July 42)
23	1942	E.Front Feb 43-May 45
24	pre-1939	Poland Sept 39; France May-June 40; E.Front June 41-May 45
25	pre-1939	Poland Sept 39; France June 40. (Became 25 Mot Oct 40)
26/26VG	pre-1939/1944	France June 40; E.Front June 41-Sept 44. Destroyed. Reformed as VG Oct 44. N.W.Europe Nov 44-May 45
27	pre-1939	Poland Sept 39; France May-June 40. (Became 17 Pz Oct 40)
28	pre-1939	Poland Sept 39; France May-June 40; E.Front June-Nov 41. (Became 28 Jäger)
29	pre-1939	(Became 29 Mot 1938)
30	pre-1939	Poland Sept 39; France May-June 40; E.Front June 41-May 45
30SS*	1944	N.W.Europe Nov 44-March 45; E.Front March-May 45
31/31VG	pre-1939/1944	Poland Sept 39; France May-June 40; E.Front June 41-July 44. Destroyed. E.Front Sept 44-May 45
32	pre-1939	Poland Sept 39; France May-June 40; E.Front June 41-May 45
33	pre-1939	France May-June 40. (Became 15 Pz Oct 40)
34	pre-1939	France May-June 40; E.Front June 41-July 44
35/35VG	pre-1939/1944	France May-June 40; E.Front June 41-July 44. Destroyed. Reformed as VG Oct 44. E.Front Oct 44-May 45
36/36VG	pre-1939/1944	France May-June 40. (Became 36 Mot Oct 40.) (Became 36 Inf again May 44.) E.Front May-July 44. Destroyed. Reformed as VG Sept 44. N.W.Europe Sept 44-May 45
38	1941	E.Front April-Dec 43. Disbanded

* SS Grenadier and *not* SS Panzer-grenadier.

† **Cavalry Divisions:** Other cavalry divisions formed but which never achieved more than regimental strength or which saw only a few days combat were 3 and 4, and 33 and 37SS.

INFANTRY DIVISIONS continued

DIVISION	FORMED	COMBAT RECORD
39	1942	E.Front April-Dec 43. Disbanded
41 Fortress	1941	Greece/Yugoslavia March 41-May 45. (Became 41 Inf Jan 45)
44	pre-1939	Poland Sept 39; France May-June 40; E.Front June 41-Feb 43. Destroyed Stalingrad. Reformed June 43. Italy Dec 43-Jan 45; E.Front Feb-May 45
45/45VG	pre-1939/1944	Poland Sept 39; France May-June 40; E.Front June 41-July 44. Destroyed. Reformed as VG Aug 44. E.Front Sept 44-May 45
46	pre-1939	Poland Sept 39; Yugoslavia April 41; E.Front July 41-May 45
47/47VG	1944	N.W.Europe June-Sept 44. Destroyed. Reformed as VG Oct 44. N.W.Europe Dec 44-May 45
48/48VG	1944/1945	N.W.Europe Aug-Nov 44. Destroyed. Reformed as VG 45 Feb 45. N.W.Europe April-May 45
49	1944	N.W.Europe Aug-Oct 44. Destroyed
50	1939	Poland Sept 39; France May-June 40; Greece April 41; E.Front June 41-May 45
52	1939	Poland Sept 39; Norway April 40; France May-June 40; E.Front June 41-Oct 43. Destroyed
56/56VG	1939/1944	Poland Sept 39; France May-June 40; E.Front June 41-July 44. Destroyed. Reformed as VG Sept 44. E.Front Oct 44-May 45
57	1939	Poland Sept 39; France May-June 40; E.Front June 41-July 44. Destroyed
58	1939	France June 40; E.Front June 41-May 45
59	1944	N.W.Europe Aug 44-April 45
60	1939	France May-June 40. (Became 6 Mot Oct 40)
61	1939	Poland Sept 39; France May-June 40; E.Front June 41-May 45
62/62VG	1939/1944	Poland Sept 39; France May-June 40; E.Front June 41-Sept 44. Destroyed. Reformed as VG Oct 44. N.W.Europe Nov 44-April 45
64	1944	N.W.Europe Aug-Nov 44
65	1942	Italy Oct 43-May 45
68	1939	Poland Sept 39; France May-June 40; E.Front June 41-May 45
69	1939	Norway April 40; E.Front April 43-April 45
70	1944	N.W.Europe Nov 44. Destroyed
71	1939	France May-June 40; E.Front June 41-Feb 43. Destroyed Stalingrad. Reformed April 43. Italy Sept 43-Dec 44; E.Front Dec 44-May 45
72	1939	France May-June 40; Yugoslavia April 41; E.Front June 41-May 45
73	1939	Poland Sept 39; France May-June 40; Yugoslavia April 41; E.Front July 41-May 45
75	1939	France May-June 40; E.Front June 41-May 45
76	1939	France May-June 40; E.Front June 41-Feb 43. Destroyed Stalingrad. Reformed April 43. E.Front Nov 43-May 45
77	1944	N.W.Europe June-Sept 44. Destroyed
78	1939	France May-June 40; E.Front June 41-July 44. Destroyed. Reformed Sept 44. E.Front Sept 44-May 45
79/79VG	1939/1944	France June 40; E.Front June 41-Feb 43. Destroyed Stalingrad. Reformed April 43. E.Front July 43-Aug 44. Destroyed. Reformed as VG Oct 44. N.W.Europe Dec 44-April 45. Disbanded
81	1939	France May-June 40; E.Front Dec 41-May 45
82	1939	E.Front May 42-May 44. Destroyed
83	1939	Poland Sept 39; France May-June 40; E.Front Dec 41-May 45

DIVISION	FORMED	COMBAT RECORD
84	1944	N.W.Europe Aug 44-March 45. Destroyed
85	1944	N.W.Europe June 44-May 45
86	1939	France May-June 40; E.Front June 41-July 44. Almost destroyed. Disbanded Oct 44
87	1939	France May-June 40; E.Front June 41-May 45
88	1939	France May-June 40; E.Front Feb 42-April 45
89	1944	N.W.Europe late June 44-May 45
92	1943	Italy Jan-June 44. Disbanded
93	1939	France May-June 40; E.Front July 41-March 45. Destroyed
94	1939	France May-June 40; E.Front July 41-Feb 43. Destroyed Stalingrad. Reformed April 43. Italy Nov 43-May 45
95/95VG	1939/1944	E.Front June 41-July 44. Destroyed. Reformed as VG Sept 44. E.Front Oct 44-May 45
96	1939	France May-June 40; E.Front July 41- May 45
97	1939	(Became 97 Jäger Dec 40)
98	1939	France May-June 40; E.Front June 41-May 44; Yugoslavia June-Sept 44; Italy Sept 44-May 45
100	1939	(Became 100 Jäger Dec 40)
101	1939	(Became 101 Jäger Dec 40)
102	1940	E.Front June 41-Jan 42 and April 42-May 45
106	1940	E.Front June 41-April 42 and April 43-Aug 44. Destroyed. Reformed Jan 45. N.W.Europe March-May 45
110	1940	E.Front June 41-July 44. Destroyed
111	1940	E.Front June 41-May 44. Destroyed
112	1940	E.Front June 41-March 44. Disbanded
113	1940	Yugoslavia Nov 41-April 42; E.Front May 42-Feb 43. Destroyed Stalingrad. Reformed April 43. E.Front Aug-Oct 43. Disbanded
121	1940	E.Front June 41-May 45
122	1940	E.Front June 41-May 45
123	1940	E.Front June 41-Feb 44. Disbanded
125	1940	Yugoslavia April 41; E.Front June 41-April 44. Disbanded
126	1940	E.Front June 41-May 45
129	1940	E.Front June 41-Sept 44. Disbanded (though HQ remained intact)
131	1940	E.Front June 41-May 45
132	1940	Yugoslavia April 41; E.Front June 41-May 45
134	1940	E.Front June 41-July 44. Destroyed
137	1940	E.Front June 41-Dec 43. Disbanded
148	1944	Italy Oct 44-May 45
153	1944	E.Front Feb 44-May 45
154 Reserve	1942	E.Front March 44-May 45

INFANTRY DIVISIONS continued		
DIVISION	FORMED	COMBAT RECORD
159	1944	N.W.Europe Sept 44-May 45
161	1940	E.Front June 41-Nov 42 and Feb 43- May 44. Disbanded
162	1940	E.Front June 41-April 42; Yugoslavia Oct 43-Feb 44.Italy June and Oct 44.
163	1940	Norway April 40; Finland June 41-Feb 45; E.Front Feb-March 45. Destroyed
166 Reserve	1943	N.W.Europe Jan-April 45
167/167VG	1940/1944	France May-June 40; E.Front June 41-May 42 and March 43-Feb 44. Disbanded. Reformed as VG Oct 44.N.W.Europe Dec 44-April 45
168	1940	E.Front June 41-May 45
169	1940	France May-June 40; Finland/Norway June 41-May 45
170	1940	Denmark April 40; E.Front June 41-May 45
174 Reserve	1943	E.Front March 44-May 45
176	?	N.W.Europe Sept 44-April 45
181	1940	Norway April 40; Yugoslavia Oct 43-May 45
182 Reserve	1942	E.Front Nov 44-May 45
183/183VG	1940/1944	Yugoslavia April 41; E.Front July 41-July 44. Destroyed. Reformed as VG Sept 44; N.W.Europe Sept 44-April 45
189	1944	S.France Aug 44; N.W.Europe Sept 44-May 45
190	1944	N.W.Europe Sept 44-April 45
196	1940	Denmark/Norway April 40; E.Front July-Sept 44. Disbanded
197	1940	E.Front June 41-July 44. Destroyed
198	1940	Denmark April 40; E.Front June 41-May 44; S.France Aug 44; N.W.Europe Sept 44-May 45
199	1939	Poland Sept 39; Norway Dec 40-May 45
203 Sec.	1942	E.Front Nov 43-May 45
205	1940	E.Front Feb 42-May 45
206	1939	Poland Sept 39; E.Front June 41-July 44. Disbanded
207	1939	Poland Sept 39. (Became Security Division 1940)
208	1939	Poland Sept 39; France May-June 40; E.Front Jan 42-May 45
210 Coastal Defence	1942	Lapland/Norway Nov 42-May 45
211/211VG	1939/1944	E.Front Jan 42-Dec 44. Destroyed. Reformed as VG Dec 44. E.Front Jan 45-May 45
212/212VG	1939/1944	France May-June 40; E.Front Jan 42-Sept 44. Destroyed. Reformed as VG Oct 44. N.W.Europe Dec 44-May 45
213 Security	1940	E.Front Oct 43-Jan 45. Disbanded
214	1939	Norway April 40; E.Front Feb 44-Jan 45. Disbanded
215	1939	France May-June 40; E.Front Jan 42-May 45
216	1939	Poland Sept 39; France May-June 40; E.Front Dec 41-Dec 43. Destroyed
217/217VG	1939/1944	Poland Sept 39; France May-June 40; E.Front June 41-Dec 43. Destroyed. Rebuilt as VG Feb 44. E.Front April-Dec 44. Disbanded

DIVISION	FORMED	COMBAT RECORD
218	1939	Poland Sept 39; France May-June 40; E.Front Feb 42-May 45
221 Security	1939	Poland Sept 39; France May-June 40; E.Front Jan-Dec 42 and May 43-July 44. Destroyed
223	1939	France May-June 40; E.Front Dec 41-Dec 43. Destroyed
225	1939	Holland May 40; E.Front Jan 42-May 45
226	1944	N.W.Europe (Dunkirk) Aug 44-May 45
227	1939	France May-June 40; E.Front Jan 42-May 45
228	1939	Poland Sept 39; E.Front July-Aug 41. Disbanded
232	1944	Italy Oct 44-May 45
239	1939	France May-June 40; E.Front June-Nov 41. Disbanded
242	1943	S.France Aug 44. Destroyed
243	1943	N.W.Europe June-Aug 44. Destroyed
244	1943	S.France Aug 44. Destroyed
245	1943	N.W.Europe Sept 44-March 45. Disbanded
246/246VG	1939/1944	France May-June 40; E.Front Jan 42-July 44. Destroyed. Reformed as VG Sept 44. N.W.Europe Sept 44-March 45. (Oct 44 merged with 49 Inf)
250*	1941	E.Front Sept 41-Jan 44
251/251VG	1939/1944	France May-June 40; E.Front June 41-July 44. Destroyed. Reformed as VG Sept 44. E.Front Sept 44-May 45
252	1939	Poland Sept 39; France May-June 40; E.Front June 41-May 45
253	1939	France May-June 40; E.Front June 41-May 45
254	1939	France May-June 40; E.Front June 41-May 45
255	1939	France May-June 40; E.Front June 41-Dec 43. Disbanded
256/256VG	1939/1944	France May-June 40; E.Front June 41-July 44. Destroyed. Reformed as VG Sept 44. N.W.Europe Oct 44-May 45
257/257VG	1939/1944	E.Front June 41-Aug 42 and April 43-Sept 44. Destroyed. Reformed as VG Oct 44. N.W.Europe Dec 44-May 45
258	1939	France May-June 40; E.Front June 41-Aug 44. Destroyed
260	1939	E.Front July 41- July 44. Destroyed
262	1939	E.Front June 41- Nov 43. Destroyed
263	1939	France May-June 40; E.Front June 41-May 45
265	1943	N.W.Europe (Lorient) June 44-May 45
266	1943	N.W.Europe June 44-Sept 44. Destroyed
267	1939	E.Front June 41- July 44. Destroyed
268	1939	E.Front June 41- Oct 43. Disbanded
269	1939	France May-June 40; E.Front June 41-Dec 42; N.W.Europe Oct 44-Jan 45; E.Front Jan-May 45
271/271VG	1940/1944	N.W.Europe July 44. Destroyed. Reformed as VG Sept 44. E.Front Dec 44-May 45
272/272VG	1943†/1944	N.W.Europe July 44. Destroyed. Reformed as VG Sept 44. N.W.Europe Nov 44-April 45
275	1943	N.W.Europe July-Dec 44. Destroyed. Reformed Jan 45. E.Front March-April 45. Disbanded

* Spanish 'Blue Division'.

† Reformed after being dissolved in 1940.

† Reformed after being dissolved in 1940.

INFANTRY DIVISIONS continued		
DIVISION	FORMED	COMBAT RECORD
276/276VG	1943†/1944	N.W.Europe June-Aug 44. Destroyed. Reformed as VG Sept 44. N.W.Europe Dec 44-April 45
277/277VG	1943†/1944	N.W.Europe June-Aug 44. Destroyed. Reformed as VG Sept 44. N.W.Europe Dec 44-April 45
278	1943†	Italy May 44-May 45
281 Sec.	1941	E.Front Jan 42 Dec 44. Disbanded
282	1942	E.Front April 43-Aug 44. Destroyed
290	1940	France May-June 40; E.Front June 41-May 45
291	1940	France May-June 40; E.Front June 41-Feb 45. Destroyed
292	1940	France May-June 40; E.Front June 41-May 45
293	1940	France May-June 40; E.Front June 41-Dec 43. Destroyed
294	1940	France May-June 40; Yugoslavia April 41; E.Front July 41-Aug 44. Destroyed
295	1940	E.Front June 41-Feb 43. Destroyed Stalingrad
296	1940	France May-June 40; E.Front June 41-May 45
297	1940	E.Front June 41-Feb 43. Destroyed Stalingrad. Reformed July 43. Balkans Sept 43-May 45
298	1940	E.Front June 41-Feb 43. Destroyed
299/299VG	1940/1944	France May-June 40; E.Front June 41-July 44. Destroyed. Reformed as VG Oct 44. E.Front Dec44-May 45
302	1940	Dieppe Aug 42; E.Front Jan 43-Aug 44. Destroyed
304	1940	E.Front Dec 42-May 45
305	1940	E.Front May 42-Feb 43. Destroyed Stalingrad. Reformed May 43. Italy Sept 43-May 45
306	1940	E.Front Dec 42-Aug 44. Destroyed
320/320VG	1940/1944	E.Front Feb 43-Aug 44. Destroyed. Reformed as VG Nov 44. E.Front Jan-May 45
321	1940	E.Front Dec 42-Oct 43. Destroyed
323	1940	E.Front May 42-Dec 43. Disbanded
326/326VG	1942/1944	N.W.Europe July-Aug 44. Destroyed. Reformed as VG Oct 44. N.W.Europe Dec 44-April 45
327	1940	E.Front March-Dec 43. Destroyed
328	1941	E.Front March 42-April 43 and June-Dec 43. Destroyed
329	1941	E.Front March 42-May 45
330	1941	E.Front Feb 42-Oct 43. Disbanded
331	1941	E.Front Feb 42-April 44; N.W.Europe June 44-May 45
332	1941	E.Front Feb 43-March 44. Disbanded
333	1941	E.Front March-Dec 43. Disbanded
334	1942	N.Africa (Tunisia) Dec 42-May 43. Destroyed. Reformed Aug 43. Italy Nov 43-May 45
335	1941	E.Front March 43-Aug 44. Destroyed
336	1941	E.Front May 42-May 44. Destroyed

DIVISION	FORMED	COMBAT RECORD
337/337VG	1941/1944	E.Front Nov 42-July 44. Destroyed. Reformed as VG Sept 44. E.Front Sept 44-Dec 44. Disbanded
338	1942	S.France Aug 44. Destroyed. Reformed Sept 44. N.W.Europe Sept 44-April 45
339	1941	E.Front Sept 41-July 44. Disbanded
340/340VG	1941/1944	E.Front June 42-July 44. Destroyed. Reformed as VG Sept 44. N.W.Europe Nov 44-May 45
342	1941	Yugoslavia Oct 41-Feb 42; E.Front Feb 42-May 45
343	1942	N.W.Europe (Brest) Aug-Sept 44. Destroyed
344/344VG	1942/1944	N.W.Europe June-Sept 44. Destroyed. Reformed as VG Oct 44. N.W.Europe Nov-Dec 44; E.Front Jan-May 45
346	1942	N.W.Europe June 44-May 45
347	1942	N.W.Europe June 44-May 45
348	1942	N.W.Europe Sept 44. Destroyed
349/349VG	1943/1944	E.Front April-July 44. Destroyed. Reformed as VG Sept 44. E.Front Sept 44-May 45
352/352VG	1943/1944	N.W.Europe June-July 44. Disbanded. Reformed as VG Aug 44. N.W.Europe Oct 44-May 45
353	1943	N.W.Europe June 44-May 45
355	1943	E.Front Aug 43. Disbanded
356	1943	Italy May 44-Jan 45; E.Front Jan-May 45
357	1943	E.Front March 44-May 45
359	1943	E.Front March 44-May 45
361/361VG	1943/1944	E.Front March-July 44. Destroyed. Reformed as VG Sept 44. N.W.Europe Oct 44-Jan 45. Disbanded
362	1943	Italy Jan 44-May 45
363/363VG	1943/1944	N.W.Europe July-Aug 44. Destroyed. Reformed as VG Sept 44. N.W.Europe Sept 44-April 45
367	1943	Yugoslavia Dec 43-March 44; E.Front March 44-March 45. Destroyed
369	1943	Yugoslavia Jan 43-May 45
370	1942	E.Front June 42-Aug 44. Destroyed
371	1942	E.Front July 42-Feb 43. Destroyed Stalingrad. Reformed May 43. E.Front Jan 44-May 45
373	1943	Yugoslavia Feb 43-May 45
376	1942	E.Front July 42-Feb 43. Destroyed Stalingrad. Reformed May 43. E.Front Nov 43-Aug 44. Destroyed
377	1942	E.Front June 42-April 44. Disbanded
383	1942	E.Front June 42-July 44. Destroyed
384	1942	E.Front May 42-Feb 43. Destroyed Stalingrad. Reformed 43. E.Front Dec 43-Aug 44. Destroyed
385	1942	E.Front Jan 42-Feb 43. Disbanded
387	1942	E.Front June 42-March 44. Disbanded
389	1942	E.Front June 42-Feb 43. Destroyed Stalingrad. Reformed July 43. E.Front Oct 43-Feb 44. Destroyed. Reformed July 44. E.Front Oct 44-May 45
392	1943	Yugoslavia Jan 44-May 45
402	1945	E.Front Jan-May 45

INFANTRY DIVISIONS continued		
DIVISION	FORMED	COMBAT RECORD
416	1942	N.W.Europe Oct 44-May 45
433RDS	1943	E.Front Jan-May 45
462VG	1944	N.W.Europe Aug-Dec 44. Disbanded
541VG	1944	E.Front July 44-May 45
542VG	1944	E.Front July 44-May 45
544VG	1944	E.Front July 44-May 45
545VG	1944	E.Front July 44-May 45
547VG	1944	E.Front July 44-May 45
548VG	1944	E.Front July 44-May 45
549VG	1944	E.Front July 44-May 45
551VG	1944	E.Front July 44-May 45
552VG	1944	E.Front July-Sept 44. Disbanded
553VG	1944	N.W.Europe Sept-Nov 44. Destroyed. Reformed Dec 44. N.W.Europe Jan-May 45
558VG	1944	E.Front July 44-May 45
559VG	1944	N.W.Europe Sept 44-March 45. Destroyed
560VG	1944	N.W.Europe Dec 44-April 45
561VG	1944	E.Front July 44-May 45
562VG	1944	E.Front July 44-May 45
563VG	1944	E.Front July 44-May 45
704	1941	Yugoslavia May 41-April 43. (Became 104 Jäger April 43)
707	1941	E.Front July 43-July 44. Destroyed
708/708VG	1941/1944	E.Front Oct 43-Feb 44; N.W.Europe June-Aug 44. Destroyed. Reformed as VG Sept 44. N.W.Europe Nov 44-Feb 45. Disbanded
709	1941	N.W.Europe June 44. Destroyed
710	1941	Italy Dec 44-Jan 45; E.Front Jan-May 45
711	1941	N.W.Europe June-Dec 44; E.Front Dec 44-May 45
712	1941	N.W.Europe June-Dec 44; E.Front Jan-May 45
714	1941	Yugoslavia Nov 41-April 43. (Became 114 Jäger April 43)
715	1941	Italy Jan-Dec 44; E.Front Jan-May 45
716	1941	N.W.Europe June-Aug 44 and Jan-May 45
717	1941	Yugoslavia Nov 41-April 43. (Became 117 Jäger April 43)
718	1941	Yugoslavia Nov 41-April 43. (Became 118 Jäger April 43)
719	1941	N.W.Europe Sept 44-May 45

The following divisions were also formed but for various reasons saw no or very little combat or remained well below divisional establishment. (Most of the proper infantry divisions below were dissolved during the war without ever having been sent into the line.)

INFANTRY 120, 209, 231, 236, 237, 270, 273, 274, 280, 285, 286, 307, 309, 310, 311, 317, 319, 341, 351, 358, 364, 365, 386, 393, 395, 399, 406, 554, 555, 556, 557, 713, Bärwalde, Berlin, Doberitz, Führer Begleit, Pomerania, Pommerland.

VG 16, 564, 582–588.

GRENADIER 25SS, 29SS, 31SS, 33SS, 35SS, 543, 546, 550, 565–81.

SECURITY 52, 201, 213, 284, 325, 390, 403, 444, 454, 455.

RESERVE 141, 143, 151, 156, 157, 158, 160, 165, 171, 172, 173, 187, 191.

REPLMNT 192, 193, 401, 404, 405, 407, 408, 409, 410, 413, 418, 419, 421, 431, 432, 461, 463, 464, 465, 467, 471, 487, 526.

FIELD TR. 147, 155, 382, 388.

SP. ADMIN. 411, 412, 417, 428, 429, 430, 442.

SP. DIV. 606, 607, 608, 609, 610, 613, 614, 615.

FORTRESS 133.

FR. GUARD 537, 538, 539, 540.

COASTAL 230, 441.

ASSAULT 440.

SP. PURP. 140.

L/W. FIELD 14.

LIGHT & JÄGER DIVISIONS (total = 17)		
DIVISION	FORMED	COMBAT RECORD
1 Ski Jäger	1944	E.Front Jan 44-May 45
5 Jäger	1941	E.Front Feb 42-May 45
5 Light	1941	N.Africa Feb 41-July 41. (Became 21 Pz July 41)
8 Jäger	1942	E.Front March 42-May 45
28 Jäger	1941	E.Front March 42-May 45
42 Jäger	1944	Yugoslavia May-Aug 44; Italy Aug 44-May 45
90 Light	1941	N.Africa Aug 41-May 43. Destroyed
97 Jäger	1940	E.Front June 41-May 45
99 Light	1940	E.Front June-Nov 41. (Became 7 Mt.)
100 Jäger	1940	E.Front June 41-Feb 43. Destroyed Stalingrad. Reformed May 43. Albania July 43-Feb 44; E.Front March 44-May 45
101 Jäger	1940	E.Front June 41-May 45
104 Jäger	1943	Greece/Yugoslavia June 43-May 45
114 Jäger	1943	Yugoslavia March-Dec 43; Italy Jan 44-May 45
117 Jäger	1943	Yugoslavia/Greece April 43-May 45
118 Jäger	1943	Yugoslavia March 43-Dec 44; E.Front Jan-May 45
164 Lt. Afrika	1942	N.Africa Aug 42-May 43. Destroyed
999 Lt. Afrika	1943	N.Africa (Tunisia) March-May 43. Destroyed

MOUNTAIN DIVISIONS (total = 13)

DIVISION	FORMED	COMBAT RECORD
1	pre-1939	Poland Sept 39; France May-June 40; Yugoslavia April 41; E.Front June 41-March 43; Yugoslavia March 43-May 45
2	pre-1939	Poland Sept 39; Norway April 40; Lapland Oct 40-Nov 44; N.W.Europe Feb-May 45
3	1939	Poland Sept 39; Norway April 40; E.Front Dec 41-May 45
4	1940	Yugoslavia April 41; E.Front June 41-May 45
5	1940	Greece April 41; Crete May 41; E.Front Oct 41-Nov 43; Italy Nov 43-May 45
6	1940	Greece April 41; Lapland/Norway Nov 41-May 45
6SS	1941	E.Front Feb 42-Dec 44; N.W.Europe Dec 44-May 45
7	1941	Lapland/Norway April 42-May 45
7SS	1942	Yugoslavia Nov 42-May 45
8	1945	Italy Feb-May 45
9	1945	Norway 45
13SS	1943	Yugoslavia Feb 44-May 45
21SS	1941	Albania April 44-May 45

Also formed, though they remained much understrength and saw hardly any combat, were 23SS and 24SS Divisions.

AIRBORNE DIVISIONS (total = 11)

DIVISION	FORMED	COMBAT RECORD
1	1943	Sicily July-Aug 43; Italy Sept 43-May 45
2	1943	E.Front Dec 43-May 44; N.W.Europe June 44-April 45
3	1943	N.W.Europe June 44-April 45
4	1943	Italy Jan 44-May 45
5	1943	N.W.Europe June 44-April 45
6	1944	N.W.Europe June 44-May 45
7	1944	N.W.Europe Sept 44-May 45
7 Flieger	pre-1939	France May-June 40; Greece April 41; Crete May 41; E.Front June 41-March 43. (Remnants used to form 1 Para.)
9	1944	E. Front March-May 45
11	1945	N.W.Europe March-May 45
22 Air Landing	pre-1939	Poland Sept 39 (part); Holland May 40; E.Front June 41-July 42; N.Africa (Tunisia) Nov 42-May 43 (part); Greece/Yugoslavia Nov 44-May 45
91 Air Landing	1944	N.W.Europe June-Aug 44. Destroyed

Also formed, though they never attained more than regimental size, were 8 and 10 Parachute Divisions.

* Also known as the 'M' Division or the 1 Armoured Division of the CCNN. A Blackshirt formation.

LUFTWAFFE FIELD DIVISIONS (total = 21)

Infantry divisions but, like the airborne divisions, they remained under Luftwaffe control

DIVISION	FORMED	COMBAT RECORD
1	1942	E.Front Oct 42-Jan 44. Disbanded
2	1942	E.Front Oct 42-Jan 44. Disbanded
3	1942	E.Front Oct 42-Jan 44. Disbanded
4	1942	E.Front Oct 42-July 44. Destroyed
5	1942	E.Front Dec 42-April 44. Disbanded
6	1942	E.Front Jan 43-July 44. Destroyed
7	1942	E.Front Jan-May 43. Disbanded
8	1942	E.Front Jan-March 43. Disbanded
9	1942	E.Front Jan 43-Feb 44. Disbanded
10	1942	E.Front Jan 43-Feb 44. Disbanded
11	1942	Yugoslavia Feb 44-May 45
12	1942	E.Front March 43-May 45
13	1942	E.Front Feb 43-Feb 44. Disbanded
15	1942	E.Front Jan-Nov 43. Disbanded
16	1942	N.W.Europe July 44. Destroyed
17	1942	N.W.Europe Aug 44. Destroyed
18	1942	N.W.Europe Aug 44. Destroyed
19	1943	Italy June-Aug 44. Destroyed
20	1943	Italy June-Nov 44. Disbanded Jan 45
21	1943	E.Front Jan 43-May 45

22 Division never completed its formation.

Italy

ARMOURED DIVISIONS (total = 5)

DIVISION	FORMED	COMBAT RECORD
131 Centauro	1939	France June 40; N.Africa Jan 41-Dec 42. Destroyed
132 Ariete	1939	Balkans June 40-Nov 42; N.Africa Nov 42-April 43. Destroyed
133 Littorio	1939	Balkans April-May 41; N.Africa Jan-Nov 42. Destroyed
135 Ariete	1943	Reformation of original Ariete as Arm. Cav. Div. April 43. Remained in Italy
Centauro Legion Arm. Div.*	1943	Italy June-Sept 43

An attempt was also made to form 134 Frecchia Armoured Division (from 2 Cavalry Division) in May 1942 but this process was soon halted and the Division became 2 Celere Division (see below).

MOBILE (CELERE) DIVISIONS (total = 3)

Formed from cavalry divisions of the same title April 1942.

DIVISION	FORMED	COMBAT RECORD
1 Eugenio di Savoia	pre-War	Balkans April 41-Sept 43
2 Emanuele Filiberto Testa di Ferro	pre-War	Italy/France June 40-April 41; Balkans April-? 41; France/Italy to Sept 43
3 Principe Amadeo Duca d'Aosta	pre-War	E.Front July 41-Jan 43. Largely destroyed. Italy Jan-Sept 43

MOTORISED DIVISIONS (total = 2)

DIVISION	FORMED	COMBAT RECORD
101 Trieste	pre-War	France June 40; Balkans Nov 40-Aug 41; N.Africa Aug 41-April 43. Destroyed
102 Trento	pre-War	France June 40; N.Africa Jan 41-April 43. Destroyed

INFANTRY DIVISIONS (total = 69)

It should be noted that only those divisions that served in N. Africa, on the Eastern Front or in Greece in 1941 (see also relevant Orders of Battle in next CAMPAIGNS sub-section) saw any prolonged combat. Balkan and island service usually involved garrison duties and limited counter-insurgency operations.

DIVISION	FORMED	COMBAT RECORD
1 Superga	pre-War	France June 40; N.Africa Nov 42-April 43. Destroyed
2 Sforzesca		Balkans Feb 41-July 42; E.Front July 42-Jan 43. Largely destroyed. Merged with 157 Novara June 43
3 Ravenna		France June 40; E.Front July 42-Jan 43. Largely destroyed. Italy Jan-Sept 43
4 Livorno *		France June 40; Italy July 40-Feb 43; Sicily Feb-July 43. Destroyed
5 Cosseria		France June 40; E.Front July 42-Jan 43. Largely destroyed. Italy Jan-Sept 43
6 Cuneo		France June 40; Balkans Dec 40-July 41; Aegean July 41-Sept 43
7 Lupi di Toscana		France June 40; Balkans Jan 41-?; Italy/France ?42-Sept 43
9 Pasubio †		France June 40; E.Front July 41-Jan 43. Largely destroyed. Italy Jan-Sept 43
10 Piave †		France June 40; Italy/France July 40-Sept 43
11 Brennero †		France June 40; Balkans Dec 40-Sept 43
12 Sassari		Balkans July 41-Jan 43; Italy Jan-Sept 43
13 Re		Balkans July 41-Jan 43; Italy Jan-Sept 43
14 Isonzo		Balkans July 41-Sept 43
15 Bergamo		Balkans July 41-Sept 43
16 Pistoia		France June 40; N.Africa July 42-April 43. Destroyed
17 Pavia •		N.Africa June 40-April 43. Destroyed
18 Messina		Balkans April 41-Sept 43
19 Venezia •		Balkans Oct 40-Sept 43
20 Friuli		France June 40; Italy/Corsica July 40-Sept 43

DIVISION	FORMED	COMBAT RECORD
21 Granatieri di Sardegna	pre-War	France June 40; Balkans July 41-Dec 42; Italy Dec 42-Sept 43
22 Cacciatori delli Alpi		France June 40; Balkans Jan 41-Sept 43
23 Ferrara		Balkans Oct 40-Sept 43
24 Pinerolo		Balkans Jan 41-Sept 43
25 Bologna •		N.Africa Dec 40-April 43. Destroyed
26 Assietta		Italy/Sicily June 40-Aug 43. Destroyed
27 Brescia •		N.Africa June 40-April 43. Destroyed
28 Aosta		Sicily June 40-Aug 43. Destroyed
29 Piemonte		Balkans/Aegean Jan 41-Sept 43
30 Sabauda		Sardinia June 40-Sept 43
31 Calabria		Sardinia June 40-Sept 43
32 Marche		Balkans April 41-Sept 43
33 Acqui		France June 40; Balkans/Aegean Dec 40-Sept 43
36 Forli		France June 40; Balkans Jan 41-Sept 43
37 Modena		France June 40; Balkans Nov 40-Sept 43
38 Puglie		Balkans March 41-Sept 43
41 Firenze		France June 40; Balkans April 41-Sept 43
44 Cremona		France June 40; Sardinia/Corsica Nov 41-Sept 43
47 Bari		Corfu June-Nov 40; Balkans Nov 40-March 43; Sardinia March-Sept 43
48 Taro		France June 40; Balkans Nov 40-Nov 42; Italy/France Nov 42-Sept 43
49 Parma		Balkans Oct 40-Sept 43
50 Regina		Aegean June 40-Sept 43
51 Sienna		Balkans/Aegean Oct 40-Sept 43
52 Torino		E.Front July 41-Jan 43. Largely destroyed. Merged with 159 Veneto June 43
53 Arezzo		Balkans Oct 40-Sept 43
54 Napoli		Italy/Sicily June 40-Aug 43. Destroyed
55 Savona •		N.Africa Dec 40-Jan 42. Destroyed
56 Casale		Balkans March 41-Sept 43
57 Lombardia		Balkans June 41-Sept 43
58 Legnano		France June 40; Balkans Jan-June 41; France Nov 42-July 43; Italy July-Sept 43
59 Cagliari		France June 40; Balkans Jan 41-Sept 43
60 Sabratha •		N.Africa June 40-late 42. Disbanded
61 Sirte •		N.Africa June 40-Jan 41. Destroyed Tobruk
62 Marmarica •		N.Africa June-Dec 40. Destroyed Bardia

* Designated Assault Landing Division June 1940 but never undertook one.

† Designated 'autotransportabile' – 'lorried' rather than 'motorised' infantry.

• Designated 'autotransportabile tipo A(frica) S(ettentriole)'.

INFANTRY DIVISIONS continued

DIVISION	FORMED	COMBAT RECORD
63 Cirene †	pre-War	N.Africa June-Dec 40. Destroyed Bardia
64 Catanzaro †		N.Africa June-Dec 40. Destroyed Bardia
65 Grenatiere di Savoia		E.Africa June 40-May 41. Destroyed
80 La Spezia •	1941	N.Africa Oct 42-April 43. Destroyed
103 Piacenza *	1942	Italy March 42-Sept 43
104 Mantova *	1942	Italy/Sicily March 42-Sept 43
105 Rovigo *	1942	Italy March 42-Sept 43
151 Perugia	1941	Balkans Dec 41-Sept 43
152 Piceno	1942	Italy April 42-Sept 43
153 Masserata	1941	Balkans June 42-Sept 43
154 Murge	1942	Balkans May 42-Sept 43
155 Emilia	1941	Balkans March 42-Sept 43
156 Vicenza	1942	E.Front July 42-Jan 43. Destroyed
157 Novara	1942	Italy March 42-Sept 43. Absorbed by 2 Sforzesca June 43
158 Zara	1942	Balkans March 42-Sept 43
159 Veneto	1942	Italy March 42-Sept 43. Merged with 52 Torino June 43

† Designated 'autotransportabile tipo A(frica) S(ettentriole)'.

• Trained, in early 1942, as an Air Landing ('Aviotransportabile') Division, though it never saw combat in this role.

* Designated 'autotransportabile' — 'lorried' rather than 'motorised' infantry.

The following Coastal Divisions were also formed but because of incomplete establishments and/or extremely poor quality personnel and equipment they were very much divisions in name only. (Those in italics did see some limited combat in Sicily in July 1943). 201, *202*, 203-5, *206*, *207*, *208*, 209-12, *213*, 214-16, 220-27, 230.

PARACHUTE DIVISIONS (total = 2)

DIVISION	FORMED	COMBAT RECORD
185 Folgore	1942	N.Africa July 42-April 43. Destroyed
184 Nembo	1943	Italy Feb-Sept 43

Also formed was the 183 Ciclone Division but it never contained more than four battalions.

MOUNTAIN DIVISIONS (total = 6)

DIVISION	FORMED	COMBAT RECORD
1 Taurinense	pre-War	France June 40; Balkans Jan 42-Sept 43
2 Tridentina	pre-War	France June 40; Balkans Nov 40-June 41; E.Front Aug 42-Jan 43. Largely destroyed. Balkans Feb-Sept 43
3 Julia	pre-War	Balkans Oct 40-March 42; E.Front Aug 42-Jan 43. Largely destroyed. Italy Jan-Sept 43
4 Cuneense	pre-War	France June 40; Balkans Dec 40-June 41; E.Front Aug 42-Jan 43. Largely destroyed. Italy Jan-Sept 43
5 Val Pusteria	pre-War	France June 40; Balkans Nov 40-Aug 42; Italy/France to Sept 43
6 Alpi Graie	1941	Balkans March-Dec 42; Italy to Sept 43

BLACKSHIRT DIVISIONS (total = 5)

DIVISION	FORMED	COMBAT RECORD
Africa	1940	E.Africa March-May 41. Destroyed
Cacchatorie d'Africa	1941	N.Africa Jan 42-May 43. Destroyed Bardia
1 23rd Marzo	pre-War	N.Africa June-Dec 40. Destroyed Bardia
2 28th Ottobre	pre-War	N.Africa June-Dec 40. Destroyed Bardia
4 3rd Gennaio	pre-War	E.Africa March-May 41. Destroyed Sidi Barrani

Also formed was 3(21 Aprile) Division but it never achieved more than regimental strength.

AFRICAN DIVISIONS (total = 7)

For 21-26 Colonial 'Divisions' see Part II of this Section on page 155.

DIVISION	FORMED	COMBAT RECORD
1 Colonial	pre-War	E.Africa June 40-May 41. Destroyed
2 Colonial	pre-War	E.Africa June 40-May 41. Destroyed
4 Colonial	pre-War	E.Africa June 40-May 41. Destroyed
101 Colonial	pre-War	E.Africa June 40-March 41. Destroyed
102 Colonial	pre-War	E.Africa June 40-March 41. Partly dissolved and rest destroyed
1 Libyan	pre-War	Libya June 40-Jan 41. Destroyed
2 Libyan	pre-War	Libya June 40-Jan 41. Destroyed

Also formed was 3 Libyan Division though it always remained well below establishment.

Hungary

ARMOURED DIVISIONS (total = 2)

DIVISION	FORMED	COMBAT RECORD
1	1942	E.Front June 42-March 43. Largely destroyed. May 44-Feb 45. Destroyed Budapest
2	1943	E.Front June 44-May 45

LIGHT DIVISIONS (total = 1)

DIVISION	FORMED	COMBAT RECORD
27	1943	E.Front May 44-May 45

CAVALRY DIVISIONS (total = 1)

DIVISION	FORMED	COMBAT RECORD
1	1942	E.Front Spring 44-March 45. Destroyed

INFANTRY DIVISIONS (total = 28 [12 saw combat])

In the following list divisions which saw no combat are included with those that did simply because this makes it much easier to describe subsequent amalgamations.

DIVISION	FORMED	COMBAT RECORD
1	1940	E.Front March-June 43. Became part of 26 Res. Inf. Div. June 43
2		No combat * Became part of 25 Mixed Inf. Div. June 43
4		No combat. Became part 6 Mixed and 5 Res. Inf. Divs. †
5		E.Front March-June 43. Became part 6 Mixed and 5 Res. Inf. Divs. †
6		E.Front June 42-March 43. Largely destroyed. Became part 6 Mixed and 5 Res. Inf. Divs. †
7		E.Front June 42-March 43. Largely destroyed. Became part 7 Mixed and 9 Res. Inf. Divs.
8		E.Front March-June 43. Became part 7 Mixed and 9 Res. Inf. Divs.
9		E.Front June 42-June 43. Largely destroyed by March. Became part 7 Mixed and 9 Res. Inf. Divs.
10		E.Front June 42-March 43. Largely destroyed. Became part 10 Mixed and 12 Res. Inf. Divs.
11		No combat. Became part 10 Mixed and 12 Res. Inf. Divs.
12		E.Front June 42-June 43. Largely destroyed by March. Became part 10 Mixed and 12 Res. Inf. Divs.
13		E.Front June 42-March 43. Largely destroyed. Became part 13 Mixed and 15 Res. Inf. Divs.
14		No combat. Became part 13 Mixed and 15 Res. Inf. Divs.
15		No combat. Became part 13 Mixed and 15 Res. Inf. Divs.
16		No combat. Became part 16 Mixed and 18 Res. Inf. Divs.
17		No combat. Became part 16 Mixed and 18 Res. Inf. Divs.
18		No combat. Became part 16 Mixed and 18 Res. Inf. Divs.
19		E.Front June 42-June 43. Largely destroyed by March. Became part 20 Mixed and 19 Res. Inf. Divs.
20		E.Front June 42-June 43. Largely destroyed. Became part 20 Mixed and 19 Res. Inf. Divs.
21		E.Front March-June 43. Became part 20 Mixed and 19 Res. Inf. Divs.
22		No combat. Became part 24 Mixed and 23 Res. Inf. Divs.
23		E.Front June 42-June 43. Largely destroyed by March. Became part 24 Mixed and 23 Res. Inf. Divs.
24		No combat. Became part 24 Mixed and 23 Res. Inf. Divs.
25		No combat. Became part of 25 Mixed and 26 Res. Inf. Divs.
26		No combat. Became part of 25 Mixed and 26 Res. Inf. Divs.
27		No combat. Became part 27 Light Div. June 43
Kossuth	1944	No combat (?)

MIXED DIVISIONS (total = 8)

DIVISION	FORMED	COMBAT RECORD
6	1943	E.Front Aug 44-?

DIVISION	FORMED	COMBAT RECORD
7	1943	E.Front May 44-?
10	1943	E.Front Aug 44-Feb 45. Destroyed Budapest
13	1943	E.Front Aug 44-?
16	1943	E.Front May 44-March 45. Destroyed
20	1943	E.Front May 44-May 45
24	1943	E.Front May 44-March 45. Destroyed
25	1943	E.Front May 44-March 45. Destroyed

RESERVE DIVISIONS (total = 8)

DIVISION	FORMED	COMBAT RECORD
5	1943/1944	E.Front Spring 44-March 45. Destroyed
9	1943/1944	E.Front Spring 44-?
12	1943/1944	E.Front Spring 44-Feb 45. Destroyed Budapest
15	1943/1944	No combat (?)
18	1943/1944	E.Front Spring 44-?
19	1943/1944	E.Front Spring 44-?
23	1943/1944	E.Front Spring 44-March 45. Destroyed
26	1943/1944	No combat (?)

Also formed were five small Security Divisions (102, 105, 108, 121, 124) in 1941, all of which served on the Eastern Front, though mainly on line of communications and counter-insurgency duties.

The ten 'Depot' Divisions formed (Cavalry, and nos. 2-9) also served on the Eastern Front but none of them ever comprised more than two battalions.

Rumania

ARMOURED DIVISIONS (total = 1)

DIVISION	FORMED	COMBAT RECORD
1 Greater Rumania	1940	E.Front Oct 42-Jan/Feb 43 and Spring-Aug 44. Disbanded Oct 44

Also formed was 2 Armoured Division in August 1944 but this was in the same month that the Rumanians quit the alliance with Germany.

CAVALRY DIVISIONS (total = 6)

All formed March 1942 from existing brigades. Combat record dates include brigade service.

DIVISION	FORMED	COMBAT RECORD
1	1942	E.Front Aug 41-Nov 42. Largely destroyed. E.Front ?-Aug 44
5	1942	E.Front July 41-Nov 42. Largely destroyed. Became 5 Motorised 1943 (see below)

* Most of the 'no combat' divisions were little more than cadre formations.

† In this and all the amalgamations mentioned below, one regiment from each of the original (two-regiment) divisions went to form either a new Mixed or Reserve (three-regiment) Division. Thus 7 Mixed Infantry Division, for example, had only one regiment from the old 7 Infantry Division.

CAVALRY DIVISIONS continued

DIVISION	FORMED	COMBAT RECORD
6	1942	E.Front July 41-Aug 44
7	1942	E.Front July 41-Nov 42. Largely destroyed. Disbanded
8	1942	E.Front July 41-Nov 42. Largely destroyed. Became 8 Motorised 1943 (see below)
9	1942	E.Front Sept 41-Aug 44

MOTORISED DIVISIONS (total = 1)

DIVISION	FORMED	COMBAT RECORD
8	1943	E.Front ? Absorbed into short-lived Moto-Mechanised Corps Sept 44

Also formed in 1943 was 5 Motorised Division but it never received adequate equipment and soon reverted to its original form as 5 Cavalry Division, as which it fought on until August 1944.

INFANTRY DIVISIONS (total = 19)

DIVISION	FORMED	COMBAT RECORD
1 Guards	pre-War	E.Front July-Oct 41 and Spring-Aug 44
1 Frontier	pre-War	E.Front 1941. Disbanded 1943
1		E.Front Sept-Dec 41, Spring 42-Jan/Feb 43 and Spring-Aug 44
2		E.Front Sept-Dec 41, Spring 42-Jan/Feb 43 and Spring-Aug 44
3		E.Front July/Aug-Oct 41 and Spring-Aug 44
4		E.Front Spring 42-Jan/Feb 43 and Spring-Aug 44
5		E.Front July-Oct 41 and Oct-Nov 42. Largely destroyed. E.Front Spring-Aug 44
6		E.Front July-Oct 41 and Oct-Nov 42. Largely destroyed. E.Front Spring-Aug 44
7		E.Front July-Oct 41 and Oct 42-Jan/Feb 43
8		E.Front July-Oct 41
9		E.Front Oct 42-Jan/Feb 43
10		E.Front Sept-Dec 41 and Spring 42-April 44. Largely destroyed Crimea
11		E.Front July/Aug-Oct 41, Oct 42-Jan/Feb 43 and Spring-Aug 44
13		E.Front July-Oct 41 and Aug-Nov 42. Largely destroyed. E.Front Spring-Aug 44
14		E.Front July-Oct 41, Oct 42-Jan/Feb 43 and Spring-Aug 44
15		E.Front July/Aug-Oct 41; Oct-Nov 42. Largely destroyed
18		E.Front Sept 41-Jan/Feb 43
19		E.Front Spring 42-April 44. Largely destroyed Crimea
20		E.Front Spring 42-Feb 43. Destroyed Stalingrad. Reformed. E.Front Spring-Aug 44
21		E.Front July/Aug-Oct 41

Also formed were 2 Guards in 1942 and 24 Division in 1943. The former was disbanded in 1943 without seeing combat and the latter undertook security duties until being merged with 4 Mountain Division in September 1943.

Other divisions that undertook security and garrison duties only were 1 Fortress and 2 Security, both pre-war divisions, and 1 and 3 Security, raised in 1942.

Raised just prior to BARBAROSSA in 1941 were six Reserve Divisions (25, 27, 30, 31, 32, 35) but only the latter saw any combat and all were soon broken up to provide replacements for the existing divisions.

MOUNTAIN DIVISIONS (total = 4)

All formed March 1942 from existing brigades. Combat record dates include brigade service.

DIVISION	FORMED	COMBAT RECORD
1	1942	E.Front July 41-Aug 44
2	1942	E.Front July 41-Aug 44
3	1942	E.Front July 41-Aug 44
4	1942	E.Front July 41-Aug 44

Bulgaria

On the outbreak of war Bulgaria could field thirteen infantry divisions (1-12, 14) and two Mobile (1 & 2). During the war nine more Reserve divisions were raised (13, 15, 16, 17, 21, 22, 24, 25 and 27). Of these, three were later disbanded and none of the remainder were much more than cadre formations. Throughout the war, moreover, the government refused to commit its troops outside Bulgaria or those territories it regarded as being historically Bulgarian. No division, therefore, saw any combat beyond sporadic counter-insurgency operations in northern Greece, Macedonia and Serbia.

Finland

In October 1939, the Finnish Army comprised only three divisions (1-3) but by the end of the war with Russia in 1939-40, the Winter War, nine more infantry divisions had been raised (4-6, 8-13, 21 and 23), all of which had been heavily engaged with the Russians.

In May 1940, the Army was reorganised into sixteen infantry divisions (1-8, 10-12, 14, 15, 17-19) all but one of which (12) took part in the German attack on Russia, in July 1941. From December 1941 to June 1944 the Finns were forced on to the defensive, although an armoured division had been formed in August 1943. After a major Russian offensive in June 1944 the Finns determined to make peace, which they did in the following August. In this third and final phase of the war, until December 1944, five divisions (1, 3, 6, 11 and the Armoured) were involved, pursuing German forces into northern Norway.

Japan

ARMOURED DIVISIONS (total = 3)

DIVISION	FORMED	COMBAT RECORD
1	1942	Manchuria Aug 42-March 45; Marianas March-Aug 44 (part); Japan March-Aug 45
2	1942	Manchuria Aug 42-Aug 44; Philippines Aug 44-June 45. Destroyed Luzon
3	1942	China ? 42-Aug 45

Also formed was 4 Armoured Division which never left Japan.

DIVISION	FORMED	COMBAT RECORD
2 Gds. ✱✱	1942/3	Indo-China Dec 41; Malaya Dec 41-March 42; Sumatra March 42-Aug 45
1	pre-1942	Manchuria Dec 41-Sept 44; Philippines Sept 44-Feb 45. Destroyed Leyte
2		Dutch E.Indies Dec 41-March 42; Guadalcanal Sept 42-Feb 43; Burma March-Aug 45. Indo-China Jan-Aug 45 (part)
3		China Dec 41-Aug 45
4		China Dec 41-Aug 43; Japan Aug 43-Aug 44; Sumatra Aug 44-Dec 44; Siam Dec 44-Aug 45
5		Malaya Dec 41-Feb 42; Dutch E.Indies Aug 43-Aug 45
6		China Dec 41-Jan 43; Bougainville Jan 43-May 44. Sealed off
8		Manchuria Dec 41-Aug 44; Philippines Aug 44-June 45. Destroyed Luzon
9 ✱		Manchuria Dec 41-April 44; Okinawa April 44-Feb 45; Formosa Feb-Aug 45
10		Manchuria Dec 41-Nov 44; Philippines Nov 44-June 45. Destroyed Luzon
11 ✱		Manchuria Dec 41-April 45; Japan April-Aug 45
12 ✱		Manchuria Dec 41-Nov 44; Formosa Nov 44-Aug 45
13		China Dec 41-Aug 45
14		Manchuria Dec 41-April 44; Palaus April-Nov 44. Destroyed on Petelieu or sealed off on Babelthuap
15		China Dec 41-Aug 43; Siam Aug 43-Feb 44; Burma Feb 44-Aug 45
16		Philippines Dec 41-Feb 45. Destroyed Leyte
17		China Dec 41-Sept 43; Solomons/New Britain Sept 43-Jan 44. Sealed off on New Britain
18		Malaya Dec 41-Feb 42; Burma April 42-Aug 45
19		Korea Dec 41-Dec 44; Philippines Dec 44-June 45. Destroyed Luzon
20		Korea Dec 41-Jan 43; New Guinea Jan 43-Aug 44. Destroyed
21		China Dec 41-Aug 43; Indo-China Aug 43-Aug 45
22		China Dec 41-Jan 45; Indo-China Jan-Aug 45
23		Manchuria Dec 41-Nov 44; Philippines Nov 44-June 45. Destroyed Luzon
24		Manchuria Dec 41-April 44; Okinawa April 44-June 45. Destroyed
25		Manchuria Dec 41-March 45; Japan March-Aug 45
26		China Dec 41-Aug 44; Philippines Aug 44-Feb 45. Destroyed Leyte
27		China/Manchuria Dec 41-Aug 45
28 ✱		Manchuria Dec 41-July 44; Ryukyu Is./Sakashima Is. July 44-Aug 45
29	↓	Manchuria Dec 41-Feb 44; Marianas Feb-Aug 44. Destroyed Guam
30	1943	Korea June 43-May 44; Philippines May 44-Aug 45. Destroyed Leyte and Mindanao
31	1943	Burma July 43-Aug 45
32	pre-1942	China Dec 41-April 44; Dutch E.Indies (Halmahera) April 44-Aug 45
33	↓	Burma Dec 41-Aug 45

DIVISION	FORMED	COMBAT RECORD
34	pre-1942	China Dec 41-Aug 45
35		China Dec 41- April 44; (one regt. to Palaus Feb 44.) New Guinea April 44-June 45. Destroyed
36		China Dec 41-Dec 43; New Guinea Dec 43-June 45. Destroyed
37		China Dec 41-Jan 45; Indo-China Jan-Aug 45
38		Hong Kong Dec 41; Dutch E.Indies Jan-March 42; Guadalcanal Oct 42-Feb 43; New Britain/New Ireland Feb 43-Jan 44. Sealed off
39		China Dec 41-July 45; Manchuria July-Aug 45
40		China Dec 41-Aug 45
41		China Dec 41-Feb 43; New Guinea Feb 43-Aug 44. Destroyed
43	1944/45	Marianas March-July 44. Destroyed Saipan
46 ✱	1943	Dutch E.Indies Dec 43-Dec 44; Malaya Dec 44-Aug 45
47	1943	China Sept 44-Aug 45
48 ✱	pre-1942	Philippines Dec 41-March 42; Dutch E.Indies (Celebes/Timor) April 42-Aug 45
49	1944	Burma June 44-Aug 45
50 ✱	1944	Formosa June 44-Aug 45
51	pre-1942	China Dec 41-Jan 43; New Guinea Jan 43-Aug 44. Destroyed
52 ✱		Truk Dec 43-Aug 45
53		Burma Jan 44-Aug 45
54		Burma Aug 43-Aug 45
55		Burma Dec 41-Aug 45
56		Burma Dec 41-Aug 45
57 ✱	↓	Manchuria Dec 41-April 45; Japan April-Aug 45
58	1942	China Feb 42-Aug 45
59	1942	China Feb 42-June 45; Korea/Manchuria July-Aug 45
60	1942	China April 42-Aug 45
61	1943	China April 43-Aug 45
62	1943	China June 43-April 44; Okinawa April 44-June 45. Destroyed
63	1943	China June 43-Aug 45; Korea/Manchuria July-Aug 45
64	1943	China June 43-Aug 45
65	1943	China June 43-Aug 45
66 ✱	1944	Formosa July 44-Aug 45
68 – 70	1942	China April 42-Aug 45
71 ✱	1942	Manchuria April 42-March 45; Japan March-Aug 45
79	1944	Korea ?-April 45; Manchuria April-Aug 45
94 ✱	1944	Malaya Oct 44-Aug 45

INFANTRY DIVISIONS (total = 107)

✱✱ Known as the Guards Division until June 1943.

✱ These divisions never saw any combat.

INFANTRY DIVISIONS continued		
DIVISION	FORMED	COMBAT RECORD
96 *	1944	Korea ?-Aug 45
100	1944	Philippines July 44-Aug 45. Destroyed Mindanao
102	1944	Philippines July 44-Aug 45. Destroyed Leyte and Cebu
103	1944	Philippines July 44-June 45. Destroyed Luzon
104	pre-1942	China Dec 41-Aug 45
105	1944	Philippines July 44-June 45. Destroyed Luzon
107	1944	Manchuria July 44-Aug 45
108	1944	Manchuria ? 44-Aug 45
109	1944	Iwo Jima Feb 44-March 45. Destroyed
110	pre-1942	China Dec 41-Aug 45
111 *	1944	Manchuria July 44-April 45; Korea April-Aug 45
112	1944	Manchuria July 44-Aug 45
114	1944	China Sept 44-Aug 45
115	1944	China July 44-Aug 45
116	pre-1942	China Dec 41-Aug 45
117	1944	China July 44-July 45; Korea/Manchuria July-Aug 45
118	1944	China Sept 44-Aug 45
119	1944	Manchuria Sept 44-Aug 45
120 *	1944	Manchuria Nov 44-April 45; Korea April-Aug 45
121 *	1944	Manchuria ? 44-April 45; Korea April-Aug 45
122 – 128	1945?	Manchuria ?-Aug 45
129 – 133	1945	China March-Aug 45
138	1945	Manchuria Aug 45
148	1945	Manchuria Aug 45
150 *	1945	Korea Feb-Aug 45
160 *	1945	Korea Feb-Aug 45
161	1945	China Feb-Aug 45
320 *	1945	Korea March-Aug 45

* These divisions never saw any combat.

Also formed were the following infantry divisions, none of which ever left Japan:

1 & 3 Gds., 7, 42, 44, 72, 73, 77, 81, 84, 86, 88, 89, 91, 93, 140, 142-147, 151-157, 201, 202, 205, 206, 207, 212, 214, 216, 221, 222, 224, 225, 229-231, 234, 303, 308, 312, 316, 321, 322, 344, 351, 354, 355.

PART II CAMPAIGNS

The organigrams on the following pages can be usefully supplemented by reference to the relevant maps in Section 1, which give the geographical location of army groups and armies, and those parts of Section 2 which list army group and army commanders for each country.

The Polish Campaign 1939

The Polish Mobilisation Plan 1 September 1939

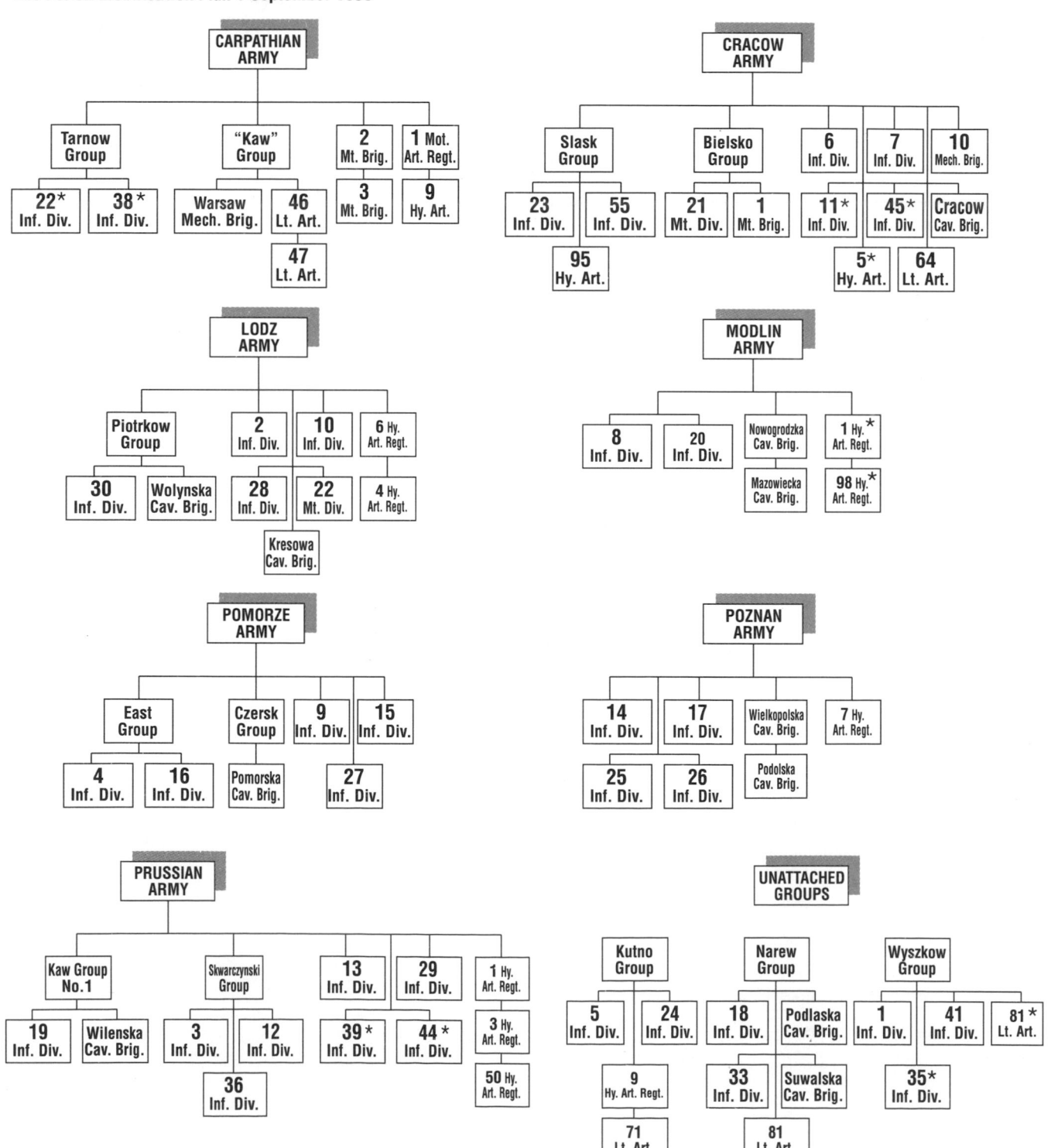

* Never fought with this particuilar formation, though supposed to do so in mobilisation plan.

The German Army in Poland 1 September 1939

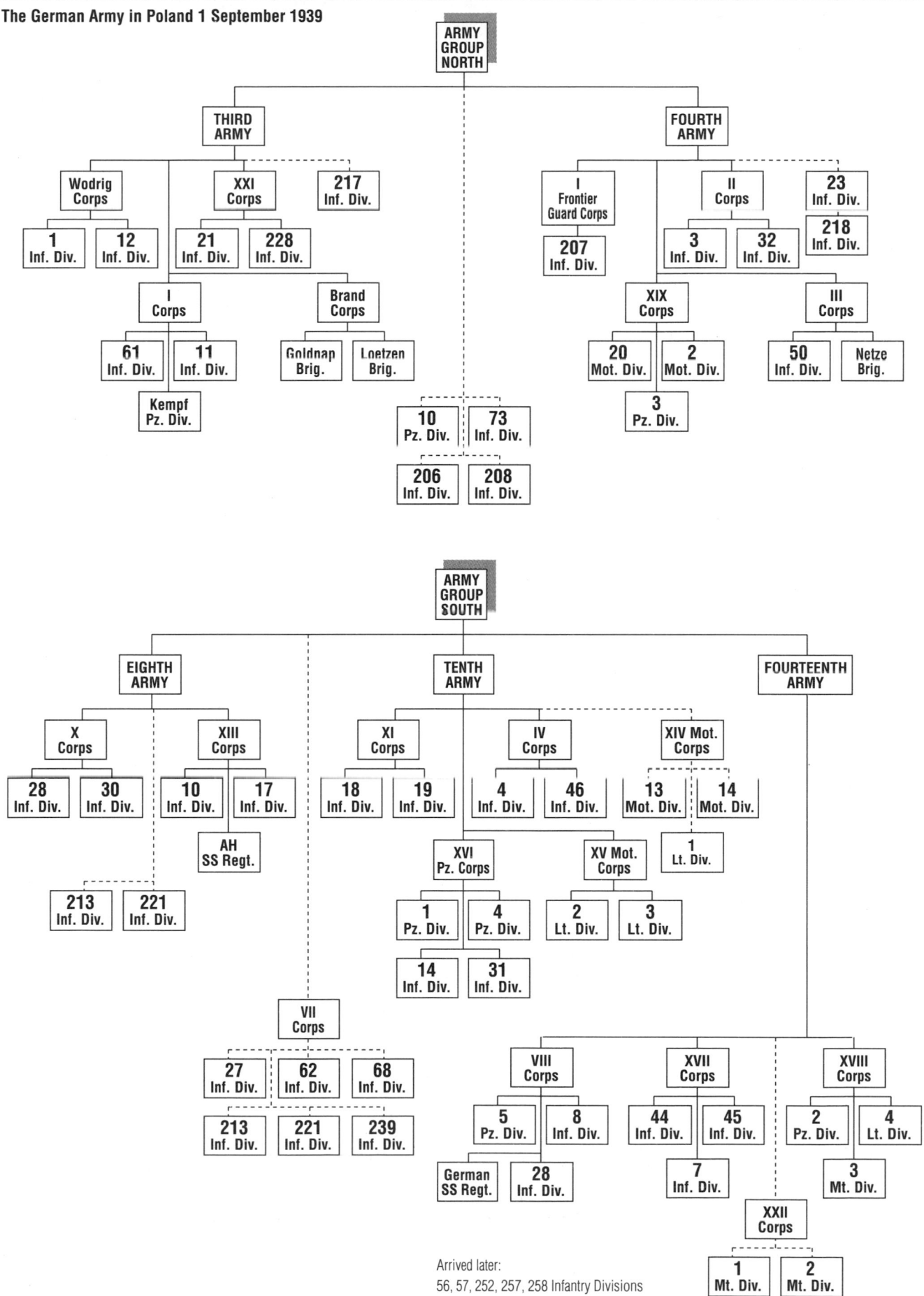

Arrived later:
56, 57, 252, 257, 258 Infantry Divisions

The Red Army in Poland 17 September 1939

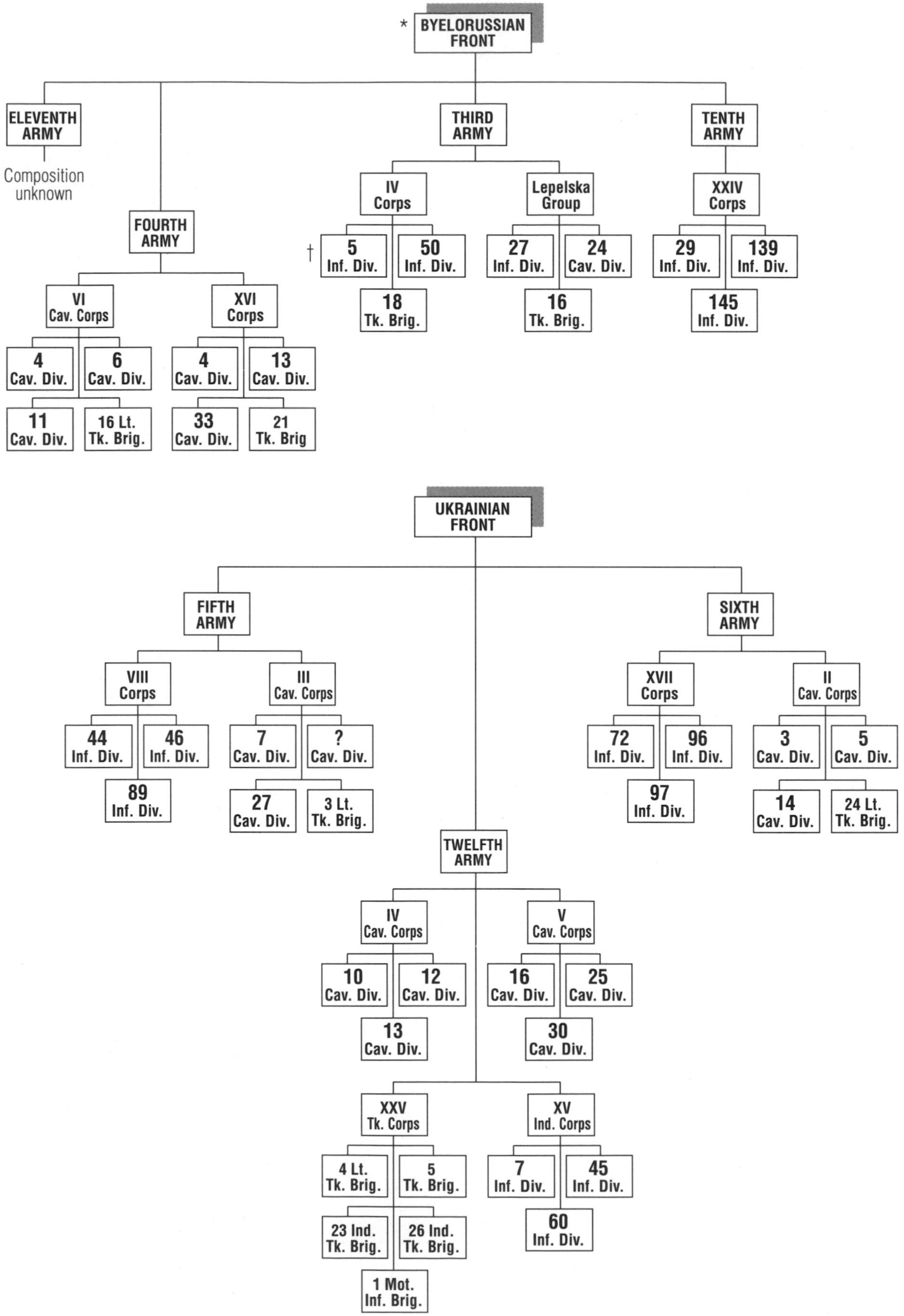

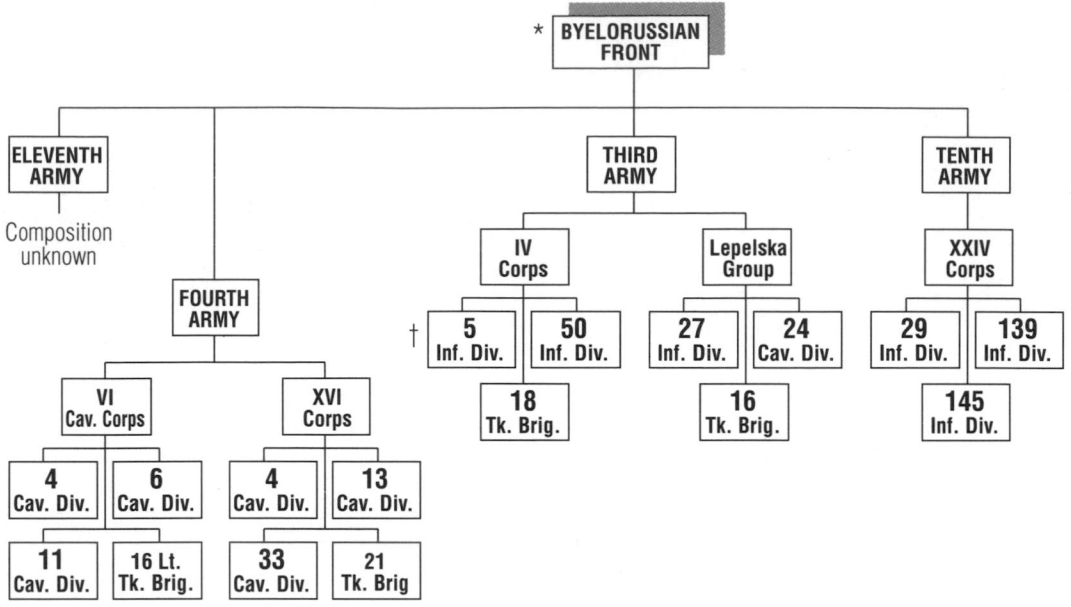

* A *Front* was a Soviet Army Group.

† Soviet infantry divisions were officially known as rifle divisions.

BYELORUSSIAN FRONT

ELEVENTH ARMY

Composition unknown

THIRD ARMY

TENTH ARMY

FOURTH ARMY

IV Corps

Lepelska Group

XXIV Corps

† 5 Inf. Div. | 50 Inf. Div.

27 Inf. Div. | 24 Cav. Div.

29 Inf. Div. | 139 Inf. Div.

18 Tk. Brig.

16 Tk. Brig.

145 Inf. Div.

VI Cav. Corps

XVI Corps

4 Cav. Div. | 6 Cav. Div.

4 Cav. Div. | 13 Cav. Div.

11 Cav. Div. | 16 Lt. Tk. Brig.

33 Cav. Div. | 21 Tk. Brig

UKRAINIAN FRONT

FIFTH ARMY

SIXTH ARMY

VIII Corps

III Cav. Corps

XVII Corps

II Cav. Corps

44 Inf. Div. | 46 Inf. Div.

7 Cav. Div. | ? Cav. Div.

72 Inf. Div. | 96 Inf. Div.

3 Cav. Div. | 5 Cav. Div.

89 Inf. Div.

27 Cav. Div. | 3 Lt. Tk. Brig.

97 Inf. Div.

14 Cav. Div. | 24 Lt. Tk. Brig.

TWELFTH ARMY

IV Cav. Corps

V Cav. Corps

10 Cav. Div. | 12 Cav. Div.

16 Cav. Div. | 25 Cav. Div.

13 Cav. Div.

30 Cav. Div.

XXV Tk. Corps

XV Ind. Corps

4 Lt. Tk. Brig. | 5 Tk. Brig.

7 Inf. Div. | 45 Inf. Div.

23 Ind. Tk. Brig. | 26 Ind. Tk. Brig.

60 Inf. Div.

1 Mot. Inf. Brig.

The Norwegian and Danish Campaigns 1940

German, Norwegian and Danish Forces 9 April 1940 and Allied Forces Norway April-June 1940

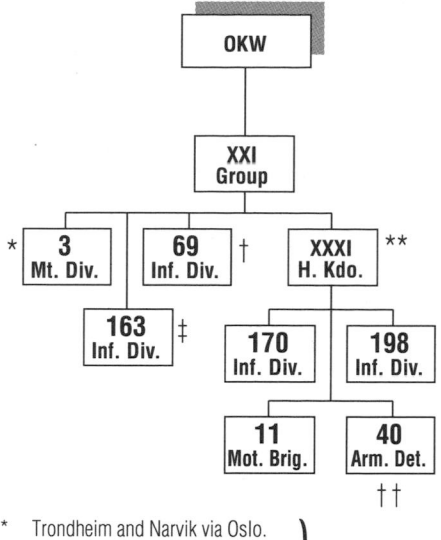

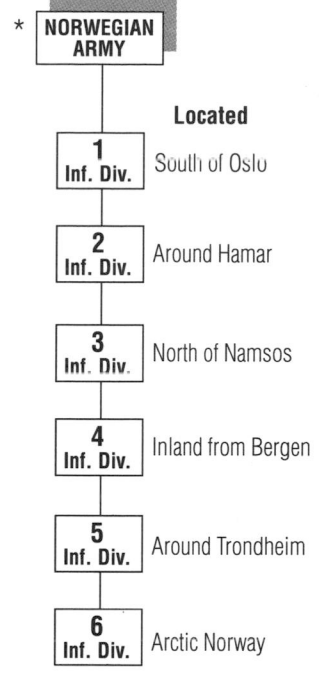

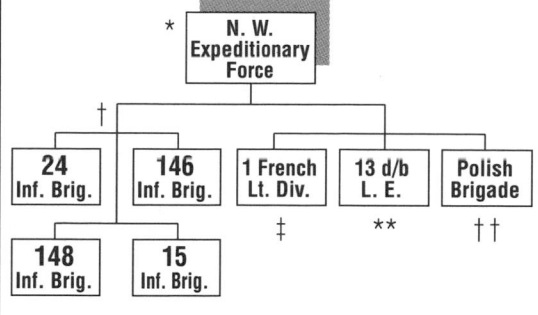

Located

1 Inf. Div. — South of Oslo

2 Inf. Div. — Around Hamar

3 Inf. Div. — North of Namsos

4 Inf. Div. — Inland from Bergen

5 Inf. Div. — Around Trondheim

6 Inf. Div. — Arctic Norway

* Trondheim and Narvik via Oslo.
† Bergen and Stavanger via Bergen. Two regts. only.
‡ Oslo and Christiansand via Oslo. Two regts. only. } 9 April 1940.
** Denmark. Reverted to OKH control 10 April.
†† Joined Norway Forces late April.

Between 11 and 14 April a second wave of troops landed at Oslo comprising 196 and 181 Inf. Divs. as well as the third regts. of 69 and 163 Divs.

On 17 April 214 Inf. Div. landed at Stavanger.

On 4 May 2 Mt. Div. landed at Trondheim.

* Except for 6 Div. the Norwegian Army was never anything like fully mobilised.

* So called from 19 April.
† All British brigades:
– 24 Brig. was an independent Guards formation and landed at Horstad on 15 April. Part of Rupert force it later moved to Narvik whence it was evacuated by 8 June.
– 146 Brig. was normally part of 49 Div. but operated independently in Norway. Part of Maurice force it landed at Namsos on 16 April and was evacuated by 3 May.
– 148 Brig. originated as 146. Part of Sickle force it landed at Aandalsnes on 18 April and was evacuated by 2 May.
– 15 Brig. was part of 5 Div. in France. It arrived at Aandalsnes on 23 April, as part of Sickle force, and was evacuated by 2 May.
‡ Organised in two *chasseur alpin* demi-brigades:
– 5th which landed at Namsos 30 April and evacuated 4 June.
– 27th which landed at Narvik 27 April and evacuated mid-June.
** Landed at Narvik 28 April and evacuated with 27th demi-brigade.
†† Landed at Horstad 7 May and evacuated from Narvik early June.

The Campaign in Holland, Belgium and France 1940

The French Army 10 May 1940

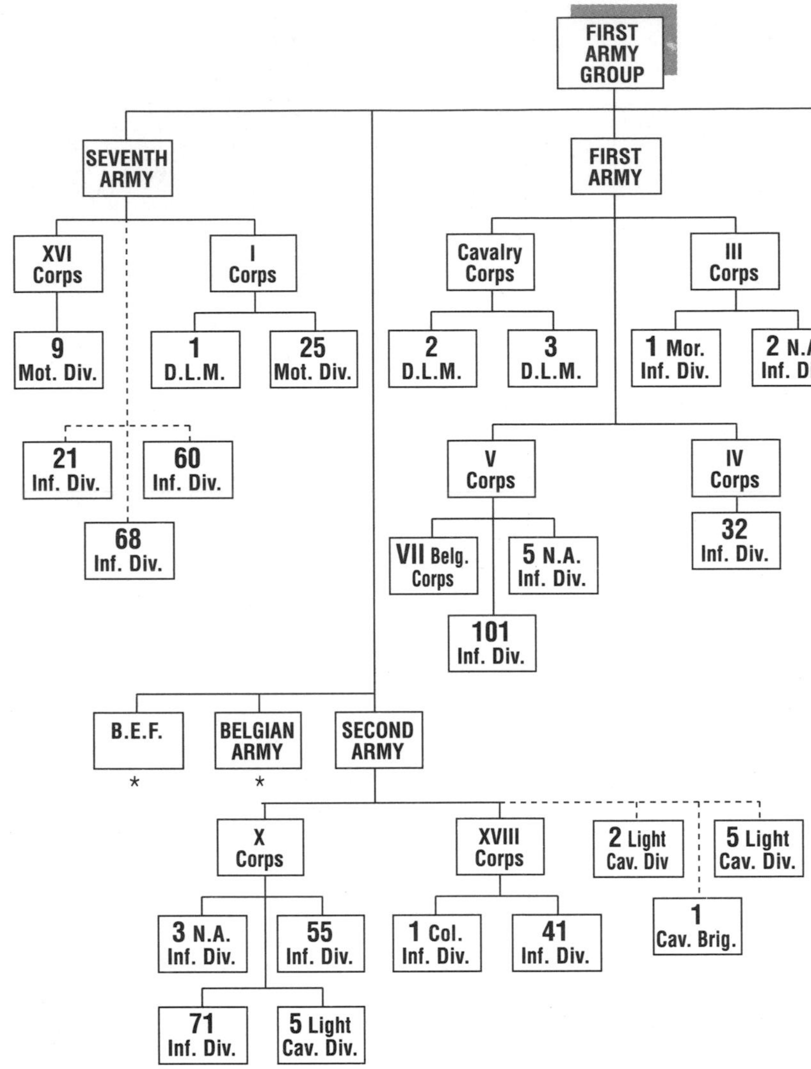

```
                              FIRST
                              ARMY
                              GROUP
   ┌──────────────────────────────┼──────────────────────────────┐
SEVENTH                          FIRST                          NINTH
ARMY                             ARMY                           ARMY
 ┌────────┐                 ┌──────────┐                    ┌──────────┐
XVI       I               Cavalry      III                 XI          II
Corps     Corps           Corps        Corps               Corps       Corps
 │      ┌────┴────┐       ┌────┴────┐   ┌────┴────┐        ┌────┴────┐  ┌────┴────┐
 9      1         25      2         3   1 Mor.    2 N.A.   1 Light   18 5        4 Light
Mot.    D.L.M.    Mot.    D.L.M.   D.L.M. Inf.    Inf.     Cav. Div. Inf. Mot.   Cav. Div.
Div.              Div.                    Div.    Div.               Div. Div.
    ┌────┴────┐              ┌────┴────┐                      22
   21        60              V         IV                    Inf. Div.
   Inf.      Inf.            Corps     Corps             ┌────┴──────────┬──────────┐
   Div.      Div.         ┌────┴────┐    │              XLI           4 N.A.    53
       68                VII Belg.  5 N.A. 32            Corps         Inf.      Inf.
      Inf. Div.          Corps     Inf.   Inf.       ┌────┴────┐       Div.      Div.
                             101   Div.   Div.      102       61
                            Inf. Div.              Fort. Div. Inf. Div.
                                                        3 Spahi
                                                        Brig.
```

* For further details see page 148.

```
 ┌──────────┬──────────┐
B.E.F.    BELGIAN    SECOND
          ARMY       ARMY
  *         *     ┌──────┴──────────────┬──────────┬──────────┐
                  X         XVIII       2 Light    5 Light
                  Corps     Corps       Cav. Div   Cav. Div.
              ┌────┴────┐  ┌────┴────┐        1
              3 N.A.   55  1 Col.   41        Cav. Brig.
              Inf.     Inf. Inf.    Inf.
              Div.     Div. Div.    Div.
          ┌────┴────┐
          71        5 Light
          Inf.      Cav. Div.
          Div.
```

In GHQ Reserve, behind First Army Group:

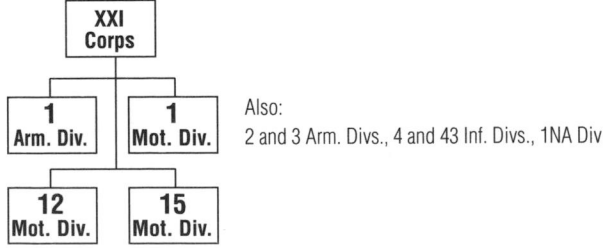

```
        XXI
        Corps
   ┌─────┴─────┐
   1           1
   Arm. Div.   Mot. Div.
   ┌─┴─┐     ┌─┴─┐
   12        15
   Mot. Div. Mot. Div.
```

Also:
2 and 3 Arm. Divs., 4 and 43 Inf. Divs., 1NA Div.

The French Army 10 May 1940

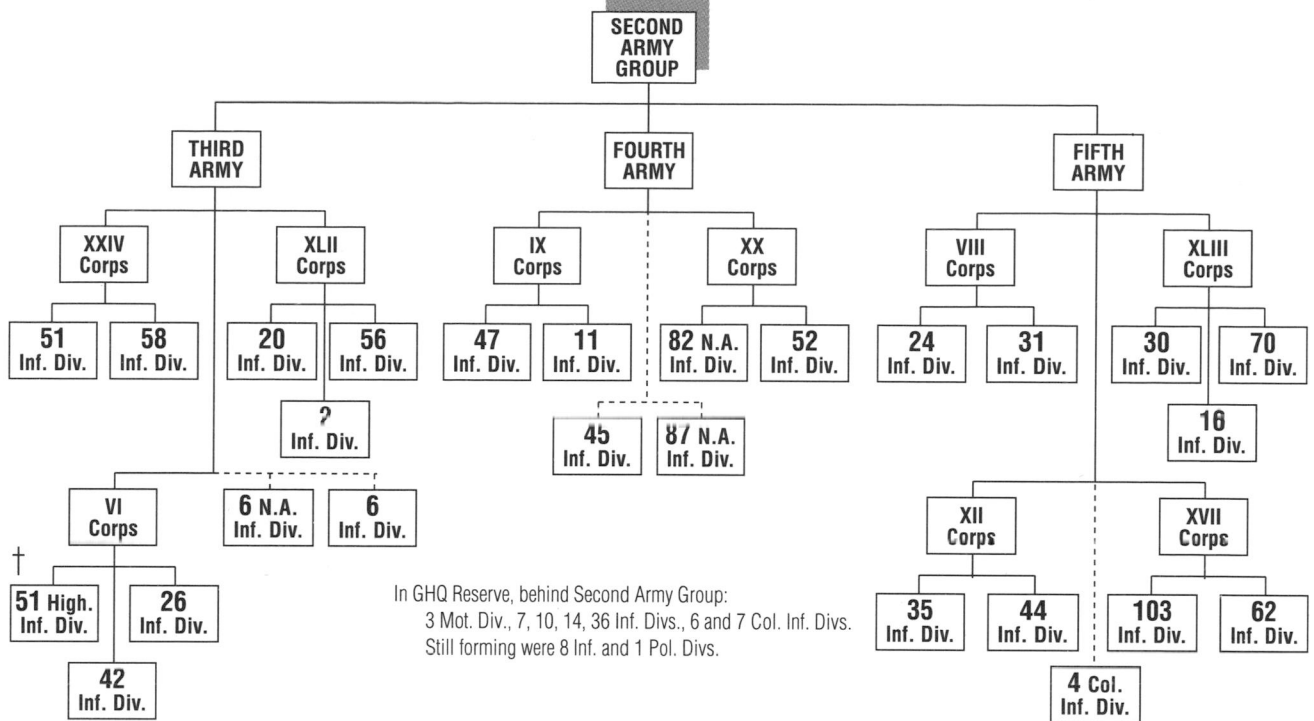

In GHQ Reserve, behind Second Army Group:
3 Mot. Div., 7, 10, 14, 36 Inf. Divs., 6 and 7 Col. Inf. Divs.
Still forming were 8 Inf. and 1 Pol. Divs.

† Part of B.E.F.

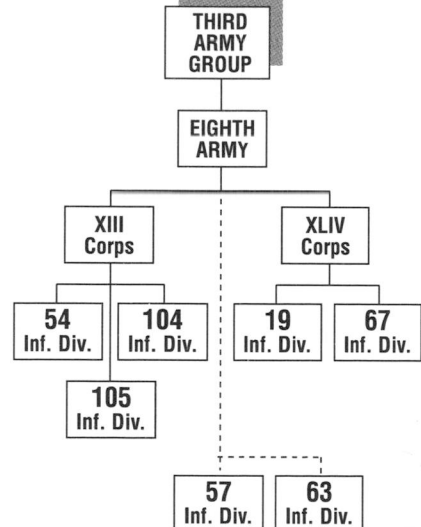

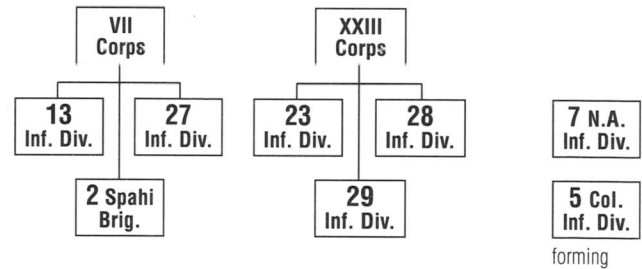

In GHQ Reserve, behind Second and Third Army Groups:

a) To the south of Third Army Group was the Army of the Alps (ex-Sixth Army) defending the frontier with Italy. This comprised four infantry divisions, 2 Col. and 64, 65, 66 Alpine, as well as seven fortress demi-brigades.

b) During the course of the campaign a further 18 divisions arrived at the front. These were: 4 Arm., 17 and 40 Inf., 3, 53, 59 and 235-241 Light, 2 Pol. Inf., 7NA, 8 Col., 84 and 85 African.

The Dutch and Belgian Armies and the British Expeditionary Force 10 May 1940

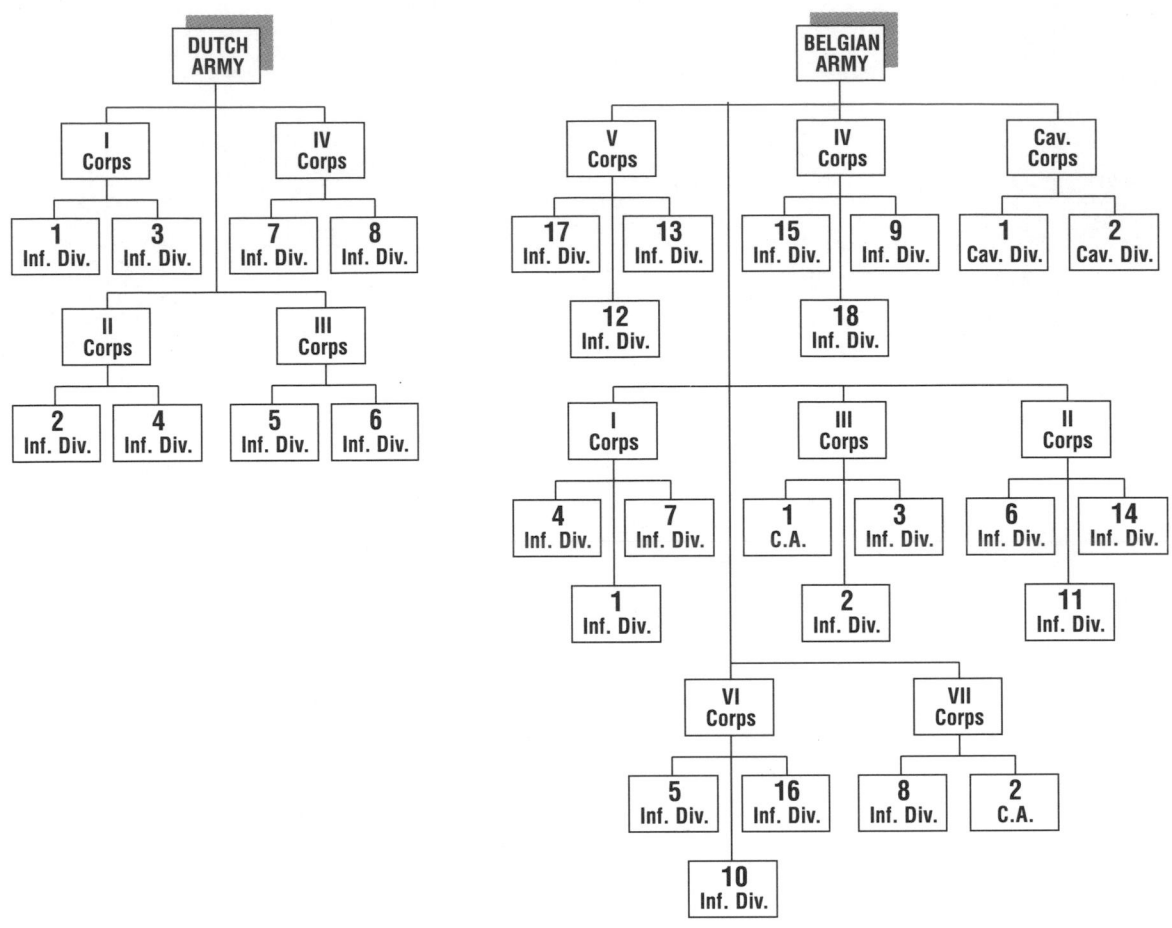

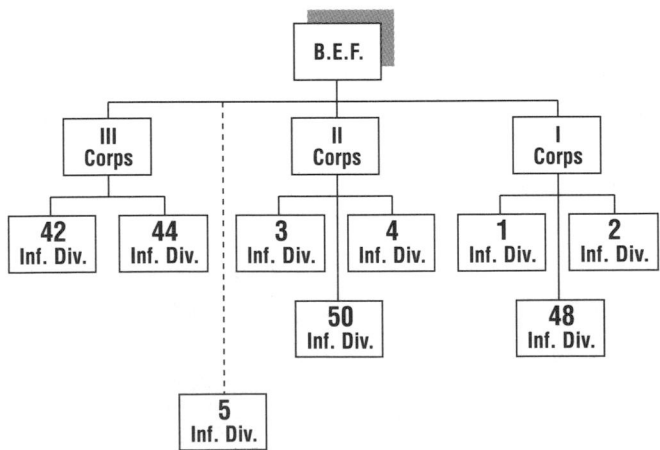

a) Also present, on labouring duties, were three Territorial Divisions, 12, 23 and
    46, which became involved in the fighting, in a piecemeal fashion, from 17 May.
b) The following divisions arrived in France after 10 May:
    1 Arm., 52 Inf., 1 Can. Inf. (elements).

The German Army in the West 10 May 1940 (also next page).

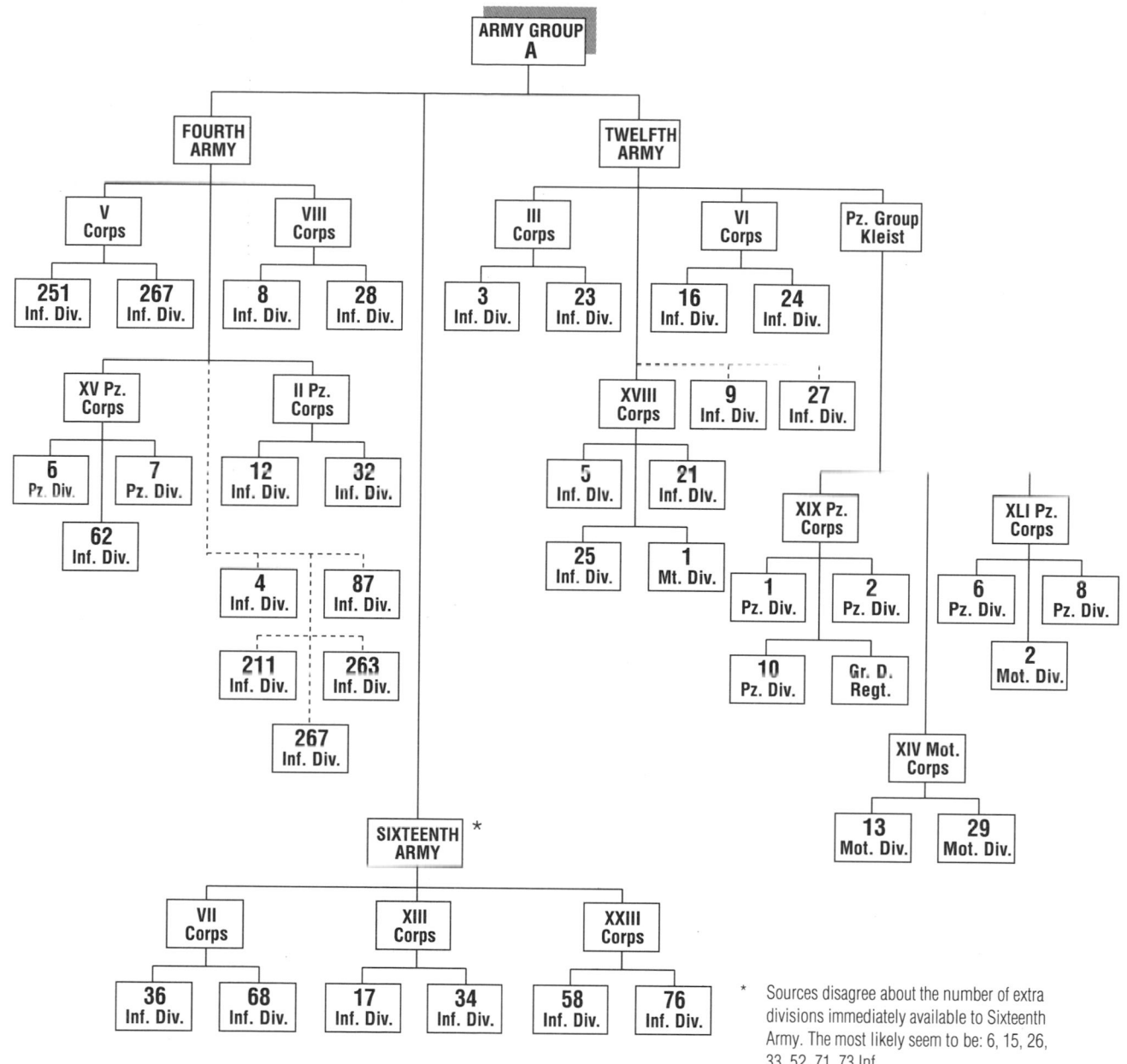

* Sources disagree about the number of extra divisions immediately available to Sixteenth Army. The most likely seem to be: 6, 15, 26, 33, 52, 71, 73 Inf.

In OKH Reserve on 10 May:

Army HQ: Second, Ninth.

Corps HQ: (Armee Korps) XVII, XXXVIII, XL, XLII, XLIII, XLIV; (Heeres Korps) XXXVI, XLV.

Divisions: (Infantry) 10, 44, 45, 46, 50, 57, 60, 72, 78, 81, 82, 83, 86, 88, 96, 161, 162, 164, 167, 168, 169, 170, 183, 197, 205, 206, 212, 213, 217, 218, 221, 260, 290, 291, 292, 293, 294, 295, 296, 297, 298, 299, 1SS, SS-Pol., 1 Pol.

The German Army in the West 10 May 1940 (also previous page).

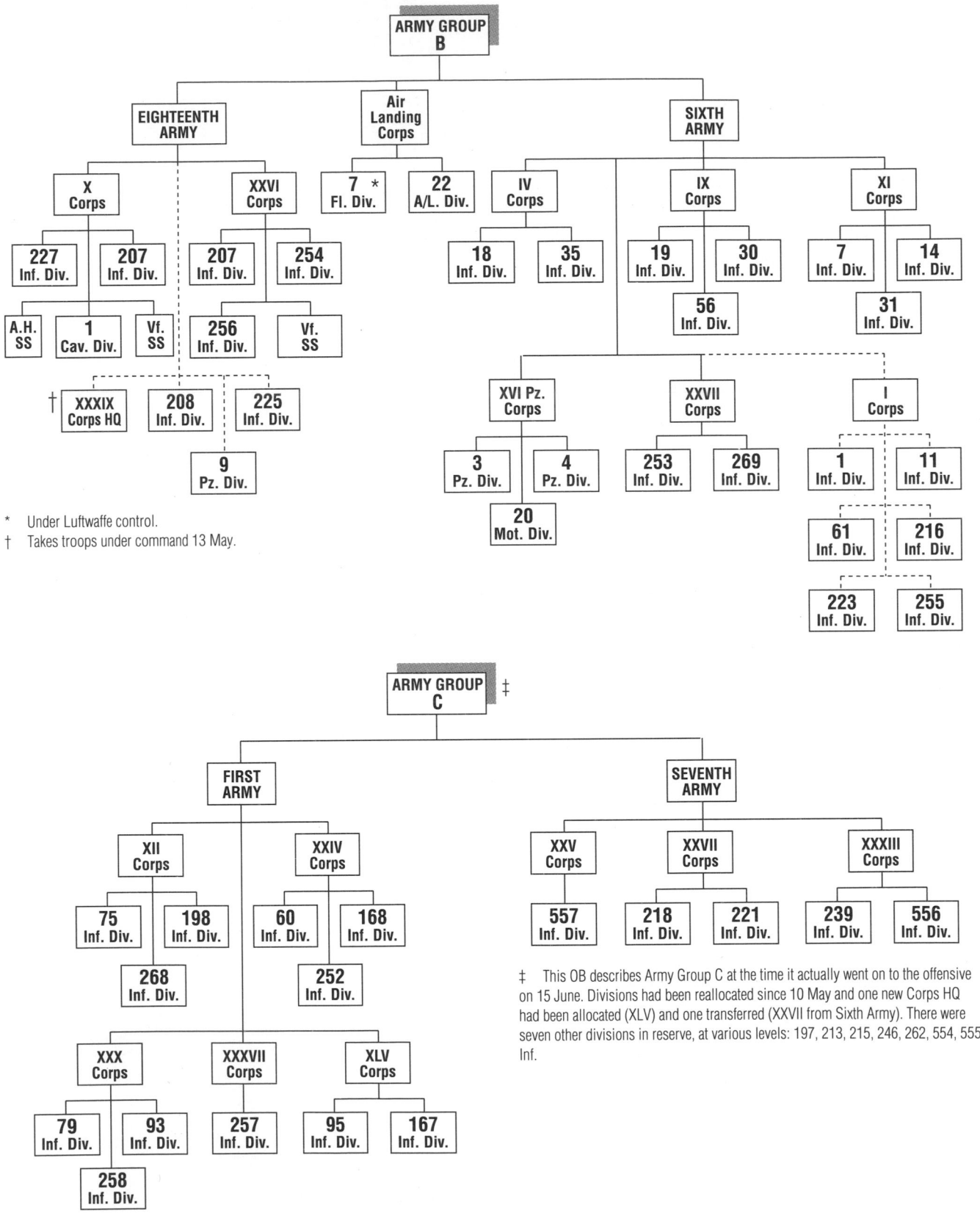

*   Under Luftwaffe control.
†   Takes troops under command 13 May.

‡   This OB describes Army Group C at the time it actually went on to the offensive on 15 June. Divisions had been reallocated since 10 May and one new Corps HQ had been allocated (XLV) and one transferred (XXVII from Sixth Army). There were seven other divisions in reserve, at various levels: 197, 213, 215, 246, 262, 554, 555 Inf.

Forces on the Franco-Italian Frontier 20 June 1940

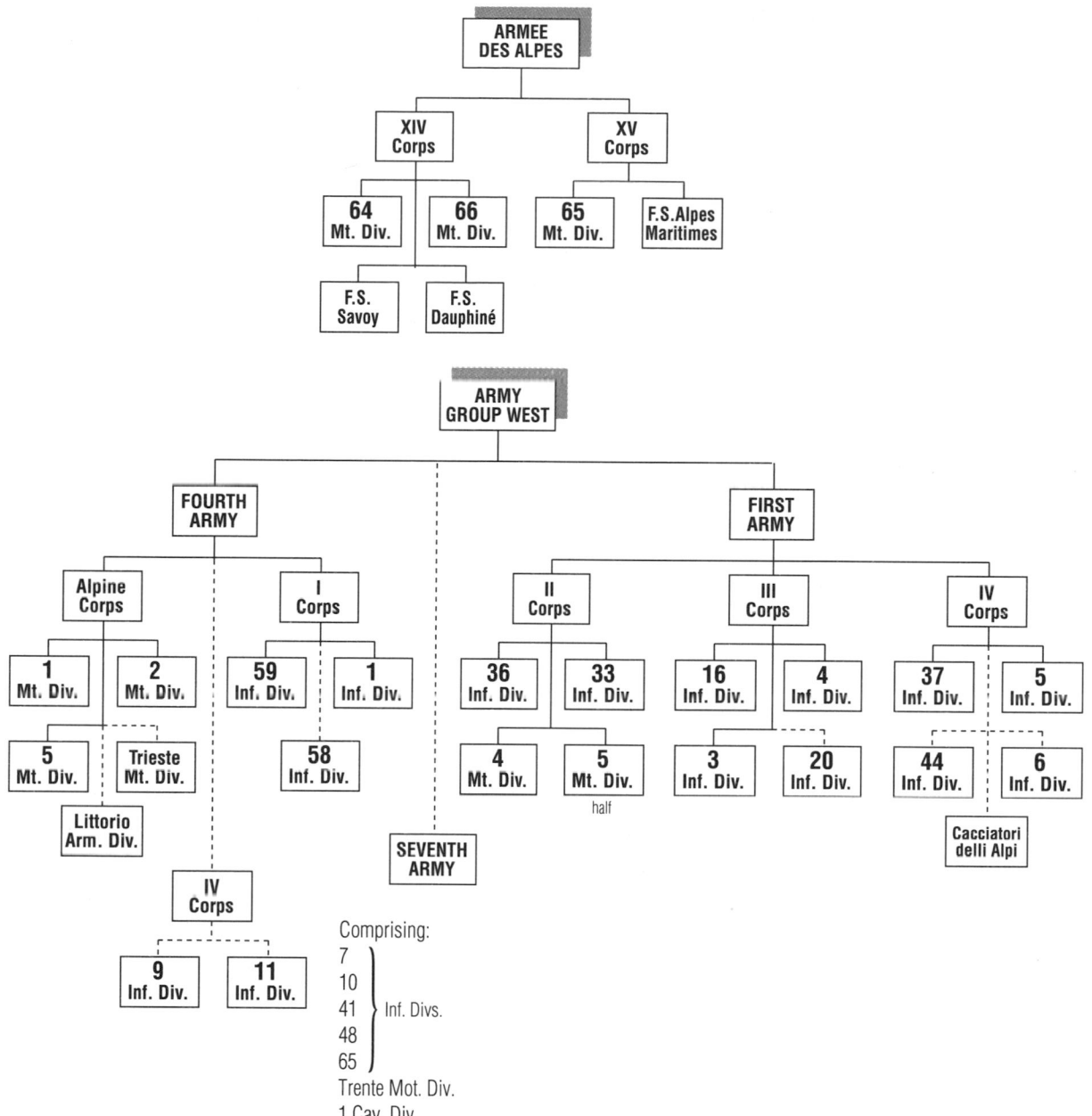

The Balkans 1940-41

The Italian Army in Albania 28 October 1940

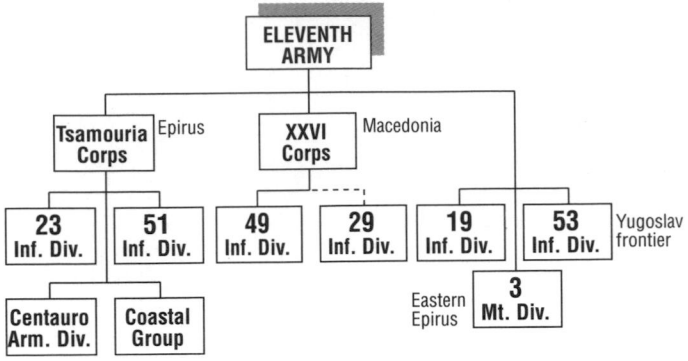

```
                    ELEVENTH
                      ARMY
        ┌───────────────┴──────────────────────────────────┐
   Tsamouria  Epirus              XXVI    Macedonia
    Corps                         Corps
   ┌───┴───┐              ┌────┬────┼──────────┬──────────┐
  23      51            49     29    19        53    Yugoslav
 Inf.    Inf.          Inf.   Inf.  Inf.      Inf.   frontier
 Div.    Div.          Div.   Div.  Div.      Div.
   │       │                            Eastern   3
Centauro  Coastal                       Epirus   Mt. Div.
Arm. Div. Group
```

Between November 1940 and January 1941 the following divisions arrived in Albania/Greece (all infantry divisions unless otherwise stated).
November 1940: 37, 47, 48, 2 Mt, 5 Mt, 101 Mot.
December 1940: 6, 11, 33, 4 Mt.
January 1941: 7, 22, 24, 36, 58, 59.

By early March the following divisions had also arrived in Albania/Greece: 2, 38, 41, 56.

The Greek Army

On 28 October the Greeks had one division, 8 Infantry, stationed in Epirus and another, 9 Infantry, in western Macedonia. Each was reinforced by an infantry brigade and in Macedonia there were also several reinforced independent infantry battalions. Another infantry division, 1st, was available in reserve.

The subsequent build-up of forces produced, on the Albanian front:
7 infantry divisions by 14 November.
11 infantry divisions by 30 November.
13 infantry divisions by 15 December.
13 infantry divisions by 15 January 1941.

The German Army in the Invasion of Yugoslavia and Greece April 1941

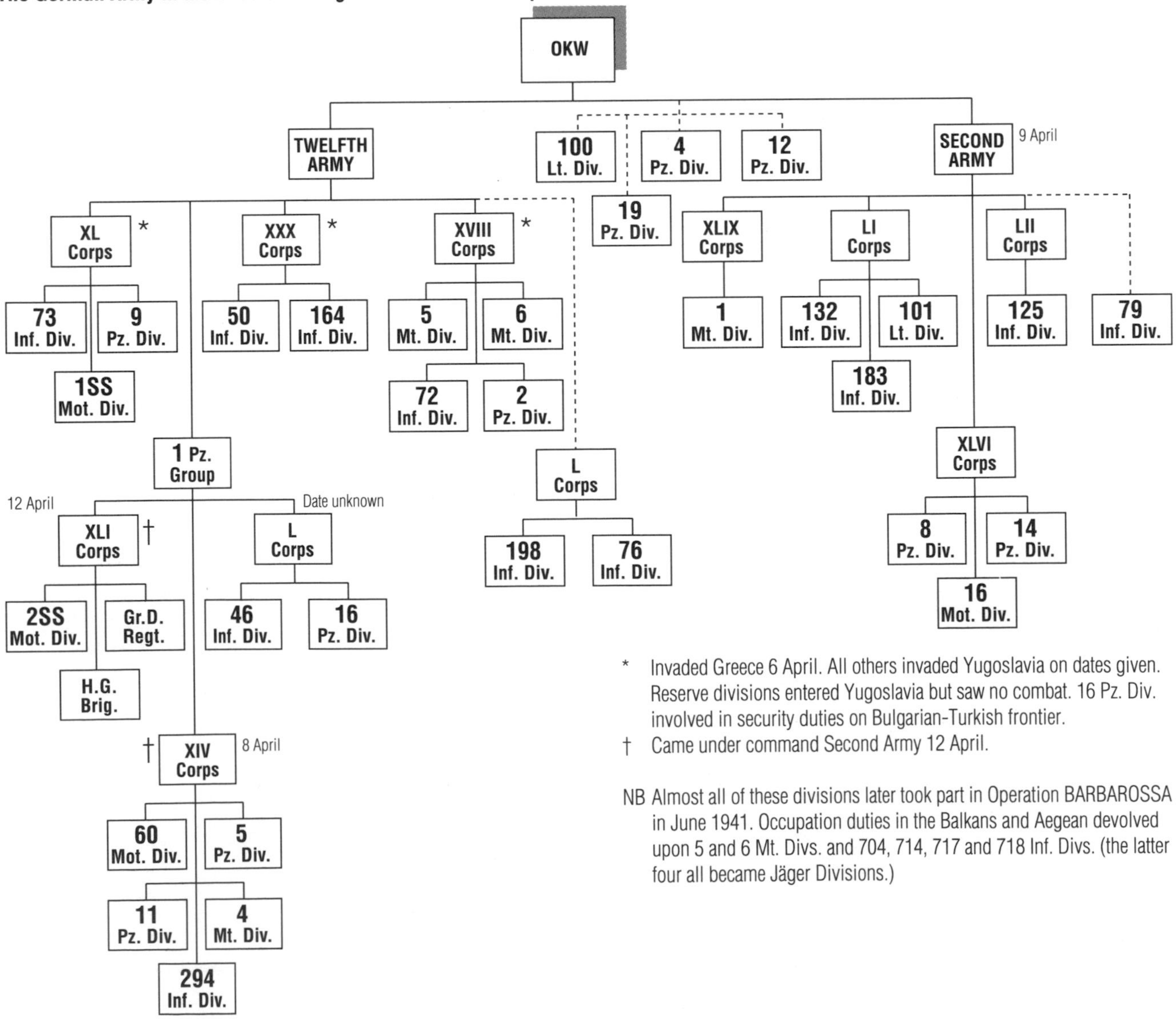

```
                                    OKW
        ┌──────────────────┬──────┬──────┬──────────────────┐
   TWELFTH            100      4      12           SECOND   9 April
    ARMY             Lt. Div. Pz.Div. Pz.Div.       ARMY
                          19
                        Pz. Div.
  ┌────────┬────────┬──────┬──────┬──────┬──────┐
 XL *     XXX *    XVIII *        XLIX    LI      LII
Corps     Corps    Corps          Corps  Corps   Corps
┌──┴─┐   ┌──┴──┐  ┌──┴──┐          1     ┌──┴──┐  ┌──┴──┐
73   9   50  164  5     6        Mt.Div. 132  101 125   79
Inf. Pz. Inf.Inf. Mt.   Mt.              Inf. Lt. Inf. Inf.
Div. Div.Div.Div. Div.  Div.             Div. Div.Div. Div.
 1SS            72    2                      183
Mot.Div.       Inf.  Pz.                    Inf. Div.
               Div.  Div.
 1 Pz.                L                      XLVI
 Group              Corps                    Corps
12 April  Date unknown ┌──┴──┐             ┌──┴──┐
 XLI †     L          198   76             8     14
Corps    Corps       Inf.  Inf.           Pz.   Pz.
┌──┴──┐  ┌──┴──┐      Div.  Div.           Div.  Div.
2SS   Gr.D. 46   16                           16
Mot.  Regt.Inf. Pz.                          Mot. Div.
Div.      Div. Div.
 H.G.
 Brig.
 † XIV   8 April
  Corps
 ┌──┴──┐
 60    5
Mot.  Pz.
Div.  Div.
 11    4
Pz.   Mt.
Div.  Div.
 294
Inf. Div.
```

* Invaded Greece 6 April. All others invaded Yugoslavia on dates given. Reserve divisions entered Yugoslavia but saw no combat. 16 Pz. Div. involved in security duties on Bulgarian-Turkish frontier.

† Came under command Second Army 12 April.

NB Almost all of these divisions later took part in Operation BARBAROSSA in June 1941. Occupation duties in the Balkans and Aegean devolved upon 5 and 6 Mt. Divs. and 704, 714, 717 and 718 Inf. Divs. (the latter four all became Jäger Divisions.)

The Italian Army in Albania April 1941

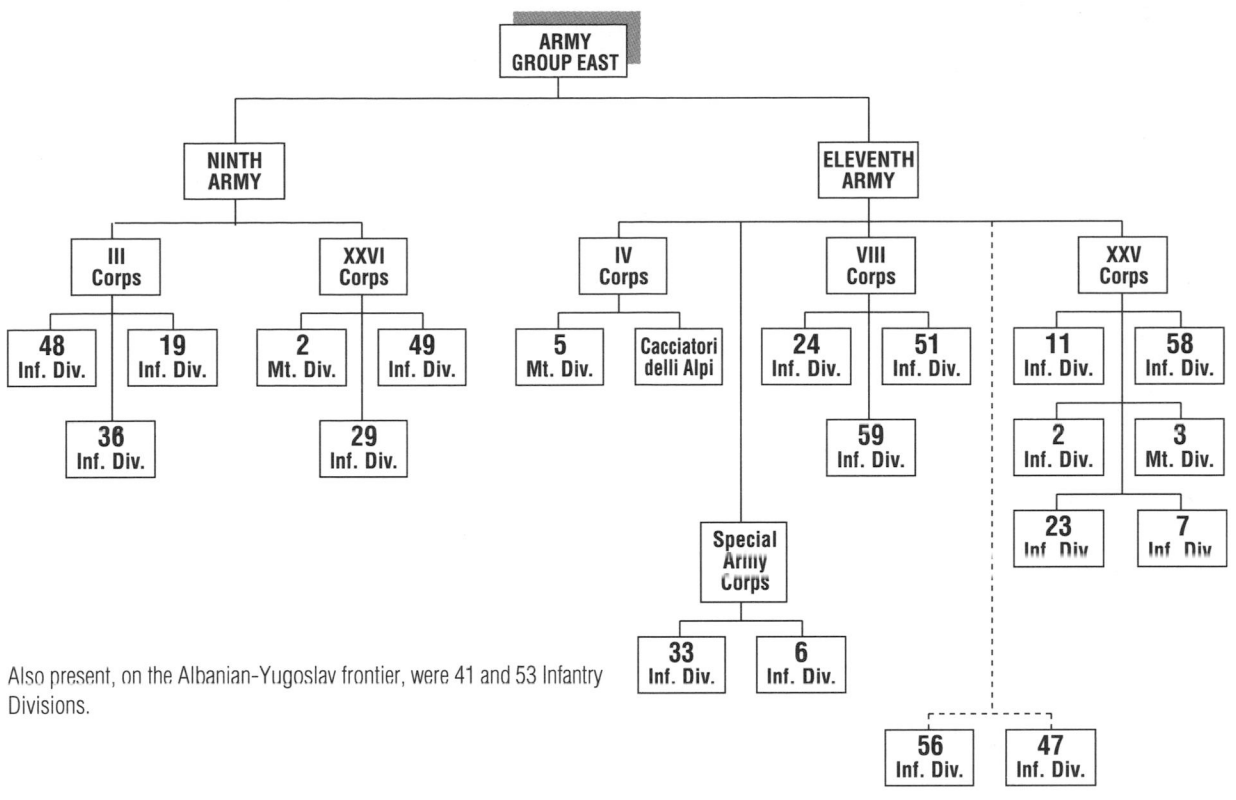

Also present, on the Albanian-Yugoslav frontier, were 41 and 53 Infantry Divisions.

Greek and Allied Forces April 1941

Greek forces on the Albanian Front were divided between two Armies, Epirus and Western Macedonian, which controlled I, II and III Corps. Within these Corps were grouped 2, 3, 4, 5, 6, 8, 9, 10, 13, 16, 17 Infantry Divisions and the Cavalry Division. 1st and 11 Infantry Divisions were held in reserve.

On the rest of the front, along the Metaxas and Aliakhmon Lines, the Greek and British forces (from N. Africa) were organised as follows:

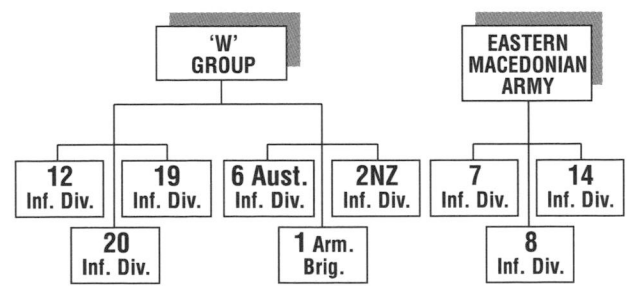

The Yugoslav Army April 1941

The administrative organisation of the Yugoslav Army was fairly clear cut, there being six armies and sixteen divisions plus one division of Royal Guards. The building blocks for the divisions were fifty-two infantry regiments numbered 1-8, 10-26, 29-36, 38-42, 44-49 and 53-56. There were also ten cavalry regiments of which two were Royal Guards.

The non-Guards divisions were named after the territories in which they were based and were: Bitoliska, Bosanska, Bregalnicka, Dravska, Drinska, Dunavska, Jadranska, Moravska, Osecka, Potiska, Savska, Sumadiska, Timocka, Vardarska, Vrbaska, Zetka.

However, the sources I have been able to consult leave it very unclear as to just how many of these troops were available in April 1941 and how many actually came into contact with the Germans. According to General Simovic, the Prime Minister, only five infantry divisions and some cavalry regiments managed to engage the enemy.

The Russo-Finnish War 1939-40

The Finnish Army 30 November 1939

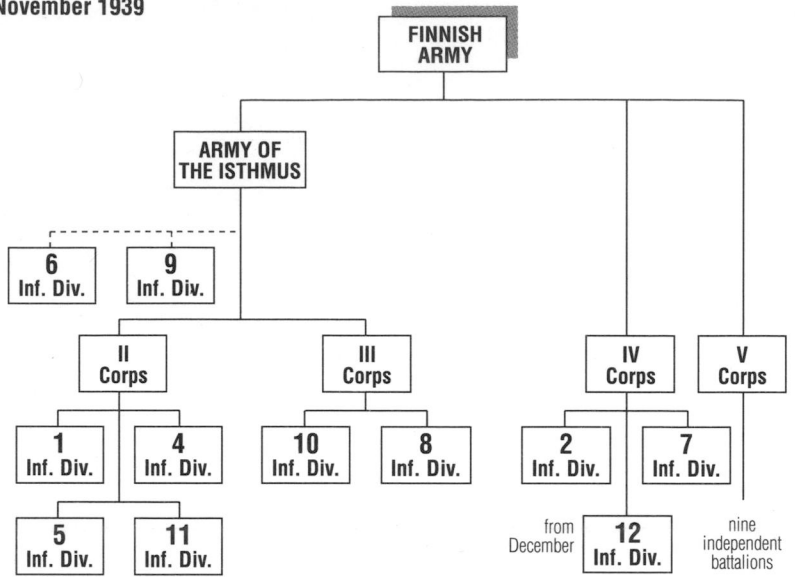

Russian Forces on the Finnish Front 30 November 1939

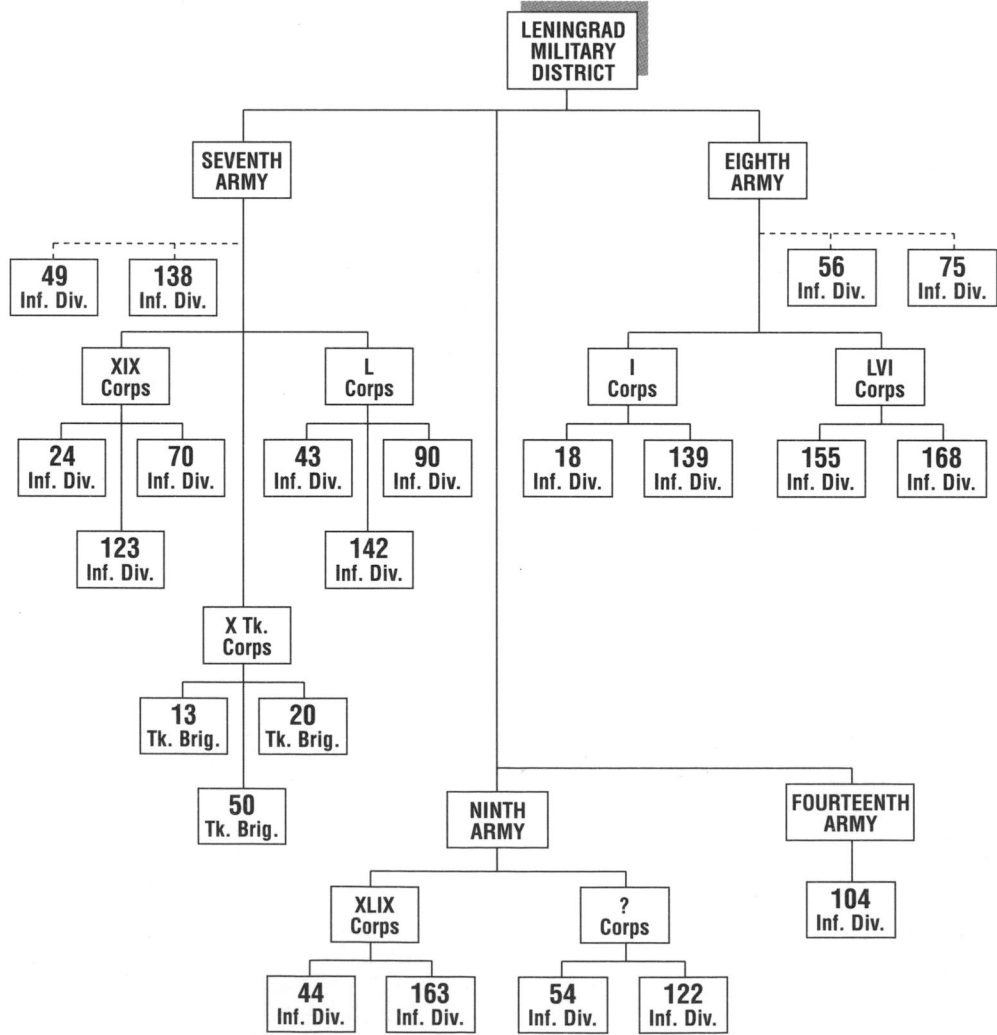

Prior to the armistice on 13 March 1940, Soviet reinforcements into Finland included the following divisions (infantry unless otherwise stated):
3, 4, 9, 14, 17, 25, 42, 43, 51, 53, 73, 80, 84, 86, 88, 90, 100, 103 Mot., 113, 136, 138, 142, 144, 150.

North Africa and the Middle East 1940-43

The Italian Army in Libya December 1940

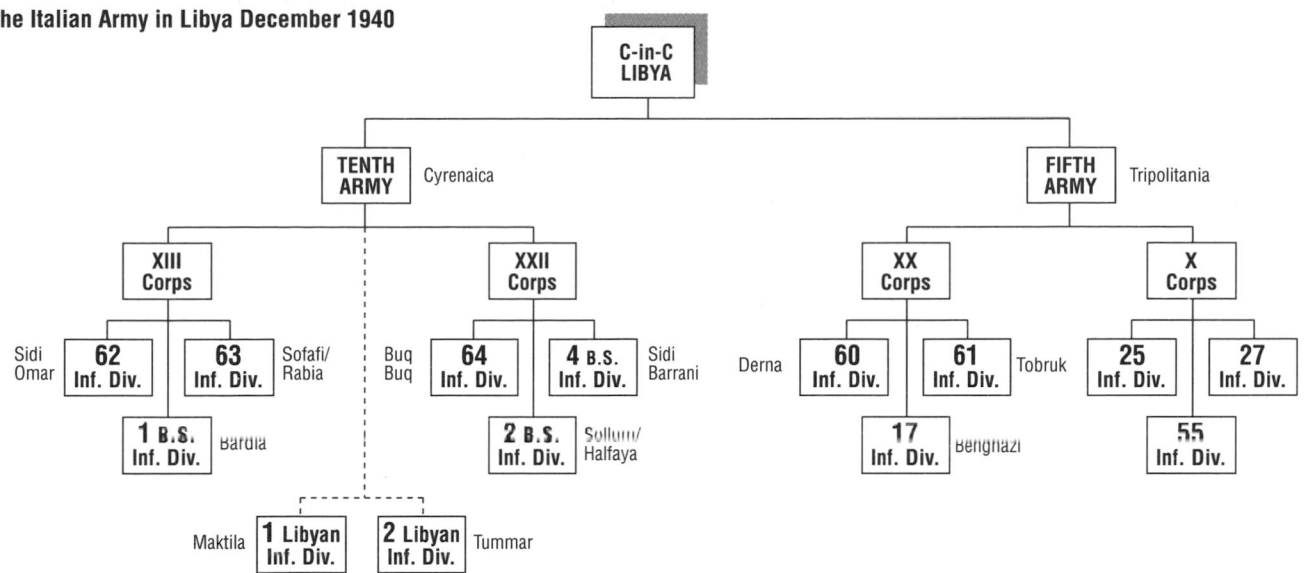

The British Army in Egypt 9 December 1940

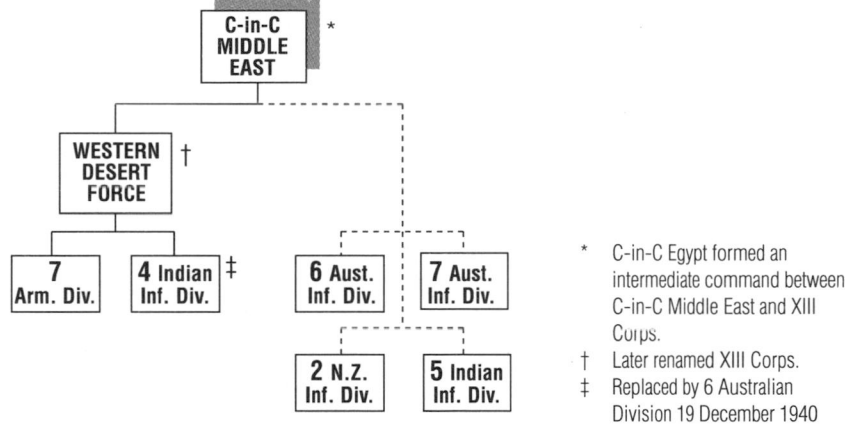

* C-in-C Egypt formed an intermediate command between C-in-C Middle East and XIII Corps.

† Later renamed XIII Corps.

‡ Replaced by 6 Australian Division 19 December 1940.

Italian and British Forces for the East African Campaign 19 January 1941

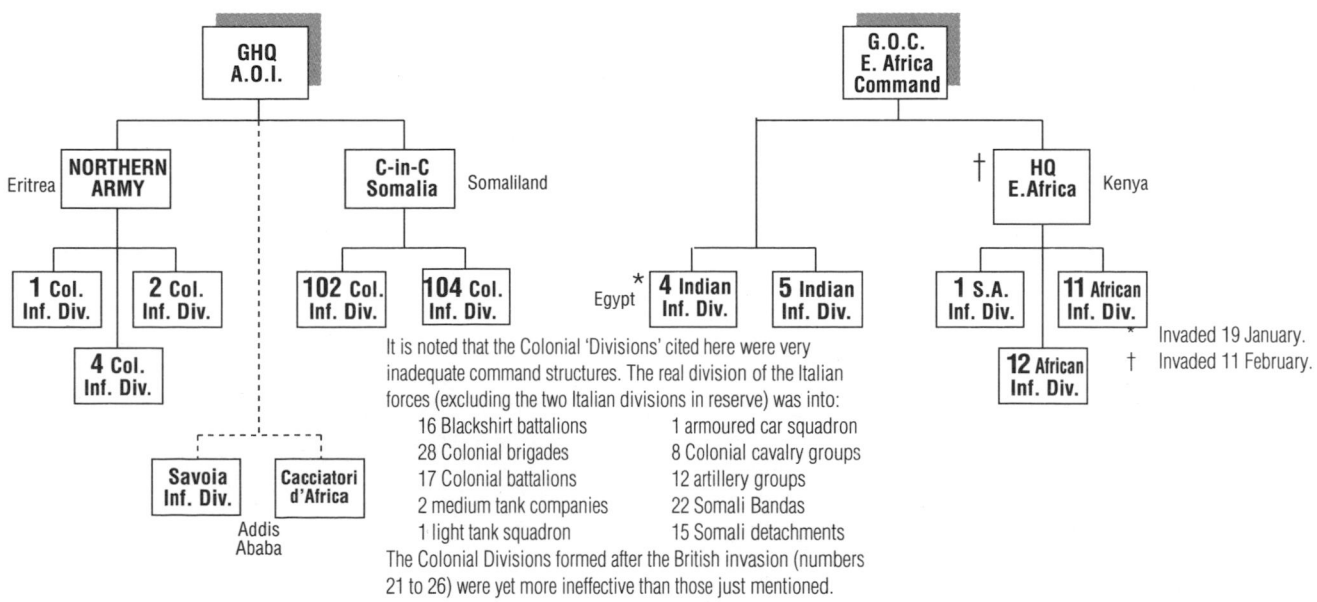

It is noted that the Colonial 'Divisions' cited here were very inadequate command structures. The real division of the Italian forces (excluding the two Italian divisions in reserve) was into:

16 Blackshirt battalions	1 armoured car squadron
28 Colonial brigades	8 Colonial cavalry groups
17 Colonial battalions	12 artillery groups
2 medium tank companies	22 Somali Bandas
1 light tank squadron	15 Somali detachments

The Colonial Divisions formed after the British invasion (numbers 21 to 26) were yet more ineffective than those just mentioned.

* Invaded 19 January.
† Invaded 11 February.

British and Iraqi Forces in the Iraq Campaign 11 May 1941

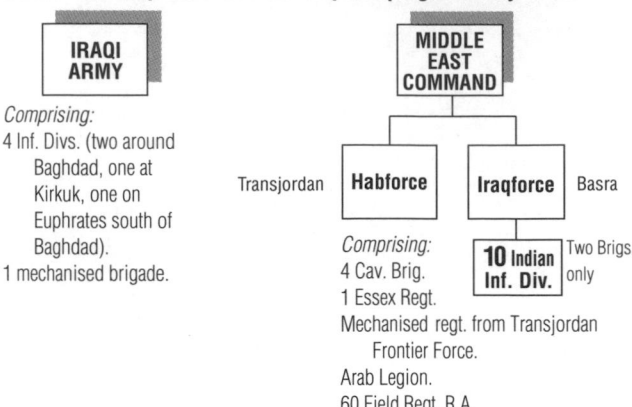

IRAQI ARMY

Comprising:
4 Inf. Divs. (two around Baghdad, one at Kirkuk, one on Euphrates south of Baghdad).
1 mechanised brigade.

MIDDLE EAST COMMAND

Transjordan **Habforce** **Iraqforce** Basra

Comprising:
4 Cav. Brig.
1 Essex Regt.
Mechanised regt. from Transjordan Frontier Force.
Arab Legion.
60 Field Regt. R.A.

10 Indian Inf. Div. Two Brigs. only

British and French Forces in the Syrian Campaign 8 June 1941

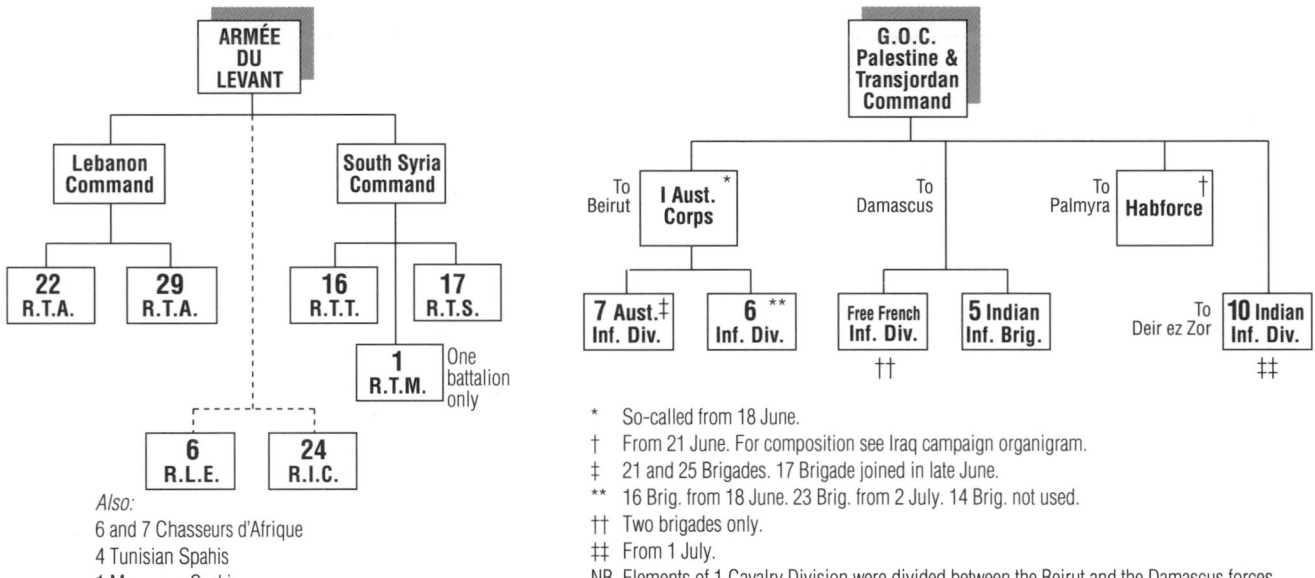

ARMÉE DU LEVANT

Lebanon Command

22 R.T.A. **29 R.T.A.**

South Syria Command

16 R.T.T. **17 R.T.S.**

1 R.T.M. One battalion only

6 R.L.E. **24 R.I.C.**

Also:
6 and 7 Chasseurs d'Afrique
4 Tunisian Spahis
1 Moroccan Spahis
8 Algerian Spahis
1, 2, 3 Compagnies Légères du Désert
Eleven batts. local levies (Troupes spéciales).

G.O.C. Palestine & Transjordan Command

To Beirut **I Aust. Corps** *

To Damascus

To Palmyra **Habforce** †

7 Aust. Inf. Div. ‡ **6 Inf. Div.** **

Free French Inf. Div. †† **5 Indian Inf. Brig.**

To Deir ez Zor **10 Indian Inf. Div.** ‡‡

* So-called from 18 June.
† From 21 June. For composition see Iraq campaign organigram.
‡ 21 and 25 Brigades. 17 Brigade joined in late June.
** 16 Brig. from 18 June. 23 Brig. from 2 July. 14 Brig. not used.
†† Two brigades only.
‡‡ From 1 July.
NB Elements of 1 Cavalry Division were divided between the Beirut and the Damascus forces.

British and Iranian Forces in the Invasion of Iran 25 August 1941

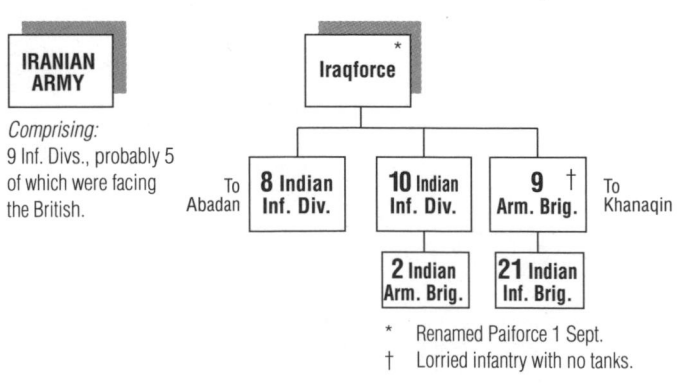

IRANIAN ARMY

Comprising:
9 Inf. Divs., probably 5 of which were facing the British.

Iraqforce *

To Abadan **8 Indian Inf. Div.** **10 Indian Inf. Div.** **9 Arm. Brig.** † To Khanaqin

2 Indian Arm. Brig. **21 Indian Inf. Brig.**

* Renamed Paiforce 1 Sept.
† Lorried infantry with no tanks.

French and British Forces for the Invasion of Madagascar 5 May 1942

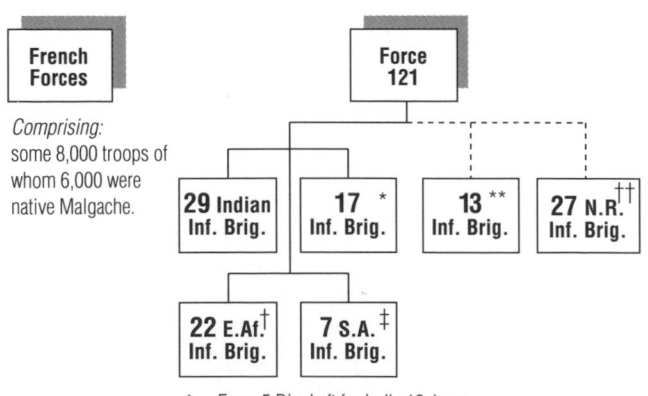

French Forces

Comprising:
some 8,000 troops of whom 6,000 were native Malgache.

Force 121

29 Indian Inf. Brig. **17 Inf. Brig.** * **13 Inf. Brig.** ** **27 N.R. Inf. Brig.** ††

22 E.Af. Inf. Brig. † **7 S.A. Inf. Brig.** ‡

* From 5 Div. Left for India 12 June.
† Replaced 17 Brig. 12 June.
‡ Arrived 24 June. Not fully committed.
** Left for India 20 May.
†† Arrived late August.

British and Axis Forces at the Battle of El Alamein 24 October 1942

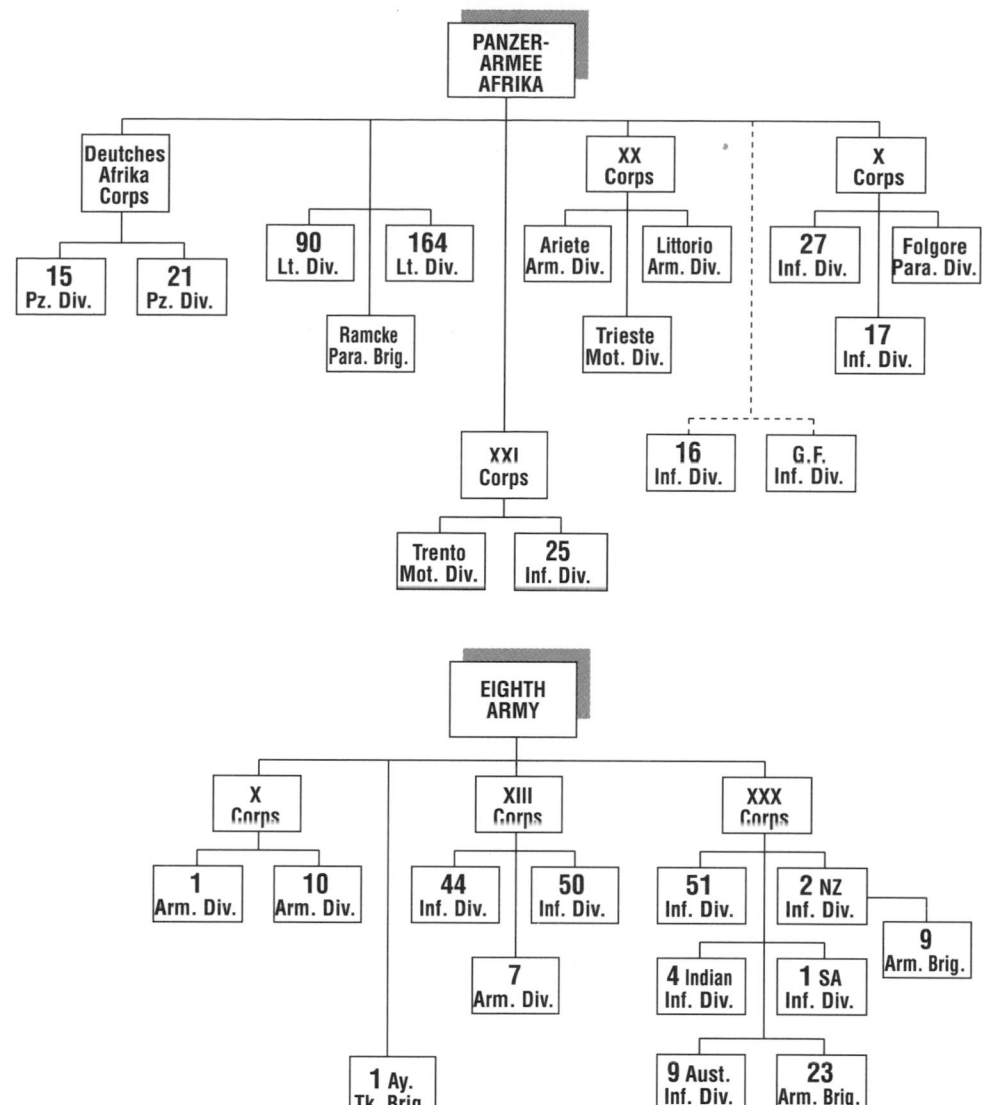

British and Axis Forces in Tunisia April 1943

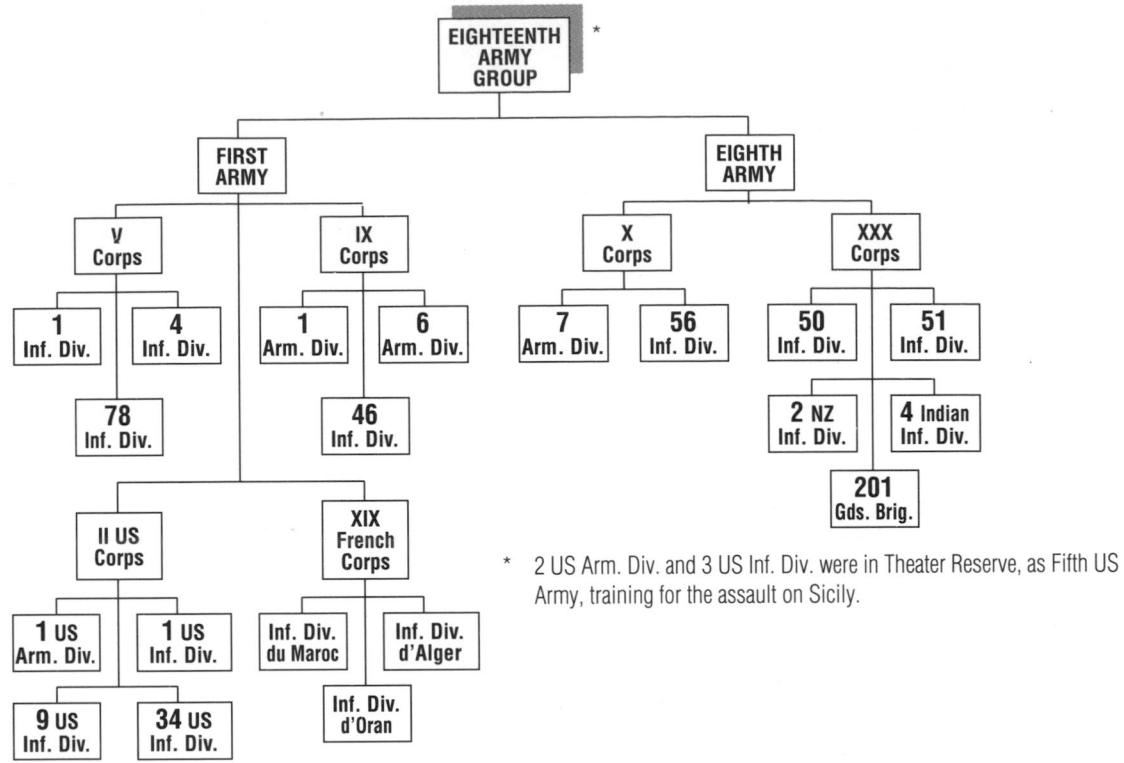

* 2 US Arm. Div. and 3 US Inf. Div. were in Theater Reserve, as Fifth US Army, training for the assault on Sicily.

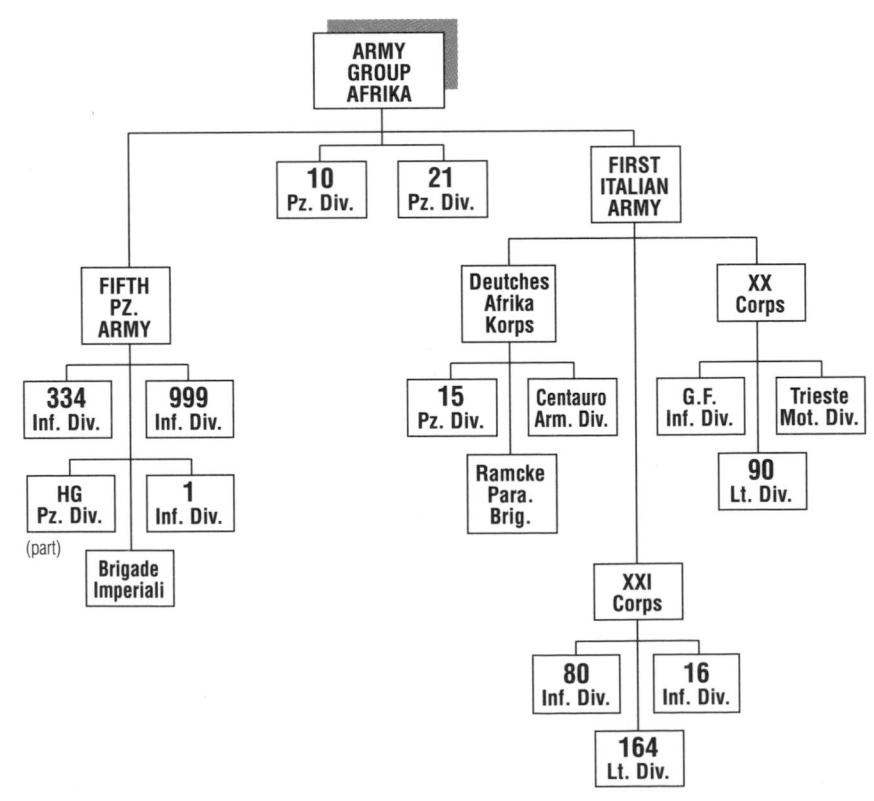

North Africa: The Ebb and Flow of Divisions*

* It should be emphasised that this chart covers only divisions in North Africa (Egypt to Tunisia) and not in the Middle East theatre as a whole. Many of the to-ings and fro-ings detailed above are in fact divisions leaving for or returning from Greece, Palestine, Syria, Iraq and Iran.

† The figure in brackets indicates the number of independent armoured brigades, in addition to the armoured divisions.

‡ Arrived as 5 Light. Changed name July.

AXIS — DEPARTED/DESTROYED						AXIS — ARRIVED						AXIS — PRESENT AT END OF MONTH								DATE	ALLIES — PRESENT AT END OF MONTH			ALLIES — ARRIVED		ALLIES — DEPARTED	
Pz G	Pz It	Mot G	Mot It	Inf G	Inf It	Pz G	Pz It	Mot G	Mot It	Inf G	Inf It	Pz G	Pz It	Mot G	Mot It	Inf G	Inf It	Tot G	Tot It		Total †	Arm †	Inf	Arm †	Inf	Arm †	Inf
												0	0	0	0	0	14	0	14	**1940** November	4	1	3	7	4 Ind. 6 Aust. 7 Aust.		
0		0		0	3	0	0	0	0	0	0	0	0	0	0	0	11	0	11	December	3	1	2	0	0	0	1
					1 Lib 2 Lib 4 B/s																						4 Ind.
0	0	0	0	0	6	0	1	0	1	0	0	0	1	0	1	0	5	0	7	**1941** January	4	2	2	1	0	0	0
					61 61 63 64 1 B/s 2 B/s		Ar.		Tre.															2			
0	0	0	0	0	0	1	0	0	0	0	0	1	1	0	1	0	5	1	7	February	4	2	2	0	0	0	0
						21 †																					
0	0	0	0	0	0	0	0	0	0	0	0	1	1	0	1	0	5	1	7	March	4	2	2	0	1	0	1
																									9 Aust.		6 Aust.
0	0	0	0	0	0	1	0	0	0	0	0	2	1	0	1	0	5	2	7	April	5	2	3	0	2	0	1
						15																			70 4 Ind.		7 Aust.
0	0	0	0	0	0	0	0	0	0	0	0	2	1	0	1	0	5	2	7	May	4 (1)	1 (1)	3	(1)	0	1	0
																								I			2
0	0	0	0	0	0	0	0	0	0	0	0	2	1	0	1	0	5	2	7	June	4 (2)	1 (2)	3	(1)	1	0	1
																								1 Ay Tk	1 SA		70
0	0	0	0	0	0	0	0	0	0	0	0	2	1	0	1	0	5	2	7	July	4 (1)	1 (1)	3	0	0	(1)	0
																											1 Ay Tk
0	0	0	0	0	0	0	0	1	1	0	0	2	1	1	2	0	5	3	8	August	5 (1)	1 (1)	4	0	1	0	0
								90Lt.	Tri.																2 SA		
0	0	0	0	0	0	0	0	0	0	0	0	2	1	1	2	0	5	3	8	September	6 (2)	1 (2)	5	(1)	1	0	0
																								32AyTk	70		
0	0	0	0	0	0	0	0	0	0	0	0	2	1	1	2	0	5	3	8	October	5 (2)	1 (2)	4	0	0	0	1
																											9 Aust.
0	0	0	0	0	0	0	0	0	0	0	0	2	1	1	2	0	5	3	8	November	7 (4)	2 (4)	5	1 (2)	1	0	0
																								1 Brigs: 7 1 AyTk	2 NZ		
0	0	0	0	0	0	0	0	0	0	0	0	2	1	1	2	0	5	3	8	December	6 (4)	2 (4)	4	0	0	0	1
																											2 NZ
0	0	0	0	0	0	0	1	0	0	0	0	2	2	1	2	0	5	3	9	**1942** January	6 (4)	2 (4)	4	0	0	0	0
							Litt.																				
0	0	0	0	0	1	0	0	0	0	0	0	2	2	1	2	0	4	3	8	February	6 (3)	2 (3)	4	0	0	(1)	0
					55																						7
0	0	0	0	0	0	0	0	0	0	0	0	2	2	1	2	0	4	3	8	March	5 (5)	2 (5)	3	(2)	0	0	1
																								9 21AyTk			70
0	0	0	0	0	0	0	0	0	0	0	0	2	2	1	2	0	4	3	8	April	6 (5)	2 (5)	4	0	1	0	0
																									5 Ind		
0	0	0	0	0	0	0	0	0	0	0	0	2	2	1	2	0	4	3	8	May	7 (5)	2 (5)	5	0	1	0	0
																									50		

DEP Pz G	DEP Pz lt	DEP Mot G	DEP Mot lt	DEP Inf G	DEP Inf lt	ARR Pz G	ARR Pz lt	ARR Mot G	ARR Mot lt	ARR Inf G	ARR Inf lt	PRES Pz G	PRES Pz lt	PRES Mot G	PRES Mot lt	PRES Inf G	PRES Inf lt	TOT G	TOT lt	DATE	Allies TOTAL†	Arm†	Inf	ARR Arm†	ARR Inf	DEP Arm†	DEP Inf
0	0	0	0	0	0	0	0	0	0	0	0	2	2	1	2	0	4	3	8	**1942** June	8 (5)	2 (5)	6	(2)	2	(2)	1
																								23 4Lt Arm	10 Ind 2 NZ	1 32AyTk	2 SA
0	0	0	0	0	0	0	0	0	0	0	2	2	2	1	2	0	6	3	10	July	10 (5)	2 (5)	8	0	3	0	1
											Fol. 16														41, 51 9 Aust		10 Ind
0	0	0	0	0	0	0	0	1	0	0	0	2	2	2	2	0	6	4	10	August	10 (5)	3 (5)	7	1	0	0	1
								164 Lt																10			5 Ind
0	0	0	0	0	1	0	0	0	0	0	0	2	2	2	2	0	5	4	9	September	10 (6)	3 (6)	7	(1)	0	0	0
					60																			24			
0	0	0	0	0	0	0	0	0	0	0	2	2	2	2	2	0	7	4	11	October	10 (5)	3 (5)	7	0	0	(1)	0
											80 Y.F.															1AyTk	
0	1	0	0	0	0	0	1	0	0	0	1	2	2	2	2	0	8	4	12	November ‡	9 (5)	2 (5)	7	(1)	0	1 (1)	0
	Litt.						Cent				1										5	1	4	1	4	0	0
																								8			10 Brigs: 9
																								6	1 US 3 US 9 US 78		
0	1	0	0	0	0	1	0	0	0	1	0	3	1	2	2	1	8	6	11	December ‡	8 (5)	2 (5)	6	0	0	0	1
	Ar.					10				334										7	3	4	2	0	0	0
																								1 US 2 US			1SA
0	0	0	1	0	4	1	0	0	0	0	0	4	1	2	1	1	4	7	6	**1943** January ‡	6 (5)	2 (5)	4	0	0	0	2
		Tre.		27 25 Fol 17		HG														9	3	6	0	2	0	0
																									34 US 46		9 Aust. 44
0	0	0	0	0	0	0	0	0	0	0	0	4	1	2	1	1	4	7	6	February	15 (5)	5 (5)	10	0	0	0	0
0	0	0	0	0	0	0	0	0	0	1	0	4	1	2	1	2	4	8	6	March	18 (5)	5 (5)	13	(1)	3	(1)	0
										999														25AyTk	1, 4, 56	24	
4	1	2	1	2	4	0	0	0	0	0	0	0	0	0	0	0	0	0	0	April/May	19 (5)	5 (5)	14	0	1	0	0
10 15 21 HG	Cent	90Lt 164Lt	Tri	334 999	80 16 1 Y.F.																				36 US		

† The figure in brackets indicates the number of independent armoured brigades, in addition to the armoured divisions.

‡ Lower line of totals gives divisions present/arriving French North Africa. Fronts joined by Feb 43.

Italy 1943-45

German Forces in Italy 3 September 1943

Allied Forces Landed in Italy 3-9 September 1943

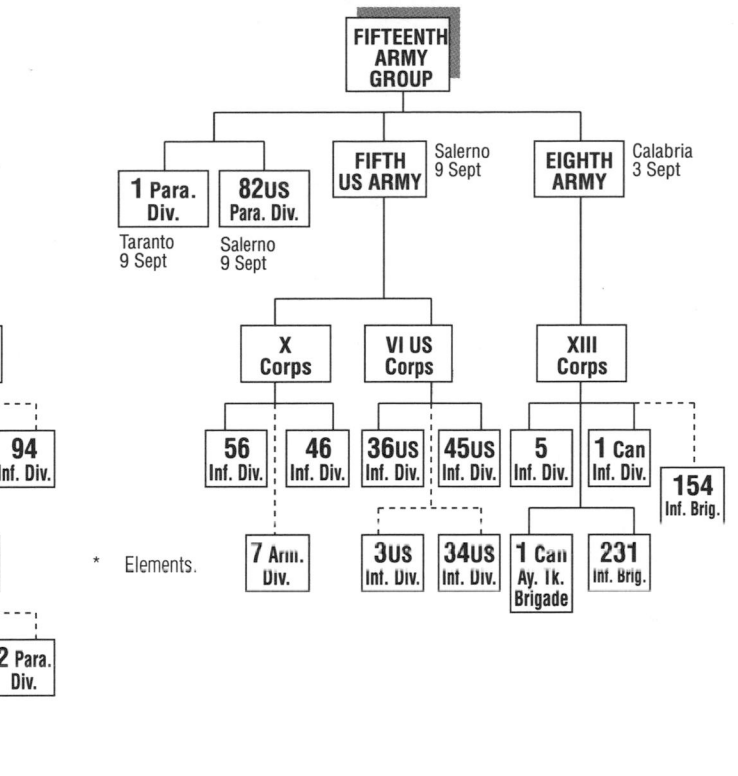

```
                                    OKW

        OB          South          North        ARMY
        SÜD    of line Pisa-Arezzo-Ancona    GROUP B

        TENTH
        ARMY

    XIV         LXXVI           IISS        LXXXVII
  Pz. Corps   Pz. Corps      Pz. Corps    Pz. Corps

  15    16    29    26    24    1SS    76    94
PG Div. Pz.Div. PG Div. Pz.Div. Pz.Div. PG Div. Inf.Div. Inf.Div.

       HG          1 Para.
     Pz. Div.       Div.

                              LI           XI Flieger-
                            Mt. Corps        korps

                          65    305      3     2 Para.
                        Inf.Div. Inf.Div. PG Div.  Div.

                              44     71
                           Inf.Div. Inf.Div.

   *  Elements.    *  16SS   4 Para. †
   †  Forming.        PG Div.  Div.
```

```
                           FIFTEENTH
                             ARMY
                             GROUP

      1 Para.   82US        FIFTH      Salerno    EIGHTH    Calabria
       Div.   Para. Div.   US ARMY     9 Sept     ARMY      3 Sept

     Taranto   Salerno
     9 Sept    9 Sept

                          X         VI US           XIII
                        Corps      Corps           Corps

                     56    46    36US   45US    5      1 Can
                   Inf.Div. Inf.Div. Inf.Div. Inf.Div. Inf.Div. Inf.Div.
                                                              154
                                                            Inf. Brig.

    *  Elements.    7 Arm.   3US    34US   1 Can    231
                     Div.  Inf.Div. Inf.Div. Ay. Tk.  Inf. Brig.
                                            Brigade
```

Allied and German Armies Before the Fourth Battle of Cassino 11 May 1944

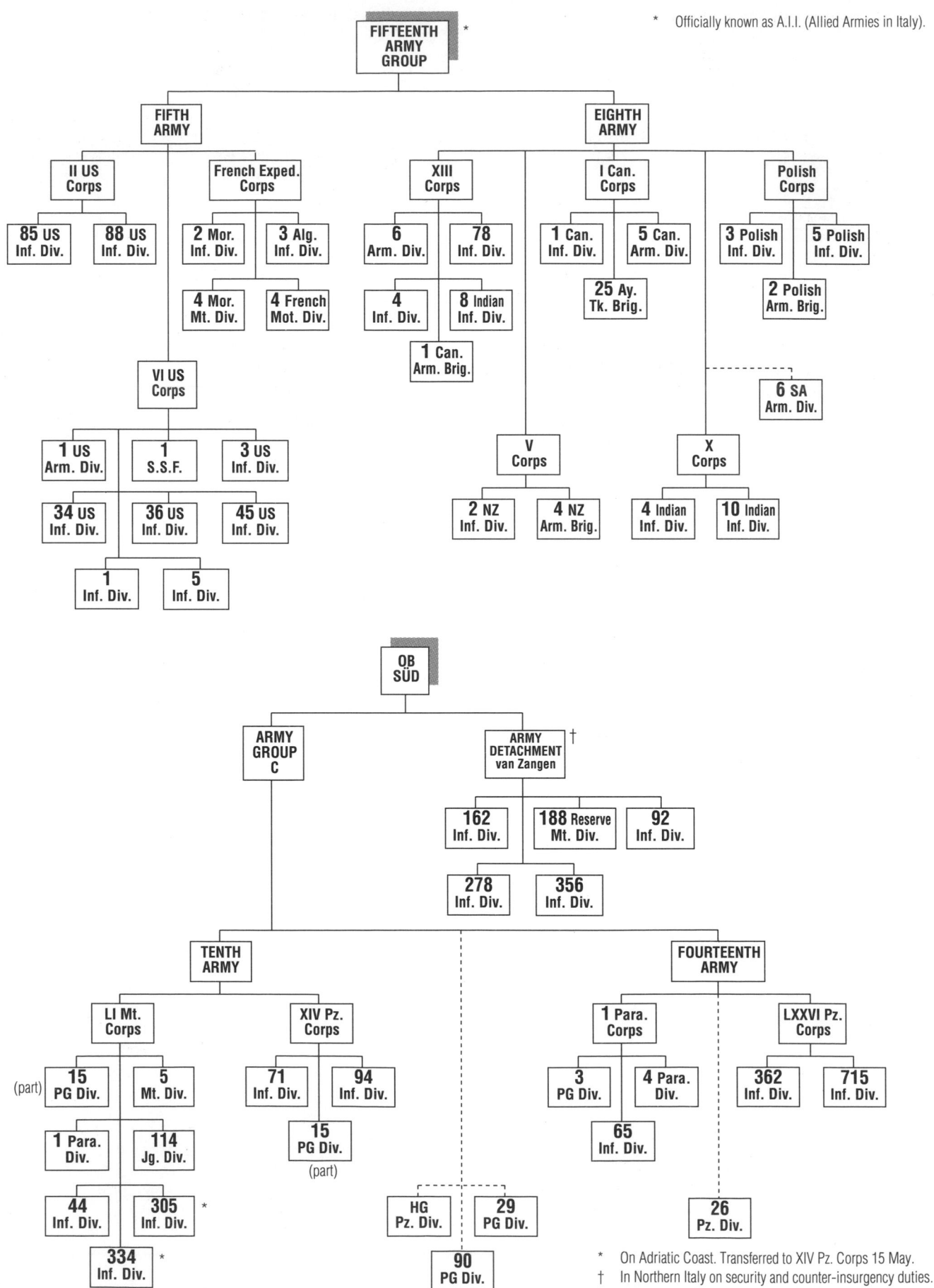

* Officially known as A.I.I. (Allied Armies in Italy).

* On Adriatic Coast. Transferred to XIV Pz. Corps 15 May.

† In Northern Italy on security and counter-insurgency duties.

Allied and German Armies in Italy 9/12 April 1945

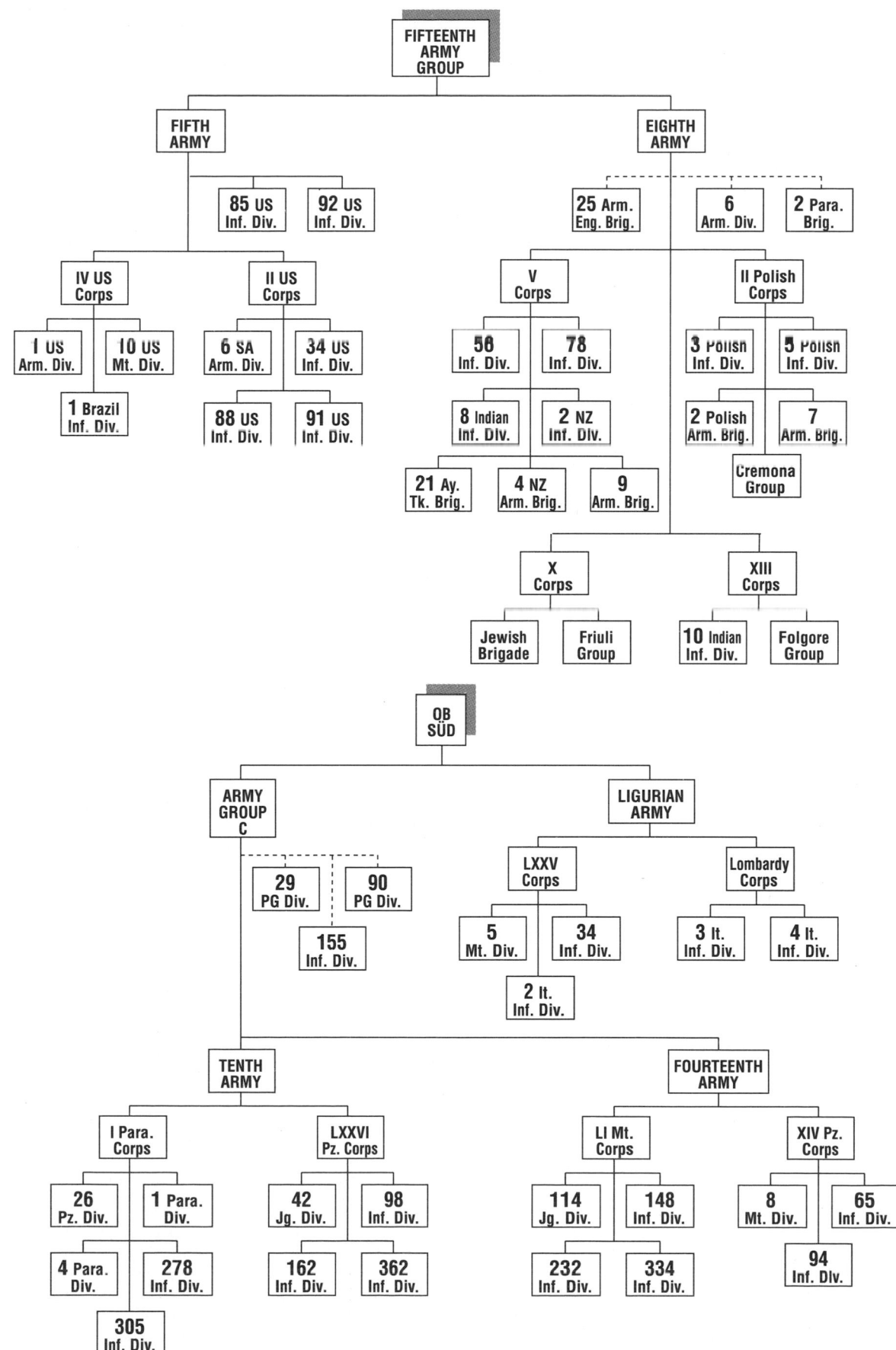

Italy: The Ebb and Flow of Divisions*

GERMANS — DEPARTED/DISBANDED Pz	Mot	Inf	ARRIVED Pz	Mot	Inf	PRESENT AT END OF MONTH Pz	Mot	Inf	TOTAL	COMBAT	DATE	ALLIES — PRESENT AT END OF MONTH TOTAL†	Arm†	Inf	ARRIVED Arm†	Inf	DEPARTED Arm†	Inf
						1	2	1	4		**1943** July ‡	11(3)	1(3)	10	1(3)	10	0	0
			HG	15PG 29PG	1 Para										2US Brigs: 4 23 1 Can	1US 3US 9US 45US 5; 50; 51; 78; 1 A/b 1 Can		
						4	5	9	18	7	September	13(3)	1(3)	12	1(3)	12	0	0
															1US Brigs: 4 23 1 Can	82US A/b 3US 34US 36US 45US 1 A/b 5; 46; 56; 78; 8 Ind 1 Can		
1	1	0	0	0	2	3	4	11	18	9	October	14(3)	2(3)	12	1	0	0	0
24	1SS PG				188 Res. Mt. 356										1US			
1	0	0	0	1	2	2	5	13	20	13	November	17(4)	3(4)	14	1(1)	2	0	0
16			90PG	5Mt 334											5 Can Brigs: 4NZ	2 NZ 2Mor		
0	1	2	0	0	0	2	4	11	17	14	December	17(4)	2(4)	15	0	3	1	2
	16SS PG	2Para 76														1 4 Ind 3 Pol	7	82US A/b 1 A/b
0	0	0	0	0	4	2	4	15	21	19	**1944** January	18(3)	2(3)	16	0	1	(1)	0
					92 114Jg 362 715											3Alg	4	
0	0	0	0	0	2	2	4	17	23	19	February	21(3)	2(3)	19	0	3	0	0
					162 278											88US 4 5Pol		
0	0	0	0	0	0	2	4	17	23	19	March	25(4)	3(4)	22	1(1)	3	0	0
															6 Brigs: 2Pol	85US 10 Ind 4MM		
0	0	0	0	0	0	2	4	17	23	19	April	25(5)	4(5)	21	1(1)	1	0	2
															6SA Brigs: 7	1Fr		46 56
0	0	0	0	0	0	2	4	17	23	21	May	26(7)	5(7)	21	1(3)	0	(1)	0
															1 Brigs: 9 21AyTk 25AyTk		23	

* Italian Gruppi that fought with the Allies not included but see Italy in Part I of this section, page 128.

† The figure in brackets indicates the number of independent armoured brigades, in addition to the armoured divisions.

‡ Divisions in Sicily only.

† The figure in brackets indicates the number of independent armoured brigades, in addition to the armoured divisions.

GERMANS											DATE	ALLIES						
DEPARTED/ DISBANDED			ARRIVED			PRESENT AT END OF MONTH						PRESENT AT END OF MONTH			ARRIVED		DEPARTED	
Pz	Mot	Inf	Pz	Mot	Inf	Pz	Mot	Inf	TOTAL	COMBAT		TOTAL†	Arm†	Inf	Arm†	Inf	Arm†	Inf
0	0	1	0	1	2	2	5	18	25	23	**1944** June	27(7)	5(7)	22	0	2	0	1
		92		16SS PG	19L/w 20L/w											91US 56		5
1	0	0	0	0	1	1	5	19	25	22	July	29(7)	5(7)	24	0	2	0	0
HG					34											46 1 Braz		
0	1	1	0	0	1	1	4	19	24	21	August	21(7)	5(7)	16	0	0	0	8
	3PG	19L/w			42Jg													3US 36US 45US 78 1Fr 2Mor 3Alg 4MM
0	1	0	0	0	2	1	3	21	25	21	September	22(7)	5(7)	17	0	1	0	0
	15PG				98 237											78		
0	0	0	0	0	2	1	3	23	27	23	October	22(7)	5(7)	17	0	1	0	1
					148 232											92US		4Ind
0	0	1	0	0	0	1	3	22	26	22	November	22(7)	5(7)	17	0	0	0	0
		44																
0	0	3	0	0	2	1	3	21	25	21	December	21(7)	5(7)	16	0	0	0	1
		71 188Res 715			155FT 710													4
0	0	2	0	0	0	1	3	19	23	19	**1945** January	20(7)	5(7)	15	0	1	0	2
		356 710														10 US Mt		1 46
0	0	0	0	0	1	1	3	20	24	20	February	21(7)	5(7)	16	0	1	0	0
					8Mt											5		
0	1	1	0	0	0	1	2	19	22	18	March	18(6)	4(6)	14	0	0	1(1)	2
	16SS PG	237															5 Can Brigs: 1 Can	5 1 Can
0	0	0	0	0	0	1	2	18	21	18	April	19(6)	4(6)	15	0	1	0	0
																46		

The Eastern Front 1941-45

German Forces for the Invasion of Russia 22 June 1941 (i) (and facing page)

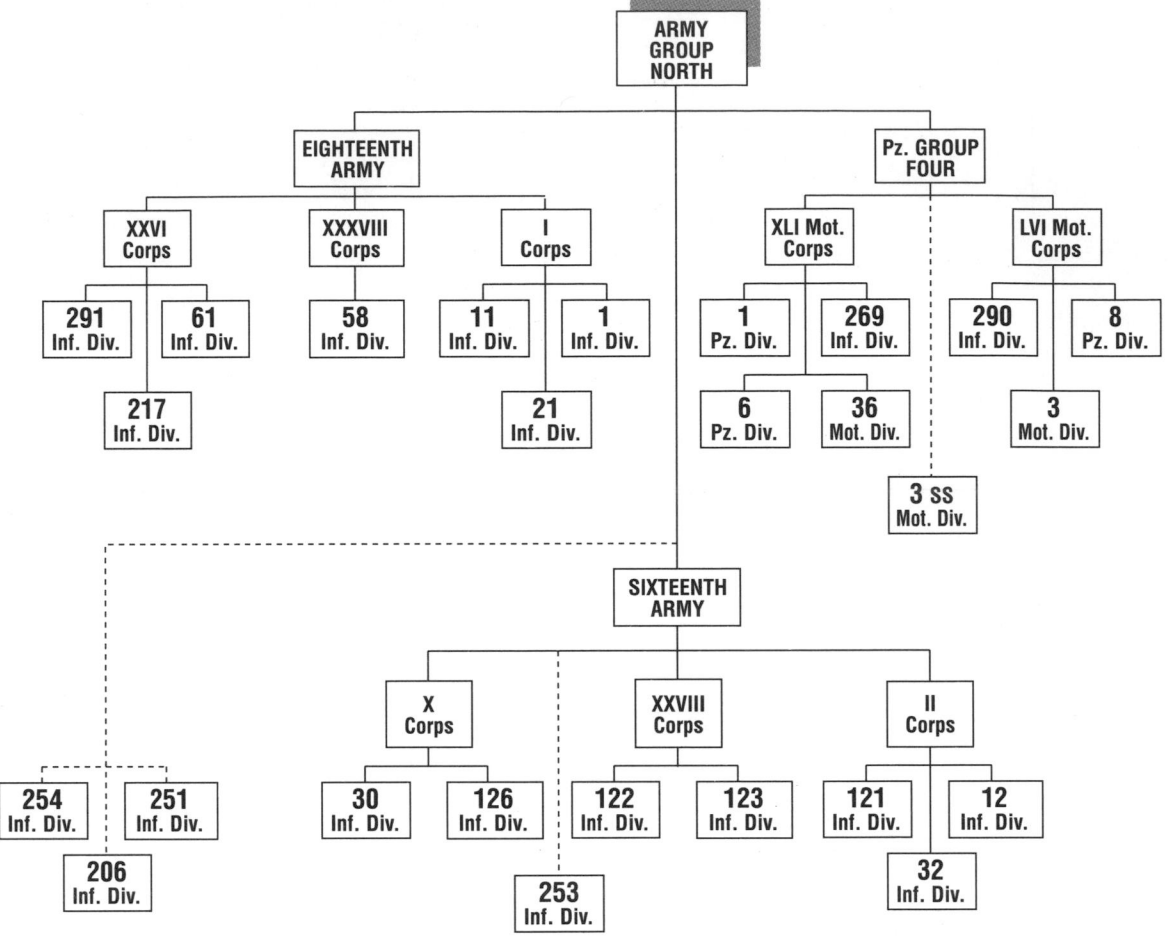

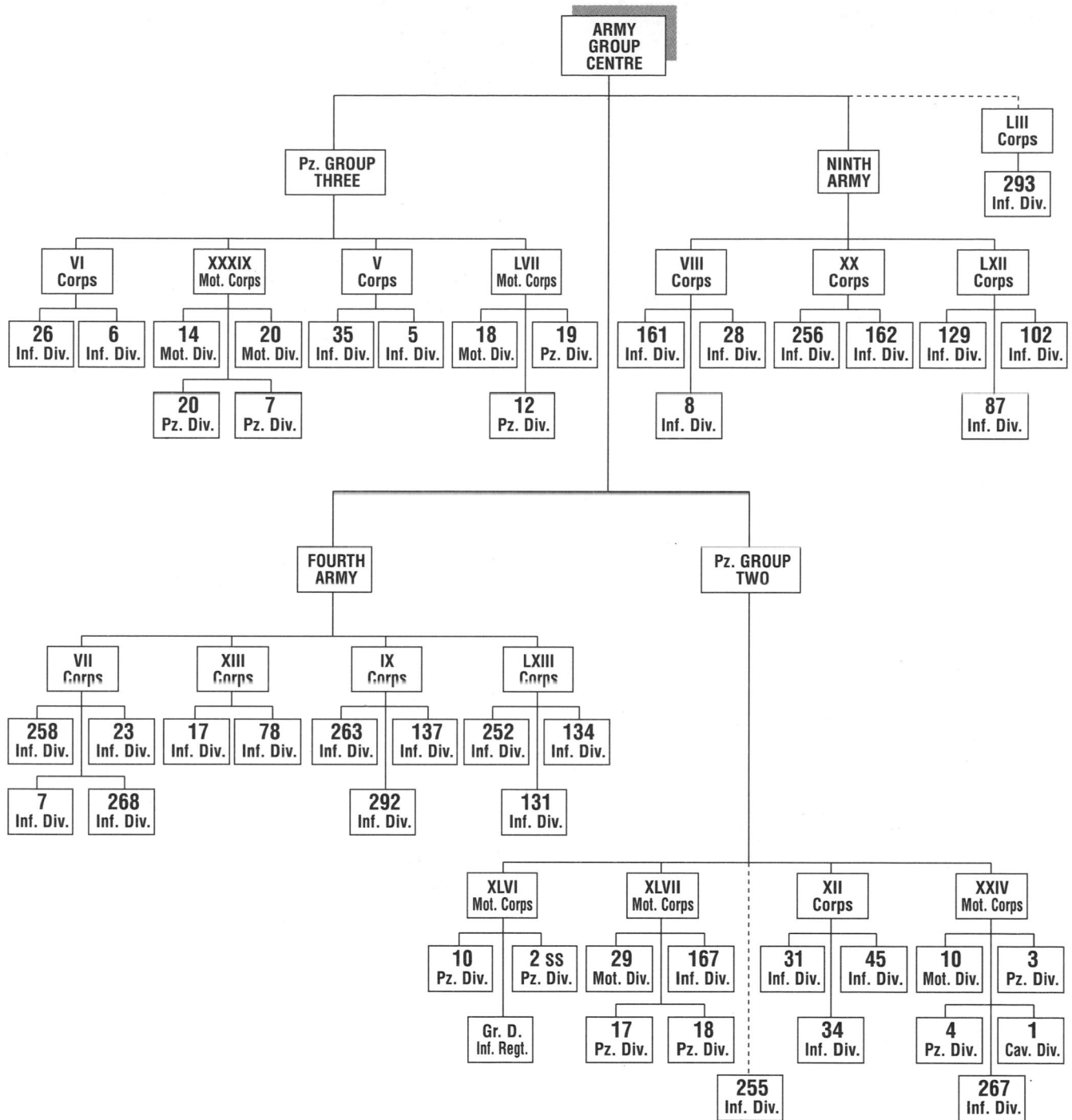

German Forces for the Invasion of Russia 22 June 1941 (ii)

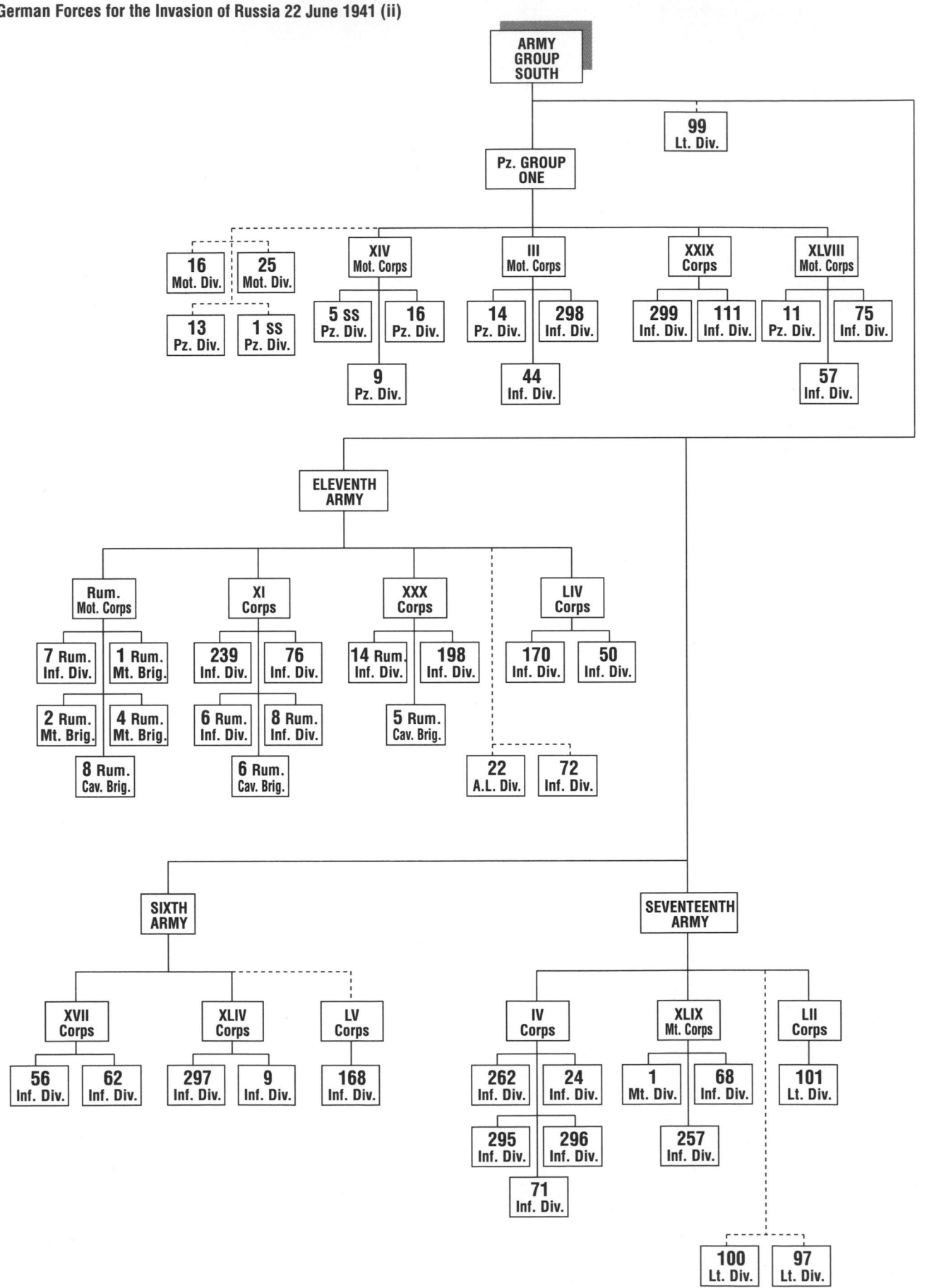

German Forces for the Invasion of Russia 22 June 1941 (iii)

The following formations, in OKH reserve, moved into Army Group sectors
on the dates specified:

Army Group North

L Corps
86 Infantry Divisions 19-26 June
4 SS Motorised Divisions 24 June-1July

Army Group Centre

XXXV Corps
52 Infantry Division 20-26 June
197 Infantry Division 20-26 June
15 Infantry Division 26 June-3 July
112 Infantry Division 25 June-1 July

XLII Corps
110 Infantry Division 21-26 June
106 Infantry Division 25 June-1 July
Lehr Motorised Brigade from 22 June

* See The German
Army in the Invasion
of Yugoslavia and
Greece, page 152.

Army Group South

XXXIV Corps
4 Mountain Division arrived by 22 June
125 Infantry Division arrived by 22 June
113 Infantry Division 23-29 June (not committed)
132 Infantry Division 28 June-4 July

LI Corps
79 Infantry Division 22-27 June
95 Infantry Division 27 June-3 July

The following divisions made up Second Army, held in OKH reserve, most of
which arrived after 4 July having travelled from the Balkans:*
2 Pz, 5 Pz, 60 Mot, 46 Inf, 73 Inf, 93 Inf, 94 Inf, 96 Inf, 98 Inf, 183 Inf, 260
Inf, 294 Inf, 707 Inf (not committed), 713 Inf (not committed).

By the end of September 1941, Fourth Rumanian Army had been reinforced
with a further twelve divisions (1, 2, 3, 8, 10, 13, 14, 15, 18, 21 Inf. Divs.
and 35 Reserve Div.) as well as 1, 7, 9 Cav. Brigs., but after the fall of
Odessa in October Fourth Army was withdrawn except for 1, 2, 10, 18 Inf.
Divs.

There were also extra formations deployed at each end of the German front.
In the south were Rumanian Third and Fourth Armies (which were in addition
to the Rumanian divisions in Army Group South) which were not at this date
under OKH control. On 22 June these Armies were organised thus:

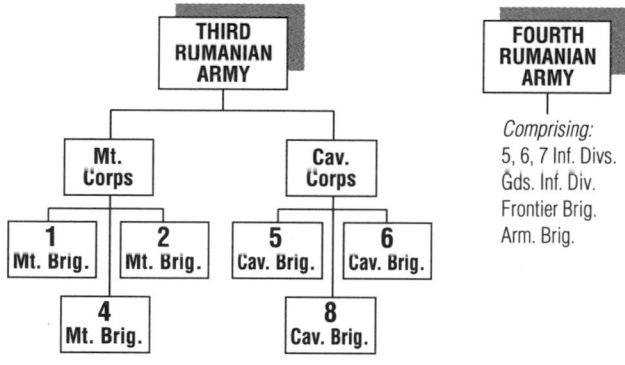

At the northern end of the front was the Finnish army together with certain
German divisions under the command of the Army of Norway. On 22 June
1941 these were deployed thus:

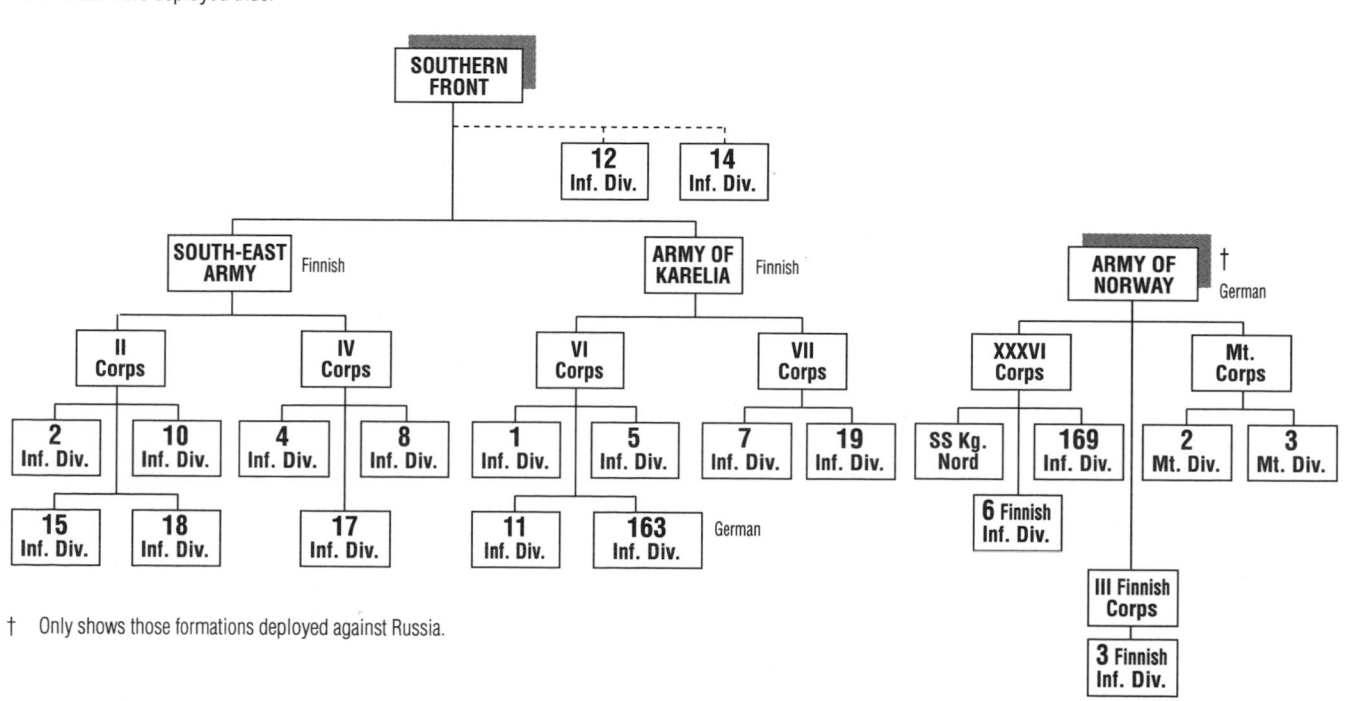

†   Only shows those formations deployed against Russia.

Russian Forces in the West 22 June 1941

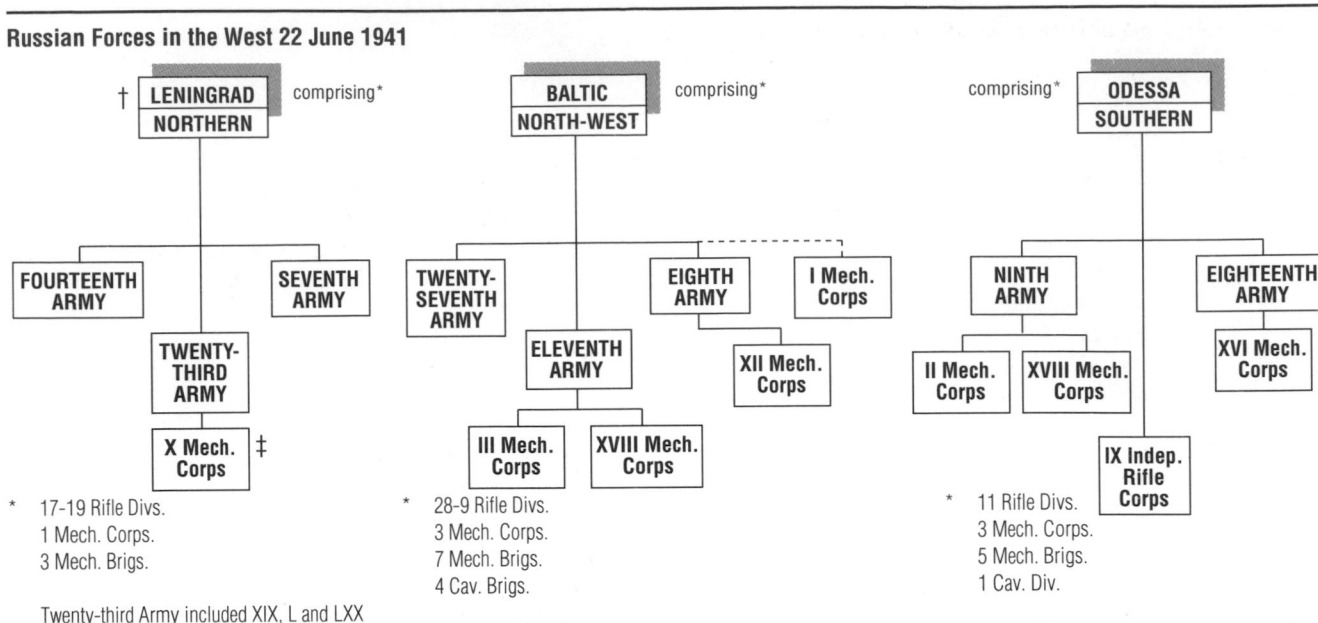

† Top name is the military district, bottom the Front HQ (Army Group) to be used in the event of hostilities.

‡ For all the Fronts except Western it has only been possible to positively identify the attached Mechanised Corps. Information on Infantry Corps and divisions is incomplete and contradictory.

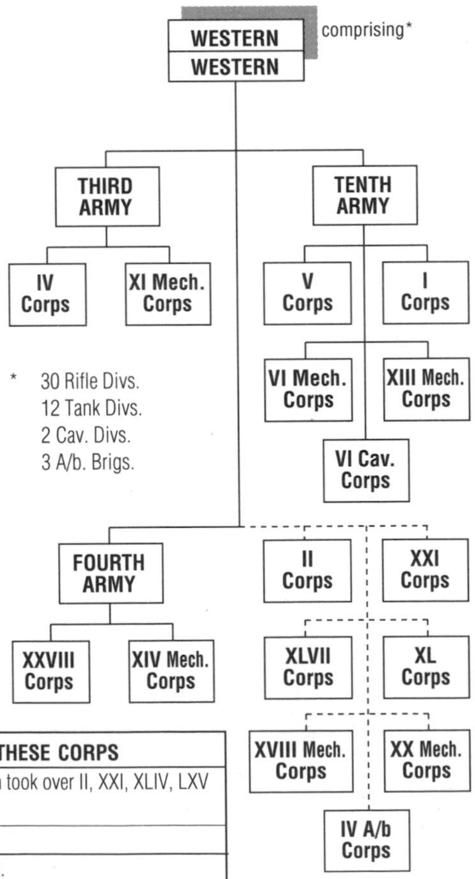

LENINGRAD / NORTHERN — comprising*
- FOURTEENTH ARMY
- SEVENTH ARMY
- TWENTY-THIRD ARMY
  - X Mech. Corps ‡

* 17-19 Rifle Divs.
1 Mech. Corps.
3 Mech. Brigs.

Twenty-third Army included XIX, L and LXX Rifle Corps.

BALTIC / NORTH-WEST — comprising*
- TWENTY-SEVENTH ARMY
- ELEVENTH ARMY
  - III Mech. Corps
  - XVIII Mech. Corps
- EIGHTH ARMY
  - XII Mech. Corps
- I Mech. Corps

* 28-9 Rifle Divs.
3 Mech. Corps.
7 Mech. Brigs.
4 Cav. Brigs.

Twenty-seventh Army included XXII, XXIV and LXI Rifle Corps.
Eighth Army included X and XI Rifle Corps.
Eleventh Army included XVI and XXIX Rifle Corps.

comprising* — **ODESSA / SOUTHERN**
- NINTH ARMY
  - II Mech. Corps
  - XVIII Mech. Corps
  - IX Indep. Rifle Corps
- EIGHTEENTH ARMY
  - XVI Mech. Corps

* 11 Rifle Divs.
3 Mech. Corps.
5 Mech. Brigs.
1 Cav. Div.

Ninth Army included XIV and XXXV Rifle, XLVIII Independent Rifle and II Cav. Corps.
Eighteenth Army included XVII Rifle Corps

WESTERN / WESTERN — comprising*
- THIRD ARMY
  - IV Corps
  - XI Mech. Corps
- TENTH ARMY
  - V Corps
    - VI Mech. Corps
  - I Corps
    - XIII Mech. Corps
  - VI Cav. Corps
- FOURTH ARMY
  - XXVIII Corps
  - XIV Mech. Corps
- II Corps
- XXI Corps
- XLVII Corps
- XL Corps
- XVIII Mech. Corps
- XX Mech. Corps
- IV A/b Corps

* 30 Rifle Divs.
12 Tank Divs.
2 Cav. Divs.
3 A/b. Brigs.

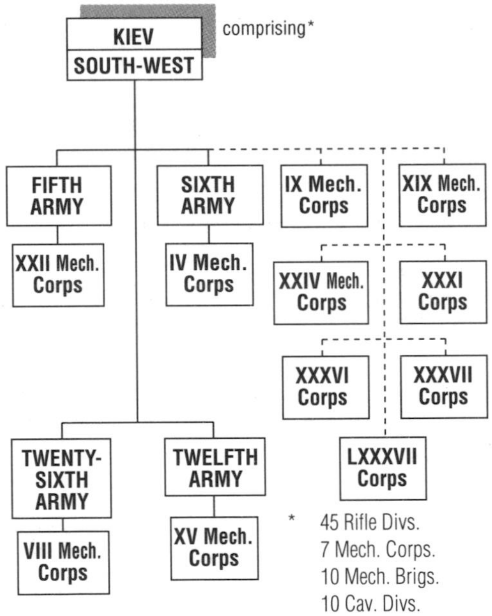

KIEV / SOUTH-WEST — comprising*
- FIFTH ARMY
  - XXII Mech. Corps
- SIXTH ARMY
  - IV Mech. Corps
- IX Mech. Corps
- XIX Mech. Corps
- XXIV Mech. Corps
- XXXI Corps
- XXXVI Corps
- XXXVII Corps
- TWENTY-SIXTH ARMY
  - VIII Mech. Corps
- TWELFTH ARMY
  - XV Mech. Corps
- LXXXVII Corps

* 45 Rifle Divs.
7 Mech. Corps.
10 Mech. Brigs.
10 Cav. Divs.

Fifth Army included XV and XXVII Rifle Corps.
Sixth Army included VI Rifle and II Cav. Corps.
Twenty-sixth Army included VIII Rifle and IV Cav. Corps.
Twelfth Army included XIII Mt. and XLIV Rifle Corps.

RESERVES

ARMY	LOCATION	INCLUDING THESE CORPS
13	Mogilev	H.Q.only. Soon took over II, XXI, XLIV, LXV Corps.
15	Birobidzhan	?
16	?	V Mech. Corps.
17	Mongolia	?
19	?	XXXIV Rifle, XXV Indep. Rifle, XXIII, XXVI Mech. Corps.
20	Orel	LXI, LXIX Rifle Corps. VII Mech. Corps.
21	Chernigov-Konitop	LXIII, LXVI Rifle Corps. XXV Mech. Corps.
22	Velikiye Luki	LI, LXII Rifle Corps.
24	Siberia	LII, LIII Rifle Corps.
28	Archangel	XXX, XXXII, XXXIII Rifle Corps.

German Forces on the Eastern Front 1 March 1945 (i)

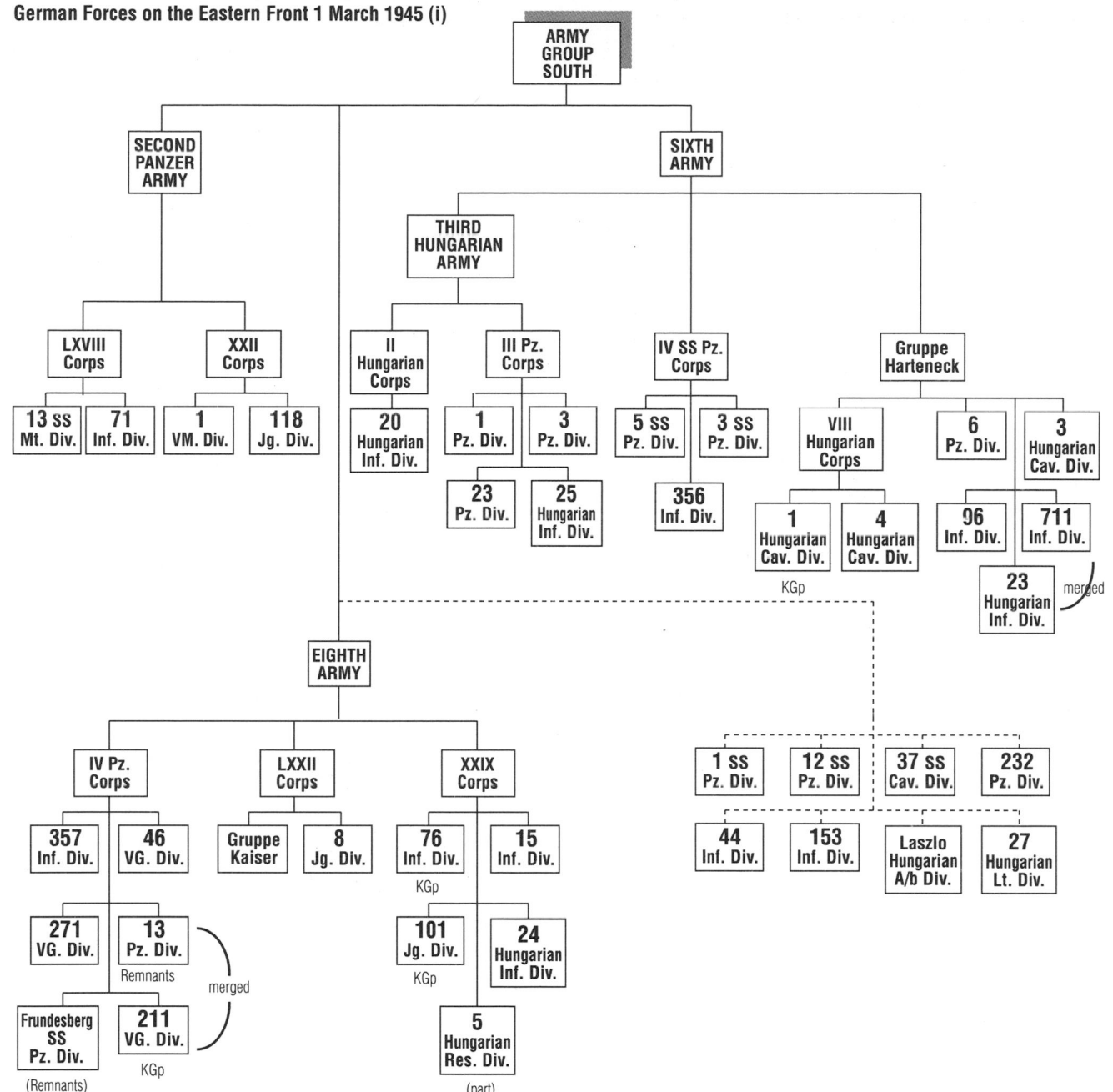

German Forces on the Eastern Front 1 March 1945 (ii)

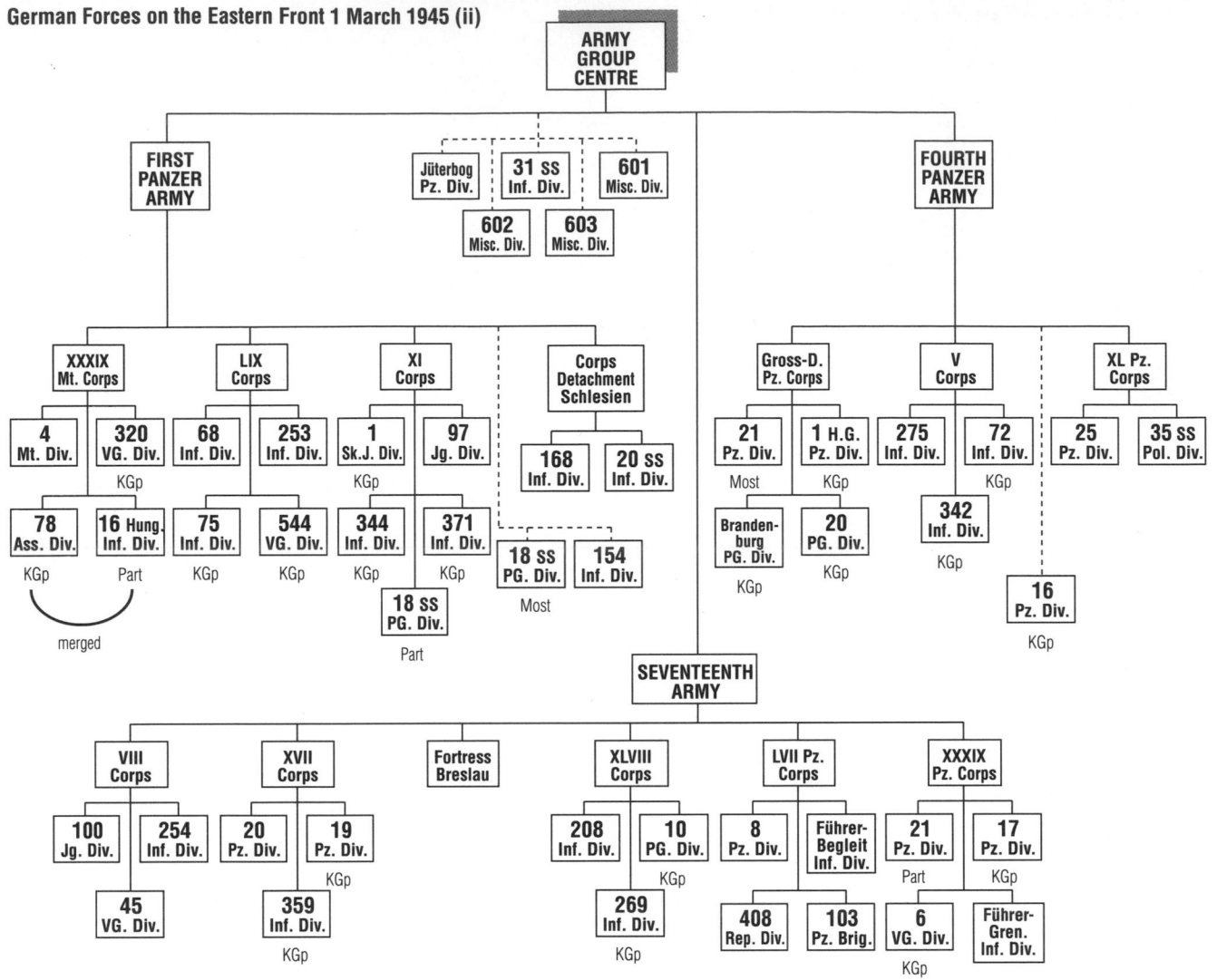

German Forces on the Eastern Front 1 March 1945 (iii)

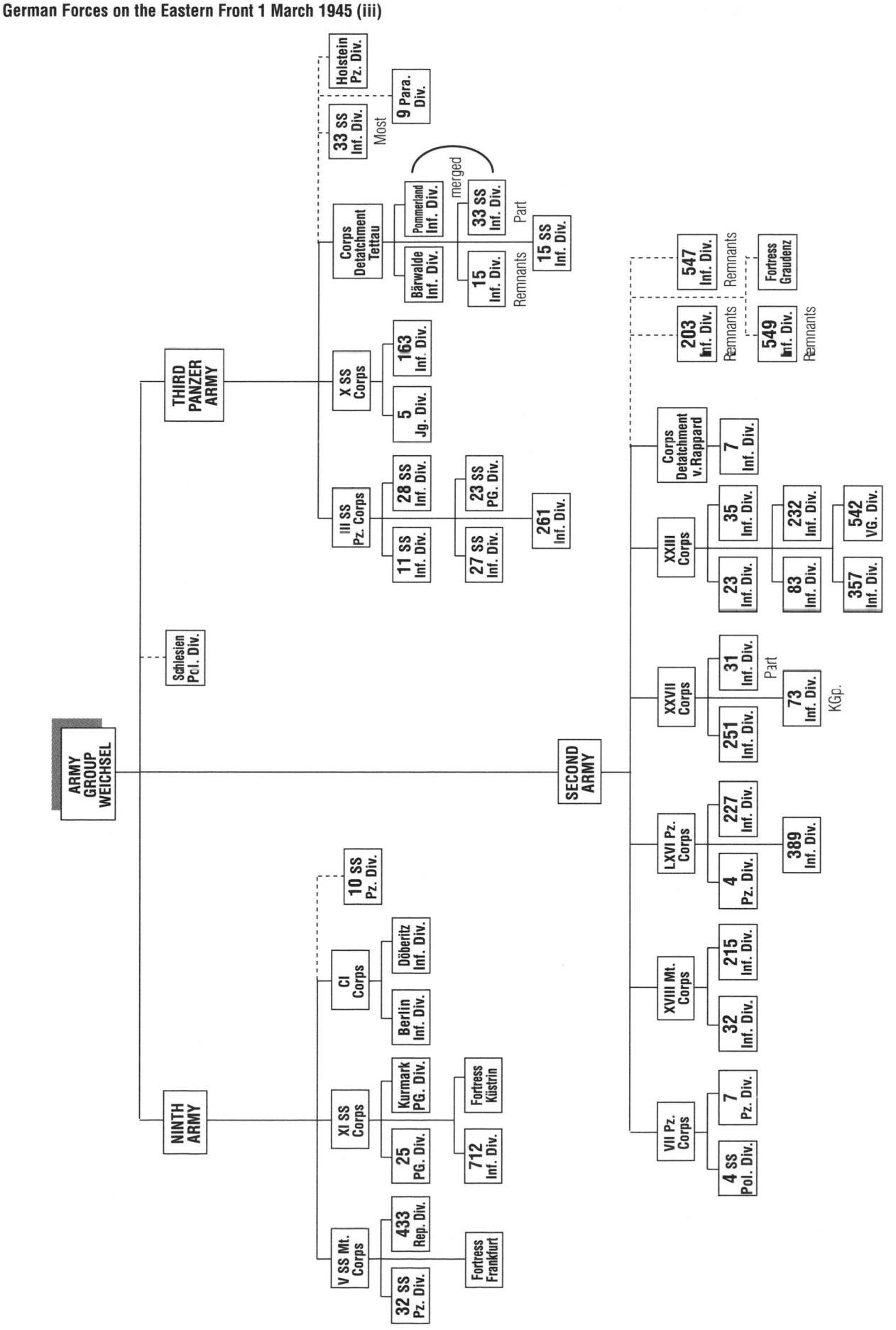

German Forces on the Eastern Front 1 March 1945 (iv)

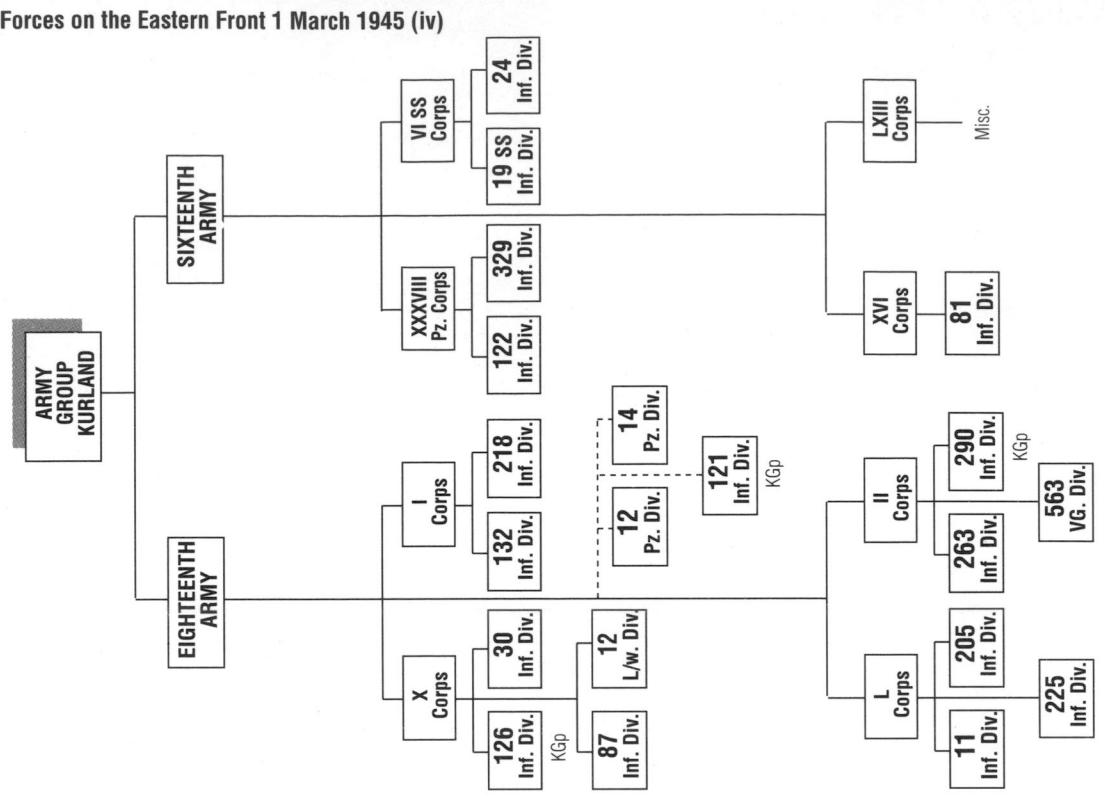

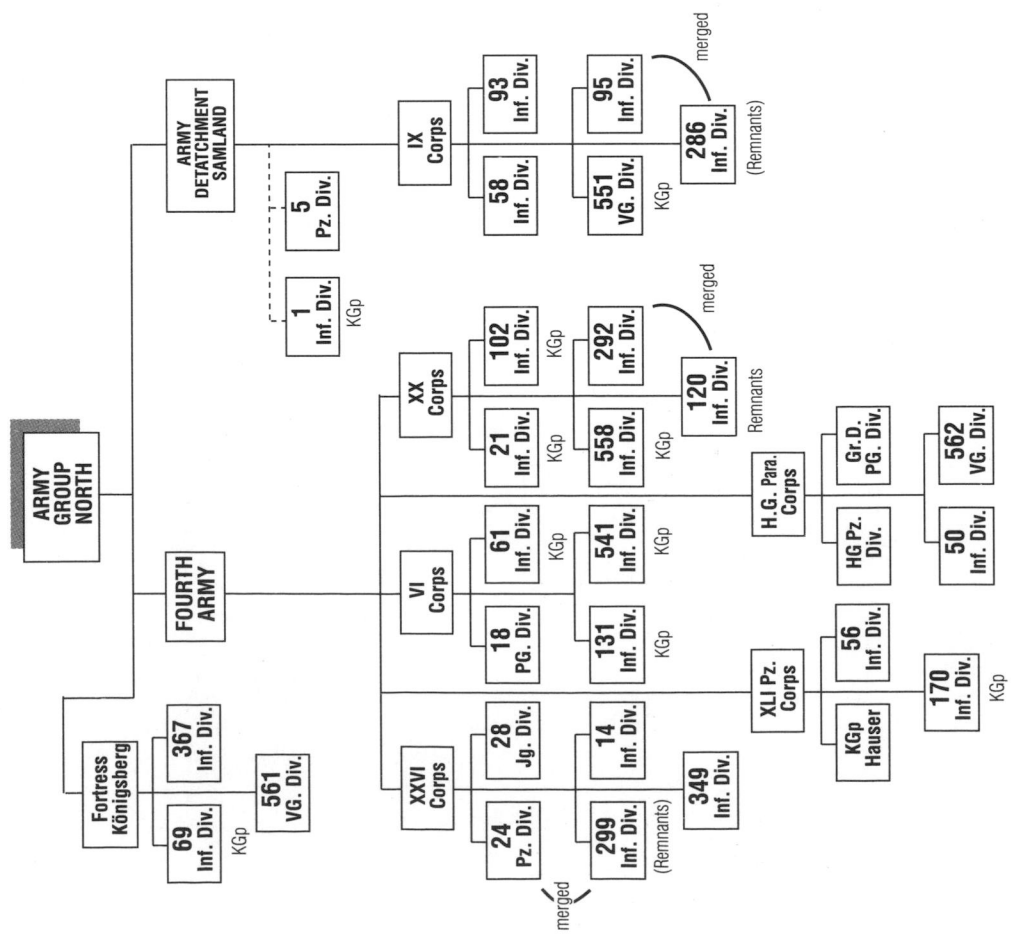

The Red Army 1 January 1945

* The relative paucity of information has made it impossible to include either Red Army or Germany's allies' divisions in this chart. For German divisions in Norway and Finland see page 169.

† Comprising 83 Infantry divisions, 4 light, 2 mountain and one air-landing. Security divisions only appear in the totals when they become involved in combat.

‡ Also present was 1 Cavalry Division but this is not included in the total until it becomes 24 Pz. Div. in February 1942.

Once again a divisional organigram of the Russian forces at this date is simply not possible and so I have had to limit myself below to a simple listing of army groups (Fronts) and their component armies. *Where known* tank and mechanised corps fighting with an army are given in brackets. Available details about the composition of the Guards tank armies are also given. The list of Fronts runs north to south as on Map 17.

Leningrad Front
    Fourteenth, Twenty-third and Thirty-second Armies.
2 Baltic Front
    First Shock, Eighth, Twenty-second and Forty-second Armies.
1 Baltic Front
    Fourth Shock, Sixth Guards, Forty-third, Fifty-first and Sixty-first (I Guards Tank) Armies.
3 Byelorussian Front
    Second Guards, Fifth, Eleventh Guards (II Guards Independent Tank), Twentieth, Thirty-first and Thirty-ninth Armies.
2 Byelorussian Front
    Second Shock, Third, Fifth Guards Tank (VIII Guards Tank, VIII Mechanised, XXIX Tank), Forty-eighth, Forty-ninth, Fiftieth, Sixty-fifth and Seventieth Armies.
1 Byelorussian Front
    First Polish, First Guards Tank (VIII Guards Mechanised, XI Guards Tank), Third Shock, Fifth Shock (II Mechanised), Eighth Guards, Thirty-third, Forty-seventh and Sixty-ninth Armies.
1 Ukrainian Front
    Third Guards (XXV Tank), Fourth Guards Tank (VI Guards Mechanised, X Guards Tank), Fifth Guards (XXXI Independent Tank), Sixth, Thirteenth, Twenty-first, Fifty-second, Fifty-ninth (IV Guards Tank), and Sixtieth Armies.
4 Ukrainian Front
    First Guards, Eighteenth and Thirty-eighth Armies.
2 Ukrainian Front
    Sixth Guards Tank (V Guards Tank, VII Mechanised, IX Guards Mechanised), Seventh Guards (IV Guards Mechanised), Twenty-seventh, Fortieth, Forty-sixth (II Guards Mechanised), and Fifty-third Armies.
3 Ukrainian Front
    Fourth Guards, Twenty-sixth, Thirty-seventh and Fifty-seventh Armies.

IN IRAN
    Forty-fifth Army.

IN THE CRIMEA
    Independent Coastal Army.

IN THE FAR EAST
    First Special Red Banner, Second Independent Red Banner, Sixteenth, Seventeenth and Thirty-second Armies.

IN SUPREME COMMAND RESERVE
    Nineteenth Army.

BEING FORMED
    Ninth Guards Army (from Independent Airborne Army).

UNACCOUNTED FOR
    Tenth Guards and Sixty-seventh Armies.

Eastern Front: The Ebb and Flow of German Divisions*

GERMANY										DATE
DEPARTED/ DESTROYED			ARRIVED			PRESENT AT END OF MONTH				
Pz	Mot	Inf	Pz	Mot	Inf	Pz	Mot	Inf	TOTAL	
						17	14	90†	121‡	**1941** June
0	0	0	2	1	12	19	15	102	136	July
			2, 5	60	15; 46 73; 93 94; 95 96; 98 132; 183 260; 294					
0	0	0	0	0	0	19	15	102	136	August
0	0	1	0	0	2	19	15	103	137	September
	228				250 339					
0	0	0	0	0	1	19	15	104	138	October
					5 Mt.					
0	0	1	0	0	0	19	15	103	137	November
	239									
0	0	0	0	0	3	19	15	106	140	December
					81, 216 223					
0	0	0	0	0	9	19	15	115	149	**1942** January
					208; 211 212; 215 221 Sec. 225; 227 246 281 Sec.					
0	0	0	0	0	8	19	15	123	157	February
					5Jg; 8Jg 88; 205 218; 330 331; 342					
0	0	0	2	0	4	21	15	127	163	March
			22, 23		8Lt;28Jg 328; 329					
1	0	1	0	0	0	20	15	126	161	April
10		162								
1	0	3	0	0	6	19	15	129	163	May
6		15; 106 167			82; 113 305; 323 336; 384					
0	0	1	1	1	7	20	16	135	171	June
		17	24	GD	340; 370 377; 383 385; 387 389					
1	1	2	0	0	2	19	15	135	169	July
7	2SS	22, 23			371; 376					
0	0	1	0	0	0	19	15	134	168	August
		257								
0	0	0	1	0	1	20	15	135	170	September
				27	3Mt.					
0	1	0	0	0	4	20	14	139	173	October
	3SS				1 L/w 2 L/w 3 L/w 4 L/w					
0	0	1	0	0	1	20	14	139	173	November
	161				337					
1	0	1	2	0	4	21	14	142	177	December
22		269	6, 7		304; 306 321; 5Lw					

GERMANY (left table)

DEPARTED/DESTROYED Pz	Mot	Inf	ARRIVED Pz	Mot	Inf	PRESENT Pz	Mot	Inf	TOTAL	DATE
2	0	1	0	1	8	19	15	149	183	**1943** January
1, 27		328		2 SS	302; 6 L/w; 7 L/w; 8 L/w; 9 L/w; 10 L/w; 15 L/w; 21 L/w					
3	3	16	0	3	7	16	15	140	171	February
14, 16, 24	3, 29, 60	44;71 76;79 94 100 Jg 113;295 297;298 305;371 376;384 385;389	1SS 3SS 4SS		15;17 23;161 320;332 13 L/w					
0	0	2	0	0	5	16	15	143	174	March
		1Mt. 8 L/w			167;327 333;335 12 L/w					
0	0	1	0	0	4	16	15	146	177	April
		328			39;106 257;282					
0	1	1	0	0	1	16	14	146	176	May
	4SS	7 L/w			79					
0	0	0	0	0	1	16	14	147	177	June
					328					
0	2	0	0	1	3	16	13	150	179	July
	14★ 36			3	14;36 707					
0	1	1	0	0	2	16	12	151	179	August
	1SS	79			113;355					
0	0	0	0	0	0	16	12	151	179	September
0	3	4	6	0	3	22	9	150	181	October
	2SS† 3SS 5SS	52;162 268;330	1SS;2SS† 3SS;5SS 24;25		389 708 213 Sec.					
1	0	3	3	1	4	24	10	151	185	November
18		5 Mt. 262 15 L/w	1, 14, 16	11SS	15SS 76;376 203 Sec.					
0	1	13	0	0	2	24	9	140	173	December
	4SS	39;38 137;216 217;223 255;293 321;323 327;328 333			2 Para. 384					
1	0	3	0	1	2	23	10	139	172	**1944** January
2		250 2 L/w 3 L/w		23SS	371 1Ski-J					
0	0	8	0	0	3	23	10	134	167	February
		123;167 389;708 1 L/w;9 L/w 10 L/w 13 L/w			20SS 153Gren. 214					
3	1	3	3	0	9	23	9	140	172	March
9 1SS 2SS	16‡	332;112 387	9SS 10SS 116‡		14SS 19SS 100Jg 154 Res 174 Res 361;357 359;367					
1	0	4	0	1	1	22	10	137	169	April
25		125;331 377;5Lw		8SS	349					

GERMANY (right table)

DEPARTED/DESTROYED Pz	Mot	Inf	ARRIVED Pz	Mot	Inf	PRESENT Pz	Mot	Inf	TOTAL	DATE
1	1	6	0	0	3	21	9	134	164	May
5SS	36	82;98 111;161 198;336			36;52 217VG					
3	0	1	0	0	0	18	9	133	160	June
11 9SS 10SS		339								
0	1	34	2	0	9	20	8	108	136	July
	18	6;12 14SS 31;34 35;36 45;56 57;78 85;95 110;134 183;197 206;221 246;251 256;260 267;296 299;337 340;349 361;383 707;4 L/w 6 L/w	HG 5SS		196 541VG 542VG 45VG 56VG 299VG 563VG 552VG 286 Sec.					
0	0	13	0	1	10	20	9	105	134	August
		9;79VG 258;282 294;302 306;320 335;355 370;376 384		18SS	6VG 544VG 545VG 547VG 548VG 549VG 551VG 558VG 561VG 562VG					
0	0	7	1	1	5	21	10	103	134	September
		26;62 129;196 212;257 384	25	4SS	31VG 78 251VG 337VG 349VG					
0	0	0	0	1	3	21	11	106	138	October
				22SS	35VG 95VG 389					
0	0	0	0	0	1	21	11	107	139	November
					182 Res					
0	1	4	0	3	4	21	13	107	141	December
	25	211 217VG 281 Sec. 337VG		Bran 34SS 18	71 271VG 299VG 711					
0	0	1	4	0	10	25	13	116	154	**1945** January
		214	2SS 12SS 21 Kurmark		118Jg 211VG 269VG 320VG 344VG 356;402 433RDS 712;715					
0	0	1	3	1	16•	28	14	131	173	February
		291	1SS 9SS 232	25	1Mt 7SS Mt 13SS Mt 21SS Mt 104Jg 117Jg 22AL 44;181 297;369 373;392 438zbV 11 L/w 41Fort					

* 14 and 36 Mot Divs became 14 and 36 Inf Divs.

† 2, 3 and 5SS Mot Divs became Pz Divs. 1SS arrived from Italy as a Pz Div.

‡ 16 PG. became 116 Pz Div.

• All but one of the mountain divisions were formations in Greece and the Balkans which now linked up with the Eastern Front Forces.

GERMANY										DATE
DEPARTED/ DESTROYED			ARRIVED			PRESENT AT END OF MONTH				
Pz	Mot	Inf	Pz	Mot	Inf	Pz	Mot	Inf	TOTAL	
0	0	2	4	1	3	32	15	132	179	**1945** March
		93 367	10SS Holstein Münch Jüterbog	16SS	9 Para 10 Para 1 Mar					
0	0	1	0	0	3	32	15	134	181	April
		88			9 Mt 14SS 48VG					

German Divisions in Norway and Finland

At the northern end of the Eastern front the Germans maintained several divisions in Norway and Finland, some of the latter being involved in combat with the Russians. These troops were commanded by various headquarters including 21 Armeegruppe, Army of Norway, Army of Lappland, Twentieth Mountain Army, and for a while at the end of 1942 formed part of Army Group North. The divisions concerned are detailed below. Those that saw combat against the Russians in Finland are marked with an asterisk.

25 Pz
Norway occupation May 42-Aug 43. Understrength.

Pz Div 'Norway'
Norway occupation Oct 43-May 45. Less than 50 tanks.

2 Mt*
Invasion of Norway April-June 40. Combat Finland June 41-Jan 45.

3 Mt*
Invasion of Norway April-June 40. Combat Finland June 41-Aug 42.

5 Mt
Norway occupation Sept 41-Jan 42.

6 Mt*
Combat Finland Oct 41-Jan 45. Norway occupation Jan-May 45.

6SS Mt*
Combat Finland June 41-Oct 44.

7 Mt*
Combat Finland May 42-Jan 45. Norway occupation Jan-May 45.

69 Inf
Invasion of Norway April-June 40. Norway occupation June 40-April 43.

163 Inf*
Invasion of Norway April-June 40. Norway occupation June 40-June 41. Combat Finland June 41-Jan 45.

169 Inf*
Combat Finland June 41-Jan 45. Norway training Jan-May 45.

181 Inf
Invasion of Norway April-June 40. Norway occupation June 40-Oct 43.

196 Inf
Invasion of Norway April-June 40. Norway occupation June 40-July 43.

199 Inf
Norway occupation Nov 40-May 45.

210 Inf
Norway coastal defence June 42-Dec(?) 42. Finland Jan(?) 43-Jan 45. Little combat. Norway coastal defence Jan-May 45.

214 Inf
Invasion of Norway April-June 40. Norway occupation June 40-Feb 44.

230 Inf
Norway coastal defence April 42-May 45.

269 Inf
Norway occupation Dec 42-Oct 44.

270 Inf
Norway occupation June 42-May 44. Finland May-Oct 44. No combat. Norway occupation Oct 44-May 45.

274 Inf
Norway occupation July 43-May 45.

280 Inf
Norway coastal defence April 42-May 45.

295 Inf
Norway occupation Nov 43-May 45.

560VG
Norway being formed Aug-Dec 44.

702 Inf
Norway occupation May 41-May 45.

710 Inf
Norway occupation May 41-Dec 44.

14 L/w Fld
Norway occupation Jan 43-May 45. (Two months in Denmark mid-44.)

German Divisions in the Aegean and the Balkans

The other significant German commitment in the east was in the Aegean and the Balkans and this theatre did in fact link up with the Eastern Front proper in February 1945. Divisions that served in this theatre are listed below but it should be noted that the list does *not* include formations involved in the invasion of Greece and Yugoslavia in April 1940 as most of these were soon diverted to Russia. (These divisions can, however, be identified in the relevant Orders of Battle (Campaigns) organigram on page 152).

1 Pz
Greece May-Nov 43.

1 Coss Cav
Yugoslavia Oct 43-Jan 45.

1 Mt
Greece and Yugoslavia March 43-Feb 45.

5 Mt
Crete May-Sept 41.

6 Mt
Greece April-Oct 41.

7SS Mt
Yugoslavia May 42-Feb 45.

13SS Mt
Yugoslavia Feb-Oct 44.

21SS Mt
Yugoslavia Sept-Nov 44.

11SS PG
Yugoslavia Oct 43-Jan 44.

42 Jg
Yugoslavia Oct 42-March 44 and May-Aug 44.

100 Jg
Yugoslavia May-July 43. Albania Aug 43-March 44.

104 Jg
Yugoslavia May 41-June 43. Greece June 43-Oct 44. Yugoslavia Oct 44-Feb 45.

114 Jg
Yugoslavia July 41-Dec 43.

117 Jg
Yugoslavia May 41-May 43. Greece May 43-Sept 44. Yugoslavia Sept 44-Feb 45.

118 Jg
Yugoslavia May 41-Feb 45.

4SS Pol
Greece June-Sept 44. Yugoslavia Sept -Nov 44.

22 Air Lan
Crete Aug 42-Nov 44. Greece and Yugoslavia Nov 44-Feb 45.

31SS Gren
Balkans Sept-Nov 44.

41 Fort
Greece May 41-Sept 44. Yugoslavia Oct 44-Feb 45.

113 Inf
   Yugoslavia Jan-April 42.
133 Fort
   See 713 Inf Div below.
164 Inf
   Greece April 41-Aug 42.
173 Res
   Yugoslavia Sept 43-Jan 44.
181 Inf
   Yugoslavia Oct 43-Feb 45.
187 Res
   Became 42 Jg March 44. See that entry above.
264 Inf
   Yugoslavia Oct 43-Feb 45.
277 Inf
   Yugoslavia Dec 43-Jan 44.
297 Inf
   Yugoslavia June-Sept 43. Albania Sept 43-Oct 44. Yugoslavia Oct 44-Feb 45.
342 Inf
   Yugoslavia Oct 41-Feb 42.
367 Inf
   Yugoslavia Dec 43-March 44.

369 Inf
   Yugoslavia Jan 43-Feb 45.
371 Inf
   Yugoslavia Nov 43-Jan 44.
373 Inf
   Yugoslavia Feb 43-Feb 45.
392 Inf
   Yugoslavia Jan 44-Feb 45.
704 Inf
   Became 104 Jg April 43. See that entry above.
713 Inf
   Greece Sept 41-Jan 42. Became Fortress Div. Crete Jan 42. Crete Jan 42-Dec 44. Converted to 133 Fort Jan 44.
714 Inf
   Became 114 Jg April 43. See that entry above.
717 Inf
   Became 117 Jg April 43. See that entry above.
718 Inf
   Became 118 Jg April 43. See that entry above.
11 L/w Fld
   Greece March 43-Sept 44. Yugoslavia Oct 44-Feb 45.
Fortress or Sturm Div. Rhodes
   Rhodes Sept 43-?

German Allies

Details on Allied divisions on the Eastern Front have already been given under the various country headings in Orders of Battle: Combat Divisions, as well as in the preceding Eastern Front organigrams. Supplementary information is provided below showing the number and nationality of the various Allied divisions at selected dates and an organigram for Army Group B on 15 Nov 42, which contained probably the greatest concentration of non-German divisions throughout the whole war.

Number of Allied Divisions Fighting with the Germans on the Eastern Front June 1941-March 1945

DATE	NUMBER OF DIVISIONS*								
	RUMANIA	HUNGARY	ITALY	SLOVAKIA	SPAIN	FINLAND	TOTAL ALLIED	GERMAN	% OF ALLIED DIVISIONS
22 June 1941	9(13)	—	—	(1)	—	16	25(14)	121	20.9
3 Sept 1941	11(9)	(3)	3	2	1	16	33(12)	137	22.2
2 Jan 1942	4(6)	3	3	2	1	16	29(6)	149	17.7
24 June 1942	13†	9	3(1)	1	1	16	43(1)	171	20.5
15 Nov 1942‡	27	12	10(3)	1	1	16	67(3)	173	28.5‡
9 April 1943	10	5	—	1	1	16	33	177	15.7
26 Dec 1943	9	9	—	1	1	16	36	173	17.2
16 Sept 1944	—	19(4)	—	—	—	—	19(4)	134	13.5
26 Nov 1944	—	15(3)	—	—	—	—	15(3)	139	10.9
1 March 1945	—	11	—	—	—	—	11	179	5.8

* The numbers in brackets are the extra brigades. These are deemed to be half a division in the computation for the last column.

† Rumanian brigades later formed into divisions though they remained the same size. They are counted as divisions in the computation for the last column.

‡ On this date Allied divisions made up 47.7 per cent of Army Group B's divisional strength.

Preponderance of Allied Divisions in Army Group B on the Eastern Front 15 November 1942

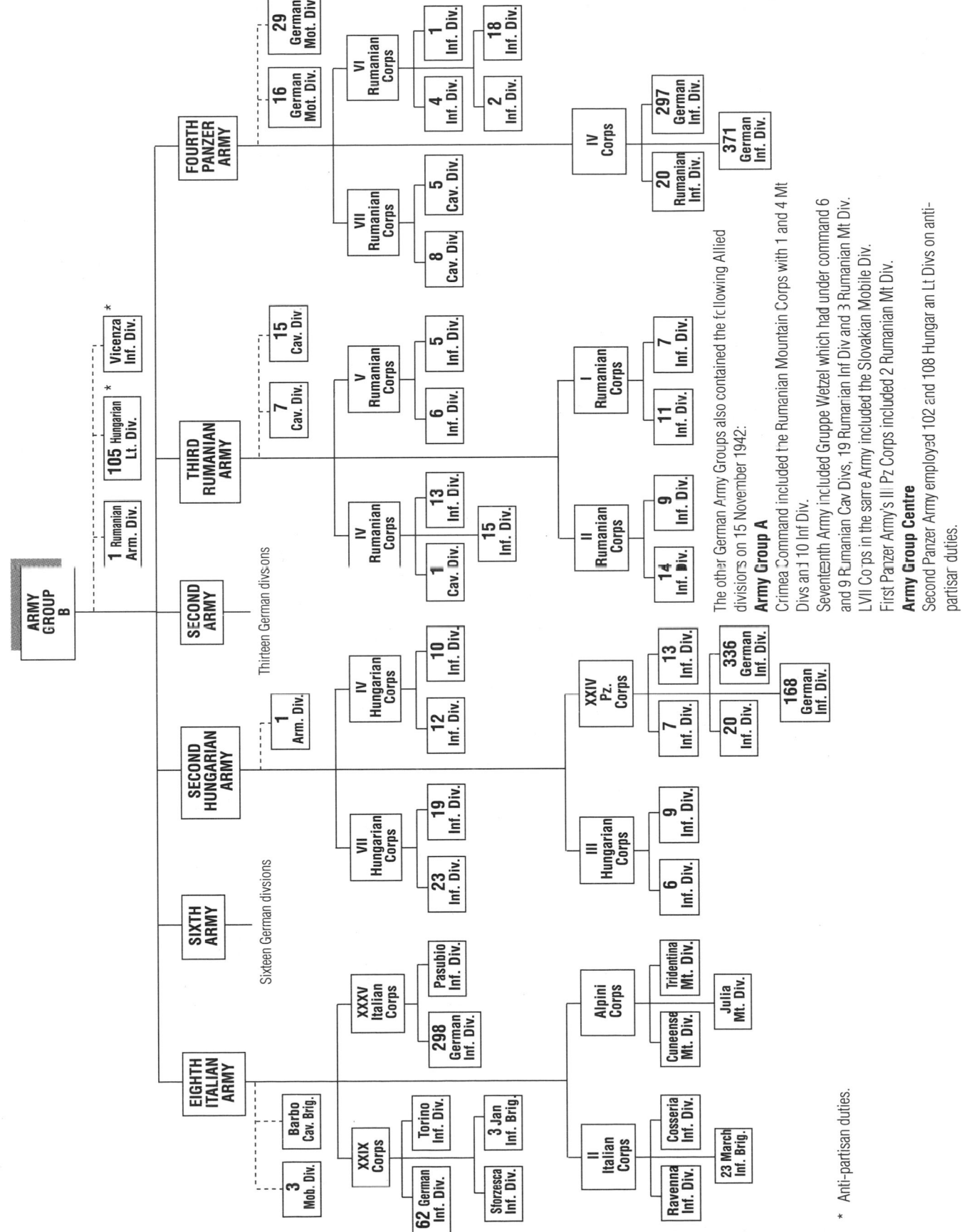

The other German Army Groups also contained the following Allied divisions on 15 November 1942:

Army Group A

Crimea Command included the Rumanian Mountain Corps with 1 and 4 Mt Divs and 10 Inf Div.

Seventeenth Army included Gruppe Wetzel which had under command 6 and 9 Rumanian Cav Divs, 19 Rumanian Inf Div and 3 Rumanian Mt Div. LVII Corps in the same Army included the Slovakian Mobile Div.

First Panzer Army's III Pz Corps included 2 Rumanian Mt Div.

Army Group Centre

Second Panzer Army employed 102 and 108 Hungarian Lt Divs on anti-partisan duties.

* Anti-partisan duties.

North-West Europe 1944-45

The German Army in the West 6 June 1944

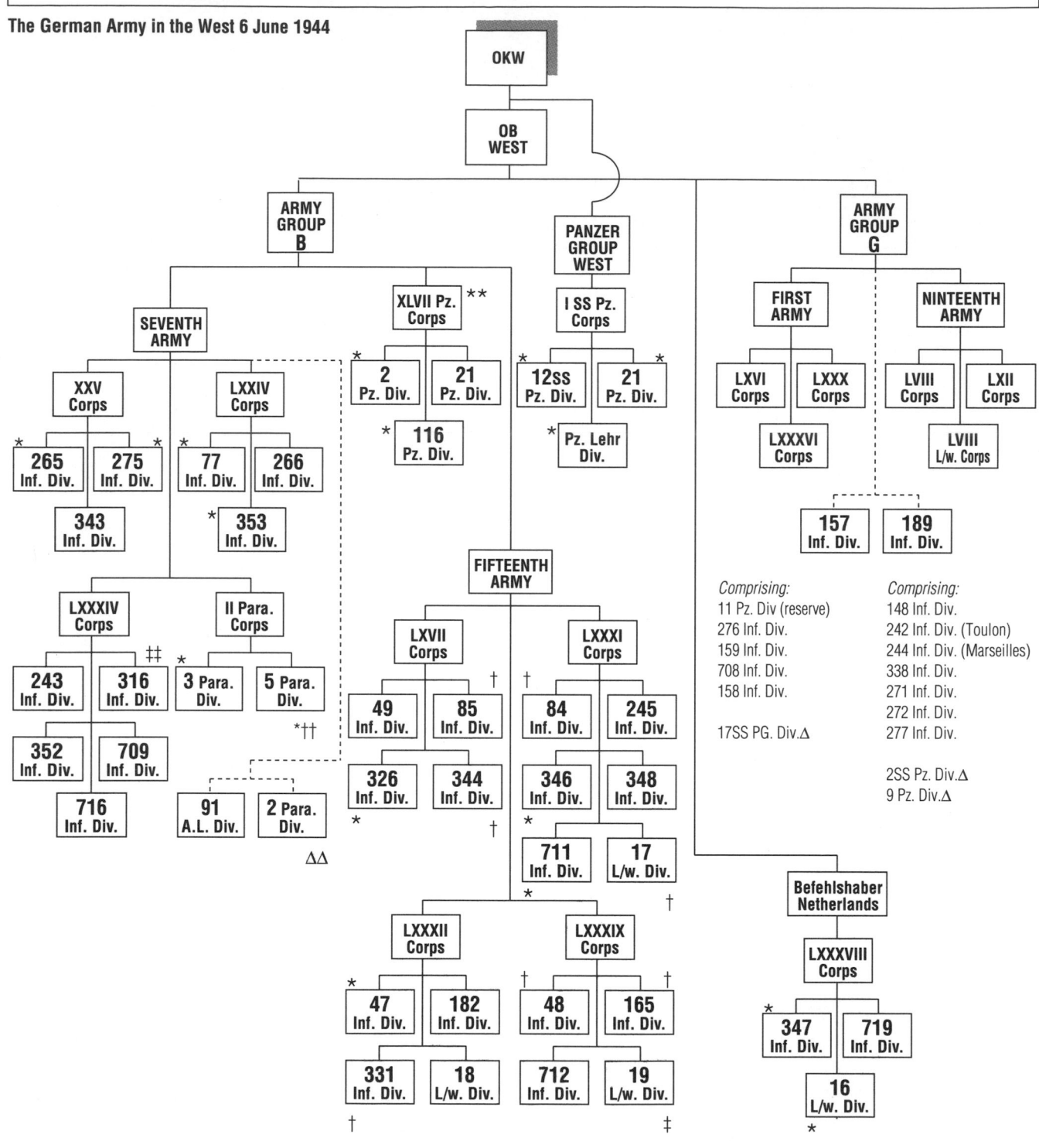

Comprising:
11 Pz. Div (reserve)
276 Inf. Div.
159 Inf. Div.
708 Inf. Div.
158 Inf. Div.

17SS PG. Div.△

Comprising:
148 Inf. Div.
242 Inf. Div. (Toulon)
244 Inf. Div. (Marseilles)
338 Inf. Div.
271 Inf. Div.
272 Inf. Div.
277 Inf. Div.

2SS Pz. Div.△
9 Pz. Div.△

* Left for Normandy 7 June-24 July 1944. (only half 265 Inf. Div.).
† Left for Normandy 25 July-25 August 1944.
‡ Left for Italy June 1944.
△ Under O.K.W. control.
** HQ only just arrived.
†† Forming.
‡‡ In Channel Islands.
△△ 6 Para Regt with 91 A.L.Div; 2 and 7 Para Regts in Brittanny.

Allied Armies in France 7 July 1944

The German Army in the West 30 April 1945

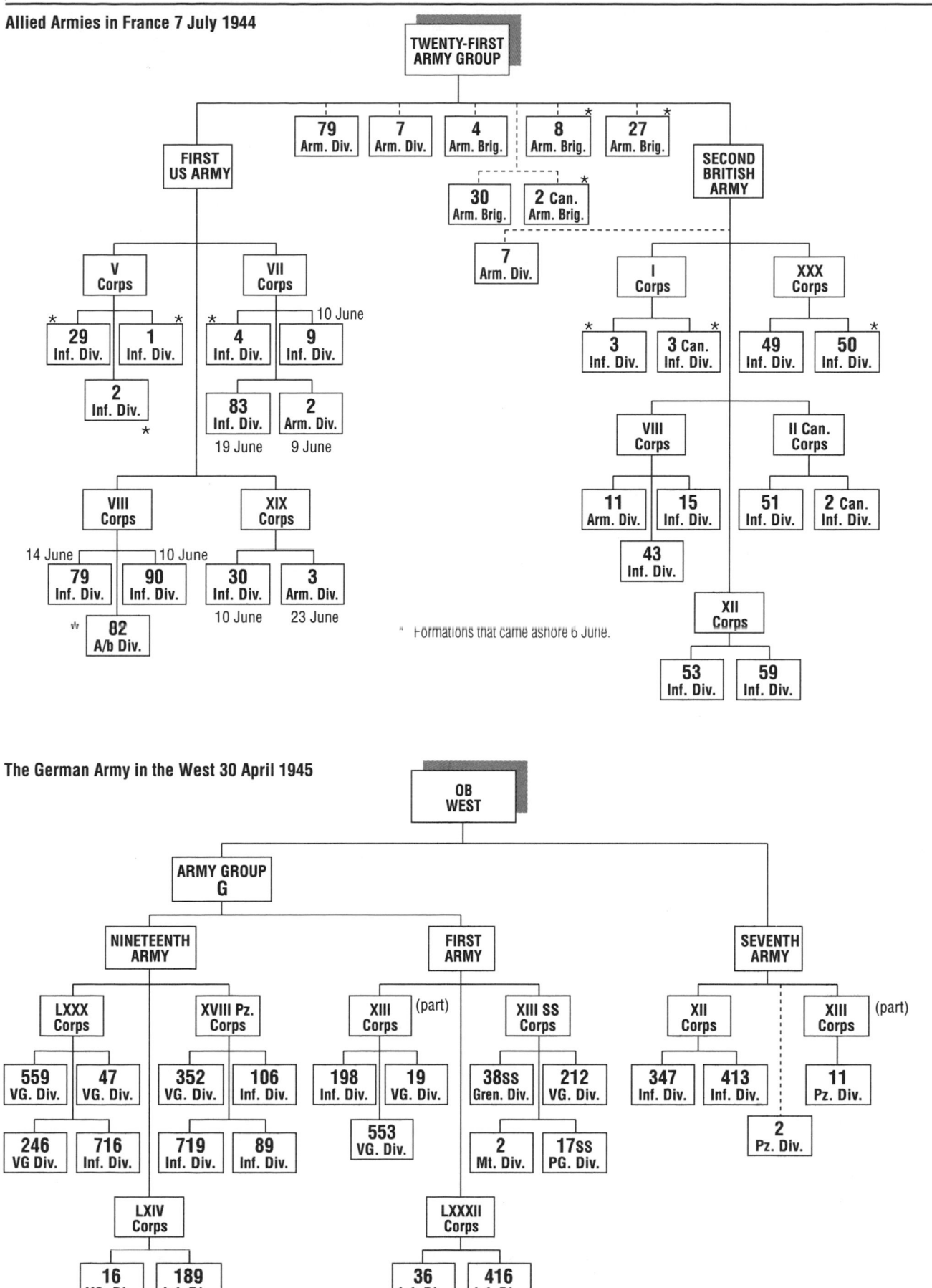

Allied Armies in North-West Europe 30 April 1945 (i)

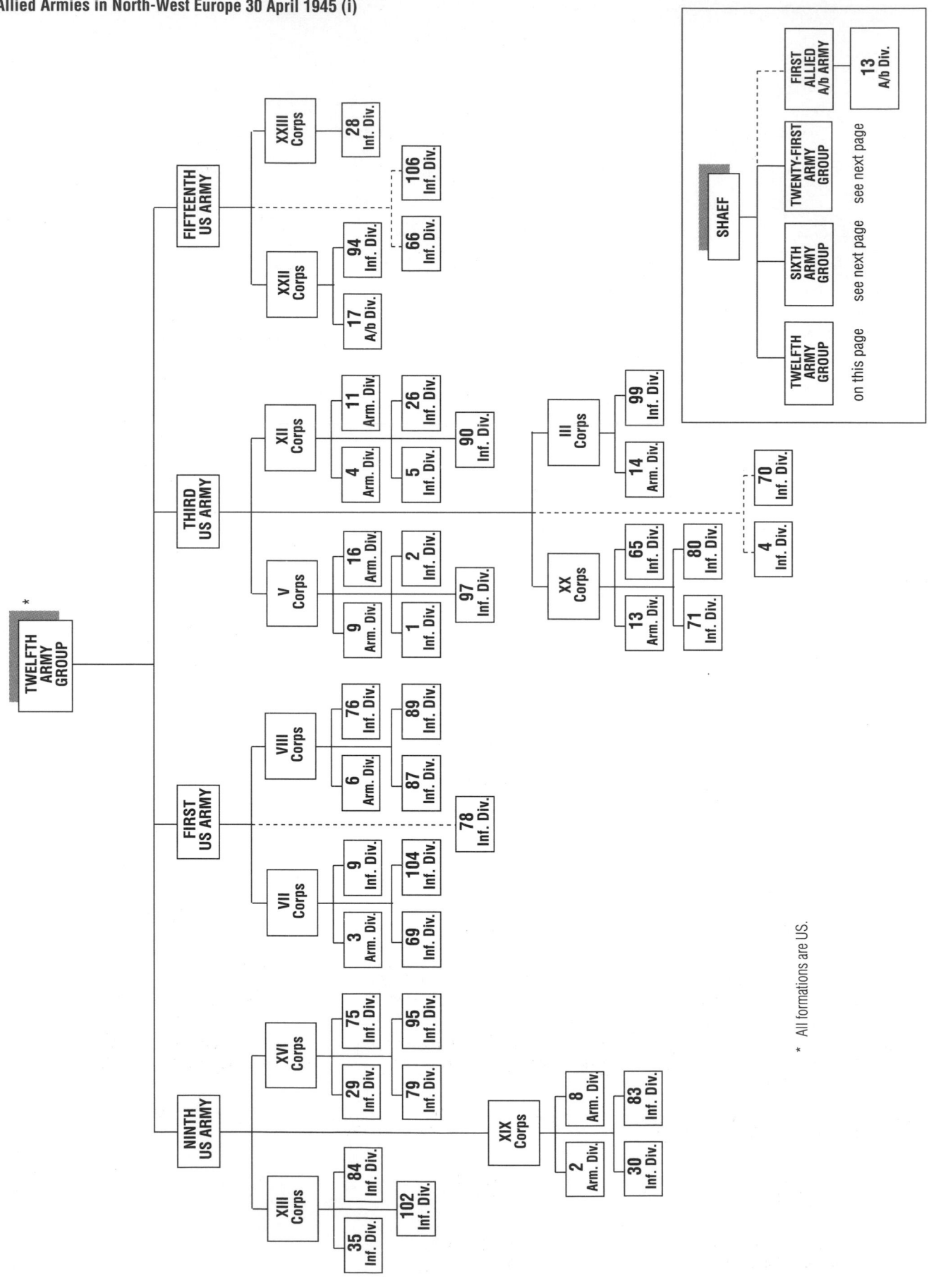

* All formations are US.

Allied Armies in North-West Europe 30 April 1945 (ii)

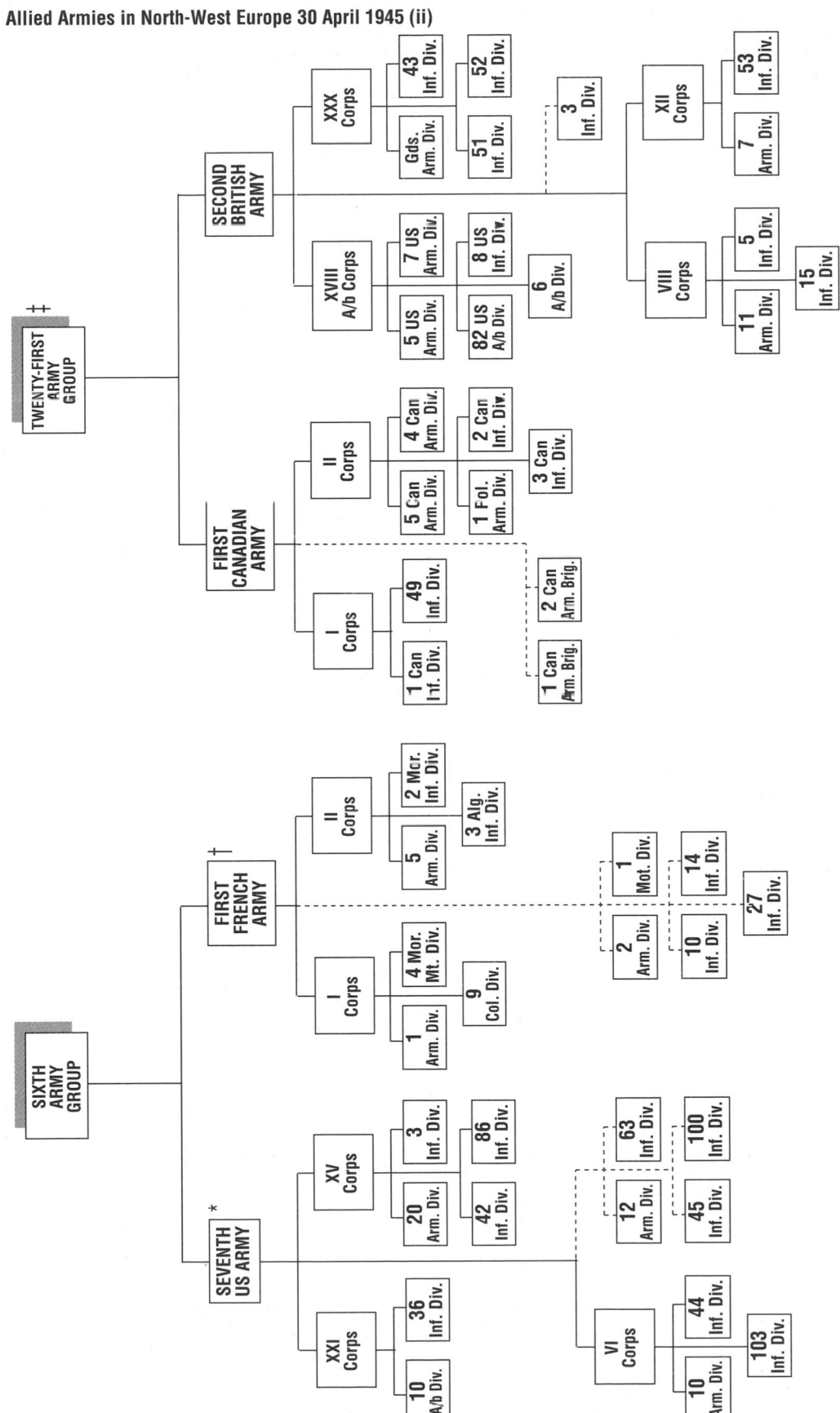

* All formations are US.
† All formations are French or N.African.
‡ All formations are British unless otherwise stated.
‡ Twenty-first Army Group had under direct command 79 Arm. Div., 4, 8, 34 and Czech Arm. Brigs., and 34 Ay. Tk. Brig.

North-West Europe: The Ebb and Flow of Divisions

GERMANS DEPARTED/DESTROYED Pz	Mot	Inf	GERMANS ARRIVED Pz	Mot	Inf	GERMANS PRESENT AT END OF MONTH Pz	Mot	Inf	TOTAL	DATE	ALLIES PRESENT AT END OF MONTH TOTAL†	Arm†	Inf	ALLIES ARRIVED Arm†	Inf	ALLIES DEPARTED Arm†	Inf
						8	2	45	55	**1944** 6 June							
0	0	1	2	0	2	10	2	46	58	June	25(5)	5(5)	20	5(5)	21	0	1
		709	9SS Pz 10SS Pz		89 363									2US 3US 7, 11, 79 Brigs: 4, 8, 27 2 Can Czech	82 US A/b 101 US A/b 6 A/b 1 US 2US 4 US 9 US 29 US 30 US 79 US 83 US 90 US 3, 15, 4 49, 50 51, 53 59 3 Can		101 US A/b
0	0	0	0	0	4	10	2	50	62	July	33(7)	9(7)	24	4(2)	5	0	1
					6 Para 16, 198, 363									4 US 5 US 6 US 4 Can Brigs: 6 Gds. Tk. 34 Ay. Tk.	5 US 8 US 28 US 35 US 2 Can		82 US A/b
0	0	14	0	0	4	10	2	40	52	August *	37(6)	13(6)	24	4	1	(1)	1
											8	0	8	0	8	0	0
		242, 243 244, 271 272, 276 277, 326 331, 344 363, 708 16 L/w 17 L/w			59 64 226 462 VG									Normandy		27	6 A/b
														7 US 2 Fr. 1 Pol. Gds. Arm.	80 US		
														S. France			
														—	1 Sp. Ser. 3 US 36 US 45 US 1 Fr. Mot. 2 Mor. 3 Alg. 4 MM		
0	0	8	0	2	9	10	4	42	56	September	55(6)	16(6)	39	3	7	0	0
		16, 47, 77, 266, 343, 348, 363 VG, 18 L/w	3 PG 15 PG		7 Para 12 VG 36 VG 159, 176 183 VG 190 246 VG 553 VG 559 VG									10 US 1 Fr. 5 Fr.	26 US 44 US 94 US 95 US 102 US 104 US 9 Col.		
0	0	2	0	0	8	10	4	48	62	October	58(6)	17(6)	41	1	3	0	1
		49 148			16 VG 18 Vg 256 269 272 VG 361 VG 416 zbV 416									14 US	100 US 103 US 52		59
0	0	4	0	0	5	10	4	49	63	November	52(6)	18(6)	44	1	3	0	0
		48 64 70 553 VG			26 VG 30SS 62 VG 340 VG 708 VG									12 US	78 US 84 US 99 US		

† The figures in brackets represent the number of independent armoured divisions ~~BGES~~ in addition to the armoured divisions.

* The American and French divisions that landed in the south of France in August 1944 are differentiated here but henceforth are included in the overall totals.

† The figures in brackets represent the number of independent armoured divisions in addition to the armoured divisions.

GERMANS										DATE	ALLIES						
DEPARTED/ DESTROYED			ARRIVED			PRESENT AT END OF MONTH					PRESENT AT END OF MONTH			ARRIVED		DEPARTED	
Pz	Mot	Inf	Pz	Mot	Inf	Pz	Mot	Inf	TOTAL		TOTAL†	Arm†	Inf	Arm†	Inf	Arm†	Inf
0	0	4	0	0	13	10	4	58	72	**1944** December	68(6)	20(6)	48	2	5	0	1
		275 462 711 712			6SS Mt. 8 Para 9 VG 47 VG 79 VG 167 VG 212 VG 257 VG 276 VG 277 VG 326 VG 344 VG 560 VG									9 US 11 US	17 US A/b 66 US 75 US 87 US 106 US		50
3	0	3	1	0	2	8	4	57	69	**1945** January	77(6)	22(6)	55	2	7	0	0
		2SS 12SS 21			269 344 VG 361 VG	Pz Claus		166 Res 553 VG						8 US 13 US	63 US 65 US 69 US 70 US 76 US 89 US 10 Fr.		
2	0	1	0	0	1	6	4	57	67	February	83(5)	24(5)	59	2	4	(1)	0
		1SS Pz 9SS Pz			708 VG			2 Mt.						16 US 20 US	13 US A/b 71 US 27 Fr. 14 Fr.	6 Gds. Tk.	
1	0	4	0	0	2	5	4	55	64	March	88(7)	25(7)	63	1(2)	4	0	0
		10SS			30SS 84, 245 559 VG			11 Para 106						5 Can Brigs: 34 1 Can	86 US 97 US 5 1 Can		
3	1	19	0	0	0	2	3	36	41	April	88(7)	25(7)	63	0	0	0	0
		9 116 Pz Lehr			2 Para 3 Para 5 Para 12 VG 59 62 VG 79 VG 166 Res 167 VG 176 183 VG 190 272 VG 276 VG 277 VG 326 VG 338 363 VG 560 VG												

The Pacific and South-East Asia 1941-45

British Forces in Malaya, Hong Kong and Burma December 1941-February 1942 and in India 21 April 1942

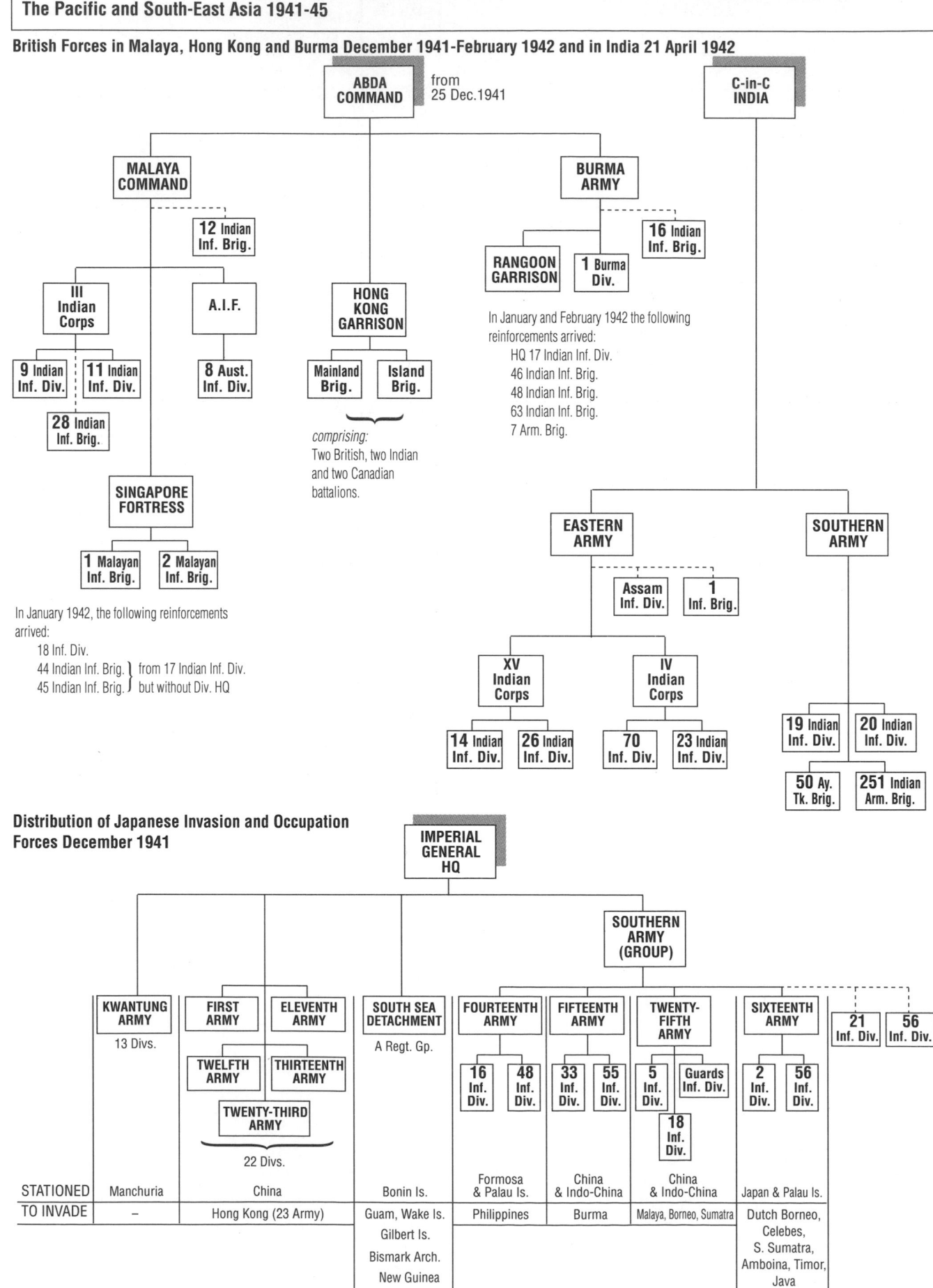

ABDA COMMAND from 25 Dec. 1941

C-in-C INDIA

MALAYA COMMAND

12 Indian Inf. Brig.

III Indian Corps

A.I.F.

HONG KONG GARRISON

9 Indian Inf. Div.

11 Indian Inf. Div.

8 Aust. Inf. Div.

Mainland Brig.

Island Brig.

28 Indian Inf. Brig.

comprising:
Two British, two Indian and two Canadian battalions.

SINGAPORE FORTRESS

1 Malayan Inf. Brig.

2 Malayan Inf. Brig.

In January 1942, the following reinforcements arrived:
18 Inf. Div.
44 Indian Inf. Brig. } from 17 Indian Inf. Div.
45 Indian Inf. Brig. } but without Div. HQ

BURMA ARMY

16 Indian Inf. Brig.

RANGOON GARRISON

1 Burma Div.

In January and February 1942 the following reinforcements arrived:
HQ 17 Indian Inf. Div.
46 Indian Inf. Brig.
48 Indian Inf. Brig.
63 Indian Inf. Brig.
7 Arm. Brig.

EASTERN ARMY

SOUTHERN ARMY

Assam Inf. Div.

1 Inf. Brig.

XV Indian Corps

IV Indian Corps

14 Indian Inf. Div.

26 Indian Inf. Div.

70 Inf. Div.

23 Indian Inf. Div.

19 Indian Inf. Div.

20 Indian Inf. Div.

50 Ay. Tk. Brig.

251 Indian Arm. Brig.

Distribution of Japanese Invasion and Occupation Forces December 1941

IMPERIAL GENERAL HQ

SOUTHERN ARMY (GROUP)

KWANTUNG ARMY — 13 Divs.

FIRST ARMY

ELEVENTH ARMY

SOUTH SEA DETACHMENT — A Regt. Gp.

FOURTEENTH ARMY

FIFTEENTH ARMY

TWENTY-FIFTH ARMY

SIXTEENTH ARMY

21 Inf. Div.

56 Inf. Div.

TWELFTH ARMY

THIRTEENTH ARMY

16 Inf. Div.

48 Inf. Div.

33 Inf. Div.

55 Inf. Div.

5 Inf. Div.

Guards Inf. Div.

2 Inf. Div.

56 Inf. Div.

TWENTY-THIRD ARMY

18 Inf. Div.

22 Divs.

	STATIONED	TO INVADE
Kwantung	Manchuria	–
First/Eleventh	China	Hong Kong (23 Army)
South Sea Det.	Bonin Is.	Guam, Wake Is. Gilbert Is. Bismark Arch. New Guinea
Fourteenth	Formosa & Palau Is.	Philippines
Fifteenth	China & Indo-China	Burma
Twenty-Fifth	China & Indo-China	Malaya, Borneo, Sumatra
Sixteenth	Japan & Palau Is.	Dutch Borneo, Celebes, S. Sumatra, Amboina, Timor, Java

Distribution of Japanese Occupation Forces August 1943

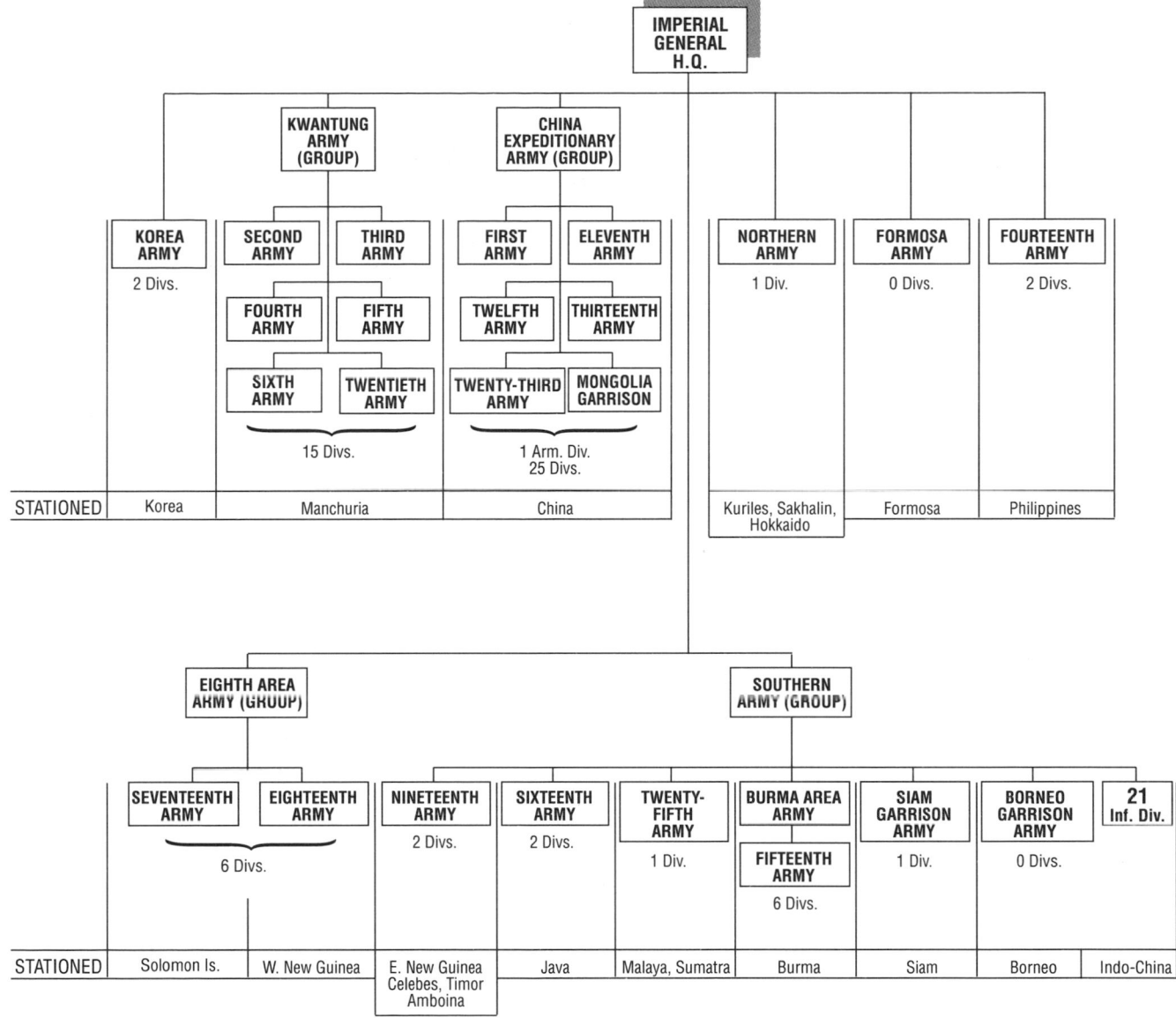

Allied Forces in South-East Asia April 1945

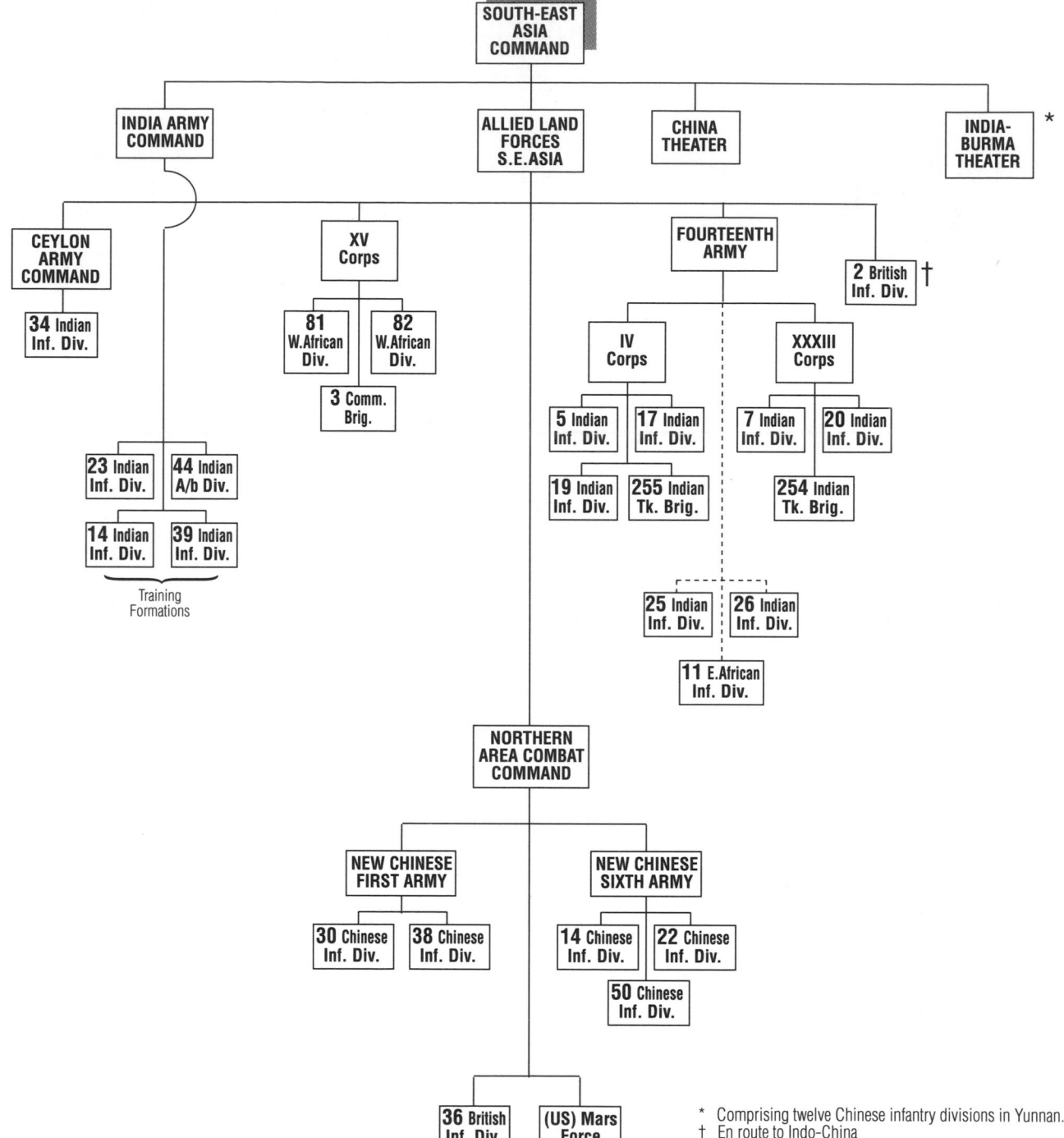

SOUTH-EAST ASIA COMMAND

INDIA ARMY COMMAND

ALLIED LAND FORCES S.E.ASIA

CHINA THEATER

INDIA-BURMA THEATER *

CEYLON ARMY COMMAND

XV Corps

FOURTEENTH ARMY

2 British Inf. Div. †

34 Indian Inf. Div.

81 W.African Div.

82 W.African Div.

3 Comm. Brig.

IV Corps

XXXIII Corps

23 Indian Inf. Div.

44 Indian A/b Div.

5 Indian Inf. Div.

17 Indian Inf. Div.

7 Indian Inf. Div.

20 Indian Inf. Div.

14 Indian Inf. Div.

39 Indian Inf. Div.

19 Indian Inf. Div.

255 Indian Tk. Brig.

254 Indian Tk. Brig.

Training Formations

25 Indian Inf. Div.

26 Indian Inf. Div.

11 E.African Inf. Div.

NORTHERN AREA COMBAT COMMAND

NEW CHINESE FIRST ARMY

NEW CHINESE SIXTH ARMY

30 Chinese Inf. Div.

38 Chinese Inf. Div.

14 Chinese Inf. Div.

22 Chinese Inf. Div.

50 Chinese Inf. Div.

36 British Inf. Div.

(US) Mars Force

* Comprising twelve Chinese infantry divisions in Yunnan.
† En route to Indo-China

US Army and Marine Corps in the Pacific 14 August 1945

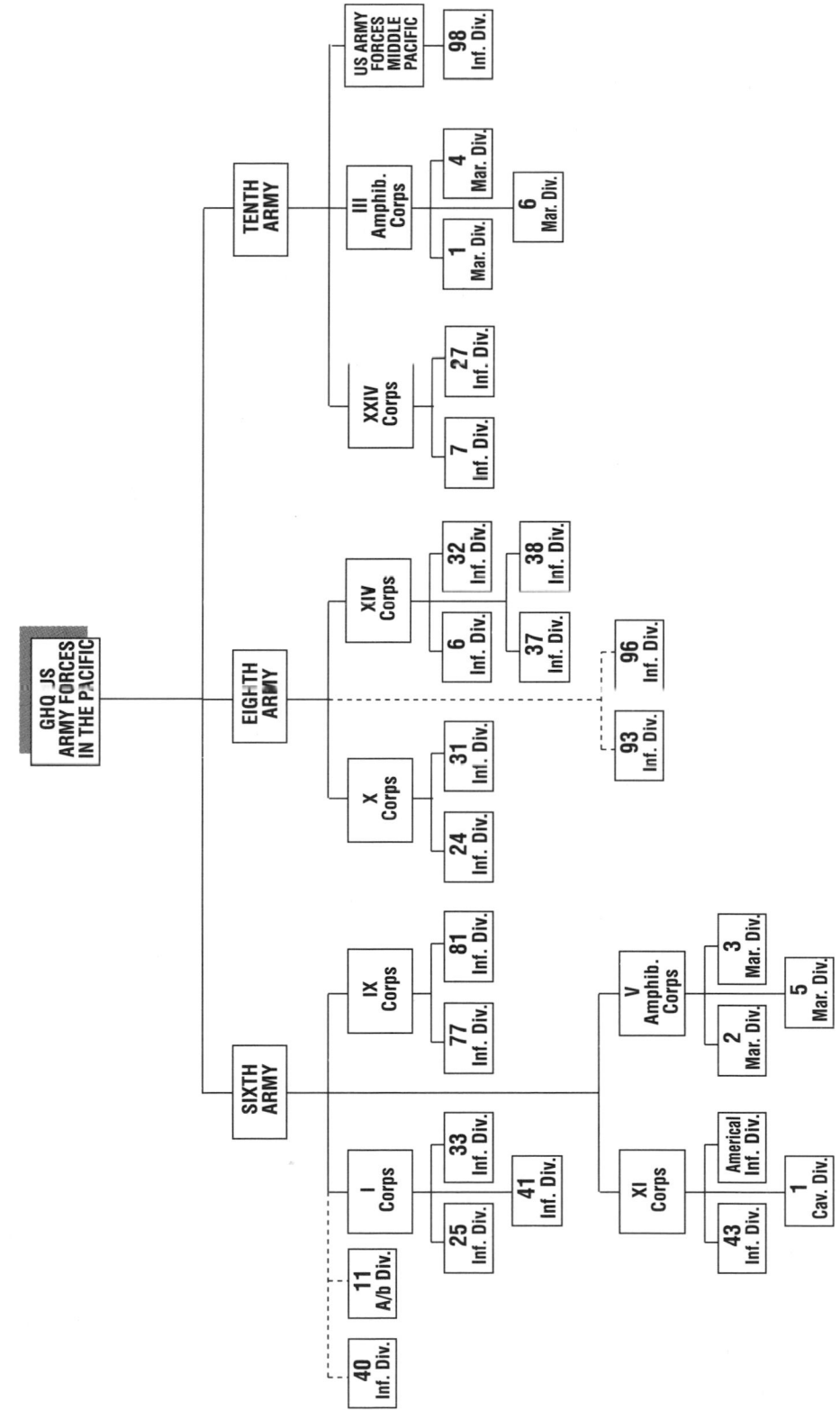

Distribution of Japanese Occupation Forces August 1945

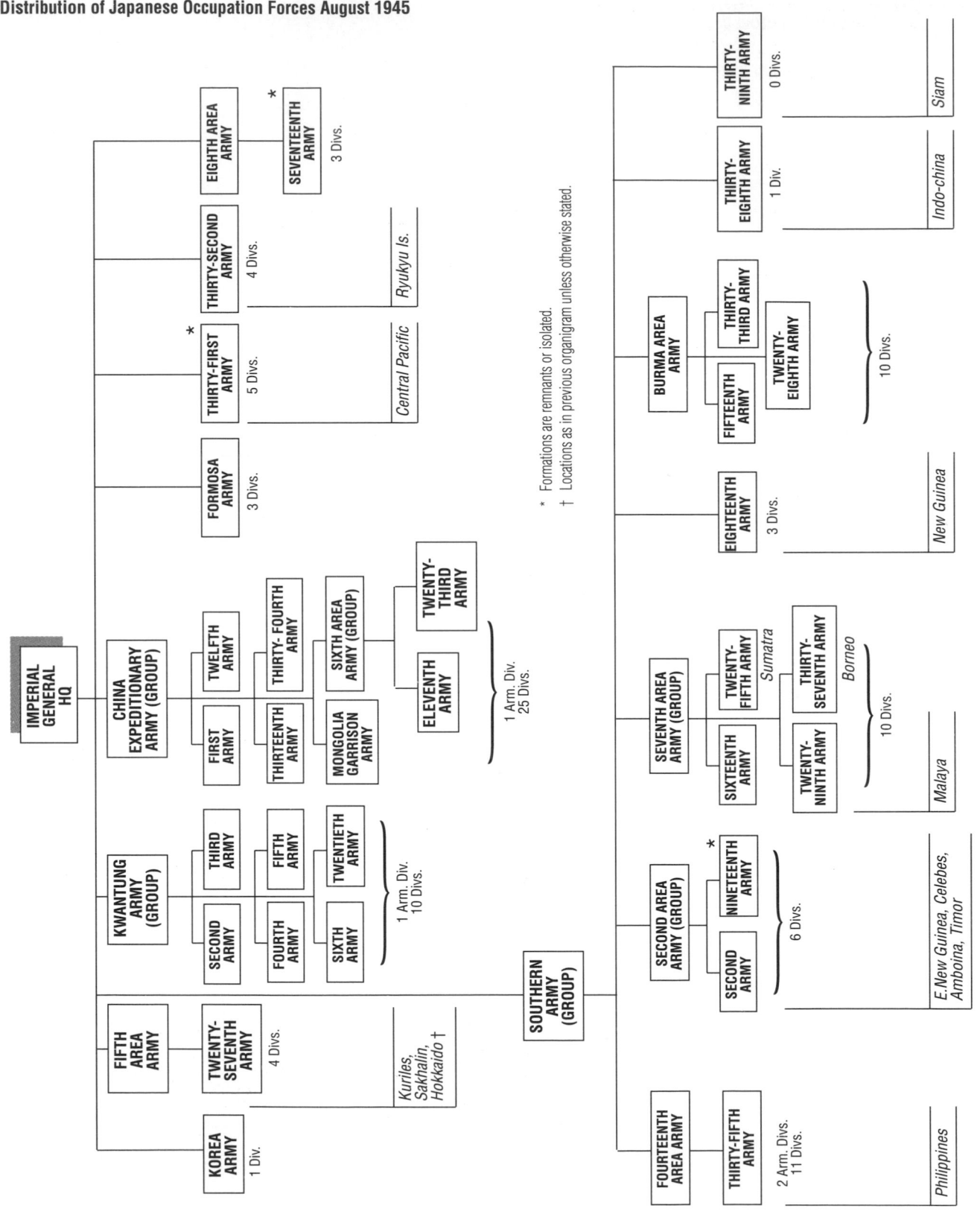

* Formations are remnants or isolated.

† Locations as in previous organigram unless otherwise stated.

The Pacific: The Ebb and Flow of Divisions

* Does not include units on Sumatra, Java and Formosa.

† All divisions are infantry.

‡ 'Destroyed' includes divisions trapped on outflanked islands.

** Number of USMC divisions in brackets.

†† Never involved in combat.

JAPANESE *† DEPARTED/ DESTROYED ‡	ARRIVED	PRESENT AT END OF MONTH	DATE	ALLIES † PRESENT AT END OF MONTH TOTAL	US**	ANZAC	ARRIVED US**	ANZAC	DEPARTED US	ANZAC
		4	**1942** August	2	1(1)	1	1(1)	1		
		2, 16, 38, 48					1 USMC	7 Aust		
0	0	4	September	5	3(2)	2	2(1)	1	0	0
							32, 2 USMC	6 Aust		
0	0	4	October	6	4(2)	2	1	0	0	0
							American			
0	0	4	November	6	4(2)	2	0	0	0	0
0	0	4	December	8	6(2)	2	2	0	0	0
							25, 41			
0	4	8	**1943** January	8	6(2)	2	0	0	0	0
	6, 20, 41, 51									
0	0	8	February	8	6(2)	2	0	0	0	0
0	1	9	March	9	7(2)	2	1	0	0	0
	5						43			
0	0	9	April	11	8(2)	3	1	1	0	0
							37	3 Aust		
0	0	9	May	12	9(2)	3	1	0	0	0
							7			
0	0	9	June	12	9(2)	3	0	0	0	0
0	0	9	July	12	9(2)	3	0	0	0	0
0	0	9	August	13	9(2)	4	0	1	0	0
								5 Aust		
0	1	10	September	15	9(2)	6	0	2	0	0
	17							9 Aust 3NZ		
0	1	11	October	16	10(3)	6	1(1)	0	0	0
	52						3 USMC			
0	0	11	November	17	11(3)	6	1	0	0	0
							27			
0	2	13	December	19	13(3)	6	2	0	0	0
	36, 46						40, 1 Cav			
2	0	11	**1944** January	22	16(4)	6	3(1)	0	0	0
17, 38							6, 93†† 4 USMC			
0	1	12	February	22	16(4)	6	0	0	0	0
	29									
1	1	12	March	23	17(4)	6	1	0	0	0
2	43						31			
0	6	18	April	26	19(4)	7	2	1	0	0
	9, 14, 24, 32, 35, 62						24, 98††	11 Aust		
1	0	17	May	28	21(4)	7	2	0	0	0
6							33, 11 A/b			
0	3	20	June	28	21(4)	7	0	0	0	0
	30, 100, 102									
2	4	22	July	29	22(4)	7	1	0	0	0
43, 52	28, 103, 105, 109						77			

DEPARTED/ DESTROYED ‡	JAPANESE*† ARRIVED	PRESENT AT END OF MONTH	DATE	ALLIES † PRESENT AT END OF MONTH TOTAL	US**	ANZAC	ARRIVED US**	ANZAC	DEPARTED US	ANZAC
1	3	24	**1944** August	29	22(4)	7	0	0	0	0
29	2 Arm., 8, 26									
5	1	20	September	30	23(4)	7	1	0	0	0
20, 35, 36, 41, 51	1						81			
1	0	19	October	31	24(4)	7	1	0	0	0
32							96			
1	2	20	November	31	24(4)	7	0	0	0	0
14	10, 23									
7	1	14	December	32	25(4)	7	1	0	0	0
1, 9, 16, 26, 30, 46, 102	19						38			
0	0	14	**1945** January	32	25(4)	7	0	0	0	0
0	0	14	February	33	26(5)	7	1(1)	0	0	0
							5 USMC			
1	0	13	March	34	27(6)	7	1(1)	0	0	0
109							6 USMC			
0	0	13	April	34	27(6)	7	0	0	0	0
0	0	13	May	34	27(6)	7	0	0	0	0
10	0	3	June	34	27(6)	7	0	0	0	0
2 Arm., 8, 10, 19, 23, 24, 48, 62, 103, 105										
3	0	0	July/ August	34	27(6)	7	0	0	0	0
5, 28, 100										

* Does not include units on Sumatra, Java and Formosa.

† All divisions are infantry.

‡ 'Destroyed' includes divisions trapped on outflanked islands.

** Number of USMC divisions in brackets.

The Pacific Campaign: US and Japanese Forces Island by Island

S.W. PACIFIC AXIS (MacArthur)				CENTRAL PACIFIC AXIS (Nimitz)			
PLACE	DATES	ALLIED FORCES	JAPANESE FORCES	PLACE	DATES	US FORCES	JAPANESE FORCES
GUADAL-CANAL	7 Aug 42 to 8 Feb 43	1 US Marine Div. 2 US Marine Div. (from 18 Sept 42) American Inf. Div. (from 13 Oct 42) 25 Inf. Div. (from 2 Jan 43)	Yosuka SNLF (from 17 Aug 42) Ichiki Detachment (from 18 Aug 42) 35 Brig (from 28 Aug 42) 2 Inf. Div. (from Sept 42) 230 Inf. Regt. (from ? 42) Δ 228 Inf. Regt. (from 2 Nov 42) Δ (island evacuated 1-8 Feb 43)				
NEW GUINEA	March 42 to Sept 44	New Guinea Force 7 Aust. Inf. Div. (from Aug 42) 32 US Inf. Div. (from Sept 42) 6 Aust. Inf. Div. (from Oct 42) 41 US Inf. Div. (from Jan 43) 3 Aust. Inf. Div. (from April 43) 5 Aust. Inf. Div. (from Aug 43) 9 Aust. Inf. Div. (from Sept 43) 6 US Inf. Div. (from Jan 44) (cont.)	South Sea Detachment (from 8 March 42) 7 Naval Base Force (from March 42) 51 Inf. Div. (from July 42) 20 Inf. Div. (from July 42) 41 Inf. Div. (from Jan 43) 5 Sasebo SNLF (from Aug 43) 2 Maizeru SNLF (from ? 43) 5 Yokosuka SNLF (from ? 43)				

Δ both from 38 Inf. Div.

The Pacific Campaign: US and Japanese Forces Island by Island (continued)

S.W.PACIFIC AXIS (MacArthur)				CENTRAL PACIFIC AXIS (Nimitz)			
PLACE	**DATES**	**ALLIED FORCES**	**JAPANESE FORCES**	**PLACE**	**DATES**	**US FORCES**	**JAPANESE FORCES**
NEW GUINEA continued	March 42 to Sept 44	31 US Inf. Div. (from March 44) 24 US Inf. Div. (from April 44) 43 US Inf. Div. (from Aug 44)	36 Inf. Div. (from Dec 43) 35 Inf. Div. (from April 44)				
Individual Landing Operations:							
Saidor	2 Jan 44	126 US R.C.T.	(bypassing 12,000 troops at Sio)				
Aitape	22 April to late Aug 44	163 US R.C.T. 43 US Inf. Div. (from July 44) 124 US Regt. (from July 44)	1,000 troops				
Hollandia	22 April to 6 June 44	24 US Inf. Div. (landing aborted) 41 US Inf. Div.	11,000 troops				
Wakde Is./ Sarmi	17-20 May 44	163 US Inf. Regt.	800 Japanese (on Wakde Is.) 36 Inf. Div. (most) (on mainland)				
Biak	27 May to 22 June 44	41 US Inf. Div. (two regts.) 41 US Inf. Div. (third regt.) (from 31 May 44) 34 US Inf. Regt. (from 13 June 44)	11,000 troops				
Noemfoor	2 July to 31 Aug 44	158 US Inf. Regt. Gp.	2,000 troops				
Sansapor	30 July 44	6 US Inf. Div.	unopposed				
Morotai	15 Sept 44	31 US Inf. Div. 126 US Inf. Regt.	little opposition				
NEW GEORGIA	30 June to 20 Sept 43	43 US Inf. Div. + other elements (see below)	6 Kure SNLF 229 Inf. Regt. (38 Inf. Div.)				
Individual Landing Operations: Munda	30 June to 5 Aug 43	27 US Inf. Regt. 169 US Inf. Regt. (two coys) 148 US Inf. Regt. (one batt.) 43 US Inf. Div. (from 2 July 43)	5,000 troops				
Rendova	30 June 43	172 US R.C.T.	140 naval personnel 229 Inf. Regt. (one coy.)				
Segi/Viru	30 June 43	4 US Marine Raiders	300 troops				
Arundel Is.	27 Aug to 20 Sept 43	172 US Inf. Regt. 27 US Inf. Regt. (two batts.)	200 troops				
VELLA LAVELLA	15 Aug to 7 Oct 43	35 US R.C.T. 3 NZ Inf. Div. (part) (from 18 Sept 43)	Two Army coys. One Navy plat. (evacuated 7 Oct 43)				
KOLOM-BANGARA	Sept 43	not attacked	13 Inf. Regt. (part) 229 Inf. Regt. (one batt.) 7 Yokosuka SNLF (evacuated 29 Sept-3 Oct 43)				

The Pacific Campaign: US and Japanese Forces Island by Island (continued)

\<S.W.PACIFIC AXIS (MacArthur)\>				\<CENTRAL PACIFIC AXIS (Nimitz)\>			
PLACE	DATES	ALLIED FORCES	JAPANESE FORCES	PLACE	DATES	US FORCES	JAPANESE FORCES
BOUGAIN-VILLE	2 Nov 43 to 1 May 44	3 US Marine Div. 37 US Inf. Div. 3 NZ Inf. Div. (one brig.) Americal Inf. Div. (from 25 Dec 43)	38 Inf. Brig. 6 Inf. Div. Kolombangara evacuees (see above) Guadalcanal evacuees (see above) (there were still 40,000 Japanese troops sealed off on the island in October 44)				
TREASURY Is.	27 Oct 43 to 6 Nov 43	3 NZ Inf. Div. (part)	250 Japanese				
NEW BRITAIN	15 Dec 43 to 16 Jan 44	see below	17 Inf. Div. 38 Inf. Div. 39 Inf. Brig. 65 Inf. Brig. 40 Inf. Brig. (on New Ireland)	**GILBERT Is.**	20-28 Nov 43	see below	Naval personnel only. See below
Individual Landing Operations:				**Individual Landing Operations:**			
Arawe	15-27 Dec 43	112 US Cav. Regt.	c. 500 troops	**Makin**	20-23 Nov 43	165 US R.C.T. 105 US Inf. Regt. (one batt.)	800 troops inc. 6 Yokosuka SNLF (one coy.) 6 Defence Force (one coy.) 111 Pioneers (part) 4 Construction Unit (part)
Cape Gloucester	26 Dec to 16 Jan 44	1 US Marine Div.	7,500 troops (mainly from 17 Inf. Div. and 65 Inf. Brig.) (there were still 93,000 Japanese troops sealed off on the island in Oct 44)	**Tarawa**	20-28 Nov 43	2 US Marine Div.	6 Yokosuka SNLF (most) 7 Sasebo SNLF 111 Pioneers (most) 4 Construction Unit (most)
GREEN Is./ NISSAN Is.	15-20 Feb 44	3 NZ Inf. Div. (one brig.)	102 troops	**MARSHALL Is.**	31 Jan 44 to 22 Feb 44	see below	
ADMIRALTY Is.	29 Feb 44 to 31 Mar 44	see below	4,600 Japanese	**Individual Landing Operations:**			
Individual Landing Operations:				**Kwajalein Atoll:**			8,000 personnel (2,200 troops)
Los Negros	29 Feb to 24 Mar 44	5 US Cav. Regt. 7 US Cav. Regt. (from 3 Mar 44) 12 US Cav. Regt. (from ? Mar 44)		**Roi Namur**	31 Jan to 2 Feb 44	4 US Marine Div.	3,800
				Kwajalein	1-4 Feb 44	7 US Inf. Div.	3,800
Manus	15-25 Mar 44	8 US Cav. Regt.		**Ebeye**	3-4 Feb 44	17 US R.C.T.	400
Pytilu	30-31 Mar 44	7 US Cav. Regt.		**Eniwetok**	17-21 Feb 44	22 US Marine Regt. 106 US R.C.T.	1 Amphib. Brig. (part)
EMIRAU	20 Mar 44	4 US Marine Regt.	unopposed	**Parry Is.**	22 Feb 44	22 US Marine Regt. (two batts.)	1 Amphib. Brig. (part)
MOROTAI	15 Sept 44 to 4 Oct 44	31 US Inf. Div. 126 US R.C.T.	500 troops (there were 37,000 Japanese on nearby Halmahera, which was not attacked)	**MARIANA Is.**	15 June 44 to 10 Aug 44	see below	see below
				Individual Landing Operations:			
				Saipan	15 June to 9 July 44	2 US Marine Div. 4 US Marine Div.	43 Inf. Div. 1 Yokosuka SNLF 47 IMB 3 Art. Regt. 55 Naval Guard Unit
				Tinian	24 July to 1 Aug 44 (mopping up until end Oct 44)	2 US Marine Div. 4 US Marine Div.	9,000 troops inc.: 50 Inf. Regt. 135 Inf. Regt. (one batt.)

The Pacific Campaign: US and Japanese Forces Island by Island (continued)

	S.W.PACIFIC AXIS (MacArthur)			CENTRAL PACIFIC AXIS (Nimitz)			
PLACE	**DATES**	**ALLIED FORCES**	**JAPANESE FORCES**	**PLACE**	**DATES**	**US FORCES**	**JAPANESE FORCES**
PHILIPPINE Is.	20 Oct 44 to 15 Aug 45	see below	see below	**Guam**	21 July to 10 Aug 44	3 US Marine Div. 77 US Inf. Div. 1 US Marine Provisional Brig.	29 Inf. Div. 6 Expeditionary Force 3,000 naval guardsmen
Individual Landing Operations:				**PALAU Is.**	15 Sept 44 to 25 Nov 44	see below	14 Inf. Div. (majority cut off on Babelthuap, which was not attacked)
				Individual Landing Operations:			
Leyte	20 Oct to 25 Dec 44 (mopping up until 10 Feb 45)	1 US Cav. Div. 7 US Inf. Div. 24 US Inf. Div. 96 US Inf. Div. 21 US R.C.T. (to Panaon Is.) 32 US Inf. Div. (from 14 Nov 44) 11 US A/b. Div. (from 18 Nov 44) 77 US Inf. Div. (from 7 Dec 44)	16 Inf. Div. 30 Inf. Div. (arrives 26 Oct-9 Dec 44) 102 Inf. Div. (arrives 26 Oct-17 Nov 44) 1 Inf. Div. (arrives 1-10 Nov 44) 26 Inf. Div. (arrives 1-10 Nov 44) 8 Inf. Div. (one regt.) (from 11 Dec 44) 68 IMB	**Peleliu**	15 Sept to 25 Nov 44	1 US Marine Div. 81 US Inf. Div. (from 23 Sept 44)	2 Inf. Regt.
				Angaur	17-20 Sept 44 (mopping up until 23 Oct 44)	81 US Inf. Div. (two regts.)	1,600 troops
Samar	24 Oct to 19 Dec 44	1 US Cav. Div. (part)	?	**IWO JIMA (Bonin Is.)**	19 Feb 45 to 26 Mar 45	4 US Marine Div. 5 US Marine Div. 3 US Marine Div. (from 21 Feb 45) 147 US Inf. Regt. (from 21 Mar 45)	109 Inf. Div. Iwo Jima Naval Guard Force 204 Naval Construction Batt.
Mindoro	15 Dec 44 to 11 Jan 45	24 US Inf. Div. (two regts.) 503 US Para. Regt.	500 troops				
Luzon	9 Jan to 30 June 45	6 US Inf. Div. 25 US Inf. Div. 37 US Inf. Div. 40 US Inf. Div. 43 US Inf. Div. 32 US Inf. Div. (from 27 Jan 45) 1 US Cav. Div. (from 27 Jan 45) 38 US Inf. Div. (from 29 Jan 45) 11 US A/b. Div. (from 31 Jan 45) 33 US Inf. Div. (from 10 Feb 45)	2 Arm. Div. 8 Inf. Div. 10 Inf. Div. 19 Inf. Div. 23 Inf. Div. 103 Inf. Div. 105 Inf. Div. 39 Inf. Div. (part) 58 IMB 31 Manila Naval Defence Force 2 Mobile Inf. (part) 1 Raiding Gp.	**OKINAWA (Ryukyu Is.)**	1 April 45 to 22 June 45	7 US Inf. Div. 96 US Inf. Div. 1 US Marine Div. 6 US Marine Div. 27 US Inf. Div. (from 9 April 45) 77 US Inf. Div. (from 27 April 45) 2 US Marine Div. (from early June 45) (This was a joint MacArthur-Nimitz operation, at the convergence of their two axes.)	62 Inf. Div. 24 Inf. Div. 44 IMB 27 Tk. Regt. 1, 23, 26, 27, 28, 29 indep. inf. batts. 1 specially established Boeitai Regt.
Palawan	28 Feb to 22 April 45	186 US R.C.T.	2,700 troops				
Zamboanga	10 Mar to 15 Aug 45	41 US Inf. Div. (two regts.)	8,300 troops				
Panay/ W. Negros	18 Mar to 4 June 45	40 US Inf. Div. (two regts.)	(Panay) 2,300 troops (W.Negros) 16,000 troops } 102 Inf. Div. (part)				
Cebu	26 Mar to 18 April 45	Americal Inf. Div.	102 Inf. Div. (part)				
S.E.Negros	26 April to 12 June 45	164 US Inf. Regt.	102 Inf. Div. (part)				
Mindanao	17 April to 15 Aug 45	24 US Inf. Div. 31 US Inf. Div. (from 22 April 45)	30 Inf. Div. (part) 100 Inf. Div. 54 IMB 32 Naval Base Force				

The Pacific Campaign: US and Japanese Forces Island by Island (continued)

PLACE	DATES	ALLIED FORCES	JAPANESE FORCES	PLACE	DATES	US FORCES	JAPANESE FORCES
		S.W.PACIFIC AXIS (MacArthur)				**CENTRAL PACIFIC AXIS (Nimitz)**	
BORNEO	1 May 45 to 22 July 45	see below	see below				
Individual Landing Operations:							
Tarakan	1-30 May 45	26 Aust. Inf. Brig.	455 Inf. Batt. 2 Naval Garrison Force ? Kure SNLF (one coy.)				
Brunei Bay	10 June to 1 July 45	9 Aust. Inf. Div. (two brigs.)	56 IMB 25 Indep. Inf. Regt. 4 Indep. Mixed Regt.				
Balikpapan	1-22 July 45	7 Aust. Inf. Div.	71 IMB				

Burma: The Ebb and Flow of Divisions

DEPARTED	ARRIVED	PRESENT AT END OF MONTH	DATE	TOTAL†	Arm †	Inf	Arm †	Inf	Arm †	Inf
	JAPANESE *				PRESENT AT END OF MONTH		ARRIVED		DEPARTED	
		4	**1942** September	4	0	4				
		18, 33, 55, 56		2, 14 Ind, 17 Ind, 23 Ind						
0	0	4	October	4	0	4	0	0	0	0
0	0	4	November	4	0	4	0	0	0	0
0	0	4	December	4	0	4	0	0	0	0
0	0	4	**1943** January	4	0	4	0	0	0	0
0	0	4	February	5	0	5	0	1	0	0
								26 Ind		
0	0	4	March	5	0	5	0	0	0	0
0	0	4	April	5	0	5	0	0	0	0
0	0	4	May	4	0	4	0	0	0	1
										14 Ind
0	0	4	June	4	0	4	0	0	0	0
0	1	5	July	4	0	4	0	0	0	0
	31									
0	1	6	August	4	0	4	0	0	0	0
	54									
0	0	6	September	6	0	6	0	2	0	0
								70 ‡ 7 Ind		
0	0	6	October	7(1)	(1)	7	(1)	1	0	0
							254 Ind Tk	20 Ind		
0	0	6	November	6(1)	(1)	6	0	0	0	1
										70 **
0	0	6	December	7(1)	(1)	7	1	0	0	0
							81 WA			
0	1	7	**1944** January	7(1)	(1)	7	0	0	0	0
	53									
0	1	8	February	7(1)	(1)	7	0	0	0	0
	15									

* All divisions are infantry.

† Number in brackets is armoured brigades.

‡ Assigned to Wingate's Special Force.

** Disbanded qua division.

Burma: The Ebb and Flow of Divisions (continued)

* Became 36 Div. September 1944.

† Emergency HQ only. Not included in total.

JAPANESE			DATE	ALLIES						
DEPARTED	ARRIVED	PRESENT AT END OF MONTH		PRESENT AT END OF MONTH			ARRIVED		DEPARTED	
				TOTAL	Arm	Inf	Arm	Inf	Arm	Inf
0	1	9	**1944** March	9(1)	(1)	9	2	0	0	0
	2						25 Ind 36 Ind*			
0	0	9	April	9(1)	(1)	9	0	0	0	0
0	0	9	May	9(1)	(1)	9	1	0	0	0
							21 Ind †			
0	1	10	June	9(1)	(1)	9	0	0	0	0
	49									
0	0	10	July	10(1)	(1)	10	1	0	1	0
							11 EA		21 Ind †	
0	0	10	August	9(1)	(1)	9	0	0	1	0
									23 Ind	
0	0	10	September	9(1)	(1)	9	0	0	0	0
0	0	10	October	11(2)	(2)	11	2	(1)	0	0
							19 Ind 82 WA	255 Ind Tk		
0	0	10	November	11(2)	(2)	11	0	0	0	0
1	0	9	December	11(2)	(2)	11	0	0	0	0
2										
0	0	0	**1945** January	11(?)	(?)	11	0	0	0	0
0	0	9	February	11(2)	(2)	11	0	0	0	0
0	0	9	March	11(2)	(2)	11	0	0	0	0
0	0	9	April	10(2)	(2)	10	0	0	1	0
									2	
0	0	9	May	10(2)	(2)	9	0	0	1	0
									36	
0	0	9	June/ August	10(2)	(2)	9	0	0	0	0

Manchuria 1945

Russian and Japanese Armies in Manchuria and China 9 August 1945

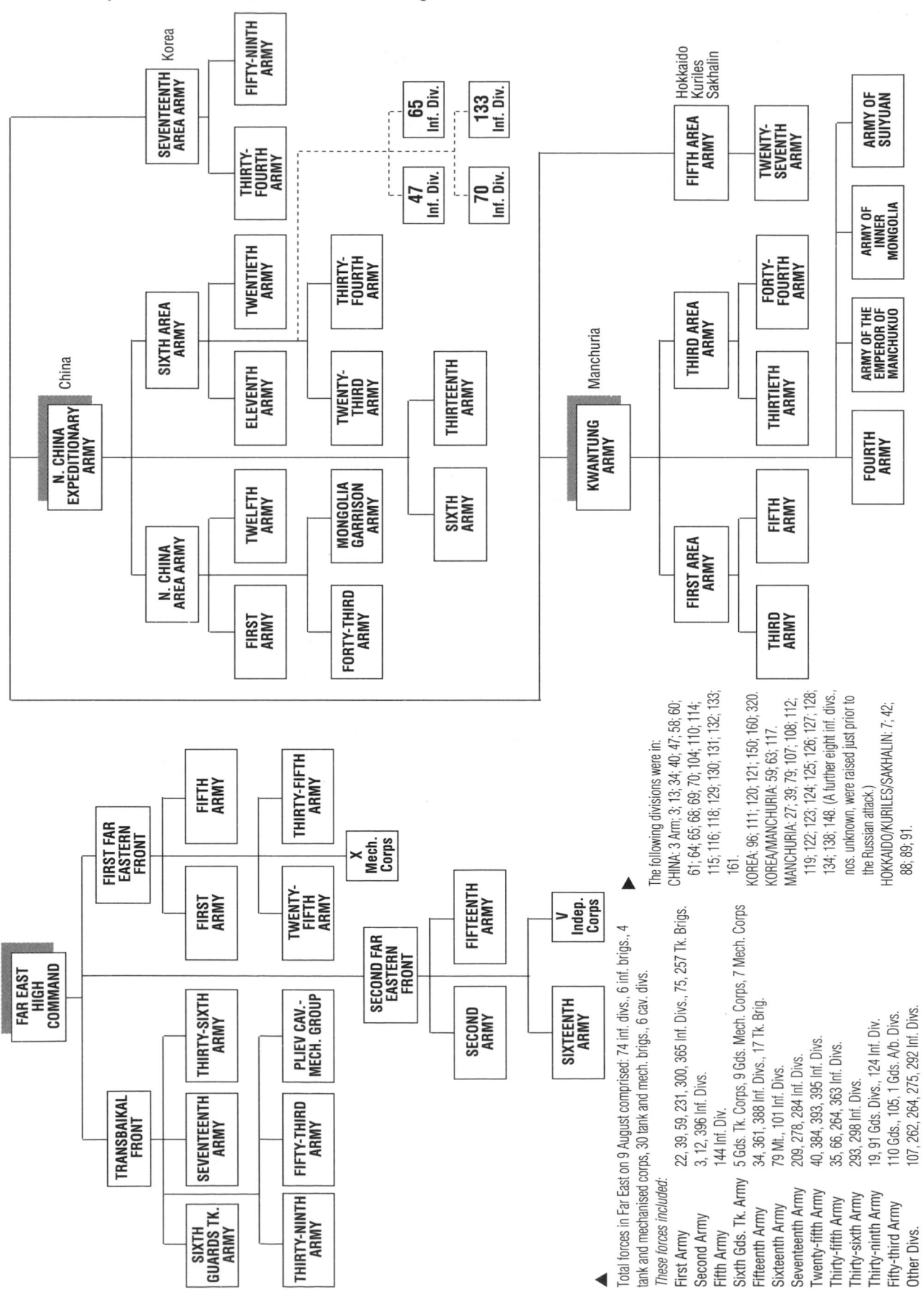

Total forces in Far East on 9 August comprised: 74 inf. divs, 6 inf. brigs., 4 tank and mechanised corps, 30 tank and mech. brigs., 6 cav. divs.

These forces included:

First Army	22, 39, 59, 231, 300, 365 Inf. Divs., 75, 257 Tk. Brigs.
Second Army	3, 12, 396 Inf. Divs.
Fifth Army	144 Inf. Div.
Sixth Gds. Tk. Army	5 Gds. Tk. Corps, 9 Gds. Mech. Corps, 7 Mech. Corps
Fifteenth Army	34, 361, 388 Inf. Divs., 17 Tk. Brig.
Sixteenth Army	79 Mt., 101 Inf. Divs.
Seventeenth Army	209, 278, 284 Inf. Divs.
Twenty-fifth Army	40, 384, 393, 395 Inf. Divs.
Thirty-fifth Army	35, 66, 264, 363 Inf. Divs.
Thirty-sixth Army	293, 298 Inf. Divs.
Thirty-ninth Army	19, 91 Gds. Divs., 124 Inf. Div.
Fifty-third Army	110 Gds., 105, 1 Gds. A/b. Divs.
Other Divs.	107, 262, 264, 275, 292 Inf. Divs.

The following divisions were in:

CHINA: 3 Arm; 3; 13; 34; 40; 47; 58; 60; 61; 64; 65; 66; 69; 70; 104; 110; 114; 115; 116; 118; 129; 130; 131; 132; 133; 161.

KOREA: 96; 111; 120; 121; 150; 160; 320.

KOREA/MANCHURIA: 59; 63; 117.

MANCHURIA: 27; 39; 79; 107; 108; 112; 119; 122; 123; 124; 125; 126; 127; 128; 134; 138; 148. (A further eight inf. divs., nos. unknown, were raised just prior to the Russian attack.)

HOKKAIDO/KURILES/SAKHALIN: 7; 42; 88; 89; 91.

SECTION 4

TABLES OF ORGANISATION AND EQUIPMENT

The organigrams and data listed below outline the structure and equipment of the different belligerent countries' most important fighting units and formations. Information on ground forces focuses on the various types of division, the main building block for all armies, and that on air forces takes the squadron as the basic unit. Naval formations are too *ad hoc* to permit useful generalisation.

AUSTRALIA

Australian forces were organised and equipped in the same way as UK forces. See that section for details.

BELGIUM
Army

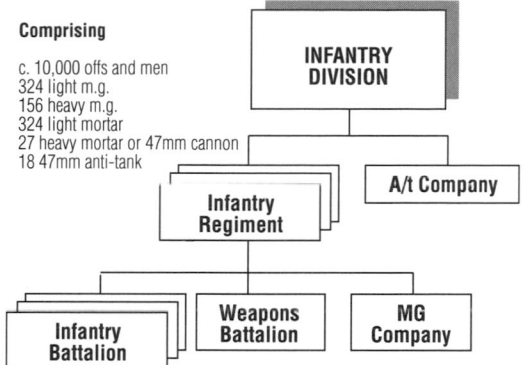

Comprising

c. 10,000 offs and men
324 light m.g.
156 heavy m.g.
324 light mortar
27 heavy mortar or 47mm cannon
18 47mm anti-tank

The Belgian Army was unusual in that corps were of a fixed size i.e. two divisions. The main artillery support was provided at corps level, comprising 8 105mm howitzers, 8 120mm field guns and 16 155mm howitzers.

Air Force

The Belgian Air Force comprised three Air Regiments, two of six squadrons, one of four. Each squadron contained between 10 and 13 aircraft.

BULGARIA

Details not available.

CANADA

Canadian forces were organised and equipped in the same way as UK forces. See that entry for details.

CHINA
Army

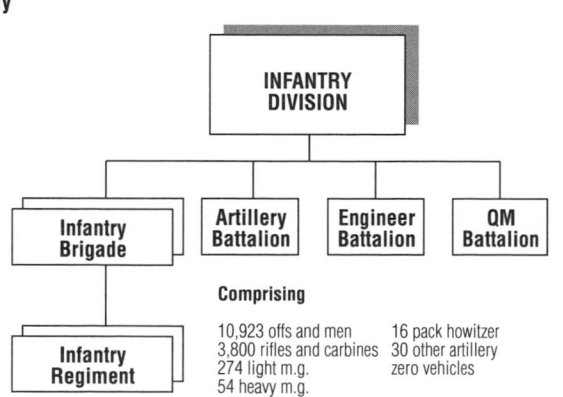

Comprising

10,923 offs and men   16 pack howitzer
3,800 rifles and carbines   30 other artillery
274 light m.g.   zero vehicles
54 heavy m.g.

It should be noted that this TO & E only applied to the ten divisions reorganised in 1937. The rest of the 170 or so divisions were lucky to be at 50 per cent of the above strengths. Moreover, ever fearful of warlordism, Chiang Kai-shek retained control of the artillery himself in a central park.

Five infantry divisions (see Allied Forces in the Pacific and South-East Asia 1945 in Section 3, page 188) were trained by the Americans in 1943-44 and these did have much more generous allocations of equipment, though not to the level of actual US divisions.

The Chinese Communists, by 1945, had organised some 16 infantry divisions in their base areas scattered all over China. Though supposedly organised on a rigidly triangular system (three regiments in a division, three battalions in a regiment etc.), they seem to have varied in size between 5,000 and as much as 30,000 men. Levels of equipment fluctuated but were always less than lavish. Between 1937 and 1944 these divisions mainly drew their equipment from the 310,000 rifles and pistols, 5,800 machine guns and 590 guns and mortars they captured from the enemy, equipment that they had to share with 150,000 local guerrillas and much of which was damaged beyond repair.

Air Force

I have been unable to find any specific details about Chinese Air Force organisation.

DENMARK
Army

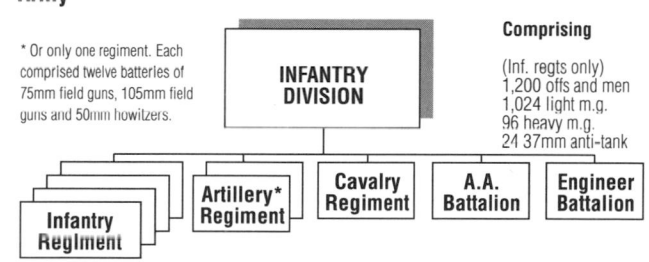

* Or only one regiment. Each comprised twelve batteries of 75mm field guns, 105mm field guns and 50mm howitzers.

Comprising

(Inf. regts only)
1,200 offs and men
1,024 light m.g.
96 heavy m.g.
24 37mm anti-tank

Air Force

Danish air force squadrons contained around a dozen airplanes. Two squadrons made up a battalion.

FINLAND
Army

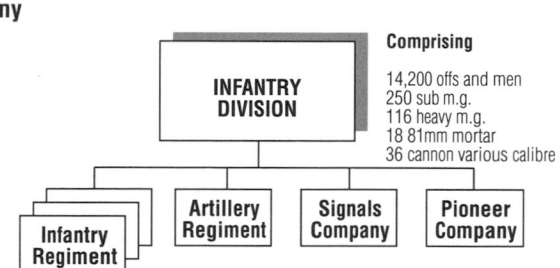

Comprising

14,200 offs and men
250 sub m.g.
116 heavy m.g.
18 81mm mortar
36 cannon various calibre

The whole Finnish Army in 1939 possessed only 112 37mm anti-tank guns and 110 anti-aircraft guns.

Air Force

A Finnish Air Force squadron contained 12 airplanes. Four squadrons made up a Flying Regiment.

FRANCE
Army

INFANTRY DIVISION

- Infantry Regiment
  - Infantry Battalion
    - HQ Company
    - Weapons Company
      6 x 25mm a/tank
      2 x 81mm mortar
- Artillery Regiment
  1 Regt=36 x 75mm
  1 Regt=12 x 105mm
  12 x 155mm
- Recce Group
  - HQ Squadron
  - M/cycle Squadron
  - Weapons Squadron
    4 x 25mm a/tank
    10 x heavy m.g.
    24 x light m.g.
  - Horsed Squadron
- Telephone Radio Company
- Engineer Company
- A/t Company
  12 x 25mm
  6 x 47mm

Comprising

17,500 offs & men
360 light m.g.
154 heavy m.g.
27 light mortar
24 heavy mortar
34 25mm anti-tank
6 47mm anti-tank
36 75mm field gun
12 105mm howitzer
12 155mm field gun

ARMOURED DIVISION

- Brigade de Combat
  - Demi-Brigade
    - Tank Battalion
- Artillery Regiment
- Chasseur Battalion
  - Weapons Company
    12 x 25mm a/tank
    4 x 81mm mortar
  - Rifle Company
- Engineer Company

Comprising

6,510 offs and men
68 tanks Char 'B'
90 tanks Hotchkiss
12 25mm anti-tank
84 37mm anti-tank
71 47mm anti-tank
25 105mm howitzer*
c. 1,100 motor vehicles
400 motorcycles

* One source also numbers 65 75mm field guns though I remain uncertain as to which unit these were supposed to have been attached.

LIGHT MECHANISED DIVISION

- Brigade de Combat
  - Demi-Brigade
    - Tank Squadron
- Artillery Regiment
- Recce Brigade
  - Recce Regiment
    - M/cycle Squadron
    - A/Car Squadron
  - Dismounted Dragoon Regiment
    - Battalion
      - A/Car Squadron
      - Weapons Squadron
      - Rifle Squadron
- Engineer Battalion

Comprising

10,400 offs and men
80 tanks Somua
80 tanks Hotchkiss
60 tanks Renault*
40 armoured cars
100 25mm anti-tank
80 37mm anti-tank
90 47mm anti-tank
24 75mm field gun
12 105mm howitzer
c. 1,800 motor vehicles
1,500 motorcycles

* Light tanks known as *automitrailleuses de reconnaissance*.

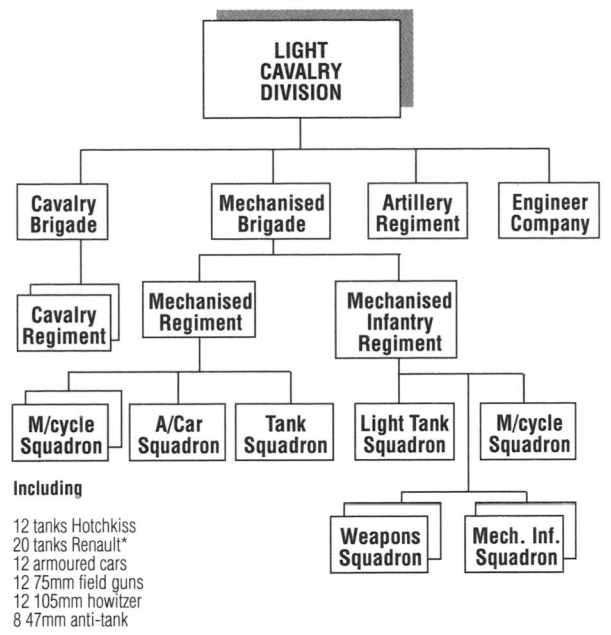

Including

12 tanks Hotchkiss
20 tanks Renault*
12 armoured cars
12 75mm field guns
12 105mm howitzer
8 47mm anti-tank

*Light tanks known as *automitrailleuses de reconnaissance*.*

Other types of division not detailed here were motorised infantry (7), Alpine (8), North African (10), Colonial (7) and Fortress (5).

When the French Army reformed in North Africa in 1942-43 the divisions were organised and equipped in the same way as US forces. See that section for details.

Air Force

The most important subdivision of the French Air Force was the *groupe*, with a theoretical establishment of 26 to 30 fighters (34 in reinforced group) and 13 to 19 bombers and reconnaissance aircraft. Some special duty and foreign units were grouped in *escadrilles* of 12 to 16 aircraft. Administratively, *groupes* were sub-divisions of *escadres* (e.g. *Groupe* II/54 would be the second *groupe* of the 54th *escadre*) but operationally they were usually joined together in *groupements*, containing anything from two to six *groupes*.

Free French units that flew with the RAF were organised accordingly (see United Kingdom, Air Force below) but after the liberation of North Africa and later Southern France many Vichy units came over to the Allies and these, though mostly re-equipped with British and American aircraft, retained their original organisation. A few squadrons also fought with the Russians and these were organised as for the host air force (see USSR below).

GERMANY
Army, SS and Luftwaffe Ground Forces

With the German Army above all it has to be remembered that the establishments given below are what the divisions ought to have contained. From 1941 onwards the gulf between theory and actuality increasingly widened so that by 1944 and 1945 having even 50 per cent of the TO&E actually available was an exception.

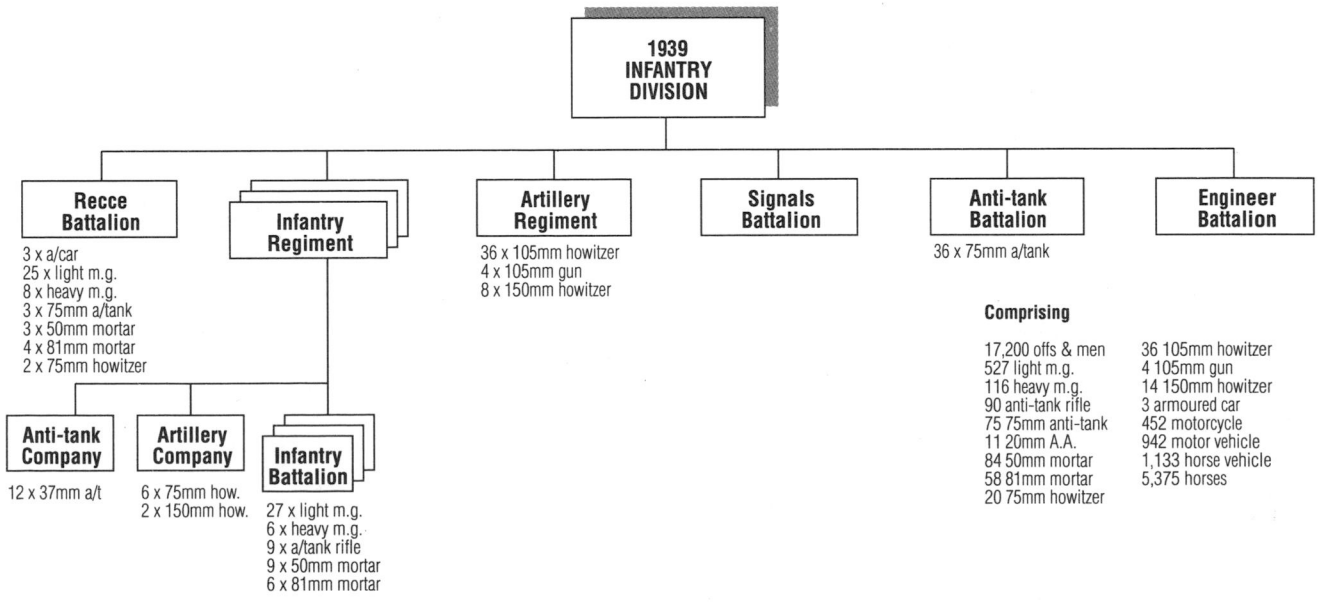

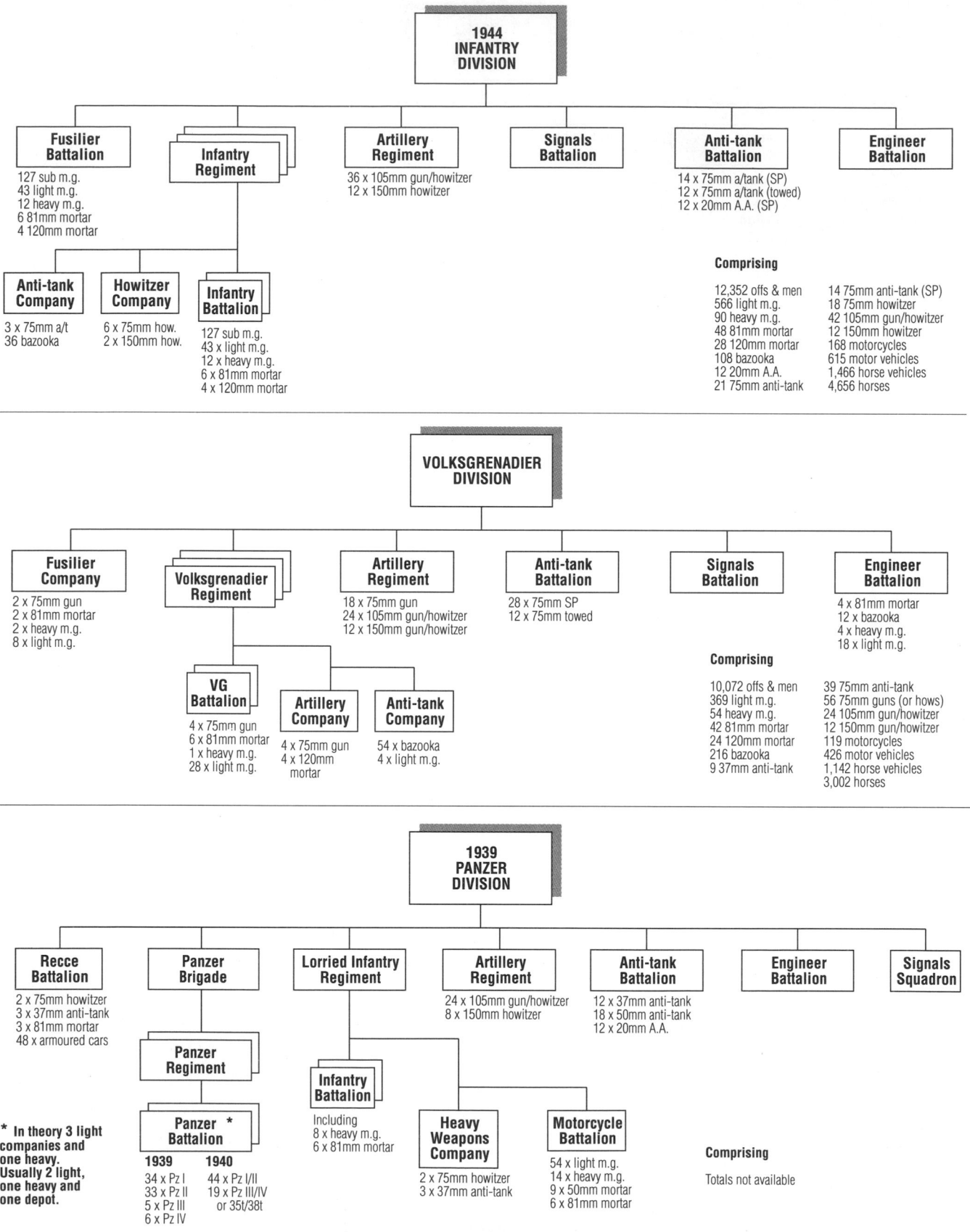

1944 INFANTRY DIVISION

Fusilier Battalion
127 sub m.g.
43 light m.g.
12 heavy m.g.
6 81mm mortar
4 120mm mortar

Infantry Regiment

Anti-tank Company
3 x 75mm a/t
36 bazooka

Howitzer Company
6 x 75mm how.
2 x 150mm how.

Infantry Battalion
127 sub m.g.
43 x light m.g.
12 x heavy m.g.
6 x 81mm mortar
4 x 120mm mortar

Artillery Regiment
36 x 105mm gun/howitzer
12 x 150mm howitzer

Signals Battalion

Anti-tank Battalion
14 x 75mm a/tank (SP)
12 x 75mm a/tank (towed)
12 x 20mm A.A. (SP)

Engineer Battalion

Comprising

12,352 offs & men	14 75mm anti-tank (SP)
566 light m.g.	18 75mm howitzer
90 heavy m.g.	42 105mm gun/howitzer
48 81mm mortar	12 150mm howitzer
28 120mm mortar	168 motorcycles
108 bazooka	615 motor vehicles
12 20mm A.A.	1,466 horse vehicles
21 75mm anti-tank	4,656 horses

VOLKSGRENADIER DIVISION

Fusilier Company
2 x 75mm gun
2 x 81mm mortar
2 x heavy m.g.
8 x light m.g.

Volksgrenadier Regiment

VG Battalion
4 x 75mm gun
6 x 81mm mortar
1 x heavy m.g.
28 x light m.g.

Artillery Company
4 x 75mm gun
4 x 120mm mortar

Anti-tank Company
54 x bazooka
4 x light m.g.

Artillery Regiment
18 x 75mm gun
24 x 105mm gun/howitzer
12 x 150mm gun/howitzer

Anti-tank Battalion
28 x 75mm SP
12 x 75mm towed

Signals Battalion

Engineer Battalion
4 x 81mm mortar
12 x bazooka
4 x heavy m.g.
18 x light m.g.

Comprising

10,072 offs & men	39 75mm anti-tank
369 light m.g.	56 75mm guns (or hows)
54 heavy m.g.	24 105mm gun/howitzer
42 81mm mortar	12 150mm gun/howitzer
24 120mm mortar	119 motorcycles
216 bazooka	426 motor vehicles
9 37mm anti-tank	1,142 horse vehicles
	3,002 horses

1939 PANZER DIVISION

Recce Battalion
2 x 75mm howitzer
3 x 37mm anti-tank
3 x 81mm mortar
48 x armoured cars

Panzer Brigade

Panzer Regiment

Panzer Battalion *

1939	1940
34 x Pz I	44 x Pz I/II
33 x Pz II	19 x Pz III/IV
5 x Pz III	or 35t/38t
6 x Pz IV	

Lorried Infantry Regiment

Infantry Battalion
Including
8 x heavy m.g.
6 x 81mm mortar

Heavy Weapons Company
2 x 75mm howitzer
3 x 37mm anti-tank

Motorcycle Battalion
54 x light m.g.
14 x heavy m.g.
9 x 50mm mortar
6 x 81mm mortar

Artillery Regiment
24 x 105mm gun/howitzer
8 x 150mm howitzer

Anti-tank Battalion
12 x 37mm anti-tank
18 x 50mm anti-tank
12 x 20mm A.A.

Engineer Battalion

Signals Squadron

* In theory 3 light companies and one heavy. Usually 2 light, one heavy and one depot.

Comprising

Totals not available

1941 PANZER DIVISION

- ### Recce Battalion
  2 x 75mm howitzer
  3 x 37mm anti-tank
  3 x 81mm mortar
  48 x armoured car

- ### Panzer Regiment
  - #### Panzer Battalion
    1941 15 x Pz II
    34 x Pz III
    10 x Pz IV

    1942 44 x Pz III
    22 x Pz IV

- ### Panzer-Grenadier Brigade
  - #### Panzer-Grenadier Regiment
    - ##### Panzer-Grenadier Battalion
      2 x 75mm field
      3 x 37mm anti-tank
      9 x bazooka
      62 x light m.g.
      14 x heavy m.g.
      9 x 50mm mortar
      6 x 81mm mortar

    - ##### Artillery
      6 x 150mm SP *or*
      6 x 150mm towed

- ### Artillery Regiment
  24 x 105mm gun/howitzer
  8 x 150mm howitzer

- ### Anti-tank Battalion
  12 x 37mm anti-tank
  18 x 50mm anti-tank

- ### Engineer Battalion

- ### Signals Squadron

Comprising

15,600 offs. and men.
(Sources on other totals extremely contradictory.)

1944 PANZER DIVISION

- ### Recce Battalion
  8 x 75mm field
  23 x 20mm A.A.
  10 x 81mm mortar
  4 x heavy m.g.
  106 x light m.g.

- ### Panzer Regiment
  - #### Panzer Battalion
    88 x Pz IV in one†
    88 x Pz V in other†

- ### Panzer-Grenadier Brigade
  - #### Panzer-Grenadier Regiment *
    - ##### Artillery
      6 x 150mm SP

    - ##### PG Battalion
      (lorries)
      6 x 20mm A.A.
      6 x 81mm mortar
      4 x 120mm mortar
      14 x heavy m.g.
      54 x light m.g.

    - ##### PG Battalion
      (half-tracks)
      12 x 75mm field
      21 x 20mm A.A.
      6 x 81mm mortar
      4 x 120mm mortar
      14 x heavy m.g.
      91 x light m.g.

- ### Artillery Regiment
  6 x 150mm SP
  12 x 150mm towed
  12 x 105mm SP
  12 x 105mm towed

- ### Anti-tank Battalion
  28 x assault gun
  12 x 75mm anti-tank

- ### A.A. Battalion
  12 x 88m
  6 x 37mm

- ### Engineer Battalion

- ### Signals Battalion

Comprising

13,276 offs & men	8 37mm anti-tank
For Tanks see 1941 Pz	40 75mm anti-tank
Battalion above	12 88mm A.A.
1,543 sub m.g.	20 75mm howitzer‡
1,157 light m.g.	24 105mm howitzer
64 heavy m.g.	24 150mm howitzer
46 81mm mortar	480 motorcycles
16 120mm mortar	2,685 motor vehicles
74 20mm A.A.	

* One of the regiments comprised two lorried battalions.
† Soon reduced to 52 of each.
‡ Some sources give all 75mm guns as anti-tank.

SS PANZER DIVISION

These were organised pretty much on the lines of the ordinary Army 1944 Panzer division, though they often had two extra panzer-grenadier battalions and a whole battalion of assault guns as well as a towed anti-tank battalion. Their official establishment of men, heavy weapons and motor transport was about 25 per cent higher than Army divisions and during periods of heavy fighting they were often, though depleted, twice as strong in men and equipment.

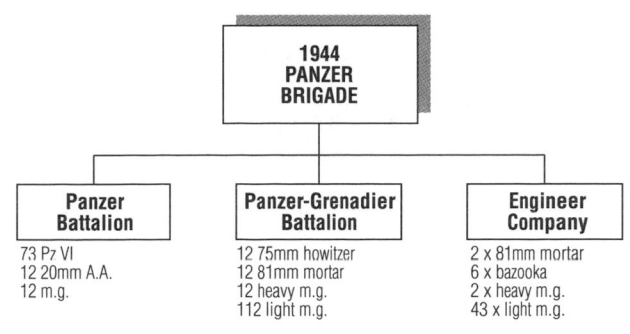

1944 PANZER BRIGADE

- ### Panzer Battalion
  73 Pz VI
  12 20mm A.A.
  12 m.g.

- ### Panzer-Grenadier Battalion
  12 75mm howitzer
  12 81mm mortar
  12 heavy m.g.
  112 light m.g.

- ### Engineer Company
  2 x 81mm mortar
  6 x bazooka
  2 x heavy m.g.
  43 x light m.g.

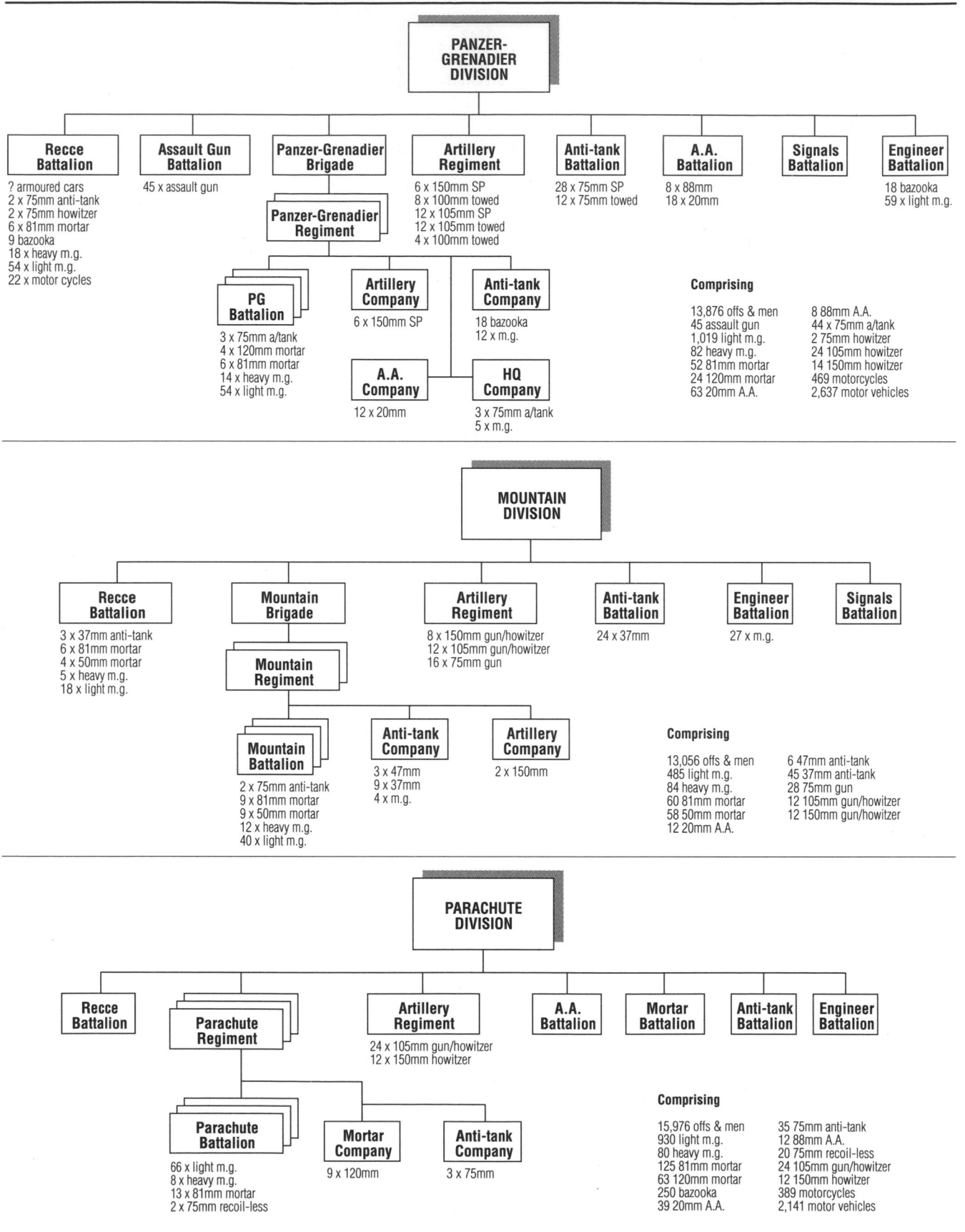

PANZER-GRENADIER DIVISION

Recce Battalion
? armoured cars
2 x 75mm anti-tank
2 x 75mm howitzer
6 x 81mm mortar
9 bazooka
18 x heavy m.g.
54 x light m.g.
22 x motor cycles

Assault Gun Battalion
45 x assault gun

Panzer-Grenadier Brigade

Panzer-Grenadier Regiment

PG Battalion
3 x 75mm a/tank
4 x 120mm mortar
6 x 81mm mortar
14 x heavy m.g.
54 x light m.g.

Artillery Company
6 x 150mm SP

Anti-tank Company
18 bazooka
12 x m.g.

A.A. Company
12 x 20mm

HQ Company
3 x 75mm a/tank
5 x m.g.

Artillery Regiment
6 x 150mm SP
8 x 100mm towed
12 x 105mm SP
12 x 105mm towed
4 x 100mm towed

Anti-tank Battalion
28 x 75mm SP
12 x 75mm towed

A.A. Battalion
8 x 88mm
18 x 20mm

Signals Battalion

Engineer Battalion
18 bazooka
59 x light m.g.

Comprising

13,876 offs & men
45 assault gun
1,019 light m.g.
82 heavy m.g.
52 81mm mortar
24 120mm mortar
63 20mm A.A.

8 88mm A.A.
44 x 75mm a/tank
2 75mm howitzer
24 105mm howitzer
14 150mm howitzer
469 motorcycles
2,637 motor vehicles

MOUNTAIN DIVISION

Recce Battalion
3 x 37mm anti-tank
6 x 81mm mortar
4 x 50mm mortar
5 x heavy m.g.
18 x light m.g.

Mountain Brigade

Mountain Regiment

Mountain Battalion
2 x 75mm anti-tank
9 x 81mm mortar
9 x 50mm mortar
12 x heavy m.g.
40 x light m.g.

Anti-tank Company
3 x 47mm
9 x 37mm
4 x m.g.

Artillery Company
2 x 150mm

Artillery Regiment
8 x 150mm gun/howitzer
12 x 105mm gun/howitzer
16 x 75mm gun

Anti-tank Battalion
24 x 37mm

Engineer Battalion
27 x m.g.

Signals Battalion

Comprising

13,056 offs & men
485 light m.g.
84 heavy m.g.
60 81mm mortar
58 50mm mortar
12 20mm A.A.

6 47mm anti-tank
45 37mm anti-tank
28 75mm gun
12 105mm gun/howitzer
12 150mm gun/howitzer

PARACHUTE DIVISION

Recce Battalion

Parachute Regiment

Parachute Battalion
66 x light m.g.
8 x heavy m.g.
13 x 81mm mortar
2 x 75mm recoil-less

Mortar Company
9 x 120mm

Anti-tank Company
3 x 75mm

Artillery Regiment
24 x 105mm gun/howitzer
12 x 150mm howitzer

A.A. Battalion

Mortar Battalion

Anti-tank Battalion

Engineer Battalion

Comprising

15,976 offs & men
930 light m.g.
80 heavy m.g.
125 81mm mortar
63 120mm mortar
250 bazooka
39 20mm A.A.

35 75mm anti-tank
12 88mm A.A.
20 75mm recoil-less
24 105mm gun/howitzer
12 150mm howitzer
389 motorcycles
2,141 motor vehicles

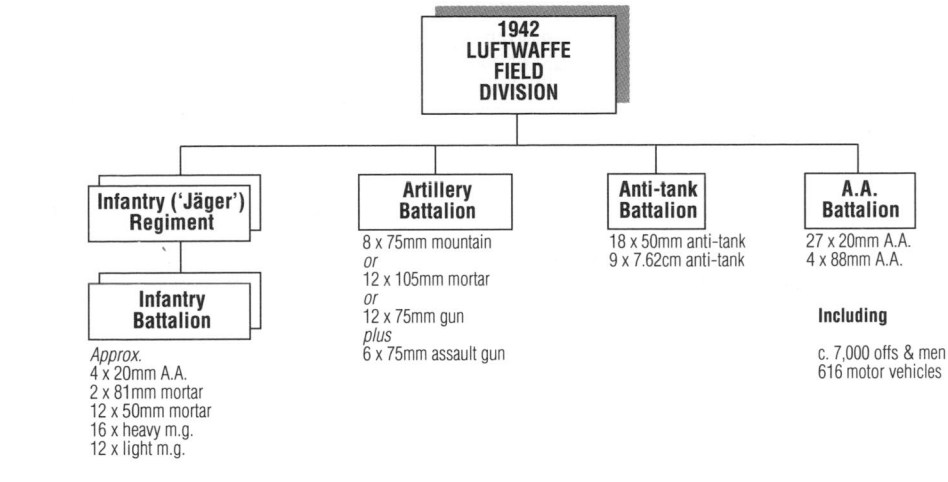

1942 LUFTWAFFE FIELD DIVISION

Infantry ('Jäger') Regiment

Infantry Battalion

Approx.
4 x 20mm A.A.
2 x 81mm mortar
12 x 50mm mortar
16 x heavy m.g.
12 x light m.g.

Artillery Battalion

8 x 75mm mountain
or
12 x 105mm mortar
or
12 x 75mm gun
plus
6 x 75mm assault gun

Anti-tank Battalion

18 x 50mm anti-tank
9 x 7.62cm anti-tank

A.A. Battalion

27 x 20mm A.A.
4 x 88mm A.A.

Including

c. 7,000 offs & men
616 motor vehicles

1944 LUFTWAFFE FIELD DIVISION

In November 1943 the Luftwaffe Field Divisions were taken over by the Army and were reorganised according to 1944 Army Infantry Division TO&E. The main differences were:
– a reconnaissance company instead of a battalion.
– the artillery regiment had 75mm guns instead of 105mm gun-howitzers.
– the A.A. guns were beefed up into a separate battalion though ironically these divisions often had no A.A. component at all as the Luftwaffe was loath to give up its guns to the Army.

Other types of division not included here, because there were very few of them, because they were short-lived or because they were not combat-worthy, were Cavalry; Coastal Defence; Cossack; Frontier; Jäger; Light; Police; Reserve; Security and *Sturm*.

Air Force*

* See previous section for Parachute and Luftwaffe Field Divisions.

Within a Luftflotte (see supplement to Table 5, page 94), Luftwaffe units were, in theory at least, organised as shown in the chart on the right.

Geschwader were numbered by type, for example Jagdgeschwader 52, abbreviated to JG 52. There were also Nachtjagd-(NJG), nightfighters; Zerstörer-(ZG), twin-engined fighters; Kampf-(KG), bombers; Sturtzkampf-(StG), dive-bombers; Schlacht-(SG), ground attack and transport (TG). Gruppen were assigned Roman numerals within the Geschwader, e.g. II/JG 52. The nine Staffeln of a Gruppe were numbered in Arabic numerals from 1 to 9. The first three were always assigned to Gruppe I, the next three to Gruppe II and so on. Thus the designation 8/JG 52 also implicitly informs us that this Staffel was part of number III Gruppe.

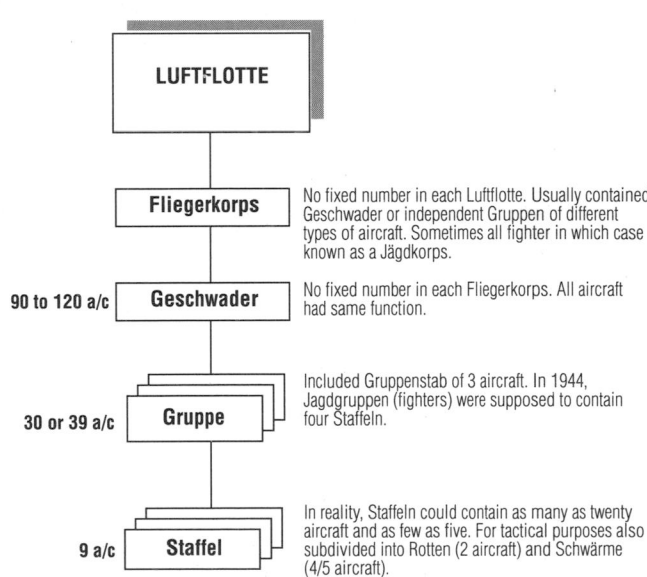

LUFTFLOTTE

Fliegerkorps — No fixed number in each Luftflotte. Usually contained Geschwader or independent Gruppen of different types of aircraft. Sometimes all fighter in which case known as a Jagdkorps.

90 to 120 a/c **Geschwader** — No fixed number in each Fliegerkorps. All aircraft had same function.

30 or 39 a/c **Gruppe** — Included Gruppenstab of 3 aircraft. In 1944, Jagdgruppen (fighters) were supposed to contain four Staffeln.

9 a/c **Staffel** — In reality, Staffeln could contain as many as twenty aircraft and as few as five. For tactical purposes also subdivided into Rotten (2 aircraft) and Schwärme (4/5 aircraft).

HUNGARY
Army

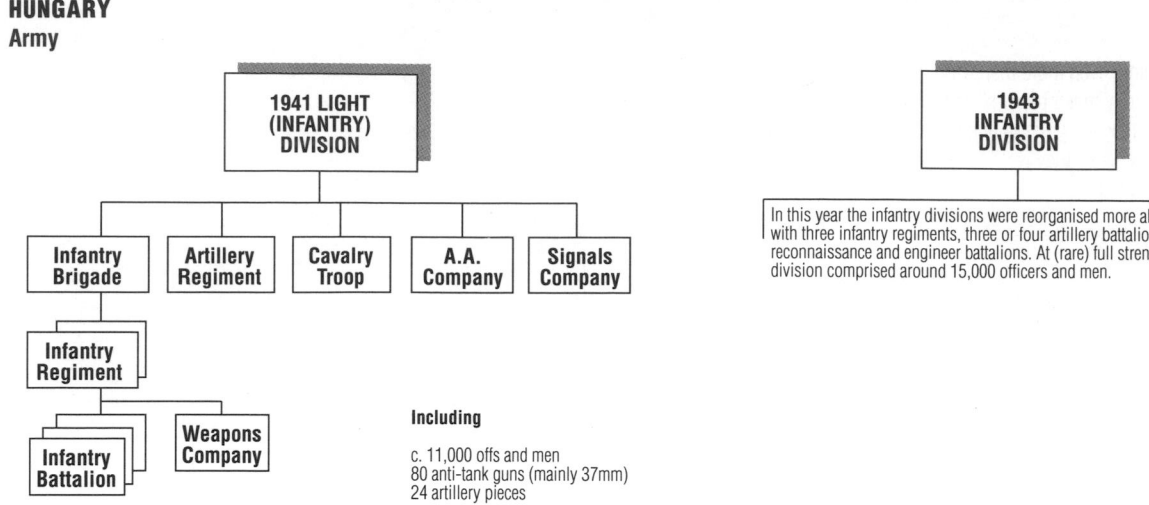

1941 LIGHT (INFANTRY) DIVISION
- Infantry Brigade
  - Infantry Regiment
    - Infantry Battalion
    - Weapons Company
- Artillery Regiment
- Cavalry Troop
- A.A. Company
- Signals Company

Including

c. 11,000 offs and men
80 anti-tank guns (mainly 37mm)
24 artillery pieces

1943 INFANTRY DIVISION

In this year the infantry divisions were reorganised more along German lines with three infantry regiments, three or four artillery battalions as well as reconnaissance and engineer battalions. At (rare) full strength an infantry division comprised around 15,000 officers and men.

In October 1942 a reconnaissance battalion was also included in the Light Divisions.

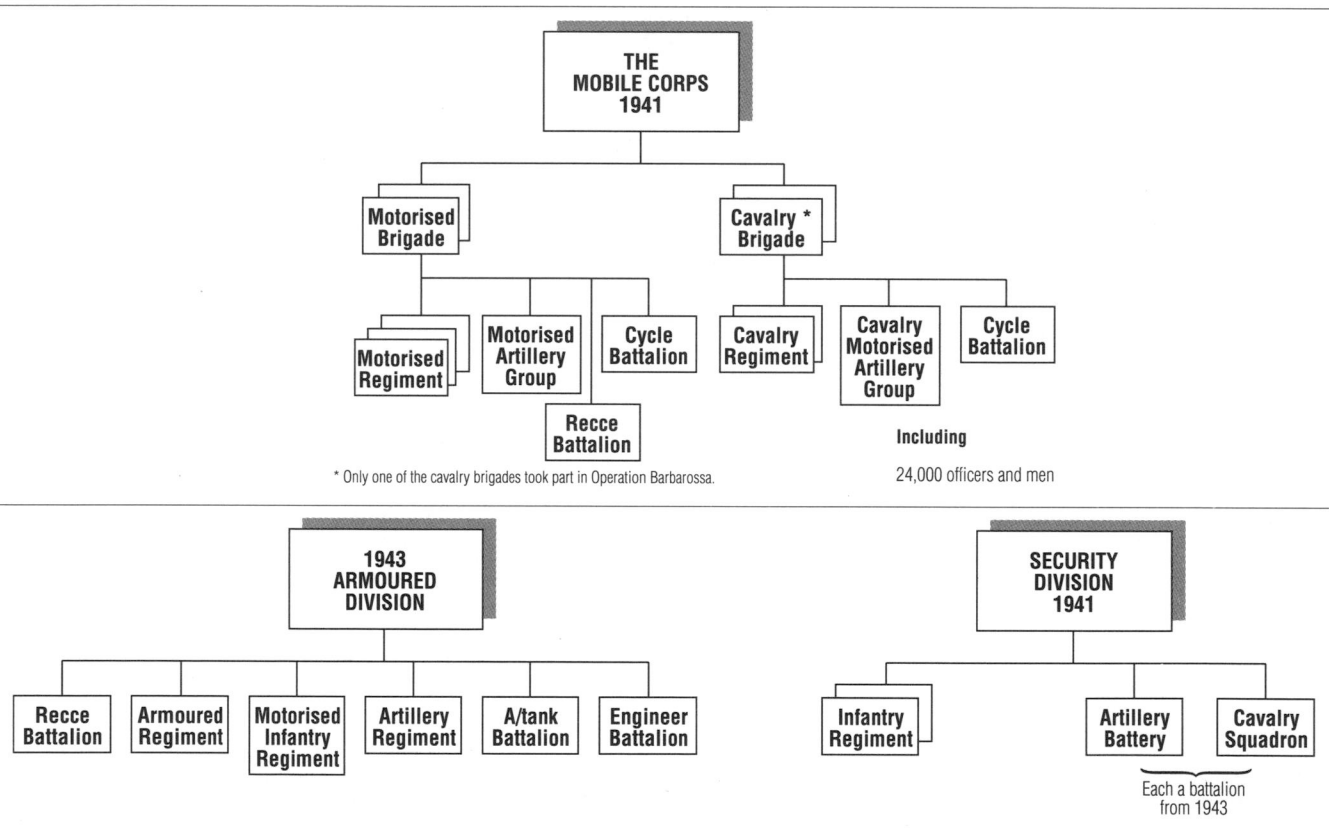

THE MOBILE CORPS 1941
- Motorised Brigade
  - Motorised Regiment
  - Motorised Artillery Group
  - Cycle Battalion
  - Recce Battalion
- Cavalry * Brigade
  - Cavalry Regiment
  - Cavalry Motorised Artillery Group
  - Cycle Battalion

* Only one of the cavalry brigades took part in Operation Barbarossa.

Including

24,000 officers and men

1943 ARMOURED DIVISION
- Recce Battalion
- Armoured Regiment
- Motorised Infantry Regiment
- Artillery Regiment
- A/tank Battalion
- Engineer Battalion

SECURITY DIVISION 1941
- Infantry Regiment
- Artillery Battery
- Cavalry Squadron

Each a battalion from 1943

Air Force
Hungarian aircraft were divided by type into Air Regiments. These were each subdivided into two groups, each of two squadrons. A squadron usually comprised four flights each of three aircraft. The group was the main operational unit, often being named after the base from which it originally operated.

INDIA
Indian forces were organised and equipped in the same way as UK forces and the reader is referred to that entry for details. An important exception was that in Indian infantry divisions each regiment contained one British and two Indian battalions.

ITALY
Army

It should be borne in mind, even more than with other armies, that the TO&Es given below are very much paper strengths. In the Balkans the Italians could not afford to keep garrison and counter-insurgency divisions up to strength whilst in N.Africa they were never able to replace the enormous losses of men and materiel.

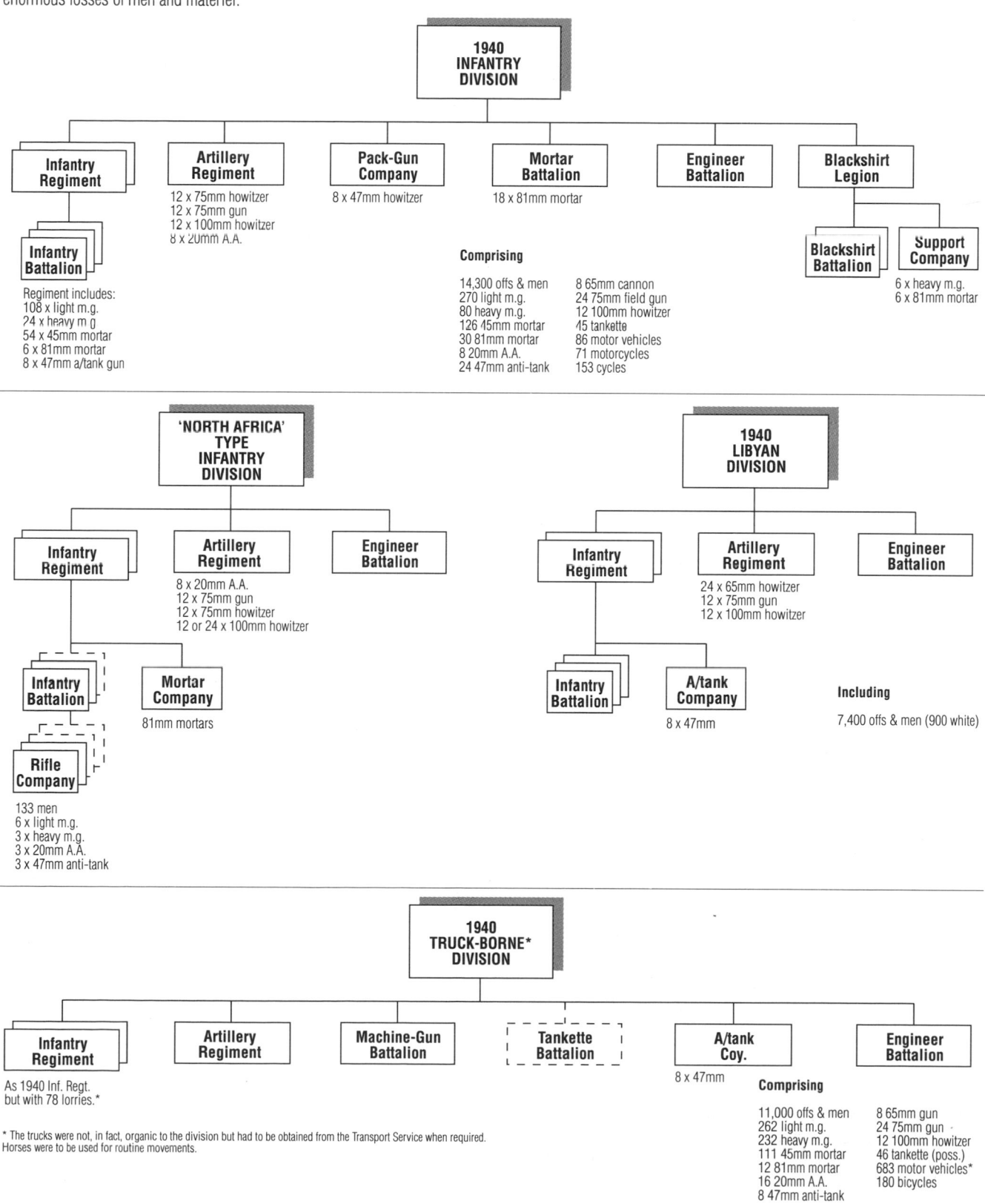

1940 INFANTRY DIVISION

Infantry Regiment

Infantry Battalion

Regiment includes:
108 x light m.g.
24 x heavy m.g
54 x 45mm mortar
6 x 81mm mortar
8 x 47mm a/tank gun

Artillery Regiment

12 x 75mm howitzer
12 x 75mm gun
12 x 100mm howitzer
8 x 20mm A.A.

Pack-Gun Company

8 x 47mm howitzer

Mortar Battalion

18 x 81mm mortar

Engineer Battalion

Blackshirt Legion

Blackshirt Battalion

Support Company

6 x heavy m.g.
6 x 81mm mortar

Comprising

14,300 offs & men
270 light m.g.
80 heavy m.g.
126 45mm mortar
30 81mm mortar
8 20mm A.A.
24 47mm anti-tank

8 65mm cannon
24 75mm field gun
12 100mm howitzer
45 tankette
86 motor vehicles
71 motorcycles
153 cycles

'NORTH AFRICA' TYPE INFANTRY DIVISION

Infantry Regiment

Artillery Regiment

8 x 20mm A.A.
12 x 75mm gun
12 x 75mm howitzer
12 or 24 x 100mm howitzer

Engineer Battalion

Infantry Battalion

Mortar Company

81mm mortars

Rifle Company

133 men
6 x light m.g.
3 x heavy m.g.
3 x 20mm A.A.
3 x 47mm anti-tank

1940 LIBYAN DIVISION

Infantry Regiment

Artillery Regiment

24 x 65mm howitzer
12 x 75mm gun
12 x 100mm howitzer

Engineer Battalion

Infantry Battalion

A/tank Company

8 x 47mm

Including

7,400 offs & men (900 white)

1940 TRUCK-BORNE* DIVISION

Infantry Regiment

As 1940 Inf. Regt.
but with 78 lorries.*

Artillery Regiment

Machine-Gun Battalion

Tankette Battalion

A/tank Coy.

8 x 47mm

Engineer Battalion

Comprising

11,000 offs & men
262 light m.g.
232 heavy m.g.
111 45mm mortar
12 81mm mortar
16 20mm A.A.
8 47mm anti-tank

8 65mm gun
24 75mm gun
12 100mm howitzer
46 tankette (poss.)
683 motor vehicles*
180 bicycles

* The trucks were not, in fact, organic to the division but had to be obtained from the Transport Service when required. Horses were to be used for routine movements.

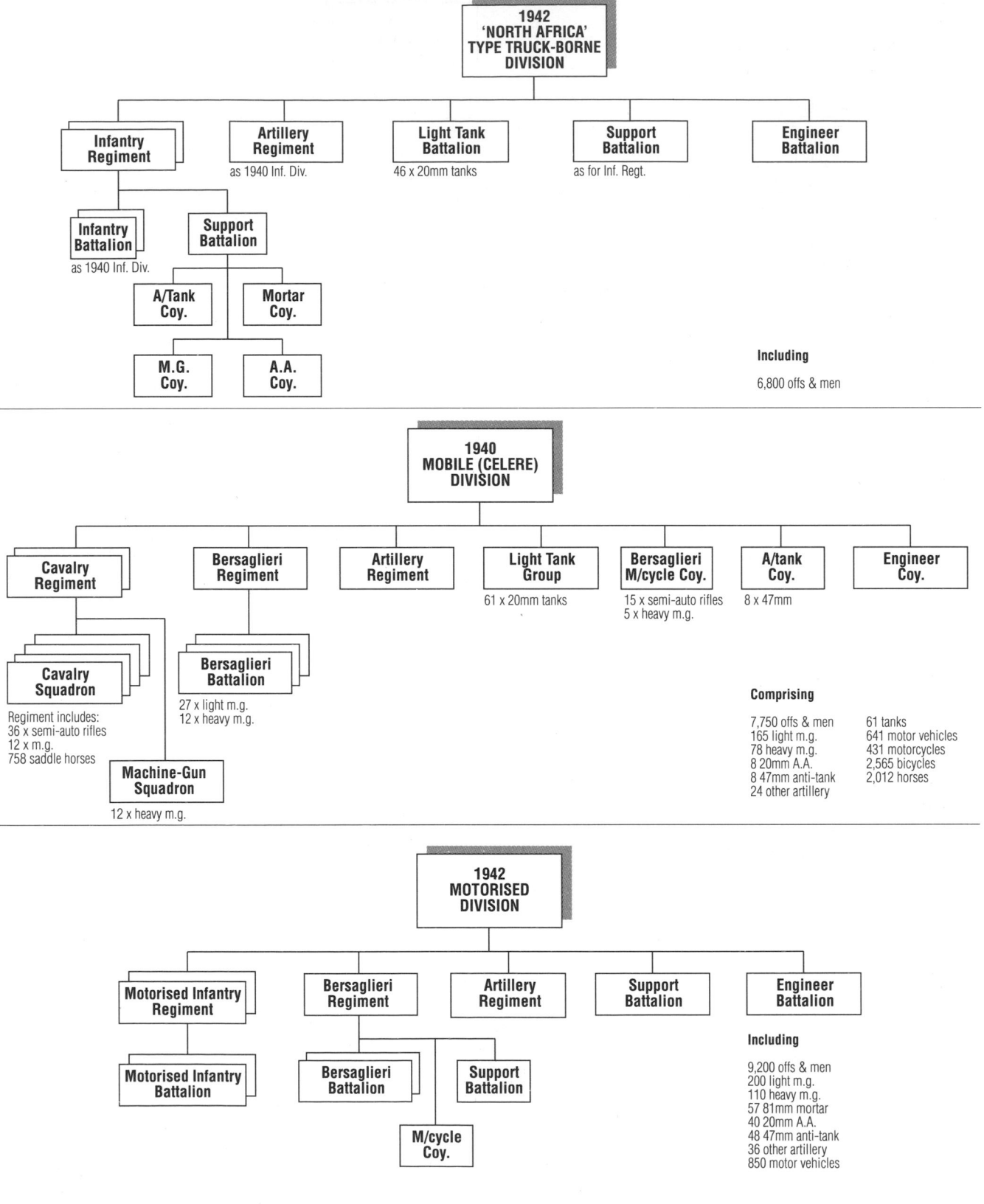

1942 'NORTH AFRICA' TYPE TRUCK-BORNE DIVISION

- **Infantry Regiment**
  - **Infantry Battalion** — as 1940 Inf. Div.
  - **Support Battalion**
    - **A/Tank Coy.**
    - **Mortar Coy.**
    - **M.G. Coy.**
    - **A.A. Coy.**
- **Artillery Regiment** — as 1940 Inf. Div.
- **Light Tank Battalion** — 46 x 20mm tanks
- **Support Battalion** — as for Inf. Regt.
- **Engineer Battalion**

Including
6,800 offs & men

1940 MOBILE (CELERE) DIVISION

- **Cavalry Regiment**
  - **Cavalry Squadron**

    Regiment includes:
    36 x semi-auto rifles
    12 x m.g.
    758 saddle horses
  - **Machine-Gun Squadron** — 12 x heavy m.g.
- **Bersaglieri Regiment**
  - **Bersaglieri Battalion** — 27 x light m.g. / 12 x heavy m.g.
- **Artillery Regiment**
- **Light Tank Group** — 61 x 20mm tanks
- **Bersaglieri M/cycle Coy.** — 15 x semi-auto rifles / 5 x heavy m.g.
- **A/tank Coy.** — 8 x 47mm
- **Engineer Coy.**

Comprising

7,750 offs & men	61 tanks
165 light m.g.	641 motor vehicles
78 heavy m.g.	431 motorcycles
8 20mm A.A.	2,565 bicycles
8 47mm anti-tank	2,012 horses
24 other artillery	

1942 MOTORISED DIVISION

- **Motorised Infantry Regiment**
  - **Motorised Infantry Battalion**
- **Bersaglieri Regiment**
  - **Bersaglieri Battalion**
  - **Support Battalion**
    - **M/cycle Coy.**
- **Artillery Regiment**
- **Support Battalion**
- **Engineer Battalion**

Including

9,200 offs & men
200 light m.g.
110 heavy m.g.
57 81mm mortar
40 20mm A.A.
48 47mm anti-tank
36 other artillery
850 motor vehicles

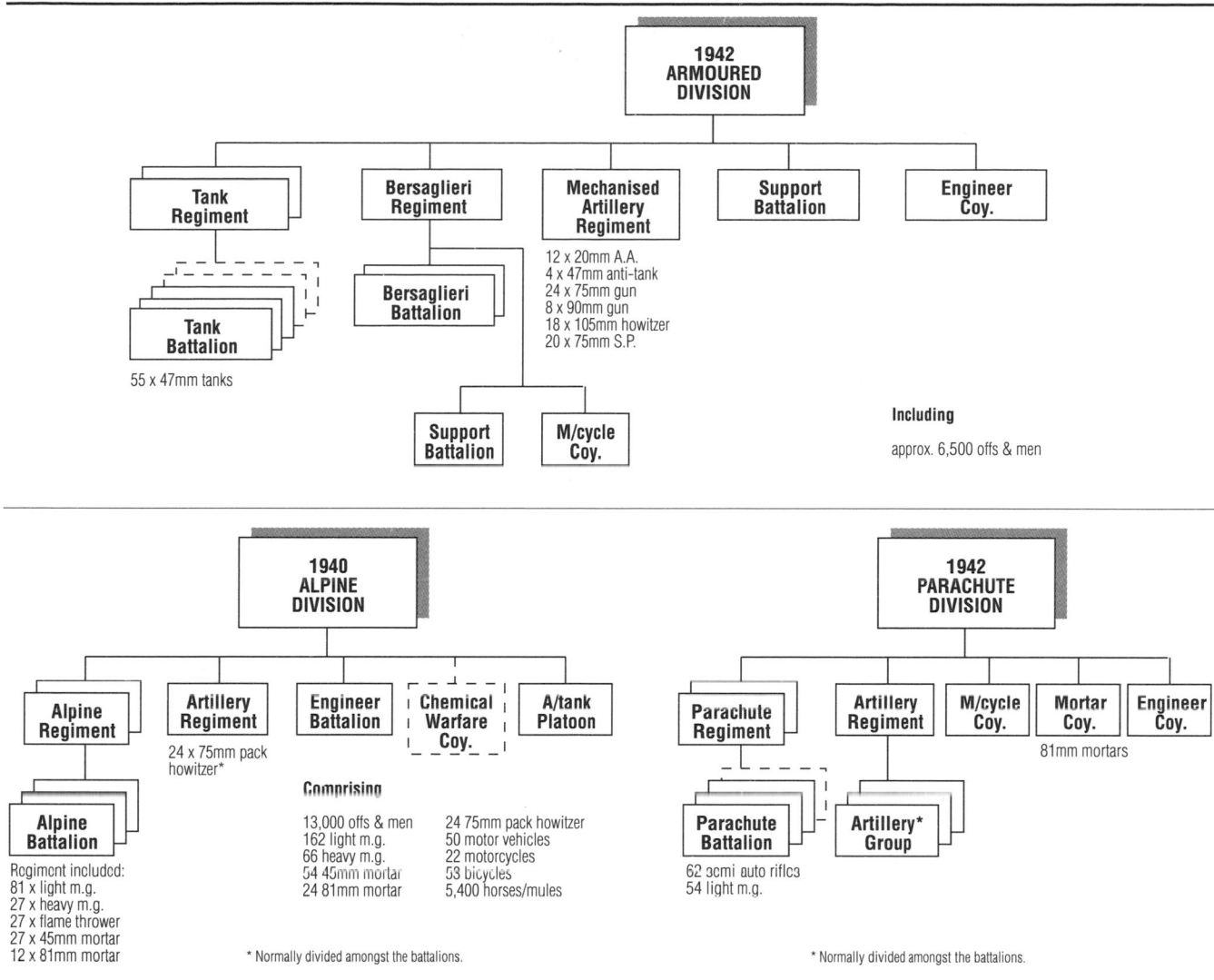

Air Force

The basic tactical and administrative formation of the Italian Air Force was the Gruppo, comprising two bomber or three fighter Squadriglie each containing six frontline bombers or nine frontline fighters, in each case with three aircraft in reserve. Two or more Gruppi made up a Stormo and in larger commands these were grouped into Air Brigades and/or Air Divisions. Whether or not in brigades and divisions, the Gruppi and Stormo came under the command of the various types of territorial command listed in the supplement to Table 6, page 97.

JAPAN
Army Ground Forces

It should be borne in mind that the TO&Es given below are mainly appropriate to the mainland campaigns of the Japanese Army. More than most, this army contained an enormous number of independent units not organic to any division and it was such units (see Section 3, The Pacific Campaign, page 192) that tended to be thrown together in *ad hoc* garrison groups to defend the various Pacific islands and atolls.

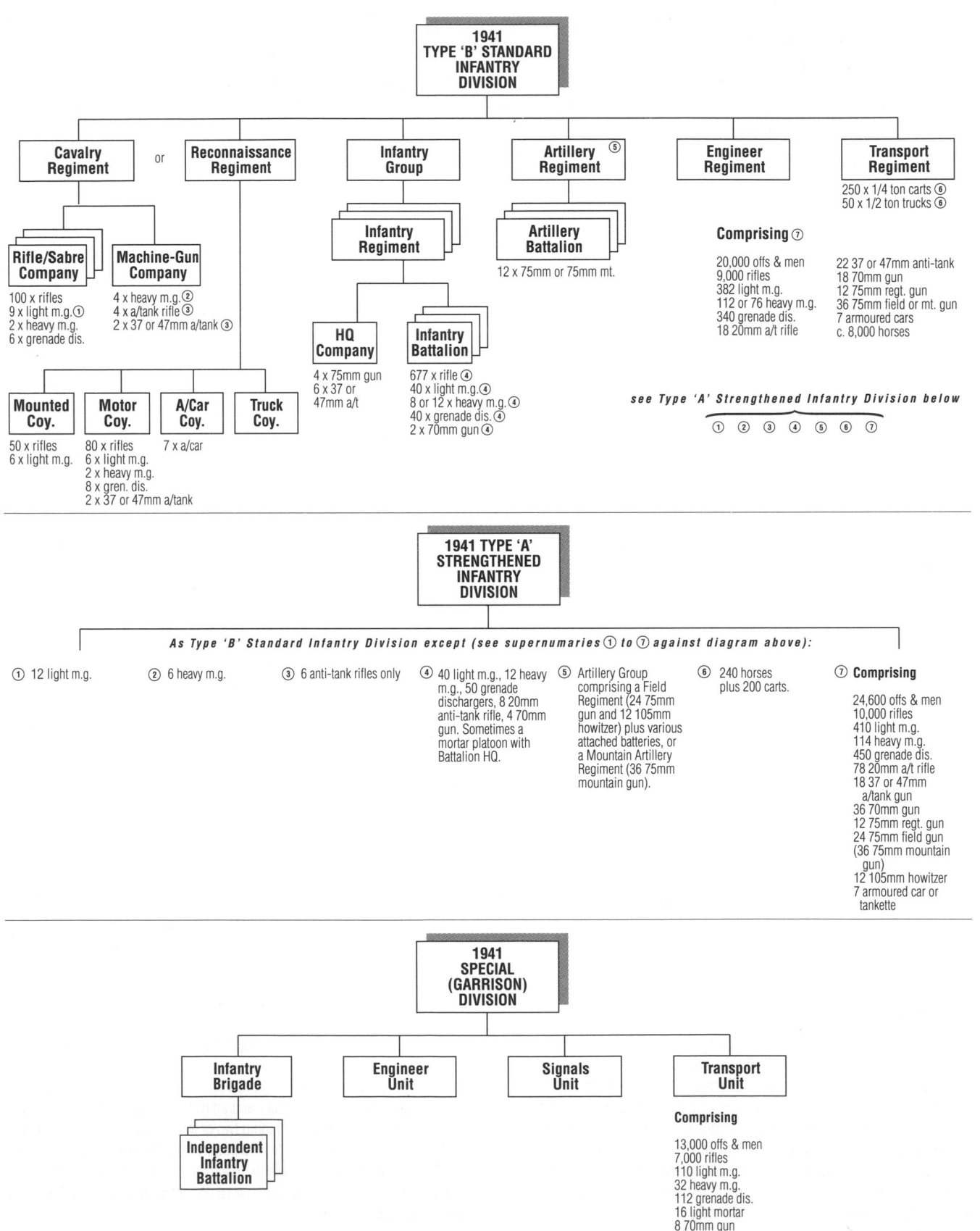

1941 TYPE 'B' STANDARD INFANTRY DIVISION

Cavalry Regiment or **Reconnaissance Regiment**

Infantry Group

Artillery Regiment ⑤

Engineer Regiment

Transport Regiment
250 x 1/4 ton carts ⑥
50 x 1/2 ton trucks ⑥

Rifle/Sabre Company
100 x rifles
9 x light m.g. ①
2 x heavy m.g.
6 x grenade dis.

Machine-Gun Company
4 x heavy m.g. ②
4 x a/tank rifle ③
2 x 37 or 47mm a/tank ③

Infantry Regiment

Artillery Battalion
12 x 75mm or 75mm mt.

Comprising ⑦

20,000 offs & men
9,000 rifles
382 light m.g.
112 or 76 heavy m.g.
340 grenade dis.
18 20mm a/t rifle

22 37 or 47mm anti-tank
18 70mm gun
12 75mm regt. gun
36 75mm field or mt. gun
7 armoured cars
c. 8,000 horses

HQ Company
4 x 75mm gun
6 x 37 or 47mm a/t

Infantry Battalion
677 x rifle ④
40 x light m.g. ④
8 or 12 x heavy m.g. ④
40 x grenade dis. ④
2 x 70mm gun ④

see Type 'A' Strengthened Infantry Division below
① ② ③ ④ ⑤ ⑥ ⑦

Mounted Coy.
50 x rifles
6 x light m.g.

Motor Coy.
80 x rifles
6 x light m.g.
2 x heavy m.g.
8 x gren. dis.
2 x 37 or 47mm a/tank

A/Car Coy.
7 x a/car

Truck Coy.

1941 TYPE 'A' STRENGTHENED INFANTRY DIVISION

As Type 'B' Standard Infantry Division except (see supernumaries ① to ⑦ against diagram above):

① 12 light m.g.

② 6 heavy m.g.

③ 6 anti-tank rifles only

④ 40 light m.g., 12 heavy m.g., 50 grenade dischargers, 8 20mm anti-tank rifle, 4 70mm gun. Sometimes a mortar platoon with Battalion HQ.

⑤ Artillery Group comprising a Field Regiment (24 75mm gun and 12 105mm howitzer) plus various attached batteries, or a Mountain Artillery Regiment (36 75mm mountain gun).

⑥ 240 horses plus 200 carts.

⑦ **Comprising**

24,600 offs & men
10,000 rifles
410 light m.g.
114 heavy m.g.
450 grenade dis.
78 20mm a/t rifle
18 37 or 47mm a/tank gun
36 70mm gun
12 75mm regt. gun
24 75mm field gun (36 75mm mountain gun)
12 105mm howitzer
7 armoured car or tankette

1941 SPECIAL (GARRISON) DIVISION

Infantry Brigade

Engineer Unit

Signals Unit

Transport Unit

Independent Infantry Battalion

Comprising

13,000 offs & men
7,000 rifles
110 light m.g.
32 heavy m.g.
112 grenade dis.
16 light mortar
8 70mm gun
2,700 horses

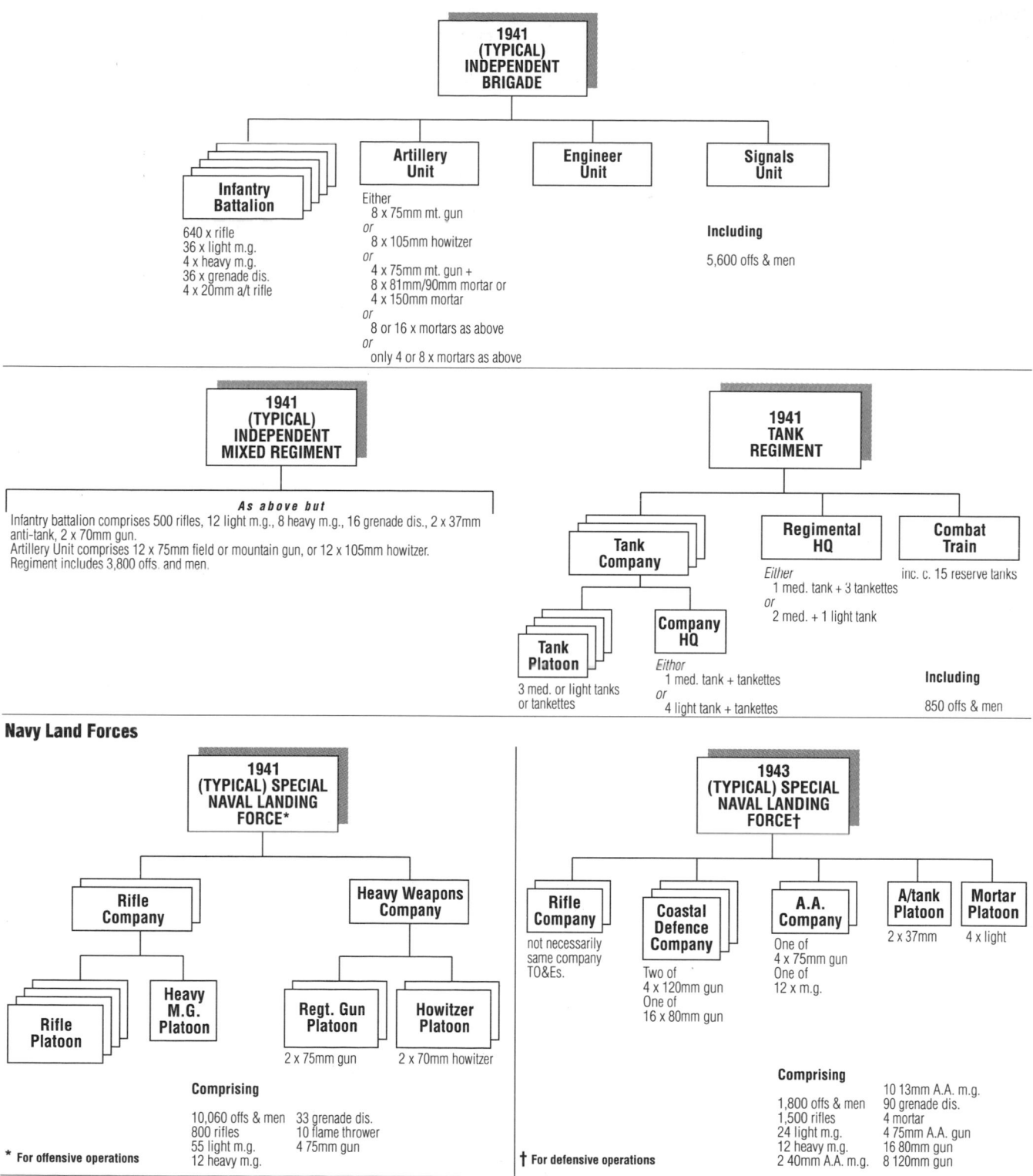

1941 (TYPICAL) INDEPENDENT BRIGADE

Infantry Battalion

640 x rifle
36 x light m.g.
4 x heavy m.g.
36 x grenade dis.
4 x 20mm a/t rifle

Artillery Unit

Either
 8 x 75mm mt. gun
or
 8 x 105mm howitzer
or
 4 x 75mm mt. gun +
 8 x 81mm/90mm mortar or
 4 x 150mm mortar
or
 8 or 16 x mortars as above
or
 only 4 or 8 x mortars as above

Engineer Unit

Signals Unit

Including

5,600 offs & men

1941 (TYPICAL) INDEPENDENT MIXED REGIMENT

As above but

Infantry battalion comprises 500 rifles, 12 light m.g., 8 heavy m.g., 16 grenade dis., 2 x 37mm anti-tank, 2 x 70mm gun.
Artillery Unit comprises 12 x 75mm field or mountain gun, or 12 x 105mm howitzer.
Regiment includes 3,800 offs. and men.

1941 TANK REGIMENT

Tank Company

Tank Platoon

3 med. or light tanks
or tankettes

Company HQ

Either
 1 med. tank + tankettes
or
 4 light tank + tankettes

Regimental HQ

Either
 1 med. tank + 3 tankettes
or
 2 med. + 1 light tank

Combat Train

inc. c. 15 reserve tanks

Including

850 offs & men

Navy Land Forces

1941 (TYPICAL) SPECIAL NAVAL LANDING FORCE*

Rifle Company

Rifle Platoon

Heavy M.G. Platoon

Heavy Weapons Company

Regt. Gun Platoon

2 x 75mm gun

Howitzer Platoon

2 x 70mm howitzer

Comprising

10,060 offs & men   33 grenade dis.
800 rifles   10 flame thrower
55 light m.g.   4 75mm gun
12 heavy m.g.

* For offensive operations

1943 (TYPICAL) SPECIAL NAVAL LANDING FORCE†

Rifle Company

not necessarily
same company
TO&Es.

Coastal Defence Company

Two of
4 x 120mm gun
One of
16 x 80mm gun

A.A. Company

One of
4 x 75mm gun
One of
12 x m.g.

A/tank Platoon

2 x 37mm

Mortar Platoon

4 x light

Comprising

1,800 offs & men   10 13mm A.A. m.g.
1,500 rifles   90 grenade dis.
24 light m.g.   4 mortar
12 heavy m.g.   4 75mm A.A. gun
2 40mm A.A. m.g.   16 80mm gun
                     8 120mm gun

† For defensive operations

Air Forces

The major subdivisions of an Army Air Force Air Army (see Table 7, page 98) were two or more air divisions (*hikoshidan*) each made up (usually) of two air brigades (*hikodan*). These latter comprised three to four air regiments (*hikosentai*) of the same type of aircraft, which in turn comprised three squadrons (*daitai*), each of three sections. The size of the squadron and its subdivisions depended on the type of aircraft flown – fighter squadrons comprised 42 or 49 aircraft, light bomber 27 or 42, medium bomber 27 or 37, reconnaissance 27 or 18. In operations later in the war these figures tended to be very much counsels of perfection.

The major subdivisions of a Naval Air Force Air Fleet or Base Air Force (see Table 7) were the air groups. Carrier air groups (*hikokitai*) usually comprised three squadrons, one each of fighters, bombers and torpedo aircraft. Land-based air groups (*kokutai*) comprised one *hikotai* (no English equivalent) for each major aircraft type in the group (usually two or three), each of these latter containing two or three squadrons (*daitai*) of 18 or 27 aircraft. These were subdivided into three-aircraft sections (*shotai*). In 1944 and 1945, squadrons were all 16 aircraft strong and sections 4 aircraft. Moreover, a group's *hikotai* were now often equipped with the same type of aircraft.

NETHERLANDS
Army

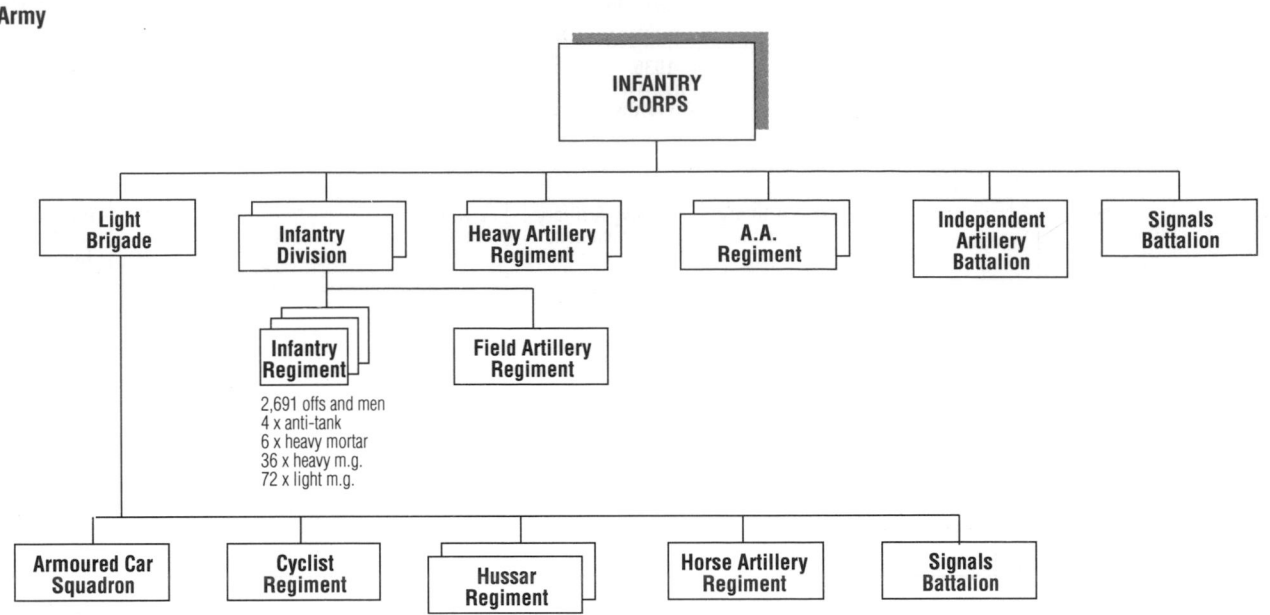

2,691 offs and men
4 x anti-tank
6 x heavy mortar
36 x heavy m.g.
72 x light m.g.

Air Force

The Dutch Army Air Service in May 1940 comprised two air regiments, the
1st with four fighter, one bomber and one reconnaissance squadron, the
2nd with two fighter and four reconnaissance squadrons.

NEW ZEALAND

New Zealand forces were organised and equipped in the same way as UK
forces. See that entry for details.

NORWAY
Army

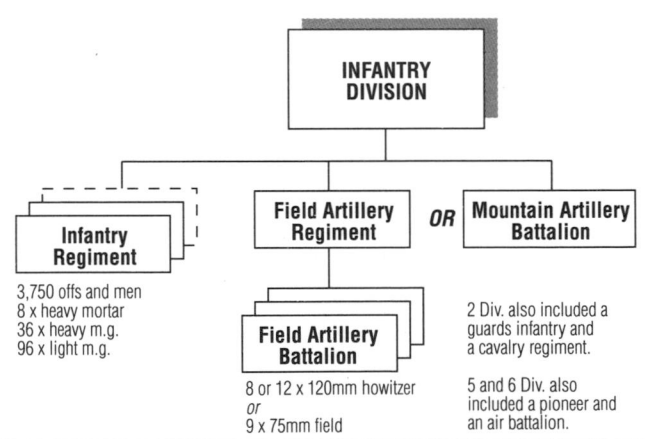

3,750 offs and men
8 x heavy mortar
36 x heavy m.g.
96 x light m.g.

8 or 12 x 120mm howitzer
or
9 x 75mm field

2 Div. also included a
guards infantry and
a cavalry regiment.

5 and 6 Div. also
included a pioneer and
an air battalion.

Air Force

Organised into a flight each of fighters, bombers and reconnaissance
aircraft.

POLAND
Army

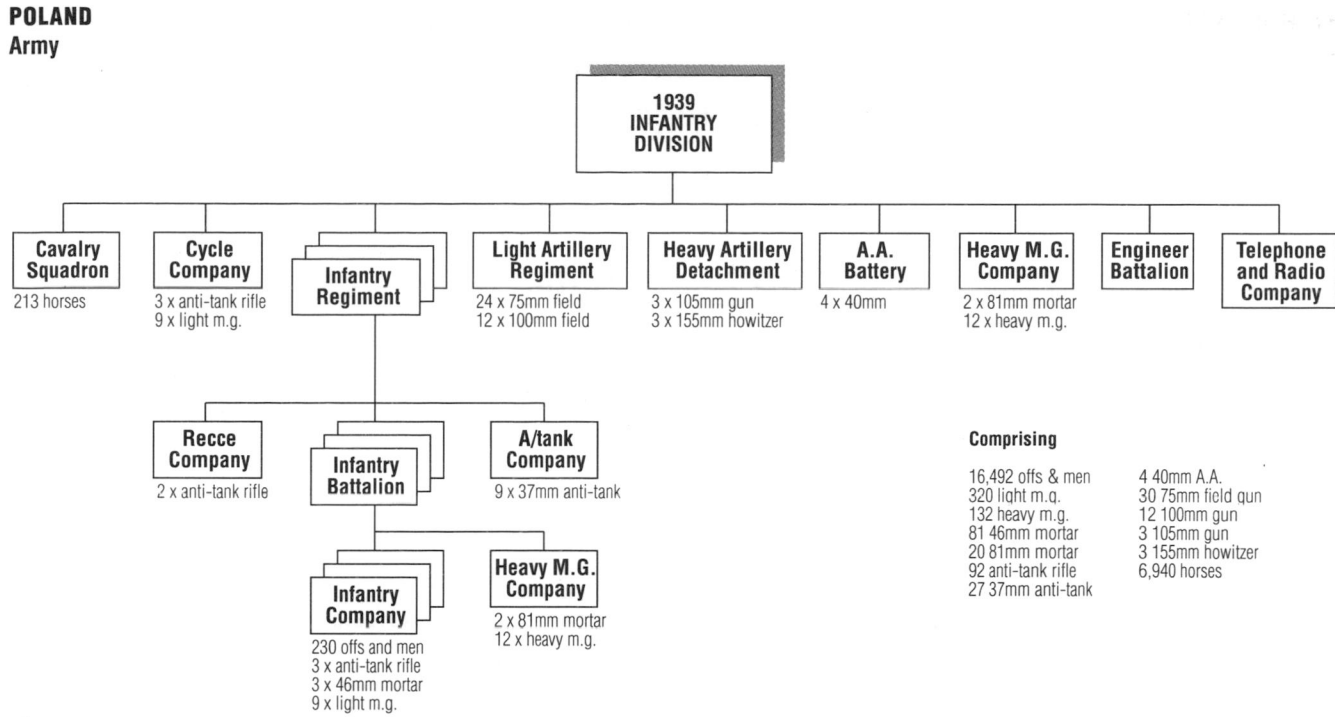

Polish divisions that fought with the British or Russian armies later in the war were organised and equipped in the same way as the parent forces. See those entries for details.

Air Force

In September 1939 Polish aircraft were organised into fighter, bomber and reconnaissance squadrons of between 10 and 12 aircraft each. Most of these were attached, two to five at a time, to the various Armies (see the relevant table in Orders of Battle: Campaigns) but some were grouped into Brigades under the control of the High Command. Five squadrons formed the Fighter Brigade and eight the Bomber Brigade.

Polish squadrons that later fought with the Royal Air Force and the Red Air Force were organised in the same way as the parent forces and reference should be made to these entries for details.

RUMANIA
Army

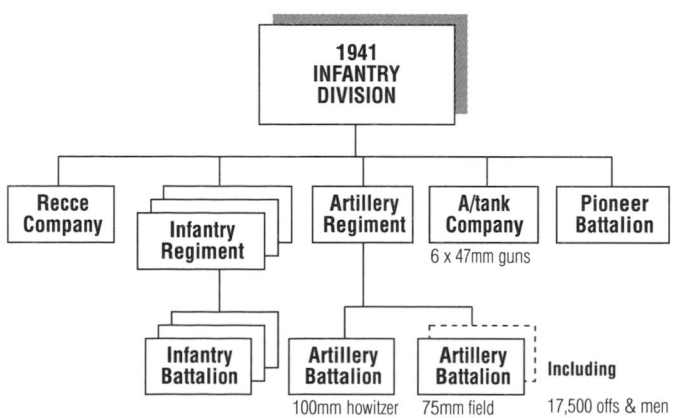

In 1942 infantry divisions numbered 13,500 officers and men, regiments having been reduced to two battalions each. There was, however, an extra company of six 75mm anti-tank guns.

By 1944 divisions were back to an official establishment of over 17,000 officers and men and once again had three battalions per infantry regiment. A further six 75mm anti-tank guns had also been added.

The divisions that fought with the Russians in 1945 had only some 9,000 officers and men, with two battalions per infantry regiment and only one artillery regiment, though the latter included Russian 120mm mortars.

RUMANIA continued
Army

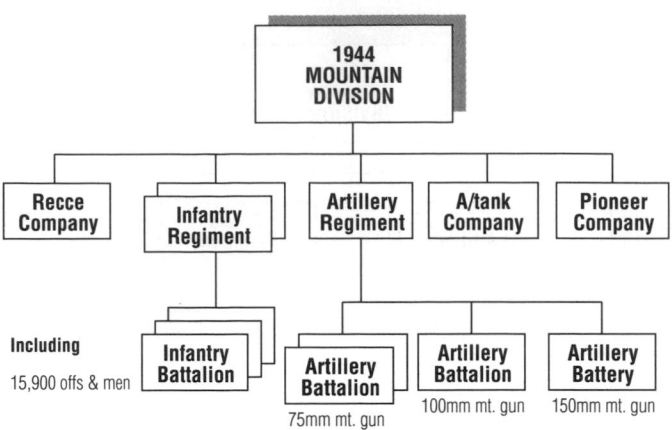

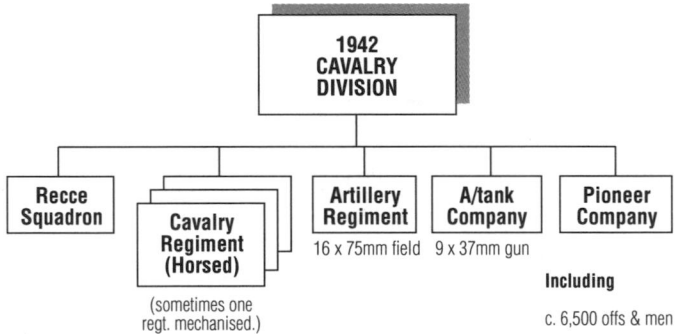

By 1944 these divisions comprised four cavalry regiments (though the number horsed, lorried or even on foot varied from division to division) and had a strength of about 10,000 officers and men. The anti-tank complement had also been doubled.

Air Force

In early 1941, Rumania was divided into three Regions for the purposes of air defence. Each region was assigned two or more air flotillas (sometimes called brigades), each made up of three wings (sometimes called groups) of fighter or bomber aircraft. Fighter and bomber groups were both made up of three squadrons which in turn comprised from two to four flights of between three and ten aircraft each.

SOUTH AFRICA

South African forces were organised pretty much along British lines and reference should be made that entry for details.

UNITED KINGDOM
Army

1939 INFANTRY DIVISION

- Cavalry Regiment
- Infantry Brigade
  - Infantry Battalion
    - 813 offs and men
    - 50 x light m.g.
    - 4 x 2in mortar
    - 2 x 3in mortar
    - 4 x anti-tank rifle
  - A/tank Company
- Field Artillery Regiment
  - 24 x 18/25 pdr.
- A/tank Regiment
- R.E.
  - Field Company
  - Field Park Company
- Divisional Signals

Comprising

13,863 offs & men	48 2 pdr anti-tank
644 light m.g.	670 motor cycle
56 heavy m.g.	140 carriers
108 2in mortar	864 vans/trucks
18 3in mortar	844 lorries/tractors
72 18/25 pdr	28 light tanks
27 25mm anti-tank	

1941 INFANTRY DIVISION

- Armoured Recce Regiment
- M.G. Battalion
- Infantry Brigade
  - Infantry Battalion
- Field Artillery Regiment
  - 24 x 25 pdr.
- A/tank Regiment
  - 48 x 2 pdr.
  - 48 x 6 pdr. (1942)
- Light A.A. Regiment
  - 48 x 40mm
- R.E.
  - Field Company
  - Field Park Company
- Divisional Signals

Comprising

17,298 offs & men	48 40mm A.A.
819 light m.g.	1,064 motor cycles
48 medium m.g.	256 carriers
162 2in mortar	994 vans/trucks
56 3in mortar	1,164 lorries/tractors
72 25 pdr.	6 armoured cars
48 2 pdr. a/tank	

1944 INFANTRY DIVISION

- Recce Regiment
  - 8 x 6 pdr. anti-tank
  - 6 x 3in mortar
  - 24 x armoured car
- M.G. Battalion
  - 42 x heavy m.g.
  - 16 x 4.2in mortar
- Infantry Brigade
  - Infantry Battalion
    - 821 offs and men
    - 49 x light m.g.
    - 12 x 2in mortar
    - 6 x 3in mortar
    - 12 x PIAT
    - 6 x 6 pdr. anti-tank
- Field Artillery Regiment
  - 18 x 25 pdr.
- A/tank Regiment
  - 32 x 17 pdr.
  - 16 x 6 pdr.
- Light A.A. Regiment
  - 36 x 40mm
  - 18 x 20mm
- R.E.
  - Field Company
  - Field Park Company
  - Bridging Platoon
- Divisional Signals

Comprising

18,347 offs & men	71 20mm A.A.
1,262 light m.g.	54 40mm A.A.
48 medium m.g.	983 motorcycles
283 2in mortar	595 carriers
60 3in mortar	881 trucks
16 4.2in mortar	1,261 lorries/tractors
436 PIAT	31 armoured cars

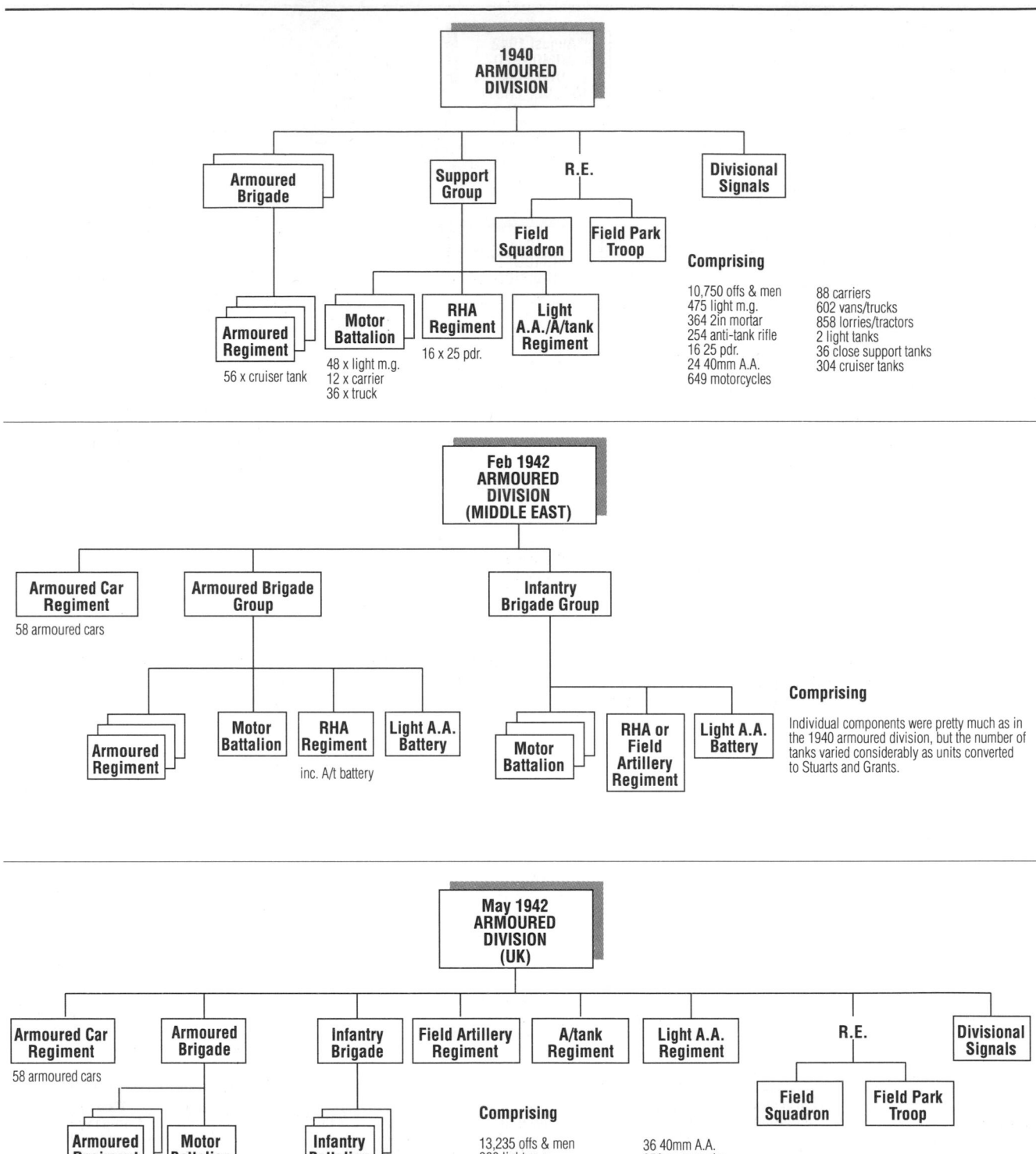

1940 ARMOURED DIVISION

- Armoured Brigade
  - Armoured Regiment — 56 x cruiser tank
- Support Group
  - Motor Battalion — 48 x light m.g. / 12 x carrier / 36 x truck
  - RHA Regiment — 16 x 25 pdr.
  - Light A.A./A/tank Regiment
- R.E.
  - Field Squadron
  - Field Park Troop
- Divisional Signals

Comprising

10,750 offs & men	88 carriers
475 light m.g.	602 vans/trucks
364 2in mortar	858 lorries/tractors
254 anti-tank rifle	2 light tanks
16 25 pdr.	36 close support tanks
24 40mm A.A.	304 cruiser tanks
649 motorcycles	

Feb 1942 ARMOURED DIVISION (MIDDLE EAST)

- Armoured Car Regiment — 58 armoured cars
- Armoured Brigade Group
  - Armoured Regiment
  - Motor Battalion
  - RHA Regiment
  - Light A.A. Battery
  - inc. A/t battery
- Infantry Brigade Group
  - Motor Battalion
  - RHA or Field Artillery Regiment
  - Light A.A. Battery

Comprising

Individual components were pretty much as in the 1940 armoured division, but the number of tanks varied considerably as units converted to Stuarts and Grants.

May 1942 ARMOURED DIVISION (UK)

- Armoured Car Regiment — 58 armoured cars
- Armoured Brigade
  - Armoured Regiment — 24 Stuarts and 24 Grants *or* 44 Crusaders and 12 Grants
  - Motor Battalion — 70 x light m.g. / 12 x medium m.g. / 6 x 3in mortar / 16 x 2 or 6 pdr. anti-tank
- Infantry Brigade
  - Infantry Battalion — 96 x light m.g. / 4 x 2in mortar / 6 x 3in mortar / 6 x 2 or 6 pdr. anti-tank
- Field Artillery Regiment
- A/tank Regiment
- Light A.A. Regiment
- R.E.
  - Field Squadron
  - Field Park Troop
- Divisional Signals

Comprising

13,235 offs & men	36 40mm A.A.
860 light m.g.	956 motorcycles
60 2in mortar	64 armoured cars
18 3in mortar	151 carriers
48 25 pdr.	417 vans/trucks
220 2 and/or 6 pdr. anti-tank	1,051 lorries/tractors
52 20mm A.A.	c. 200 light/cruiser tanks

**August 1942
ARMOURED
DIVISION
(MIDDLE EAST)**

As May 1942 UK, except that there were three Field Regiments of artillery and the infantry battalions were all motorised or lorried. These divisions were also reequipped with Sherman tanks, the full complement of these being 172.

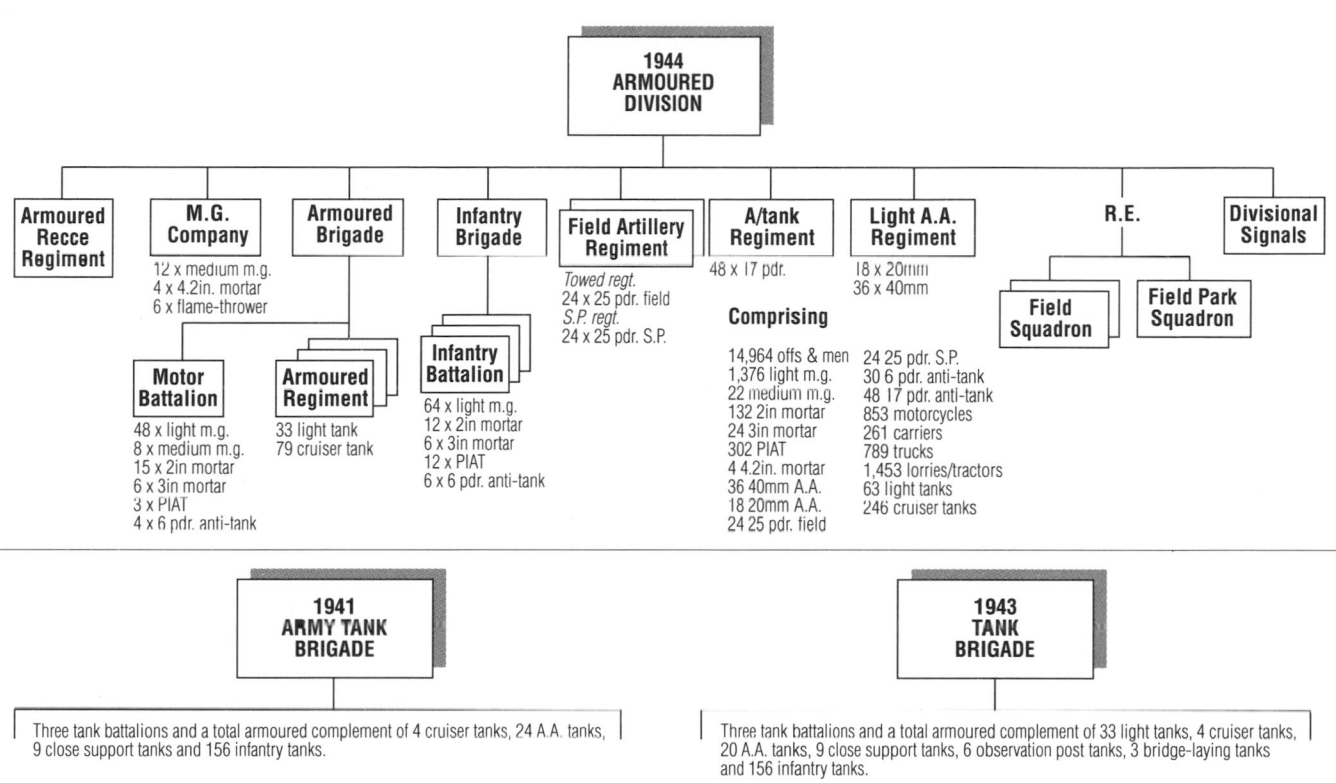

**1944
ARMOURED
DIVISION**

Armoured Recce Regiment

M.G. Company
12 x medium m.g.
4 x 4.2in. mortar
6 x flame-thrower

Armoured Brigade

Infantry Brigade

Field Artillery Regiment
Towed regt.
24 x 25 pdr. field
S.P. regt.
24 x 25 pdr. S.P.

A/tank Regiment
48 x 17 pdr.

Light A.A. Regiment
18 x 20mm
36 x 40mm

R.E.

Divisional Signals

Motor Battalion
48 x light m.g.
8 x medium m.g.
15 x 2in mortar
6 x 3in mortar
3 x PIAT
4 x 6 pdr. anti-tank

Armoured Regiment
33 light tank
79 cruiser tank

Infantry Battalion
64 x light m.g.
12 x 2in mortar
6 x 3in mortar
12 x PIAT
6 x 6 pdr. anti-tank

Field Squadron

Field Park Squadron

Comprising

14,964 offs & men
1,376 light m.g.
22 medium m.g.
132 2in mortar
24 3in mortar
302 PIAT
4 4.2in. mortar
36 40mm A.A.
18 20mm A.A.
24 25 pdr. field

24 25 pdr. S.P.
30 6 pdr. anti-tank
48 17 pdr. anti-tank
853 motorcycles
261 carriers
789 trucks
1,453 lorries/tractors
63 light tanks
246 cruiser tanks

**1941
ARMY TANK
BRIGADE**

Three tank battalions and a total armoured complement of 4 cruiser tanks, 24 A.A. tanks, 9 close support tanks and 156 infantry tanks.

**1943
TANK
BRIGADE**

Three tank battalions and a total armoured complement of 33 light tanks, 4 cruiser tanks, 20 A.A. tanks, 9 close support tanks, 6 observation post tanks, 3 bridge-laying tanks and 156 infantry tanks.

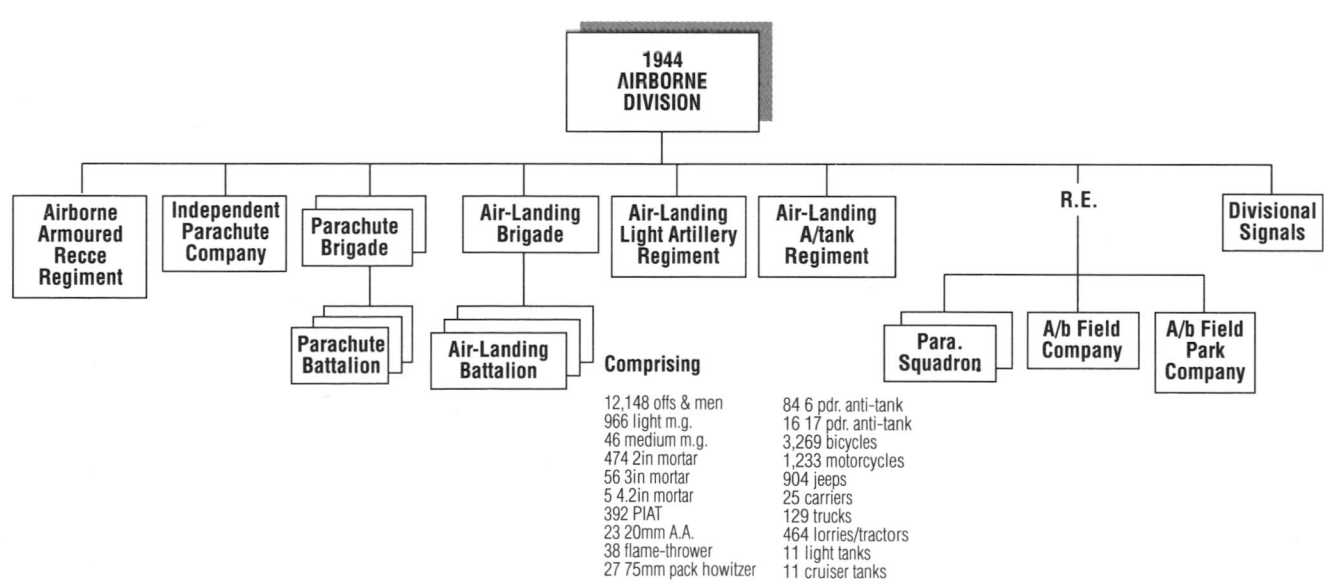

**1944
AIRBORNE
DIVISION**

Airborne Armoured Recce Regiment

Independent Parachute Company

Parachute Brigade

Air-Landing Brigade

Air-Landing Light Artillery Regiment

Air-Landing A/tank Regiment

R.E.

Divisional Signals

Parachute Battalion

Air-Landing Battalion

Para. Squadron

A/b Field Company

A/b Field Park Company

Comprising

12,148 offs & men
966 light m.g.
46 medium m.g.
474 2in mortar
56 3in mortar
5 4.2in mortar
392 PIAT
23 20mm A.A.
38 flame-thrower
27 75mm pack howitzer

84 6 pdr. anti-tank
16 17 pdr. anti-tank
3,269 bicycles
1,233 motorcycles
904 jeeps
25 carriers
129 trucks
464 lorries/tractors
11 light tanks
11 cruiser tanks

Air Force

The exact deployment of squadrons, the basic building-block of the RAF, was in continual flux throughout the war but the following shows the main chain of command and sub-groupings.

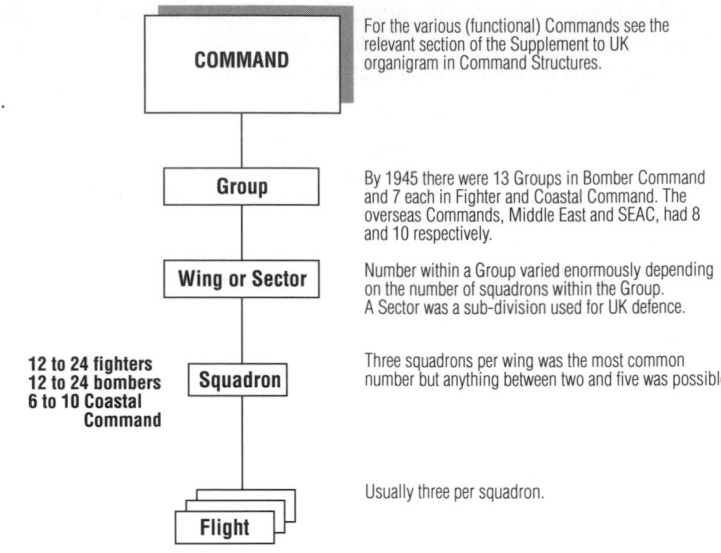

For the various (functional) Commands see the relevant section of the Supplement to UK organigram in Command Structures.

By 1945 there were 13 Groups in Bomber Command and 7 each in Fighter and Coastal Command. The overseas Commands, Middle East and SEAC, had 8 and 10 respectively.

Number within a Group varied enormously depending on the number of squadrons within the Group. A Sector was a sub-division used for UK defence.

Three squadrons per wing was the most common number but anything between two and five was possible.

Usually three per squadron.

USA
Army and Marine Corps

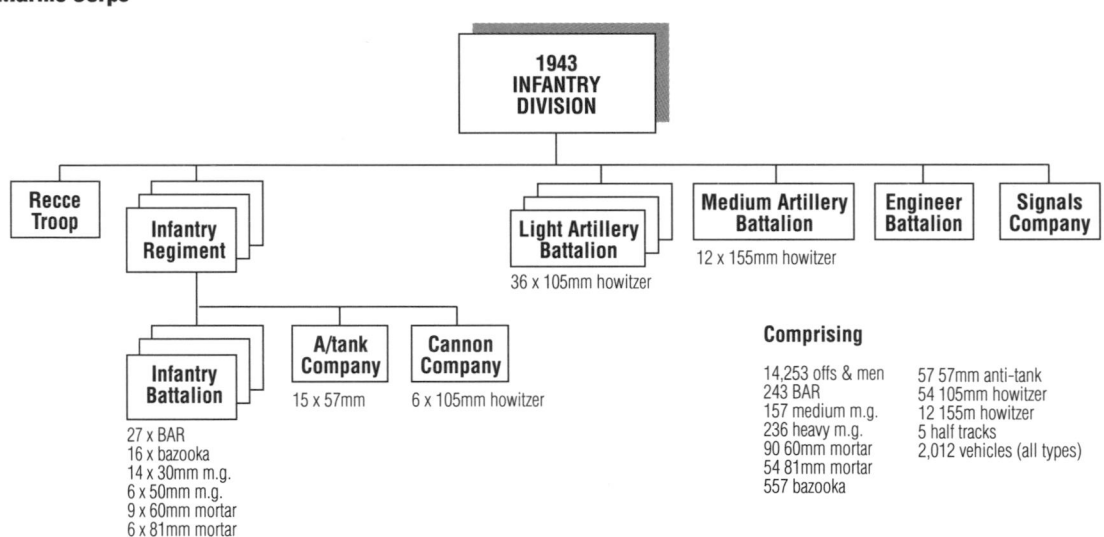

Light Artillery Battalion
36 x 105mm howitzer

Medium Artillery Battalion
12 x 155mm howitzer

Infantry Battalion
27 x BAR
16 x bazooka
14 x 30mm m.g.
6 x 50mm m.g.
9 x 60mm mortar
6 x 81mm mortar

A/tank Company
15 x 57mm

Cannon Company
6 x 105mm howitzer

Comprising

14,253 offs & men
243 BAR
157 medium m.g.
236 heavy m.g.
90 60mm mortar
54 81mm mortar
557 bazooka

57 57mm anti-tank
54 105mm howitzer
12 155m howitzer
5 half tracks
2,012 vehicles (all types)

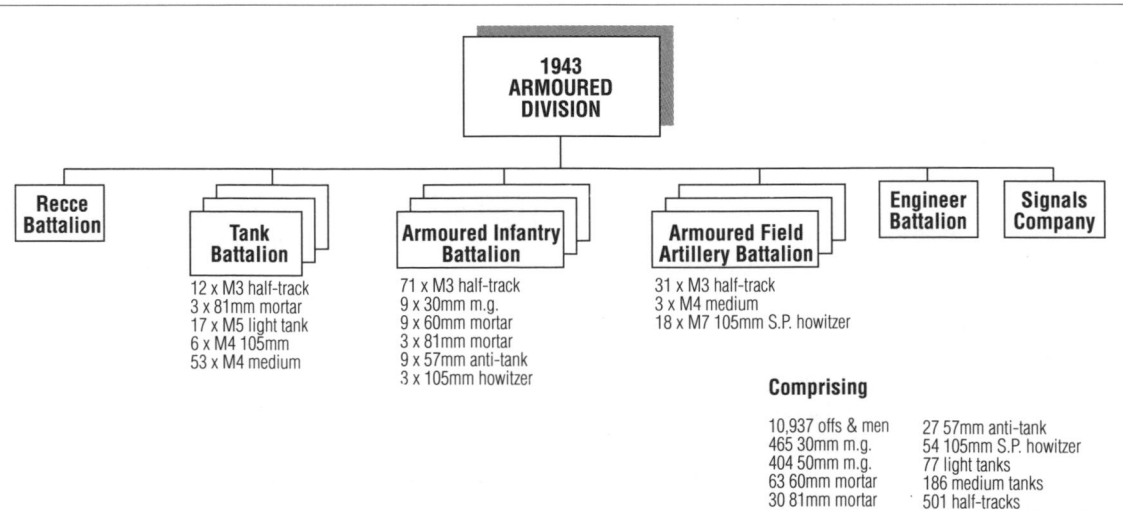

Tank Battalion
12 x M3 half-track
3 x 81mm mortar
17 x M5 light tank
6 x M4 105mm
53 x M4 medium

Armoured Infantry Battalion
71 x M3 half-track
9 x 30mm m.g.
9 x 60mm mortar
3 x 81mm mortar
9 x 57mm anti-tank
3 x 105mm howitzer

Armoured Field Artillery Battalion
31 x M3 half-track
3 x M4 medium
18 x M7 105mm S.P. howitzer

Comprising

10,937 offs & men
465 30mm m.g.
404 50mm m.g.
63 60mm mortar
30 81mm mortar
607 bazooka

27 57mm anti-tank
54 105mm S.P. howitzer
77 light tanks
186 medium tanks
501 half-tracks
2,653 vehicles (all types)

Though they were not part of the official Table of Organisation and Equipment, it became standard US practice to attach an independent tank battalion to each infantry division and an independent tank destroyer battalion to each armoured division. These units were made up as follows:

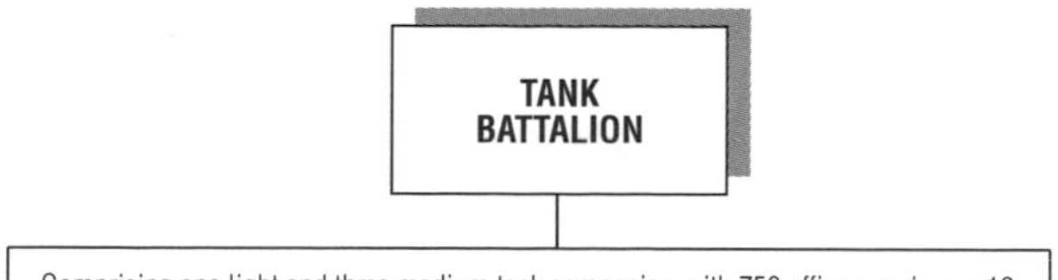

TANK BATTALION

Comprising one light and three medium tank companies, with 750 officers and men, 18 30mm m.g., 26 50mm m.g., 25 bazooka, 6 81mm mortar, 6 M4 105mm howitzer, 53 M4 medium tank, 17 M5 light tank, 13 M3 half-track and 64 trucks.

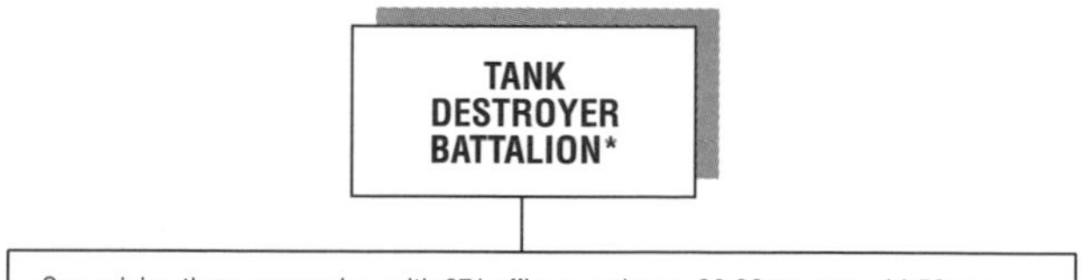

TANK DESTROYER BATTALION*

Comprising three companies, with 671 officers and men, 30 30mm m.g., 44 50mm m.g., 62 bazooka, 3 81mm mortar, 36 76 or 90mm S.P. guns, 36 armoured cars, and 82 trucks.
* Self-propelled battalions, as of March 1944.

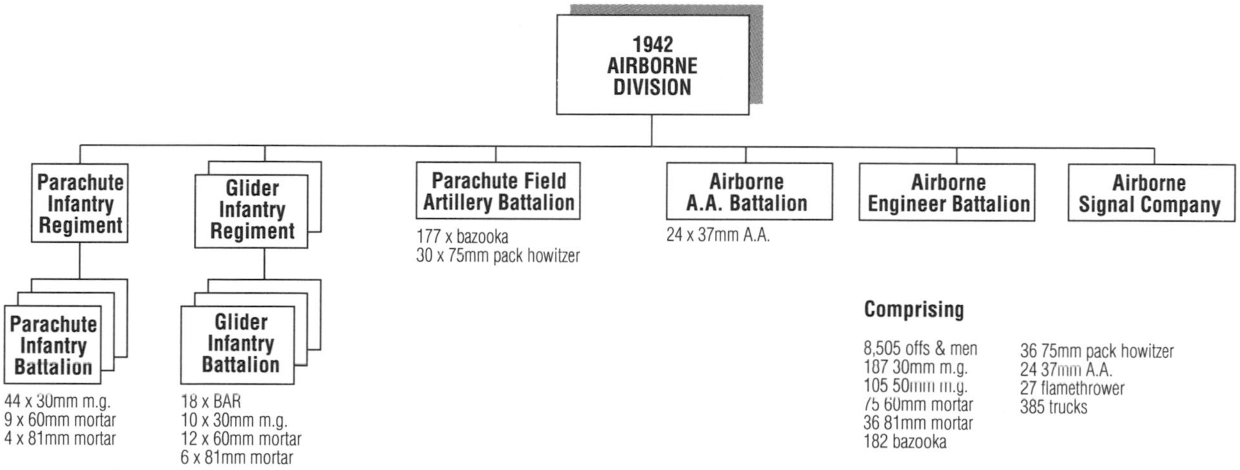

1942 AIRBORNE DIVISION

- **Parachute Infantry Regiment**
  - **Parachute Infantry Battalion**
    44 x 30mm m.g.
    9 x 60mm mortar
    4 x 81mm mortar
- **Glider Infantry Regiment**
  - **Glider Infantry Battalion**
    18 x BAR
    10 x 30mm m.g.
    12 x 60mm mortar
    6 x 81mm mortar
- **Parachute Field Artillery Battalion**
  177 x bazooka
  30 x 75mm pack howitzer
- **Airborne A.A. Battalion**
  24 x 37mm A.A.
- **Airborne Engineer Battalion**
- **Airborne Signal Company**

Comprising

8,505 offs & men
107 30mm m.g.
105 50mm m.g.
75 60mm mortar
36 81mm mortar
182 bazooka

36 75mm pack howitzer
24 37mm A.A.
27 flamethrower
385 trucks

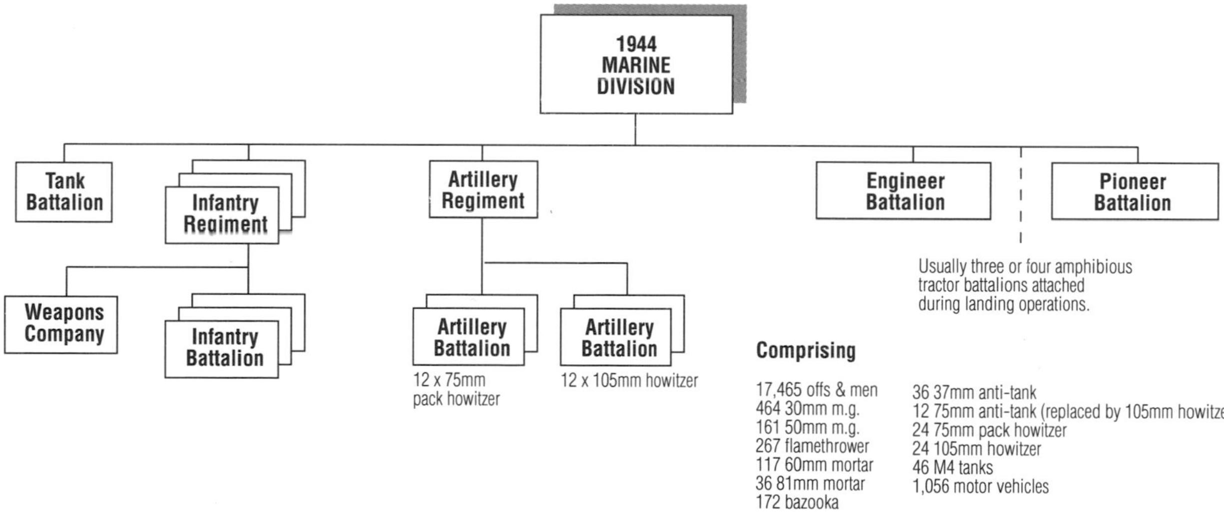

1944 MARINE DIVISION

- **Tank Battalion**
- **Infantry Regiment**
  - **Weapons Company**
  - **Infantry Battalion**
- **Artillery Regiment**
  - **Artillery Battalion**
    12 x 75mm pack howitzer
  - **Artillery Battalion**
    12 x 105mm howitzer
- **Engineer Battalion**
- **Pioneer Battalion**

Usually three or four amphibious tractor battalions attached during landing operations.

Comprising

17,465 offs & men
464 30mm m.g.
161 50mm m.g.
267 flamethrower
117 60mm mortar
36 81mm mortar
172 bazooka

36 37mm anti-tank
12 75mm anti-tank (replaced by 105mm howitzer)
24 75mm pack howitzer
24 105mm howitzer
46 M4 tanks
1,056 motor vehicles

Air Force

The highest operational formation in the USAAF was the Air Force, these were allocated by theatre as detailed in the supplement to Table 1, page 77. Most of these were sub-divided into functional commands (usually fighter, bomber and air service) and within these the main tactical formation was the Group*. Groups were in turn usually sub-divided into three or four squadrons. The table here gives the aircraft strength norms for the various types of group (including the allowance for a reserve of aircraft).

* Though wings, usually of two groups, were sometimes an important focus for tactical co-ordination, and on occasion a particularly large command was split into air divisions to facilitate tactical control.

TYPE OF GROUP	MAIN TYPE OF PLANE	NUMBER OF PLANES	NUMBER OF CREWS
Very Heavy Bombardment	B-29	45	60
Heavy Bombardment	B-17 B-24	72	96
Medium Bombardment	B-25 B-26	96	96
Light Bombardment	A-20 A-26	96	96
S/Engine Fighter	P-40 P-47 P-51	110-125	108-125
T/Engine Fighter	P-38	110-125	108-125
Troop Carrier	C-47	80-110	128
Combat Cargo	C-46 C-47	125	150

Air Force (continued)

It is difficult to generalise about group size for the following types of aircraft and therefore the totals for squadrons are given instead.

TYPE OF SQUADRON	MAIN TYPE OF PLANE	NUMBER OF PLANES	NUMBER OF CREWS
Night Fighter	P-61 P-70	18	16
Tactical Reconnaissance	P-39 P-40	27	23
	P-51		
	L-4 L-5		
Photo-Reconnaissance	P-38	24	21
Combat Mapping	B-24 B-17	18	16

USSR
Army

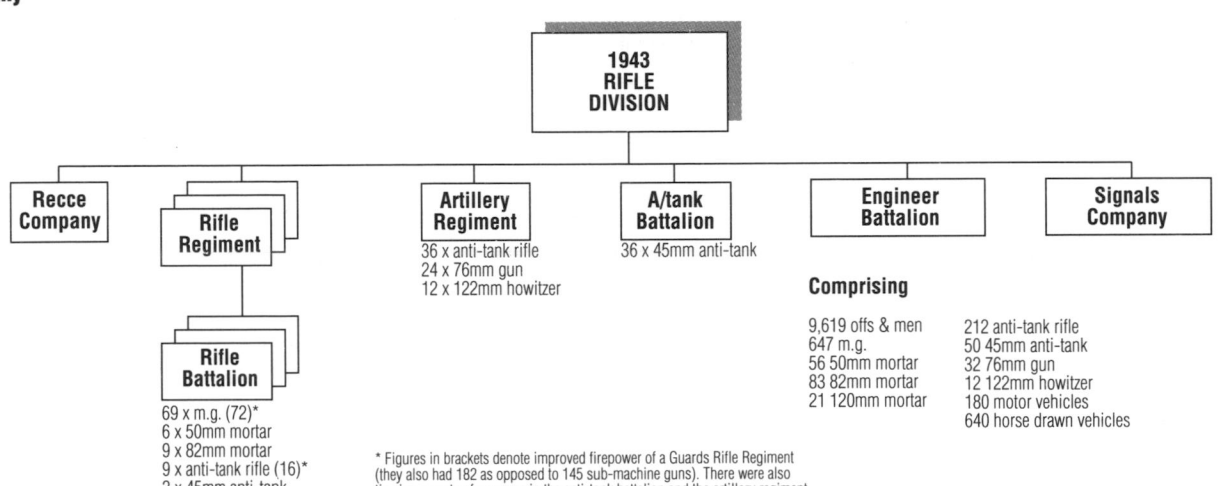

1943 RIFLE DIVISION

Recce Company

Rifle Regiment

Artillery Regiment
36 x anti-tank rifle
24 x 76mm gun
12 x 122mm howitzer

A/tank Battalion
36 x 45mm anti-tank

Engineer Battalion

Signals Company

Rifle Battalion
69 x m.g. (72)*
6 x 50mm mortar
9 x 82mm mortar
9 x anti-tank rifle (16)*
2 x 45mm anti-tank

Comprising

9,619 offs & men
647 m.g.
56 50mm mortar
83 82mm mortar
21 120mm mortar

212 anti-tank rifle
50 45mm anti-tank
32 76mm gun
12 122mm howitzer
180 motor vehicles
640 horse drawn vehicles

* Figures in brackets denote improved firepower of a Guards Rifle Regiment (they also had 182 as opposed to 145 sub-machine guns). There were also tiny increments of weapons in the anti-tank battalion and the artillery regiment.

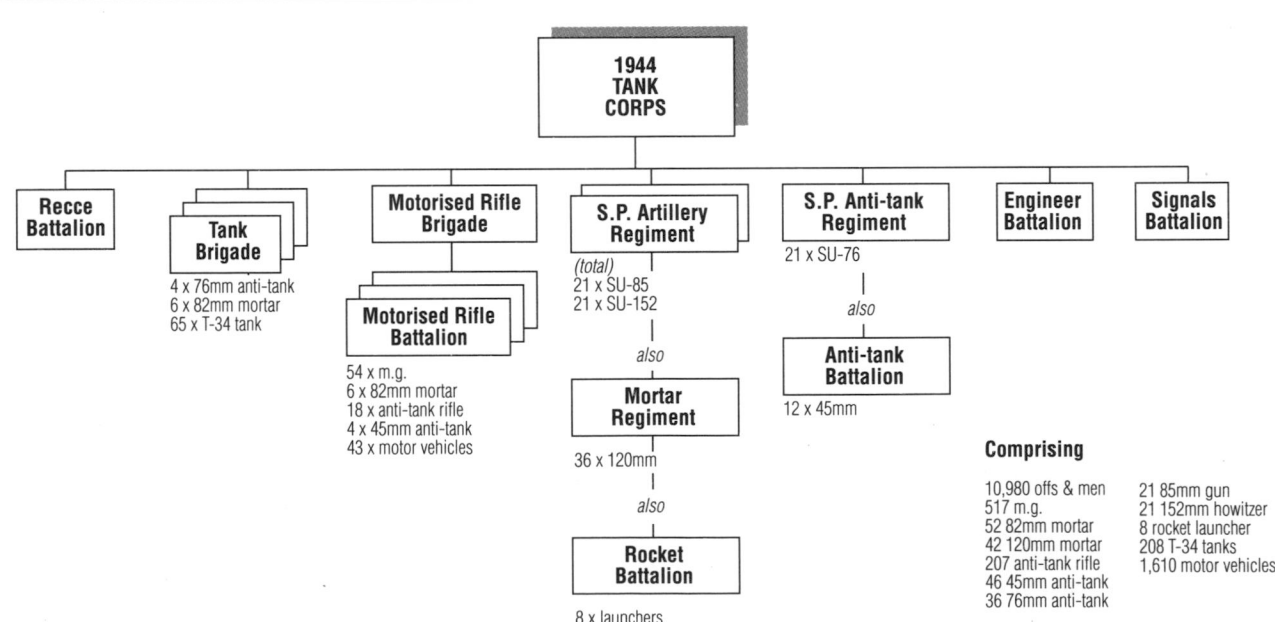

1944 TANK CORPS

Recce Battalion

Tank Brigade
4 x 76mm anti-tank
6 x 82mm mortar
65 x T-34 tank

Motorised Rifle Brigade

Motorised Rifle Battalion
54 x m.g.
6 x 82mm mortar
18 x anti-tank rifle
4 x 45mm anti-tank
43 x motor vehicles

S.P. Artillery Regiment
(total)
21 x SU-85
21 x SU-152

also

Mortar Regiment
36 x 120mm

also

Rocket Battalion
8 x launchers

S.P. Anti-tank Regiment
21 x SU-76

also

Anti-tank Battalion
12 x 45mm

Engineer Battalion

Signals Battalion

Comprising

10,980 offs & men
517 m.g.
52 82mm mortar
42 120mm mortar
207 anti-tank rifle
46 45mm anti-tank
36 76mm anti-tank

21 85mm gun
21 152mm howitzer
8 rocket launcher
208 T-34 tanks
1,610 motor vehicles

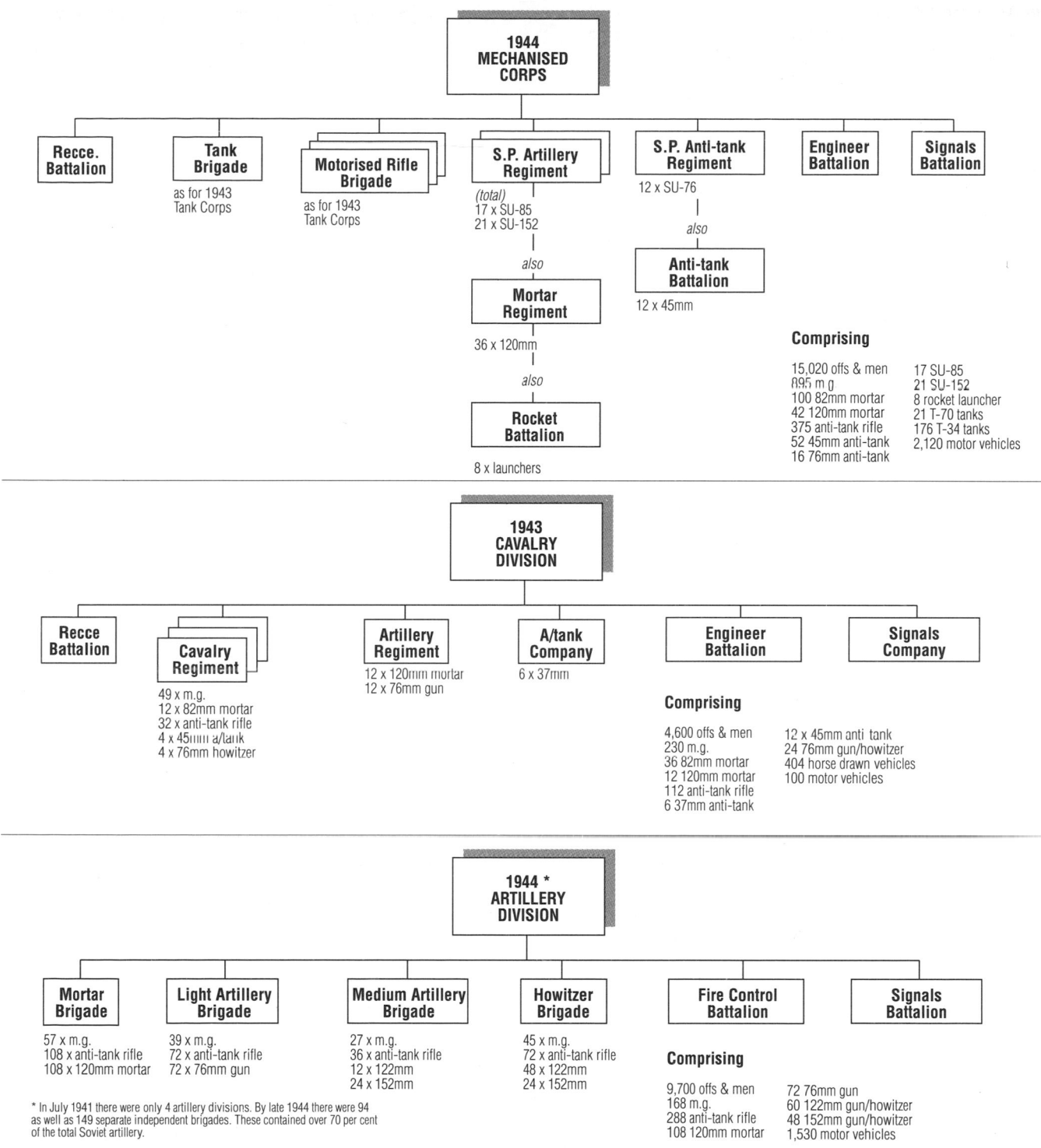

1944 MECHANISED CORPS

Recce. Battalion

Tank Brigade
as for 1943 Tank Corps

Motorised Rifle Brigade
as for 1943 Tank Corps

S.P. Artillery Regiment
(total)
17 x SU-85
21 x SU-152

also

Mortar Regiment
36 x 120mm

also

Rocket Battalion
8 x launchers

S.P. Anti-tank Regiment
12 x SU-76

also

Anti-tank Battalion
12 x 45mm

Engineer Battalion

Signals Battalion

Comprising

15,020 offs & men
895 m g
100 82mm mortar
42 120mm mortar
375 anti-tank rifle
52 45mm anti-tank
16 76mm anti-tank

17 SU-85
21 SU-152
8 rocket launcher
21 T-70 tanks
176 T-34 tanks
2,120 motor vehicles

1943 CAVALRY DIVISION

Recce Battalion

Cavalry Regiment
49 x m.g.
12 x 82mm mortar
32 x anti-tank rifle
4 x 45mm a/tank
4 x 76mm howitzer

Artillery Regiment
12 x 120mm mortar
12 x 76mm gun

A/tank Company
6 x 37mm

Engineer Battalion

Signals Company

Comprising

4,600 offs & men
230 m.g.
36 82mm mortar
12 120mm mortar
112 anti-tank rifle
6 37mm anti-tank

12 x 45mm anti tank
24 76mm gun/howitzer
404 horse drawn vehicles
100 motor vehicles

1944 * ARTILLERY DIVISION

Mortar Brigade
57 x m.g.
108 x anti-tank rifle
108 x 120mm mortar

Light Artillery Brigade
39 x m.g.
72 x anti-tank rifle
72 x 76mm gun

Medium Artillery Brigade
27 x m.g.
36 x anti-tank rifle
12 x 122mm
24 x 152mm

Howitzer Brigade
45 x m.g.
72 x anti-tank rifle
48 x 122mm
24 x 152mm

Fire Control Battalion

Signals Battalion

Comprising

9,700 offs & men
168 m.g.
288 anti-tank rifle
108 120mm mortar

72 76mm gun
60 122mm gun/howitzer
48 152mm gun/howitzer
1,530 motor vehicles

* In July 1941 there were only 4 artillery divisions. By late 1944 there were 94 as well as 149 separate independent brigades. These contained over 70 per cent of the total Soviet artillery.

Air Force

By 1943 the Red Air Force had reached its mature form. The core tactical unit was the air regiment (40 planes) made up of three 12-plane squadrons. Three to four regiments made up an air division and two to four divisions a corps. Corps were usually of the same type of aircraft, except in ground attack corps where two to three ground attack divisions would be supplemented by a fighter division. (Bomber squadrons usually contained only nine planes, and regiments thirty.)

Squadrons were sub-divided into three four-plane flights (*zveno*) but for operational purposes these were further sub-divided into pairs (*para*). Where necessary pairs could then be grouped together into a (tactical) *zveno*, still of four planes or a group (*gruppa*) of six.

Air corps were grouped together into multi-type air armies, a list of which will be found in the supplement to Table 2, page 81.

YUGOSLAVIA

Army

A Yugoslavian infantry division in 1941 comprised two to four infantry regiments and one or two artillery regiments. Each infantry regiment contained some 2,400 men and the main support weapons were 170 machine guns and four field guns.

Air Force

This comprised eight Air Regiments with a total of 48 squadrons. These had an average paper strength of 7 to 8 aircraft each.

SECTION 5

STRENGTHS

PART I MILITARY MANPOWER

The three tables following deal mainly with the ground forces of the Second World War belligerents, though air force and naval personnel strengths are also given for those countries which had significant such arms. Table 9 gives details on all the countries involved, whilst the following table lists selected countries and shows what proportion of their ground forces actually served overseas. (Air forces and navies are too mobile to allow this kind of distinction to be made.) Where possible this table also distinguishes between the theatres to which the soldiers were posted. With this latter point in mind, Table 11 deals with Germany only and attempts to compute the military effort expended on the Eastern Front as opposed to the other theatres.

The following points should be borne in mind when consulting these tables:
— In Table 9, especially, the data given for certain countries can only be an informed approximation.
— The overall figures for ground forces given below are not an accurate reflection of the number of men actually in the firing line. This figure, both for the war as a whole or for an individual campaign, is best arrived at by combining the data on divisions in the Orders of Battle and the Tables of Organisation and Equipment sections.
— Where a dash is given in Table 9 it indicates that the figure for that column is not significantly different from that in the previous completed column.

Table 9 Military Manpower Raised, by Each of the Belligerent Nations, 1939-45

* Only given when significantly different from preceding columns.

† Numbers in brackets denote theoretical figure.

‡ Active Army only.

†† There were also 1,640,000 men in the Army of the Interior.

Δ Figures in brackets are Waffen-SS numbers.

** Some sources give between 1.5 million and 1.8 million.

COUNTRY		ON ENTRY INTO WAR	END OF WAR	PEAK NUMBER *	TOTAL MOBILISED †
Albania		13,000	—	—	—
Australia	Armed Forces	91,700	575,100	—	993,000
	Army	82,800	380,700	—	727,200
	Air Force	3,500	154,500	—	216,900
	Navy	5,400	39,900	—	48,900
Belgium		600,000	650,000	—	(900,000)
Bulgaria		160,000 ‡	450,000 (with Soviets)	—	1,011,000
Canada	Armed Forces	63,100	759,800	—	1,100,000
	Army	55,600	474,000	—	690,000
	Air Force	3,100	193,000	—	222,500
	Navy	4,400	92,800	—	99,400
China		2,500,000 (1937)	5,000,000	5,700,000	14,000,000
Denmark		6,600	—	—	—
Finland	1939-40	127,800	200,000	—	?
	1941-44	400,000	270,000	—	?
France	Sept 1939	900,000	—	—	—
	1940	2,680,000 ††	—	—	—
	1943-44 Italy	15,000	98,000	113,000	160,000
	1944-45 N.W.E.	?	437,000	—	?
Germany	Armed Forces	3,180,000	7,800,000	9,500,000	17,900,000
	Δ Army	2,730,000 (30,000)	6,100,000 (800,000)	6,500,000	?
	Air Force	400,000	1,000,000 **	2,100,000	?
	Navy	50,000	700,000	800,000	?
Greece	Oct 1940	430,000	—	—	?
	April 1941	540,000	—	—	?
Hungary		80,000 (1939)	210,000	?	?
India	Armed Forces	197,000	2,159,700	—	2,581,800
	Army	194,900	2,100,000	—	2,500,000
	Air Force	300	29,200	—	52,800
	Navy	1,800	30,500	—	29,000

Table 9 **Military Manpower Raised, by Each of the Belligerent Nations, 1939-45 continued**

COUNTRY		ON ENTRY INTO WAR	END OF WAR	PEAK NUMBER *	TOTAL MOBILISED †
Italy	Armed Forces	1,899,600	?	?	9,100,000
	Army	1,630,000	?	2,563,000	?
	Air Force	101,000	(May 43) 200,000	—	?
	Navy	168,600	(Sept 43) 259,100	—	?
Japan	Armed Forces	1,700,000	7,200,000	—	9,100,000
	Army	1,500,000	5,500,000	—	?
	Navy	200,000	1,700,000	—	?
Netherlands		270,000	400,000	—	400,000
New Zealand	Armed Forces	13,800	192,800	—	?
	Army	11,300	157,000	—	?
	Air Force	1,200	c. 27,000	—	?
	Navy	1,300	5,800	—	?
Norway		25,000	—	—	(90,000)
Poland	1939	1,200,000	250,000	?	(2,400,000)
	1943-45 Italy	8,600	50,000	—	?
	1944-45 N.W.E.	28,000	—	—	?
	1941-45 E.Front	30,000	?	?	200,000
Rumania	1941-44	686,000	1,225,000	—	?
	1944-45 with Red Army	?	370,000	—	539,000
S.Africa	Armed Forces	?	?	?	250,000
	Army	18,000	?	198,000	208,000
	Air Force	1,000	?	?	38,000
	Navy	?	?	?	4,000
UK	Armed Forces	681,000	4,683,000	—	5,896,000
	Army	402,000	2,931,000	—	3,778,000
	Air Force	118,000	963,000	1,012,000	1,185,000
	Navy	161,000	789,000	—	923,000
USA	Armed Forces	5,413,000	11,877,000	—	16,354,000
	†† Army	4,602,000	5,851,000	—	} 11,260,000
	Air Force	354,000	2,282,000	—	
	Navy	382,000	3,288,000	—	4,183,000
	US M.C.	75,000	456,000	—	669,000
USSR	Armed Forces	9,000,000	12,400,000	13,200,000	?
	‡‡ Army	2,900,000	6,000,000	—	?
	Air Force	?	?	?	?
	Navy	?	?	266,000	?
Yugoslavia	1941	150,000	?	—	(1,500,000)
	1941-45 Partisans	(Dec) 2,000	800,000	—	?

* Only given when significantly different from preceding columns.

† Numbers in brackets denote theoretical figure.

†† Not including USAAF.

‡‡ With army groups on the German front. German sources give a figure in excess of 4.5 million for June 1941.

Table 10 Numbers of Army Troops Who Served Overseas and in Main Theatres (Selected Countries)

COUNTRY	SERVED	SERVED OVERSEAS	SERVED IN MAIN THEATRES	
Australia	727,000	397,000	Middle East	c. 130,000
			Malaya	18,000
			Pacific	?
Canada	691,000	371,000	Italy	92,000
			N.W.Europe	c. 215,000
India	3,698,000	399,000	?	
New Zealand	138,000	115,000	Mediterranean	76,000
			Pacific	c. 40,000
UK	3,788,000	2,640,000	Far East	390,000
			Other	2,250,000
			of which:	
			N.W.Europe	c. 275,000
USA *	8,291,000	5,407,000	N.W.Europe †	3,021,000
			Mediterranean	446,000
			Pacific	
			S.W.Pacific	840,000
			Pacific Ocean	456,000
			C.B.I.	199,000
			Other	891,000
Japan	3,400,000	2,100,000 ‡	China	1,100,000
			Pacific	700,000
			S.E.Asia	300,000

* This entry includes USAAF personnel. Moreover it shows not aggregate figures but those for 31/5/45. However, as these represent close to peak US Army strength figures, when combined with casualty figures from Table 52 they are not too short of the aggregate figures.

† Includes US personnel in UK.

‡ Does not include Korea or Manchuria.

This book does not usually attempt to draw conclusions from the data presented and even less to be didactic about any of it. Nevertheless, it does seem to be logical to follow the table above with some information on the distribution of German ground troops during the war, and In so doing one cannot forbear to make at least passing comment on the clear proof these figures give of the enormous burden borne by the *Russians* throughout the last four years of the war.

In the following table German military effort is defined in terms of the aggregate months spent by various types of division in different combat theatres. Prolonged periods out of the line or on internal security duties are not included.

Table 11 Military Effort Expended by Germans, by Type of Division (Army and SS) and by Theatre 1939-45

TYPE OF DIVISION	THEATRE						GRAND TOTAL
	E.Front	N.W. Europe	Italy	N.Africa	Other	TOTAL Non-E.Front	
Panzer	1,029	85	34	65	24	208	**1,237**
Motorised/ Pz. Gren.	493	27	78	0	49	154	**647**
Light/ Jäger	277	0	27	13	122	162	**439**
Mountain	175	6	23	0	108	137	**312**
Parachute	45	66	38	7	8	119	**164**
Infantry	5,127	453	193	6	454	1,106	**6,233**
TOTAL	7,146	637	393	91	665	1,884	**9,032**

PART II ARMOUR

It would be appropriate at this point to be able to include some comparative figures on armoured fighting vehicle strengths for various belligerents and theatres at various dates. Sadly, however, one must follow King Lear in warning that 'that way madness lies'. For though the Second World War was usually a very well 'accounted' conflict, in the matter of armour hardly any consistently or usefully consistent figures seem to exist, for any of the belligerents. Many are overoptimistic or guesswork; some refer to tanks only, some to tanks and self-propelled guns, others to all kinds of armoured, tracked vehicle; some refer to tanks etc. with fighting units, others to all such vehicles within a theatre; some refer only to tanks fit for action, others to those in any sort of repair. •

Thus, though some figures for various theatres are presented below, it should be made clear that these are only fragmentary and must without exception be treated with the utmost caution. Though they do have the virtue of underlining one of the basic points to emerge from much of the data included in this book – that as the war progressed the Germans were simply swamped by the productive capacities of their opponents.

Table 12 Axis and British Tank Strengths at the Beginning of Selected Battles in North Africa November 1941-October 1942

DATE	18 Nov 41	26 May 42	1 July 42	30 Aug 42	23 Oct 42
BATTLE	Crusader	Gazala	Alamein	Alam Halfa	2 Alamein
GERMAN					
Light	70	50	}54	31	31
Medium	174	280		234	211
TOTAL	244	330	54	265	242
ITALIAN	146	228	30	243	279
AXIS TOTAL	390	558	84	508	521
BRITISH					
Light	173	149	93	169	119
Medium	339	424	106	361	716
Heavy	199	276	53	163	194
TOTAL	711	849	252	693	1,029
RESERVES					
Axis	50	77	?	?	22
British	495	450	220	250	1,200
RATIO △	3.1:1	2.5:1	3.1:1	2.2:1	4.3:1

• However, a rough and ready figure for Allied tank holdings in a particular theatre, at the end of any month, can be got by multiplying the number of armoured formations given as present in the Ebb and Flow Charts (in the Order of Battle Section) by the relevant establishment figures in the Tables of Organisation and Equipment. Reducing the resulting figure by 20% will then give a rough idea of serviceable front-line tanks on hand. This calculation does *not* work for the Germans as establishments were always *well* below paper levels.

△ Of front-line British medium and heavy to German medium.

Table 13 Eighth Army and Axis* Tank Strengths October 1942-January 1943

* With Rommel
i.e. not in Tunisia

DATE		23 Oct 42	5 Nov 42	15 Nov 42	25 Nov 42	11 Dec 42	30 Dec 42	15 Jan 43
AXIS	German	238	35	35	54	c. 60	60	34
	Italian	279	0	45	42	c. 30	?	57
	TOTAL	**517**	**35**	**80**	**96**	**c. 90**	**?**	**91**
BRITISH	Front-line	1,029	537	395	418	454	367	532
	Fwd. Res.	200	67	105	144	105	180	91
	TOTAL	**1,229**	**604**	**500**	**562**	**559**	**547**	**623**

Table 14 German and Russian Armoured Fighting Vehicle Strengths on the Eastern Front 1941-45†

DATE	June 41	March 42	May 42	Nov 42	March 43	Aug 43	June 44	Sept 44	Oct 44	Nov 44	Dec 44	Jan 45
GERMAN	3,671	1,503	3,981	3,133	2,374	2,555	4,470	4,186	4,917	5,202	4,785	4,881
RUSSIAN	28,800	4,690	6,190	4,940	7,200	6,200	11,600	11,200	11,900	14,000	15,000	14,200

† These figures include tanks and all kinds of self-propelled guns (see Tables 101 and 103). They are taken from Zaloga & Brandsen p. 223 (see Bibliography) with adjustments made to the Russian figures to allow for the permanent armoured force held on the Manchurian front. For the Germans, in particular, these figures give a misleading overall impression of armoured strengths. A corrective is offered in the following figures for *serviceable* tank strengths on certain dates: Feb 42 465; March 42 140; Jan 43 495; April 43 600; Oct 43 770.

The following table, detailing local tank strengths before certain major Russian offensives, gives a more realistic picture of armoured ratios in actual combat sectors.

Table 15 German and Russian Armoured Fighting Vehicle Strengths at the Beginning of Selected Major Offensives 1944-45

DATE	SECTOR	FORMATIONS		TANKS AND SELF-PROPELLED GUNS	
		GERMAN	**RUSSIAN**	**GERMAN**	**RUSSIAN**
14 Jan 44	Leningrad	18 Army	Leningrad Fr.; Volkov Fr.	200	1,200
30 Jan 44	Krivoi Rog/Nikopol	6 Army	3 Ukrainian Fr.; 4 Ukrainian Fr.	250	1,400
4 Mar 44	R. Pripet/Nikolaev	1 Pz Army; 4 Pz Army; 6 Army; 8 Army	1 Ukrainian Fr.; 2 Ukrainian Fr. 3 Ukrainian Fr.	1,300	6,400
5 Mar 44	Uman/Kirovgrad	8 Army	2 Ukrainian Fr.	310	2,400
8 April 44	Crimea	17 Army	4 Ukrainian Fr.; Ind. Cst. Army	70	900
22 Jun 44	Vitebsk/R. Pripet	Army Group Centre	1 Baltic Fr.; 1 Byelo. Fr. 2 Byelo. Fr.; 3 Byelo. Fr.	800	4,100
12 July 44	Kovel/Tarnopol	A. Group N. Ukraine	1 Ukrainian Fr.	700	2,040
18 July 44	Chelm/Rava Russkaya	4 Pz Army	3 Gds Army; 13 Army; 1 Gds Tk Army	174	550
19 July 44	Mariampol/Daugavpils	3 Pz Army	1 Baltic Fr.; 3 Byelo. Fr. (parts)	95	1,100
20 Aug 44	Bendory/Chemovitsy	A. Group S.Ukraine	2 Ukrainian Fr.; 3 Ukrainian Fr.	400	1,880
14 Sep 44	Narva	Army Group North	Leningrad Fr.; 1 Baltic Fr,; 2 Baltic Fr.; 3 Baltic Fr.	400	3,000
12 Jan 45	Warsaw/Tarnow	Army Group A	1 Byelo. Fr.; 1 Ukrainian Fr.	770	6,460
13 Jan 45	E.Prussia	Army Group Centre	2 Byelo. Fr.; 3 Byelo. Fr.	750	3,300
1 Mar 45	Pomerania	3 Pz Army	1 Byelo. Fr. (part)	70	1,600
16 Apr 45	Oder/Neisse confluence to Stettin	A. Group Vistula	1 Byelo. Fr.; 2 Byelo. Fr.	750	4,100
16 Apr 45	R.Neisse	4 Pz Army	1 Ukrainian Fr.	200	2,150

Table 16 Tank strengths of Panzer Divisions in Normandy, on Dates Known, June-August 1944

DIVISION	21 Pz	12SS Pz	Pz Lehr	2 Pz	2SS Pz	1SS Pz	9SS Pz	10SS Pz	116 Pz
MONTH **June**	6th 127 7th 70	6th 177 7th 90	6th 182 25th 66	6th 161	1st 69	1st 88			
July	1st 40	1st 51 8th 85	7th 30 25th 45 26th 14		23rd 57	2nd 80			30th 62
August	 23rd 10	7th 54 8th 48 10th 39 15th 15 23rd 10	5th 13 6th 9	7th 45 13th 25 19th 15 23rd 0	 23rd 15	7th 60 13th 30 23rd 0	 21st 25 23rd 22	 23rd 0	7th 60 23rd 12

During June and July 1944, the Allies committed a little over 5,000 tanks in this theatre, and even that figure only includes tanks actually with the combat units.

PART III AIR FORCES

The air forces of the Second World War present a particular problem in a book of this nature. Except for production figures (see Section 7) and figures on strategic bombing (see the later tables in this section) the available figures are sporadic and imprecise such that it is rarely possible to compile detailed comparative tables. A particular problem is that even when figures are given they do not specify the category of aircraft involved e.g. combat or non-combat, first-line or second-line, full establishment or actually operational, serviceable or non-serviceable. Sadly, therefore, this section contains only a few comparative tables, presented first, and is perforce mainly taken up with a listing of available data country by country.

Comparative Strengths

Table 17 German and Allied Front-line Combat Aircraft At Selected Dates September 1939-April 1945

DATE	GERMANY	USA*	USSR†	UK	TOTAL ALLIED
September 1939	2,916	—	—	1,660	1,660
August 1940	3,015	—	—	2,913	2,913
December 1940	2,885	—	—	1,064 ‡	1,064
June 1941	3,451	—	8,105	3,106	11,211
December 1941	2,561	4,000 Δ 957	2,495	4,287	6,782**
June 1942	3,573	? 1,902	3,160	4,500††	9,562
December 1942	3,440	10,885 4,695	3,088	5,257	13,040 ‡‡
June 1943	5,003	? 8,586	8,290	6,026	22,902
December 1943	4,667	23,807 11,917	8,500	6,646	27,063 ‡‡
June 1944	4,637	? 19,342	11,800	8,339	39,481
December 1944	5,041	33,179 19,892	14,500	8,395	42,787 ‡‡
April 1945	2,175	31,335 21,572	17,000	8,000 ‡	46,752 ‡‡

* US Army Air Force only.
† Includes *Stavka* Reserve, which was apportioned among key army groups prior to a major offensive. At other times front-line strengths were some 25 per cent less e.g. Dec 43 5,775; June 44 8,798; Dec 44 11,530.
‡ Fighters only.

Δ In the USA column the top figure is total aircraft available, the bottom figure total aircraft overseas.
** Does not include USA.
†† Estimate.
‡‡ Includes US aircraft overseas only.

Table 18 British and German Serviceable Aircraft Available for the Battle of Britain 6 July-28 September 1940

WEEK ENDING	RAF			LUFTWAFFE *			
	Single-engined	S.E. Aircraft in Storage		Single-engined fighters	Twin-engined fighters	Dive-bombers	Bombers
		Immediately Available	Delayed Availability				
1940 July 6	644	373	181	760 †	220 †	280 †	1,200 †
13	666	355	161				
20	658	333	213	656	168	248	769
27	651	312	217				
August 3	708	336	267				
10	749	372	292	805	224	261	998
17	704	289	258				
24	758	249	259				
31	764	191	291				
September 7	746	194	196	623	129	180	772
14	725	208	152				
21	715	192	197				
28	732	225	244	276	230	343	750

* Luftflotten 2 and 3 only.

† Actual strength. Only 50 per cent or so of aircraft were serviceable.

Table 19 Axis and Allied Front-line Aircraft in the Mediterranean June 1940-March 1945

DATE	AXIS		ALLIED
	GERMAN	ITALIAN	
1940 June	—	1,770 in Italian Air Force‡ 300 in Libya	300 in Middle East
1941 January	410	330	208 in Middle East
June	320	376 in N. Africa and Sicily	419 in Middle East (excl. Malta)
October	642	544 in N. Africa and Sicily	780 in Middle East
1942 January	560	277 in N. Africa and Sicily	445 in Desert Air Force
June	357 in Mediterranean 183 in N. Africa	748 in Mediterranean 248 in N. Africa	803 in Mediterranean ** 463 in N. Africa **
November	940 in Mediterranean 375 in N. Africa	515 in Mediterranean 283 in N. Africa	1,500 in Middle East 920 in W. Desert
1943 April	800 in Mediterranean 200 in N. Africa	376 (not N. & Central Italy)	3,241 in Mediterranean
July	960 in central Mediterranean	300 ††	3,680 in Mediterranean
August	841 in Italy	450 operational	
October	571 in Italy	—	
December	470 in Mediterranean 341 in Italy	—	c. 4,000 in Mediterranean
1944 January	575 in Mediterranean 370 in Italy	—	
March	760 in Mediterranean 566 in Italy	—	3,960 combat in Mediterranean
July	300 in Mediterranean 125 in Italy	—	c. 5,000 in Mediterranean
November	104 in Italy	—	
1945 March	217 in Italy	—	c. 4,000 combat in Mediterranean

‡ Also 300 largely obsolete machines in Italian East Africa.

** Serviceable.

* Serviceable combat and non-combat.

† 45 per cent obsolete types.

‡ On all fronts.

Table 20 Russian and German Front-line Combat Aircraft on the Eastern Front at Selected Dates 1941-45

DATE	GERMAN	RUSSIAN	DATE	GERMAN	RUSSIAN
June 41	2,130	8,100	July 43	2,500	8,300
July 41	1,050*	2,500	Jan 44	1,800	8,500
Dec 41	2,500	2,500	June 44	1,710	11,800
May 42	3,400	3,160	Jan 45	1,430	14,500
Nov 42	2,450	3,100	April 45	1,500‡	17,000

Table 21 US and Japanese Front-line Combat Aircraft in the Pacific at Selected Dates 1942-45

DATE	US ARMY AIR FORCE	US NAVY and US MARINE CORPS	TOTAL US	JAPANESE ARMY and NAVY
Jan 1942	1,622	1,915	3,537	2,520
Jan 1943	3,174	8,268	11,442	3,200
Jan 1944	4,911	13,065	17,976	4,050
Jan 1945	5,827	14,576	20,403	4,100
July 1945	7,260	14,648	21,908	4,600

Bombing

Table 22 Tons Bombs Dropped and Sorties Flown by Bomber Command September 1939-July 1942

** The top figure for each month is night sorties, the bottom day. The numbers represent totals despatched, not necessarily completed.

YEAR	1939		1940		1941		1942	
Month	TONS DROPPED	NUMBER** SORTIES	TONS DROPPED	NUMBER** SORTIES	TONS DROPPED	NUMBER** SORTIES	TONS DROPPED	NUMBER** SORTIES
January			1	38 6	777	1,030 96	2,292	2,216 24
February			1	54 4	1,431	1,617 124	1,011	1,162 252
March			31	259 53	1,744	1,728 162	2,675	2,224 131
April			112	489 167	2,396	2,249 676	4,433	3,752 246
May			1,668	1,617 802	2,846	2,416 273	3,234	2,702 105
June			2,300	2,484 812	4,310	3,228 531	6,845	4,801 196
July			1,257	1,722 616	4,384	3,243 582	6,368	3,914 313
August			1,365	2,188 417	4,242	3,344 468		
September	6	83 40	2,339	3,141 98	2,889	2,621 263		
October	—	32 —	1,651	2,242 172	2,984	2,501 138		
November	—	15 4	1,316	1,894 113	1,907	1,713 43		
December	25	40 119	992	1,385 56	1,794	1,411 151		
TOTAL	**31**	**170** **163**	**13,037**	**17,513** **3,316**	**31,704**	**27,101** **3,507**	**26,858**	**20,771** **1,267**
						GRAND TOTAL	**71,630**	**65,555** **8,253**

Table 23 Tons Bombs Dropped and Sorties Flown by the Allied Air Forces in Europe August 1942-May 1945

DATE	BOMBER COMMAND		8 US AIR FORCE		15 US AIR FORCE		BALKAN AIR FORCE	
1942	TONS DROPPED	NUMBER* SORTIES	TONS DROPPED	NUMBER SORTIES	TONS DROPPED	NUMBER SORTIES	TONS DROPPED	NUMBER† SORTIES
August	4,162	2,454 186	151	114	—	—	—	—
September	5,595	3,489 127	188	183	—	—	—	—
October	3,809	2,198 406	278	284	—	—	—	—
November	2,423	2,067 127	604	519	—	—	—	—
December	2,714	1,758 200	340	353	—	—	—	—
TOTAL	**18,703**	**11,966 1,046**	**1,411**	**1,453**	**—**	**—**	**—**	**—**
1943								
January	4,345	2,556 406	594	338	—	—	—	—
February	10,959	5,030 426	568	526	—	—	—	—
March	10,591	5,174 284	1,483	956	—	—	—	—
April	11,467	5,571 316	858	449	—	—	—	—
May	12,290	5,130 360	2,555	1,672	—	—	—	—
June	15,271	5,816 —	2,330	2,107	—	—	—	—
July	16,830	6,170 —	3,475	2,829	—	—	—	—
August	20,149	7,807 —	3,999	2,265	—	—	—	—
September	14,855	5,513 —	7,369	3,259	—	—	—	—
October	13,773	4,638 —	4,548	2,831	—	—	—	—
November	14,495	5,208 —	5,751	4,157	5,392	1,785	—	—
December	11,802	4,123 —	10,655	5,973	7,752	2,039	—	—
TOTAL	**157,367**	**62,736 1,792**	**44,185**	**27,362**	**13,144**	**3,824**	**—**	**—**
1944								
January	18,428	6,278 —	10,532	6,367	11,051	4,720	—	—
February	12,054	4,263 45	16,480	9,884	6,747	3,981	—	—
March	27,698	9,031 18	19,892	11,590	10,176	5,996	—	—
April	33,496	9,873 10	22,447	14,464	21,256	10,182	—	—
May	37,252	11,353 16	32,450	19,825	30,355	14,432	—	—
June	57,267	13,592 2,371	54,204	28,925	27,466	11,761	—	—
July	57,615	11,500 6,298	40,784	23,917	32,183	12,642	132	2,509

* The top figure for each month is night sorties, the bottom day.

† All types aircraft.

Table 23 Tons Bombs Dropped and Sorties Flown by Allied Air Forces in Europe August 1942-May 1945 (continued)

* The top figure for each month is night sorties, the bottom day.

† All types aircraft.

DATE 1944	BOMBER COMMAND		8 US AIR FORCE		15 US AIR FORCE		BALKAN AIR FORCE	
	TONS DROPPED	NUMBER* SORTIES	TONS DROPPED	NUMBER SORTIES	TONS DROPPED	NUMBER SORTIES	TONS DROPPED	NUMBER† SORTIES
August	65,855	10,013 10,271	44,120	22,967	27,859	12,194	277	3,437
September	52,587	6,428 9,643	36,332	18,268	20,856	10,056	480	3,698
October	61,204	10,193 6,713	38,961	19,082	16,257	9,567	430	3,416
November	53,022	9,589 5,055	36,091	17,003	17,297	9,259	342	4,604
December	49,040	11,239 3,656	36,826	18,252	18,757	10,050	761	4,653
TOTAL	**525,518**	**113,352 44,096**	**389,119**	**210,544**	**240,260**	**114,840**	**2,422**	**22,317**
1945								
January	32,923	9,603 1,304	34,891	16,702	6,784	4,002	395	2,460
February	45,889	13,715 3,685	46,088	22,884	24,508	13,444	1,085	4,690
March	67,637	11,585 9,606	65,962	31,169	30,265	14,939	1,086	3,954
April	34,954	8,822 5,001	41,632	20,514	29,258	15,846	1,561	4,546
May	337	349 1,068	—	2,276	84	42	101	373
TOTAL	**181,740**	**44,074 20,664**	**188,573**	**93,545**	**90,899**	**48,273**	**4,228**	**16,023**
GRAND TOTAL	**883,328**	**232,128 67,598**	**623,288**	**332,904**	**344,303**	**166,937**	**6,650**	**38,340**

Table 24 Tons Bombs Dropped and Sorties Flown Against Japan by 20 US Air Force June 1944-August 1945‡

MONTH	NUMBER SORTIES FLOWN	TONS BOMBS DROPPED	
		H.E.	INCENDIARY
1944 June		501	46
July		209	—
August		184	68
September		521	—
October		1,023	646
November		1,758	447
December		3,051	610
TOTAL	**2,102**	**7,247**	**1,817**

MONTH	NUMBER SORTIES FLOWN	TONS BOMBS DROPPED	
		H.E.	INCENDIARY
1945 January		2,511	899
February		2,401	1,619
March		4,105	11,138
April		13,209	4,283
May		6,937	17,348
June		9,954	22,588
July		9,388	33,163
August		8,438	12,591
TOTAL	**26,724**	**56,943**	**103,629**
GRAND TOTAL	**28,826**	**64,190**	**105,446**

‡ 20 US Air Force was by far the most important formation attacking Japan proper. Other Air Forces achieved only the following modest tonnages against this target:

US Navy	6,788
7 US Air Force	5,102
5 US Air Force	1,905
13 US Air Force	6
TOTAL	13,801

| Table 25 Tons of Bombs (including V-Weapons) Dropped by Germany on the UK 1940-45 |

YEAR	1940	1941	1942	1943	1944	1945	TOTAL
TONNAGE	36,844	21,858	3,260	2,298	9,151	761	**74,172**

| Table 26 Tons Bombs Dropped and Sorties Flown by Luftwaffe During the Blitz September 1940-February 1941 |

MONTH	1940				1941		TOTAL
	Sept	Oct	Nov	Dec	Jan	Feb	
NUMBER OF SORTIES	7,260	9,911	c. 6,000	3,844	2,465	1,401	**30,881**
TONS DROPPED	7,044	9,113	6,510	4,323	2,424	1,127	**30,541**

National Air Forces

AUSTRALIA

The Australian Air Force comprised the RAAF proper, based in Australia, and the squadrons that fought overseas as part of the Royal Air Force.

These latter were Squadrons 450 through 464 and 466 and 467, comprising six fighter squadrons (one night), nine bomber and two flying-boat. Of these, eight were raised in 1941, eight in 1942 and one in 1943.

During the war the RAAF fielded 55 squadrons, of which 21 were (at the end of the war) equipped with fighters, 16 with bombers, 7 with amphibious aircraft, 6 with transport aircraft and 5 with trainers. In September 1939, RAAF front-line strength consisted of 164 combat aircraft, mainly Avro Ansons and Hawker Demons. In December 1941, front-line strength was 177 combat aircraft, mainly Lockheed Hudsons and Commonwealth Wirraways. In April 1943, the RAAF operated all told 1,015 combat aircraft, of which 473 were serviceable. In April 1945 there were 3,187 front-line RAAF aircraft in the Pacific.

BELGIUM

In May 1940, the Belgian Air Force could deploy 180 front-line aircraft, mainly Fairey Foxes.

Two Belgian fighter squadrons, 349 and 350, formed in 1943 and 1941 respectively, fought with the RAF.

BULGARIA

In September 1939, the Bulgarian Air Force's front-line combat squadrons were almost entirely equipped with Polish aircraft i.e. 101 P.Z.L. P.-24 fighters and 45 P.Z.L. P.-43 single-engined bombers. By the time of the invasion of Russia, in which the Bulgarians declined to participate, they had partially re-equipped, the 18 combat squadrons comprising 60 Avia B-534 and 10 Messerschmitt Bf 109E-3 fighters and 60 Letov S-328, 25 Avia B-71, 12 P.Z.L. P.-43 and 11 Dornier Do 17M bombers.

For the rest of the war replacement aircraft came via the Germans, the main arrivals being 9 more Bf 109E-3s, 16 109G-2s and 128 109G-6s; 100 Dewoitine D.520 and 24 Avia B-135 fighters; 48 Junkers Ju 87 dive bombers and 12 Dornier Do 17M bombers.

CANADA

The RCAF began the war with 270 aircraft, few of them front-line, organised in six bomber and four fighter squadrons as well as nine others.

During the war 84 Canadian squadrons were formed, 49 of which served with the RCAF proper in Canada and 44 with the RAF (the discrepancy in the figures indicates that nine squadrons served with both air forces). Of the 49 RCAF squadrons, 14 of which were disbanded and later reformed, 15 ended up as fighter squadrons, 7 as bomber, 7 as flying

boat and 20 as other. These squadrons' first formation occurred as follows:

1939	1940	1941	1942	1943	1944	1945
19	2	1	17	6	2	—

17 of these squadrons were disbanded for good before the end of the war.

The 44 squadrons that served overseas with the RAF took the numbers 400 through 443. 19 were equipped with fighters (4 night), 15 with bombers, 5 with flying boats and 5 with other. These squadrons' formation or conversion to the RAF occurred as follows:

1941	1942	1943	1944
21	4	16	3

CHINA

At the start of the Sino-Japanese War, in August 1937, the Chinese Air Force comprised some 230 aircraft of all types*. The main combat types were Curtiss F6-C Hawks and Boeing P-26s, both fighters. In November, the Chinese received a consignment of Russian planes, Polikarpov I-15 and I-16 fighters as well as Tupolev SB-2 bombers. There were also some deliveries of Gloster Gladiators and Dewoitine D510s.

Between 1938 and 1941 peak air force strength was around 300 fighters and 100 bombers, though it fell at one stage in 1939 to only 135 aircraft and in 1940 to a mere 65. Another Russian consignment of 250 aircraft in early 1941 and a purchase shortly therafter of 100 Curtiss P-40s brought the strength in December 1941 back up to 364 aircraft.

A year later there were 337 combat aircraft on hand and over the rest of the war, thanks to a steady stream of US replacements (notably P-40 and P-51 fighters and B-25 bombers), air force strength was greatly increased, though Chinese official sources give no actual figures. Probably the most important source of air power in China was US Fourteenth Air Force. Formed in March 1943, it numbered over 700 aircraft by January 1945.

* According to the Chinese; Japanese sources talk of 650-700.

CZECHOSLOVAKIA

When German troops occupied Bohemia and Moravia in March 1939, the Czech Army Air Force comprised over 1,000 aircraft, some 570 of which were considered to be front-line. Main combat types were Avia B.H.33 fighters and Fokker F-VII and F-IX bombers. The Slovakian Air Force established by the Germans was much reduced in strength, never more than 70 first-line aircraft, though these did include, by 1942, three Messerschmitt Bf 109 Squadrons.

Czech airmen who fled to Britain provided three fighter squadrons (Nos. 310, 312 and 313) for the RAF, these becoming operational in August and October 1940 and June 1941. They later made up an independent Czech Fighter Wing. There was also one bomber squadron formed, No. 311, in

August 1940. On the Eastern Front, in June 1944, a Czech Air Regiment was formed, flying fighters and light bombers.

DENMARK
When the Germans invaded Denmark in April 1940, the main element of the Danish Army Air Force was two squadrons of Bristol Bulldogs and Gloster Gladiators. Together with the Danish Naval Air Service (mainly one squadron of Hawker Nimrod fighters and one of Hawker Horsley torpedo-bombers) it made up a force of little more than 100 aircraft in all.

FINLAND
In November 1939, at the beginning of the Winter War, the Finnish Air Force comprised 2 fighter, 2 bomber, 2 dive-bomber and 3 other squadrons, totalling 145 aircraft, 114 of which were serviceable. 107 of these were modern types, namely 56 Fokker D.XXI and Bristol Bulldog fighters, 34 Fokker C.X recce/dive-bombers and 17 Blenheim I bombers. During the war a further two reconnaissance, one fighter and one bomber squadrons were formed and at the time of the armistice air force strength was 196 operational planes, of which only 112 were serviceable (111/71 fighters, 29/11 bombers and 56/30 others).

From June 1941 the Finns fought with the Germans and at that date the air force consisted of around 280 operational aircraft formed into 5 fighter, 3 bomber and 4 other squadrons. These included 40 Brewster 239s, 25 Fiat G.50s, 29 Morane Saulnier 406s and 24 Bristol Blenheim Is. Just before the Finnish surrender, in September 1944, they fielded 6 fighter squadrons, 4 bomber and 3 reconnaissance. The most common fighter was now the Messerschmitt Bf 109G-6, of which 114 were delivered all told. But when the Finns actually began fighting alongside the Russians, in the following month, they had only 70 operational combat aircraft.

FRANCE
In September 1939 the *Armée de l'Air* comprised 24 front-line fighter squadrons (*groupes*), 34 bomber and 17 reconnaissance. These included some 550 fighters (440 of which were modern) and 400 bombers (hardly any modern). In May 1940, in France itself, there were 22 front-line fighter squadrons, 6 fighter *escadrilles*, 10 bomber squadrons, 2 assault squadrons and 11 reconnaissance squadrons. The total number of aircraft available in all home units (not just front-line) was 1,368. This comprised 637 fighters (37 Bloch 151, 93 Bloch 152, 98 Curtiss Hawk 75, 38 Dewoitine D.520, 278 Morane Saulnier 406, 67 Potez 631, 28 obsolete), 242 bombers (45 Breguet 691 and 693, 54 Leo 451, 23 miscellaneous modern, 120 obsolete), and 489 reconnaissance (24 Bloch 174, 257 Potez 637 and 63-11, 208 obsolete). This was a total of 1,012 modern and 356 obsolete aircraft. The total number of aircraft in operational units was somewhat less – 1,145 (of which 243 were obsolete), breaking down into 585 fighters (28 obsolete), 140 bombers (65), and 420 reconnaissance (150). By the time of the Armistice the French actually had more planes than on 10 May 1940 but the great proportion of the new production was not yet operational.

After the Armistice 12 almost wholly French squadrons fought with the RAF. These comprised 7 fighter (Nos. 326 to 329, 340 and 341 and 345), 4 bomber (342, 344, 346 and 347) and one flying boat (343). One of these squadrons was formed in 1941, 7 in 1943 and 4 in 1944. Two USAAF bomber groups were also French (Nos. 31 and 34) and one fighter squadron (*Groupe de Chasse 3*) fought with the Red Air Force. After June 1944 several autonomous *Armée de l'Air* units were formed. Eight were fighter and ground attack (*Groupes de Chasse* II/3, III/3, I/4, I/5, II/5, III/6, I/18 and II/18), 6 were bomber (II/22, II/23, I/25, I/31, I/34 and II/52) 2 were reconnaissance (I/33 and III/33) and 3 were transport (II/15, Artois and Picardy).

GERMANY
The table below gives quarterly Luftwaffe strengths of the main types of aircraft, both operational and serviceable.

Table 27 Quarterly Luftwaffe Aircraft Strengths by Type (Operational and Serviceable) 1939-45

DATE		SINGLE-ENGINE FIGHTERS		TWIN-ENGINE FIGHTERS		NIGHT FIGHTERS		DIVE-BOMBER & GROUND ATTACK		BOMBERS		TRANSPORT	
		Strength	Serviceable	Strength	Serviceable	Strength	Serviceable	Strength	Serviceable	Strength	Serviceable	Strength	Serviceable
1939	Sept	1,125	870	194	141	—	—	384	267	1,213	1,014	552	
	Dec	1,022	769	410	299	—	—	459	356	1,367	1,000	?	
1940	Mar	1,258	817	325	222	—	—	453	368	1,656	1,102	466	
	June	1,107	856	357	261	—	—	483	337	1,380	841	357	
	Sept	932	721	181	114	—	—	482	401	1,420	818	365	
	Dec	832	587	241	168	165	104	482	375	1,330	722	415	
1941	Mar	1,158	846	322	224	199	124	444	353	1,460	932	713	
	June	1,266	885	210	131	244	172	410	278	1,321	763	?	
	Sept	1,226	774	155	83	245	140	397	280	1,538	630	?	
	Dec	1,116	670	48	21	223	132	256	132	918	383	991	
1942	Mar	1,129	747	112	61	248	134	406	205	977	480	?	
	June	1,277	901	362	210	244	162	461	300	1,381	885	957	
	Sept	1,491	1,024	297	166	350	245	413	273	1,416	741	?	
	Dec	1,360	908	212	111	389	278	286	160	1,193	611	881	
1943	Mar	1,535	1,006	401	206	493	360	469	325	1,522	844	?	
	June	1,849	1,361	414	305	554	371	523	444	1,663	1,070	850	
	Sept	1,646	1,080	392	243	574	248	562	395	1,080	639	?	
	Dec	1,561	1,095	290	199	611	405	601	466	1,604	1,078	903	
1944	Mar	1,696	1,188	251	148	565	361	776	516	1,331	825	?	
	June	1,523	895	242	124	778	528	1,005	751	1,089	694	944	
	Sept	1,984	1,413	142	122	1,018	854	816	606	929	644	?	
	Dec	2,260	1,521	105	85	1,256	913	892	637	528	359	500	
1945	April	1,637	? *	?	?	498	? *	?	?	?	?	(Feb) 505	

Transport "Serviceable" column note: not available

* It is certain that the vast majority of planes at this date would have had no fuel, and like as not no competent pilot.

Listed below are the number of planes specifically allocated to certain major campaigns. The figures usually represent strengths on the first day, but may include reserves.

Table 28 Luftwaffe Aircraft Strengths Allocated at the Beginning of Major Campaigns, by Type

CAMPAIGN	Fighters		Dive-Bomber & Ground Attack	Bomber	Recce	Transport	Other *	TOTAL	TOTAL COMBAT
	Single-Engine	Twin-Engine							
POLAND Sept 1939	210		249	648	474		—	1,581	1,107
NORWAY April 1940 †	50	70	50	360	60	570	120 Coastal	1,280	530
FRANCE May 1940	860	355	410	1,120	640	475	45 Gliders	3,905	2,745
BATTLE OF BRITAIN July 1940 ‡	893 †† / c.700	246 / 168	316 / 248	1,260 / 864	115 / 81	—	—	2,830 / 2,061	2,715 / 1,980
BALKANS April 1941	30	70	40	290	40	500	—	970	430
BARBAROSSA June 1941	965 †† / 735	102 / 64	465 / 360	952 / 757	61 / 39	292 / 175	—	2,837 / 2,130	2,484 / 1,916
NORMANDY June 1944	172		—	88	59	—	—	319	260

* If a significant component.

† Peak strength, in May.

‡ See also Table 18.

†† Top left figure gives operational strength, lower right gives serviceable.

Finally, in the table below, will be found details on the number of fighters (day and night) assigned to the defence of the Reich at various dates. Figures refer to operational aircraft with numbers serviceable, where known, given in brackets.

Table 29 Luftwaffe Fighter Strength For Home Defence at Selected Dates August 1940-April 1945

DATE		Day-Fighters		Night-Fighters
		Single-Engine	Twin-Engine	
1940	Aug			43
	Dec			164 (97)
1941	Sept			263 (174)
1942	Feb			265 (159)
	June			255 (167)
	Aug			322 (214)
	Nov	221 (144)	144 (80)	
	Dec			375 (282)
1943	Jan	635	?	
	Feb			477 (330)
	July	c. 800		
	Aug			627 (421)
	Sept			? (308)

DATE		Day-Fighters		Night-Fighters
		Single-Engine	Twin-Engine	
1943	Oct	975	175	? (166)
	Nov			? (258)
	Dec			? (247)
1944	Feb	863 (517)		? (223)
	April	850		
	June	982 (534)	116 (53)	
	July			849 (614)
	Sept	1,260	—	959 (792)
	Oct	900	—	
	Dec	400	—	1,355 (982)
1945	March	c. 500	—	
	April	451	96 (Jet)	600

GREECE

In November 1940, at the time of the Italian invasion, the Royal Hellenic Air Force comprised seven front-line combat squadrons. These were four fighter and three bomber, made up of 36 P.Z.L. P-24-F and 9 Bloch M.B.151 single-seat fighters as well as 12 Bristol Blenheim I, 12 Fairey Battle and 12 Potez 63 bombers.

After the surrender to the Germans in April 1941, the RHAF evacuated to North Africa. There it came under RAF command and provided two fighter squadrons, 335 and 336 formed in October 1941 and February 1943, and part of one bomber, I3, formed in February 1943.

HUNGARY

In June 1941, the Hungarian Air Force consisted of 8 fighter, 8 bomber and 13 reconnaissance squadrons, equipped mainly with Fiat C.R.42 fighters, Caproni Ca.135bis bombers and Heinkel He 70s. All in all it comprised

about 350 aircraft. Only a proportion of these fought in Russia, however, as can be seen below:
- July 1941: 1 fighter, 1 bomber and 2 short-range reconnaissance squadrons.
- June 1942: 2 fighter, 2 bomber, 2 long-range and 1 short-range reconnaissance squadrons. (Approximately 100 aircraft.)
- June 1943: 2 fighter, 1 bomber, 1 dive-bomber, 1 long-range and 1 short-range reconnaissance squadrons.

By mid-1944 the Hungarian Air Force, now largely German-equipped, was mainly concerned with home defence against Allied bombers. Here it comprised:
- April 1944: 2 fighter and 1 night-fighter squadrons.
- July 1944: 6 fighter and 1 night-fighter squadrons.
- Nov 1944: 8 fighter, 1 night-fighter, 2 ground-attack and 3 bomber squadrons. (Peak strength of c. 600 aircraft.)

INDIA

At the beginning of the war the Indian Air Force ('Royal' from March 1945) had only one fighter squadron and this was not brought up to strength until July 1940 and not equipped with modern fighters (Hawker Hurricanes) until 1942. By the end of the war, however, the Air Force had 2 fighter, 3 fighter reconnaissance, 2 ground-attack and 2 light bomber squadrons.

ITALY

The following were the strengths and deployment of the *Regia Aeronautica* on Italy's declaration of war, in November 1942 and at the time of the Armistice.

Table 30 Italian Air Force Combat Aircraft Strengths, by Location, June 1940, November 1942 and September 1943

DATE	June 1940†			Nov 1942‡			Sept 1943#		
LOCATION					Type*				
	f.	d/b g/a	b.	f.	d/b g/a	b.	f.	d/b g/a	b.
Mainland	7St.	1Gp.	11St.	264 (186)	20 —	209 (83)	260	48	139
Sicily	1St. 1Gp.	1Gp.	5St.	184 (24)	— —	84 (53)	—	—	—
Sardinia	3St.	1Gp.	1Gp.	33 (27)	— —	72 (52)	—	—	—
E.Africa	see Note † below			—	—	—	—	—	—
Libya	3St.	1St.	4St.	147 (95)	85 (45)	61 (38)	—	—	—
Aegean	2St.	—	1St.	46 (34)	— —	41 (26)	45	—	13
Greece	—	—	—	81 (34)	—	—	23	—	6
Albania	1St.	—	1St.	15 (9)	—	17 (12)	25	18	31
Slovenia-Dalmalla	—	—	—	—	—	17 (16)	—	22	14
Russia	—	—	—	40 (30)	—	—	—	—	—

* f = fighter; d/b = dive-bomber; g/a = ground-attack; b = bomber.
† Number of formations given: St. = Stormo; Gp. = Gruppo. The number of front-line planes was 2,350 of which 1,796 were immediately available. These included 759 (594) fighters and ground-attack, 1,064 (783) bombers, 337 (268) reconnaissance and 190 (151) naval floatplanes. In Italian East Africa there were a further 325 aircraft, only 183 of which were serviceable front-line. Combat aircraft comprised 45 fighters and 36 bombers.
‡ Top figure = aircraft operational, figure in brackets = aircraft serviceable.
# Not included in these aircraft totals are 14 squadrons of fighters, 5 of dive-bomber/ground-attack, and 6 of bombers that were in the process of re-equipping with more modern types.

The aircraft which most impinged upon Allied operations in Africa and the Mediterranean were those stationed in Libya, Sicily, Sardinia and, later, Tunisia. Figures for the average quarterly serviceability of aircraft in these locations are given in the next table, covering the period January 1941 to April 1943:

Table 31 Quarterly Totals of Serviceable Italian Combat Aircraft in Sicily, Sardinia and North Africa January 1941-April 1943

AREA	Sicily			Sardinia			Libya			Tunisia		
					Type							
1941 First quarter	f	d/b	b	f	d/b	b	f	d/b	b	f	d/b	b
	56	—	19	?	?	?	85	10	20	—	—	—
2	88	16	39	?	?	?	90	10	28	—	—	—
3	99	14	62	?	?	?	112	19	56	—	—	—
4	110	8	55	?	?	?	179	11	59	—	—	—
1942 1	68	—	42	53	—	36	131	14	25	—	—	—
2	114	15	58	51	—	32	159	25	32	—	—	—
3	79	13	66	33	—	41	131	34	35	—	—	—
4	96	6	49	55	—	65	82	55	26	—	—	—
1943 1	96	—	30	46	—	48	102	—	13	37	—	—
April	95	—	13	41	—	31	—	—	—	55	—	—

JAPAN

Figures for both the Japanese Army and Navy Air Forces are extremely fragmentary and contradictory, at least in English sources. Overall figures are particularly scarce and so, except for referring the reader back to Table 21, all that can be added here are some more detailed figures at the outbreak of war and almost at the end. Aircraft strengths in major naval battles will be found in Table 48. Also included are some figures on kamikaze sorties and on aircraft strengths and bombing sorties in China.

Table 32 Japanese Combat Aircraft Available 8 December 1941

TYPE	Army*	Navy †	
		Carrier	Land
Fighter	550	371	
Bomber	660	320	324
Reconnaissance	290	—	30
Other	70	334	
TOTAL	1,570	1,379	

* Operational. † First Line.

The Army deployed 725 of its aircraft in the initial campaigns in Malaya and the Philippines, whilst the Navy utilised 371 aircraft in the attack on Pearl Harbour, 556 in Malaya and the Philippines and between 50 and 100 at Wake and Guam. Army aircraft not used in the drive south (81 out of 150 squadrons) were grouped in 56 squadrons in Manchuria, 16 in China and 9 in Japan, Korea and Formosa.

Table 33 Deployment of Combat Aircraft for the Defence of Japan and its Approaches March 1945

LOCATION	Army					Navy					GRAND TOTAL
	fighter	bomber	recce.	kami-kaze	TOTAL	fighter	bomber	recce.	kami-kaze	TOTAL	
Japan*	550	120	110	400	1,180	600	530	30	3,100	4,260	5,440
China	105	120	16	200	441	—	—	—	—	—	441
Indo-China	25	15	—	—	40	—	—	—	—	—	40
Formosa	120	60	10	250	440	40	40	5	—	85	525
TOTAL	800	315	136	850	2,101	640	570	35	3,100	4,345	6,456

* Army figures include some reserve aircraft.

Table 34 Kamikaze Sorties October 1944-August 1945

MONTH		SORTIES	MONTH		SORTIES
1944	Oct	55	1945	April	1,162
	Nov	143		May	596
	Dec	232		June	210
1945	Jan	230		July	20
	Feb	196		August	59
	March	37	TOTAL		2,940

Table 35 Japanese Air Raids in China and their Effects 1939-45*

YEAR	Raids	Sorties	No. Bombs Dropped	Deaths	Injured	Houses Destroyed
1939	2,603	14,138	60,174	28,463	31,546	138,171
1940	2,069	12,767	50,118	18,829	21,830	107,750
1941	1,858	12,211	43,308	14,121	16,902	97,714
1942	828	3,297	12,435	6,718	3,853	17,609
1943	664	3,543	13,642	2,333	3,406	14,161
1944	917	2,071	17,266	557	766	1,173
1945	49	131	3,718	84	91	151
TOTAL	8,988	48,140	197,661	71,105	78,394	376,729

* These figures should be treated with extra caution. They will not, for example, include raids and losses in Communist-held areas. They are best treated as an indicator of the tempo of activity.

Chinese sources give the following figures for the number of planes stationed in China at various dates:

Oct 1939	Oct 1940	Dec 1941	1942 average	July 1945
600	800	750	275	310

NETHERLANDS

In May 1940, the Royal Netherlands Air Force comprised 132 serviceable aircraft, of which only 72 could be regarded as being modern. 78 of the total were combat aircraft, namely 29 Fokker D.XXI and 6 D.XVIII fighters, 23 Fokker G.I twin-engined fighters, and 11 Douglas DB-8A-3N and 9 Fokker T.V. bombers.

The Dutch air force in the East Indies survived the fall of metropolitan Holland and in December 1941 its combat component comprised 59 Curtiss 75A-7 Hawk, CW-218 Interceptor and Brewster B-3390 Buffalo fighters, and 58 Martin B-10 bombers. The naval air arm also provided 73 Dornier Do 24K and Convair Catalina flying boats. On 1 February 1942, the whole air force was concentrated in Java and still numbered 52 fighters and 45 bombers. In the next weeks a further 48 Hurricane I and IIAs and 30 Curtiss P-40 Kittyhawks were delivered by the Allies.

After the collapse in Europe Dutch fliers manned three RAF squadrons: 320 Coastal Command (Bomber Command from July 1943) formed in June 1940, 321 Coastal Command formed in March 1942*, and 322 fighter squadron formed in June 1943. There was also an 860 aircraft carrier squadron serving with the Royal Netherlands Navy from June 1943. After the collapse in the Pacific Dutch fliers manned two RAAF squadrons: 18, flying bombers and formed in 1942, and 20, flying Kittyhawks and formed in December 1943.

NEW ZEALAND

The Royal New Zealand Air Force fought in the Pacific, where 25 squadrons were raised, and New Zealanders also manned seven RAF squadrons, six of which fought in Europe and one in West Africa.

The RNZAF squadrons were raised as follows:

	1940	1941	1942	1943	1944	1945	TOTAL
Bomber-Recce	2	2	1	—	1	—	6
Recce	—	—	—	2	—	—	2
Fighter-Bomber	—	1	—	2	—	—	3
Torpedo-Bomber	—	—	—	2	—	—	2
Fighter	—	—	4	2	6	1	13
Transport	—	—	—	1	1	—	2
TOTAL	2	3	5	9	8	1	28†

The RAF squadrons comprised one bomber (75, formed 1940), one fighter (485, 1941), one fighter/fighter-bomber (486, 1942), three bomber-reconnaissance (487-489, 1941/42) and one flying boat (490, 1943).

† One squadron was renumbered and two more were raised twice. Two squadrons were disbanded before the end of the war.

NORWAY

In April 1940 the Army Air Force comprised one fighter and three reconnaissance squadrons which could deploy 7 Gloster Gladiators, 40 Fokker C.V. and C.VD reconnaissance planes and 4 Caproni Ca 310 light bombers. The Naval Air Service comprised 21 M.F.11 and Heinkel He 115 reconnaissance seaplanes as well as 7 Douglas DT-2B and C torpedo-bombers.

After the fall of Norway five squadrons were formed for service with the RAF. Two of these were flying boat (330 and 333, formed 1940 and 1942), two fighter (331 and 332, 1941 and 1942) and one Mosquito (334, 1945).

POLAND

In September 1939 the air force comprised 16 bomber squadrons, 15 fighter, 12 reconnaissance, 1 torpedo-bomber and 1 transport. These contained 678 operational aircraft of which 388 were serviceable. These included 266 bombers (156 serviceable), 202 fighters (serviceable total not available), 210 reconnaissance (not available) and 9 transport (not available).

In France in 1940, Polish pilots manned I, II, III and IV/145 fighter squadrons, though only 1½ of these were fully formed and trained in May, containing something like 50 serviceable fighters.

The Polish component of the RAF was considerable, 14 squadrons in all being formed. 9 of these were fighter (302-303, formed in 1940; 306, 308-309 and 315-317 in 1941 and 318 in 1943), 4 bomber (300-301, 1940; and 304-305, 1941), and one Mosquito (307, 1941).

Finally, the Poles also provided 3 Russian air regiments, all formed in 1944, of which one was fighter, one ground attack and one night bomber.

RUMANIA

In September 1939 the air force contained some 500 operational aircraft, including 11 fighter squadrons, 4 bomber and 4 reconnaissance. By June 1942 there were 700 operational aircraft, half of them fighters, a veritable *pot pourri* of Polish, French, Italian, British and German types. Strength declined inexorably thereafter despite the acquisition, all told, of about 200 German aircraft (half of them Bf 109E and Gs). Domestic production never exceeded 350 aircraft per year.

SOUTH AFRICA

At the beginning of the war the South African fighter force comprised 4 Hawker Hurricanes, 6 Hawker Furies and one Bristol Blenheim, whilst for bombing and reconnaissance there were 63 Hawker Hartebeestes and 18 converted Junkers Ju 86 airliners. By June 1940 the South African Air Force had assembled 46 combat aircraft for operations against the Italians and these were organised into two bomber squadrons (Nos. 11 and 12) and one fighter (No.1).

Over the war as a whole the SAAF underwent a remarkable expansion (there were no S.African RAF squadrons) and the following table shows the number and type of squadrons deployed in the Mediterranean at three dates:

* After a brief existence in 1940 and early 1941 as a depot squadron.

Table 36 Number of South African Air Force Squadrons Deployed in the Mediterranean, by Type, October 1942, April 1943 and May 1944

DATE	Fighter	Tank Destroyer	Bomber	Recce	Coastal	Other	TOTAL
October 1942	5	2	4	6	—	—	**17**
April 1943	6	—	3	5	—	—	**14**
May 1944	6*	—	4	2	1	1	**14**

* One also had a reconniassance role.

UNITED KINGDOM

Details on numbers of RAF aircraft are suprisingly fragmentary and most of the figures that are available can be found in Table 17 above. However, full records of RAF squadrons are available and from these the following comparative figures on squadron location by type have been assembled.

They are followed by three tables giving extra details on the numbers of aircraft available to Bomber and Coastal Commands and the Fleet Air Arm at certain dates.

Table 37 Number of RAF Combat Squadrons, by Type and Theatre, at Selected Dates 1939-45

• Includes twin-engined.

† Typhoons only.

‡ 'Resistance' squadrons excluded.

** Mainly Coastal Command. Includes Iceland.

DATE	Fighter •					Ground Attack †					Bomber ‡ Command	Other Medium and Heavy Bomber				
	UK	NWE	Med	FE	TOTAL	UK	NWE	Med	FE	TOTAL	TOTAL	UK**	NWE	Med	FE	TOTAL
Sept 1939	41	4	6	4	**55**	—	—	—	—	—	37	3	—	2	2	**7**
July 1940	65	—	8	4	**77**	—	—	—	—	—	38	3	—	2	2	**7**
Dec 1941	114	—	29	13	**156**	—	—	—	—	—	50	12	—	7	3	**22**
Dec 1942	93	—	47	19	**159**	12	—	—	—	**12**	60	17	—	14	7	**38**
Dec 1943	83	—	49	29	**161**	19	—	—	—	**19**	72	19	—	21	8	**48**
Sept 1944	58	48	41	29	**176**	1	19	—	—	**20**	86	23	1	19	9	**52**
March 1945	46	51	33	30	**160**	4	20	—	—	**24**	96	30	2	16	15	**63**

DATE	Light Bomber					Torpedo Bomber					Flying Boat					TOTAL COMBAT SQUADRONS				
	UK	NWE	Med	FE	TOTAL	UK	NWE	Med	FE	TOTAL	UK	NWE	Med	FE	TOTAL	UK	NWE	Med	FE	TOTAL
Sept 1939	12	6	8	5	**31**	1	—	1	—	**2**	4	—	1	2	**7**	98	10	18	13	**139**
July 1940	19	—	9	4	**32**	3	—	—	—	**3**	4	—	2	1	**7**	132	—	21	11	**164**
Dec 1941	22	—	10	2	**34**	9	—	2	1	**12**	7	—	3	1	**11**	214	—	51	20	**285**
Dec 1942	8	—	17	9	**34**	8	—	8	2	**18**	9	—	6	4	**19**	207	—	92	41	**340**
Dec 1943	17	—	13	5	**35**	11	—	9	5	**25**	10	—	8	6	**24**	231	—	100	53	**384**
Sept 1944	12	3	7	6	**28**	7	—	3	6	**16**	12	—	8	8	**28**	199	71	78	58	**406**
March 1945	8	9	6	5	**28**	4	—	2	4	**10**	12	—	9	6	**27**	200	82	66	60	**408**

Table 38 Bomber Command Aircraft Strengths, by Type, and Availability with Crews at Selected Dates September 1939-April 1945

DATE	Hampdens	Blenheims	Mosquitos	Wellingtons	Whitleys	Stirlings	Halifaxes	Manchesters	Lancasters	US Types	Total with Crews
Sept 1939	71	140	—	77	61	—	—	—	—	—	280
Nov 1941	150	79	—	250	62	18	17	31	—	3	506
May 1942	27	29	—	214	15	45	62	15	29	44	417
Jan 1943	—	—	17	128	—	56	104	—	178	99	515
Mar 1944	—	—	58	—	—	63	328	—	594	—	974
April 1945	—	—	203	—	—	—	353	—	1,087	—	1,609

Table 39 Coastal Command Squadron and Aircraft Strengths, by Type, at Selected Dates September 1939-May 1945

| DATE | Type of Squadron/Aircraft | | | | | | | | | | | TOTAL | |
| | VLR Recce | | LR Recce | | Other Recce | | Flying Boat | | Torpedo/Fighter | | | | |
	Sqds.	A/c	Sqds.	A/c	Sqds.	A/c	Sqds.	A/c	Sqds.	A/c		Sqds.	A/c
Sept 1939	—	—	—	—	10	209	5	40	1	16		16	265
July 1940	—	—	—	—	13	267	7	46	8$^1/_2$	177		28$^1/_2$	490
July 1941	1	9	—	—	17	324	10	81	12	262		40	676
July 1942	1	16	1	12	19	370	10	91	11	220		42	709
July 1943	7	105	3	45	9	186	10	120	10$^1/_2$	208		39$^1/_2$	664
June 1944	3	45	11	166	10	137	10$^1/_2$	127	15	278		49$^1/_2$	753
Jan 1945	2	30	11	163	8$^1/_2$	125	10$^1/_2$	127	15$^1/_2$	290		46$^3/_2$	735
May 1945	—	—	15	225	10$^1/_2$	155	11	131	14$^1/_2$	274		50$^2/_2$	785

Table 40 Fleet Air Arm Combat Squadron and Combat Aircraft Strengths, by Type, September 1939-September 1945

| DATE | Fighters and Dive-Bombers | | No. A/c * | Torpedo-Planes | | No. A/c * | TOTAL | | No. A/c * |
| | No. Squadrons | | | No. Squadrons | | | No. Squadrons | | |
	Total	FE†		Total	FE†		Total	FE†	
Sept 1939	3	—	36	12	2	140	15	2	176
Sept 1940	7	—	78	19	—	169	26	—	247
Sept 1941	13	—	129	20	—	198	33	—	327
Sept 1942	27	—	252	28	1	209	55	1	461
Sept 1943	32	—	339	29	1	349	61	1	688
Sept 1944	37	4	645	37	6	549	74	10	1,194
April 1945	39	26	826	27	8	500	66	34	1,326
Sept 1945	40	32	739	27	14	205	67	46	945

† Aircraft with front-line units only.

* Portion of total stationed in Far East.

USA

As usual, the data on American air forces is fuller than for other countries and the tables that follow give a fairly complete picture of total numbers of aircraft available at various dates, as well as a breakdown of theatre allocation of the various types of combat group. The last three tables provide extra details on US Navy and Marine Corps deployments in the Pacific.

Table 41 US Army Air Force Aircraft Strengths, by Year by Type 1939-45

| DATE | Combat | | | | | Non-combat | | | | | GRAND TOTAL |
	Heavy Bomber	Med. & Lt. Bomber	TOTAL BOMBER	Fighter	TOTAL COMBAT	Recce	Transport	Trainer	Comms	TOTAL NON-COM.	
Dec 1939	39	738	777	492	1,269	378	131	761	7	1,277	2,546
Dec 1940	92	639	731	625	1,356	404	124	2,069	8	2,605	3,961
Dec 1941	288	1,544	1,832	2,170	4,002	475	254	7,340	226	8,295	12,297
Dec 1942	2,079	3,757	5,836	5,303	11,139	468	1,857	17,044	2,796	22,165	33,304
Dec 1943	8,118	6,741	14,859	11,875	26,734	714	6,466	26,051	4,267	37,498	64,232
Dec 1944	13,790	9,169	22,959	17,198	40,157	1,804	10,456	17,060	3,249	32,569	72,726
Aug 1945	13,930	8,463	22,393	16,799	39,192	1,971	9,561	9,588	3,433	24,553	63,745

Table 42 US Army Air Force Combat Aircraft, Total Strengths and Strengths Overseas 1941-45

DATE	December 1941	December 1942	December 1943	December 1944	August 1945
Total First-Line Combat	4,000	10,885	23,807	33,179	31,235
Total Combat Overseas	1,105	4,798	12,719	22,876	17,315
Total First-Line Combat Overseas	957	4,695	11,917	19,892	15,100

Table 43 Number of US Army Air Force Combat Groups Stationed Overseas, by Type and by Theatre, December 1941-August 1945

DATE/THEATRE	FIGHTERS	BOMBERS					TOTAL GROUPS
DECEMBER 1941		Light	Medium	Heavy	Very Heavy	TOTAL BOMBERS	
Pacific	4	—	—	3	—	3	7
DECEMBER 1942							
Pacific	7	1	2	5	—	8	15
CBI	2	—	1	1	—	2	4
UK	4	—	1	10	—	11	15
Med	10	1	5	3	—	9	19
TOTAL	23	2	9	19	—	30	53
DECEMBER 1943							
Pacific	10	2	5	7	—	14	24
CBI	4	—	1	2	—	3	7
UK	17	—	3	31	—	34	51
Med	13	1	7	9	—	17	30
TOTAL	44	3	16	49	—	68	112
SEPTEMBER 1944							
Pacific	9	3	3	9	4	19	28
CBI	6	—	1	2	4	7	13
UK	16	—	—	44	—	44	60
NWE	17	3	6	—	—	9	26
Med	12	1	7	19	—	27	39
TOTAL	60	7	17	74	8	106	166
MARCH 1945							
Pacific	12	3	4	9	14	30	42
CBI	6	—	1	2	3	6	12
UK	9	—	—	43	—	43	52
NWE	21	3	6	—	—	9	30
Med	10	1	7	19	—	27	37
TOTAL	58	7	18	73	17	115	173
AUGUST 1945							
Pacific	16	2	4	10	23	39	55
CBI	6	—	2	2	—	4	10
TOTAL	22	2	6	12	23	43	65

Table 44 Total US Navy Aircraft Strengths (including Marine Corps), by Type, and Total First Line Combat Strengths in the Pacific 1941-45

DATE	Combat	Transport	Trainer	Other	TOTAL	Total First-Line Combat in Pacific *
Dec 1941	2,471	303	2,459	27	**5,260**	?
Dec 1942	5,434	624	5,714	41	**11,813**	1,915
Dec 1943	15,164	1,367	9,057	304	**25,892**	8,268
Dec 1944	25,780	2,437	7,883	621	**36,721**	13,065
Dec 1945	19,402	2,876	7,280	977	**30,535**	14,648†

* Hawaii to India.

† Aug 45.

Table 45 Total US Marine Corps Squadrons at End of Year and Totals, by Type, Involved in Combat Operations, 1940-45

YEAR	Total Squadrons available by end of year	Total Combat Squadrons Starting Combat Operations				
		Fighter	Torpedo Bomber	Scout Bomber	Medium Bomber	Cumulative Total
1940	10	—	—	—	—	—
1941	13	1	2	—	—	**3**
1942	41	9	4	2	—	**18**
1943	88	12(1)‡	4	6	—	**40**
1944	145*	13(5)	2	4	6	**65**
1945	132†	11(1)	1	—	—	77
TOTAL	—	**46(7)**	**13**	**12**	**6**	**77**
NUMBER SAW NO COMBAT	?	20(1)	10	10	4	**44**

* Sept 30.

† Aug 31.

‡ Figure in brackets denotes number of total which were night-fighter squadrons.

Table 46 Sorties Flown in Pacific by US Forces 1941-45

YEAR	USAAF (excluding 20 US Air Force)	20 US Air Force	US Navy and Marine Air	TOTAL
1941/2	7,447	—	3,023	**10,470**
1943	102,092	—	16,132	**118,224**
1944	195,879	2,102	128,942	**326,923**
1945	170,365	26,724	110,012	**307,101**
TOTAL	**475,783**	**28,826**	**258,109**	**762,718**

USSR

Details on Red Air Force organisation are meagre and such figures as are available have already appeared in other Tables. Therefore, see Supplement to Table 2 for the growth of the Air Armies and Table 20 for aircraft strengths at certain dates. Table 93, listing aircraft production, gives some idea of the proportions of different types of aircraft.

YUGOSLAVIA

In March 1941, the paper front-line strength of the Yugoslav Air Force was 400 aircraft. Only 235 of these were in any sense modern i.e. 135 fighters (70 Bf 109E, 30 Hurricanes, 30 Hawker Furies, 5 Ikarus IK-2), 160 bombers (70 Dornier Do 171C, 40 Savoia Marchetti S.M. 79, 50 Blenheim I) and 40 reconnaissance (30 Breguet 19, 10 Caproni Ca 30). These were organised into 8 Air Regiments of 48 squadrons.

In 1944 two Yugoslav squadrons were formed within the RAF. Both flew fighters with the Balkan Air Force, 351 Squadron formed July and 352 formed April. There were also a fighter and a ground attack squadron fighting with the Red Air Force.

PART IV NAVIES

The first Table gives the naval strengths of all the belligerents at the beginning of the war. Though there is no Table giving comparative strengths for subsequent years, it should be noted that, for the major powers, these strengths can be deduced by combining the Table below with Tables 95 (Naval Production) and 65 (Naval Losses). The second Table in this section gives comparative naval strengths at all the major naval battles of the war. It combines exactly with Table 65 which lists comparative naval losses. The final Table gives some details on the strengths of the Commonwealth and government-in-exile navies throughout the war.

Table 47 **Naval Strengths of the Belligerent Nations on Entry into the War**

	AIRCRAFT CARRIERS	BATTLESHIPS	CRUISERS	DESTROYERS	ESCORTS	SUBMARINES
Australia	—	—	6	—	7	—
Brazil	—	2	2	13	—	4
Canada	—	—	—	6	—	—
China	—	—	6	—	?	—
Denmark	—	2*	1	—	—	12
Finland	—	2*	—	—	—	5
France	1	7	19	70	—	77
Germany	—	5	6	17†	—	57
Greece	—	—	2‡	10	—	6
India	—	—	—	—	5	—
Italy	—	2	22	59	—	115
Japan**	10	10	36	113	—	63
Netherlands	—	—	5	8	—	21
New Zealand††	—	—	2	—	—	—
Norway	—	—	—	8	—	5
Poland	—	—	—	4	—	5
Rumania	—	—	—	4	—	—
UK	8	12	50	94	87	38
USA**	8	17	36	171		112
USSR	—	2	2	47	—	75
Yugoslavia	—	—	1+1‡	3	—	4

* Coastal Defence.

† Serviceable.

‡ Antiquated.

** December 1941.

†† The Royal New Zealand Navy was created 1.10.41. Prior to that it was New Zealand Division, Royal Navy.

Table 48 **Comparative Strengths in Major Naval Engagements 1939-45**

Mediterranean and Atlantic

△ Includes battlecruisers.

BATTLE AND DATE		SHIPS PRESENT				NOTES
		A/Cr.	B/s.△	Cr.	Dest.	
RIVER PLATE						
13/12/39	British	—	—	3	—	
	Germans	—	1	—	—	
NARVIK						Total Fleets available during the whole period of the Norway Campaign were:
9-13/4/40	British	1	1	—	14	British: 3 aircraft carriers; 7 battleships; 19 cruisers; c. 30 destroyers
	Germans	—	—	—	10	German: 3 battleships; 6 cruisers; 18 destroyers
NORWAY EVACUATION						
4-9/6/40	British	2	—	3	10	
	Germans	—	2	1	4	
MERS EL-KEBIR						The French ships were in harbour.
3/7/40	British	1	3	2	11	
	French	—	4	—	11	

Table 48 Comparative Strengths in Major Naval Engagements 1939-45 (continued)

Mediterranean and Atlantic (continued)

BATTLE AND DATE		SHIPS PRESENT				NOTES
		A/Cr.	B/s.△	Cr.	Dest.	
PUNTA STILO						
9/7/40	British	1	3	5	16	
	Italians	—	2	19	24	
DAKAR						Most French ships remained in harbour. Battleship unfit to put to sea.
23-25/9/40	British	1	2	3	6	
	French	—	1	2	2	
TARANTO						Italian ships in harbour.
11-12/11/40	British	1	—	4	4	
	Italians	—	6	9	12	
CAPE TEULADA						
27/11/40	British	1	2	5	14	
	Italians	—	2	6	14	
CAPE MATAPAN						
28/3/41	British	1	3	4	13	
	Italians	—	1	7	14	
HUNT FOR BISMARK						Actually in combat with the Bismark, at one time or another were 2 aircraft carriers; 4 battleships; 3 cruisers; 5 destroyers.
18-28/5/41	British	2	7	12	?	
	Germans	—	1	1	—	
CRETE						German force consisted of 670 fighters and bombers.
20/5-1/6/41	British	1	4	11	32	
	Germans	—	—	—	—	
FIRST SYRTE						
17/12/41	British	—	—	5	20	
	Italians	—	4	5	20	
SECOND SYRTE						
23/3/42	British	—	—	5	11	
	Italians	—	1	3	10	
CONVOY 'HARPOON'						Convoy also heavily attacked by aircraft.
	British	2(–)	1(–)	3(1)	8(9)	
12-16/6/42	Italians	—	—	2	5	British figures are: Covering Force (Close Escort).
CONVOY 'VIGOROUS'						British force also included virtually unarmed battleship. Convoy also heavily attacked by E-Boats, submarines and aircraft.
	British	—	—	7	26	
12-16/6/42	Italians	—	2	4	12	
CONVOY PQ17						No Fleet action.
	British	1(–)	2(–)	2(4)	14(3)	
2-13/7/42	Germans	—	1	3	—	British figures are: Covering Force (Close Escort).
CONVOY 'PEDESTAL'						Axis force consists of E-Boats, submarines and aircraft.
	British	4	2	7	27	
10-15/8/42	Axis	—	—	—	—	
NORTH CAPE						
	British	—	1	4	18	
26/12/43	Germans	—	1	—	5	

△ Includes battlecruisers.

Table 48 Comparative Strengths in Major Naval Engagements 1939-45 (continued)

Pacific and Indian Ocean

Δ Includes battlecruisers.

† First figure is fleet carriers; figure in brackets is escort carriers.

BATTLE AND DATE		SHIPS PRESENT				NOTES
		A/Cr.†	B/s.Δ	Cr.	Dest.	
JAVA SEA 27/2/42	Allies	—	—	5	9	
	Japanese	—	—	4	14	
INDIAN OCEAN 5-9/4/42	Allies	3	5	7	16	
	Japanese	5	4	4	8	
CORAL SEA 3-8/5/42	US	2	—	8	11	The Americans deployed 141 naval aircraft and the Japanese 125.
	Japanese	2(1)	—	6	7	
MIDWAY 3-7/6/42	US	3	—	8	15	The Americans deployed 230 naval and 50 land-based aircraft and the Japanese 262 naval.
	Japanese	5(1)	11	16	46	
SAVO ISLAND 8-9/8/42	US	—	—	5	6	
	Japanese	—	—	7	1	
SOLOMON ISLANDS 23-25/8/42	US	2	1	4	11	The Americans deployed 176 naval aircraft and the Japanese 168.
	Japanese	2(1)	3	11	23	
CAPE ESPERANCE 11-12/10/42	US	—	—	4	5	
	Japanese	—	—	3	8	
SANTA CRUZ ISLANDS 26-27/10/42	US	2(—)	1	6	14	The Americans deployed 171 naval and 60 land-based aircraft and the Japanese 212 naval.
	Japanese	2(2)	4	10	29	
FIRST GUADALCANAL 12-13/11/42	US	—	—	5	8	
	Japanese	—	2	1	11	
SECOND GUADALCANAL 14-15/11/42	US	—	2	—	4	
	Japanese	—	1	4	9	
TASSAFARONGA 30/11-1/12/42	US	—	—	5	6	
	Japanese	—	—	—	8	
KOMANDORSKI ISLANDS 26/3/43	US	—	—	2	4	
	Japanese	—	—	4	4	
KULA GULF 5-6/7/43	US	—	—	3	4	
	Japanese	—	—	—	10	
KOLOMBANGARA 12-13/7/43	US	—	—	3	10	
	Japanese	—	—	1	9	

Table 48 Comparative Strengths in Major Naval Engagements 1939-45 (continued)

Pacific and Indian Ocean (continued)

BATTLE AND DATE		SHIPS PRESENT				NOTES
		A/Cr.†	B/s.△	Cr.	Dest.	
EMPRESS AUGUSTA BAY						
2/11/43	US	—	—	4	8	
	Japanese	—	—	4	6	
PHILIPPINE SEA						
19-20/6/44	US	7(8)	7	21	67	The Americans deployed 890 naval aircraft, the Japanese 430 naval and 540 land-based.
	Japanese	5(4)	5	13	28	
LEYTE GULF Comprising: (i) Sibuyan Sea 24/10/44	US	5(5)	—	—	—	The Americans deployed 530 naval aircraft, the Japanese 116 naval and 300 land-based.
	Japanese	1(3)	5	9	15	
(ii) Suriago Straits 25/10/44	US	—	6	8	9	
	Japanese	—	2	4	11	
(iii) Samar 25/10/44	US	—(16)	—	—	21	The Americans deployed 400 naval aircraft.
	Japanese	—	4	8	11	
(iv) Cape Engano 25/10/44	US	5(5)	6	8	41	The Americans deployed 527 naval aircraft, the Japanese 29.
	Japanese	1(3)	2	3	9	
TOTAL	US	8(26)	12	29	111	The Americans deployed 1,400 naval aircraft, the Japanese 116 naval and 300 land-based.
	Japanese	1(3)	9	19	35	

△ Includes battlecruisers.

† First figure is fleet carriers; figure in brackets is escort carriers.

Table 49 Strengths of British Empire and Government-in-Exile Navies 1939-45

COUNTRY	TYPE OF SHIP	TOTAL DEPLOYED	PERIOD IN SERVICE
Australia	**Cruiser**	7	3 x 1939-45; 2 x 1939-42; 1 x 1939-41; 1 x 1942-45
	Destroyer	12	2 x 1940-45; 3 x 1941-45; 5 x 1942-45; 1 x 1943-45; 1 x 1945
	Escort	16	1 x 1939-45; 1 x 1940-45; 1 x 1939-42; 1 x 1939-41; 4 x 1943-45; 7 x 1944-45; 1 x 1945
Canada	**Cruiser**	1	1 x 1945
	Destroyer	21	7 x 1939-45; 2 x 1941-45; 2 x 1942-45; 1 x 1941-44; 5 x 1943-45; 5 x 1944-45
	Escort	172	33 x 1940-45; 1 x 1940-44; 2 x 1940-41; 1 x 1940-42; 38 x 1941-45; 1 x 1941-42; 2 x 1941-43; 2 x 1941-44; 6 x 1942-45; 45 x 1943-45; 1 x 1943-44; 53 x 1944-45
France	In July 1940 such French ships as had managed to escape to British ports comprised 2 battleships, 8 destroyers, 15 escort vessels and 7 submarines. By September 1940, 2 destroyers, 5 escort vessels and 3 submarines had actually been commissioned in the Free French Navy. In August 1943 the Free French Navy and the Vichy Navy amalgamated. At this time the Free French Navy comprised several destroyers, 12 escort ships and 4 submarines whilst Vichy ships numbered 1 aircraft carrier, 3 battleships (one uncompleted), 11 cruisers, 11 destroyers, 23 escort vessels and 19 submarines. Between the amalgamation and the end of the war a further 3 destroyers, 13 escort vessels and 4 submarines were acquired.		
Greece	**Destroyer**	2	2 x 1944-45
	Escort	4	4 x 1943-45
India	**Escort**	11	1 x 1939-45; 1 x 1939-42; 4 x 1940-45; 2 x 1943-45; 3 x 1945
Netherlands	**Destroyer**	6	2 x 1942-45; 4 x 1945
	Escort	2	2 x 1943-45
New Zealand	**Cruiser**	3	1 x 1939-45; 1 x 1939-43; 1 x 1943-45
	Escort	2	2 x 1944-45
Norway	**Destroyer**	2	1 x 1943-44; 1 x 1944
	Escort	11	2 x 1941-45; 1 x 1941-44; 4 x 1942-45; 2 x 1942-43; 1 x 1942-44; 1 x 1944
Poland	**Cruiser**	2	1 x 1944-45; 1 x 1944
	Destroyer	6	2 x 1939-45; 1 x 1939-?; 1 x 1940-45; 1 x 1941-45; 1 x 1941-42
Yugoslavia	**Escort**	1	1 x 1944-45

MERCHANT MARINE

Table 50 gives the size of all major merchant fleets in 1939. It should be noted that the annual size of the most important merchant fleets during the war itself can be computed by combining the Table below with the construction figures in Table 96 and the figures for losses in Table 72 (Casualties and Losses Section).

Table 50 **Size of the Merchant Fleets of the Major Belligerent Nations and Total World Shipping 1939**

COUNTRY	NUMBER	TONNAGE
Belgium	200	408,014
Commonwealth	2,255	3,110,791
Denmark	705	1,174,944
France	1,231	2,933,933
Germany	2,159	4,482,662
Greece	607	1,780,666
Italy	1,227	3,424,804
Japan*	1,609	5,996,607
Netherlands	1,523	2,969,578
Norway	1,987	4,833,813
UK	6,722	17,891,134
USA†	2,345	8,909,892
USSR	?	?
Whole World	29,763	68,509,432

* December 1941.

† Sea-going.

SECTION 6

CASUALTIES AND LOSSES

In this section losses both in men and materiel are covered, with the data being subdivided into overall, ground, air and naval losses. Most of the tables, as elsewhere, try to present a complete picture over the whole war but it will be noticed that a few of the tables below give figures applying to one or two countries only but which are presented as being typical of the experience of armed forces as a whole.

PART I OVERALL CASUALTIES

Table 51 Military and Civilian Casualties of the Belligerent Nations 1939-45

| COUNTRY | POPULATION | No. SERVED IN FORCES | FORCES CASUALTIES | | | | TOTAL CIVILIAN CASUALTIES |
			KILLED & MISSING	WOUNDED	P.O.W.	TOTAL KILLED & WOUNDED	
ALBANIA	1,100,000	?	?	?	?	?	?
AUSTRALIA	6,900,000	1,340,000	29,400	39,800	26,400	69,200	–
BELGIUM 1940	8,300,000	650,000	7,500	15,900	200,000	23,400	12,000
BELGIUM in exile		3,500	500	?	?	?	
BULGARIA with Axis	6,300,000	?	?	?	?	?	50,000 killed inc. 40,000 Jews
BULGARIA with Russians		500,000	32,000		?	32,000	
CANADA	11,100,000	1,100,000	39,300	53,200	9,000	92,500	–
CHINA	450,000,000	14,000,000	1,400,000	1,800,000	?	?	8,000,000
CZECHOSLOVAKIA (in exile)	10,300,000	c. 5,000	?	?	?	?	215,000 killed
DENMARK	3,800,000	6,600	?	?	?	?	1,000 killed
FINLAND Winter War	3,800,000	?	24,900	43,600	?	78,500	3,400 killed
FINLAND 1941-44		?	65,000	158,000	?	223,000	
FRANCE 1940	42,000,000	c. 4,000,000	92,000	250,000	1,450,000	342,000	470,000
FRANCE in exile		c. 600,000	c. 30,000	c. 85,000	6,500	c. 115,000	
GERMANY	(1938) 78,000,000	17,900,000	3,250,000	4,606,600	?	7,856,600	2,050,000 killed by Allies * 300,000 by Germans
GREECE	7,000,000	?	18,300	60,000	?	78,300	415,000 dead inc. 260,000 from famine
HUNGARY	(Nov 1938) 10,000,000	?	136,000	c. 250,000	?	c. 386,000	300,000
INDIA	359,000,000	2,582,000	36,100	64,300	79,500	100,400	–
ITALY	43,800,000	?	226,900	?	?	?	60,000 killed
JAPAN	from 1937 72,200,000	9,100,000	1,740,000	94,000	41,000 †	1,834,000	393,400 killed 275,000 wounded/missing
NETHERLANDS 1940	8,700,000	400,000	2,900	6,900	?	9,800	150,000 killed or missing (inc. Asia)
NETHERLANDS in exile		?	10,800	?	?	?	
NEW ZEALAND	1,600,000	?	12,200	19,300	8,500	31,500	–
NORWAY	2,900,000	25,000	2,000	?	?	?	3,800 killed
POLAND 1939	34,800,000	1,200,000	66,300	133,700	787,000	200,000	4,800,000 killed in camps plus c. 500,000 other dead
POLAND in W.Europe		c. 90,000	4,500	13,000	?	27,500	
POLAND with Russians		200,000	at least 40,000		?	at least 40,000	
RUMANIA with Axis	(Dec 1937) 19,600,000	?	381,000‡	243,000	?	624,000	340,000 killed
RUMANIA with Russians		540,000	170,000		?	170,000	

* There were also 2,010,000 wounded or permanently disabled.

† Also 300,000 in Manchuria Aug 1945.

‡ Includes 310,000 missing.

Table 51 Military and Civilian Casualties of the Belligerent Nations 1939-45 (continued)

| COUNTRY | POPULATION | No. SERVED IN FORCES | FORCES CASUALTIES | | | | TOTAL CIVILIAN CASUALTIES |
			KILLED & MISSING	WOUNDED	P.O.W.	TOTAL KILLED & WOUNDED	
S. AFRICA	10,000,000 (inc. 2.1 m. white)	250,000	8,700	14,400	14,600	23,100	–
UK	47,500,000	5,896,000	305,800	277,100	172,600	582,900	146,800 inc. 60,600 killed
USA	129,200,000	16,354,000	405,400	670,800	139,700	1,076,200	–
USSR	194,100,000	c. 30,000,000	11,000,000	?	c. 6,000,000	?	6,700,000
YUGOSLAVIA	15,400,000	?	Estimates of total Yugoslav deaths 1941-45 1.5 to 1.7 million.				

Table 52 Battle Casualties by Service of the Armed Forces of the Major Belligerents 1939-45

COUNTRY		No. SERVED	KILLED & MISSING	WOUNDED	P.O.W.
USA	Army *	c. 7,900,000 †	165,800	574,300	79,800
	Air Force *	c. 3,400,000	54,700	17,900	40,200
	Navy	4,183,000	36,900	37,800	?
	Marines	669,000	19,600	67,200	?
USSR‡		Forces breakdown not available			
UK	Army	3,778,000†	177,800	239,600	152,076
	Air Force △	1,185,000	76,300	22,800	13,100
	Navy ◊	923,000	51,600	14,700	7,400
GERMANY **	Army	c. 13,000,000	1,622,600	4,188,000	1,646,300††
	Air Force	c. 3,400,000	294,900‡‡	216,600‡‡	?
	Navy △△	c. 1,500,000	149,200	25,300	?
JAPAN ◊◊	Army	c. 6,300,000†	1,526,000	85,600	} 41,500
	Navy	c. 2,100,000	414,900	8,900	

* The Army Air Force was technically part of the US Army and it should be borne in mind that many sources lump their casualty figures together.

† Of these 4,950,000 US Army personnel served overseas and 2,640,000 British Army, and 2,100,000 Japanese Army. It is these troops who sustained the battle casualties.

‡ See Table 51 for the aggregate forces figure. The Red Army accounted for the vast proportion of these casualties. In December 1943, for example, the total strength of the Navy was only 266,000 men and the Air Force 483,000.

△ Bomber Command's aircrew losses were 59,423 killed and missing out of 125,000 served, a mortality rate of 47.5 per cent.

◊ Not including the Merchant Navy, whose casualties were 34,902 killed and missing, 4,707 wounded and 5,720 p.o.w.

** To 31 January 1945 only.

†† The p.o.w. figure includes all missing, most of whom perished.

△△ The Navy's U-Boat offensive involved 39,000 officers and men. Of these 32,000 were killed and missing (82 per cent) and 5,000 p.o.w.s.

‡‡ Most of these were members of the Luftwaffe Field Divisions. Aircrew losses (to 31/1/45) were 69,623 killed and missing, and 27,294 wounded.

◊◊ The Japanese Army and Navy each had their own air force.

PART II GROUND FORCES

Table 52 in the preceding subsection gives details on total army casualties for the major belligerents, and so the table below breaks these figures down by individual campaign. Figures for the lesser participants in these campaigns are also included and it should be remembered that many of these e.g., France 1940 (Belgians) or Eastern Front (Hungarians) represent the larger portion of a country's ground casualties throughout the war. The subsequent tables (54-60) present data relating to one or two countries only but are included because that data can be taken as fairly typical of the combat experience of most of the belligerents.

Table 53 **Army Battle Casualties in Major Campaigns 1939-45**

CAMPAIGN		BATTLE CASUALTIES		
		KILLED & MISSING	WOUNDED	P.O.W.
POLAND				
	Poles	66,300	133,700	787,000
	Germans	13,110	27,280	—
	Russians	900	?	?
DENMARK/NORWAY				
	Danes	—	—	—
	Norwegians	2,000	?	?
	Germans *	3,692	1,600	—
FRANCE 1940				
	Dutch	2,890	6,900	?
	Belgians	7,500	15,850	200,000
	French	120,000	250,000	1,450,000
	British †	11,010	14,070	41,340
	Germans	43,110	111,640	—
	Italians	1,250	4,780	—
BALKANS 1941				
	Yugoslavs	?	?	?
	Greeks •	19,000	70,000	?
	Germans △	3,674		—
	Italians #	38,830	50,870	—
EASTERN FRONT				
	Russians	c. 11,000,000	?	c. 6,000,000
	Germans ◊	2,415,690	3,498,060	?
	Italians	84,830	30,000	?
	Rumanians I‡	381,000	243,000	?
	Rumanians II‡	170,000		?
	Hungarians	136,000	c. 250,000	?
	Poles	at least 40,000		?
	Bulgarians	32,000		?

CAMPAIGN		BATTLE CASUALTIES		
		KILLED & MISSING	WOUNDED	P.O.W.
W. DESERT				
	British	c. 7,000	?	?
	Indians	1,720	3,740	9,790
	Australians	3,150	8,320	9,250
••	N. Zealanders	6,340	32,870	8,520
	S. Africans	2,100	3,930	14,250
	Germans	12,010	?	}266,600 ††
	Italians	20,720	?	
TUNISIA				
	Americans	3,620	9,250	4,640
	British	6,230	21,260	10,600
	Indians	included in W. Desert		
	N. Zealanders	included in W. Desert		
	French	total military casualties= 12,920		
	Germans	included in W. Desert		
	Italians	included in W. Desert		
ITALY				
	Americans	29,560	82,180	7,410
	British	89,440		?
	Indians ‡‡	4,720	17,310	46
	Canadians	5,400	19,490	1,000
	N. Zealanders	included in W. Desert		
	Poles	2,460	8,640	?
	S. Africans	710	2,670	160
	French	8,660	23,510	?
	Brazilians	510	1,900	?
	Germans##	59,940	163,600	357,090

Table continues on following page

* Includes Navy and Air Force.

† Evacuated wounded only.

• Figure is for the whole war.

△ German battle casualties in the Balkans up to 31 December 1944 were 34,040 killed and missing and 55,070 wounded.

Figures for Greece October 1940-April 1941. In April 1941 the Italians lost a further 3,330 killed and wounded in Yugoslavia, whilst anti-Partisan operations in that country, up to the Armistice of September 1943, cost another 30,360 men killed and wounded.

◊ From September 1939 to 31 December 1944. Prisoners-of-war are included in KILLED & MISSING. Figures include SS and foreign volunteers. Another set of figures, for the Field Army only, between 22 June 1941 and 10 March 1945, gives 1,001,680 killed, 1,287,140 missing and 3,968,260 wounded.

‡ I = fighting with Germans; II = fighting with Russians.

•• Includes casualties in Tunisia and Italy.

†† Prisoners-of-war in Tunisia only.

‡‡ To February 1945.

From September 1939 to 31 December 1944. German killed and missing is killed only. Figures include SS and foreign volunteers. Another set of figures, for the Field Army only, between June 1941 and 10 April 1945 gives 46,800 killed, 208,240 missing and 168,570 wounded.

Table 53 Army Battle Casualties in Major Campaigns 1939-45 (continued)

CAMPAIGN		BATTLE CASUALTIES		
		KILLED & MISSING	WOUNDED	P.O.W.
N.W.EUROPE				
	Americans	109,820	356,660	56,630
	British	30,280	96,670	14,700
	Canadians	10,740	30,910	2,250
	French	12,590	49,510	4,730
	Poles	1,160	3,840	370
	Germans ◊◊	128,030	399,860	7,614,790
PACIFIC ***				
	Americans	55,060	162,230	30,000
	Japanese	685,230	?	37,280
S.E.ASIA				
	British †††	5,670	12,840	53,230
	Indian	6,860	24,200	68,890
	African	860	3,210	200
	Australian	1,820	1,370	18,130
	American	3,650	2,600	680
	Japanese	210,830	?	3,100
CHINA				
	Chinese	Total Military casualties= 3,211,420		
	Japanese	388,600	?	1,060

◊◊ From September 1939 to 31 December 1944. KILLED & MISSING is killed only. The prisoner-of-war figures include 3,404,950 disarmed after the surrender and applies only to the Western Front. Figures include SS and foreign volunteers. Another set of figures, for the Field Army only, between June 1941 and 10 April 1945, gives 80,820 killed, 490,260 missing and 265,526 wounded.

*** These figures, it should be borne in mind, are for the Army (and Marines) only. The Japanese Navy lost a further 414,880 men killed whilst the major portion of the 36,950 US Navy men killed and 37,780 wounded in the war were serving in the Pacific.

††† Missing included in prisoners-of-war.

Casualty figures given thus far can be somewhat misleading in that they give a false impression of the lot of the *fighting* soldier in the Second World War. If data from Table 52, for example, were rendered into simple percentages of soldiers killed per number that served overall (even including only all those who served overseas) then it would seem that we were dealing with a much 'cheaper' conflict than, say, the First World War on the Western Front. And it is true that a soldier *just* inducted in 1941, for example, did stand, at that particular moment, a much greater chance of coming through the war unscathed than a predecessor in 1915. But, if he were unlucky enough to be posted to a rifle company, the men who did most of the actual fighting, then his chances of survival were not much better than an equivalent 'Tommy' or 'Doughboy'. The tables following show this fairly clearly, using casualty data on certain British and US infantry divisions that fought in N.W.Europe in 1944-45. Appalling though they are, these figures are not exceptionally severe. Only the Japanese in the Pacific and S.E.Asia, thanks to their disinclination to surrender, endured worse casualty rates and in no theatre of war were the rifleman's expectations much better.

Table 54 Battle Casualties of Selected US Infantry Divisions in North-West Europe 1944-45 and Percentage Riflemen who Became Casualties

DIVISION	MONTHS IN EUROPE	TOTAL CASUALTIES		PERCENTAGE†	
		DEAD	WOUNDED	DEAD	WOUNDED
4	11	4,834	17,371	18.1	65.1
29	11	3,786	15,541	15.9	56.3
30	11	3,516	13,376	16.5	62.7
79	11	2,943	10,971	16.1	59.8
83	11	3,620	11,807	19.2	62.5
90	11	3,930	14,386	17.3	63.2
5	10	2,656	9,549	15.9	60.3
8	10	2,820	10,057	16.3	60.8
35	10	2,947	11,526	15.6	61.0
28	9	2,683	9,609	16.1	57.7
80	9	3,480	12,484	17.0	61.0

† Percentage of a Division's riflemen (including replacements) who became casualties assuming 90% all casualties were amongst the riflemen and an 85% replacement rate.

Table 55 Percentage of Officer and Other Rank Casualties in Selected British Rifle Battalions in North-West Europe 1944-45

| UNIT | % HIT | | % KILLED | |
	Officers	ORs	Officers	ORs
50 (Northumbrian) Division*	65.9	50.0	16.5	8.7
15 (Scottish) Division *	72.2	62.9	28.7	16.8
6 K.O.S.B.	67.5	62.5	17.5	8.9
1 Royal Norfolk	72.1	64.5	17.4	17.0
1 Dorsetshire	70.6	62.0	25.9	13.2

* The nine rifle battalions only.

The following two tables also offer only sample data, relating in these cases to the location on the body of battle wounds and to the percentages of wounds caused by different weapons.

Table 56 Percentage Distribution of Battle Wounds over Human Body in Various US, British and Soviet Samples from World War II.

TYPE OF DATA	Head, Face & Neck	Chest	Abdominal	Arms & Shoulders	Legs
Body Area	12	16	11	2	39
Total Hits (Bougainville sample)	21	13	8	23	35
Fatal Hits (Bougainville sample)	47	25	15	5	8
Major Wounds (Europe sample)	15	10	6	28	41
(British M.E. sample)	14	11	6	69	
(Soviet sample)	9	12	6	28	45

Table 57 Percentage of Battle Wounds to British Soldiers Caused by Different Weapons 1939-45

CAUSAL AGENT	% OF WOUNDS
Mortar, grenade, aerial bomb, shell	75
Bullet, anti-tank mine*	10
Landmine, booby trap	10
Blast, crush	2
Chemical	2
Other	1

* Many smaller samples from individual theatres give a significantly higher proportion of wounds from bullets. Two British divisional samples from N.W.Europe in 1944 give 25.2 and 31.5 per cent, an El Alamein (Oct 1942) corps sample gives 42.8 per cent and a US Bougainville/New Georgia/Burma sample gives 38.4 per cent.

Of course, the physically wounded are not the only battle casualties and a considerable problem in the Second World War, as it had been in the First, was that of combat fatigue/neurosis, the updated appellation for 'shell shock'. The table below gives some idea of its prevalence in relation to 'ordinary' battle casualties in the US, Canadian and British armies.

Table 58 US, British and Canadian Army Battle Casualties (Wounded and Psychoneurotic) in Selected Theatres and Years 1943-44. (Number of Hospital Admissions per 1000 Ration Strength)

THEATRE	WOUNDED	PSYCHONEUROTIC	RATIO
US (1944)			
All Overseas	87	42	2.0:1
N.W.Europe	135	52	2.6:1
Mediterranean	113	42	2.7:1
S.W.Pacific	32	47	0.7:1
Pacific Ocean	26	28	0.9:1
China/Burma/India	10	20	0.5:1
UK (All Troops)			
Middle East 1943	22	9	2.4:1
Mediterranean 1944	55	21	2.6:1
N.W.Europe 1944*	65	12	5.9:1
India/Burma 1944	47	6	8.8:1
Canadian Italy Nov 43-June 44	3,102†	940†	3.3:1

* Average quarterly admissions per 1000 ration strength.
† Canadian totals are gross figures.

The last two tables in this subsection give some British and American figures on the relative incidence of battle and non-battle casualties and on the diseases which were the main causes of the latter.

Table 59 Relative Incidence of US and British Army Battle and Non-battle Casualties in Selected Theatres 1942-45. (Average Annual Number of Hospital Admissions per 1000 Ration Strength)

THEATRE	WOUNDS	INJURY	DISEASE
US Total	27	90	666
Total Overseas	68	113	689
Europe	94	111	696
Pacific	39	122	785
UK Europe	119	85	545
India/Burma (British)	81*	49	1,118
India/Burma (All)	43*	45	873

* 1944 and 1945 only.

Table 60 Incidence in British Army of Five Most Common Diseases in Selected Theatres in 1942 and 1944. (Annual Hospitalisations per 1000 Ration Strength)

DISEASE	INCIDENCE
Middle East 1942	
Digestive System	86.5
Inflammation Areolar Tissue and Skin Diseases	47.6
Venereal	45.9
Dysentry	30.4
Hepatitis	28.4
Mediterranean 1944	
Digestive System	74.2
Inflammation Areolar Tissue and Skin Diseases	66.0
Malaria	50.6
Venereal	39.0
Respiratory	36.1
India/Burma 1944	
Malaria	364.2
Pyrexia of Unknown Origins and Undiagnosed Fever	151.6
Dysentry	92.5
Diarrhoea	84.9
Venereal	59.0

PART III AIR FORCES LOSSES

With regard to aircraft, it is impossible to be anything like as precise as with personnel and naval losses. There are various reasons for this. Firstly, some countries have made public hardly any figures at all. Secondly, such figures as are available usually fail to make it clear whether an aircraft 'loss' refers to one completely destroyed or only damaged. The Germans, for example, classified their casualties by the percentage of damage sustained. One hundred per cent was obviously a total loss, but in fact the Luftwaffe wrote off any aircraft with 60 per cent or more damage, the exact figure indicating the extent of cannibalisation possible. 'Losses' with less than 60 per cent damage were repairable, though the time required would vary greatly. Thirdly, most available figures do not make it clear whether the losses were from all causes or whether they do not include aircraft destroyed on the ground, refer only to air combat losses, refer only to 'operational' losses (combat plus accidents taking off and landing whilst on mission), do or do not include all accidental losses, including those in training and whilst ferrying aircraft from one front to another.

It is therefore not possible to give any sort of overall table of aircraft losses, even for the major belligerents. What is given below is an alphabetical list, by country, giving such figures as have been made available and, where possible, specifying the exact type of loss referred to.

However, more detailed figures about Allied bomber losses are available and these are given in separate tables at the end of this section.

Figures on casualties amongst air force personnel of the major belligerents will be found in Table 52 at the beginning of this Section, whilst Table 64, at the end of this subsection, gives some details on the incidence of injuries and diseases amongst RAF flying personnel.

FINLAND

During the Winter War, November 1939-March 1940, the Finns lost 67 aircraft destroyed, 42 of them on operations.

During the Continuation War, June 1941-September 1944, they lost 536 aircraft, 209 of them on operations.

FRANCE 1940

	In Action	Air Attack on Ground	Accident	TOTAL
Fighter	250	135	123	**508**
Bomber	106	43	69	**218**
Recce	57	56	53	**166**
TOTAL	**413**	**234**	**245**	**892**

GERMANY*

All losses down to 10 per cent damage, between 1 September 1939 and 10 January 1945:

	Total Loss	Damaged	TOTAL
Combat	40,613	20,492	**61,105**
Other operational	10,457	15,171	**25,628**
Training	11,442	9,931	**21,373**
TOTAL	**62,512**	**45,594**	**108,106**

Between 10 January and 31 March 1945 there were a further 8,478 combat losses, giving an (almost complete) total loss for the whole war to April 1945 of 116,584 aircraft. This figure was broken down by type as follows:

41,452 fighters	6,141 transport
10,221 night fighters †	6,733 reconnaissance
8,548 ground attack	15,428 trainers
22,037 bombers	

ITALY

Combat	Accident	Scrapped	TOTAL ‡
3,269	1,771	232	**5,272**

* See also UK for figures on aircraft losses in the Battle of Britain.

† Includes all twin-engined fighter losses.

‡ Another source gives 6,483 total losses and another mentions 3,380 fighters and 3,110 bombers lost.

JAPAN

One source gives 38,105 aircraft (17,760 Army and 20,345 Navy) lost 'in combat'. This presumably means operational losses, including aircraft destroyed on the ground.*

Another source gives total losses of around 50,000 aircraft, 40 per cent lost on operations and 60 per cent in training, ferrying etc. accidents.

NETHERLANDS 1940

In May 1940 the Dutch Air Force lost 81 aircraft.

POLAND 1939

Aircraft destroyed totalled 398, divided by type into:

116 fighters	9 transport
112 dive-bombers	21 sea-planes
36 bombers	23 other
81 reconnaissance	

UNITED KINGDOM

Remarkably few figures have been made available about RAF losses. One source gives the following figures for combat aircraft (operational only?), in Europe only.

Fighters	10,045
Bombers	11,965
TOTAL	**22,010**

One of the very few air campaigns for which accurate loss figures have been compiled is the Battle of Britain and the available figures on aircraft totally destroyed are presented below.

USA

Operational losses (combat and other):

	EUROPE	PACIFIC	TOTAL
1942	141	344	**485**
1943	3,028	819	**3,847**
1944	11,618	1,671	**13,289**
1945	3,631	1,699	**5,330**
TOTAL	**18,418**	**4,533**[†]	**22,951**

Non-operational losses were c. 22,000 aircraft, giving a total of just under 45,000 for the whole war.

According to another source these (operational?) losses included 8,420 fighters and 9,949 bombers in Europe only.

USSR

The figures below must be treated with particular caution as they include estimated losses from all causes including withdrawal of aircraft from front-line formations to the rear.

Period	Combat Aircraft Lost
21 June 1941-31 November 1941	12,652
1 December 1941-30 April 1942	7,099
1 May 1942-31 October 1942	14,601
1 November 1942-30 June 1943	17,690
1 July 1943-31 December 1943	20,741
1 January 1944-31 May 1944	13,386
1 June 1944-31 December 1944	20,283
1 January 1945-8 May 1945	?
TOTAL	**106,652**

Margin notes:

* US naval aviation, for example, claimed only 9,000 Japanese planes actually shot down.

† Another source speaks of 8,700 'combat' losses in the Pacific and 18,300 'other'.

∆ 'Totally Destroyed' denotes Category 3 damage to RAF aircraft and 60 per cent damage to Luftwaffe aircraft.

◊ These figures differ from those given in other published sources but are compiled from daily casualty figures given in F.K.Mason, *Battle Over Britain* (McWhirter Twins, 1969).

‡ Figures in brackets denote number of accidents included in total.

Table 61 British and German Aircraft Totally Destroyed∆ During the Battle of Britain 10 July-31 October 1940◊

DATE	RAF ‡		LUFTWAFFE ‡				
	Fighter	Other	Fighter	Me 110	Ju 87	Bomber	Other
10-16 July	25 (10)	0	11 (2)	3 (1)	3 (1)	37 (4)	3
17-23 July	23 (9)	7	9 (1)	2	3 (1)	34 (11)	5
24-30 July	27 (8)	1 (1)	20	4 (2)	2	37 (14)	6 (1)
TOTAL	**75 (27)**	**8 (1)**	**40 (3)**	**9 (3)**	**8 (2)**	**108 (29)**	**14 (1)**
31 July-6 Aug	16 (11)	2 (2)	8 (3)	4 (1)	2 (1)	33 (18)	6 (4)
7-13 Aug	88 (9)	3 (2)	52 (11)	38 (3)	17 (1)	54 (15)	4 (1)
14-20 Aug	110 (6)	12 (1)	52 (6)	50 (0)	39	92 (11)	7 (3)
21-27 Aug	70 (4)	13 (2)	48 (9)	16 (2)	—	69 (7)	4 (1)
TOTAL	**284 (30)**	**30 (7)**	**160 (29)**	**108 (6)**	**58 (2)**	**248 (51)**	**21 (9)**
28 Aug-3 Sept	136 (6)	5 (1)	93 (16)	28 (1)	4 (4)	59 (18)	6 (4)
4-10 Sept	125 (9)	1 (1)	85 (5)	26 (2)	1 (1)	76 (18)	4 (3)
11-17 Sept	85 (6)	4 (2)	42 (5)	12 (1)	4 (4)	74 (8)	9 (8)
18-24 Sept	41 (5)	—	21 (4)	3	1 (1)	62 (11)	3 (1)
25 Sept-1 Oct	84 (6)	2 (1)	59 (5)	31 (2)	—	64 (13)	6 (2)
TOTAL	**471 (32)**	**12 (5)**	**300 (35)**	**100 (6)**	**10 (10)**	**335 (68)**	**28 (18)**
2-8 Oct	34 (11)	3 (3)	31 (5)	12 (3)	2 (2)	53 (15)	5 (2)
9-15 Oct	57 (14)	4 (2)	28 (9)	3 (1)	—	24 (11)	5 (3)
16-22 Oct	26 (13)	2	21 (5)	6 (5)	2 (2)	58 (21)	2 (1)
23-29 Oct	49 (18)	2 (2)	52 (5)	5 (3)	—	50 (13)	5 (2)
30-31 Oct	8 (1)	—	4	—	—	5 (4)	2 (1)
TOTAL	**174 (57)**	**11 (7)**	**136 (24)**	**26 (12)**	**4 (4)**	**190 (64)**	**19 (9)**
GRAND TOTAL	**1,004 (146)**	**61 (20)**	**636 (91)**	**243 (27)**	**80 (18)**	**881 (212)**	**82 (37)**

Table 62 Bomber Command and 8 US Air Force Losses 1939-45

DATE		BOMBER COMMAND		8 US AIR FORCE	
		Planes lost	As % No. Sorties	Planes lost	As % No. Sorties
1939	Sept	17	13.8	—	—
	Oct	4	12.5	—	—
	Nov	1	5.3	—	—
	Dec	19	11.9	—	—
1940	Jan	—	—	—	—
	Feb	3	5.2	—	—
	Mar	12	4.1	—	—
	April	41	6.2	—	—
	May	73	3.0	—	—
	June	65	2.0	—	—
	July	79	3.4	—	—
	Aug	81	3.1	—	—
	Sept	87	2.7	—	—
	Oct	60	2.5	—	—
	Nov	86	4.3	—	—
	Dec	62	4.3	—	—
1941	Jan	28	2.5	—	—
	Feb	52	3.0	—	—
	Mar	75	4.0	—	—
	April	98	3.3	—	—
	May	76	2.8	—	—
	June	116	3.1	—	—
	July	188	4.9	—	—
	Aug	206	5.4	—	—
	Sept	153	5.3	—	—
	Oct	126	4.8	—	—
	Nov	104	5.9	—	—
	Dec	51	3.3	—	—
1942	Jan	88	3.9	—	—
	Feb	33	2.3	—	—
	Mar	80	3.4	—	—
	April	143	3.6	—	—
	May	115	4.1	—	—
	June	201	4.0	—	—
	July	190	4.5	—	—
	Aug	152	5.8	—	—
	Sept	175	4.8	2	1.1
	Oct	103	4.0	10	3.5
	Nov	64	2.9	13	2.5
1942	Dec	88	4.5	17	4.8
1943	Jan	101	3.4	18	5.3
	Feb	107	2.0	23	4.4
	Mar	168	3.1	21	2.2
	April	265	4.5	29	6.5
	May	253	4.6	69	4.1
	June	275	4.7	90	4.3
	July	188	3.0	118	4.2
	Aug	275	3.5	117	5.2
	Sept	191	3.5	98	3.0
	Oct	159	3.4	186	6.6
	Nov	162	3.1	95	2.3
	Dec	170	4.1	172	2.9
1944	Jan	314	5.0	203	3.2
	Feb	199	4.6	271	2.7
	Mar	283	2.8	345	3.0
	April	214	2.2	420	2.9
	May	274	2.4	376	1.9
	June	305	1.9	320	1.1
	July	241	1.4	352	1.5
	Aug	221	1.1	331	1.4
	Sept	137	0.9	374	2.0
	Oct	127	0.8	177	0.9
	Nov	139	0.9	209	1.2
	Dec	119	0.8	119	0.6
1945	Jan	133	1.2	314	1.9
	Feb	173	1.0	196	0.9
	Mar	215	1.0	266	0.9
	April	73	0.5	190	0.9

Table 63 15 US Air Force Bomber Losses 1943-45

DATE		Planes lost	As % No. Sorties	DATE		Planes lost	As % No. Sorties
1943	Nov	28	1.6	**1944**	Aug	254	2.1
	Dec	36	1.8		Sept	94	0.9
1944	Jan	54	1.1		Oct	140	1.5
	Feb	128	3.2		Nov	132	1.4
	Mar	85	1.4		Dec	205	2.0
	April	194	1.9	**1945**	Jan	88	2.2
	May	175	1.2		Feb	147	1.1
	June	196	1.7		Mar	149	1.0
	July	317	2.5		April	83	0.5

Table 64 Incidence of Diseases, Psychoneurosis and Combat and Non-Combat Injuries Amongst RAF General Duties Officers and Aircrew 1939-45. (Annual Number Hospital Admissions per 1000 Ration Strength)

YEAR		ALL DISEASES	UPPER RESPIRATORY TRACT	ALIMENTARY	EAR, NOSE & THROAT	VENEREAL	PSYCHO-NEUROSIS	ALL INJURIES
1939	Gen. duties Officers	245	99	24	15	6	3	91
	Aircrew	142	55	10	5	8	1	64
1940	Gen. duties Officers	468	209	30	22	9	9	304
	Aircrew	342	153	19	12	7	4	188
1941	Gen. duties Officers	490	158	39	35	15	19	338
	Aircrew	255	97	15	12	7	7	144
1942	Gen. duties Officers	410	116	44	30	12	13	225
	Aircrew	389	135	37	13	11	6	146
1943	Gen. duties Officers	403	131	48	27	8	10	196
	Aircrew	492	203	46	16	12	7	165
1944	Gen. duties Officers	408	103	54	31	11	15	186
	Aircrew	540	181	56	19	18	9	159
1945	Gen. duties Officers	322	80	46	23	14	8	85
	Aircrew	349	88	45	15	23	9	86

PART IV NAVAL LOSSES

Some details on the personnel losses in the major navies of the Second World War will be found in Table 52, at the beginning of this section, and some figures on merchant navy crewmen lost are given in Tables 74 and 75 below. The main emphasis, however, is on ships lost and the manner of their sinking and it should be noted that additional figures on ship losses, by type and class, can be found in Table 100 in Section 8 on HARDWARE.

Table 65 Naval Losses of the Major Belligerents 1939-45

* Includes 3 cruiser-minelayers.

† Figures in brackets represent number scuttled. A further 221 U-Boats were scuttled after the surrender.

‡ Includes equivalents to destroyer escorts.

∆ Three other battleships which foundered in port are regarded by US statisticians as having been sunk in air attacks.

		AIRCRAFT CARRIERS	BATTLE-SHIPS	CRUISERS	DESTROYERS	ESCORT	SUBMARINES
USA	Total	11	2	10	71	10	53
	In Pacific	10	2	10	56	5	49
UK	Total	8	5	30*	110	58	77
	In Mediterranean	2	1	19	45	19	41
USSR		—	1	3	33	—	c. 100
AUSTRALIA		—	—	3	4	2	—
CANADA		—	—	—	6	11	—
JAPAN		19	8 ∆	37	134 ‡	—	130
GERMANY †		—	9 (3)	7 (3)	44 (6) ‡	—	785 (17)
ITALY		—	1	11	84 ‡	—	84

Table 66 US and Japanese Naval Losses in the Pacific 1941-45

		AIRCRAFT CARRIERS	BATTLESHIPS	CRUISERS	DESTROYERS	SUBMARINES
1941	USA	—	2	—	1	1
	JAPAN	—	—	—	4	3
1942	USA	4	—	7	21	7
	JAPAN	6	2	6	19	19
1943	USA	1	—	2	9	17
	JAPAN	1	1	2	34	23
1944	USA	3	—	—	11	20
	JAPAN	12	4	23	61	56
1945	USA	2	—	1	15	8
	JAPAN	—	1	5	15	29

Table 67 Causes of Warship Losses of the Major Belligerents 1939-45

AGENT	USA A/cr	USA B/s	USA Cr	USA Dest	USA E/Des	UK A/cr	UK B/s	UK Cr	UK Dest	UK Esct‡	OTHER* Cr	OTHER* Dest	OTHER* Esct‡	GERMANY B/s	GERMANY Cr	GERMANY Dest Δ	ITALY† B/s	ITALY† Cr	ITALY† Dest Δ	JAPAN A/cr	JAPAN B/s	JAPAN Cr	JAPAN Dest Δ	TOTAL minus Germany	TOTAL plus Germany
BOMB	2	1	—	11	—	1	3◊	11	36	12	—	4	2	••	••		—	2	18	9††	2††	15††	44††	173	217
AIR TORPEDO	2	1	1	4	1	—	—	—	5	—	—	—	—	6	4	11	1	—	1	2	1	1	3	23	
KAMIKAZE	3	—	—	10	1	—	—	—	—	—	—	—	—	—	—	—	—	—	—	—	—	—	—	—	14
SURFACE GUNFIRE	1	—	5	12	1	1	1	1	10	—	—	—	1				—	3	12	—	1	3	15	67	129
SURFACE TORPEDO	—	—	2	8	—	—	—	2	6	3	3	2	1	1	2	11	—	3	1	—	2	2	13	48	
SUBMARINE	3	—	2	8	7	5	2	10	28	33	—	4	11	—	1	—	—	3	11	8	1	16	42	—	189
MINE	—	—	—	5	1	—	—	2	15	7	—	—	6	1	—	7	—	—	15	—	—	—	7	—	66
OTHER & UNKNOWN	—	—	—	13	—	1	1	4	10	3	1	4	2	1	—	15	—	1	26	—	1	—	10	—	93
TOTAL	11	2	10	71	11	8	7	30	110	58	4	14	23	9	7	44	1	12	84	19	8‡‡	37	134	—	708

* Comprises Canada, Australia, India, Free France, Poland and Norway.

† These figures are taken from the Italian official history. The British one gives Air = 26; Surface = 16; Submarines = 12; Mines = 19 and Other = 12.

‡ Comprises escort destroyers, sloops, frigates and corvettes.

Δ Includes equivalent of escort destroyers.

◊ Two of which were also hit by air torpedos.

•• Five of the battleships and four of the cruisers were in harbour.

†† Three of the aircaft carriers, two of the battleships, eight of the cruisers and twelve of the destroyers were also hit by air torpedos.

‡‡ A further three battleships foundered in port in July 1945 and US statisticians regard these as having been sunk in air attacks.

Table 68 Losses of Warships in Major Engagements 1939-45

Mediterranean and Atlantic

*d = very badly damaged.

† includes battlecruisers.

BATTLE AND DATE		Aircraft Carriers	Battleships†	Cruisers	Destroyers	NOTES
RIVER PLATE 13/12/39	British	—	—	—	—	*Graf Spee* was scuttled shortly after the actual battle.
	Germans	—	1	—	—	
NARVIK 9-13/4/40	British	—	—	—	2	Total Fleets available during the whole period of the Norway Campaign were: British: 3 aircraft carriers; 7 battleships; 19 cruisers; c. 30 destroyers German: 3 battleships; 6 cruisers; 18 destroyers Other losses during the Norway Campaign were: British: 3 destroyers German: 3 cruisers
	Germans	—	—	—	10	
NORWAY EVACUATION 10/6/40	British	1	—	—	2	
	Germans	—	—	—	—	
MERS EL-KEBIR 3/7/40	British	—	—	—	—	Despite there being only one actual sinking, only 1 of 3 battleships and 6 of 11 destroyers got away to Toulon.
	French	—	1	—	—	
PUNTA STILO 9/7/40	British	—	—	—	—	
	Italians	—	—	—	—	
DAKAR 23-25/9/40	British	—	—	1d	—	
	French	—	—	—	1	
TARANTO 11-12/11/40	British	—	—	—	—	One of the Italian battleships was out of action for the rest of the war. The British lost only two carrier aircraft.
	Italians	—	3d	—	—	
CAPE TEULADA 27/11/40	British	—	—	1d	—	
	Italians	—	—	—	1d	
CAPE MATAPAN 28/3/41	British	—	—	—	—	
	Italians	—	—	3	2	
HUNT FOR *BISMARK* 18-28/5/41	British	—	—	1	1	
	Germans	—	1	—	—	
CRETE 20/5-1/6/41	British	—	—	3	8	The main enemy were 670 German fighters and bombers.
	Germans	—	—	—	—	
FIRST SYRTE 17/12/41	British	—	—	—	—	
	Italians	—	—	—	—	
SECOND SYRTE 23/3/42	British	—	—	—	2d	Two Italian destroyers sank in a storm immediately after the battle.
	Italians	—	—	—	—	
CONVOYS 'HARPOON'/ 'VIGOROUS' 12-14/6/42	British	—	—	1	5	The damage was done by aircraft and submarines as the two opposing fleets did not engage.
	Italians	—	—	1	—	

Table 68 **Losses of Warships in Major Engagements 1939-45 (continued)**

Mediterranean and Atlantic (continued)

BATTLE AND DATE		SHIPS LOST *				NOTES
		Aircraft Carriers	Battleships†	Cruisers	Destroyers	
CONVOY PQ17 2-13/7/42	British	—	—	—	—	There was no fleet action as both turned back but 30 of 34 British merchant ships were lost to aircraft and U-Boats.
	Germans	—	—	—	—	
CONVOY 'PEDESTAL' 10-15/8/42	British	1	—	2	1	
	Axis	—	—	—	—	
NORTH CAPE 26/12/43	British	—	—	—	—	
	Germans	—	1	—	—	

* d = very badly damaged.

† includes battlecruisers.

Pacific and Indian Ocean

BATTLE AND DATE		SHIPS LOST *				NOTES
		Aircraft Carriers	Battleships†	Cruisers	Destroyers	
JAVA SEA 27/2/42	Allies	—	—	2	3	
	Japanese	—	—	—	—	
INDIAN OCEAN 5-9/4/42	Allies	1	—	2	1	The Allies lost c. 300 aircraft of all types and the Japanese 90 carrier aircraft.
	Japanese	—	—	—	—	
CORAL SEA 3-8/5/42	US	1	—	—	—	The Americans lost 33 carrier aircraft and the Japanese 43.
	Japanese	1 + 1d	—	—	1	
MIDWAY 3-7/6/42	US	1	—	—	1	The Americans lost 180 carrier and other aircraft, the Japanese 262 carrier aircraft and a further 70 being shipped to Midway Island.
	Japanese	4	—	1	—	
SAVO ISLAND 8-9/8/42	US	—	—	2 (sic)	—	4 CA
	Japanese	—	—	—	—	
SOLOMON ISLANDS 23-25/8/42	US	—	—	—	—	The Americans lost 20 carrier aircraft and the Japanese 90.
	Japanese	1	—	—	1	
CAPE ESPERANCE 11-12/10/42	US	—	—	1d	1	
	Japanese	—	—	1	1	
SANTA CRUZ ISLANDS 26-27/10/42	US	1	—	—	—	The Americans lost 75 carrier aircraft and the Japanese c. 100
	Japanese	2d	—	—	—	
FIRST GUADALCANAL 12-13/11/42	US	—	—	2	4	
	Japanese	—	1	—	2	

Table 68 Losses of Warships in Major Engagements 1939-45 (continued)

Pacific and Indian Ocean (continued)

* d = very badly damaged.

† includes battlecruisers.

BATTLE AND DATE		Aircraft Carriers	Battleships†	Cruisers	Destroyers	NOTES
SECOND GUADALCANAL						
14-15/11/42	US	—	1d	—	3	
	Japanese	—	1	—	1	
TASSAFARONGA						
30/11-1/12/42	US	—	—	1	—	
	Japanese	—	—	—	1	
KOMANDORSKI Is.						
26/3/43	US	—	—	1d	1d	
	Japanese	—	—	1d	—	
KULA GULF						
5-6/7/43	US	—	—	1	—	
	Japanese	—	—	—	2	
KOLOMBANGARA						
12-13/7/43	US	—	—	3d	1	
	Japanese	—	—	1	—	
EMPRESS AUGUSTA BAY						
2/11/43	US	—	—	2d	—	
	Japanese	—	—	1	1	
PHILIPPINE SEA						Two of the Japanese carriers were sunk by submarines. The Americans lost 130 carrier planes and the Japanese 400.
19-20/6/44	US	—	—	—	—	
	Japanese	3	—	—	—	
LEYTE GULF comprising:						
(i) Sibuyan Sea						
24/10/44	US	1	—	—	—	
	Japanese	—	1	1d	—	
(ii) Suriago Straits						
25/10/44	US	—	—	—	—	
	Japanese	—	2	2	3	
(iii) Samar						
25/10/44	US	2	—	—	3	
	Japanese	—	—	3	6	
(iv) Cape Engano						
25/10/44	US	—	—	—	—	
	Japanese	4	—	3	—	
TOTAL						
	US	**3**	**—**	**—**	**3**	Includes two Japanese cruisers sunk by submarines 23/10/44
	Japanese	**4**	**3**	**10**	**9**	

Table 69 Annual Submarine Losses of the Major Belligerents 1939-45

YEAR	UK	USA	GERMANY	ITALY	JAPAN
1939	1	—	9	—	—
1940	24	—	23	20	—
1941	11	1	35	18	3
1942	20	7	87	22	19
1943	14	17	237	24	23
1944	6	20	242	—	56
1945	1	8	151	—	29
TOTAL	77	53	785*	84	130

* Does not include 221 U-Boats scuttled after the surrender.

Table 70 Cause of Submarine Losses of the Major Belligerents 1939-45

AGENT	UK	USA	GER.	ITALY	JAPAN	TOTAL
BOMBED FROM AIR AT SEA	4	6	} 290	} 9	} 14	} 323
TORPEDOED FROM AIR	—	—				
SURFACE GUNFIRE	1	2	} 246	} 34	} 70	} 394
SURFACE DEPTH-CHARGE	27	14				
MINE	12	7	25	—	4	48
SUBMARINE	5	1	21	14	25	66
AIR & SURFACE	—	7	48	5	8	68
RAMMED	2	—	—	—	—	2
BOMBED IN HARBOUR	—	—	62	2	—	64
OTHER & UNKNOWN	26	16	93	20	9	164
TOTAL	77	53	785	84	130	1029

Table 71 Monthly Sinkings of U-Boats in the Atlantic, Arctic and Baltic 1939-45

DATE	JAN	FEB	MARCH	APRIL	MAY	JUNE	JULY	AUG	SEPT	OCT	NOV	DEC
1939									2	5	1	1
1940	2	4	3	5	1	—	2	3	—	1	2	—
1941	—	—	5	2	1	3	1	3	2	2	3	6
1942	1	2	5	3	1	3	11	9	11	15	8	5
1943	4	15	13	14	37	16	34	24	9	24	19	6
1944	14	19	20	19	17	25	22	25	14	11	6	11
1945	12	22	36	55	10							

PART V MERCHANT MARINE

Table 72 Merchant Shipping Losses in Major Theatres 1939-45

DATE		ALLIED in ATLANTIC		ALLIED ELSEWHERE		AXIS in MEDITERRANEAN		JAPANESE in PACIFIC	
		TONS	No.	TONS	No.	TONS	No.	TONS	No.
1939	Sept	194,845	53	—	—	—	—	—	—
	Oct	196,355	46	—	—	—	—	—	—
	Nov	173,563	49	706	1	—	—	—	—
	Dec	190,768	72	—	—	—	—	—	—
TOTAL		**755,531**	**220**	**706**	**1**	**—**	**—**	**—**	**—**
1940	Jan	214,506	73	—	—	—	—	—	—
	Feb	226,920	63	—	—	—	—	—	—
	Mar	107,009	45	—	—	—	—	—	—
	April	158,218	58	—	—	—	—	—	—
	May	285,893	100	2,568	1	—	—	—	—
	June	505,453	130	268,075	10	32,380	10	—	—
	July	365,074	101	21,839	4	30,677	5	—	—
	Aug	353,004	84	44,225	8	10,064	4	—	—
	Sept	403,504	92	45,117	8	21,466	6	—	—
	Oct	418, 264	99	24,721	4	19,968	6	—	—

Table 72 Merchant Shipping Losses in Major Theatres 1939-45 (continued)

DATE		ALLIED in ATLANTIC		ALLIED ELSEWHERE		AXIS in MEDITERRANEAN		JAPANESE in PACIFIC	
		TONS	No.	TONS	No.	TONS	No.	TONS	No.
1940	Nov	294,054	86	91,661	11	16,938	4	—	—
	Dec	322,612	76	26,956	6	55,138	11	—	—
TOTAL		**3,654,511**	**1,007**	**525,162**	**52**	**186,631**	**46**	**—**	**—**
1941	Jan	309,942	74	13,478	2	23,129	8	—	—
	Feb	368,759	95	34,634	7	38,784	10	—	—
	Mar	517,551	136	12,155	3	30,536	10	—	—
	April	381,289	88	306,512	107	152,129	32	—	—
	May	436,544	119	74,498	20	85,360	20	—	—
	June	415,255	104	16,770	5	58,425	17	—	—
	July	113,078	41	7,897	2	47,055	12	—	—
	Aug	103,452	36	27,247	5	52,538	11	—	—
	Sept	254,761	76	31,091	8	41,868	11	—	—
	Oct	195,886	45	22,403	6	49,565	12	—	—
	Nov	85,500	31	19,140	4	73,940	21	—	—
	Dec	113,802	30	469,904	255	61,081	14	57,758	12
TOTAL		**3,295,819**	**875**	**1,035,729**	**424**	**714,410**	**178**	**57,758**	**12**
1942	Jan	296,136	62	123,771	44	40,274	8	73,865	17
	Feb	440,989	78	238,743	76	34,889	9	37,291	9
	Mar	562,336	106	271,828	167	37,453	9	103,095	20
	April	493,810	88	180,647	44	18,411	6	42,796	9
	May	644,827	136	60,223	15	23,819	8	105,128	24
	June	652,487	131	181,709	42	19,028	6	38,519	10
	July	533,494	110	84,919	18	15,386	7	62,331	12
	Aug	543,920	106	117,213	17	72,420	13	114,281	23
	Sept	533,274	103	34,053	11	33,791	11	54,478	14
	Oct	560,590	88	77,243	13	56,303	17	176,997	36
	Nov	573,732	98	234,022	36	72,693	20	168,253	30
	Dec	314,745	64	34,157	9	97,615	34	88,364	25
TOTAL		**6,150,340**	**1,170**	**1,638,528**	**492**	**522,082**	**148**	**1,065,398**	**229**
1943	Jan	204,626	34	56,733	16	123,918	34	158,885	34
	Feb	315,206	52	87,856	21	96,257	26	92,662	21
	Mar	538,695	92	154,694	28	96,763	31	147,540	37
	April	252,533	45	92,147	19	101,996	34	132,724	26
	May	205,598	41	93,830	17	110,086	42	134,661	34
	June	30,115	18	93,710	20	72,909	19	105,108	26
	July	187,877	30	177,521	31	78,055	19	84,361	25
	Aug	25,573	5	64,228	20	86,313	18	100,064	24
	Sept	54,545	11	101,874	18	1,437	2	178,966	45
	Oct	61,085	13	78,776	16	—	—	158,093	39
	Nov	40,686	14	103,705	15	—	—	320,807	70
	Dec	53,871	8	114,653	23	—	—	207,048	53
TOTAL		**2,170,410**	**363**	**1,219,724**	**244**	**767,734**	**225**	**1,820,919**	**434**

Table 72 Merchant Shipping Losses in Major Theatres 1939-45 (continued)

DATE		ALLIED in ATLANTIC		ALLIED ELSEWHERE		AXIS in MEDITERRANEAN		JAPANESE in PACIFIC	
		TONS	No.	TONS	No.	TONS	No.	TONS	No.
1944	Jan	43,009	13	87,626	13	—	—	355,368	95
	Feb	16,628	5	100,227	18	—	—	518,697	112
	Mar	41,562	8	116,398	17	—	—	263,805	67
	April	48,231	8	34,141	5	—	—	128,328	38
	May	17,277	3	10,020	2	—	—	258,591	64
	June	82,728	22	21,356	4	—	—	278,484	71
	July	48,580	12	30,176	5	—	—	251,921	66
	Aug	60,519	13	57,785	10	—	—	295,022	66
	Sept	37,698	6	7,107	2	—	—	419,112	120
	Oct	1,722	2	9,946	2	—	—	512,378	130
	Nov	16,708	6	21,272	3	—	—	421,026	97
	Dec	91,097	19	43,816	7	—	—	188,287	43
TOTAL		**505,759**	**117**	**539,870**	**88**	**—**	**—**	**3,891,019**	**969**
1945	Jan	75,721	17	7,176	1	—	—	434,648	101
	Feb	88,140	25	7,176	1	—	—	101,541	33
	March	111,204	27	—	—	—	—	194,649	81
	April	81,690	19	22,822	3	—	—	125,673	52
	May	10,022	3	7,176	1	—	—	270,703	118
	June	—	—	18,615	2	—	—	245,930	123
	July	—	—	7,237	3	—	—	309,902	145
	Aug	—	—	36	1	—	—	99,094	48
TOTAL		**366,777**	**91**	**70,238**	**12**	**—**	**—**	**1,782,140**	**701**
GRAND TOTAL		**16,899,147**	**3,843**	**5,029,957**	**1,250**	**2,190,857**	**597**	**8,617,234**	**2,345**

Table 73 Percentage of Major Belligerents' Merchant Shipping Sunk by Agent 1939-45

DATE	SUBMARINES			AIRCRAFT			MINES			SURFACE			OTHER		
	ALLIED	AXIS IN MED.	JAP	ALLIED	AXIS IN MED.	JAP*	ALLIED	AXIS IN MED.	JAP	ALLIED	AXIS IN MED.	JAP	ALLIED	AXIS IN MED.	JAP
1939	55.8	—	—	0.4	—	—	34.8	—	—	8.1	—	—	0.9	—	—
1940	54.8	26.8	—	14.5	21.8	—	12.8	20.2	—	12.8	11.4	—	5.1	19.8	—
1941	50.1	41.0	56.5	23.5	26.1	30.1	5.3	10.6	—	11.2	13.7	—	9.9	8.6	22.3
1942	80.4	47.5	59.8	10.0	39.2	24.6	1.3	6.0	2.8	5.1	3.1	5.3	3.2	4.2	7.5
1943	80.3	29.7	76.2	13.2	36.5	18.5	3.4	3.8	0.3	2.5	3.3	0.2	0.6	26.7	4.8
1944	74.0	—	64.1	11.5	—	31.7	9.2	—	0.9	3.3	—	0.4	2.0	—	2.9
1945	64.2	—	19.9	10.1	—	41.7	21.3	—	33.3	2.3	—	0.4	2.1	—	4.7
TOTAL	**68.1**	**36.2**	**54.8**	**13.4**	**33.2**	**30.8**	**6.5**	**7.2**	**9.2**	**7.3**	**6.7**	**0.9**	**4.7**	**16.7**	**4.5**

* Of the total tonnage sunk by US aircraft, 33.1 per cent were sunk by Army planes, 13.8 per cent by land-based Navy planes and 53.1 per cent by carrier planes. These figures are derived from the USAAF Strategic Bombing Survey. Curiously, another source that might be assumed to be more sympathetic to the Navy attributes only 58.7 per cent of aircraft successes to the Navy.

Figures on comparative losses of merchant navy crewmen of the major belligerents are not available, but the figures below, for merchant navy crews sailing under the British flag, give some idea of the heavy losses suffered.

Another official source gives the following figures for total British registered merchant navy losses:

Table 74 Merchant Navy Crewmen Casualties in British Registered Ships 1939-45. (a)

YEAR	Col. A No. ships lost to enemy action in which crew also lost	Total No. crew in ships in Col. A	Total No. crew lost in ships in Col. A	Percentage of crew lost in ships in Col.A
1939	53	1,466	490	33.4
1940	363	12,206	5,553	45.5
1941	416	12,756	6,873	53.9
1942	427	17,927	7,622	42.5
1943	202	8,148	3,923	48.1
1944	71	2,380	1,087	45.7
1945	33	998	316	31.7
TOTAL	1,565	55,882	25,864	46.3

Table 75 Merchant Navy Crewmen Casualties in British Registered Ships 1939-45. (b)

	NUMBER	% OF TOTAL SERVED*
Killed	30,248	13.4
Wounded	4,707	2.1
Missing	530	0.2
P.O.W.	5,720	2.5
TOTAL	41,205	18.3

* Approximately 225,000 crew served in British registered merchant vessels during the Second World War.

SECTION 7

PRODUCTION

This section deals mainly with comparative production figures for various strategically vital raw materials as well as for the major munitions. But it also touches upon the availability of raw materials and foodstuffs, with Tables 76 and 77 highlighting major producers and levels of self-sufficiency and the concluding Table 98 detailing UK and Japanese dependence on maritime imports and their success in maintaining the flow thereof.

Table 76 Strategic Raw Materials and Foodstuffs: Total World Production 1937 and Percentage Produced by Major Countries

* Metal content.

† Inc. Austria and Czechoslovakia.

‡ Inc. Korea, Kwantung, Manchukuo, Mandates.

** Totals for China not known and therefore not included in aggregate base for percentages. This skews percentages given somewhat.

	COAL	OIL	IRON ORE*	COPPER ORE*	LEAD ORE*	TIN ORE*	ZINC ORE*	NICKEL ORE*	BAUXITE	MANGANESE ORE*	TUNGSTEN ORE*	CHROME ORE*	MOLYBDENUM	SULPHUR	PYRITES	PHOSPHATES	POTASH	MAGNESITE	RUBBER	WHEAT	RICE	MAIZE	SUGAR CANE	SUGAR BEET	MEAT
TOTAL WORLD PRODUCTION (million metric tons)	1,247.4	272.0	98.0	2.3	1.7	0.2	1.9	1.1	4.0	3.0	0.2	0.6	0.016	3.4	10.6	14.5	3.2	1.8	0.92	167.0	93.9	117.4	17.3	9.7	30.0
USA	34.2	60.4	38.0	32.4	24.7	—	30.6	0.2	10.7	0.7	8.8	0.2	92.5	81.9	5.6	29.8	8.1	10.6	0.1	15.2	3.7	55.2	18.3	15.7	23.8
USSR	9.3	10.6	14.3	4.0	3.3	—	3.8	1.8	6.2	40.5	?	15.3	—	—	5.8	24.5	7.3	27.2	—	26.5	2.4	2.4	—	22.7	15.0
UK	18.6	—	4.4	—	1.6	1.3	0.4	—	—	—	0.4	—	—	—	—	—	—	—	—	1.2	—	—	—	3.0	4.5
British Empire	5.0	2.0	5.9	24.8	33.5	39.1	27.9	90.6	10.0	36.6	22.4	41.2	0.2	—	9.2	8.7	0.6	6.0	52.2	16.5	51.9	3.5	32.2	1.3	8.8
... of which	—	—	—	Can. 10.2 N.R. 10.6	Can. 10.9 Aust. 14.7	Maly. 27.8	Aust. 11.1 Can. 9.1	Can. 89.5	B.G. 9.1	India 17.9 G.C. 9.4 S.A. 9.0	Burma 15.3	S.R. 22.9 S.A. 12.8	—	—	Cyprs. 7.3	Pc. Is. 8.7	—	Aust. 3.1	Maly. 41.2	India 6.6 Can. 5.7	India 43.5	—	India 18.7 Aust. 4.5	—	Aust. 3.2 Can. 2.5
France	3.4	—	11.7	—	0.3	—	—	—	17.2	0.1	—	—	—	—	1.4	0.7	15.5	—	—	5.6	—	0.4	—	8.2	4.8
French Empire	0.2	—	1.8	—	2.0	1.1	0.9	4.4	0.2	0.3	1.8	4.1	0.6	—	0.4	28.3	—	—	6.7	1.6	7.8	1.1	1.4	—	0.8
... of which	—	—	—	—	—	—	—	N.Cal. 4.3	—	—	—	N.Cal. 4.1	—	—	—	M/Tu. 22.5	—	—	I/c 6.4	—	I/c 6.7	—	—	—	—
Netherlands	1.1	—	—	—	—	—	—	—	—	—	—	—	—	—	—	—	—	—	—	0.2	—	—	—	2.0	1.3
Dutch E.Indies /Dutch Guiana	0.1	2.7	—	—	—	17.5	—	—	14.8	0.2	—	—	—	0.4	—	0.9	—	—	33.0	—	6.3	1.7	8.1	—	—
Italy	0.1		0.5	—	2.0	—	4.3	—	9.6	0.4	—	—	—	—	8.6	—	—	0.2	—	4.8	0.8	2.9	—	3.7	2.1
Greater Germany†	15.3	0.2	4.1	1.3	5.4	0.1	9.4	—	2.3	8.4	—	—	—	—	4.2	—	61.5	27.9	—	4.7	—	0.6	—	24.7	13.6
Norway	0.1	—	0.7	0.9	—	—	0.5	0.8	—	—	—	—	—	—	9.9	—	—	0.2	—	—	—	—	—	—	0.3
Sweden	—	—	9.3	0.3	0.5	—	1.9	—	—	0.1	0.4	—	—	—	1.6	—	—	—	—	0.5	—	—	—	2.7	0.7
Hungary	0.1	—	0.1	—	—	—	—	—	13.3	0.3	—	—	—	—	—	—	—	—	—	1.6	—	2.4	—	1.3	—
Yugoslavia	—	—	0.3	1.7	4.2	—	2.6	—	8.9	0.1	—	4.8	—	—	1.3	—	—	3.9	—	1.8	—	4.5	—	0.8	—
Rumania	—	2.4	0.1	—	0.5	—	0.4	—	0.3	0.6	—	—	—	—	0.1	—	—	—	—	2.9	—	4.0	—	1.4	0.7
Greece	—	—	0.1	—	—	—	0.5	0.9	3.4	0.2	—	3.4	—	—	1.9	—	—	6.6	—	0.6	—	0.3	—	—	—
Turkey	0.2	—	—	—	0.4	—	0.6	—	—	—	—	16.3	—	0.1	—	—	—	0.1	—	2.5	0.1	0.5	—	0.5	0.2
Iran & Iraq	—	5.4	—	—	—	—	—	—	—	—	—	—	—	—	—	—	—	—	—	—	0.2	—	—	—	—
Japanese Empire‡	4.9	0.1	2.2	4.0	0.9	1.4	1.1	—	—	1.1	5.3	2.6	0.2	5.8	17.2	1.4	0.1	13.5	—	1.4	20.9	2.1	6.7	0.7	0.9
China	1.1	—	0.2	—	0.2	5.7	0.2	—	—	0.8	0.6	—	—	0.2	0.7	—	—	—	—	?**	?**	?**	—	—	—
Latin America	0.3	15.3	1.4	21.8	16.4	17.8	10.2	0.1	0.2	6.0	7.6	5.3	3.6	0.7	—	—	—	—	—	6.0	1.6	11.5	31.8	—	12.5

Abbreviations:
Aust. = Australia; B.G. = British Guiana; Cyprs. = Cyprus; I/c = Indochina; Maly. = Malaya; M/Tu. = Morocco/Tunisia; N.Cal. = New Caledonia; N.R. = Northern Rhodesia; Pc. Is. = Pacific Islands (inc. Nauru); S.A. = South Africa; S.R. = Southern Rhodesia.

Table 77 Levels of Self-Sufficiency/Deficiency in Strategic Raw Materials and Foodstuffs for the Major Belligerents (1937 Figures)

	Coal	Oil	Iron	Copper	Lead	Zinc	Tin	Nickel	Bauxite	Manganese	Tungsten	Chromium	Molybdenum	Magnesite	Sulphur & Pyrites	Phosphates	Potash	Rubber	Wheat	Rice	Maize	Potatoes	Sugar	Meat
USA	Ex.	Ex.	SS	Ex.	SS	SS	Def.	Def.	NSS	Def.	Def.	Def.	Ex.	NSS	Ex.	Ex.	Def.	Def.	SS	Ex.	SS	SS	Def.	SS
USSR	SS	Ex.	SS	NSS	NSS	SS	Def.	Def.	SS	Ex.	Def.	SS	Def.	SS	SS	SS	Def.	Def.	Ex.	NSS	SS	SS	SS	SS
UK	Ex.	Def.	NSS	Def.	Def.	Def.	NSS	Def.	Def.	Def.	Def.	Def.	Def.	Def.	Def.	Def.	Def.	Def.	Def.	Def.	Def.	SS	NSS	NSS
GERMANY*	Ex.	Def.	Def.	Def.	NSS	NSS	Def.	Def.	Def.	Def.	Def.	Def.	Def.	Ex.	Def.	Def.	Ex.	Def.	NSS	Def.	Def.	SS	Ex.	NSS
ITALY	Def.	Def.	NSS	Def.	SS	SS	Def.	Def.	Ex.	Def.	Def.	Def.	Def.	NSS	Ex.	Def.	Def.	Def.	NSS	Ex.	SS	SS	SS	NSS
JAPAN†	NSS	Def.	NSS	Def.	Def.	Def.	Def.	Def.	Def.	Def.	Def.	Def.	NSS	Ex.	Ex.	Def.	Def.	Def.	NSS	SS	SS	SS	SS	NSS

* Inc. Austria and Czechoslavakia.

† Inc. Korea, Kwantung, Manchukuo, Mandates.

KEY:
Ex. = Export surplus; SS = Self-Sufficient; NSS = Not Self-Sufficient; Def. = Largely or Entirely Deficient.

Table 78 The Uses of Raw Materials in the Munitions Industry 1939-45

RAW MATERIAL	DERIVATIVE	USES
COAL		Fuel for power stations
	Coke	Fuel for iron and steel furnaces
	Coal tar (partic. benzene)	Synthetic rubber; DDT; motor fuel additive; sufa drugs; aspirin; explosives (RDX)
	Coal gas	Dyes; explosives; fertilisers
	Methane	Methyl alcohol/methanol (industrial solvent)
	Light oils	Explosives (toluol/toluene for TNT)
	Artificial fuel	When combined with hydrogen (partic. Germany)
PETROLEUM	Gasoline	Auto and aviation fuel
	Fuel oil	Marine furnaces
	Kerosene	Lamps and heating
	Lubricating oil	
	Paraffins	Wax (sealing and waterproofing)
	Ethene/Ethylene	Industrial solvent
IRON ORE	Pig-iron	Ore with oxygen removed
	Cast iron	Pig-iron with impurities removed and then moulded
	Steel	Iron ore minus carbon. Also alloyed. (a) Cast steel: moulded; (b) Forged/rolled steel: cast steel re-rolled into blooms/billets; (c) Hot or cold finished into end product
ASBESTOS		Brake shoes and clutch linings
BAUXITE (also Cryolite)	Aluminium	Electric cables; aircraft parts; moving parts in engines; explosives
COPPER		Electric wires and cables; boiler and condenser parts; armatures and electro-magnets in dynamos, motors and magnetos
	Brass	Alloyed with zinc. Cartridge and shell cases
GLYCERINE	Nitroglycerine	When treated with nitric and sulphuric acid, explosives
	Cordite	Nitroglycerine plus nitrocellulose (paper and wood shavings treated with nitric and sulphuric acid). Propellant
GRAPHITE		Electrodes; electric motor brushes
LEAD		Batteries to store electricity. Alloyed with bronze for bearings
	Lead azide	Explosives
	Lead oxide	Anti-rusting paint
	Lead tetraethyl	Anti-knock agent in gasoline
MAGNESITE		Brick for furnaces
	Magnesium	Light steel alloys
MANGANESE		Steel alloys: vital if short of quality iron ore
MOLYBDENUM		Steel alloys
NICKEL		Steel alloys. Gears; shafts; engine parts
NITROGEN	Nitric acid	Explosives; fertilisers
POTASSIUM	Potash/Potassium Carbonate	Fertilisers
RUBBER		(Useless unless vulcanised with heat and sulphur.) Tyres; sealing rings
SODIUM*	Carbonate	Manufacturing glass and paper
	Chloride	Explosives; chemicals; oil refining
	Hydroxide	Chemicals; aluminium; oil refining

* Sodium is never found in a pure form.

* Includes imports

Table 79 Annual Allied and Axis Coal Production 1939-45* (m. metric tons)

DATE	USA	USSR	UK	CANADA	TOTAL	GERMANY	ITALY	HUNGARY	RUMANIA	JAPAN	TOTAL
1939	—	—	231.3	13.3	**244.6**	332.8	—	—	—	—	**332.8**
1940	—	—	224.3	14.9	**239.2**	364.8	4.4	1.2	0.3	—	**370.7**
1941	—	151.4	206.3	15.3	**373.0**	402.8	4.4	1.3	0.2	—	**408.8**
1942	528.5	75.5	204.9	15.9	**824.8**	407.8	4.8	1.3	0.3	61.3	**475.4**
1943	535.3	93.1	198.9	14.7	**842.0**	429.0	3.3	1.4	0.3	60.5	**494.5**
1944	562.0	121.5	192.7	14.2	**890.4**	432.8	—	1.4	0.2	51.7	**486.2**
1945	523.9	149.3	182.8	13.6	**869.6**	50.3	—	?	?	11.0	**61.5**
TOTAL	**2,149.7**	**590.8**	**1,441.2**	**101.9**	**4,283.6**	**2,420.3**	**16.9**	**6.6**	**1.6**	**184.5**	**2,629.9**

Table 80 Annual Allied and Axis Iron Ore Production 1939-45 (m. metric tons)

DATE	USA	USSR	UK	CANADA	TOTAL	GERMANY	ITALY	HUNGARY	RUMANIA	JAPAN	TOTAL
1939	—	—	14.5	0.1	**14.6**	18.5	—	—	—	—	**18.5**
1940	—	—	17.7	0.4	**18.1**	29.5	1.2	1.9	2.1	—	**34.7**
1941	—	24.7	19.0	0.5	**44.2**	53.3	1.3	2.4	2.4	—	**59.4**
1942	107.6	9.7	19.9	0.5	**137.7**	50.6	1.1	2.5	3.0	7.4	**64.6**
1943	103.1	9.3	18.5	0.6	**131.5**	56.2	0.8	2.6	3.3	6.7	**69.6**
1944	96.0	11.7	15.5	0.5	**123.7**	32.6	—	4.7	?	6.0	**43.3**
1945	90.2	15.9	14.2	1.0	**121.3**	?	?	?	?	0.0	**?**
TOTAL	**396.9**	**71.3**	**119.3**	**3.6**	**591.1**	**240.7**	**4.4**	**14.1**	**10.8**	**21.0**	**291.0**

† Excludes imports from outside Greater Germany.

‡ Very low. Production of aviation fuel, for example, had fallen to 1.1 per cent of the 1944 figure.

Table 81 Annual Allied and Axis Crude Oil Production 1939-45 (m. metric tons)

DATE	USA	USSR	UK	CANADA	TOTAL	GERMANY†	Germany synthetic oil only	ITALY	HUNGARY	RUMANIA	JAPAN	TOTAL
1939	—	—	?	1.0	**?**	3.1	2.2	—	—	—	—	**3.1**
1940	—	—	11.9	1.1	**13.0**	4.8	3.2	0.01	0.3	5.0	—	**10.1**
1941	—	33.0	13.9	1.3	**48.2**	5.7	3.9	0.12	0.4	5.5	—	**11.7**
1942	183.9	22.0	11.2	1.3	**218.4**	6.6	4.6	0.01	0.7	5.7	1.8	**14.8**
1943	199.6	18.0	15.8	1.3	**234.7**	7.6	5.6	0.01	0.8	5.3	2.3	**16.0**
1944	222.5	18.2	21.4	1.3	**263.4**	5.6	3.9	—	1.0	3.5	1.0	**11.1**
1945	227.2	19.4	16.6	1.1	**264.3**	?‡	?‡	—	?	?	0.1	**?**
TOTAL	**833.2**	**110.6**	**90.8**	**8.4**	**1,043.0**	**33.4**	**23.4**	**0.17**	**3.2**	**25.0**	**5.2**	**67.0**

** The unavailability of these figures renders this table less than helpful in highlighting the great German oil crisis of late 1944/45. The table below is more forthcoming as are various fragmentary figures that show that in the first three months of 1945 synthetic oil production (hydrogenation and Fischer-Tropsch process only) was barely 6 per cent of the total for the same period in 1944. Other comparisons are diesel oil 58.1%, motor petrol 38.9% and aviation fuel 2.4%.

As oil was perhaps *the* most important strategic resource during the Second World War and the one whose lack most effectively hamstrung the Axis war effort, the following three tables provide additional detail on German and Japanese production and consumption. With regard to Japan, see also Table 97 giving details on the Japanese tanker fleet.

Table 82 Annual German Oil Production by Source, and Consumption 1939-45 (000 metric tons)

	Home Crude	Home Synthetic	Import	TOTAL	Used in Year
1939	888	2,200	5,165	**8,353**	?
1940	1,465	3,348	2,075	**6,888**	5,856
1941	1,562	4,116	2,807	**8,485**	7,305
1942	1,686	4,920	2,359	**8,965**	6,483
1943	1,883	5,748	2,766	**10,497**	6,971
1944	1,681	3,962	961	**6,504**	?
1945**	?	?	?	**?**	?

Table 83 German Production and Consumption of Key Petroleum Products* 1939-45 (000 metric tons)

	AVIATION					MOTOR					DIESEL				
	Prod.	Imports	TOTAL	Consm.	Stocks End Yr.	Prod.	Imports	TOTAL	Consm.	Stocks End Yr.	Prod.	Imports	TOTAL	Consm.	Stocks End Yr.
1939					511					280					150
1940	643	78 275†	**966**	863	613	1,138	683 309†	**2,130**	1,811	599	781	501 200†	**1,482**	1,335	296
1941	889	21	**910**	1,274	254	1,160	1,124	**2,284**	2,504	379	1,114	612	**1,726**	1,856	164
1942	1,370	102	**1,472**	1,426	324	1,002	1,021	**2,023**	2,089	313	1,285	208	**1,493**	1,519	138
1943	1,788	129	**1,917**	1,825	440	1,133	804	**1,937**	2,101	436	1,358	435	**1,793**	1,744	244
1944	998	107	**1,105**	1,403	146	935	542	**1,477**	1,805	118	889	371	**1,260**	1,435	121
1945	?	?	**12**	114	?	?	?	**139**	?	?	?	?	**180**	?	?

* Aviation, Motor and Diesel Oil accounted for (in 1943) 23.7, 15.5 and 18.6 per cent respectively of total German oil production. The other main types were Fuel Oil (13.3%), Lubricating Oils (10.6%), Liquefied Gases (5.9%), Kerosene (2.4%) and Miscellaneous (10.0%).

† Captured.

Table 84 Annual Japanese Oil Production by Source, and Consumption 1939-45 (million US barrels)

	Home Crude	Home Synthetic	Imports	TOTAL	Used in Year	Deficit	Stocks End Yr.
1941	1.9	1.2	8.4	**11.5**	22.6	-11.5	48.9
1942	1.7	1.5	10.5	**13.7**	25.8	-12.1	37.8
1943	1.8	1.0	14.5	**17.3**	27.8	-10.5	25.8
1944	1.6	1.2	5.0	**7.8**	19.4	-11.6	15.3
1945	0.8	0.2	—	**1.0**	4.6	-3.6	3.7

Table 85 Annual Allied and Axis Crude Steel Production 1939-45 (m. metric tons)

DATE	USA	USSR	UK	CANADA	TOTAL	GERMANY	ITALY	HUNGARY	RUMANIA	JAPAN	TOTAL
1939	—	—	13.2	1.4	**14.6**	23.7	—	—	—	—	**23.7**
1940	—	—	13.0	1.7	**14.7**	21.5	2.1	0.7	0.3	—	**24.6**
1941	—	17.9	12.3	2.5	**32.7**	28.2	2.1	0.8	?	—	**31.1**
1942	80.6	8.1	12.8	2.8	**104.3**	28.7	1.9	0.8	0.3	8.0	**40.5**
1943	82.2	8.5	13.3	2.7	**106.7**	30.6	1.7	0.8	0.3	8.8	**42.2**
1944	85.1	10.9	12.1	2.7	**110.8**	25.8	—	0.7	?	6.5	**33.0**
1945	86.6	12.3	11.8	2.6	**113.3**	1.4	—	?	?	0.8	**2.2**
TOTAL	**334.5**	**57.7**	**88.5**	**16.4**	**497.1**	**159.9**	**7.8**	**3.8**	**0.9**	**24.1**	**196.5**

Table 86 Annual Allied and Axis Aluminium Production 1939-45 (000 metric tons)

DATE	USA	USSR	UK	TOTAL	GERMANY	ITALY	HUNGARY	RUMANIA	JAPAN	TOTAL
1939	—	—	25.0	**25.0**	239.4	—	—	—	—	**239.4**
1940	—	—	18.9	**18.9**	265.3	?	3.2	?	—	**268.5**
1941	—	?	22.7	**22.7**	315.6	?	5.0	?	—	**320.6**
1942	751.9	51.7	46.8	**805.4**	420.0	?	6.0	?	103.0	**529.0**
1943	1,251.7	62.3	55.7	**1,369.7**	432.0	?	9.5	?	141.0	**582.5**
1944	1,092.9	82.7	35.5	**1,211.1**	470.0	—	13.2	?	110.0	**593.2**
1945	1,026.7	86.3	31.9	**1,144.9**	?	—	?	?	7.0	**?**
TOTAL	**4,123.2**	**236.5**	**283.0**	**4,642.7**	**2,142.3**	**?**	**36.9**	**?**	**361.0**	**2,540.2**

Table 87 Annual Allied and Axis Tank and Self-propelled Gun Production 1939-45 (units)

* Excludes light tanks and tankettes.

† Turan I and II tanks and Zrinyl S.P. gun.

DATE	USA	USSR	UK	CANADA	TOTAL	GERMANY	ITALY*	HUNGARY	JAPAN*	TOTAL
1939	—	2,950	969	?	**3,919**	247	40	—	—	**287**
1940	331	2,794	1,399	?	**4,524**	1,643	250	—	315	**2,208**
1941	4,052	6,590	4,841	?	**15,483**	3,790	595	—	595	**4,980**
1942	24,997	24,446	8,611	?	**58,054**	6,180	1,252	} c. 500†	557	**7,989+**
1943	29,497	24,089	7,476	?	**61,062**	12,063	336		558	**12,957+**
1944	17,565	28,963	4,600	?	**51,128**	19,002	—		353	**19,355+**
1945	11,968	15,419	?	?	**27,387**	3,932	—	—	137	**4,069**
TOTAL	**88,410**	**105,251**	**27,896**	**5,678**	**227,235**	**46,857**	**2,473**	**c. 500**	**2,515**	**c. 52,345**

‡ Main types in question are: Centaur, Cromwell IV, V, VII; Churchill IV, VI, VII; Challenger, Archer, Comet.

DATE	Tanks and S.P. Guns with 75mm guns and above			
	USA	USSR	UK‡	GERMANY
1939	—	—	—	—
1940	—	—	—	—
1941	—	3,135	—	1,028
1942	?	14,589	?	2,841
1943	?	20,091	?	11,349
1944	?	28,483	?	18,576
1945	?	26,297	?	c. 4,000
TOTAL	**71,067**	**92,595**	**?**	**37,794**

Table 88 Annual Allied and Axis Artillery Production (including Anti-tank and Anti-aircraft) 1939-45 (units)

• Australia, New Zealand, India and South Africa.

∆ Infantry guns only.

DATE	USA	USSR	UK	CANADA	EASTERN • GROUP	TOTAL	GERMANY	ITALY	HUNGARY	JAPAN ∆	TOTAL
1939	?	17,348	538	?	?	?	1,214	?	?	?	?
1940	?	15,300	4,700	?	?	?	6,730	?	?	?	?
1941	?	42,300	16,700	?	?	?	11,200	?	?	2,250	?
1942	?	127,000	43,000	?	?	?	23,200	?	?	2,550	?
1943	?	130,000	38,000	?	?	?	46,100	?	?	3,600	?
1944	?	122,400	16,000	?	?	?	70,700	—	?	3,300	?
1945	?	62,000	5,939	?	?	?	?	—	?	1,650	?
TOTAL	**257,390**	**516,648**	**124,877**	**10,552**	**5,215**	**914,682**	**159,144**	**7,200**	**447**	**13,350**	**180,141**

Table 89 Total Allied and Axis Production of Mortars 1939-45 (units)

USA	USSR	UK	CANADA	EASTERN GROUP	TOTAL		GERMANY	ITALY	JAPAN
105,054	403,300	102,950	20,619	25,395	657,318		73,484	?	?

Table 90 Total Allied and Axis Machine-Gun Production (Not Sub-machine-guns) 1939-45 (units)

USA	USSR	UK	CANADA	EASTERN GROUP	TOTAL		GERMANY	ITALY	HUNGARY	JAPAN	TOTAL
2,679,840	1,477,400	297,336	251,925	37,983	4,744,484		674,280	?	4,583	380,000	1,058,863

Table 91 Annual Allied and Axis Production of Military Trucks and Lorries 1939-45 (units)

DATE	USA	USSR	UK	TOTAL	GERMANY	ITALY	JAPAN	TOTAL
1939	}32,604	?	?	?	32,558	?	?	?
1940		?	89,582	?	53,348	?	38,056	?
1941	183,614	?	88,161	?	51,085	?	46,389	?
1942	619,735	30,400	87,499	**737,634**	58,049	?	35,386	?
1943	621,502	45,600	113,912	**781,014**	74,181	?	c. 24,000	?
1944	596,963	52,600	54,615	**704,178**	67,375	?	20,356	?
1945	327,893	68,500	47,174	**443,567**	9,318	?	1,758	?
TOTAL	**2,382,311**	**197,100**	**480,943**	**3,060,354**	**345,914**	**83,000**	**165,945**	**594,859**

Table 92 Annual Allied and Axis Military Aircraft Production 1939-45 (units)

DATE	USA	USSR	UK	CANADA	EASTERN GROUP	TOTAL	GERMANY	ITALY	HUNGARY	RUMANIA	JAPAN	TOTAL
1939	5,856	10,382	7,940	?	?	**24,178**	8,295	1,692	—	?	4,467	**14,454**
1940	12,804	10,565	15,049	?	?	**38,418**	10,826	2,142	—	?	4,768	**17,736**
1941	26,277	15,735	20,094	?	?	**62,106**	11,776	3,503	—	?	5,088	**20,367**
1942	47,836	25,436	23,672	?	?	**96,944**	15,556	2,818	6	?	8,861	**27,235**
1943	85,898	34,845	26,263	?	?	**147,006**	25,527	967	267	?	16,693	**43,454**
1944	96,318	40,246	26,461	?	?	**163,025**	39,807	—	773	?	28,180	**68,760**
1945	49,761	20,052	12,070	?	?	**81,883**	7,544	—	?	—	8,263	**15,807**
TOTAL	**324,750**	**157,261**	**131,549**	**16,431**	**3,081**	**633,072**	**189,307**	**11,122**	**1,046**	**c.1,000**	**76,320**	**89,488**

sic!

Table 93 Annual Allied and Axis Military Aircraft Production, by Type 1939-45 (units)

FIGHTERS									
DATE	USA	USSR	UK	TOTAL	GERMANY*	ITALY	JAPAN	TOTAL	
1939	–	–	1,324	**1,324**	605	?	?	?	
1940	1,162	4,574	4,283	**10,019**	2,746	1,155	?	?	
1941	4,416	7,086	7,064	**18,566**	3,744	1,339	1,080	**6,163**	
1942	10,769	9,924	9,849	**30,542**	5,515	1,488	2,935	**9,938**	
1943	23,988	14,590	10,727	**49,305**	10,898	528	7,147	**18,573**	
1944	38,873	17,913	10,730	**67,516**	26,326	—	13,811	**40,137**	
1945	20,742	c. 9,000	5,445	**35,187**	5,883	—	5,474	**11,357**	
TOTAL	**99,950**	**63,087**	**49,422**	**212,459**	**55,727**	**4,510**	**30,447**	**90,684**	

* Includes jets: 1944= 1,041; 1945= 947. Total= 1,988.

GROUND ATTACK								
DATE	USA	USSR	UK	TOTAL	GERMANY	ITALY	JAPAN	TOTAL
1939	—	—	—	**—**	134	—	—	**134**
1940	—	—	—	**—**	603	—	—	**603**
1941	—	1,543	—	**1,543**	507	—	—	**507**
1942	—	8,219	—	**8,219**	1,249	—	—	**1,249**
1943	—	11,177	—	**11,177**	3,266	—	—	**3,266**
1944	—	11,110	—	**11,110**	5,496	—	—	**5,496**
1945	—	c. 5,500	—	**c. 5,500**	1,104	—	—	**1,104**
TOTAL	**—**	**37,549**	**—**	**37,549**	**12,539**	**—**	**—**	**12,539**

BOMBERS

DATE	USA	USSR	UK	TOTAL	GERMANY	ITALY	JAPAN	TOTAL
1939	?	?	1,837	?	737	?	?	?
1940	623	3,571	3,488	7,682	2,852	640	?	?
1941	4,115	3,748	4,668	12,531	3,373	754	1,461	5,588
1942	12,627	3,537	6,253	22,417	4,502	566	2,433	7,501
1943	29,355	4,074	7,728	41,157	4,789	103	4,189	9,081
1944	35,003	4,186	7,903	47,092	1,982	—	5,100	7,082
1945	16,087	c. 2,000	2,812	20,899	—	—	1,934	1,934
TOTAL	97,810	21,116	34,689	153,615	18,235	2,063	15,117	35,415

RECONNAISSANCE

DATE	USA	USSR	UK	TOTAL	GERMANY	ITALY	JAPAN	TOTAL
1939	?	—	61	?	163	?	?	?
1940	63	—	387	450	971	351	?	?
1941	727	—	196	923	1,079	355	639	2,073
1942	1,468	—	546	2,014	1,067	276	967	2,310
1943	734	—	1,054	1,788	1,117	98	1,046	2,261
1944	259	—	1,123	1,382	1,686	—	2,147	3,833
1945	667	—	600	1,267	216	—	855	1,071
TOTAL	3,918	—	3,967	7,885	6,299	1,080	5,654	13,033

TRANSPORT

DATE	USA	USSR	UK	TOTAL	GERMANY	ITALY	JAPAN	TOTAL
1939	—	?	—	?	145	—	?	?
1940	164	1,691	—	1,855	388	—	?	?
1941	532	3,091	—	3,623	502	102	?	?
1942	1,984	3,298	—	5,282	573	249	?	?
1943	7,012	3,744	209	10,965	1,028	117	?	?
1944	9,834	5,508	889	16,231	443	—	?	?
1945	4,403	?	686	5,089	—	—	?	?
TOTAL	23,929	17,332	1,784	43,045	3,079	468	2,110	5,657

TRAINERS

DATE	USA	USSR	UK *	TOTAL	GERMANY	ITALY	JAPAN	TOTAL
1939	?	?	4,209	?	588	?	?	?
1940	1,794	549	6,415	12,819	1,870	797	?	?
1941	9,373	267	6,934	16,574	1,725	710	1,489	3,924
1942	17,631	457	5,942	24,030	1,078	160	2,171	3,409
1943	19,939	1,260	4,825	26,024	2,274	102	2,871	5,247
1944	7,577	1,528	2,877	11,982	3,693	—	6,147	9,840
1945	1,309	?	692	2,001	318	—	2,523	2,841
TOTAL	57,623	4,061	31,894	93,578	11,546	1,769	15,201	28,516

* Includes miscellaneous military types.

Table 94 British and German Production of Single-engined Fighters During the Battle of Britain June 1940-April 1941

DATE	1940								1941					GRAND TOTAL
	June	July	Aug	Sept	Oct	Nov	Dec	TOTAL	Jan	Feb	March	April	TOTAL	
Britain	446	496	476	467	469	458	413	**3,195**	313	535	609	534	**1,991**	**5,186**
Germany	164	220	173	218	144	c. 150	c. 150	**1,519**	136	255	424	446	1,261	**c.2,800**

Table 95 Annual Allied and Axis Naval Construction 1939-45 (units)

DATE	USA *						UK						USSR					CANADA						ALLIED TOTAL ••					
	A/Cr	B/s	Cr	Dest	Esc†	Sub	A/Cr	B/s	Cr	Dest	Esc†	Sub	A/Cr	B/s	Cr	Dest	Sub	A/Cr	B/s	Cr	Dest	Esc†	Sub	A/Cr	B/s	Cr	Dest	Esc†	Sub
1939	—	—	—	—	—	—	—	—	3	22	5	7	—	—	?	?	?	—	—	—	—	?	—	—	—	3	22	5	7
1940	—	—	—	—	—	—	2	1	7	27	109	15	—	—	?	?	?	—	—	—	—	?	—	2	1	7	27	109	15
1941	—	—	1	2	—	2	2	2	6	39	87	20	—	—	?	?	?	—	—	—	—	?	—	2	2	7	41	87	22
1942	18	4	8	82	—	34	—	2	6	73	71	33	—	—	?	?	?	—	—	—	—	?	—	18	6	14	155	71	67
1943	65	2	11	128	298	55	2	—	7	37	79	39	—	—	?	?	?	—	—	—	—	?	—	67	2	18	165	377	94
1944	45	2	14	74	194	81	4	—	2	31	55	39	—	—	?	?	?	—	—	—	—	?	—	49	2	16	105	249	120
1945	13	—	14	63	6	31	4	—	1	13	7	14	—	—	?	?	?	—	—	—	—	?	—	17	—	15	76	13	45
TOTAL	141	8	48	349	498	203	14	5	32	240	413	167	—	—	2	25	52	—	—	—	—	191‡	—	155	13	82	814	1,102	422

(sic) 10 15

DATE	GERMANY					ITALY					JAPAN					AXIS TOTAL				
	A/Cr	B/s	Cr	Dest	Sub	A/Cr	B/s	Cr	Dest	Sub	A/Cr	B/s	Cr	Dest	Sub	A/Cr	B/s	Cr	Dest	Sub
1939	—	—	—	—	58	—	—	—	—	—	—	—	—	—	—	—	—	—	—	58
1940	—	—	—	2	68	—	2	2	—	2	—	—	—	—	—	—	2	2	2	70
1941	—	—	—	5	129	—	1	3	—	7	1	1	—	—	—	1	2	3	5	136
1942	—	—	—	3	282	—	—	1	6	10	6	1	4	10	61	6	1	5	19	353
1943	—	—	—	7	207	—	—	—	—	9	4	—	3	12	37	4	—	3	19	253
1944	—	—	—	—	258	—	—	—	—	—	5	—	2	24	39	5	—	2	24	297
1945	—	—	—	—	139	—	—	—	—	—	—	—	—	17	30	—	—	—	17	169
TOTAL	—	—	—	17	1141	—	3	6	6	28	16	2	9	63	167	16	5	15	86	1,337

* Ships commissioned to October 1945.

† Comprises escort destroyers, frigates, sloops and corvettes.

‡ A further 12 escort ships were built in Australia.

•• USSR and Canada included only in bottom-line totals.

Table 96 Annual Allied and Axis Production of Merchant Shipping 1939-45 (gross tons)

DATE	USA*	UK*	Other Commonwealth	ALLIED TOTAL	GERMANY	ITALY*	JAPAN	AXIS TOTAL
1939	376,419	629,705	36,142	**1,042,266**	?	119,757	320,466*	?
1940	528,697	842,910	18,886	**1,390,493**	?	35,299	293,612	?
1941	1,031,974	1,185,894	90,595	**2,308,465**	?	96,999	210,373	?
1942	5,479,766	1,270,714	720,172	**7,488,652**	?	153,656	260,059	?
1943	11,448,360	1,136,804	1,002,850	**13,588,014**	?	63,895	769,085	?
1944	9,288,156	919,357	692,405	**10,899,918**	?	—	1,699,203	?
1945	5,839,858	393,515	141,893	**6,375,266**	?	—	599,563	?
TOTAL	**33,993,230**	**6,378,899**	**2,702,943**	**43,075,072**	?	469,606	4,152,361	?

* Tonnage launched.

One of the most vital components of the wartime merchant fleets were the tankers and for none was this more true than for the Japanese. The table here gives a terse history of that fleet, providing telling evidence of one of the major reasons for Japan's defeat.

Table 97 Annual Tonnage of Japanese Tankers Built, Sunk and Extant, 1941-45

	Tonnage Built	Tonnage Sunk	Tonnage Available End of Year
1941			**578,000**
1942	20,316	9,538	**686,000**
1943	254,927	169,491	**873,000**
1944	624,290	754,889	**860,000**
1945	85,651	351,028	**266,948**

The most decisive battle of the Second World War was undoubtedly that of production, as outlined in the preceding tables in this section. But a vital sector within this battle was that of the import of raw materials etc., and the following table shows the varying success in this sector of the two belligerents most dependent on maritime imports, the United Kingdom and Japan.

Table 98 Annual UK and Japanese Imports of Various Strategic Raw Materials and Foodstuffs 1939-45 (000 metric tons)

	UK							JAPAN				
	1939	1940	1941	1942	1943	1944	1945	1941	1942	1943	1944	1945
OIL	11,628*	11,270	13,130	16,280	14,790	20,340	15,620	1,090	1,360	1,880	650	—
COAL	—	—	—	—	—	—	—	6,460	6,390	5,180	2,630	548
IRON ORE	5,200	4,500	2,300	1,900	1,900	2,200	4,100	6,310	4,700	4,300	2,150	341
IRON & STEEL	1,820	3,690	4,080	2,210	2,810	1,760	314	921	993	997	1,100	170
SCRAP IRON	605	937	549	—	?	—	200	246	50	43	21	12
BAUXITE	302	112	87	48	242	172	163	150	305	909	376	15
LEAD	334	336	139	235	226	225	165	86	11	25	17	4
TIN	54	84	65	44	52	33	45	5	4	27	23	4
ZINC	167	204	210	212	188	119	97	8	8	10	6	2
RAW RUBBER	69	200	168	66	69	34	36	68	31	42	31	18
RICE	143	191	179	53	131	72	25	2,110	2,250	990	652	201
PEAS & BEANS	135	147	158	48	69	71	66	546	648	276	?	?
WHEAT	5,300	5,800	5,400	3,500	3,300	2,800	3,600	—	—	—	—	—

* 1938.

SECTION 8

HARDWARE

In this section will be found details about the weaponry of the Second World War. However, as there are many books now available devoted to just one aircraft, for example, or just one tank, it is clear that the information presented below must be ruthlessly compressed. Thus, whilst all major types of weapon system are included – combat aircraft, ships (naval and merchant), tanks, tank and anti-tank guns, and artillery (including self-propelled) – there has been space for only the most essential information about them. It should be noted, therefore, that

— There are no details on small arms (mortars, machine guns, rifles etc.).*
— Only the most widely used weapons are listed and there is hardly any mention of the very numerous failures and eccentricities that regularly cluttered up the production lines; except, that is, for a few weapons whose time was yet to come, like jet aircraft and missiles.
— Details about the weapons included are limited almost exclusively to their combat performance and to the numbers produced. Other details, most notably size specifications and external appearance, must be sought in the more compendious, specialised works listed in the Bibliography.

* Though some tactical rocketry (e.g. 'bazookas'), with the ability to 'kill' tanks, has been included.

COMBAT AICRAFT

In addition to the qualifications just noted, the following points should be borne in mind:

— Figures for range, ceiling, speed and rate of climb are usually the maxima possible. In actual operations the innumerable possible permutations of amount of fuel carried, weight of payload, height flown, weather conditions etc. would have a marked effect on aircraft performance.
— Maximum bomb-loads, especially for the dedicated bombers, also tend to be counsel of perfection. Thus despite the impressive figures for Lancasters, Flying Fortresses etc. in the ARMAMENT column below, the *average* bomb-loads carried in 1944 by 8 US Air Force and Bomber Command aircraft were 4,100 lb and 10,400 lb respectively.
— Each line entry usually gives details for one particular version of an aircraft type, e.g. the Junkers Ju-88G-7b night-fighter version of the basic Ju-88 light bomber. In most of these instances two entries are given in the DATE IN SERVICE and NUMBER PRODUCED columns, the top one giving the date/number of the type and the bottom one of the particular version.

Table 99 Combat Aircraft

Fighters

TYPE	DATE IN SERVICE	SPEED (mph at feet.)	RANGE (miles)	CEILING (feet.)	RATE OF CLIMB (min/sec. to feet.)	ARMAMENT	NUMBER PRODUCED
AUSTRALIA	No Australian aircraft went into mass production and RAAF squadrons fought under RAF or overall American command, flying British or American aircraft. The main fighters used were the Curtiss Kittyhawk (see USA below) and the Supermarine Spitfire (see UK below).						
BELGIUM	In May 1940, the Belgian Air Force was largely obsolete being equipped with Fairey Foxes and Fiat CR.42s. (For the latter see Italy below).						
BULGARIA	Bulgaria had no indigenous aircraft industry. The most common fighter at the beginning of the war was the Czech Avia B-534, replaced later by Dewoitine D520s (see France below) and some Messerschmitt Bf 109s (see Germany below).						
CANADA	No Canadian fighters went into mass production and Canadian squadrons fought under RAF command. The main types flown were Curtiss Kittyhawks (see USA below), Hawker Hurricanes, Supermarine Spitfires and de Havilland Mosquitos (see UK below).						
FINLAND	The only indigenous fighter of any note was the VL Myrsky II (see below). The other main types employed were various Fokkers, and the Fiat G.50, Brewster 239, Curtiss Hawk, Morane-Saulnier 406c (see France below), Gloster Gladiator, Hawker Hurricane (for both see UK below), and Messerschmitt Bf 109G (see Germany below).						
VL Myrsky II	1943	329 at 10,700	311	29,500	?	4 x 12.7mm m.g.	52
FRANCE 1940							
Bloch 152	1939	316 at 14,800	336	38,800	3/24 to 6,500	1 x 20mm cannon 2 x 7.5mm m.g.	483
Curtiss Hawk 75a (US)	1939	300 at 10,000	825	33,000	1 to 3,400	4 or 5 x 7.5mm m.g.	165 (delivered to France)
Dewoitine D520	1940	330 at 19,700	550	36,100	5/39 to 13,100	1 x 20mm cannon 4 x 7.9mm m.g.	910
Morane-Saulnier MS 406 C1	1939	300 at 14,700	460	30,840	6/30 to 16,400	1 x 20mm cannon 2 x 7.9mm m.g.	1,400
GERMANY							
Focke-Wulf FW 190A-8	1941 / 1943	400 at 18,000	495	33,800	1 to 2,350	2 x 20mm cannon 2 x 13mm m.g. 2 x 20mm m.g.	20,000 / 1,330 x 'A-8'
Focke-Wulf FW 190G-3 (fighter-bomber)	1941 / 1943	356 at sea-level	395	?	?	2 x 20mm cannon max bombs 2,755 lb	20,000 / ?
Junkers Ju-88C-6c (night-fighter)	1938 / 1940	300 at 19,700	1,230	32,450	12/5 to 19,700	3 x 20mm cannon 3 x 7.9mm m.g. 1 x 13mm m.g.	14,670* / 3,200 x 'C'

* Of which c. 6,000 fighters. See also Bombers (German).

Fighters (continued)

TYPE	DATE IN SERVICE	SPEED (mph at feet.)	RANGE (miles)	CEILING (feet.)	RATE OF CLIMB (min/sec. to feet.)	ARMAMENT	NUMBER PRODUCED
GERMANY							
Junkers Ju-88G-7b (night-fighter)	1938 / 1944	389 at 29,000	1,400	32,800	26/25 to 30,200	6 x 20mm cannon 1 x 13mm m.g.	14,670* / 2,800 x 'G'
Messerschmitt Bf 109E-3	1937 / 1938	350 at 14,550	410	34,450	1/6 to 3,280	3 x 20mm cannon 2 x 7.9mm m.g.	30,000 / c. 4,000 x 'E'
Messerschmitt Bf 109G-2	1937 / 1942	405 at 28,500	525	39,370	1/30 to 6,550	1 x 20mm cannon 2 x 7.9mm m.g.	30,000 / 23,500 x 'G'
Messerschmitt Bf 110C-1 (twin-engined fighter)	1938 / 1939	325 at 13,120	680	32,800	1 to 2,150	2 x 20mm cannon 5 x 7.9mm m.g.	6,000 / c. 1,500 x 'C'
Messerschmitt Bf 110G-4 (night-fighter)	1938 / 1942	340 at 22,950	1,300	26,250	1 to 2,170	as above	6,000 / c. 3,700 x 'G-4'
Messerschmitt Me 262-1a (jet fighter)	1944	540 at 19,680	525	37,560	6/50 to 19,700	4 x 30mm cannon	1,100 / ?
GREECE 1940	The main front-line fighters were the Polish P.Z.L. P-24-F and the Bloch M.B. 151.						
HUNGARY	Fought mainly with the Luftwaffe on the Eastern Front. Main types employed were the Hejja (licence-built Italian Reggiane Re 2000), Fiat C.R.42 (see Italy below), and Messerschmitt Bf 109E, F and G (see Germany above).						
INDIA	From 1943 the Indian Air Force fought pretty much as an autonomous force under overall Allied control. The main fighters employed were the Curtiss Hawk 75a (see France above), the Hawker Hurricane and the Supermarine Spitfire (see UK below for both).						
ITALY							
Fiat C.R.42AS (bi-plane)	1939	280	480	34,450	7/0 to 19,700	2 x 12.7mm m.g. max. bombs 440 lb.	c. 1,800
Macchi M.C.200	1939	310 at 14,800	540	29,200	3/25 to 9,850	2 x 12.7mm m.g.	1,153
Macchi M.C.202	1941	370 at 16,400	475	37,700	5/55 to 19,700	2 x 12.7mm m.g. provision for 2 x 7.7mm m.g.	1,100
JAPAN							
Kawanishi N1K2-J 'George 21'	1944	370 at 18,400	1,300	35,300	7/22 to 19,700	4 x 20mm cannon max. bombs 1,100 lb.	1,440 x 'N1K' / ?
Kawasaki Ki-45 KAIa 'Nick' (twin-engined)	1942	340 at 23,000	1,400	35,200	6/17 to 16,400	1 x 20mm cannon 2 x 12.7mm m.g. 1 x 7.9mm m.g.	1,700 / c. 1,200
Kawasaki Ki-45 KAIc 'Nick' (night-fighter)	1942 / 1944	340 at 23,000	1,240	32,800	6/17 to 16,400	1 x 37mm cannon 2 x 20mm cannon	1,700 / c. 500
Kawasaki Ki-61-Ib 'Tony'	1943	370 at 16,000	680	37,700	5/30 to 16,400	4 x 12.7mm m.g. or 2 x 12.7mm m.g. + 2 x 20mm cannon max bombs 1,100 lb.	3,100 / 1,380 (inc 'Ia')
Mitsubishi A6M2 'Zeke' ('Zero') (carrier-fighter)	1940	330 at 15,000	1,930	32,800	7/27 to 19,700	2 x 20mm cannon 2 x 7.7mm m.g. max bombs 265 lb.	11,720 / 6,570
Nakajima Ki-27a 'Nate'	1938	290 at 11,500	1,050	40,200	5/20 to 16,400	2 x 7.7mm m.g. max bombs 220 lb.	3,500 / ?
Nakajima Ki-43-IIa 'Oscar'	1941 / 1942	290 at sea-level	1,990	36,750	5/50 to 16,400	2 x 12.7mm m.g. max bombs 1,100 lb.	5,900 / c. 5,200
Nakajima Ki-84-Ia 'Frank'	1944	390 at 20,000	1,350	36,100	5/54 to 16,400	2 x 20mm cannon 2 x 12.7mm m.g. max bombs 1,100 lb.	3,500 / ?

* Of which c. 6,000 fighters. See also Bombers (German).

Fighters (continued)

TYPE	DATE IN SERVICE	SPEED (mph at feet.)	RANGE (miles)	CEILING (feet.)	RATE OF CLIMB (min/sec. to feet.)	ARMAMENT	NUMBER PRODUCED
NETHERLANDS 1940	Two types of fighter were available in May, the Fokker D.XXI and G.I.						
NEW ZEALAND	New Zealand squadrons fought both in Europe, under RAF command, and in the Pacific, under control of US South Pacific Command. Main types employed were Brewster Buffalos, Curtiss Kittyhawks, Chance Vought Corsairs (see USA below), Hawker Hurricanes, Supermarine Spitfires, Hawker Tempests and Typhoons (see UK below).						
NORWAY 1940	Only a few Gloster Gladiators were available when Germany attacked in April.						
POLAND							
P.Z.L. P-7a (bi-plane)	1932	200 at 13,100	350	27,100	1/38 to 3,300	2 x 7.7mm m.g.	153
P.Z.L. P-11c	pre-war	240 at 18,000	435	26,250	6/0 to 16,400	2 x 7.7mm m.g. max. bombs 110 lb.	330
RUMANIA	As well as German supplied Messerschmitt Bf 109E and Gs (see Germany above) and Heinkel He 112Bs, the Rumanians used the indigenously produced						
IAR 80A	1942	315 at 13,100	584	34,500	5/40 to 14,700	6 x 7.92mm m.g.	c. 180
SOUTH AFRICA	South African squadrons fought under Allied command in Africa and the Mediterranean, the most common fighters being the Curtiss Kittyhawk (see USA below) and the Supermarine Spitfire (see UK below).						
UNITED KINGDOM							
Bristol Beaufighter IF (night-fighter)	1940	306 at sea-level	1,500	28,900	1/0 to 1,850	4 x 20mm cannon 6 x 0.303in m.g.	5,920 / 1,150*
de Havilland Mosquito XIX (night-fighter)	1941 / 1944	380 at 13,200	1,000	33,000	1/0 to 2,700	4 x 20mm cannon	7,780† / 1,900*
de Havilland Mosquito Mk VI (fighter-bomber)	1941 / 1943	380 at 13,000	1,880	33,000	1/0 to 2,800	4 x 0.303in m.g. 4 x 20mm cannon max bombs 2,000 lb.	7,780† / 2,720
Gloster Meteor Mk III (jet)	1944	493 at 30,000	1,340	44,000	1/0 to 2,100 15/0 to 30,000	4 x 20mm cannon	316 (in war) / 280
Hawker Hurricane Mk I	1937	310 at 10,000	525	33,400	4/15 to 10,000	8 x 0.303in m.g.	14,230 / 3,900
Hawker Hurricane Mk IIC	1937 / 1940	330 at 18,000	920	35,600	1/0 to 2,700 12/30 to 30,000	4 x 20mm cannon max bombs 1,000 lb. or 8 x 3in rocket	14,230 / 6,650
Hawker Tempest Mk V (fighter-bomber)	1944	420 at 18,500	1,530	36,500	5/0 to 15,000	4 x 20mm cannon max bombs 2,000 lb. or 8 x 3in rocket	1,420 / 800
Supermarine Spitfire Mk IA	1938	360	395	31,900	1/0 to 2,500	8 x 0.303in m.g.	20,350 / 1,500
Supermarine Spitfire Mk VB	1938 / 1941	360 at 6,000	470	35,500	1/0 to 4,700	2 x 20mm cannon 4 x 0.303in m.g.	20,350 / 3,920
Supermarine Spitfire Mk IX	1938 / 1942	410 at 25,000	980	43,000	1/0 to 4,000	2 x 20mm cannon 4 x 0.303in m.g.	20,350 / 5,700
Supermarine Spitfire Mk XIV	1938 / 1944	440 at 24,500	850	43,000	1/0 to 4,600 7/0 to 20,000	2 x 20mm cannon 2 x 0.5in m.g.	20,350 / 960
USA							
Bell Airacobra P-39Q	1941 / 1943	385 at 11,000	675	35,000	4/50 to 15,000	1 x 37mm cannon 4 x 0.5in m.g. max bombs 500 lb.	9,590• / 4,900
Brewster Buffalo F2A-3	1939 / 1941	320 at 16,500	960	33,200	1/0 to 2,300	4 x 0.5in m.g.	510 / 200
Δ Curtiss Kittyhawk IA P-40E (fighter-bomber)	1939 / 1942	335 at 5,000	850	29,000	4/50 to 10,000	6 x 0.5in m.g. max bombs 500 lb.	13,740 / 2,320

* All night-fighter variants (inc. Beaufighter IIF and Mosquito II, XII, XIII, XV, XVIII and Mk 30).

† See also Mosquito under Bombers (UK).

• Over half the total production went to the USSR.

Δ In the USA, the P-40 was known as the Warhawk.

Fighters (continued)

TYPE	DATE IN SERVICE	SPEED (mph at feet.)	RANGE (miles)	CEILING (feet.)	RATE OF CLIMB (min/sec. to feet.)	ARMAMENT	NUMBER PRODUCED	
USA								
* Curtiss Kittyhawk IV P-40N-20 (fighter-bomber)	1939 / 1944	350 at 16,400	750	31,000	7/20 to 14,000	6 x 0.5in m.g. max bombs 1,500 lb.	13,740	5,200 x 'N'
Grumman Wildcat F4F-4 and FM-1 (carrier-fighter)	1940 / 1941	320 at 19,400	770	34,900	1/0 to 2,000	6 x 0.5in m.g. max bombs 200 lb.	7,350	2,310
Grumman Hellcat F6F-5 (carrier-fighter)	1943 / 1944	380 at 23,400	950	37,300	1/0 to 3,000	6 x 0.5in m.g. or 2 x 20mm cannon + 4 x 0.5in m.g. max bombs 2,000 lb.	12,270	6,436
Lockheed Lightning P-38G	1941 / 1942	345 at 5,000	1,400	39,000	1/50 to 5,000	1 x 20mm cannon 4 x 0.5in m.g. max bombs 2,000 lb.	9,390	1,080
Lockheed Lightning P-38L	1941 / 1943	410 at 25,000	2,250	44,000	2/0 to 5,000	1 x 20mm cannon 4 x 0.5in m.g. max bombs 3,200 lb.	9,390	3,920
North American Mustang P-51B/C	1942 / 1943	440 at 30,000	2,200	42,000	12/30 to 30,000	4 x 0.5in m.g. max bombs 2,000 lb.	15,470	3,750
North American Mustang P-51D	1942 / 1944	440 at 25,000	2,100	41,900	13/1 to 30,000	6 x 0.5in m.g. max bombs 2,000 lb.	15,470	7,970
Northrop Black Widow P-61A/B (night-fighter)	1944	360 at 20,000	3,000	33,100	12/0 to 20,000	4 x 20mm cannon 4 x 0.5in m.g. max bombs 6,400 lb.	740	650
Republic Thunderbolt P-47D	1942 / 1943	430 at 30,000	590	42,000	11/0 to 20,000	6 or 8 x 0.5in m.g. max bombs 2,500 lb.	15,630	12,560
Vought Corsair F4U-1 (carrier-fighter)	1943	415 at 20,000	1,015	37,000	1/0 to 3,100	6 x 0.5in m.g.	12,570	9,440†
USSR								
Lavochkin La-5FN	1941 / 1943	400 at 6,400	475	31,100	4/42 to 16,400	2 x 20mm cannon or 1 x 23mm cannon	9,920	?
Lavochkin La-7	1941 / 1944	410	395	34,450	4/30 to 16,400	2 or 3 x 20mm cannon max bombs 440 lb.		5,750
Yakovlev Yak-1	1940	360 at 16,400	530	32,810	4/30 to 16,400	1 x 20mm cannon 2 x 7.6mm m.g. max bombs 440 lb. or 6 x 82mm rocket		8,700
Yakovlev Yak-3	1943	405 at 3,300	560	35,430	4/6 to 16,400	1 x 20mm cannon 2 x 7.6mm m.g.		4,850
Yakovlev Yak-7	1942	340 at sea-level	510	33,460	4/55 to 16,400	1 x 20mm cannon 1 x 12.7mm m.g. max bombs 440 lb. or 6 x 82mm rocket		6,400
Yakovlev Yak-9D	1942	370 at 6,550	875	34,770	5/40 to 16,400	1 x 20mm cannon 1 x 12.7mm m.g.		16,800

* In the USA, the P-40 was known as the Warhawk.

† Including F4U-1, F3A-1, FG-1, FG-1D.

Dive and Torpedo Bombers and Ground Attack

TYPE	DATE IN SERVICE	SPEED (mph at feet.)	RANGE (miles)	CEILING (feet.)	RATE OF CLIMB (min/sec. to feet.)	ARMAMENT	NUMBER PRODUCED
GERMANY							
Focke-Wulf FW 190F-3 (ground-attack)	1941 / 1942	370 at 18,000	330	?	1/0 to 2,100	2 x 20mm cannon 2 x 7.9mm m.g. max bombs 550 lb.	20,000 / c. 500
Henschel Hs 129B-2 (ground-attack)	1942 / 1943	250 at 12,600	430	29,500	1/0 to 1,600	Variety of 20mm (2), 30mm (1), 37mm (1) cannon and 7.9mm (2) m.g. max bombs 770 lb.	870 / c. 450
Junkers Ju 87B-1/2 (dive-bomber)	1937 / 1938	240 at 13,400	490	26,150	4/20 to 6,600	3 x 7.9mm m.g. max bombs 1,100 lb.	5,710 / c. 1,350
Junkers Ju 87D-1 (dive-bomber)	1937 / 1941	255 at 13,500	950	23,900	19/50 to 16,400	3 x 7.9mm m.g. max bombs 4,000 lb.	5,710 / c. 3,300 x 'D'
JAPAN							
Aichi D3A2 'Val' (dive-bomber)	1937 / 1942	240 at 9,800	915	30,000	6/30 to 9,800	3 x 7.7mm m.g. max bombs 810 lb.	1,500 / 1,020
Nakajima B5N2 'Kate' (torpedo-bomber)	1938 / 1941	230 at 11,800	1,240	27,000	7/40 to 9,800	1 x 7.7mm m.g. max bombs 1,800 lb. or 1 x torpedo	1,150 / ?
Nakajima B6N2 'Jill' (torpedo-bomber)	1942 / 1944	300 at 16,000	1,900	29,700	10/25 to 16,400	2 x 7.7mm m.g. max bombs 1,800 lb. or 1 x torpedo	1,270 / 1,130
Yokosuka D4Y1 'Judy' (dive-bomber)	1942 / 1943*	340 at 15,600	980	32,500	6/15 to 0,000	2 x 7.7mm m.g. 1 x 7.92mm m.g. max bombs 680 lb.	2,040 / c. 800
UNITED KINGDOM							
Bristol Beaufourt Mk I (torpedo-bomber)	1940	265 at 6,000	1,600	16,500	?	6 x 0.303in m.g. max bombs 1,500 lb. max torpedo 1,600 lb.	1,130 / 960
Bristol Beaufighter Mk X (anti-shipping fighter)	1940 / 1942	300 at 13,000	1,470	15,000	3/30 to 5,000	4 x 20mm cannon 1 x 0.303in m.g. max bombs 1,650 lb. max torpedo 2,130 lb. or 8 x 90lb. rocket	5,920 / 2,100
Fairey Swordfish Mk I (torpedo-bomber)	1936	140 at 4,700	1,000	10,700	10/0 to 5,000	2 x 0.303in m.g. max bombs 1,500 lb. or 1 x 18" torpedo	2,390 / 990
Fairey Barracuda Mk II (torpedo/dive-bomber)	1942	230 at 1,700	1,150	16,600	6/0 to 5,000	2 x 0.303in m.g. max bombs 1,000 lb. or 1 x 1,620lb. torpedo	2,600 / 1,400
Hawker Typhoon IB (ground-attack)	1941	410 at 19,000	510	35,200	5/50 to 15,000	4 x 20mm cannon max bombs 2,000 lb. or 8 x 3" rocket	3,270 / c. 2,700
USA							
Curtiss Helldiver SB2C-4 (scout-bomber)	1943 / 1944	270 at sea-level	1,240	29,100	1/0 to 1,800	2 x 20mm cannon 2 x 0.3in m.g. max bombs 2,000 lb.	7,200 / 2,040
Douglas Dauntless SBD-5/A24-B (dive-bomber)	1940 / 1943	240 at 15,800	1,100	24,300	1/0 to 1,200	2 x 0.5in m.g. 2 x 0.3in m.g. max bombs 2,250 lb.	5,940 / 3,640
Grumman Avenger TBF-1/TBM-1 (torpedo-bomber)	1942	250 at sea-level	1,210	22,400	1/0 to 1,400	1 x 0.5in m.g. 2 x 0.3in m.g. max torpedo 1,600 lb.	9,800 / 5,170
Vultee Vengeance A-35B (dive-bomber)	1942 / 1943	280 at 13,500	2,300	22,300	11/20 to 15,000	7 x 0.5in m.g. max bombs 2,000 lb.	1,930 / 830

* qua dive-bomber. Originally reconnaissance aircraft

Dive and Torpedo Bombers and Ground Attack (continued)

TYPE	DATE IN SERVICE	SPEED (mph at feet.)	RANGE (miles)	CEILING (feet.)	RATE OF CLIMB (min/sec. to feet.)	ARMAMENT	NUMBER PRODUCED
USSR							
Ilyushin Il-2m3 'Sturmovik' (ground-attack)	1941 / 1942	250 at 4,900	475	19,700	12/0 to 16,400	2 x 23mm cannon 2 x 7.62mm m.g. 1 x 12.7mm m.g. max bombs 1,320 lb. or 8 x 82 or 132mm rocket	36,200 / most
Petlyakov Pe-2 (dive-bomber)	1941	335 at 16,400	930	29,000	7/0 to 16,400	3 x 7.62mm m.g. or 1 x 7.62mm m.g. + 2 x 12.7mm m.g. max bombs 2,650 lb.	11,000

Bombers

TYPE	DATE IN SERVICE	SPEED (mph at feet.)	RANGE (miles)	CEILING (feet.)	RATE OF CLIMB (min/sec. to feet.)	ARMAMENT	NUMBER PRODUCED
FRANCE 1940							
Amiot 143M (medium x 2)*	1936	190 at 13,100	1,240	25,900	14/20 to 13,100	4 x 7.5mm m.g. max bombs 4,000 lb.	138
Bloch 210 BN4/5 (medium x 2)	1937	200 at 11,500	1,050	32,500	12/0 to 13,100	3 x 7.5mm m.g. max bombs 3,500 lb.	281
Lioré et Olivier 451 B4 (medium x 2)	1939	300 at 15,700	1,800	29,500	14/0 to 16,400	1 x 20mm cannon 4 x 7.5mm m.g. max bombs 4,400 lb.	580
GERMANY							
Dornier Do 17Z-2 (medium x 2)	1937 / 1938	250 at 13,100	930	26,900	?	4 or 6 or 8 x 7.92mm m.g. max bombs 2,200 lb.	1,100 / c. 500 x Z-1 & Z-2
Dornier Do 217E-2 (heavy x 2)	1941	320 at 17,100	1,740	29,500	1/0 to 710	1 x 15mm m.g. 6 x 7.9mm m.g. 1 x 13mm m.g. max bombs 8,800 lb.	1,900 / 300 x '217E'
Dornier Do 217M-1 (heavy x 2)	1941 / 1942	350 at 18,700	1,550	31,200	1/0 to 690	2 x 13mm m.g. 4 x 7.9mm m.g. max bombs 8,800 lb.	1,900 / c. 550 x '217M'
Focke-Wulf FW 200C-4 'Condor' (maritime bomber x 4)	1940 / 1942	220 at 15,700	2,175	19,000	?	1 x 20mm cannon 4 x 13mm m.g. 1 x 7.9mm m.g. max bombs 3,750 lb.	c. 250 x '200C' / c. 70 x C-4
Heinkel He 111H-6 (medium x 2)	1936 / 1941	250 at 19,700	1,200	27,900	42/0 to 19,700	1 x 20mm cannon 1 x 13mm m.g. 4 x 7.9mm m.g. max bombs 7,200 lb.	7,300 / ?
Heinkel He 177A-5 'Griffon' (heavy x 4)	1943	303 at 20,000	3,400	26,200	39/0 to 20,000	1 x 20mm cannon 2 x 13mm m.g. 3 x 7.9mm m.g. max bombs 13,200lb.	1,120 / 820
Junkers Ju 88A-4 (medium x 2)	1938 / 1940	290 at 17,400	1,700	26,900	23/0 to 17,700	2 x 13mm m.g. 3 x 7.9mm m.g. max bombs 7,900 lb.	14,670† / c. 7,000 x 'A'
ITALY							
CANT Z.1007bis (medium x 3)	1938	280	1,110	24,600	16/10 to 19,700	2 x 12.7mm m.g. 2 x 7.7mm m.g. max bombs 2,650 lb.	530 / most
Fiat BR.20M (medium x 2)	1938 / 1939	270 at sea-level	1,700	26,200	25/0 to 19,700	3 x 12.7mm m.g. max bombs 3,500 lb.	600 / 260
Piaggio P.108B (heavy x 4)	1942	270 at 13,800	2,200	28,000	21/8 to 16,400	6 x 12.7mm m.g. max bombs 7,700 lb.	160
Savoia-Marchetti SM79-I (medium x 3)	1937	270 at 13,100	1,180	21,300	3/30 to 3,300	3 x 12.7mm m.g. 2 x 7.7mm m.g. max bombs 2,750 lb.	1,230 / ?

* 'x 2' indicates number of engines.

† Of which c. 9,000 bombers. See also Fighters (German).

Bombers (continued)

TYPE	DATE IN SERVICE	SPEED (mph at feet.)	RANGE (miles)	CEILING (feet.)	RATE OF CLIMB (min/sec. to feet.)	ARMAMENT	NUMBER PRODUCED
JAPAN							
Kawasaki Ki-48-II 'Lily' (light x 2)*	1940 / 1942	310 at 18,400	1,500	33,100	8/30 to 16,400	3 x 7.7mm m.g. max bombs 1,750 lb.	1,120 / 410
Mitsubishi G3M2 'Nell' (medium x 2)	1937	230 at 13,700	2,700	30,000	8/20 to 9,800	1 x 20mm cannon 4 x 7.7mm m.g. max bombs 1,760 lb.	1,050 / c. 700
Mitsubishi Ki-21-IIa/b 'Sally' (heavy x 2)	1938 / 1941	300 at 15,500	1,700	32,800	13/15 to 19,600	1 x 12.7mm m.g. 5 x 7.7mm m.g. max bombs 2,200 lb.	2,060 / 1,280
Mitsubishi G4M1-11 'Betty' (medium x 2)	1941	270 at 13,800	3,750	28,000	18/0 to 23,000	1 x 20mm cannon 4 x 7.7mm m.g. max bombs 1,750 lb.	2,450 / 1,200
Mitsubishi G4M2-22 'Betty' (medium x 2)	1941 / 1943	270 at 15,000	3,270	29,300	30/20 to 26,000	2 x 20mm cannon 6 x 7.7mm m.g. max bombs 2,200 lb.	2,450 / 1,140 x M2 and M2a
Nakajima Ki-49-IIa/b 'Helen' (heavy x 2)	1938 / ?	300 at 16,400	1,830	30,500	13/40 to 16,400	1 x 20mm cannon 5 x 7.7mm m.g. max bombs 2,500 lb.	815 / 665
Yokosuka P1Y1 'Frances' (medium x 2)	1945	340 at 19,300	3,340	30,800	4/15 to 9,800	2 x 20mm cannon max bombs 2,200 lb.	1,100
POLAND 1939							
P.Z.L. P-23-B (light x 1)	1936	185 at 6,560	780	24,000	4/40 to 6,500	3 x 7.7mm m.g. max bombs 1,540 lb.	310
P.Z.L. P-37-B (medium x 2)	1938	280 at 11,100	2,800	30,300	?	3 x 7.7mm m.g. max bombs 5,700 lb.	95
UNITED KINGDOM							
Armstrong Whitworth Whitley Mk V (heavy x 2)	1937 / 1939	230 at 16,400	1,500	26,000	16/0 to 15,000	5 x 0.303in m.g. max bombs 7,000 lb.	1,810 / 1,470
Avro Lancaster I (heavy x 4)	1942	240 at sea-level	2,530	22,000	41/0 to 20,000	8 x 0.303in m.g. max bombs 18,000 lb.	7,400 / 3,440
Bristol Blenheim IV (medium x 2)	1937 / 1939	260 at 12,000	1,460	22,000	1/0 to 1,500	2 or 4 x 0.303in m.g. max bombs 1,000 lb.	6,360 / 3,300
de Havilland Mosquito B. Mk XVI (light x 2)	1941 / 1942	410 at 26,000	1,480	37,000	1/0 to 2,800	max bombs 4,000 lb.	7,780† / 1,200
Fairey Battle Mk III (light x 1)	1937	260 at 15,000	1,000	25,000	4/0 to 5,000	2 x 0.303in m.g. max bombs 1,000 lb.	2,200 / ?
Handley Page Halifax B. Mk III (heavy x 4)	1940 / 1941	280 at 13,500	1,980	24,000	1/0 to 960	10 x 0.303in m.g. max bombs 13,000 lb.	6,180 / 2,090
Handley Page Hampden Mk I (medium x 2)	1938	260 at 16,500	1,990	22,700	19/0 to 15,000	6 x 0.303in m.g. max bombs 4,000 lb.	1,530 / 1,410
Short Stirling III (heavy x 4)	1940 / 1941	270 at 14,500	2,000	17,000	?	8 x 0.303in m.g. max bombs 14,000 lb.	2,370 / 880
Vickers Wellington IC (medium x 2)	1938	230 at 15,500	2,550	18,000	1/0 to 1,120	6 x 0.303in m.g. max bombs 4,500 lb.	11,460• / 2,680
USA							
Boeing Flying Fortress B-17F (heavy x 4)	1940 / 1942	325 at 25,000	3,800	35,000	25/40 to 20,000	12 x 0.5in m.g. 1 x 0.3in m.g. max bombs 17,600 lb.	12,700 / 3,400

* 'x 2' indicates number of engines.

† Of which c. 2,100 were bombers. See also Fighters (UK).

• Including 2,320 for Coastal Command.

Bombers (continued)

TYPE	DATE IN SERVICE	SPEED (mph at feet.)	RANGE (miles)	CEILING (feet.)	RATE OF CLIMB (min/sec. to feet.)	ARMAMENT	NUMBER PRODUCED	
USA continued								
Boeing Flying Fortress B-17G (heavy x 4)*	1940 / 1943	300 at 25,000	3,400	35,600	37/0 to 20,000	13 x 0.5in m.g. max bombs 17,600 lb.	12,700 / 6,300	* 'x 4' indicates number of engines.
Boeing Superfortress B-29 (heavy x 4)	1944	360 at 25,000	5,600	31,800	38/0 to 20,000	10 x 0.5in m.g. max bombs 20,000 lb.	3,900 / 2,460	
Consolidated Liberator B-24D (heavy x 4)	1942	300 at 25,000	2,850	32,000	22/0 to 20,000	10 x 0.5in m.g. max bombs 8,800 lb.	18,500 / 2,750	
Consolidated Liberator B-24J (heavy x 4)	1942 / 1943	300 at 30,000	2,100	28,000	25/0 to 20,000	10 x 0.5in m.g. max bombs 8,800 lb.	18,500 / 7,700	
Douglas Havoc A-20G (light x 2)	1941 / 1943	340 at 12,400	1,100	25,800	7/5 to 10,000	10 x 0.5in m.g. max bombs 4,000 lb.	7,480† / 2,850	† Many went to USSR and RAF (where known as Bostons).
Douglas Invader A-26B (light x 2)	1944	350 at 15,000	1,800	31,300	8/5 to 10,000	10 or 18 x 0.5in m.g. max bombs 6,000 lb.	2,450 / 1,350	
Lockheed Hudson A-29/IIIA ● (light x 2)	1939 / 1940	250 at 15,000	2,800	26,500	6/20 to 10,000	5 x 0.3in m.g. max bombs 1,600 lb.	2,930 / c. 800	● Mainly flown by RAF Coastal Command.
Martin Marauder B-26B (medium x 2)	1941 / 1942	320 at 14,500	1,150	23,500	12/0 to 15,000	6 x 0.5in m.g. max bombs 5,200 lb.	4,700 / 1,880	
North American Mitchell B-25J (medium x 2)	1941 / 1943	275 at 13,000	2,700	23,800	19/0 to 15,000	14 x 0.5in m.g. max bombs 3,200 lb.	9,820 / 4,320	
USSR								
Ilyushin Il-4 DB-3F (medium x 2)	1938 / 1940	270 at 22,000	2,350	31,800	12/0 to 22,000	4 x 7.62mm m.g. max bombs 5,500 lb.	6,800 / 5,260	
Tupolev Tu-2S (medium x 2)	1944	340 at 17,700	1,240	31,200	9/30 to 16,400	2 x 20mm cannon 3 x 12.7mm m.g. max bombs 6,600 lb.	c. 1,000 (pre-VJ Day)	

SHIPS

As with Combat Aircraft, the details supplied for naval ships have had to be tightly compressed. Thus:

— Except for submarines and landing craft, no ship smaller than an 'escort' has been included.
— Only details relevant to combat performance are listed. For other details, notably dimensions and a complete armaments breakdown,

recourse must be had to more specialised works, the most important of which are listed in the Bibliography.

— Only ships completed (though not necessarily commissioned) by the end of the war are included.
— For older ships the armament given is that at the beginning of the war.

Table 100 Ships

Aircraft Carriers

* For French ships to June 1940 only and Italian Ships to September 1943 only.

† Sister ships officially.

SHOKAKU + ZUIKAKU MISSING

CLASS	FIRST SHIP COMPLETED	DISPLACEMENT (Standard)	SPEED (knots)	CREW	MAIN ARMAMENT	NUMBER COMPLETED	NUMBER* SUNK
FRANCE 1940							
Béarn	1927	22,150 (unloaded)	21.5	865	Various A.A. 40 aircraft	1	To Vichy June 1940 To US June 1943
JAPAN							
Kaga	1930	38,200	28.3	2,020	10 x 8in. Various A.A. 90 aircraft	1	Sunk 4/6/42
Akagi	1938 (refit)	36,500	31.2	2,000	6 x 8in. Various A.A. 91 aircraft	1	Sunk 5/6/42
Ryujo	1931	10,600	29.0	900	8 x 5in. Various A.A. 48 aircraft	1	Sunk 24/8/42
Soryu †	1935	15,900	34.3	1,100	Various A.A. 73 aircraft	1	Sunk 5/6/42
Hiryu †	1937	17,300	34.5	1,100	Various A.A. 73 aircraft	1	Sunk 5/6/42
Shoho	1941	11,260	28.0	780	Various A.A. 30 aircraft	2	Shoho sunk 8/5/42 Zuiho sunk 25/10/44
Taiyo	1941	17,830	21.0	850	Various A.A. 27 aircraft	3	Onuyo sunk 4/12/43 Taiyo sunk 18/8/44 Unyo sunk 16/9/44
Hiyo	1942	24,140	25.5	1,225	Various A.A. 53 aircraft	2	Hiyo sunk 20/6/44
Ryuho	1942	13,360	26.5	?	8 x 5in. Various A.A. 31 aircraft	1	—
Chiyoda	1943	11,190	29.0	990	Various A.A. 30 aircraft	2	Chiyoda sunk 25/10/44 Chitosi sunk 25/10/44
Kaiyo	1943	13,600	23.8	830	Various A.A. 24 aircraft	1	Sunk 10/8/45
Shinyo	1943	17,500	22.0	950	8 x 5in. Various A.A. 33 aircraft	1	Sunk 17/11/44
Taiho	1944	29,300	33.0	1,750	Various A.A. 53 aircraft	1	Sunk 19/6/44
Shinano	1944	64,800	27.0	2,400	Various A.A. 47 aircraft	1	Sunk 29/11/44
Unryu	1944	17,150	32.0	1,500	Various A.A. 65 aircraft	3	Unryu sunk 19/12/44 Amagi sunk 27/7/45
UNITED KINGDOM							
Courageous	1928	22,500	30.5	1,215	16 x 4.7in. A.A. 48 aircraft	2	Courageous sunk 17/9/39 Glorious sunk 8/6/40
Furious	1925	14,000	20.2	375	6 x 4in. A.A. 30 aircraft	1	—
Eagle	1923	22,600	24.0	750	9 x 6in. Various A.A. 18 aircraft	1	Sunk 11/8/42

Aircraft Carriers (continued)

CLASS	FIRST SHIP COMPLETED	DISPLACEMENT (Standard)	SPEED (knots)	CREW	MAIN ARMAMENT	NUMBER COMPLETED	NUMBER SUNK
UNITED KINGDOM continued							
Hermes	1923	10,850	25.0	660	6 x 5.5in. Various A.A. 9 aircraft	1	Sunk 9/4/42
Ark Royal	1938	22,000	30.7	1,575	Various A.A. 60 aircraft	1	Sunk 14/11/41
Illustrious	1940	4 x 23,000 2 x 26,000	4 x 31.0 2 x 32.0	4 x 1,400 2 x 1,790	Various A.A. 4 x 36 aircraft/ 2 x 72 aircraft	6	—
Colossus	1944	6 x 13,200 4 x 13,350	25.0	1,080	Various A.A. 48 aircraft	10*	—
Archer	1940	4 x 8,200 1 x 9,000	4 x 17.0 1 x 16.5	555	Various A.A. 15 aircraft	5	Avenger sunk 15/11/42 Dasher sunk 27/3/43
Attacker †	1942	11,420	17.0	650	Various A.A. 18 aircraft	8	—
Ruler †	1943	11,420	17.0	650	Various A.A. 24 aircraft	23	—
USA							
Saratoga	1927	33,000	34.0	3,300	8 x 8in. Various A.A. 90 aircraft	2	Lexington sunk 8/5/42
Ranger	1934	14,500	29.5	2,000	8 x 5in. 75 aircraft	1	—
Yorktown	1937	19,900	34.0	2,200	8 x 5in. 100 aircraft	3	Yorktown sunk 7/6/42 Hornet sunk 27/10/42
Wasp	1940	14,700	29.5	1,800	8 x 5in. 85 aircraft	1	Sunk 15/9/42
Essex	1942	27,100	33.0	3,500	12 x 5in. 100 aircraft	17●	—
Independence	1943	11,000	31.6	1,560	26 x 40mm A.A. 45 aircraft	9	Princetown sunk 24/10/44
Bogue	1942	9,800	18.0	890	2 x 5in. 20 x 40mm A.A. 21 aircraft	11	Block Island sunk 29/5/44
Casablanca	1943	7,800	19.2	860	1 x 5in. 16 x 40mm A.A. 28 aircraft	50	4
Commencement Bay	1944	10,900	19.0	1,070	2 x 5in. 36 x 40mm A.A. 34 aircraft	11●	—

* Only 4 operational as combat carriers before end of war. All served in Pacific 1945.

† US built escort carriers. Only 4 escort carriers (Activity, Campania, Vindex and Nairana) were completed in the UK.

● Only those commissioned during the war.

Battleships, Pocket Battleships and Battlecruisers

CLASS	FIRST SHIP COMPLETED	DISPLACEMENT (Standard)	SPEED (knots)	CREW	MAIN ARMAMENT	NUMBER COMPLETED	NUMBER SUNK
FRANCE 1940							
Courbet	1913	23,200	16.0	1,070	12 x 12in. 22 x 5.5in.	2	—
Bretagne	1915	22,200	21.4	1,190	10 x 13.4in. 14 x 5.5in.	2	Bretagne sunk 3/7/40
Lorraine	1916	22,200	21.4	1,190	8 x 13.4in. 14 x 5.5in.	1	—
Dunkerque	1937	26,500	29.5	1,430	8 x 13in. 16 x 5.5in.	2	—
Richelieu	1940	35,000	30.0	1,670	8 x 15in. 9 x 6in.	1	—
GERMANY							
Bismark	1940	1 x 41,700 1 x 42,900	30.0	2,400	8 x 15in. 12 x 5.9in.	2	Bismark sunk 27/5/41 Tirpitz sunk in harbour 12/11/44

Battleships, Pocket Battleships and Battlecruisers (continued)

CLASS	FIRST SHIP COMPLETED	DISPLACEMENT (Standard)	SPEED (knots)	CREW	MAIN ARMAMENT	NUMBER COMPLETED	NUMBER SUNK
GERMANY							
Gneisenau	1938	32,000	31.5	1,800	9 x 11in. 12 x 5.9in.	2	Scharnhorst sunk 26/12/43
Graf Spee*	1933	2 x 12,100 1 x 11,700	26.0	1,150	6 x 11in. 8 x 5.9in.	3	Graf Spee scuttled 17/12/39 Admiral Scheer sunk in harbour 9/4/45 Lützow scuttled 4/5/45
ITALY							
Conte di Cavour	1937 (rebuilt)	26,140	26.0	1,240	10 x 12.6in. 12 x 4.7in.	2	Cavour sunk in harbour 12/11/40
Andrea Doria	1940 (rebuilt)	25,920	26.0	1,490	10 x 12.6in. 12 x 5.3in.	2	—
Littorio	1940	1 x 41,380 1 x 41,170 1 x 41,650	2 x 28.0 1 x 30.0	2 x 1,830 1 x 1,930	9 x 15in. 12 x 6in.	3	—
UNITED KINGDOM							
Queen Elizabeth	1941 (rebuilt)	2 x 31,100 1 x 30,600 2 x 32,700	24.0	1,120	8 x 15in. 8/12 x 6in. or 20 x 4.5in. D.P.	5	Barham sunk 25/11/41
Royal Sovereign †	1931 (rebuilt)	29,150	21.5	1,150	8 x 15in. 12 x 6in.	5	Royal Oak sunk 14/10/39
Repulse	1936 (rebuilt)	32,000	29.0	1,180	6 x 15in. 20 x 4.5in. D.P.	2	Repulse sunk 10/12/41
Hood	1931 (rebuilt)	42,100	31.0	1,340	8 x 15in. 12 x 5.5in.	1	Sunk 24/5/41
Nelson	1927	1 x 33,950 1 x 33,900	23.0	1,310	9 x 16in. 12 x 6in.	2	—
King George V	1940	35,000	29.0	1,560	10 x 14in. 16 x 5.5in. D.P.	5	Prince of Wales sunk 10/12/41
USA							
Arkansas	1926 (rebuilt)	26,100	21.0	1,650	12 x 12in. 16 x 5in.	1	—
Texas	1927 (rebuilt)	27,000	21.0	1,530	10 x 14in. 16 x 5in.	2	—
Oklahoma	1929 (rebuilt)	29,000	20.5	2,100	10 x 14in. 12 x 5in.	2	Nevada sunk 7/12/41, raised and repaired. Oklahoma sunk 7/12/41 ●
Pennsylvania	1931 (rebuilt)	1 x 33,000 1 x 32,600	21.0	2,290	12 x 14in. 12 x 5in.	2	Arizona sunk 7/12/41
New Mexico	1933 (rebuilt)	2 x 33,400 1 x 33,000	21.7	1,930	12 x 14in. 12 x 5in.	3	—
California	1920	32,600	21.0	2,200	12 x 14in. 12 x 5in.	2	California sunk 7/12/41, raised and repaired
Maryland	1923	1 x 31,500 1 x 32,500 1 x 31,800	21.0	2,100	8 x 16in. 10 x 5in.	3	West Virginia sunk 7/12/41, raised and repaired
North Carolina	1941	35,000	28.0	2,500	9 x 16in. 20 x 5in. D.P.	2	—
South Dakota	1942	35,000	28.0	2,500	9 x 16in. 20 x 5in. D.P.	4	—
Iowa	1943	45,000	33.0	2,700	9 x 16in. 20 x 5in. D.P.	4	—
Alaska	1944	27,500	33.0	2,200	9 x 12in. 12 x 5in.	2	—
USSR							
Poltava	1930s (rebuilt)	2 x 25,460 1 x 25,000	23.0	c. 1,300	12 x 12in. 16 x 4.7in.	3∆	—

Left margin notes:

* Lützow (ex-Deutschland) and Admiral Scheer redesignated as heavy cruisers Feb 1940.

† All training/reserve 1944-45.

● Raised but not repaired.

∆ Only 3 out of 9 built still extant 1941.

Cruisers

CLASS	FIRST SHIP COMPLETED	DISPLACEMENT (Standard)	SPEED (knots)	CREW	MAIN ARMAMENT	NUMBER COMPLETED	NUMBER SUNK
AUSTRALIA	Began the war with 3 *Leander* class cruisers (2 lost); 2 *Kent* class (1 lost) and 1 *Birmingham* class. Acquired 1 *London* class 1942. (For details on these classes see United Kingdom below).						
CANADA	Acquired 1 *Minotaur* class cruiser in 1945.						
FRANCE 1940							
Suffren	1930	9,940	33.0	605	8 x 8in. 6 x 21.7in. T.T.	4	—
Duguay-Trouin	1926	7,250	33.0	580	8 x 6.1in. 12 x 21.7in. T.T.	3	—
La Galissonnière	1935	7,600	30.0	540	9 x 6in. 4 x 21.7in. T.T.	6	—
GERMANY							
Admiral Hipper	1939	13,900	32.0	1,600	8 x 8in. 12 x 21in. T.T.	5*	2 (scuttled)
Könisberg	1927	6,650	32.0	820	9 x 5.9in. 12 x 21in. T.T.	3	3
ITALY							
Trento	1928	2 x 10,500 1 x 11,060	2 x 31.0 1 x 34.0	2 x 780 1 x 830	8 x 8in. 8 x 21in. T.T.	3	2
Zara	1931	11,500 to 11,900	29.0	830	8 x 8in. 16 x 3.9in.	4	4
da Barbiano†	1931	5,200	30.0	520	8 x 6in. 4 x 21in. T.T.	4	4
Cadorna†	1933	5,400	38.0	540	8 x 6in. 4 x 21in. T.T.	2	1
Montecuccoli†	1935	7,550	34.0	650	8 x 6in. 4 x 21in. T.T.	2	1
Aosta†	1935	8,660	34.0	690	8 x 6in. 6 x 21in. T.T.	2	—
Garibaldi†	1937	9,960	31.0	890	10 x 6in. 6 x 21in. T.T.	2	—
Capitani Romani	1941	3,750	43.0	420	8 x 5.3in. 8 x 21in. T.T.	3	—
JAPAN							
Kuma	1921	5,870	31.7	440	7 x 5.5in. 8 x 24in. T.T.	5	4
Nagara	1924	5,170	36.0	440	7 x 5.5in. 8 x 24in. T.T.	6	6
Sendai	1924	5,195	35.2	450	7 x 5.5in. 8 x 24in. T.T.	3	3
Myoko	1928	13,380	33.7	775	10 x 8in. 16 x 24in. T.T.	4	4
Takao	1931	13,160	34.2	775	10 x 8in. 16 x 24in. T.T.	4	4
Mogami	1935	12,400	34.7	850	10 x 8in. 12 x 24in. T.T.	4	4
Agano	1942	6,650	35.0	730	6 x 6.1in. 8 x 24in. T.T.	4	3
NEW ZEALAND	Began the war with 2 *Leander* class cruisers and acquired 1 *Fiji* class cruiser 1943. (For details on these classes see United Kingdom below.)						

* One sold to Russians 1940.

† All sub-groupings of the *Condottieri* class.

Cruisers (continued)

CLASS	FIRST SHIP COMPLETED	DISPLACEMENT (Standard)	SPEED (knots)	CREW	MAIN ARMAMENT	NUMBER COMPLETED	NUMBER SUNK
UNITED KINGDOM							
Ceres	1918	4,190	29.0	400	5 x 6in. 8 x 21in. T.T.	5	3
Capetown	1919	4,290	29.0	400	8 x 4in. A.A.	5	2
Birmingham	1919	9,770 to 9,860	30.5	710	5 or 7 x 7.5in. 4 or 6 x 21in. T.T.	5*	1
'D'	1918	4,850	29.0	450	6 x 6in. 12 x 21in. T.T.	8	2 (as breakwaters)
Kent	1927	9,750 to 9,870	31.5	680	8 x 8in. 8 x 21in. T.T.	7	2
London	1928	2 x 9,830 2 x 9,850	32.2	650	8 x 8in. 8 x 21in. T.T.	4	—
Leander	1932	6,830 to 7,270	32.5	550	8 x 6in. 8 x 21in. T.T.	8	3
Arethusa	1935	2 x 5,220 2 x 5,270	32.2	450	6 x 6in. 6 x 21in. T.T.	4	2
Southampton	1937	5 x 9,100 3 x 9,400 2 x 10,000	7 x 32.0 3 x 32.5	8 x 700 2 x 850	12 x 6in. 6 x 21in. T.T.	10	4
Dido	1940	11 x 5,450 5 x 5,770	33.0	11 x 530 5 x 535	8 or 10 x 5.25in. 6 x 21in. T.T.	16	5
Fiji	1940	8 x 8,000 3 x 8,800	33.0	730	9 or 12 x 6in. 6 x 21in. T.T.	11	2
USA							
Northampton	1930	4 x 9,050 1 x 9,300 1 x 9,200	32.7	1,100	9 x 8in.	6	3
Astoria	1934	9,375 to 9,975	32.7	1,050	9 x 8in.	7	3
Baltimore	1943	15 x 13,600 4 x 13,700	33.0	1,700	9 x 8in.	19	
Omaha	1921	7,050	34.0	800	10 x 6in. 6 x 21in. T.T.	10	—
Brooklyn	1937	9,475 to 10,000	34.0	1,300	15 x 6in. 8 x 5in.	9	1
Atlanta	1942	6,000	32.0	800	12/16 x 5in. D.P. 10/16 x 40mm. A.A.	11	2
Cleveland-Fargo	1942	10,000	33.0	1,200	12 x 16in. 12 x 5in.	38	—
USSR							
Kirov	1938	2 x 8,800 4 x 8,177	35.0	2 x 730 4 x 950	9 x 7.1in. 6 x 21in. T.T.	6	—

* One lost 1922

Destroyers

CLASS	FIRST SHIP COMPLETED	DISPLACEMENT (Standard)	SPEED (knots)	CREW	MAIN ARMAMENT	NUMBER COMPLETED	NUMBER SUNK
AUSTRALIA	The Royal Australian Navy possessed no destroyers at the start of the war but during its course it built or received 3 *Tribal* class (1941, 43, 45), 4 *'N'* class (1940-45), and 5 *'Q'* class (1942-45). Of these, one *'N'* class was lost (1942). For details on these classes see United Kingdom below.						
CANADA	The Royal Canadian Navy possessed 2 *'A'* class and 5 *'C'* class destroyers at the start of the war of which one *'A'* class was lost (1944) and 2 *'C'* class (1940 and 1942). During the war it acquired a further 2 of each of the *'D', 'F'* and *'V'* classes, one each of the *'E', 'G'* and *'H'* classes and 6 *Tribal* class (2 built in Canada). Of these one *'D'* class was lost (1940) and one *Tribal* (1944).						

Destroyers (continued)

CLASS	FIRST SHIP COMPLETED	DISPLACEMENT (Standard)	SPEED (knots)	CREW	MAIN ARMAMENT	NUMBER COMPLETED	NUMBER SUNK
FRANCE 1940							
Chacal	1926	2,130	35.5	195	4 x 5.1in. 6 x 21.7in. T.T.	6	2
Guepard	1929	2,436	35.5	230	5 x 5.5in. 6 x 21.7in. T.T.	6	1
Aigle	1931	2,440	36.0	230	5 x 5.5in. 6 x 21.7in. T.T.	6	—
Vauquelin	1932	2,440	36.0	230	5 x 5.5in. 7 x 21.7in. T.T.	6	1
Le Fantasque	1935	2,570	37.0	210	5 x 5.5in. 9 x 21.7in. T.T.	6	—
Bourrasque	1926	1,320	29.0	140	4 x 5.1in. 6 x 21.7in. T.T.	12	3
L'Adroit	1928	1,380	29.0	138	4 x 5.1in. 6 x 21.7in. T.T.	14	2
Le Hardi	1940	1,770	37.0	185	6 x 5.1in. 7 x 21.7in. T.T.	8	—
GERMANY							
Z23-Z34	1940	2,600	38.5	320	4 x 5.9in. 8 x 21in. T.T.	12	6
von Roeder	1938	2,400	38.0	310	4 x 5in. 8 x 21in. T.T.	6	5
Leberecht Maas	1937	2,200	30.0	315	5 x 5in. 8 x 21in. T.T.	16	10
INDIA	The Royal Indian Navy operated no destroyers during the war.						
ITALY							
Turbine	1927	1,090	33.0	180	4 x 4.7in. 6 x 21in. T.T.	8	7
Navigatori	1929	1,940	32.0	220	6 x 4.7in. 6 x 21in. T.T. (4)	12	7
Soldati	1938	1,715 to 1,845	34 or 35	220	5 x 4.7in. (4) 6 x 21in. T.T.	17	9
JAPAN							
Minekazi	1920	1,215	39.0	150	4 x 4.7in. 6 x 21in. T.T.	13	8
Mutsuki	1926	1,315	37.0	150	4 x 4.7in. 6 x 24in. T.T.	12	12
Fabuki	1930	2,090	34.0	200	6 x 5in. D.P./S.P. 9 x 24in. T.T.	19	19
Shiratsuyu	1936	1,580	34.0	180	5 x 5in. D.P. 8 x 24in. T.T.	10	10
Asashio	1937	1,960	35.0	200	5 x 6in. D.P. 8 x 24in. T.T.	10	10
Kagero	1939	2,030	35.5	240	6 x 5in. D.P. 8 x 24in. T.T.	18	17
Yagumo	1942	2,080	35.5	230	6 x 5in. D.P. 8 x 24in. T.T.	20	20
Matsu	1944	1,260	27.7	?	3 x 5in. 4 x 24in. T.T.	24	10
NEW ZEALAND	The Royal New Zealand Navy operated no destroyers during the war.						

Destroyers (continued)

CLASS	FIRST SHIP COMPLETED	DISPLACEMENT (Standard)	SPEED (knots)	CREW	MAIN ARMAMENT	NUMBER COMPLETED	NUMBER SUNK
UNITED KINGDOM*							
'C' & 'D'	1932	1,375	35.5	145	4 x 4.7in. 8 x 21in. T.T.	12	9
'E' & 'F'	1934	8 x 1,375 8 x 1,350	35.5	145	4 x 4.7in. 8 x 21in. T.T.	16	9
'G' & 'H'	1936	1,340	35.5	145	4 x 4.7in. 8 x 21in. T.T.	16	11
Tribal	1938	20 x 1,870 5 x 1,930	36.0	190 to 250	8 x 4.7in. (20)or 6 x 4.7in. (5) 4 x 21in. T.T.	25†	13
'J', 'K' & 'N'	1939	1,690	36.0	185	6 x 4.7in. 10 x 21in. T.T.	24	12
'L' & 'M'	1940	1,920	36.0	220	6 x 4.7in. D.P. 8 x 21in. T.T.	16	10
'O' & 'P'	1941	1,540	36.7	175	4 x 4.7in. 8 x 21in. T.T.	16	5
'Q' & 'R'	1942	1,705	36.7	175	4 x 4.7in. 8 x 21in. T.T.	16	2
'S' & 'T'	1943	1,710	36.7	180	4 x 4.7in. 8 x 21in. T.T.	16	2
'U' & 'V'	1943	1,710	36.7	180	4 x 4.7in. 8 x 21in. T.T.	16	1
'W' & 'Z'	1943	1,710	36.7	185	4 x 4.7in. (8)or 4 x 4.5in. D.P. (8) 8 x 21in. T.T.	16	—
USA							
'Flush-Deck'	Most of these ships that served as destroyers did so as escorts with the Royal Navy to whom 50 were transferred in 1940. See Escorts: United Kingdom: *Town* class below.						
Benson-Livermore	1940	30 x 1,620 66 x 1,630	37.0	250	4 x 5in. 10 x 21in. T.T.	96	15
Fletcher	1942	2,050	37.0	300	5 x 5in. 10 x 21in. T.T.	176	19
Allan M. Sumner	1943	2,200	36.5	350	6 x 5in. 10 x 21in. T.T.	68 ‡	4
Gearing	1944	2,425	35.0	350	6 x 5in. 10 x 21in. T.T.	28	—
USSR							
Leningrad	1936	2,150	36.0	250	5 x 5.1in. 8 x 21in. T.T.	6	2
'Type 7'	1938	1,695	38.0	240	4 x 5.1in. 6 x 21in. T.T.	29	10
'Type 7U'	1940	1,685	36.0	205	4 x 5.1in. 6 x 21in. T.T.	18	9

Escorts•

CLASS	FIRST SHIP COMPLETED	DISPLACEMENT (Standard)	SPEED (knots)	CREW	MAIN ARMAMENT	NUMBER COMPLETED	NUMBER SUNK
AUSTRALIA	Four *Grimsby* class sloops were built in Australia. Two were lost. Also built were 12 *River* class frigates. None were lost. (For details of these classes see United Kingdom below.)						
CANADA	Escort ships built in Canada comprised 80 *Flower* class corvettes, 39 modified *Flower* class and 70 *River* class frigates. The Royal Canadian Navy also received 4 modified *Flower* class and 12 *Castle* class corvettes as well as 7 *River* class frigates. It lost 8 *Flower* class and one modified *Flower* class. (For details of these classes see United Kingdom below.)						

Escorts• (continued)

CLASS	FIRST SHIP COMPLETED	DISPLACEMENT (Standard)	SPEED (knots)	CREW	MAIN ARMAMENT	NUMBER COMPLETED	NUMBER SUNK
UNITED KINGDOM							
E.D. Hunt (Type 1)	1939	910	26.0	145	4 x 4in. A.A.	20	4
E.D. Hunt (Type 2)	1940	1,050	25.0	170	6 x 4in. A.A.	36	6
E.D. Hunt (Type 3)	1941	1,090	25.0	170	4 x 4in. A.A. 2 x 21in. T.T.	28	10
S. B./H./S./F. *	1929	1,045 to 1,105	16.0	100	2 x 4in. A.A.	15	1
S. Grimsby	1934	990 to 1,060	16.5	100	2 x 4.7in. or 3/4 x 4in. A.A.	9	2
S. Black Swan	1939	13 x 1,300 24 x 1,350	13 x 19.2 24 x 20	13 x 180 24 x 190	6 x 4in. A.A.	37	5
C. Flower	1940	925	16.0	85	1 x 4in.	136	21
C. Flower (modified)	1943	980	16.0	110	1 x 4in. 1 x 'Hedgehog' A.T.W.	10	—
C. Castle	1944	1,010	16.5	120	1 x 4in. 1 x 'Squid' A.T.W.	44	3
F. River	1942	1,370	20.0	140	2 x 4in 1 x 'Hedgehog' A.T.W.	69	4
F. Loch/Bay	1945	21 x 1,435 17 x 1,580	20.0	21 x 115 17 x 155	1 x 4in. (21) or 4 x 4in. A.A. (17) 2 x 'Squid' (21) or 1 x 'Hedgehog' (17)	69	4
USA							
E.D. Evarts	1942	1,140	21.0	170	3 x 3in.	98†	6 (6)‡
E.D. Buckley	1943	1,400	23.5	220	3 x 3in. 3 x 21in. T.T.	149†**	6 (3)‡
E.D. Cannon	1943	1,240	21.0	200	3 x 3in. 3 x 21in. T.T.	66	—
E.D. Edsall	1943	1,200	21.0	200	3 x 3in. 3 x 21in. T.T.	85	3
E.D. John C. Butler	1944	1,350	24.0	200	2 x 5in. 3 x 21in. T.T.	85	4
F. Tacoma	1943	1,430	20.0	180	2 or 3 x 3in.	95†	—

Submarines

CLASS	FIRST SHIP COMPLETED	DISPLACEMENT• (Standard)	SPEED • (knots)	CREW	MAIN ARMAMENT	RADIUS OF ACTION* (miles at knots)	NUMBER COMPLETED	NUMBER LOST△
GERMANY								
VIIC	1940	769 871	17.0 7.5	44	1 x 3.5in. 5 x 21in. T.T. 14 torpedoes	6,500 at 12 80 at 4	603	482
IXC	1940	1,120 1,232	18.2 7.2	48	1 x 4.1in. 6 x 21in. T.T. 22 torpedoes	11,000 at 12 63 at 4	144◊	117
XXI	1944	1,612 1,819	15.5 16.0	57	4 x 30mm A.A. 6 x 21in. T.T. 23 torpedoes	11,150 at 12 285 at 6	124	26
ITALY								
Marcello	1938	1,063 1,317	18.1 8.3	60	2 x 3.9in. 8 x 21in. T.T. 16 torpedoes	7,500 at 9.4 120 at 3.0	9	7
Adua	1936	698 866	14.0 8.4	45	1 x 3.9in. 6 x 21in. T.T. 12 torpedoes	3,180 at 10.5 74 at 4.0	17	13
Acciaio	1941	714 871	15.0 6.7	50	1 x 3.9in. 6 x 21in. T.T. 8 torpedoes	5,000 at 8.5 80 at 3.0	13	9

• E.D.= escort destroyer
S.= sloop (minesweepers not included)
C.= corvette
F.= frigate

* *Bridgewater, Hastings, Shoreham* and *Falmouth* classes.

† These figures include the following ships transferred to the Royal Navy: *Evarts* class 30 *Buckley* class 47 *Tacoma* class 21.

‡ Figure in brackets is ships in Royal Navy.

** 37 became APD high speed transports.

* The top figure in these columns refers to surface details and the bottom to submerged.

△ Excludes scuttling at end of war.

◊ Figure includes 48 almost identical Type IXC40, introduced in 1942.

Submarines (continued)

* The top figure in these columns refers to surface details and the bottom to submerged.

† Excludes scuttling at end of war.

CLASS	FIRST SHIP COMPLETED	DISPLACEMENT* (Standard)	SPEED* (knots)	CREW	MAIN ARMAMENT	RADIUS OF ACTION* (miles at knots)	NUMBER COMPLETED	NUMBER LOST†
JAPAN								
I-15	1939	2,584 3,654	23.5 8.0	100	1 x 5.5in. 6 x 21in. T.T. 17 torpedoes	16,000 at 16 96 at 3	20	19
Ro-100	1942	601 702	14.0 8.0	75	1 x 3in. 4 x 21in. T.T. 5 torpedoes	3,500 at 12 60 at 3	18	18
I-176	1941	1,833 2,602	23.0 8.0	80	1 x 4.7in. 6 x 21in. T.T. 12 torpedoes	8,000 at 16 50 at 5	10	10
Ro-35	1942	1,115 1,447	19.7 8.0	80	1 x 3in. 4 x 21in. T.T. 10 torpedoes	5,000 at 16 45 at 5	18	17
I-361	1943	1,780 2,215	13.0 6.5	75	1 x 5.5in. (transport boats)	15,000 at 10 120 at 3	11	9
UNITED KINGDOM								
'S' (II)	1942	715 990	14.7 9.0	44	1 x 3in. 7 x 21in. T.T. 12 torpedoes	3,800 or 6,000 at 10 ?	51	9
'T'	1938	1,090 1,580	15.0 or 15.2 9.0	59 or 65	1 x 4in. 11 x 21in. T.T. 17 torpedoes	8,000 at 10 ?	52	16
'U'	1938	540 or 545 730 or 740	11.7 or 11.2 9.0	31	1 x 3in. 4 x 21in. T.T. 8 or 10 torpedoes	4,050 at 10 ?	49	20
USA								
Gato	1941	1,525 2,415	20.2 10.0	80	1 x 5in. 10 x 21in. T.T. 24 torpedoes	11,800 at 10 95 at 5	87	29

Landing Craft/Ships (US types only)

• The British Landing Craft Infantry (Small) carried 96 troops and 18 bicycles.

TYPE	SPEED (knots)	LOAD	NUMBER BUILT
Landing Craft Infantry (Large)• (LCI(L))	12.5	205 troops and 35 tons	920
Landing Craft Mechanised (LCM)	Mk. 3 ? Mk. 6 ?	30 tons 30 tons	8,630 2,720
Landing Craft Personnel (Large) (LCP(L))	9.0	36 troops	2,190
Landing Craft Personnel (Ramp) (LCP(R))	9.0	36 troops	2,630
Landing Craft Support (Large) (LCS(L))	11.5	Provided light artillery fire support	130
Landing Craft Support (Small) (LCS(S))	?	Control craft to lead in DD tanks	558
Landing Craft Tank (LCT)	Mk.5 10 Mk.6 10	4 x 40 or 3 x 50 ton tanks	470 965
Landing Craft Vehicles & Personnel (LCVP)	?	36 troops or 3 tons	23,358
Landing Ship Medium (LSM)	12.5	150 tons	539
Landing Ship Tank (LST)	9.0	300 troops and 60 tanks	1,040
Landing Vehicle Tracked (LVT)	4 knots 15 m.p.h.	20 men or 2.8 tons	15,500
Landing Vehicle Tracked (Armoured) (LVT(A))	as above	Mk.1 fire support only Rest as above	510 2,610

Merchant Ships Standardised Allied Types

CLASS	FIRST SHIP COMPLETED	TONNAGE Δ	SPEED (knots)	SHAFT HORSEPOWER	RADIUS	NUMBER COMPLETED	NUMBER LOST
C2 General Cargo	1938	3,730 8,510	15.5	6,000	16,200	} c.500	?
C3 General Cargo	1938	5,700 12,930	17.0	8,500	12,500		?
EC2 'Liberty' General Cargo	1941	4,380 10,800	11.0	2,500 ◊	17,000	2,710	200+
VC2 'Victory' General Cargo	1943	4,550 10,850	15.0 – 17.0	8,500	20,500	414	3
T2 Tanker	1941	6,107 16,765 (141,200)	14.5	6,000	12,600	636	?
T3 Tanker	1939	6,646 18,302 (133,800)	18.0	13,500	11,900	58	1

Δ First figure is net tonnage, second figure is deadweight tonnage, third figure in brackets (where appropriate) is capacity in 42-gallon barrels.

◊ Indicated horsepower.

TANKS

As with the previous sub-sections on weaponry, entries here are limited to major combat types. Two further points should be borne in mind:

— Details on tank guns' capabilities will be found in a separate sub-

section, TANK AND ANTI-TANK GUNS, following this one.
— Details on self-propelled guns and tank destroyers are also given in a separate sub-section.

Table 101 Tanks

TYPE	DATE IN* SERVICE	WEIGHT (tons)	ENGINE H.P.	MAX SPEED (m.p.h.)	RADIUS (miles)	GUN	THICKNESS OF ARMOUR (mm.)			NUMBER† PRODUCED
							Hull side	Hull front	Turret (max)	
FRANCE 1940										
FCM 21	PW	15.5	120	11	110	75mm.	max 25mm.			90
Renault R35	PW	11.0	83	12.5	50	37mm.	40	30	45	900
Renault D1	PW	14.0	100	12	60	47mm.	?	30	40	} 260
Renault D2	PW	20.0	150	14	95	47mm.	?	30	40	
Renault B1 *bis*	PW	31.0	307	18	130	75mm. + 47mm.	60	60	56	300
Somua 35S	PW	19.5	190	29	145	47mm.	40	35	56	400
GERMANY										
Panzer IA	PW	5.4	57	23	90	m.g.	13	13	13	1,500
Panzer IIC	PW	8.9	140	25	125	20mm.	14.5	14.5	14.5	650
Panzer IIF	1941	9.5	140	25	125	20mm.	15	35	30	?
Panzer IIIG	PW / 1940	20.3	300	25	110	50mm. short	30	30	30	5,500
Panzer IIIJ ('Special')	1941	22.3	300	25	110	50mm. long	30	50	30	?
Panzer IVD	PW / 1939	20.0	300	25	125	75mm. short	14.5	14.5	30	8,000
Panzer IVF² ('Special')	1942	23.6	300	25	125	75mm. long	40	50	50	?
Panzer VG	1943 / 1944	44.8	700	29	110	75mm.	50	80	100	5,500
Panzer VI 'Tiger' I	1942	55.0	700	24	65	88mm.	60	100	100	1,350
Panzer VI 'Tiger' II	1944	69.7	700	24	70	88mm.	80	100	180	380
Panzer 35(t)	PW	10.5	120	22	120	37mm.	16	25	25	160
Panzer 38(t)B	1940	9.5	150	26	155	37mm.	15	25	30	1,170
ITALY										
L3	PW	3.2	43	26	75	m.g.	8.5	13.5	?	2,500
M11/39	1940	11.0	105	21	125	37/40mm	14.5	30	30	100
M13/40	1940	14.0	125	20	125	47/32mm	25	30	40	800

* PW= pre-war. Where two dates are given, first is when type entered service and second the particular model.

† Number produced for whole series.

* PW= pre-war. Where two dates are given, first is when type entered service and second the particular model.

† Number produced for whole series.

• All medium tanks (inc. Type 89).

Δ Number in service 1939.

◊ Only 4 armoured regiments converted to Comet by end of war.

‡ Known as the Grant to British and Commonwealth forces.

** Number with 75mm or 76mm guns.

†† In 1944 both the American M4A1/2/3 (76mm) and the British Sherman IIC 'Firefly' were fitted with a 76mm gun.

•• Only twenty Pershings ever saw combat in the Second World War.

TYPE	DATE IN* SERVICE	WEIGHT (tons)	ENGINE H.P.	MAX SPEED (m.p.h.)	RADIUS (miles)	GUN	THICKNESS OF ARMOUR (mm.)			NUMBER† PRODUCED
							Hull side	Hull front	Turret (max)	
JAPAN										
95	1935	8.5	70	30	110	37mm	11	14	11	?
97 Chiha	1934	14.0	170	24	130	57mm	20	25	?	} 2,580•
97 Shinhoto Chiha	1937	15.0	170	28	130	47mm	20	25	33	
POLAND										
TKS	PW	2.6	42	25	?	m.g.	3 to 10mm			300Δ
Vickers Mk.E	PW	7.4	92	22	130	47mm	5 to 13mm			38Δ
7TPjw	PW	9.9	110	23	?	37mm	5 to 17mm			95Δ
UNITED KINGDOM										
Matilda II	1939	26.5	2 x 87	15	160	2pdr.	65	78	75	2,990
Crusader I	1941	19.0	340	27	100	2pdr.	27	40	39	4,750
Crusader II	1941	19.0	340	27	100	2pdr.	27	51	51	—
Valentine II	1941	17.5	131	15	90	2pdr.	60	60	65	8,280
Churchill VII	1942 / 1944	40.00	350	12.5	90	75mm	76	152	89	5,640
Cromwell IV	1943	27.5	600	32	170	75mm	32	63	76	c. 3,000
Comet	1944	35.0	600	29	125	77mm	32	76	101	?◊
USA										
M3 General Stuart	1941	12.2	220 or 250	36	70	37mm	25	38	38	c. 14,000
M3A1 Lee ‡	1941	26.8	340	26	120	75mm+ 37mm	38	51	57	7,400
M4A3 Sherman	1942	31.0	500	25	100	75mm	51	51	76	41,530**
M4A3 (76mm) Sherman	1944	31.7	500	25	100	76mm††	51	51	76	—
M26 Pershing	1945	46	500	30	110	90mm	76.2	101	101	?••
USSR										
KV1 Model 42	PW / 1942	47.0	600	17.5	155	76.2	90 to 130	110	120	3,010
T34 Model 42	1940 / 1942	28.5	500	34	250	76.2	47	47	65	35,120
T34/85	1944	32.0	500	34	225	85	60	47	90	29,430
IS2	1944	46.0	600	23	150	122	120	95	160	3,850

Table 102 Tank and Anti-Tank Guns

GUN	THICKNESS OF ARMOUR (mm) PENETRATED AT: (yards)					
	250	500	750	1,000	1,500	2,000
FRANCE						
25mm SA-L 1934	Muzzle velocity: 950 metres per second. Range: 1,800 metres. Weight shell: 0.3 kilograms.					
37mm short SA I8	?	?	?	30	—	—
37mm long SA 38	Muzzle velocity: 690 metres per second.					
47mm short SA 34	Muzzle velocity: ?					
47mm long SA 35	Muzzle velocity: 660 metres per second.					
47mm long SA 37 & 39	?	?	80	?	?	?
GERMANY						
37mm Kwk L/46.5	32(40)*	28(28)	—			—
50mm short Kwk 38	56(83)	53(60)	46(42)	40	28	22
50mm long Kwk 39 and PAK 38	67(109)	61(77)	56(46)	50	38	29
75mm short Kwk 37	all	46(75)	42(75)	41(75)	33	30
75mm long Kwk 40 L/43 and PAK 43	all	92(108)	?	82 (87)	72(69)	63
75mm long Kwk 40 L/48 and PAK 39	all	96(120)	?	85 (97)	74(77)	64
88mm Kwk 36 and PAK 36	all	110(156)	?	100(138)	91(123)	84(110)
ITALY						
20mm towed	29	24	—	—	—	—
37/40mm	?	?	?	32	?	?
47/32mm	?	48 (at 400yd)	38	32	?	?
JAPAN						
20mm a/t rifle Type 97	30 (at 270yd)	?	—	—	—	—
37mm Type 94	?	?	?	24	—	—
37mm Type 98	Muzzle velocity: 665 metres per second.					
47mm Type 1	?	51	?	—	—	—
57mm Type 97	Muzzle velocity: 420 metres per second.					
POLAND						
7.92mm wz. 35-Marosczet	20 (at 300m)	—	—	—	—	—
37mm wz.36	40 (at 100m)	33	?	26	—	—

GUN	THICKNESS OF ARMOUR (mm) PENETRATED AT: (yards)					
	250	500	750	1,000	1,500	2,000
UNITED KINGDOM & USA						
14mm Boys	21 (at 300yd)	?	—	—	—	—
2pdr. (shot)	58	52	46	40	—	—
2pdr. (high velocity shot)	64	57	51	45	—	—
37mm	58	53	48	47	—	—
6pdr.	all	79	72	65	52	—
17pdr.	all	all	120	113	96	82
75mm M2 firing:14AP M72	all	61	?	53	46	38
75mm M2 firing M61	all	66	?	61	56	51
75mm M3 firing M61	all	66	?	61	56	51
76mm	all	all	all	98	?	?
25pdr.(towed) firing 20AP shot	all	63	58	54	?	?
USSR						
37mm	?	38 (at 400yd)	?	?	—	—
45mm	all	80	?	50	?	—
57mm	all	140	?	?	?	?
76mm F-34 firing DS a.p.	all	92	?	60	?	?
85mm D-5	all	138	?	100	?	?
100mm D-10 firing HE a.p.	all	195	?	185	?	?
122mm M-30 firing HE a.p.	all	145	145	145	?	?

* (left-hand column) Figure in brackets is thickness pierced using *Panzergranate* 40 ammunition.

ARTILLERY

The guns dealt with in this sub-section are divided into two basic categories: towed and self-propelled. The former are all artillery types proper but the list of self-propelled guns also contains German assault guns as well as self-propelled anti-tank guns (or tank destroyers).

Table 103 Artillery

Towed

GUN	WEIGHT IN ACTION (kg)	LENGTH BORE (mm)	WEIGHT SHELL (kg)	MAXIMUM MUZZLE VELOCITY (mtrs per sec.)	MAXIMUM RANGE (metres)
FRANCE					
75mm 1897	1,140	2,587*	6.2	575	11,100
105mm 1913	1,985	2,305*	10.0	670	15,150
105mm 1934S	1,722	1,948*	15.7	465	10,700
GERMANY					
75mm 1e IG 18	400	783	6.0	210	3,375
100mm SK 18	5,642	5,173	15.1	835	19,075
105mm 1e FH 18	1,985	2,612	14.8	470	10,675
105mm 1e FH 18m	2,040	2,612	14.8 †	540	12,325
105mm 1e FH 18/40	1,955	2,710	14.8	540	12,325
150mm s FH 18	5,512	4,125	43.5	495	13,250
150mm s IG 33	1,700	1,346	38.0	240	4,700
ITALY					
47/32mm 35	277	1,328	2.4	250	4,300
65/17mm	556	905	4.2	348	6,500
75/27mm 06	1,015	1,744	6.3	502	10,240
75/27mm II	1,076	1,748	6.3	502	10,240
JAPAN					
37mm Type 94	321	1,686*	0.5	700	4,570
70mm Type 92	212	622*	3.8	198	2,745
75mm Type 38 (Improved)	1,135	2,286•	6.0	603	11,970
105mm Type 91	1,500	2,540•	15.8	546	10,771
105mm Type 92	3,732	4,681•	15.8	760	18,300
150mm Type 92	16,500	?	36.0	?	19,800
240mm Type 45	?	?	90.0	?	9,900
POLAND					
75mm wz. 97	1,200	36Δ	7.9	?	11,200
75mm wz. 02/26	1,100	30Δ	7.9	?	10,700
100mm wz. 14/19	1,500	24Δ	16.0	?	10,000
105mm wz. 29	2,800	31Δ	15.7	?	15,200
120mm wz. 09/31	3,500	27Δ	20.3	?	12,400
155mm wz. 17	3,300	15Δ	43.4	?	11,200
UNITED KINGDOM					
25pdr. Mk II	1,801	1,886	11.3	532	12,253

* Length barrel.

† With special charge.

* Length barrel.

• Length piece.

Δ x Calibre.

Towed continued

GUN	WEIGHT IN ACTION (kg)	LENGTH BORE (mm)	WEIGHT SHELL (kg)	MAXIMUM MUZZLE VELOCITY (mtrs per sec.)	MAXIMUM RANGE (metres)
UNITED KINGDOM					
5.5 inch Medium	6,141	4,166	36 or 45	585	16,290
6 inch Howitzer	4,168	2,027	38.7	423	10,260
7.2 inch Howitzer Mk II	10,242	6,048	90	577	17,640
USA					
105mm Howitzer M2A1	2,241	2,362	14.8	465	10,984
155mm Howitzer M1	5,385	3,100	42.7	555	14,720
155mm Howitzer M1A1	13,770	6,975	42.7	840	22,855
240mm Howitzer M1	29,115	?	162.0	690	22,702
USSR					
76.2mm 76-27	780	1,168	6.2	387	8,555
76.2mm 76-43	600	1,168	6.2	387	8,555
76.2mm 02/30	1,320	2,196	6.4	635	12,400
76.2mm 76-36	1,350	1,905	6.4	706	13,580
76.2mm 76-42 Zis 3	1,120	2,994*	6.2	680	13,290
85mm D-44	1,725	4,657†	9.5	793	15,500
122mm Howitzer 1938	2,450	2,800†	21.8	515	11,800
152mm Gun Howitzer 1937 (ML-20)	7,128	4,404†	43.6	655 (H/E)	17,265
152mm Field Howitzer 1938r	4,150	3,700†	51.5	432(H/E) 508(A/P)	12,400

* Length barrel.

† Length piece.

Self-propelled Guns

Included in this category are German assault guns and all self-propelled anti-tank guns (or tank destroyers). Details on the various guns' capabilities will be found in the ARTILLERY (Towed) and TANK AND ANTI-TANK GUN sub-sections above, though space has not permitted the inclusion of details of every type in the list below. Those for which details are not given are marked thus ■.

In the FUNCTION column below, AG= Assault Gun, SP=Self-propelled Artillery, TD= Tank Destroyer.

DESIGNATION	FUNCTION	GUN	CARRIAGE/ CHASSIS
GERMANY			
Marder II	TD	75mm PAK 40	Pz II
Marder III	TD	75mm PAK 40	Pz 38(t)
Sd Kfz 138	TD	75mm PAK 40	Pz 38(t) (redesigned)
Hetzer	TD	75mm PAK 39	Pz 38(t)
StuG Ausf. G	AG	75mm StuK 40■	Pz III
Sd Kfz 167	AG	75mm StuK 40■	Pz IV
Pz IV/70 (V)	TD	75mm PAK 43	Pz IV
Sd Kfz 132	TD	76.2mm PAK 36(r)•	Pz II
Marder VII/VIII	TD	76.2mm PAK 36(r)•	Pz 38(t)
Nashorn	TD	88mm PAK 43	Pz IV
Jagdpanther	TD	88mm PAK 43	Pz V

DESIGNATION	FUNCTION	GUN	CARRIAGE/ CHASSIS
GERMANY			
Ferdinand/Elefant	TD	88mm PAK 43	Pz VI (I)
StuH 42	SP	105mm StuH 42■	Pz III
Wespe	SP	105mm le FH 18	Pz II
Jagdtiger	TD	128mm PAK 44■	Pz VI (II)
Grille	SP	150mm sIG 33	Pz 38(t)
Hummel	SP	150mm sFH 18	Pz IV
ITALY			
L40	SP	47/32mm 35	L6/40
M40 M41 M42	TD	75/18mm 35■	M13/40 M14/41 M15/42

• (left-hand column) Captured models of the Russian 76mm anti-tank gun.

Self-propelled Guns continued

DESIGNATION	FUNCTION	GUN	CARRIAGE/CHASSIS
UNITED KINGDOM & USA			
M3 75mm Autocar*	SP	75mm M1897A■	M3 Half-track
M8	SP	75mm M1A1■	M5 Stuart
M18 'Hellcat'	TD	76mm M1	own
M10 Wolverine	TD	3inch M7■ †	M4 Sherman
Archer	TD	17pdr	Valentine
Sexton	SP	25pdr	M3 Ram•
M36	TD	90mm M3■	M4 Sherman
M4	SP	105mm M2A1	M4 Sherman
M7 (Priest)	SP	105mm M2A1	M3 Lee
M7 B1	SP	105mm M2A1	M4 Sherman
M12	SP	155mm M1A1	M3 Lee

DESIGNATION	FUNCTION	GUN	CARRIAGE/CHASSIS
USSR			
SU-76M	SP	76.2mm Zis-3	T-70M
SU-85	TD	85mm D-5S	T-34
SU-100	TD	100mm D-10S	T-34
SU-122	AG	122mm M30-S	T-34
SU-152	TD/SP	152mm ML-20	KV-1S
ISU-122	TD/SP	122mm A-195■	IS-1
ISU-152	TD/SP	152mm ML-20	IS-1

* British designation.

† Many British Wolverines substituted the 17pdr. anti-tank gun and were then known as Achilles.

• Canadian version of M3 Lee.

ROCKETS/MISSILES 'Strategic'

TYPE	POWER	CONTROL	MAX SPEED (m.p.h.)	RANGE (miles)	WARHEAD (lb.)	NUMBER FIRED
GERMANY						
V-1 (Fieseler FZG 76)	Pulse-jet engine	Askania autopilot	350	160	1,870	8,900 vs. UK 12,000 vs. W. Europe
V-2 (Peenemunde A-4)	Liquid-fuelled rocket motor	Gyroscopic	3,800	190	2,200	3,610 vs. UK/W. Europe

ROCKETS/MISSILES Tactical

TYPE	FUNCTION	USUAL LAUNCHER	WEIGHT (lbs.) Projectile	WEIGHT (lbs.) Warhead	VELOCITY (metre/sec)	EFFECTIVE RANGE (metres)	ARMOUR-PIERCING CAPABILITY
GERMANY							
88mm Raketen-panzerbüchse Granate 4322	A/tank	Raketen-panzerbüchse 54/1 ("Panzerschreck")	7.3	1.5	104	150	200mm
150mm Wurfgranate 41 Spreng	Artillery	150mm Nebel-Werfer 41 (6 x tubes)	70	5.5	342	7,050	—
USA							
2.36in. H.E.A.T. M6A1	A/tank	M1/M9 shoulder-launcher ("Bazooka")	3.4	0.5	82	275	?
4.5in. H.E. M8	Artillery	Various	38.5	4.3	260	4,200	—
USSR							
132mm Rocket	Artillery	M-13 launcher (16 x rails) ("Katyusha")	93.7	40.8	355	9,300	—

Two other important anti-tank weapons associated with the 'bazooka' and the 'Panzerschreck' were the German Faustpatrone ('Panzerfaust') and the British PIAT (Projectile Infantry Anti-Tank). Strictly speaking, however, neither utilised rocket propulsion, the former being a recoil-less gun and the latter a spigot mortar, both firing hollow-charged grenades. But both were fairly effective, firing 7lb. and 3lb. projectiles respectively, with an effective range of about 100 metres.

BIBLIOGRAPHY

The following are the books that I have found particularly useful whilst compiling this book. On the whole they are also the ones to which anyone wishing to look in more detail at any of the topics in this book should turn.

All books are published in London unless otherwise stated.

A

P. ABBOTT & N. THOMAS, *Germany's Eastern Front Allies 1941-45*, Osprey, 1982

G. ADERS, *History of the German Night-Fighter Force 1917-45*, Arms & Armour Press, 1979

R.H. AHRENFELDT, *Psychiatry in the British Army in the Second World War*, Routledge & Kegan Paul,1958

AIR MINISTRY, *Psychological Disorders in Flying Personnel of the Royal Air Force Investigated During the War 1939-45*, HMSO, 1947

AIR MINISTRY, *The Rise and Fall of the German Air Force 1933-45*, W E Inc., Old Greenwich, Conn., 1969 (written in 1948)

L. ALLEN, *Burma: the Longest War 1941-45*, Dent, 1984
Annual Register, 1939-46

ANON, *Germany Reports*, Press and Information Office, German Federal Republic, 1953

M. AXWORTHY & H. SERBANESCU, *The Romanian Army of World War 2*, Osprey, 1991

B

E. BAGNASCO, *Submarines of World War Two*, Arms & Armour Press, 1985

A.J. BARKER, *Japanese Army Handbook 1939-45*, Ian Allen, Shepperton, 1979

M. BAUDOT et al, *The Historical Encyclopedia of World War II*, Greenwich House, New York, 1985

E. BAUER, *The History of World War II*, Orbis, 1979

G.W. BEEBE & M.E.de BAKEY, *Battle Casualties*, C. C. Thomas, Springfield, Ill., 1952

R. BENNETT, *Ultra and Mediterranean Strategy 1941-45*, Hamish Hamilton, 1989
Ultra in the West: the Normandy Campaign of 1944-45, Hutchinson, 1979

G. BOULLE, *Le Corps Expéditionnaire Français en Italie 1943-44*, 2 vols, Imprimerie Nationale, Paris, 1971-73

C. BOWYER, *Royal Air Force Handbook 1939-45*, Ian Allen, Shepperton, 1984

M.A. BRAGADIN, *The Italian Navy in World War II*, US Naval Institute Press, Annapolis, Md., 1957

R. BRETT-SMITH, *Hitler's Generals*, Osprey, 1976

D. BUTLER & J. FREEMAN, *British Political Facts 1900-1960*, Macmillan, 1964

C

P.V. CANNISTRARO, *Historical Dictionary of Fascist Italy*, Greenwood Press, 1982

CENTRAL STATISTICAL OFFICE, *Statistical Digest of the War*, HMSO, 1947

M. CERVI, *The Hollow Legions: Mussolini's Italian Blunder 1940-41*, Chatto & Windus, 1971

P. CHAMBERLAIN & C. ELLIS, *British and American Tanks of World War II*, Arms & Armour Press, 1981
Pictorial History of Tanks of the World 1915-45, Arms & Armour Press, 1972

P. CHAMBERLAIN & H. L. DOYLE, *Encyclopedia of German Tanks of World War Two*, Arms & Armour Press, 1978

G. CHAPMAN, *Why France Collapsed*, Cassell, 1968

COMMITTEE ON RECORDS OF WAR ADMINISTRATION, *The United States at War*, Government Printing Office, Washington, (1946?)

J.B. COHEN, *Japan's Economy in War and Reconstruction*, University of Minnesota Press, Minneapolis, 1949

C. COOK & J. PAXTON, *European Political Facts 1918-73*, Macmillan, 1975

J.L. COUHAT, *French Warships of World War II*, Ian Allen, Shepperton, 1978

W.F. CRAVEN & J.L. CATE, *The Army Air Forces in World War II*, 7 vols, Chicago University Press, Chicago, 1948-78

D

W.J.K. DAVIES, *German Army Handbook 1939-45*, Ian Allen, Shepperton, 1973

A.I. DESPOTOPOULOS, La guerre Gréco-Italienne et Gréco-Allemande du 28 octobre 1940-31 mai 1941 *Revue d'histoire de la deuxieme guerre mondiale*, no. 136/1984

D. DEXTER, *The New Guinea Offensives* (Australia in the War of 1939-45), Australian War Memorial, Canberra, 1961

P.S. DULL, *A Battle History of the Imperial Japanese Navy 1941-45*, Patrick Stephens,Cambridge, 1978

J.F. DUNNIGAN (ed.), *The Russian Front: Germany's War in the East 1941-45*, Arms & Armour Press, 1978

C. DUNNING, *Combat Units of the Regia Aeronautica 1940-43*, Air Research, New Malden, 1988

E

D. EICHHOLTZ, *Geschichte der Deutschen Kriegswirtschaft 1939-45*, vol.2, Akademie Verlag, Berlin, 1985

P. ELLIOTT, *Allied Escort Ships of World War II*, Macdonald and Jane's, 1977

J. ERICKSON, *Stalin's War with Germany*, 2 vols, Weidenfeld & Nicholson, 1975-83

F

G. FORTY, *United States Tanks of World War II*, Blandford, Poole, 1983
US Army Handbook 1939-45, Ian Allen, Shepperton 1979

A. FRACCAROLI, *Italian Warships of World War II*, Ian Allen, Shepperton, 1974

M. FREEMAN, *Atlas of Nazi Germany*, Croom Helm, 1987

R.A. FREEMAN, *The Mighty Eighth War Diary*, Jane's, 1981
The US Strategic Bomber, Macdonald and Jane's, 1975

G

J. GARLINSKI, *Poland in the Second World War*, Macmillan, 1985

Great Soviet Encyclopedia (1970), 31 vols. Macmillan, New York, 1978-83

W. GREEN, *Warplanes of the Third Reich*, Macdonald & Jane's 1976

W. GREEN & J. FLICKER, *Air Forces of the World*, Macdonald, 1958

J. GREENE, *Handbook on the Italian Army in World War II* 1940-43, private, pub., Cambria, Calif., 1988

T.E. GRIESS (ed.), *Atlas for the Second World War*, 2 vols, Avery, Wayne, NJ, 1985

O. GROEHLER, *Geschichte des Luftkrieges 1910-80*, Militärverlag der DDR, Berlin, 1981

J.A. GUNSBERG, *Divided and Conquered: the French High Command and Defeat in the West*, Greenwood, 1979

B. GUNSTON, *Encyclopedia of the World's Combat Aircraft*, Salamander, 1976

H

C. HAMILTON, *Leaders and Personalities of the Third Reich*, Bender, San Jose, Calif.,1984

V. HARDESTY, *Red Phoenix: the Rise of Soviet Air Power 1941-45*, Arms & Armour Press , 1982

M. HARRISON, *Soviet Planning in Peace and War 1938-45*, CUP, 1985

I. HATA & Y. IZAWA, *Japanese Naval Aces and Fighter Units in World War II*, Airlife, Shrewsbury, 1989

P.N. HEHN (ed.), *The German Struggle Against Yugoslav Guerrillas in World War II*, Columbia University Press, New York, 1979

F. H. HINSLEY, *British Intelligence in the Second World War*, 3 vols, HMSO, 1979-88

HMSO, *The Japanese Air Forces in World War II*, Arms & Armour Press, 1979 (written in 1945)

I. HOGG, *British and American Artillery of World War Two*, Arms & Armour Press, 1978
German Artillery of World War Two, Arms & Armour Press, 1975

HSUE LONG-HSUEN & CHANG MING-KAI, *History of the Sino-Japanese War 1937-45*, Chung Wu, Taipei, 1971

I

S. IWAO, *Biographical Dictionary of Japanese History*, Kodansha International, New York, 1978

J

R. JACKSON, *Air War Over France*, Ian Allen, Shepperton, 1974

W.G.F JACKSON, *The Battle For Italy*, Batsford, 1967

H.A. JACOBSEN & H. DOLLINGER, *Der Zweite Weltkrieg*, 3 vols, Verlag Kurt Desch, Munich, 1963

C.G. JEFFORD, *R.A.F. Squadrons*, Airlife, Shrewsbury, 1988

H.F. JOSLEN, *Orders of Battle Second World War 1939-45*, HMSO, 1960

K

M.C KASER & E.A. RADICE, *The Economic History of Eastern Europe 1919-75*, Vol. 2, Clarendon, Oxford, 1986

R.M. KENNEDY, *The German Campaign in Poland 1939* (US Dept. of the Army), Government Printing Office, Washington, 1956

S.W. KIRBY *et al.*, *The War Against Japan*, 5 vols (History of the Second World War: UK Military Series), HMSO, 1956-69

B.H. KLEIN, *Germany's Economic Preparations for War*, Harvard University Press, Cambridge, Mass., 1959

M.A. KREIDBERG & M.G. HENRY, *History of Military Mobilisation in the U.S. Army 1775-1945* (US Dept. of the Army), Government Printing Office, Washington, 1955

L

E. LEFEVRE, *Panzers in Normandy Then and Now*, Battle of Britain Prints International, 1983

H. LE MASSON, *The French Navy,* 2 vols (Navies of the Second World War), Macdonald, 1969

J. LIRON & R. DANEL, The French Air Force in 1939-40, *Air Pictorial*, May/June/July 1963

F.F. LIU, *A Military History of Modern China 1924-49*, Princeton University Press, Princeton, 1956

J. LUCAS, *Panzer Army Africa*, Macdonald & Jane's, 1977

E.J. KING, *US Navy at War 1941-45: Official Reports to the Secretary of the Navy* (US Navy Dept.), Government Printing Office, Washington, 1946

H. T. LENTON & J.J. COLLEDGE, *Warships of World War II*, Ian Allen, Shepperton, 1970

M

C.A. MACARTNEY, *October Fifteenth: a History of Modern Hungary 1929-45*, 2 vols, Edinburgh University Press, Edinburgh, 1957

F. MACLEAN, *The Battle of Neretva*, Panther Books, 1970

V. MADEJ (ed.), *Italian Order of Battle 1940-44*, Valor, Allentown, Penn., 1990
Japanese Armed Forces Order of Battle 1937-45, vol.1, Game Marketing, Allentown, Penn., 1981

F. MANZO & G. FIORAVANZO, *Dati Statistici* (La Marina Italiana Nella Seconda Guerra Mondiale, Vol.1), Ufficio Storico della Marina Militare, Rome, 1972

F.K. MASON, *Battle Over Britain*, McWhirter Twins, 1969

M. MAURER, *Air Force Combat Units of World War II* (Dept. of the Air Force), Government Printing Office, Washington, 1961

D.McISAAC (ed.), *The United States Strategic Bombing Survey*, 10 vols, Garland, New York, 1976 (a selection from the original Survey reports published between 1946 and 1947)

J. MEISTER, *Soviet Warships of the Second World War*, Macdonald & Jane's, 1977

W.F. MELLOR, *Casualties and Medical Statistics* (Medical History of the Second World War), HMSO, 1972

M.MIDDLEBROOK & C. EVERITT, *The Bomber Command War Diaries*, Viking, 1985

MILITÄRGESCHICHTLICHEN FORSCHUNGSAMT, *Das Deutsche Reich und der Zweite Weltkrieg*, ongoing, Deutsche Verlags-Anstalt, Stuttgart, 1979-

B. MILLOT, *La Guerre du Pacifique*, 2 vols, Robert Laffont, Paris, 1968

J. MILSOM, *Russian Tanks 1900-1970*, Arms & Armour Press, 1970

A. MILWARD, *War, Economy and Society 1939-45*, Allen Lane, 1977

MINISTRY OF DEFENCE (NAVY), *The U-Boat War in the Atlantic 1939-45*, 2 vols, HMSO, 1989

F. MINNITI, Il problema degli armamenti nell preparazione militari italiana dal 1935 al 1943, *Storia Contemporania*, 1/1978

S.W.MITCHAM, *Hitler's Legions*, Leo Cooper, 1989

A. MOLLO, *The Armed Forces of World War II*, Macdonald, 1987

D. MONDEY, *American Aircraft of World War II* Hamlyn, 1982

S.E. MORISON, *History of United States Naval Operations in World War II*, 15 vols, OUP, 1948-62

MOUNTBATTEN OF BURMA, *Report to the Combined Chiefs of Staff by the Supreme Commander S.E. Asia 1943-45*, HMSO, 1951

P. MOYES, *Bomber Squadrons of the RAF and their Aircraft*, Macdonald & Jane's, 1976

B. MULLER-HILLEBRAND, *Das Heer 1933-45*, 3 vols, Mittler und Sohn, Frankfurt, 1954-69

K. MUNSON, *Aircraft of World War II*, Ian Allen, Shepperton, 1962

W. MURRAY, *Luftwaffe: Strategy for Defeat 1933-45*, Allen & Unwin, 1985

N

J. NOAKES & G. PRIDHAM, *Nazism 1919-45: a Documentary Reader*, vol. 3, University of Exeter Publications, 1988

O

N. ORPEN, *The East African and Abyssinian Campaigns* (South African Forces in World War II), Purnell, Cape Town, 1968

P

J.P. PALLUD, *Blitzkrieg in the West Then and Now*, Battle of Britain Prints International, 1991

PARLIAMENT, *Statistics Relating to the War Effort of the United Kingdom*, HMSO, 1945

N.M. PARNELL & C.A. LYNCH, *History of the R.A.A.F. 1909-69*, Air Pictorial, Jan 1909-March 1970

T. PARRISH (ed.), *The Encyclopaedia of World War II*, Secker & Warburg, 1978

H. PEMSEL, *Atlas of Naval Warfare*, Arms & Armour Press, 1977

I.S.O. PLAYFAIR *et al.*, *The Mediterranean and the Middle East*, 7 vols (History of the Second World War: UK Military Series), HMSO, 1954-91

R.G. POIRIER & A.Z. CONNER, *The Red Army Order of Battle in the Great Patriotic War*, Presidio, Novato, Calif., 1985

N. POLMAR & D.B. CARPENTER, *Submarines of the Imperial Japanese Navy 1904-45*, Conway, 1986

A. PRICE, *Luftwaffe Handbook 1939-45*, Ian Allen, Shepperton, 1986

PROFILE PUBLICATIONS, Armoured Fighting Vehicles of the World Series:
vol.2: British AFVs 1919-40 (1970)
vol.3: British and Commonwealth AFVs 1940-46 (1971)
vol.4: American AFVs of World War II (1972)
vol.5: AFVs of Germany (1973)

R

J.L. READY, *The Forgotten Axis: Germany's Partners and Foreign Volunteers in World War II*, McFarland, 1987

REVUE DE L'HISTOIRE DE LA DEUXIEME GUERRE MONDIALE, Campagne de France 1940, *numéro spécial,* June/Sept 1953
Sur l'aviation française 1919-40, *numéro spécial,* Jan 1969

R. RICCIO, *Italian Tanks and Fighting Vehicles of World War II*, Pique Pubs., Henley-on-Thames, 1975

J. ROBERTSON, *Australia at War 1939-45*, Heinemann, Melbourne, 1981

J. ROHWER & G. HUMMELCHEN, *Chronology of the War at Sea 1939-45,* 2 vols, Ian Allen, Shepperton, 1972

G. ROSIGNOLI, *MSVN 1929-43: Badges and Uniforms of the Italian Fascist Militia*, pvte. pub., Farnham, 1980
The Allied Forces in Italy 1943-45, David & Charles, Newton Abbot, 1989

S.W. ROSKILL, *The War at Sea 1939-45* (History of the Second World War: UK Military Series), 3 vols, HMSO, 1954-61

ROYAL INSTITUTE OF INTERNATIONAL AFFAIRS, *Raw Materials*, OUP, 1939

S

G. SANTORO, *L'Aeronautica Italiana, nella Segunda Guerra Mondiale,* Edizione Milano, Rome, 1957

L.A. SAWYER & W.H. MITCHELL, *The Liberty Ships*, David & Charles, Newton Abbot, 1970
Victory Ships and Tankers, David & Charles, Newton Abbot, 1974

W. SCHUMANN & G. HASS (eds.), *Deutschland im Zweiten Weltkriege,* Pahl-Rugenstein, Cologne, 1974

A. SEATON, *The Russo-German War 1941-45*, Arthur Barker, 1971
Stalin as Warlord, Batsford, 1976

E. SEKIGAWA, *Pictorial History of Japanese Military Aviation*, Ian Allen, Shepperton, 1974

G.A. SHEPPERD, *The Italian Campaign 1943-45*, Arthur Barker, 1968

R. SHERROD, *History of Marine Corps Aviation in World War II*, Presidio, San Rafael, Calif., 1980 (written in 1952)

C. SHORES, *History of the Royal Canadian Air Force*, Arms & Armour Press, 1984
Pictorial History of the Mediterranean Air War, 3 vols, Ian Allen, Shepperton, 1974

C. SHORES & R. WARD, *The Finnish Air Force 1918-68*, Osprey, Reading, 1968

J.P.M. SHOWELL, *The German Navy in World War Two*, Arms & Armour Press, 1979

T.A. SIEFRING, *The US Air Force in World War II*, Hamlyn, 1977

P.H. SILVERSTONE, *US Warships of World War II*, Ian Allen, Shepperton, 1965

L.L. SNYDER, *Encyclopedia of the Third Reich*, Blandford, 1989

C.P. STACEY, *The Victory Campaign* (Official History of the Canadian Army in the Second World War), Queen's Printers, Ottawa, 1960

S.L. STANTON, *Order of Battle US Army World War II*, Presidio, Novato, Calif., 1984

T

J.C. TAYLOR, *German Warships of World War II*, Ian Allen, Shepperton, 1966

M.J.H. TAYLOR, *Warplanes of the World 1918-39*, Ian Allen, Shepperton, 1981

T. TAYLOR, *The Breaking Wave: the German Defeat in the Summer of 1940*, Weidenfeld & Nicholson, 1967
The March of Conquest: German Victories in Western Europe in 1940, Hulton, 1959

D.W. THORPE, *Japanese Army Air Force Camouflage and Markings World War II*, Aero Pubs., Fallbrook, Calif., 1968
Japanese Naval Air Force Camouflage and Markings World War II, Aero Pubs., Fallbrook, Calif., 1977

P. TOUZIN, *Les Engins Blindés Français 1920-45*, vol.1, Sera, Paris, 1976

U

UNRRA, *Survey of Italy's Economy*, Rome, 1947

US DEPARTMENT OF THE ARMY (OFFICE OF THE CHIEF OF MILITARY HISTORY), The United States Army in World War II:
　　Army Ground Forces Series, 2 vols, 1947-48
　　European Theater of Operations Series, 6 vols, 1950-65
　　Mediterranean Theater of Operations Series, 4 vols, 1957-77
　　War in the Pacific Series, 11 vols, 1948-63
　　Special Studies Series, 8 vols including
　　　　Buying Aircraft: Material Procurement for the Army Air Forces, 1964
　　　　Chronology 1941-45, 1960
　　Technical Services Series, 21 vols including
　　　　Ordnance Department: Planning Munitions for War, 1955
　　　　Ordnance Department: Procurement and Supply, 1960
　　　　Quartermaster Corps: Organisation, Supply and Services, 2 vols, 1953-55
　　War Department Series, 8 vols including
　　　　The Army and Economic Mobilisation, 1959
　　　　Global Logistics and Strategy, 2 vols 1955-68

UNITED STATES STRATEGIC BOMBING SURVEY (see McISAAC above)

US WAR DEPARTMENT, *Handbook on German Military Forces*, Government Printing Office, March 1945
Handbook on the Italian Army May 1943, Athena Books, Doncaster, 1983 (first published in 1943)
Handbook on Japanese Military Forces, Greenhill, 1991 (first published in 1944)

V

B. VERNIER, Les operations Greco-Italiennes du 28 octobre 1940 au 20 avril 1941, *Revue d'Histoire de la Deuxième Guerre Mondiale*, April 1960

F.M. von SENGER UND ETTERLIN, *German Tanks of World War II*, Galahad Books, New York, 1969

W

R. WAGNER (ed.), *The Soviet Air Force in World War II: the Official History*, David & Charles, Newton Abbot, 1974

A.J. WATTS, *Japanese Warships of the World War II*, Ian Allen, Shepperton, 1974

E.C. WEAL *et al.*, *Combat Aircraft of World War Two*, Arms & Armour Press, 1977

C. WEBSTER & N. FRANKLAND, *The Strategic Air Offensive Against Germany 1939-45*, vol.4 (History of the Second World War: UK Military Series), HMSO, 1961

R.F. WEIGHLEY, *Eisenhower's Lieutenants: the Campaigns of France and Germany 1944-45*, Sidgwick & Jackson, 1981

Whitaker's Almanac, 1939-46

Who's Who, 1946-50

D. WOOD & D. DEMPSTER, *The Narrow Margin: the Battle of Britain and the Rise of Air Power 1930-40*, Arrow, 1967

D.P. WOODHALL, *Royal New Zealand Air Force*, Air Pictorial, January 1968

Y

J.M. YOUNG, *Britain's Sea War: a Diary of Ship Losses 1939-45*, Patrick Stephens, Wellingborough, 1989

P. YOUNG (ed.), *The Almanac of World War II*, Hamlyn, 1981

Z

S.J. ZALOGA & J. GRANDSEN, *Soviet Tanks and Combat Vehicles of World War Two*, Arms & Armour Press, 1984

S.J. ZALOGA & V.W. MADEJ, *The Polish Campaign 1939*, Hippocrene, New York, 1985

E.F. ZIEMKE, *The German Northern Theater of Operations 1940-45* (US Dept. of the Army), Government Printing Office, Washington, 1959 *Stalingrad to Berlin: the German Defeat in the East*, Government Printing Office, Washington, 1968

E.F. ZIEMKE & M.E. BAUER, *Moscow to Stalingrad: Decision in the East*, Government Printing Office, Washington, 1988